ONE WEE

WHY WE FOCUS ON *Effectiveness*

This sixth edition of *Advertising: Principles and Practice* brings to fruition a shift in focus started in the previous edition. Looking at the advertising landscape, what strikes us is the prevalence of accountability. While advertising agencies never had the power to ignore the client, they have not been held to such standards as they are now. To explain this shift, a major factor has been the development of measurement tools to bring this goal of accountability to life.

The Lemon Is Sweet

Award: *EFFIE Silver 2001, Automotive category*

Company: *Volkswagen of America*

Agency: *Arnold Worldwide*

Campaign: *"Volkswagen Owners Really Love Their Cars"*

Ask anyone who grew up in the 1960s and they can provide a chronology of VW ads created by the Doyle Dan Bernback advertising agency: "Think Small," "Lemon," "The Floating Car," "The Egg Car," "Ugly is Only Skin Deep." This creative genius continued through the early 1970s and VW became an advertising icon. Then the bottom dropped out of Volkswagen's marketing world, and the product disappeared from sight.

From the late 1970s into the early 1990s, Volkswagen switched agencies a few times. Clever ad campaigns were created, but they were not effective enough to drive sales compared to the ads produced in the 1960s and 1970s. Instead, U.S. sales were dropping. By 1993, less than 50,000 Volkswagens were sold in the United States per year. With so few sales, Volkswagen ~~uct line in the United States. Fortunately, howe~~ at Volkswagen between 199~~2~~ and 1994.

THE MANDATE FOR EFFECTIVENESS

Today, advertising finds itself in a serious bind. With a down economy, the tragedy of 9/11, and new technology that may threaten the way advertising operates, there is a need to rethink advertising as a strategic alternative. Advertising will only survive and grow if it focuses on being effective. All advertisers are expecting specific results, based on their stated objectives. Clients expect proof, and, for the most part, that proof must lead to or actually produce sales. It is no longer acceptable to tell a client, "Our ads work, we just don't know how, when, and with what results."

The basic premise of this book is that *advertising must be effective*; it must achieve its objectives. To that end, we teach you about advertising strategies that produce effective results. The VW campaign that introduced this chapter was an effective campaign. That doesn't mean that all VW campaigns have been effective. In fact, VW ads were considered outstanding during the 1960s, through the creative genius of Bill Bernbach. Then, for the next 30 years, VW lost its way, sales dropped, advertising was ineffective, and product development was poor. *Advertising cannot save bad products.*

Because we are so concerned about effectiveness, we will introduce most chapters with an ad that has won an EFFIE or an equivalent award. There are hundreds of major awards that are given to ads, with the CLIOs being the most famous, equivalent to the Oscar in the movie industry. The great majority of these advertising awards tend to focus on creativity, not effectiveness. The EFFIE is one exception. To quote from its Web site: "The New York American Marketing Association introduced the EFFIE Awards in 1968. It is the only national award to recognize creative achievement in meeting and exceeding advertising object~~ives. As such, it honors~~

CHAPTER OPENING Effectiveness Cases

ADVERTISING

PRINCIPLES&PRACTICE

6TH edition

WILLIAM WELLS
University of Minnesota

JOHN BURNETT
University of Denver

SANDRA MORIARTY
University of Colorado

Prentice Hall

Pearson Education International

Senior Editor: Bruce Kaplan
Editor-in-Chief: Jeff Shelstad
Director of Development: Steve Deitmer
Development Editor: Audrey Regan
Assistant Editor: Melissa Pellerano
Editorial Assistant: Danielle Rose Serra
Media Project Manager: Anthony Palmiotto
Senior Marketing Manager: Michelle O'Brien
Managing Editor (Production): Judy Leale
Production Editor: Keri Jean Miksza
Permissions Coordinator: Suzanne Grappi
Associate Director, Manufacturing: Vinnie Scelta
Buyer: Arnold Vila
Design Manager: Maria Lange
Designer: Blair Brown
Cover Design: Blair Brown
Cover Photo: Jerry Driendl
Illustrator (Interior): Electrographics
Associate Director, Media Productions: Karen Goldsmith
Manager, Print Production: Christy Mahon
Formatter: Suzanne Duda
Composition: Carlisle Communications
Project Manager (Carlisle): Lynn Steines
Printer/Binder: Phoenix/Quebecor World-Versailles

Credits and acknowledgments borrowed from other sources and reproduced, with permission, in this textbook appear on appropriate page within text and on page 575.

This book may be sold only in those countries to which it is consigned by Pearson Education International. It is not to be re-exported and it is not for sale in the U.S.A., Mexico, or Canada.

Pearson Education LTD.
Pearson Education Australia PTY, Limited
Pearson Education Singapore, Pte. Ltd
Pearson Education North Asia Ltd
Pearson Education, Canada, Ltd
Pearson Educación de Mexico, S.A. de C.V.
Pearson Education—Japan
Pearson Education Malaysia, Pte. Ltd
Pearson Education Upper Saddle River, New Jersey

10 9 8 7 6 5 4 3 2
ISBN 0-13-120206-5

I wish to dedicate this book to my wife, Nancy,
who has inspired, endured, and loved me through it all.
—John Burnett

*T*hanks to my husband, Tom Duncan,
who shares his files, as well as his thoughts and love.
—Sandra Moriarty

BRIEF CONTENTS

CONTENTS

PART II   **ADVERTISING BACKGROUND, PLANNING, AND STRATEGY**

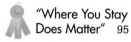

"Where You Stay Does Matter"   95

PART IV

CREATIVE ADVERTISING

PART V

INTEGRATING MARKETING COMMUNICATION ELEMENTS

ABOUT THE AUTHORS

William Wells

One of the industry's leading market and research authorities, Bill Wells is Professor of Advertising at the University of Minnesota's School of Journalism and Mass Communication. Formerly Executive Vice President and Director of Marketing Services at DDB Needharn Chicago, he is the only representative of the advertising business elected to the Attitude Research Hall of Fame. He earned a Ph.D. from Stanford University and was formerly Professor of Psychology and Marketing at the University of Chicago. He joined Needham, Harper, Chicago as Director of Corporate Research. Author of the Needham Harper Lifestyle study as well as author of more than 60 books and articles, Dr. Wells also published *Planning for ROI: Effective Advertising Strategy* (Prentice Hall, 1989).

John Burnett

A Professor of Marketing at the University of Denver, he holds a D.B.A. degree in Marketing from the University of Kentucky. John is a co-author of *Introduction to Marketing Communications: An Integrated Approach.* In addition, his numerous articles and research papers have been published in a wide variety of professional and academic journals. In particular, his research has examined the effectiveness of emotional appeals in advertising and how various segments respond to such strategies. He is an active consultant and expert witness in marketing and advertising and has served as a consultant for AT&T, Qwest, First Trust, Noel-Levitz, and others.

Sandra Moriarty

Sandra Moriarty holds a B.J. and M.S. in journalism from the University of Missouri and a Ph.D. from Kansas State University. Before moving into full-time teaching, she owned her own public relations and advertising agency. Currently, Dr. Moriarty is a professor at the University of Colorado, Boulder where she teaches in the Integrated Marketing Communication graduate program. In addition to an extensive list of articles in both scholarly and trade journals, Dr. Moriarty has authored or co-authored 9 other books, including *Driving Brand Value, Creative Advertising, The Creative Package,* and *Introduction to Marketing Communications: An Integrated Approach.*

PREFACE

Advertising is all about *Effectiveness*

This sixth edition of *Advertising: Principles and Practice* brings to fruition a shift in focus started in the previous edition. Looking at the advertising landscape, what strikes us is the prevalence of accountability. While advertising agencies never had the power to ignore the client, they have not been held to such standards as they are now. To explain this shift, a major factor has been the development of measurement tools to bring this goal of accountability to life.

So advertising has reached a stage where the memorable ad or jingle is no longer enough. It may not sell the product or build market share. It may not be *effective* advertising, as defined by the goals of the client.

Everything You Need

Award: EFFIE Gold, *Automotive category*

Company/Brand: Nissan North America/Xterra

Agency: TBWA/Chiat Day

Campaign: "Nissan Xterra Launch Campaign"

The EFFIE award–winning Xterra Launch ads, using the tagline "Everything you need. Nothing you don't," demonstrated that this rugged, no-nonsense SUV is built for the true outdoor enthusiast. Images of mud-drenched mountain bikers, outrageous skiers and snowboarders, and extreme surfers and kayakers fill the screen. The "Xtreme" theme, which was created by California-based TBWA/Chiat Day, is mirrored in the Lenny Kravitz Grammy-winning hit, "Fly Away"—a Generation X anthem.

Xterra's strategy was not to be all things to all people, but rather to be everything

The problem with making *advertising effectiveness* a hallmark of an advertising book is that it is so difficult to show. Advertising agencies have always been very guarded about goals and measures. In this situation, how does one accurately portray what advertising effectiveness is and how it can be measured?

THERE IS A WAY, AS YOU WILL SEE IN OUR

SIXTH EDITION.

HEAVY-DUTY ALUMINUM ROOF RACK

Xterra SE shown with optional accesories

HOW WE DEMONSTRATE
Advertising Effectiveness

Advertising: Principles and Practice, Sixth Edition, lifts the veil by focusing on EFFIE-award winners: advertising campaigns that have won awards for their effectiveness from the American Marketing Association of New York. Chapter-opening cases on these EFFIE award winners reveal client goals and how these goals were reached. No other book shows you how effective advertising is identified and done today. No other book shows you advertising that works and why it works.

Chapter-opening effectiveness cases

You will get a behind the scenes look at campaigns for companies such as Holiday Inn, Delta, Polaroid, drugstore.com, Nissan, and Orkin. You'll see theory embodied in the components of effective advertising campaigns. Chapter 4's case on Holiday Inn Express, for example, outlines three goals that Holiday Inn set for its "Stay Smart" campaign. The campaign won a 2001 EFFIE Gold award in the travel/tourism/destination category.

"Where You Stay Does Matter"

Award: *EFFIE Gold 2001, Travel/Tourism/Destination category*

Company: *Bass Hotels*

Agency: *Fallon Worldwide*

Campaign: *"Stay Smart"*

You've seen the commercial. The rock band Kiss runs off a raucous stage to their back room. Their gleeful manager, tinted shades popping off his face, exclaims, "That was possibly the finest rock and roll show I have ever seen! I SMELL WORLD TOUR!"

But as the performers take off their wigs and makeup, the manager despairs, "You're not Gene. You're not Paul. You guys aren't Kiss!"

"No," says Gene.

THE EFFECTIVENESS OF ADVERTISING

USA Today conducts an annual poll on which TV commercials are the most popular among its readers. For years, those clever Energizer bunny commercials topped the field in the poll. They started off like commercials for other products—but then the Energizer bunny crossed the screen, catching viewers by surprise. The campaign slogan was "It keeps going and going and going. . . ." The commercials won a number of advertising awards, but which company made the Energizer battery? (See www.Energizer.com/bunny/.)

Most people weren't quite sure. So when they got to the store, they bought the brand leader—Gillette's Duracell, instead of the Eveready Energizer. In other words, the Energizer bunny commercials did little to influence the actual sales of Eveready batteries, even though they had high levels of awareness and were well liked. Energizer has taken steps to correct

In-text examples on effectiveness

Too many to list, these examples demonstrate what effectiveness means in advertising. But to give you a glimpse here, look at Chapter 6. It examines the Energizer Bunny campaign and explains that even though the early Bunny commercials were memorable and well-liked, they weren't effective, serving to drive sales of rival Duracell rather than Energizer.

It's a Wrap At the end of the chapter, in a feature called "It's a Wrap" we loop back to the opening case and show you why it won an award—why it was effective. The "It's a Wrap" box in Chapter 4 explains how the Holiday Inn Express "Stay Smart" campaign not only met its goals but exceeded them in a big way.

IT'S A WRAP
A SEGMENT THAT RESPONDED

Throughout this chapter we have emphasized the importance of understanding the audiences. Fallon's campaign for Holiday Inn Express paid off in a big way. Let's look at the three goals it had and how the campaign performed on those goals.

1. **Generate awareness of Express as a competitor among limited-service hotel brands.**

   By 2001, Express's brand awareness had increased 27 points while competitors' brand awareness rates had barely increased. Unaided awareness [no hints provided] tripled while unaided awareness for the competitors' brands declined. In addition, Express advertising awareness doubled while competitors' performance was flat. In terms of brand awareness, Express moved from last place to first place in the limited-service hotel category.

Express Brand Awareness

84%

57%

10%

Ad Awareness Growth

51%   41%   43%

26%

*But the **Sixth Edition** is much more than a bunch of cool examples of effective advertising. It rests on a solid theoretical framework that has been carefully developed and refined throughout the book.*

It starts in Chapter 1 where we set up two key models for determining effectiveness.

THE MANDATE FOR EFFECTIVENESS

Today, advertising finds itself in a serious bind. With a down economy, the tragedy of 9/11, and new technology that may threaten the way advertising operates, there is a need to rethink advertising as a strategic alternative. Advertising will only survive and grow if it focuses on being effective. All advertisers are expecting specific results, based on their stated objectives. Clients expect proof, and, for the most part, that proof must lead to or actually produce sales. It is no longer acceptable to tell a client, "Our ads work, we just don't know how, when, and with what results."

The basic premise of this book is that *advertising must be effective*; it must achieve its objectives. To that end, we teach you about advertising strategies that produce effective results. The VW campaign that introduced this chapter was an effective campaign. That doesn't mean that all VW campaigns have been effective. In fact, VW ads were considered outstanding during the 1960s, through the creative genius of Bill Bernbach. Then, for the

Advertising Must Be Goal-Direct

Although these three conditions must be m sidered effective, they are not isolated. The hope to create in the minds of the peo

GURE 1.1

FECTIVE ADS CONNECT
REE ELEMENTS
ategy, creativity, and execution
st work in concert for an ad to be
ly effective.

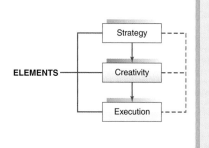

ELEMENTS — Strategy / Creativity / Execution

FIGURE 1.2
A MODEL OF KEY EFFECTS
(CATEGORIES OF EFFECTIVENESS)
First, advertisers try to get consumers to perceive—at least notice—their ads. Then advertisers hope consumers will either learn something or be persuaded by something in the ads. Finally, advertisers try to get consumers to behave in a certain way—ideally, to buy the product in the ad.

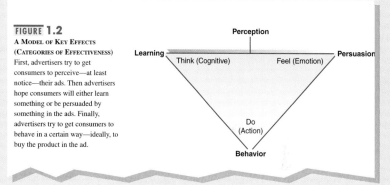

Following chapters build on these theoretical models. In particular, see Chapters 6, 7, and 11.

- **Chapter 6, How Advertising Works,** explains how effectiveness measures fit into the basic communication process.
- **Chapter 7, Advertising Planning and Strategy,** uses the effectiveness model to explain how companies formulate advertising planning objectives.
- **Chapter 11, The Creative Side of Advertising,** returns to the effectiveness model to explain how advertisers develop message strategies that are geared toward the four categories of effects.

The result? An effective presentation of what effective advertising is and how to measure it—principles enriched by practice, and practice made understandable by principles.

Enduring Strengths: *Principles*

Our focus on effective advertising rests on the solid groundwork we have established in five previous editions of *Advertising: Principles and Practice.* We have sought to present the principles of advertising clearly and concisely, while showing how current practice in advertising agencies modifies or brings these principles to fruition. With this goal in mind, we have improved both the principles and the practice parts of the book.

On the Principles side, we have made these enhancements:

Internet Audience Measurement When compared to most other media, the advantages of the Internet as a potential advertising vehicle are tremendous, with rapid, near instantaneous feedback and results chief among them. Rather than wait weeks or months to measure the success of an advertising campaign, marketers can instead run tests online, measure meaningful results within days, and quickly invest in the best performers with minimal switching costs. However, the measures of effectiveness used to evaluate off-line campaigns don't seem to transfer well to the online world.[4]

The biggest issue with measuring audience on the Internet has been the lack of standardization of the measurement tools. CASIE (a joint project of the Association of National Advertisers, Inc., and the American Association of Advertising Agencies, with the support of the Advertising Research Foundation [ARF]), created the Guiding Principles of Interactive Media Audience Measurement in 1996. This working paper focuses on supplying guidelines for providing quality audience measurement of interactive media. (See

➤ Expanded coverage of interactive advertising

We've added the latest coverage of advertising and the Web in just about every chapter. New sections include the effects of technological change on advertising agencies (Chapter 3), new coverage of Web-based promotions (Chapter 6), enhanced coverage of Internet audience measurement (Chapter 8), and new sections on writing and designing for the Web (Chapters 12 and 13). Chapter 12 takes a look at how an art director used creative copy to enhance a campaign for a SCUBA industry Web site (time2dive.com). The chapter delves into the principles of writing good banners, pop-ups, daughter windows, and side frame ads—not to mention Web sites.

➤ Streamlined discussion of copywriting, design, and production

for both print and broadcast advertising. Chapter 12 covers copywriting; Chapter 13 covers design and production. Students can better focus on the creative skills of the advertiser. And students can see what skills are needed to write and design for the Web.

Designers know that Web pages, particularly the first screen, should follow the same layout rules as posters: The graphics should be eye-catching without demanding too much downloading time; type should be simple, using one or two typefaces and avoiding all capitals and letter spacing that distorts the words. Because there is often a lot to read, black type on a high-contrast background usually is best; all the design elements—type and graphics—should be big enough to see on the smallest screen.

The Interactive Dimension

The combination of interactive navigation, live streaming video, online radio, and 360 degree camera angles creates Web pages that may be more complex than anything you see on TV. For example, Texture/Media, a Boulder Colorado–based Web design firm, create a seven-episode series over five months that detailed the journey of two men attempting t

➤ Discussion of the effects of the economic downturn and world events on advertising

Advertising revenues plummet when economic times turn sour. What can advertising agencies do, and what campaigns do they craft during such times? Chapter 14's opening case covers a campaign to increase charitable giving during an economic downturn. And what can advertising do to reassure people fearful of flying after the tragedy on September 11, 2001? Chapter 19's opener shows how the Spokane Regional Convention and Visitor's Bureau responded.

Practices

On the Practice side, we have provided updates and the latest examples. We highlight these in the following features:

New to this edition are **"A Matter of Practice"** boxes. These boxes examine effectiveness tactics, such as how advertisers try to reach the kids market and how to create good advertising campaigns for the Web. These boxes also highlight key aspects of actual campaigns that made the difference between success and failure. Companies examined include White Castle, Verizon, and EDS. Speaking of EDS, do you remember the award-winning EDS commercial that aired during the 2000 Super Bowl? Wonder how they kept all those cats in line? Chapter 13's "A Matter of Practice" box reveals EDS's goals for that commercial and the chapter explains some tricks that turned those kitties into stars.

A MATTER OF PRACTICE
Kitty Slickers and Cat Herders

> EDS, a company that essentially invented the information technology (IT) industry back in the 1960s, found itself with an unhip Old Economy image as the New Economy exploded in the late 1990s. Although a leader in such New Economy areas as Web hosting, digital supply chain management, and networking, EDS got no respect from its would-be high-tech partners.

The assignment given to the Fallon agency (Minneapolis) was to change those perceptions and infuse energy and pride into the EDS workforce. Fallon's strategy was to leverage EDS's proven experience and its rock-solid infrastructure, which enabled it to tackle enormous IT problems. The strategy came together in the positioning statement: "EDS thrives on defeating complexity."

How do you depict an organization defeating complexity? A catch phrase popular in the Silicon Valley culture—"It's like herding cats"—was the perfect metaphor for how EDS wrangles technology and manages complexity. And that's what the Fallon creative team did—it filmed a team of rugged

in the industry, EDS estimated that its $8 million investr in the ad and its supporting campaign netted an additi $12 million in PR. The campaign was also designed to ge

We've kept last edition's **"A Matter of Principle"** boxes, which are short ethics cases that address sound thorny issues as well as controversial ad campaigns. This edition takes a look at many new topics: Buzz marketing in Chapter 4; Chapter 2's box examines the latest on the Master Settlement Agreement with the tobacco industry; and Chapter 13's new box examines the relationship between effectiveness and diversity in advertising.

A MATTER OF PRINCIPLE
The Link between Diversity and Creativity

> Although stereotyped images may create ethical questions, diversity of images may be a positive factor in creative design, as the work of Sheri Broyles, a professor at the University of North Texas, has found.[2] She explains:

For decades the use of ethnic images—from Aunt Jemima to Uptown cigarettes, from Frito Bandito to taco-eating Chihuahuas—has been controversial. And the faces that appear in ads and commercials will become increasingly important as the faces across America become increasingly more diverse. One student in a creative advertising class at the University of North Texas made that point succinctly when commenting about an ad for Pantene Shampoo. The African American woman remarked that she didn't know this shampoo would work with her hair until she saw the black model.

This point—that diversity can increase the effectiveness of advertising—raises several questions: How does diversity relate to the execution of a creative strategy? And how does diversity relate to the perception, and ultimately the effectiveness, of the advertisement for younger consumers?

In a study, Professor Broyles asked echo boomers (children of baby boomers) questions concerning the faces found in magazine ads and the creative execution of the ads. She found that these echo boomers considered more diverse ads more creative, more positive, and more effective. Dr. Broyles suggests that ads showing the diverse ethnic faces of America may reach not only the growing ethnic population, but also the coveted youth market as well.

Source: This feature was provided by Professor Sheri Broyles, Assistant Professor of Advertising [...] North Texas.

Practices

THE INSIDE STORY

THE DAY-TO-DAY JOB OF AN ACCOUNT EXECUTIVE

Tammie DeGrasse Account Executive
McCann-Erickson, New York

"'So what exactly do you do in advertising?" That is by far the most common question I am asked once someone finds out I'm in Account Management. "Do you create the ads?" "Do you choose the actors?" "Do you decide which magazines to run in?" To be honest, I don't think my own mother has it figured out, yet. I've since realized that the best way to define what we, as account people, do in advertising is

thing but typical. Some highlights during my career at McCann include watching a handful of celebrities read our scripts in a recording session and even having myself featured in a national newspaper ad (Hey, anything to get the job done, right?).

Nonetheless, it's been amazing so far and a valuable learning experience every step of the way.

For those of you considering entering the advertising industry, deciding which area to concentrate in can be difficult. Every department is so equally appetizing; anyone would have trouble figuring out what the best fit for him or her might be. Being that I possess leadership qualities, enjoy strategizing, and like to get my hands in just about everything, Account Manage-

Back by popular demand is **"The Inside Story"** feature, which are boxes written by practitioners in the field who reveal advertising challenges they faced. You'll read how these professionals from agencies big and small put together new campaigns, learned how to handle hard to please clients, and managed to balance their creative drive with the realities of advertising planning. You'll especially enjoy Chapter 1's new Inside Story written by Tammie DeGrasse from the McCann-Erickson agency about her daily life as an account executive. Chapter 6's new Inside Story practitioner details his humorous campaign to get more women into Icelandic politics.

"Practical Tips" give students suggestions that they can apply on the job, in an internship, or in their coursework. Building on the Tips we have compiled over the editions, there are new Tips in this edition, including how to write e-mail pitch letters and new ways to measure PR effectiveness. From how to write compelling copy to mulling over whether you, as an advertiser, should enter foreign markets, these tips are keepers for students after they graduate.

Practical Tips

WRITING EFFECTIVE COPY

- *Be succinct.* Use short, familiar words, short sentences, and short paragraphs.
- *Be specific.* Don't waste time on generalities. The more specific the message, the more attention-getting and memorable it is.
- *Get personal.* Directly address your audience whenever possible as "you" and "your," rather than "we" or "they."
- *Keep a single focus.* Deliver a simple message instead of one that makes too many points. Focus on a single idea and support it.
- *Be conversational.* Use the language of everyday conversation. The copy should sound like two friends talking to one another, so don't shy away from incomplete sentences, thought fragments, and contractions.

Continuing **"Suggested Class Projects"** and new **"Suggested Internet Class Projects"** at the end of each chapter allow students to learn how to work in teams as advertisers do and how to use the Internet as a research and creative tool. Chapter 3's Internet Project asks students to note the differences in domestic and international advertising agency Web sites. In chapter 16, students are asked to analyze antismoking sites in terms of their effectiveness to reach a teen audience.

Suggested Class Projects

1. Working in a team, locate library materials on two organizational crises: one whose outcome was positive and the other negative. Do a short (two- to three-page) report explaining the reasons for these outcomes. Be prepared to present your findings to the class.
2. Divide the class into groups of three to four people. Each group should adopt a local cause that operates on a low budget and needs public relations help. As a team, develop a public relations plan for that nonprofit organization.

Suggested Internet Class Project

Consult the three anti-smoking Web sites mentioned in the effectiveness stories in this chapter and compare them in terms of their appeal to a teen audience. Which one do you think is the most interesting to this age group? Which one is the least interesting? Combine the best ideas from all

Practices

The "Hallmark Build-A-Campaign" feature shows students the winning brief of the American Advertising Federation's National Student Advertising Competition. Included as a model campaign in the appendix of the text, students can do advertising themselves by completing the Build-A-Campaign questions at the end of Chapters 3–19.

Hallmark BUILD•A•CAMPAIGN *Projects*

Please review the Hallmark Case Appendix at the end of the text before responding to these questions.

1. Meet in small groups to discuss how Capitol Advertising used television and radio to take advantage of each medium's key benefits and how it might have improved those uses.

2. Given the various advantages and disadvantages of television, radio, and interactive media, which of the three would best serve the needs of your local Gold Crown store? Why?

PART-ENDING CASE

Part III
Advertising Media

8 Media Planning and Buying
9 Print Media
10 Broadcast and Interactive Online Media

LOSE THAT BURGER BELLY

Chick-fil-A

A Company's Media Plan

NEW! "Part-Ending Cases."

We've kept the part-ending case format in this edition, but changed the company to the creative and irreverent advertising of Chick-fil-A. At the end of each part of the book we feature a presentation by advertising experts from Chick-fil-A. The cases focus on the fast food chain's corporate values and beliefs as well as its branding strategies. Questions at the end of each case make sure students have generally understood each part's main topic.

"Hands-on Cases" remain in the *Sixth Edition*. At the end of the chapter, students have the chance to become advertising decision makers themselves by analyzing a real-world advertising case. Students get to think critically about the many pieces of the puzzle that must fit together to create successful ads. New companies examined include Nike, John Hancock, Dodge, and Kraft.

HANDS-ON
Case 9
DODGE GOES NASCAR

There was a time when Dodge cars were the big winners in NASCAR events. But the 1970s and 1980s were not kind to Chrysler Motors and its Dodge division, and in 1981 a decision was made not to participate in NASCAR. Then in October 2000, Chrysler top management decided that there were good reasons to reenter the fray of racing. Most notably, the popularity of NASCAR and the Winston Cup circuit had skyrocketed during the 1990s. Also, Chrysler engineers had designed a turbo-charged vehicle that could compete with the current racing teams.

With only 250 days until the 2000 Daytona 500, the creative team at Chrysler's media agency, PentaCom, had the task of

television, you know that the race cars and the track are covered with ads. Dodge decided that an integrated sponsorship would be more effective than covering the car with ads. They signed on over 50 co-sponsors to leverage their marketing message. General Mills agreed to put a die-cast car from the Dodge race team in a window on the front of 14 million cereal boxes. Bill Elliott was also on the front of 3.5 million Wheaties boxes. In turn, these cereals added a new level of excitement to their products.

The final phase of the campaign occurred just a few days before the race. In addition to print ads appearing in magazines such as *Sports Illustrated* and *Field & Stream*, and newspapers such as *USA Today*, PentaCom also created an eight-page insert featuring the new Dodge team and placed it in several car-buff magazines. Finally, a 64-page custom-

SUPPLEMENTS

Our text forms a solid foundation for teaching and learning advertising principles and practices. We know, however, that in-class delivery can make or break the success of the message you want to send. Our extensive package is designed to enhance the teaching experience for the professor and the learning experience for the student.

FOR THE PROFESSOR

To teach this course effectively, you need an array of advertisements: commercials and stills, effective advertisements, and advertisements that somehow never seemed to resonate with viewers. We provide an extensive bank of advertisements, in several formats.

EFFIE award-winning commercials on video: Many of the chapter-opening EFFIE briefs are brought to life in your classroom by these actual, award-winning commercials.

New York Festivals Video: This collection of award-winning commercial advertisements from around the world is great for showing in class to emphasize advertising style and key concepts.

Additional advertisements: We have collected many advertisements to supplement those found in the book, so you never have to look anywhere else for advertisements that work—and some that do not.

As well as these commercial and still advertisements, we have provided a full range of classroom presentation resources to help you.

Instructor's Manual: The first stop in preparing for your class, the instructor's manual contains chapter overviews and objectives, plus lecture outlines and suggested answers to end-of-chapter questions. Also included are additional activities for both inside and outside the classroom.

Test Item File: This is brand new, completely revamped since the last edition. It includes over 100 questions per chapter consisting of multiple-choice, true/false, short-answer, and essay questions. Page references and difficulty level are provided for each question.

Prentice Hall Electronic Test Manager: The test item file is also available in an electronic version with our Windows-based Test Manager. Create exams and evaluate and track students' results. This test manager has been developed to be easily customizable for your individual needs.

PowerPoint Package (Now with 2 versions of slides!)

➤ PowerPoint Express: Easily customizable for even the most novice user, this presentation includes basic chapter outlines and key points from each chapter. The best option if you want to incorporate your own material.

➤ PowerPoint Expanded: Includes the basics found in the Express version but also advertisements and art from the text. This is the best option if you want a complete presentation solution!

    Both Powerpoint presentations are available from the Prentice Hall Website at **www.prenhall.com/wellsburnett** *and on the Instructor Resource CD-ROM.*

Instructor's Resource CD-ROM: The one source for all of your supplement needs. This Instructor CD contains all the print and technology supplements on a single CD-ROM. Enjoy the freedom to transport the entire supplements package from home, to office, to classroom. The Instructor CD-ROM enables you to customize any of the ancillaries, print only the chapters or materials you wish to use, or access any item from the package within the classroom.

On Location Videos: We have more than just videos of commercial advertisements. This set of videos goes behind the scenes to examine the advertising process—perfect for starting classroom discussions and an excellent basis for assignments and activities.

Overhead Transparencies: Available as acetates or PowerPoint slides. Includes important figures, advertisements, and key concepts from the text.

Expanded Companion Website:
Go beyond the text. Our acclaimed Web resource provides professors with a customized course Website that features a complete array of teaching and learning material. Instructors can download the Instructor's Resource Manual and Powerpoint slides, plus view additional resources such as current events and Internet exercises. Or, try the Syllabus Builder to plan your own course. Just go to **www.prenhall.com/wellsburnett.**

Innovative Online Courses: We provide standard Online Courses in Blackboard, WebCT, and CourseCompass. No technical expertise is needed. Teach a complete online course or a Web-enhanced course. Add your own materials, take advantage of online testing and Gradebook opportunities, and utilize the bulletin board and discussion board functions. All courses are free to your students with purchase of the text.

FOR THE STUDENT

Media Buying Role Play Simulation: This unique class-tested simulation lets students experience actual media buys and sells. Simply divide your class into "buy" or "sell" teams, and the free manual guides them through the exercise.

Expanded Companion Website: Go beyond the text with a customized course Website that features a complete array of learning material. An interactive Student Study Guide with chapter by chapter quizzes provides a way for students to test their mastery of the material. **www.prenhall.com/wellsburnett**

Advertising Adventure: Looking for additional practice in evaluating advertisements? This CD-ROM contains hundreds of award-winning ads culled from the New York Festivals. Instructors can use the teaching notes available online. Take a look at **www.prenhall.com/adventure.** The CD-ROM can be packaged with the text for a nominal fee; use ISBN 0-13-102566-X.

A FINAL WORD

Acknowledgments

Advertising: Principles and Practice, Sixth Edition, has benefited from an outstanding team of reviewers and contributors.

We especially would like to thank the following reviewers:

Laurie Babin, *University of Southern Mississippi*
Janice Bukovac, *Michigan State University*
Steve Edwards, *Michigan State University*
Thomas Kim Hixson, *University of Wisconsin-Whitewater*
Cathy Johnson, *Angelo State University, Texas*
Melissa Moore, *Mississippi State University*
Robert Moore, *Mississippi State University*
Allen Schaefer, *Southwest Missouri State University*
Dr. Richard Shainwald, *College of Charleston, South Carolina*
Michael Weigold, *University of Florida*

William Wells
John Burnett
Sandra Moriarty

CHAPTER

1

Introduction to Advertising

CHAPTER OBJECTIVES

When you have completed this chapter, you should be able to

1. Discuss the elements of effective advertising.
2. Define advertising and identify its types and roles.
3. Identify the five players in the advertising world.
4. Generally explain the evolution of the advertising industry and the current issues it faces.

The Lemon Is Sweet

Award: *EFFIE Silver 2001, Automotive category*

Company: *Volkswagen of America*

Agency: *Arnold Worldwide*

Campaign: *"Volkswagen Owners Really Love Their Cars"*

Ask anyone who grew up in the 1960s and they can provide a chronology of VW ads created by the Doyle Dan Bernback advertising agency: "Think Small," "Lemon," "The Floating Car," "The Egg Car," "Ugly is Only Skin Deep." This creative genius continued through the early 1970s and VW became an advertising icon. Then the bottom dropped out of Volkswagen's marketing world, and the product disappeared from sight.

From the late 1970s into the early 1990s, Volkswagen switched agencies a few times. Clever ad campaigns were created, but they were not effective enough to drive sales compared to the ads produced in the 1960s and 1970s. Instead, U.S. sales were dropping. By 1993, less than 50,000 Volkswagens were sold in the United States per year. With so few sales, Volkswagen was considering discontinuing its product line in the United States. Fortunately, however, there was a switch in management at Volkswagen between 1993 and 1994.

The new management spurred the search for a new ad agency to help regain sales in the United States. Arnold Communications of Boston won the bid to represent the company and successfully launched the "Drivers Wanted" campaign in 1995–1996. While the Asian competitors were advertising safe and reliable features, the VW campaign was focusing on quality German engineering and driving fun for a unique and active lifestyle, which appeared to reconnect emotionally with the target audience. From 1997 to 1999, VW engaged in extensive redesign on all its models, introducing the unbelievably successful New Beetle. VW continued to use the "Drivers Wanted" tagline as an umbrella for all of its new models. Every key measure of advertising effectiveness exceeded expectations.

So, what do you do when you have new models to introduce and you need a new campaign before the current one gets too old? Volkswagen marketers caught a lucky break. As they were formulating their grand campaign for 2000, they received the annual report from JD Powers & Associates on customer satisfaction. The report noted that Volkswagen owners are more satisfied with their cars than are other car owners. VW decided to capitalize on this information to sustain brand momentum. The idea was to use the brand's unique personality to illustrate just how much VW owners loved their cars and to thank their consumers for it.

Enter its 2000, EFFIE-award winning "VW owners really love their cars" campaign. The target audience for this new campaign was young, affluent individuals as well as the current VW consumer. Research showed that attitudinally, VW drivers are different and proud of it, and that they have a unique relationship with their cars. It was this relationship that inspired the campaign in which VW pays tribute to its consumers for appreciating their product in exaggerated ways, or "for the lengths they will go to protect their Volkswagens." The commercial pictured here shows a man tackling a wayward grocery cart before it hit his Jetta.

Just how effective was the VW campaign? Check the "It's a Wrap" box at the end of this chapter.

THE MANDATE FOR EFFECTIVENESS

Today, advertising finds itself in a serious bind. With a down economy, the tragedy of 9/11, and new technology that may threaten the way advertising operates, there is a need to rethink advertising as a strategic alternative. Advertising will only survive and grow if it focuses on being effective. All advertisers are expecting specific results, based on their stated objectives. Clients expect proof, and, for the most part, that proof must lead to or actually produce sales. It is no longer acceptable to tell a client, "Our ads work, we just don't know how, when, and with what results."

The basic premise of this book is that *advertising must be effective*; it must achieve its objectives. To that end, we teach you about advertising strategies that produce effective results. The VW campaign that introduced this chapter was an effective campaign. That doesn't mean that all VW campaigns have been effective. In fact, VW ads were considered outstanding during the 1960s, through the creative genius of Bill Bernbach. Then, for the next 30 years, VW lost its way, sales dropped, advertising was ineffective, and product development was poor. *Advertising cannot save bad products.*

Because we are so concerned about effectiveness, we will introduce most chapters with an ad that has won an EFFIE or an equivalent award. There are hundreds of major awards that are given to ads, with the CLIOs being the most famous, equivalent to the Oscar in the movie industry. The great majority of these advertising awards tend to focus on creativity, not effectiveness. The EFFIE is one exception. To quote from its Web site: "The New York American Marketing Association introduced the EFFIE Awards in 1968. It is the only national award to recognize creative achievement in meeting and exceeding advertising objectives. As such, it honors the 'real world' work of agency/client partnerships that create, manage and build brands that have become a part of the American landscape." (Visit EFFIE Worldwide at www.effie.org for more information.)

WHAT MAKES AN AD EFFECTIVE?

How and why was the 2001 VW campaign effective? Explicit objectives should drive the planning, creation, and execution of each ad. Did VW do this? Ads should work with other forms of marketing communication to reach customers. Did VW do this, too?

Only the advertiser (and the supporting ad agency) knows whether the ad campaign reached its objectives, and whether the ad truly was worth the money. Effective ads, the focus of this text, are ads that help the advertiser reach its goals.

But are all award-winning ads effective ads? Not necessarily. In August 1996, Nissan launched one of the most memorable advertising campaigns in automotive history. Lively, music-filled commercials featured dogs, dolls, a grinning Japanese man, and the friendly tagline, "Enjoy the Ride." One spot had an action figure pick up his Barbie-like date in a toy car to the tune of Van Halen's "You Really Got Me." *Time Magazine* named it the best commercial of the year. Nissan poured $330 million into the campaign.

Too bad it didn't sell cars. Nissan's U.S. sales declined steadily during the first six months of the campaign, and, more alarmingly, the number of consumers planning to buy a Nissan was at its lowest point in six years. Dealers were irate because the campaign didn't show the car. Nissan posted a $518 million loss in fiscal 1998. Needless to say, the company cancelled the campaign.

Characteristics of Effective Ads

Effective ads work on two levels. First, they should satisfy consumers' objectives by engaging them and delivering a relevant message. And, as we said, the ads must achieve the advertiser's objectives.

Initially, a consumer may be interested in watching an ad for its entertainment value or to satisfy her curiosity. If the ad is sufficiently entertaining, she may remember it. However, she may then learn that the ad relates to a personal need and provides relevant information about how to satisfy that need. The ad may also offer enough incentive for the consumer to risk change because it shows her how to satisfy her needs in a manageable way. Further, ads may reinforce her product decisions and remind her of how her needs have been satisfied.

The advertiser's objectives differ from the consumer's. Ultimately, advertisers want consumers to buy and keep buying their goods and services. To move consumers to action, they must gain their attention. They must then hold their interest long enough to convince them to change their purchasing behavior, try their product, and stick with their product.

Holiday Inn developed a campaign that strives to keep consumers' interest. Its ads grab your attention through humor and a funny cast of characters. There's Mark (the returning son), Mom, Dad, Grandma, and in some ads, an outsider. "Mark, listen, you're 37 years old," Dad says in an ad. "Thirty-seven and a half," Mark corrects him proudly. Mom takes it from there. "Mark, you're an adult. It's time to chip in around here." Mark, in a bathrobe, with morning stubble on his face, his hair tousled like a toddler just up from an afternoon nap, replies, "Grandma doesn't pay to live here." "Grandma's 93!" Mom says incredulously. "Well, there you go," says Mark, who then compares himself to Larry. "Larry's a dog!" says Mom. "Yeah, I'm a kid and kids should stay for free, and eat for free," says Mark. "What does this look like, a Holiday Inn?" Dad asks. Then the entire family, including Grandma, screams with laughter, except Mark, who can't understand their remarks.[1]

The campaign's humor means that it is likely to satisfy the viewer's curiosity and need for entertainment. The consumer will probably remember the ad, and because it is such a likeable campaign it will reinforce the good feelings/satisfaction of consumers who already stay at Holiday Inn.

The campaign also tries to undo the negative associations consumers had with Holiday Inn during the 1980s and early 1990s. They complained of dirty rooms, poor food, and outdated technology at many Holiday Inn franchises. Holiday Inn's ads take on these issues.

However, the campaign lacks detailed information. It doesn't list room rates or locations, for example. Does that mean it isn't an effective ad campaign? It depends on the advertiser's goals, but such information would increase an ad's chances of accomplishing the specific objectives.

Three broad dimensions characterize effective advertising: strategy, creativity, and execution. This book highlights these three dimensions (see Figure 1.1).

Holiday Inn has used the "Mark and His Family" campaign to increase sales as well as change customer attitudes.

Strategy Every effective ad implements a sound strategy. The advertiser develops the ad to meet specific objectives, carefully directs it to a certain audience, creates its message to speak to that audience's most important concerns, and runs it in media (print, broadcast, or the Internet, for instance) that will reach its audience most effectively.

Creativity The creative concept is the ad's central idea that grabs your attention and sticks in your memory. The lengths to which VW owners will go in order to save their cars is a strong creative concept.

A concern for creative thinking drives the entire field of advertising. Planning the strategy calls for imaginative problem solving: The research efforts need to be creative, and the buying and placing of ads in the media require creative thinking. Advertising is an exciting field because of the constant demand for imaginative solutions to media and message problems.

Execution Finally, effective ads are well executed. That means that the details, the photography, setting, printing, and the production values all have been fine-tuned. Many of these techniques are standard in the industry, such as the use of products created by Adobe, a popular computer graphics software manufacturer.

Good advertisers know that how you say something is just as important as what you say. What you say comes from strategy, whereas how you say it is a product of creativity and execution. Strategy, creativity, and execution all contribute to whether an ad wins an award. But, as noted in the "A Matter of Principle" box, winning awards is only important if advertising objectives are achieved.

Advertising Must Be Goal-Directed

Although these three conditions must be met for an advertisement/campaign to be considered effective, they are not isolated. They depend on the types of impacts advertisers hope to create in the minds of the people who read, view, or listen to the ads.

FIGURE 1.1

EFFECTIVE ADS CONNECT THREE ELEMENTS

Strategy, creativity, and execution must work in concert for an ad to be truly effective.

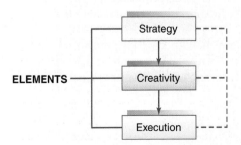

A MATTER OF PRINCIPLE

PRIZES GALORE

▶ Very few industries are more awards-conscious than the ad agency business. Visit the New York offices of Cliff Freeman & Partners and you are greeted in the reception area and escorted to the agency's presentation room. Along the entire length of an 80-foot corridor, you walk past the agency's vast collection of creative awards. Surprisingly, every award is sitting on the floor. Why? They simply ran out of room.

Creative awards are avidly sought and highly regarded by agencies for their ability to:

- raise employee morale and build teamwork
- attract new creative hires to the agency
- generate new business
- establish the agency's reputation as a creative force

Despite the casual way awards are often deployed, they do vary in importance. Cannes, the One Show, DNAD (Great Britain), the CLIOs, and the Kelly Awards from the Magazine Publishers of America top the list. The awards given by *Communication Arts* magazine, the OBIE's and the EFFIEs, are considered very important as well.

Some agencies view these awards as an opportunity to cement relationships. For instance, Howard Merree & Partners, Raleigh, NC, doesn't keep its awards. After taking a picture of the award itself, it's handed over to the client on whose behalf the work was done.

Senior Vice President Mike Ganey notes, "It's really that the agency is winning the award on behalf of the client. Our clients come to us for good strategic thinking, and what we like most are the EFFIE awards, which show that the campaigns we produce are truly effective for our clients' business."

Is the effort worth it? Ron Berger, chief executive officer and chief creative officer at Messner Vetere Berger McNamee Schmetterer/Euro RSCG New York, answers this question as follows: "Current clients may like it when their work wins an award, but if that work isn't providing the results that are most intended, it won't be a long-lived appreciation. It almost always backfires, because the agency is proud of the award-winning work, but the client is unhappy because its work isn't selling the product." Still, "winning is kinda cool," notes Ron Lawner, chairman and chief creative officer of Arnold Worldwide in Boston, "especially when it's an international show, like Cannes."

POINT TO PONDER

How do you view awards?

Source: Laurie Freeman, "Just Awards," *Agency* (Fall 2001): 11–14.

Understanding the various types of intended effects that typically are the goals of advertising is the way we evaluate whether an ad is effective. However, effectiveness only occurs to the degree that certain effects—such as the impact or results of a message—are accomplished. In order, then, to understand what effectiveness means in advertising, you need to have an idea of the key effects, or results, that advertising can typically accomplish.

Figure 1.2 is a simplified model of a set of typical effects that advertisers hope to achieve. In this model, the first level is perception, which means the advertiser hopes the ad will be noticed and remembered. Then there are two categories of effects that are either focused on learning, which means the audience will understand the message and make the correct associations, or persuasion, which means the advertiser hopes to create or change attitudes and touch emotions. The last major category of effects is behavior—getting the audience to try or buy the product, or perform some other action.

In advertising strategy and planning, we refer to these effects as objectives. Every advertiser, deep down inside, hopes or assumes that each ad will produce sales. However, we know that to get to the sale, there are communication activities that need to take place and these are often the best indicators of the success of an advertising message, because other marketing variables may have more impact on sales. The relationship may be causal—the ad created $$ in sales response—or it may only make a partial contribution or lead prospects part of the way to sales. It may also reflect the kinds of communication effects that messages can be expected to deliver, such as understanding or conviction.

In addition, two other assumptions must be considered in analyzing advertising objectives. First, advertising communication objectives are derived from the company's marketing objectives. So, if Red Robin restaurants has an objective to increase market share by 5 percent, this should have a direct impact on the stated communication objectives. In other words, the advertising objectives are designed to contribute to the accomplishment

Ground Zero, an advertising agency in Los Angeles, stores all its awards in trash cans. "It helps maintain their perspective."

of this market share objective. The second assumption is that any of the communication objectives may be legitimate, even the ones that aren't focused directly on a sale. For example, Expedia.com is a new consulting company and it views its advertising as a way to draw attention to itself, create name recognition, and create understanding of the products and services it sells.

Effectiveness Factors

The key effects from Figure 1.2, which are used to determine the effectiveness of an advertisement, are further explained in Table 1.1. Here the key categories of message

FIGURE 1.2

A MODEL OF KEY EFFECTS (CATEGORIES OF EFFECTIVENESS) First, advertisers try to get consumers to perceive—at least notice—their ads. Then advertisers hope consumers will either learn something or be persuaded by something in the ads. Finally, advertisers try to get consumers to behave in a certain way—ideally, to buy the product in the ad.

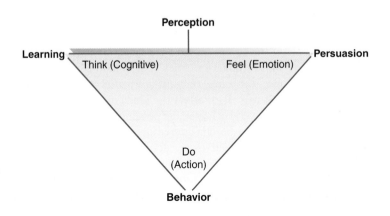

effects are listed down the left side. The second column is labeled "surrogate measures" and refers to the way advertisers evaluate how well the advertising worked—how effective the advertising was in meeting its objectives. The advertising industry, led by agencies, has developed a set of measures that are indicators of these key effects. The exact terminology will vary, but the effectiveness of most advertising is evaluated based on such factors as consumers' exposure, attention, interest, and so forth.

The next column lists the communication tool or tools that may be most appropriate for achieving the objective. Even though this book focuses on advertising, we recognize that advertising is just one part of the market communication mix, along with sales promotion, public relations, direct marketing, events, and personal selling. There are communication objectives that are more effectively accomplished through advertising, but there are situations where other communication tools may be more effective.

An examination of Table 1.1 shows that advertising is effective in accomplishing several objectives; for instance, creating exposure, attention, and awareness. It is also good at providing a reminder to the customer and encouraging repurchase. However, other marketing communication tools, such as sales promotion, are better at getting people to respond with a purchase or other types of actions.

Few ad campaigns exhibit all the elements of effective advertising and also follow the process in Figure 1.2.

One example of an effective campaign is the 1995 campaign produced by Atlanta-based Chick-fil-A restaurants. Experts in the food industry give two reasons why the sandwich maker became one of the restaurant industry's fastest-growing chains. One reason was American's shift away from red meat and toward chicken consumption. The other reason was the idea to capitalize on this shift and dramatize it through a worried-looking Holstein cow. The bovine pitchman offered three reasons to eat at Chick-fil-A: "It's good for you, it tastes good, it's not us."

The cow campaign earned Chick-fil-A many awards, thanks to those classy bovines, including a 1996 OBIE from the Outdoor Advertising Association of America, a 1997 Silver Lion from the Cannes International Advertising Festival, and a 1998 Silver EFFIE for creativity and effectiveness. The company has also sold thousands of calendars, t-shirts, and other store merchandise from the campaign.

We will explain more about the Chick-fil-A company throughout this book. A Chick-fil-A feature is found at the end of each of the five parts of the book.

TABLE 1.1   **Message Effectiveness Factors**

Key Message Effects	Surrogate Measures	Communication Tools
Perception	Exposure	Advertising Media; Public Relations
	Attention	Advertising; Sales Promotion
	Interest	Advertising; Sales Promotion; Public Relations
	Memory: Recognition/Recall	Advertising; Sales Promotion; Public Relations
Learning	Understanding	Public Relations; Personal Selling; Direct Marketing; Advertising
	Image and Association Brand Links	Advertising; Public Relations; Point of Purchase Ads
Persuasion	Attitudes: Form or Change Preference/Intention	Public Relations; Personal Selling; Sales Promotion
	Emotions and Involvement	Advertising; Public Relations; Personal Selling Events
	Conviction: Belief, Commitment	Personal Selling; Direct Marketing
Behavior	Trial	Sales Promotion; Personal Selling; Direct Marketing
	Purchase	Sales Promotion; Personal Selling; Direct Marketing
	Repeat Purchase, Use More	Sales Promotion; Personal Selling; Direct Marketing

THE WORLD OF ADVERTISING

In this section we define advertising by analyzing its six elements. Then we examine the types and roles of advertising.

Defining Advertising

What is advertising? What are its elements? The standard definition of advertising has six elements. First, advertising is a paid form of communication, although some forms of advertising, such as public service announcements (PSAs), use donated space and time. Second, not only is the message paid for, but the sponsor is identified. Third, most advertising tries to persuade or influence the consumer to do something, although in some cases the point of the message is simply to make consumers aware of the product or company. Fourth, the message is conveyed through many different kinds of mass media, and fifth, advertising reaches a large audience of potential consumers. Finally, because advertising is a form of mass communication, it is also nonpersonal. A definition of advertising, then, includes all six elements.

Advertising is paid nonpersonal communication from an identified sponsor using mass media to persuade or influence an audience.

In an ideal world every manufacturer would be able to talk one-on-one with every consumer about its product. But personal selling, a one-on-one approach, is very expensive. Today, advertisers can provide customization through interactive media such as the World Wide Web, but it is not the same as meeting with every customer individually to discuss a product or service. Still, what does this have to do with defining advertising? The key point is that interactive advertising reaches a large audience, just like traditional advertising.

The costs for time in broadcast media, for space in print media, and for time and space in interactive and support media are spread over the tremendous number of people that these media reach. For example, $2 million may sound like a lot of money for one Super

This ad uses humor to create brand awareness.

Bowl ad, but when you consider that the advertisers are reaching over 500 million people, the cost is not so extreme.

Types of Advertising

Advertising is complex because so many different advertisers try to reach so many different types of audiences. Let's examine nine major types of advertising.

Brand Advertising The most visible type of advertising is national consumer, or brand advertising. Brand advertising focuses on the development of a long-term brand identity and image. One of the TV commercials for Worldspan illustrates how an ad can use humor to create brand awareness.

Retail or Local Advertising A great deal of advertising focuses on retailers or manufacturers that sell their merchandise in a restricted area. In the case of retail advertising, the message announces facts about products that are available in nearby stores. The objectives tend to focus on stimulating store traffic, and creating a distinctive image for the retailer. Local advertising can refer to a retailer or a manufacturer or distributor who offers products in a fairly restricted geographic area. White Wave, who manufactures Silk brand soy milk in Boulder, Colorado, will likely be a national brand by the time you read this line.

Political Advertising Politicians use advertising to persuade people to vote for them or their ideas, so it is an important part of the political process in the United States and other countries that permit candidate advertising. Critics worry that political advertising tends to focus more on image than on issues, meaning that voters concentrate on the emotional part of the message or candidate, often overlooking important differences.

Directory Advertising Another type of advertising is called directory advertising because people refer to it to find out how to buy a product or service. The best-known form of directory advertising is the Yellow Pages, although there are many other kinds of directories such as trade directories, organization directories, and so forth.

Direct-Response Advertising Direct-response advertising can use any advertising medium, including direct mail, but the message is different from that of national and retail advertising in that it tries to stimulate a sale directly. The consumer can respond by

Silk Soymilk is advertising started as a local campaign.

telephone or mail, and the product is delivered directly to the consumer by mail or some other carrier. Of particular importance has been the evolution of the Internet as an advertising medium.

Business-to-Business Advertising Business-to-business advertising includes only messages directed at retailers, wholesalers, and distributors, and from industrial purchasers and professionals such as lawyers and physicians to other businesses, but not to general consumers. Advertisers place most business advertising in publications or professional journals. One ad for Interland is an example of a typical business-to-business ad.

Institutional Advertising Institutional advertising is also called corporate advertising. These messages focus on establishing a corporate identity or winning the public over to the organization's point of view. Many of the tobacco companies are running ads that focus on the positive things they are now doing, and ads for America's Pharmaceutical Companies are also adopting that focus.

Public Service Advertising Public service announcements (PSAs) communicate a message on behalf of some good cause, such as stopping drunk driving (Mothers Against Drunk Driving) or preventing child abuse. These advertisements are usually created by advertising professionals free of charge and the media often donate the space and time.

Interactive Advertising Interactive advertising is delivered to individual consumers who have access to a computer and the Internet. Advertisers use Web pages, banner ads, and e-mail to deliver their messages. In this instance, the consumer can respond to the ad or ignore it.

Business-to-Business advertising is a big market.

We all know about the tremendous growth in Internet usage. Today, some 100 million U.S. households are dialing into the Internet, up from just 6 million in 1994. Total U.S. purchasing on the Web is expected to skyrocket from zero in 1994 to about $1.7 trillion in 2003.[2] Companies spent almost $2 billion in Web advertising in 2000, and spending is expected to increase to almost $9 billion in 2003.

We see, then, that there isn't just one kind of advertising. In fact, advertising is a large and varied industry. All types of advertising demand creative, original messages that are strategically sound and well executed. In upcoming chapters, we discuss each type of advertising in greater depth.

Roles of Advertising

Advertising also can be explained in terms of the four roles it plays in business and in society:

1. Marketing
2. Communication
3. Economic
4. Societal

Let's briefly explore each of these roles.

The Marketing Role **Marketing** is the process a business uses to satisfy consumer needs and wants through goods and services. The particular consumers at whom the company directs its marketing effort constitute the *target market*. The tools available to marketing include the *product*, its *price*, and the means used to deliver the product, or the *place*. Marketing also includes a method for communicating this information to the consumer called *marketing communication*, or *promotion*. These four tools are collectively referred to as the marketing mix or the four Ps.

Marketing communication consists of several related communication techniques, including advertising, sales promotion, public relations, and personal selling. The role of

This institutional ad for a trade association uses a heart-tugging visual and copy to show consumers the value of the organization's activities: producing pharmaceutical drugs that help save lives.

This ad campaign for America's Beef Producers was a critical part of their marketing effort.

advertising, within marketing, is to carry persuasive messages to actual and potential customers. One advertising campaign that has been very effective is the "It's What's for Dinner" campaign, started over 20 years ago when the America's Beef Producers trade association decided that the decline in beef consumption, due to consumers' concern for personal health, had to be reversed. Starting with a TV commercial, featuring the voice of actor Robert Mitchum, America learned that beef went along with mom and apple pie. Since that initial ad, beef consumption has stabilized and increased 12 percent.

The Communication Role Advertising is a form of mass communication. It transmits different types of market information to match buyers and sellers in the marketplace. Advertising both informs and transforms the product by creating an image that goes beyond straightforward facts.

The Economic Role There are two points of view about how advertising affects an economy. In the first, advertising is so persuasive that it decreases the likelihood that a consumer will switch to an alternative product, regardless of the price charged. By featuring other positive attributes, and avoiding price, the consumer makes a decision on these various nonprice benefits.

The second approach views advertising as a vehicle for helping consumers assess value, through price as well as other elements such as quality, location, and reputation. Rather than diminishing the importance of price as a basis for comparison, advocates of this school view the role of advertising as a means to objectively provide price/value information, thereby creating a more rational economy.[3] It should be noted that neither perspective has been verified, and it is presumed that advertising likely represents both economic models.

The Societal Role Advertising also has a number of social roles. It informs us about new and improved products and helps us compare products and features and make informed consumer decisions. It mirrors fashion and design trends and adds to our aesthetic sense. Advertising tends to flourish in societies that enjoy some level of economic abundance, in which supply exceeds demand. In these societies, advertising moves from being informational only to creating a demand for a particular brand.

The question is: Does advertising follow trends or does it lead them? At what point does advertising cross the line between *reflecting* social values and *creating* social values? Critics argue that advertising repeatedly has crossed this line, influencing vulnerable groups, such as young teenagers, too strongly. The increasing power of advertising, both in terms of money (we spend more annually educating consumers than we spend educating our children) and in terms of communication dominance (the mass media can no longer survive without advertising support), has made these concerns more prominent than ever.

Can advertising manipulate people? Some critics argue that advertising has the power to dictate how people behave. They believe that even if an individual ad cannot control our behavior, the cumulative effects of nonstop television, radio, print, and outdoor ads can be overwhelming.

The evidence demonstrating the manipulative power of advertising is shaky because so many other factors contribute to the choices we make. Still, advertisers are not objective and often slant or omit information to their benefit. In the next chapter we delve into manipulation and other ethical issues.

Functions of Advertising

Even though each ad or campaign tries to accomplish goals unique to its sponsor, advertising performs three basic functions.

- *Provides product and brand information.* Although many ads are devoid of information, providing the consumer with relevant information that will aid decision making is still the main function of advertising. The information given depends on the needs of the target audience. In the case of purchasing a new suit, needed information might be price and outlet location. For technical products, the information is likely to be very detailed. For VW, the information was both technical and motivational.
- *Provides incentives to take action.* In most instances, consumers are reluctant to change their buying behavior. Even if they are somewhat dissatisfied with their current product, a habit has been established and learning about a new product is difficult. Advertising sometimes gives the consumer reasons to switch brands, if that's the goal. Convenience, high quality, lower price, warranties—these all might be stressed in advertising.
- *Provides reminders and reinforcement.* Much advertising is directed at keeping current customers. Consumers forget why they bought a particular brand of microwave or automobile. Advertising must constantly remind the consumer about the name of the brand, its benefits, its value, and so forth. These same messages help reinforce the consumer's decision. Most TV advertising provides this function.

Table 1.2 summarizes the types, roles, and functions of advertising that we have just examined. In the next section we examine the five players in advertising.

TABLE 1.2 Advertising Types, Roles, and Functions: A Summary

Types	Roles
Brand	Marketing
Retail/local	Communication
Political	Economic
Directory	Societal
Direct-response	
Business-to-business	**Functions**
Institutional	Product/brand information
Public service	Incentives to take action
Interactive	Reminder/reinforcement

THE FIVE PLAYERS OF ADVERTISING

In addition to the types of advertising and their various roles and functions, advertising can be defined in terms of those who play important roles in bringing ads to the consumer. Here are the five key players in the advertising world:

1. The advertiser
2. The advertising agency
3. The media
4. The vendor
5. The audience

Let's look at each of these players and what they do.

The Advertiser

Advertising begins with the **advertiser**, the person or organization that "needs to get out a message." The advertiser also makes the final decisions about the target audience, the media that will carry the advertising, the size of the advertising budget, and the length of the campaign. Finally, the advertiser pays the bills. The 25 leading U.S. advertisers, in respect to media spending, are displayed in Table 1.3.

TABLE 1.3   25 Leaders by U.S. Advertising Spending

Rank 2000	Rank 1999	Advertiser	Headquarters	Total U.S. Ad Spending 2000	Total U.S. Ad Spending 1999
1	1	General Motors Corp.	Detroit	$3,934.8	$4,118.4
2	3	Philip Morris Cos.	New York	2,602.9	2,527.3
3	2	Procter & Gamble Co.	Cincinnati	2,363.5	2,694.0
4	5	Ford Motor Co.	Dearborn, Mich.	2,345.2	2,111.1
5	4	Pfizer	New York	2,265.3	2,142.7
6	6	PepsiCo	Purchase, N.Y.	2,100.7	2,010.4
7	7	DaimlerChrysler	Auburn Hills, Mich./Stuttgart, Germany	1,984.0	1,801.8
8	10	AOL Time Warner	New York	1,770.1	1,523.0
9	9	Walt Disney Co.	Burbank, Calif.	1,757.5	1,545.2
10	26	Verizon Communications	New York	1,612.9	977.5
11	8	Johnson & Johnson	New Brunswick, N.J.	1,601.2	1,666.7
12	11	Sears, Roebuck & Co.	Hoffman Estates, Ill.	1,455.4	1,460.2
13	13	Unilever	London/Rotterdam	1,453.6	1,225.9
14	12	AT&T Corp.	Basking Ridge, N.J.	1,415.7	1,430.6
15	19	General Electric Co.	Fairfield, Conn.	1,310.1	1,111.1
16	18	Toyota Motor Corp.	Toyota City, Japan	1,273.9	1,124.4
17	14	McDonald's Corp.	Oak Brook, Ill.	1,273.9	1,203.8
18	24	U.S. Government	Washington	1,246.3	1,010.8
19	28	Sprint Corp.	Westwood, Kan.	1,227.3	932.9
20	16	Viacom	New York	1,220.9	1,189.7
21	25	Bristol-Myers Squibb Co.	New York	1,190.7	1,009.6
22	17	IBM Corp.	Armonk, N.Y.	1,189.0	1,130.9
23	21	Federated Department Stores	Cincinnati	1,127.6	1,054.6
24	27	GlaxoSmithKline	Greenford, Middlesex, U.K.	1,126.4	969.4
25	15	Diageo	London	1,112.1	1,199.2

Note: Dollars are in millions. 1999 rankings represent data compiled in 2001.

Source: Reprinted with permission from the September 24, 2001, issue of *Advertising Age.* Copyright ©, Crain Communications Inc. 2001.

THE INSIDE STORY

THE DAY-TO-DAY JOB OF AN ACCOUNT EXECUTIVE

Tammie DeGrasse Account Executive
McCann-Erickson, New York

"So what exactly do you do in advertising?" That is by far the most common question I am asked once someone finds out I'm in Account Management. "Do you create the ads?" "Do you choose the actors?" "Do you decide which magazines to run in?" To be honest, I don't think my own mother has it figured out, yet. I've since realized that the best way to define what we, as account people, do in advertising is . . . make it all happen. To use a simple analogy, an account manager is like the supervisor in a car factory's assembly line. We don't physically connect part A to part B; but we do make sure every department fully understands what the car is supposed to look like and how it should run to ensure that it will be created effectively and efficiently, so it can sell.

That's just the big picture; my day-to-day duties aren't so lofty. Now, I could break it down and give you an idea of my typical 9 to 5 day; but to be honest, in advertising there's no such thing as "typical" or "9 to 5." My day entails anything and everything to make sure the job gets done. Whether it's literally running tapes to NBC, viewing casting reels for the next commercial, researching our clients' top competitors, watching focus groups describe what they think makes a good ad (that's always fun), or attending television shoots . . . my days are any-

thing but typical. Some highlights during my career at McCann include watching a handful of celebrities read our scripts in a recording session and even having myself featured in a national newspaper ad (Hey, anything to get the job done, right?).

Nonetheless, it's been amazing so far and a valuable learning experience every step of the way.

For those of you considering entering the advertising industry, deciding which area to concentrate in can be difficult. Every department is so equally appetizing; anyone would have trouble figuring out what the best fit for him or her might be. Being that I possess leadership qualities, enjoy strategizing, and like to get my hands in just about everything, Account Management seemed like my perfect fit. For others it may not be so easy, so I strongly suggest learning more about the specifics of every group. Keep in mind that there are pros and cons to each and only you can decipher which end of the factory assembly line you would be best to work on. That's all for now—have to run . . . client dinner in ten minutes. Best of luck to all of you! "

Tammie DeGrasse graduated Magna Cum Laude from Florida State University, in the spring of 2000. She then began her career at McCann-Erickson as an Assistant Account Executive, working on two multimillion-dollar accounts (Gateway and Burger King) and was promoted to Account Executive after a little more than a year on the job.

Nominated by Professor Kartik Pashupati, Florida State University.

The Advertising Agency

The second player in the advertising world is the advertising agency. Advertisers hire independent agencies to plan and implement part or all of their advertising efforts. This working arrangement is known as the agency–client partnership. See "The Inside Story" for a look at how ad agencies function.

In 2000, ad agency gross income was $32.6 billion worldwide, on billing of $295 billion among U.S. agencies, according to *Advertising Age*'s annual agency report. The big three ad organizations were Omnicom Group, WPP Group, and Interpublic Group of Companies. The top three U.S. ad agencies were Grey Worldwide, J. Walter Thompson, and McCann-Erickson Worldwide. Arnold Worldwide of Boston is the agency that produced the EFFIE-winning campaign for VW; it is ranked twenty-first among U.S. agencies and had billings of $1.3 billion in 2000.[4]

An advertiser uses an outside agency because it believes the agency will be more efficient in creating an individual commercial or a complete campaign. Successful agencies typically have strategic and creative expertise, media knowledge, workforce talent, and the ability to negotiate good deals for clients.

Large advertisers, either companies or organizations, participate in the advertising process either through their advertising departments or through their in-house agencies, as we see in Figure 1.3.

WHEN THE ADVERTISER HAS AN IN-HOUSE AGENCY

WHEN THE ADVERTISER DOESN'T HAVE AN IN-HOUSE AGENCY

```
Advertising          Internal Advertising
Organization    →        Department
                             ↓
                    In-House Agency
                    • Research/Planning
                    • Creative Development
                    • Media
                    • Production
```

```
Advertising              Advertising
Organization    →        Department
                             ↓
                    External Agencies
                    • Full-Service Agency
                    • Media Specialists
                    • Creative Boutiques
                    • Vendors (freelance writers,
                      lighting specialists, etc.)
```

FIGURE 1.3   SAMPLE STRUCTURES OF THE ADVERTISING PROCESS

Large advertisers have two choices when it comes to producing ads: Use their own internal advertising department or hire an outside agency.

The Advertising Department Most large businesses have advertising departments. Their primary responsibility is to act as a liaison between the marketing department and the advertising agency (or agencies) and other vendors. Depending on the business, the involvement of the marketing department can vary tremendously from company to company; and committees are quite common. The individual in charge of the advertising department may carry a title such as Director of Advertising or Advertising Manager. Typically, that person has extensive experience in all the facets of advertising. In fact, many have had jobs on the agency side, so they may have worked with advertisers in various capacities and are familiar with their operations.

As indicated, the task of the advertising manager and the staff is to facilitate the interaction between the company's marketing department and the agencies. Many companies may have hundreds of agencies working for them, although they normally have an **agency-of-record**, which does most of their business and may even manage the other agencies. Tasks performed by the advertising department include the following: it selects the agencies; coordinates activities with vendors, such as media, production, photography, fulfillment; makes sure the work gets done as scheduled; and determines whether the work has achieved prescribed objectives.

The In-House Agency Companies that need closer control over the advertising have their own in-house agencies. Large retailers, for example, find that doing their own advertising provides cost savings as well as the ability to meet deadlines. An **in-house agency** performs most, and sometimes all, of the functions of an outside advertising agency.

The Media

The third player in the advertising world is the media. The **media** is composed of the channels of communication that carry the message from the advertiser to the audience, and in the case of the Internet, it carries the response from the audience back to the advertiser. Each medium has an organization structure in place that is responsible for selling ad space or time. Each medium also has the capability to assist advertisers in making comparisons between media as well as making the optimum choice within a particular media category. Finally, many of the media will assist advertisers in the design and production of advertisements.

A media representative typically meets the advertiser or the advertiser's representative (probably an ad agency) and tries to convince him that the medium is a good delivery vehicle for the advertiser's message. For example, a marketing representative for media provider *Qwest Dex* (Yellow Pages directory) calls on hundreds of prospective users of the

Dex directory. The purpose of the call is to describe the research supporting the use of this medium, discuss the various advertising designs, offer assistance in designing an ad, and outline the conditions of buying space in the directory.

Media delivers advertising messages in a way that is consistent with the creative effort. Volvo Cars of North America used two different media during the 2001 NCAA men's basketball tournament to send consumers to its Web site, where they could enter a contest to win a Volvo S60. Basketball fans were able to participate in the contest using two entry points: Those who were checking scores on their cell phones via CBS Sports Line and 602.com could access an entry application; those watching the basketball games on Web TV were directed to the Volvo Web site.[5] All these elements were consistent with Volvo's creative effort.

Vendors

The fourth player in the world of advertising is the group of service organizations that assist advertisers, advertising agencies, and the media: the **vendors**. Members of this group are also called freelancers, consultants, and self-employed professionals. The array of vendors mirrors the variety of tasks that it takes to put together an ad. Examples include freelance copywriters and graphic artists, photographers, songwriters, printers, market researchers, direct-mail production houses, telemarketers, and public relations consultants.

Why would the other advertising players hire a vendor? For many reasons. The advertisers may not have expertise in that area; they may be overloaded, or they may want a fresh perspective. Another reason to rely on vendors is cost: Vendors' services are often cheaper than the services of someone in-house.

The Target Audience

The final player in the advertising world is the target audience. All strategy starts with the customer.

Focus targets the very young ages of 18–24.

In a marketing strategy, the term **target market** denotes the customer, the person who purchases the product. In the case of cold cereal, for example, parents may purchase the product but kids consume it and definitely influence purchase. Kellogg might design one version of an ad for the kids' target audience and another for the parents' target audience. It's critical then, that advertisers recognize the various target audiences they are talking to and know as much about them as possible.

The target audience has a direct bearing on the overall advertising strategy, especially the creative strategy and the media strategy. The task of learning about the target audience is laborious and may take thousands of hours and millions of dollars to accomplish. Fortunately, we now have data-gathering technology that not only reduces the time and cost of doing the research but also improves accuracy of information. This information is collected every time you buy products using a scanner, complete a warranty target audience/guarantee card, sign up for a book or CD club, or sign up for America Online.

Despite the tremendous availability of information, it is possible that ads will be created that speak to no one or reach no one. Interactive technology has improved this situation, and ads can now be customized to individual consumers to some extent. This customization is growing and will make it even more important to know the target audience and create ads that speak to individual needs.

THE EVOLUTION OF ADVERTISING

Now that we have discussed the types, functions, and players in advertising, let's investigate how these roles and players developed historically.[6] The history of advertising has been dynamic and unpredictable, as noted in Figure 1.4.

The figure divides the history of advertising into four stages. The first stage is the "Age of Print." Ads were primarily classified in format and print media carried them. The culmination of this age was the development of the newspaper.

FIGURE 1.4   ADVERTISING TIMELINE

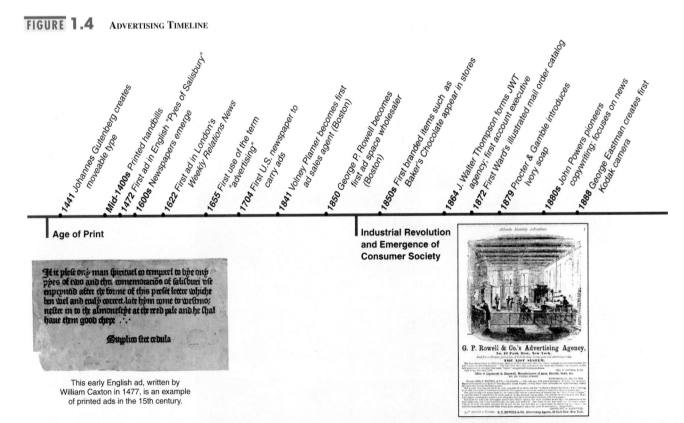

This early English ad, written by William Caxton in 1477, is an example of printed ads in the 15th century.

In this 1869 ad, George P. Rowell's Ad-Wholesaling agency used testimonial from a satisfied customer to promote the agency.

The second stage we label "The Industrial Revolution and Emergence of Consumer Society," a period when advertising grew in importance and size because of numerous social and technological developments. The purpose of advertising was to devise an effective, efficient communication system that could sell products to a widely dispersed marketplace. National media developed as the country's transportation system grew.

"Modern Advertising: Agencies, Science and Creativity" is the third stage in the evolution of advertising. The advertising industry grew to a remarkable $500 million in media billing and as a result, attracted the development of organizations specializing in advertising (agencies, established research techniques) and moved into an era of more creativity.

Starting in the early 1970s, the "Accountability Era" began. Clients wanted ads that produced sales and implemented technology, so they hired experts that could produce such results. In the early 1990s, the advertising industry recognized that its fate was linked to the global business environment. Advertising had to learn to pay its own way.

Finally, as this book prepares to go to press, the tragedy of September 11, 2001 is still very much on the minds of citizens around the world. How this event will ultimately change advertising is yet to be determined, but it has changed already. Immediately following the attacks, the advertising industry rushed to change any ads that were distasteful. Also, advertisers ran less ads, as the economy faltered.

CURRENT ADVERTISING ISSUES

Aside from our change in worldview since the 2001 terrorist attacks, there are some pretty forceful issues affecting advertising today. Let's take a look at these issues now.

Interactive Advertising

Some experts believe that technology, especially interactive technology, will change the face of advertising completely. Others contend that the promise of technology is exaggerated

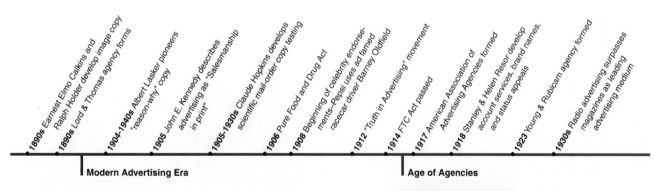

Modern Advertising Era

Age of Agencies

After WW1, "I wanted to be happy" was the call of consumer, and jazz and dancing became popular, as this ad for Victor Talking Machine Co. illustrates.

(continued)

and that advertising will retain its basic characteristics. The truth probably lies somewhere between these two opinions.

The meltdown of the dot-com industry has changed our perceptions of Internet advertising. It seemed a good idea in theory: The dot-coms would provide free access to opportunities to surf, chat, and buy, and advertisers would run banner ads, gain sales, and pay the dot-coms' operating costs. Expectations were high, but the results proved disappointing.

What went wrong? Static banners with big letters and little information have not attracted customers. Making them move or pop up just created an irritant.

Consequently, some advertisers are going back to old-fashioned TV spots to drive traffic directly to their Web sites. Other companies are signing up with sites that essentially pay consumers to engage with an electronic mall full of marketers. At mypoints.com, for example, surfers collect points and prizes for agreeing to visit companies' sites, read their e-mail, or buy their products online. There is another advertising tactic: bidding for prime spots on search engines. By paying to top the list of results for users who search for, say, "banking" on GoTo.com, a marketer such as Citicorp ensures that it is searching live prospects.

Even so, banner ads are not going away. Web sites are now willing to offer advertisers more shapes and sizes to play with, pop-up ads are developing a following, and rollout of broadband technology will bring streaming videos with grabbier messages. And while banner ads could capture some data about clickers before, agencies are helping marketers track customers' profiles more minutely.

Integrated Marketing Communication

The 1990s and 2000s brought us **integrated marketing communication (IMC)**. IMC is the practice of unifying all marketing communication tools so they send a consistent, persuasive message promoting company goals to target audiences. Marketing communication tools

FIGURE 1.4   Continued

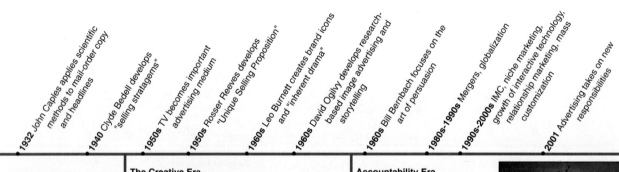

In the 1950's – TV becomes an important advertising medium.

This ad created by Bill Bernbach reflects his appeal to emotions.

Who can forget Pepsi's use of celebrity endorsements in the 1980's?

Due to the 9/11 attacks, advertising takes on a new responsiblilty.

This homepage for AOL is a host for many advertisements

include advertising, sales promotion, direct marketing, public relations, packaging, and personal selling. In companies that use IMC, marketers coordinate all marketing communication messages to create synergy, which means each individual message has more impact working jointly to promote a product than it would working on its own.

According to Don E. Schultz, Professor of Advertising at Northwestern University, IMC starts with the consumer's needs and wants. He contends that marketers now have the ability to capture data about consumers that allows them to shift from inside-out to outside-in advertising planning. Inside-out planning means marketers plan advertising messages based on what they believe is important. For example, this would be a company that employs the same creative format regardless of changes in its target audience.[7] Outside-in planning means that marketers start with data about customers and prospects to plan the advertising message. For example, Microsoft engaged in thousands of surveys of target audiences before it designed ads introducing its XP software.

Consumer Power

With these technological changes, consumers have more information to give them muscle in the marketplace. Today consumers don't have to endure the harangues of car dealers. Instead, they can visit a car manufacturer's Web site or an Internet auto dealer's site, find a fair car price, and order the car to specification. Retailers and manufacturers respond to consumer demands for information access or they risk losing business. In addition to the power of information, consumers are basically smarter and they know they have many more choices; this gives them additional leverage over the advertiser.

Two other concepts have emerged as a result of the new power base shared by consumers. The first, **permission marketing**, is a term coined by Seth Goden, Vice President of Direct Marketing for Yahoo! Goden argues that most advertising has been interruptive. Consumers don't request the ad so they aren't pleased by it, and that's a major hurdle for advertisers to get over before they can actually sell something. Permission marketing is different. It's based on three main principles:

1. The consumers, or recipients, control the process.
2. They agree to receive communications.
3. They consciously sign up (or "opt-in").

Participation marketing, a term offered by Alan Rosenspan, an expert in direct marketing, is a concept that goes beyond permission marketing. The five principles of participation marketing are:

1. You really know your customers.
2. You generate feedback at every opportunity.
3. You involve customers and prospects as much as possible.
4. You market on their schedule—not yours.
5. You make them feel vested in your success.[8]

Clearly, consumers will not tolerate being bombarded with unwanted ads.

Globalization

Another trend that continues to affect advertising is **globalization**. In the early 1990s the trade barriers throughout much of Europe came down, making it the largest contiguous market in

A MATTER OF PRACTICE
WHY ADVERTISING MATTERS MORE THAN EVER

➤ How much does advertising matter? That's the question that marketers are asking themselves as the worldwide economy slows and budgets tighten. When times are good, the corporate commitment to long-range brand building knows few bounds; but when profits drop, the ad budgets become an irresistible target for the budget slashers.

It's dangerous, though, to give in to that temptation. "People who starve their brands now will be paying for it in the future," warns Kevin Lane Keller, marketing professor at Dartmouth University's Amos Tuck School of Business. After all, in an era of wide consumer choice among roughly comparable products, marketers have learned to think of their brands not so much as a list of features or a logo or an advertising tagline, but as a relationship with the consumer. And just as one's friendships need to be kept in good repair, customer relationships can be maintained only through consistency. The marketing budget pays for much of that needed face time.

So what's the ad-spending outlook like this time? Certainly, ad agencies and media sales staffs have been doing their best to remind advertisers that history has a way of repeating itself. They point to the last downturn, in the early 1990s, when private-label products leaped to prominence while packaged-goods marketers slashed their budgets. And while it's not definitive, some research suggests that the best way to gain share is to sustain your spending during a downturn as your rivals are cutting back. That's how cereal maker Kellogg leapfrogged C. W. Post during the Depression, and how Pizza Hut and Taco Bell grabbed share from McDonald's during the early 1990s' dip. "Smart companies look to these environments, when other people go darker, to advance their proposition," says Donald R. Uzzi, senior vice-president of global advertising, marketing, and communications for information-systems company Electronic Data Systems.

That sounds logical, but lots of companies take the short view. With unrelenting pressure from Wall Street to meet earnings forecasts, it's not hard to see why. Cutting

back on ad spending for a quarter or two seems like an easy way to make the numbers. Some, including Delta Air Lines and General Motors, reacted quickly to slowing growth in the beginning of 2001 by slashing marketing budgets. Overall, U.S. spending for the first four months of 2001 dropped 5.7 percent from the previous year, according to ad tracker *Competitive Media Reporting.*

Marketers outside of traditional consumer goods have shown less willingness to support their brands. As a result, they risk losing their pricing power—and more important, their connection with their customers. Technology, which has led the downturn, is where marketers most need to stay the course. Skittish customers need reassurance that the investments they have made will pay off and that the supplier will be there to support them.

Besides, those that cut back risk ceding ground to a few well-funded players eager to grab market share from weaker rivals. That's why third-ranked IBM, with a $650 million media budget, is "absolutely going to stay the course," says Maureen McGuire, vice president for integrated marketing communications. "Successful companies try to use the downturn to solidify their position and take some share. We see it as an opportunity." That kind of long-term thinking may well be one reason why IBM lost only 1 percent of brand value last year, compared with bigger declines at some other high-tech companies.

Will IBM and similar opportunists show the grit to maintain these commitments? As Dartmouth's Keller points out, marketers tamper with their core commitment to their brands at the gravest risk. Those who don't burnish their brands in the downturn may find their good names are worth a whole lot less when the tough times end.

POINT TO PONDER

Is there a right or wrong answer to this dilemma?

Sources: Gerry Khermouch, "Why Advertising Matters More Than Ever," *Marketing News* (October 17, 2001): 56, 57; Jeff Neff, "Wall Street Advice: Ad Don't Subtract," *Advertising Age* (November 12, 2001): 1, 56.

the world. Eastern Europe, Russia, and China have at least partially opened their markets to Western businesses. Advertisers are moving into these markets, and ad agencies are forming huge multinational operations with international research and media-buying capabilities.

The advertising question is whether to practice global or local advertising: Should advertisers standardize ads across all cultures—**mass customization**—or customize ads for each culture? The answer to that strategic question is still open to debate. Because of the importance of understanding the underlying cultural issues that affect advertising, we devote Chapter 18 to this topic and weave a global perspective into features and discussion throughout the text.

Niche Marketing

Although advertising has gone global, many advertisers have moved toward tighter and tighter **niche markets**. Instead of marketing to the masses, they target market segments. New technologies enable advertisers to reach groups of consumers by using selective media, such as the Internet, databases, and e-mail.

Knowledge is power. Retailers such as Nordstrom's have gained an advantage over Dillard's because they have more information about credit card users. The retailer has taken a more active role in the communication effort. Retailers have taken this role partly because they are often closest to the niches they serve.

The bywords for advertising in the future will be accountability and adaptability. Advertising will be forced to walk the precarious tightrope between creativity and profitability, and survival will go to the fittest. Still, the future is not guaranteed. This is discussed in the "A Matter of Practice" box, which in the remaining chapters will present applications of advertising concepts.

IT'S A WRAP

A LEMON NO MORE

This chapter highlighted the various elements of advertising—past, present, and future. It also focused on the importance of effectiveness as the guiding principle of all advertising. Advertising must be goal-driven and ads that do not achieve their objectives are a failure.

The award-winning Volkswagen campaign introduced at the beginning of this chapter shows this effectiveness process. Like the VW ads produced in the 1950s and 1960s, the current campaign reached its objectives. The VW profits in 2000 reached an all-time high of $1.8 billion on sales of $76 billion, and advertising effectiveness measures such as unaided recall, intention to buy, and total ad recall all exceeded expectations. Overall, the campaign has been a huge success and it created a great deal of positive momentum going into the new millennium.

Summary

1. **Discuss the elements of effective advertising**. Effective ads work on two levels: They engage the mind of the consumer and at the same time deliver a selling message. Such ads have three characteristics. First, they are strategically sound; that is, they are directed at a specific audience and, driven by specific objectives. The messages are crafted to speak to that audience's most important concerns and are placed in media that will most effectively reach that audience. Second, these ads have a creative concept that gets the audi-

ence's attention and is remembered. Third, they use the right execution for the message and the audience.

2. **Define advertising and identify nine types and four roles of advertising**. The definition of advertising has six elements: (1) it is paid communication, (2) that is nonpersonal, (3) from an identified sponsor, (4) using mass media, (5) to persuade or influence, and (6) to reach a large audience. There are nine types of advertising, each appropriate for certain distinct

strategies: (1) brand, (2) retail, (3) political,
(4) directory, (5) direct-response, (6) business-to-business,
(7) institutional, (8) public service, and (9) interactive.
Advertising fulfills (1) a marketing role, (2) a communication
role, (3) an economic role, and (4) a societal role.

3. **Identify the five players in the advertising world**. The
five key players in the advertising industry are advertisers,
advertising agencies, media, vendors, and the target audience. A firm's advertising can be handled either internally
by an in-house agency or externally by an advertising
agency. Companies often have advertising departments to
either handle their own work or work with an agency.

4. **Explain how key figures and events in advertising history affect advertising today**. The evolution of advertising
has gone through many creative peaks and valleys, influenced largely by societal factors and the creative capabilities
of the people working in advertising at the time.

5. **Summarize current advertising issues**. Today, advertising
is strongly affected by changes in the business environment
such as technology, globalization, and marketing practice.
Some current issues that advertisers grapple with are: online
advertising and its role, integrated marketing communication, globalization, niche marketing, consumer power, relationship marketing, and mass customization.

Key Terms

advertiser, p. 16
advertising, p. 10
agency-of-record, p. 18
globalization, p. 24

in-house agency, p. 18
integrated marketing communication (IMC), p. 22
marketing, p. 12

marketing communication, p. 12
mass customization, p. 25
media, p. 18
niche markets, p. 25

participation marketing, p. 24
permission marketing, p. 23
target market, p. 20
vendors, p. 19

Questions

1. Critics charge that advertising seeks to manipulate its
audience, whereas advertising's supporters claim that it
merely seeks to persuade. Which interpretation do you
agree with? Why?

2. "I'll tell you what great advertising means," Bill Slater, a
finance major, said during a heated discussion. "Great
advertising is the ability to capture the imagination of the
public—the stuff that sticks in the memory, like Dancing
Raisins, Levi's jeans commercials, Budweiser Frogs, or that
rabbit with the drum—that's what great is," he says. "Bill,
you missed the point," says Phil Graham, a marketing major.
"Advertising is a promotional weapon. Greatness means
commanding attention and persuading people to buy something. No frills, no cuteness—great advertising has to sell
the public and keep them sold," he adds. How would you
enter this argument? How do you define great advertising?

3. Chris Jameson has just joined the advertising department
faculty in a university after a long professional career. In an
informal talk with the campus advertising club, she is put on
the spot about career choices. The students want to know
which is the best place to start: with an advertiser (a company) or with an advertising agency. How should she
respond? Should she base her answer on the current situation or on how she reads the future?

4. A strong debate continues at Telcom, a supplier of telephone
communication systems for business. The issue is whether
the company will do a better communication job with its
budget of $15 million by using an in-house advertising
agency or by assigning the business to an independent
advertising agency. What are the major issues Telcom
should consider?

5. This chapter discussed a number of creative approaches that
are honored in the history of advertising. When you think of
Reeves, Burnett, Ogilvy, and Bernbach, do any of their
styles seem suited to today's business world? Do the years
ahead seem to require hard-sell or soft-sell advertising
strategies? Explain your reasons.

6. Identify five major figures in the history of advertising and
explain their contributions to the field.

7. How did the advertising field change after the invention of
movable type, radio, and television? How is advertising
changing in response to the development of the Internet?

8. This chapter discussed a Nissan ad that, while it received
awards from the advertising industry, failed to satisfy advertising objectives. Sure, consumers liked the ad, but it did not
motivate them to buy Nissan cars. It seems that the ad succeeded in creativity, but failed in strategy and execution. Do
you agree? Why, or why not? Reflecting on the characteristics of effective ads, what could have been done differently?

9. Recently, advertisers have turned to feature films to promote their products. James Bond drives a particular foreign
car and uses a certain company's cell phone. Characters in
other films drink a particular brand of soda or beer. Does
this approach fulfill the three basic functions of advertising? How are the four roles advertising plays influenced by
this approach?

10. Most, if not all, companies have budget allocations for
advertising expenses. How do companies determine which
of the nine types of advertising to use to reach their target
audience? What are the trade-offs involved in selecting one
type over another? How can companies ensure that the
type(s) chosen will meet advertising objectives?

Suggested Class Project

Form groups of five or six students. Have a spokesperson contact one or two advertising agencies. Question one or more key people about the changes that have taken place in their agencies and the industry during the last five years. (Prepare a list of questions ahead of time). What kinds of changes do they expect in the next five years? Meet to write a three- to five-page report.

Suggested Internet Class Project

Examine three Web sites that contain banner ads. Do any of these ads appear to achieve the criteria for effective ads? Write a short report on two such banner ads.

HANDS-ON   Case 1

FOR SKIERS WHO CARE

Tenica Ski Company makes some of the finest ski boots in the world. Its top-of-the-line boot is the Icon RX, manufactured in Italy, and then sold through Tenica USA. The boot features a variety of adjustments to fit it to the customer's foot, resulting in a superior fit that leads to higher levels of comfort on the ski slope. Another feature is a carbon cuff that stiffens up the boot for racers who need to put a lot of pressure it, and the cuff can be injected with foam in order to form the liner to the wearer's foot. Colored bright orange, which has been the color of Tenica's past top-end boots, this one can effectively compete with any top-of-the-line boot.

The target market for the Icon RX is the expert skier or racer. These individuals usually look for a high performance boot to supplement their other high-end equipment and their superior skills. People who ski and buy their own equipment usually have a significant amount of disposable income; they often live in an area of the country that provides them with opportunities to ski, such as a mountainous region. The skier who buys this type of boot is a moderate to heavy user, usually someone who skis 20-plus times each season. While these boots are not made to perform better with one type of ski, it would benefit the company as a whole if they were bought in tandem with Volkl skis, another high-end Tenica Product. Tenica would like the boots to be viewed as a complement to the whole elite ski package.

The product is positioned as the high-end boot that feels good. The advertising campaign being considered focuses on all the benefits of a tight-fitting race boot, with the added bonus of comfort. ■

IT'S YOUR TURN

1. What category of advertising would Tenica most likely employ?
2. What should be the tone of this campaign?

Notes

1. Peter McHugh, "Wake-Up Calls," *Agency* (Fall 2001): 6–8.

2. Wendy Tanaka, "Public Buys into E-Shopping," *Denver Post* (August 5, 2001): 3K.

3. Anusree Mitra and John G. Lynch Jr., "Toward a Reconciliation of Market Power and Information Theories of Advertising Effects on Price Elasticity," *Journal of Consumer Research* 21 (March 1995): 44–59.

4. Seth Sutel, "Soft Landing Seen for Ad Spending amid Slowing Economy," *Denver Post* (December 24, 2000): 4K.

5. Suzanne Vranica, "Volvo Campaign Tests New-Media Waters," *Wall Street Journal* (March 16, 2001): B5.

6. Much of this historical review was adapted from Stephen Fox, *The Mirror Makers* (New York: Vintage Books, 1985).

7. Tom Duncan and Steve Everett, "Client Perceptions of Integrated Marketing Communications," *Journal of Advertising Research* 33(3) (May/June 1993): 30–39; Clarke Caywood, Don Schultz, and Paul Wang, "Integrated Marketing Communications: A Survey of National Consumer Goods Advertisers," *Northwestern University Report* (June 1991).

8. Alan Rosenspan, "Participation Marketing," *Direct Marketing* (June 2001): 54–55.

Help.

It's never too early to start planning for retirement. But how do you know if the financial decisions you make are the right ones? At CIGNA, we know how difficult this can be. That's why we created the Academy by CIGNA®† workshops to help educate employees about retirement options so the choices they make will be ones they can live with. At CIGNA we believe everyone shouldn't just have retirement dreams, but the tools to make them real.

CIGNA
A Business of Caring.

www.cigna.com

CHAPTER 2

Advertising and Society: Ethics, Regulation, and Social Responsibility

CHAPTER OBJECTIVES

When you have completed this chapter, you should be able to

1. Discuss the social issues advertisers face.
2. List the key ethical issues that affect advertising.
3. Identify the main factors in advertising's legal and regulatory environment.
4. Outline how federal case law affects advertising.
5. Summarize how the FTC and other federal agencies govern advertising.
6. Debate whether advertising self-regulation fulfills advertisers' responsibility to society.

Cigna Shows It Cares

Award: *EFFIE Bronze 2001, Corporate Reputation/Image/Identity Category*

Company: *Cigna Inc.*

Agency: *DDB Needham Worldwide Communications Group, New York*

Campaign: *"The Power of Caring"*

Even before the events of 9/11, companies knew that consumers are more likely to patronize businesses that support charitable causes. This strategy, known as *cause marketing*, can take many forms, including providing money or product to the beneficiary, supporting certain agencies such as the Red Cross or the United Way, or even setting up spaces where victims of a disaster can be fed and housed. Literally thousands of companies engaged in these various forms of cause marketing after the 9/11 disaster. Getting the word out about these programs is often one of the responsibilities of advertising, along with other communication-related tasks.

CIGNA Inc. has been around for many years and certainly has done its part in supporting various charitable causes. Yet it wasn't until late 1999 that the executives at CIGNA decided to promote its good services at a higher level. Let's face it, not many consumers have much empathy for insurance companies. They view the insurance industry as one that takes your money, gives back reluctantly, and raises premiums when its costs go up.

Top management at CIGNA conducted survey research and found that consumers pretty much viewed CIGNA in terms of these negative characteristics. Additional research, recommended by several executives in marketing, discovered that the majority of those surveyed, especially married women, viewed companies that supported charities in a very positive light. So CIGNA executives asked these questions: How can we engage in a cause marketing program that benefits both various charities and CIGNA? How can we direct consumers' attention toward CIGNA and, ultimately, increase sales?

The answer was a new creative strategy entitled "The Power of Caring." It was a philanthropic sponsorship program that featured well-known personalities and their charitable causes, all brought to you by CIGNA (in partnership with CNN and AOL Time Warner). This partnership was deemed necessary in order to share the cost of the program and give it more credibility.

The new campaign was combined with CIGNA's long-running, award-winning corporate campaign entitled "Business of Caring." Building on the equity of the latter, TV commercials were created that paired "news" vignettes, which featured such people as Mary Tyler Moore, Colin Powell, and Derek Jeter touting their favorite charities. Mary Tyler Moore, for instance, provided news on medical advances in the cure for diabetes, and gave addresses and phone numbers for making donations. Single-page print ads featured screen shots, which delivered the core message along with the donation information. Finally, the company established a "Power of Caring" Web site to mirror the off-line program, with banner ads directing traffic to the cigna.com site.

This program not only cost CIGNA several million dollars; it also carried the risk that consumers would view CIGNA's efforts as insincere. How did CIGNA do? Check the "It's a Wrap" box at the end of this chapter.

ADVERTISING AND SOCIAL RESPONSIBILITY

Because advertising is so visible, and is often considered manipulative and controversial, it draws attention from citizens, the media, government, and competitors. In this chapter we investigate the ethical and social responsibility questions that advertisers face. We also examine government and self-regulation issues that affect advertising.

Advertising takes place in a public forum in which business interests, creativity, consumer needs, and government regulations meet; and its visible social role makes it a target for criticism. As a result, today's consumers believe that a great deal of advertising is unethical. These people say it raises the prices of products, is untruthful, tricks people, or targets the vulnerable.

Let's examine the social issues facing advertisers so that we can see whether the negative perceptions of advertising are valid. The issues are complex, often revolving around public welfare and freedom-of-speech debates. Consumers and the advertising industry—including agencies, advertisers, and the media—have an important stake in how the public and regulators of the industry view these social issues.

Ethical Issues

Although many laws govern advertising, not all advertising is regulated. Numerous advertising-related issues are left to the discretion of the advertisers and are based on ethical concerns.

For instance, many people complain that society is becoming overrun with advertising, and in many respects this criticism is valid. Ads are everywhere these days: on beaches and in public restrooms; in sports arenas and on supermarket receipts; on municipal garbage cans and granny apples. Already there are advertisements on ATM screens and cell phone screens. "It's endless," says Mark Crispin Miller, Professor of Media Studies at New York University. "The clutter keeps rising. And what is the clutter? The clutter is advertising. It aspires to total domination of the environment." A recent *Advertising Age* study found that we (Americans) are exposed to 5,000 commercial messages a day, most of which we never notice.[1]

The following issues are central to a discussion of ethics in advertising: advocacy, accuracy, and acquisitiveness.

Advocacy The first ethical issue is advocacy. Advertising, by its very nature, tries to persuade its audience to do something. As a result, it is not objective or neutral, which disturbs critics who think it should be. Most people, however, are aware that advertising tries to sell something, whether it is a product, a service, or an idea. Think about presidential elections. Whoever runs for president, you can be sure that the campaign ads will portray the candidate positively.

Accuracy The second ethical issue is accuracy. Beyond the easily verifiable claims in an advertising message (for example, does the sedan in the ad have a sunroof, a CD player, and antilock brakes?) are matters of perception. Will buying the automobile make me the envy of my neighbors? Will it make me more attractive to the opposite sex? Such messages may be implied by the ads.

Ads on the beach, ads on baggage conveyors . . . all contribute to the increased clutter of advertising.

An Alliance Capital TV spot titled "Rude Awakenings" portrays a couple who are disappointed because their poor financial investments didn't meet their expectations. Is that an accurate portrayal of the concerns of the typical preretirement couple?

Most of us know that buying a car or drinking a certain brand of soft drink won't make us a new person, but innuendoes in the messages we see or hear cause concern among advertising critics. The subtle messages are more troubling when they are aimed at particular groups with limited experiences, such as children and teenagers, or people with limited resources, such as the elderly or disabled.

Acquisitiveness   The third ethical issue is acquisitiveness. Some critics maintain that advertising is a symbol of our society's preoccupation with accumulating material objects. Because we are continually exposed to an array of changing, newer, and better products, critics claim we become convinced that we must have these products. The rebuttal of this criticism is that advertising allows society to see and choose among different products. It offers choices and incentives that we can strive for if we want to.

Ultimately, consumers make the final decisions. Will an American Express Financial services ad lure female consumers (Am Ex's hope) simply because it features a young, highly successful spokeswoman? Maybe. Maybe not. In addition, if a consumer has Charles Schwab or Aetna handling her investments, it is unlikely that an ad will change her mind because of its spokesperson. Decisions about advertising campaigns start with advertisers, so they have the social responsibility of communicating ethically.

Determining What Is Ethical

Although advertisers can seek help in making decisions from such sources as codes of ethics, these codes provide only general guidance. When advertising questions are not clearly covered by a code, a rule, or a regulation, someone must make a decision.

Even though an ad might increase product sales, do you use copy that has an offensive double meaning or illustrations that portray people in stereotypical situations? Do you

The Alliance Capital commercial suggests that pre-retirement people are concerned about having enough money to retire comfortably. Do you think this portrayal is accurate?

Despite the appeal of highlighting a success story, readers still make the final decision to buy.

Practical Tips #1

QUESTIONS FOR ETHICAL ADVERTISING

Advertising people must address these five questions to ensure ethical advertising:

1. Who should and should not be the target of an advertisement?
2. What should and should not be advertised?
3. What should and should not be the symbolic tone of the advertising message? Humor, sincerity, and sarcasm are all examples of the symbolic tone an ad can convey.
4. What should and should not be the relationship between advertising and the mass media? Clearly, ads containing sexual innuendo should not be run on Saturday morning television during the cartoon hours.
5. What should and should not be advertising's conscious obligation to society?

stretch the truth when making a claim about a product? Do you malign the competitor's product even though you know it is basically the same as your own?

These questions can be complex and uncomfortable. Essentially, advertisers must make conscious decisions to adhere to either a high moral standard or something less. Will white lies be allowed? Once the decision is made, the agency must conduct the necessary research that verifies facts about the messages of the advertisers as well as competitors. Having customers view and report on their perceptions of ads will prove helpful in assessing what is ethical.

A serious ethical problem facing many advertising agencies today is whether they will represent clients that sell tobacco products.

Several agencies have resigned from profitable tobacco advertising accounts because of the medical evidence about the harm that these products cause.

Unfortunately, answers to these questions are not always straightforward. The advertiser must consider a number of related factors, such as the nature of the company and its mission, marketing objectives, reputation, available resources, and competition. Even then, what is or is not ethical is still a judgment call made by imperfect people.

Some calls, however, are clear breaches of ethics. Volvo lost credibility with consumers for years because of misleading advertising about its primary benefit—safety. Volvo was running a series of TV commercials showing a monster truck running over a line of Volvos and then a line of competitors' cars. The Volvos withstood the crunch, while the competitors' cars were smashed. Fortunately, a reporter who was at the filming witnessed a group of technicians cutting the roof support of competitors' cars and reinforcing the roof supports of the Volvos. Volvo blamed the agency. The agency blamed Volvo. We still don't know who gave the order.

For advertisers such as Volvo, weak management, poor products, and unexciting message possibilities may all lead to unethical practices, but none of these factors is an excuse for such behavior.

Social Responsibility

Advertising can help to improve society. An example of this is public service announcements (PSAs) for a good cause that run free of charge on broadcast media. The United Way and the Red Cross are two nonprofit organizations that produce PSAs.

The largest organization to focus on social responsibility in the industry is the Ad Council, a private, nonprofit group of advertising agencies and media that adopts good causes and develops free advertising campaigns on their behalf. The most famous is "Smokey the Bear" for the Forest Service. The Partnership for a Drug-Free America and its "Just Say No" campaign is a part of the Ad Council.

Companies, government agencies, and nonprofit organizations can also use advertising to disseminate information about their social programs and motivate their target

CONNECTICUT DEPARTMENT OF PUBLIC HEALTH "WHAT IS A WOMAN?" :30 TELEVISION

YOU'RE A MOTHER. A DAUGHTER. A SISTER. A WIFE. YOU'D RATHER DO WITHOUT THAN HAVE YOUR FAMILY DO WITHOUT.

BUT HOW WILL YOUR FAMILY DO WITHOUT YOU? IF YOU'RE A WOMAN OVER THE AGE OF 40, YOU'RE AT GREATER RISK FOR BREAST CANCER. BUT EARLY DETECTION CAN SAVE YOUR LIFE.

1-800-203-1234

CALL INFOLINE TO SEE IF YOU QUALIFY FOR A FREE MAMMOGRAM. 1-800-203-1234. CARE ENOUGH TO CARE FOR YOURSELF. CALL TODAY.

TV commercials, brochures, and posters all used the "Care Enough to Care for Yourself" theme, a social responsibility campaign designed to overcome motivation issues among women in the target audience.

La detección temprana
del cáncer de seno y
del cuello del útero le
puede salvar la vida.

Early detection of breast
and cervical cancer can
save your life.

"Care Enough" brochures contained information about breast cancer risk, the early detection program, and the toll-free number for information about the breast cancer screenings.

audiences to respond; this is called **social marketing**. The Connecticut Breast Cancer Awareness campaign from the Cronin agency illustrates this type of advertising effort. The Breast Cancer campaign's objectives were to create an awareness of free mammogram screenings in the target group, to make all women aware that they are at risk for breast cancer, and to generate calls to a toll-free information number. To accomplish those objectives, the Cronin agency used television and radio commercials along with outdoor billboards, brochures, free coupons, and reminder cards in both English and Spanish. The ethical orientation is easier to see in public information efforts such as the Connecticut Breast Cancer Awareness campaign. That campaign was successful because it made women in the low-income target audience realize how important they were to their families. The campaign message asked them to think about what their families would do without them, using the campaign slogan, "Care Enough to Care for Yourself." With a modest budget, the Cronin agency overcame women's barriers to action and inspired a large number of them to call for a free mammogram.

SIX KEY ISSUES IN ADVERTISING

Six key issues of ethics in advertising are puffery, taste, stereotyping, children's advertising, advertising controversial products, and subliminal advertising.

Puffery

Puffery is defined as "advertising or other sales representations, which praise the item to be sold with subjective opinions, superlatives, or exaggerations, vaguely and generally, stating no specific facts."[2]

Because obviously exaggerated "puffing" claims are legal, the question of puffery is mainly an ethical one. According to the courts, consumers expect exaggerations and inflated claims in advertising, so reasonable people wouldn't believe that these statements ("puffs") are literal facts. Virtually everyone is familiar with puffery claims for certain products: Sugar Frosted Flakes are "g-r-eat," send Hallmark cards if you "want to send the very best," and "nothing outlasts an Eveready battery."

However, the empirical evidence on the effectiveness of puffery is mixed. Some research suggests that the public might expect advertisers to be able to prove the truth of superlative claims, and other research indicates that reasonable people do not believe such claims. Advertisers must decide what claims are and are not socially responsible.[3]

The Uniform Commercial Code (UCC), a set of laws that govern sales and other commercial matters, distinguishes between mere "puffing" and statements about a product's performance or qualities that create an "express warranty." Under the UCC, a general statement praising the value of a product (such as "the Best Seafood Restaurant") does not create an express warranty. More concrete representations, however, might (for instance, "our fish are never frozen").

The UCC recognizes that advertisers cannot be expected to prove or live up to every general, glorifying statement made about a product. After all, it's only a company's opinion that its product is the best on the market. No one would want to, or could, prove the reasonableness or rationality of such opinions.

However, a proposed draft of UCC sections relating to express warranties would make all statements about a product part of the sale agreement. This could mean that all product statements create an express warranty, which could transform advertising as we know it.

Taste and Advertising

We all have our own ideas as to what constitutes good taste. Unfortunately, these ideas vary so much that creating general guidelines for good taste in advertising is difficult. Different things offend different people.

For example, an ad for Texas Instruments shows a close-up of a woman's face with enormous flames shooting from her eyelashes. Her metallic-toned face looks as if it's on fire, yet she's not the least bit concerned. Although the purpose of the ad is to promote the

A MATTER OF PRINCIPLE
BAD TASTE IN FRANCE

➤ If we believe the rumors, nudity is something the French enjoy and promote. However, it appears that everything has its limits. Recently, billboards along the most popular boulevards in Paris featured provocative photos that made even the French blush. Examples include Yves St. Laurent ads posted on bus shelters that feature a ghostly white naked woman caressing herself. A billboard just up the street, for the fashion house La City, showed a woman, wearing only underpants, suggestively posed next to a sheep. Sound degrading? Well the French thought so, too.

There actually was a strategy behind what many French citizens are calling "porno chic." But clearly, the companies behind these messaging strategies missed the state of the French moral mind. According to *BusinessWeek,* a poll of several thousand citizens conducted by the French government found that 70 percent reported being "more shocked than ever" by the new sexual ads, and two-thirds found (at least some of) them "objectionable." In addition, thousands of letters expressing displeasure with these ads were received by the Department of Communication Standards

from irate pedestrians who tore down several posters and covered others with mud and paint. It's not that they objected to the nudity—indeed France is a liberal and open society—it was the degradation of women that so enraged the public.

Those in favor of the porno chic type of campaign argue that this approach to advertising is necessary to break through the clutter. There's already a lot of "skin" in French ads. One way to do this is through shock value. Of course, if competitors buy into this approach, and the French government allows it, one risk is porno one-upsmanship.

POINT TO PONDER

Besides unhappy consumers, especially women, what other risks would you take following a porno chic strategy? Do you think advertisers could use shock as a tactic, without offending one group or another?

Sources: Stephen Baker and Christina White, "Why 'Porno Chic' is Riling the French," *BusinessWeek* (July 30, 2001): 47; Danielle Fox, "Skin Trade," *Business and Management Practices* (February 26, 2001): 50; Bob Garfield, "Publicity Monster Turns on Klein," *AdAge.com* (September 4, 2001).

---

company's computer chips, the creative approach is to attract attention by focusing on the unusual and bizarre. However, if targeted viewers are frightened or disturbed by such visuals, and consider them tasteless and inappropriate,[4] the company risks losing sales in the end. This notion of bad taste is further illustrated in the "A Matter of Principle" box.

Product Categories and Taste One dimension of taste concerns the product itself. Television advertising for certain products, such as designer jeans, pantyhose, bras, laxatives, and feminine hygiene aids, produces higher levels of distaste than do ads for other product categories.[5] Television has the ability to bring a spokesperson into our living rooms to "talk" to us about topics that embarrass many people, who then complain that the ads lack taste.

Although certain ads might be in bad taste in any circumstance, viewer reactions are affected by such factors as sensitivity to the product category, the time the message is received (for example, in the middle of dinner), and whether the person is alone or with others when viewing the message. Also, questionable ads become offensive in the wrong media context. Parents, for example, may object to a racy ad in Sports Illustrated for Kids or in a prime-time family program. Advertisers and media outlets must try to be sensitive to such objections.

In addition, taste changes over time. What was offensive yesterday may not be considered offensive today. A 1919 *Ladies' Home Journal* deodorant advertisement that asked the question, "Are you one of the many women who are troubled with excess perspiration?" was so controversial that 200 readers immediately canceled their subscriptions.[6] By today's standards that advertisement seems pretty tame.

Current Issues in Taste and Advertising Today's questions of taste center on the use of sexual innuendo, nudity, vulgarity, and violence. Although the use of sex in advertising is not new, the blatancy of its use is.

An example of this is the recent campaign rolled out in Europe and Asia from SSL International PLC, the world's number-one condom maker. The campaign featured the Durex brand, and was targeted to an audience of 16- to 24-year-olds. McCann-Erickson of Manchester, England, decided to use humor rather than a traditionally "preachy" approach. Both television and print ads showed men dressed in white sperm costumes blockaded in a city street by a giant Durex condom. While offensive to parents, young people found this creative approach very appealing: Awareness scores increased by 12 percent and sales by 5 percent.[7]

JC Penney, the retailer, did provoke the wrath of parents. In its TV spot, a mother and daughter are shown in a retail store with the daughter trying on hip-hugging jeans. "You're not going to school dressed like that, are you?" Mom demands. Unexpectedly, the mother yanks the jeans lower to reveal the daughter's bare midriff. Mothers seeing the spot complained that the campaign was promoting the wrong values. The ad was pulled in four days.[8]

Advertisers would be wise to conduct the necessary research for gauging the standards of taste for the general population as well as a target audience. Because mass media are seen or read by people outside the target audience, such testing can be tricky. The two examples just discussed indicate that the target audiences were probably not offended by the commercials, while parents were. But if you aim to satisfy parents, you may not connect with the primary target audience. This is a serious dilemma in creating advertising, and one not easily resolved.

CIGNA Inc. did extensive research before introducing the "Power of Caring" campaign. CIGNA's primary research question was: "What is a conscientious consumer?" A conscientious consumer is someone who:

- shows higher propensity for action and involvement in areas such as family and health.
- is usually the decision maker in the purchase of CIGNA's health, financial, and insurance products.
- is more inclined to purchase from companies that support charitable causes.
- has a higher propensity for community volunteer work.
- represents approximately 30 percent of the U.S. population.

Having this information kept CIGNA from inadvertently putting out a campaign that its target audience might have found distasteful.

Stereotyping in Advertising

Over the years people have accused advertisers of stereotyping large segments of the population, particularly women, minorities, and the elderly. In advertising, **stereotyping** is presenting a group of people in an unvarying pattern that lacks individuality. The issue of stereotyping raises the question of whether advertising shapes society's values or simply mirrors them.

Either way, the issue is crucial. If we believe that advertising has the ability to shape our values and our view of the world, then it is essential that advertisers become aware of how they portray different groups. Conversely, if we believe that advertising mirrors society, advertisers have a responsibility to ensure that what is portrayed is accurate and representative. Advertisers struggle with this issue every time they use people in an ad.

Women in Advertisements The portrayal of women in advertisements has received much attention over time, especially recently. Initially, critics complained that ads showed women as preoccupied with beauty, household duties, and motherhood. Although there is still concern about this stereotype, more advertisers are recognizing the diversity of women's roles. However, with the effort to portray women as more than housewives came a different problem. Beginning in the 1980s, advertisements focused on briefcase-toting professional women. Consider the commercial in which a NASA engineer, who is also a working mother, tells us the benefits of serving her children a powdered breakfast drink. The image of Supermom has been displaced by the image of Superwoman.

Historically, advertising has portrayed gender in distinct and predictable stereotypes. Men are shown as strong, independent, and achievement oriented; women are shown as nurturing and empathetic, but softer and more dependent, and they are told that the products being advertised will make their lives less stressful and more manageable.[9]

Even women's body language in advertising can infer certain traits. One research study of print ads found that women were often depicted as "shy, dreamy, gentle, likely to be manipulated, and helpless." Men were shown as expressing a level of power, control, and dominance.[10] Hopefully, these gender stereotypes are changing.

Racial and Ethnic Stereotypes Critics charge that racial and ethnic groups are stereotyped in advertising. The root of most complaints is that certain groups are shown in subservient, unflattering ways. Many times minorities are the basis of a joke or consigned to a spot in the background. Advertising has been accused of perpetuating some of the myths associated with certain minorities.

One myth is that members of minority groups are all the same. The Hispanic market is a case in point. In 2000, the Hispanic population in the United States was over 30 million, 15 percent of the total. Still, there is a misconception that all Hispanic consumers are alike, and nothing could be farther from the truth.

Experts agree that advertising efforts must portray cultural nuances of the local market to succeed with Hispanic consumers. "When marketers go through the exercise of marketing to Hispanics they need to recognize the culture and the set of needs of the Hispanic consumer, or else they're wasting their money," notes Isabel Valdez, president of Cultural Access Worldwide's market connections consultancy unit. "Spanish is more than a language issue."[11]

This ad speaks to a specific segment of the older consumer market.

Senior Citizens Another group that critics say is often subject to stereotyping is senior citizens, a growing segment of the population with increasing disposable income. Critics often object to the use of older people in roles that portray them negatively.

Barbara Champion, president of Champion & Associates, a research firm specializing in the maturing market, made the following observation: "The needs of maturing consumers, depending on mental and physical acuity as well as life-stage factors, are often different from one another. Whether a consumer is an empty-nester, a grandparent, a retiree, a widow, or in need of assisted living, for example, will greatly affect how, when, and why goods and services are purchased."[12] Many of the ads for Viagra speak to a specific segment of the population, and do so in a tasteful, tactful way.

Gay and Lesbian Consumers Dubbed in the early 1990s as the "Dream Market," the gay and lesbian community is still considered today to be an untapped goldmine, with U.S. population estimates reaching 19 million, and estimates of spending power topping $350 billion. Businesses targeting gays and lesbians have expanded beyond clubs and bookstores to comprise a full-service market that includes media, merchandise catalogs, vacation companies, and legal, medical, financial, and communication services.

A few adventurous companies have even begun to show images suggesting homosexuality in advertising to general audiences through mass media. Such images have appeared fairly extensively in mainstream fashion advertising for brands such as Calvin Klein, Benetton, and Banana Republic. The coming-out episode of ABC's *Ellen* was groundbreaking in more ways than just programming—it was the first time advertisers used prime-time network TV to reach gay and lesbian viewers.

Although ads that specifically target the gay market tend to be more effective in the gay media, companies such as Subaru are attempting to reach this market through the usual channels by employing less specific copy and visuals.[13] This is quite difficult because the advertiser wants to portray gay life accurately, yet does not want to lose the straight consumer market, which may be uncomfortable with that lifestyle. Commercial Closet is a non-profit journalistic and educational organization that seeks to raise awareness about how the gay community is portrayed in advertising. Its Web site primarily analyzes mainstream commercials that represent the gay community as a minority. The Commercial Closet is a Web site devoted to "raising awareness of something no one has thought of before: How the gay community is portrayed as a minority group in advertising."

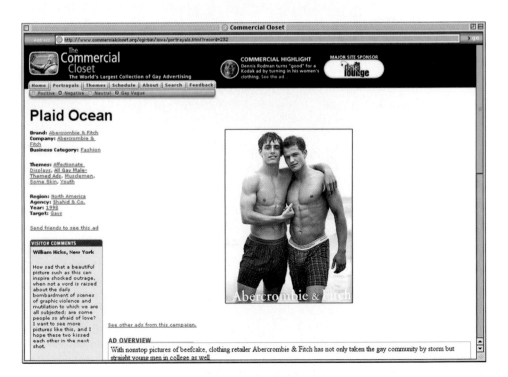

The Commercial Closet Web site analyzes ads targeting the homosexual consumer.

Advertising to Children

Advertising to children continues to be one of the most controversial topics in the industry. After a 1988 study found that the average child saw over 20,000 TV commercials per year, a heated debate ensued.[14] One side favored regulation because of children's inability to evaluate advertising messages and make purchase decisions. The other side opposed regulation because members of that group believed many self-regulatory mechanisms already existed and the proper place for restricting advertising to children was in the home.[15]

In response, the Federal Trade Commission (FTC) initiated proceedings to study possible regulations of children's television. Despite the FTC's recommendations, the proceedings did not result in new federal regulations until 1990. In the interim, self-regulation in the advertising industry tried to fill this void. The National Advertising Division (NAD) of the Council of Better Business Bureaus, Inc., set up a group charged with helping advertisers deal with children's advertising in a manner sensitive to children's special needs. The Children's Advertising Review Unit (CARU), established in 1974, evaluates advertising directed at children under the age of 12.

In 1990 Congress passed the Children's Television Advertising Practice Act, which placed 10.5-minute-per-hour ceilings for commercials in children's weekend television programming and 12-minute-per-hour limits for weekday programs. The act also set rules requiring that commercial breaks be clearly distinguished from programming, barring the use of program characters to promote products.

Advocates for children's television continued to argue that many stations made little effort to comply with the 1990 act and petitioned the Federal Communications Commission (FCC) to increase the required number of educational programs to be shown daily. In 1996, broadcasters, children's advocates, and the federal government reached an agreement requiring all TV stations to air three hours of children's educational shows a week.

Advertising Controversial Products

Over time, products that were once considered not suitable to advertise, such as those related to feminine hygiene, foot problems, and hemorrhoids, have become acceptable. There are still some things, however, that have not been accepted by the majority of consumers.

Tobacco One of the most heated advertising issues in recent years has been the proposed restrictions on the advertising of tobacco. Restrictions on products thought to be unhealthy or unsafe are not new. Cigarette advertising on television and radio has been banned since January 1, 1971.

Proponents of the ban on cigarette advertising argue that since cigarettes have been shown to cause cancer as well as other illnesses, encouraging tobacco use promotes sickness, injury, or death for the smoker and those inhaling second-hand smoke. The restriction of advertising on those products would result in fewer sales and fewer health problems for America as a whole.

Opponents of an advertising ban counter that prohibiting truthful, nondeceptive advertising for a legal product is unconstitutional. They feel the same as attorney and First Amendment authority Floyd Abrams: "Censorship is contagious and habit-forming even for commercial speech. What we need is more speech, not less." Opponents of the ban also cite statistics demonstrating that similar bans in other countries have proven unsuccessful in reducing tobacco sales.

In 1996 the Food and Drug Administration (FDA) established a set of restrictions applicable to tobacco advertisers. Among these were a ban on outdoor ads within 1,000 feet of a school or playground; and they limited ads to black-and-white, text only, in magazines with 55 percent readership under the age of 18. The restrictions also stipulated that $150 million be provided to fund antismoking ads targeting children.[16]

Since then, 46 states have received initial payments from the $206 billion Master Settlement Agreement to be supplied by tobacco companies over a 25-year period. Approximately half the money goes to fund TV and print ads warning children about the dangers of smoking; the other half pays for promotions such as loyalty cards, all-expenses-paid teen summits, and various events. As indicated in the "A Matter of Principle" box, there is some doubt that all this money is producing effective results.

A second issue deals with attempts by the tobacco industry to reverse the decision in Massachusetts to ban ads near schools and playgrounds. The Supreme Court heard the case in April 2001, and determined that the ban on tobacco advertising limited commercial speech and violated First Amendment rights. Essentially, the Court ruled in favor of the tobacco industry. The Court has also reviewed a trifecta of ads bans: liquor (1996), casino gambling (1999), and tobacco (2001), and all have been struck down. Still, as noted in the Philip Morris ads, tobacco companies have tried to educate.

Banning tobacco advertising is not unique to the United States. Malaysia, for example, has banned most forms of tobacco advertising, including print, TV, radio, and billboards. However, these bans are fairly ineffective as the result of **indirect advertising**. Indirect advertising is advertising that features one product instead of the primary (controversial) product. Examples of these techniques in Malaysia are quite plentiful. Billboards with the Salem, Benson & Hedges, and Winston names dot the landscape, but they're not advertising cigarettes. They're advertising their travel, clothing, and restaurant businesses.

In Hong Kong, outdoor display advertising of tobacco products was recently banned, but small shops that sell cigarettes were exempted from the regulation. Since then, some shop signs for cigarettes have gotten so big, approaching 10 feet long, that the industry itself has voluntarily agreed to limit their size.

Thailand has three laws banning tobacco ads. Two exceptions include ads in international magazines and on live TV shown from abroad.[17]

Alcohol Liquor executives contend that they will follow voluntary advertising guidelines to avoid images and time slots that appeal to kids. That promise has been hard to keep because every major brand is trying to win over young consumers. Consider *Spin* magazine. Forty-eight percent of the music magazine's readers are under the legal drinking age of 21, according to data used by ad executives. That audience is much younger than the nation as a whole, in which 30 percent are under age 21. However, in one representative issue the back cover carries an ad for V.O. Seagram Co.'s Absolut Vodka, and inside pages are filled with rival ads. Liquor advertising in *Allure* (with 44 percent underage readers), *Rolling Stone* (35 percent), and other publications prove that *Spin* is hardly the exception.[18]

The beer industry has been the target of strong criticism for several years. Anheuser-Busch pulled its beer advertising from MTV to avoid drawing fire for marketing to underage drinkers, and moved its spots to VH-1, a similar network that targets 25- to 49-year-olds. This decision was partly the result of a study by *Advertising Age* that tracked MTV commercial viewership and found that 50 percent of the viewers were underage.[19] Although it is unlikely that beer advertising will be banned, some companies sensitive to public opinion have initiated proactive programs that educate and discourage underage drinkers.

NBC angered many people in December 2001 when, after a 50-year self-imposed industry ban, it decided to air hard liquor ads on prime-time television. Bowing to the pressure from Congress and a strong backlash from advocacy groups such as Mothers Against Drunk Driving (MADD), the network removed the commercials about three months later.

Gambling Gambling is a serious addiction for millions of people. Thanks to marketing databases, advertisers can target people who have a history of gambling (and losing). Recently, advertising has triggered a debate in the United States about the proliferation of gambling, particularly casino gambling and its effect.

Just as gambling businesses have become cash-cow clients for many ad agencies, a grassroots antigambling movement has been gaining momentum in many states. Activists such as Reverend Thomas Grey of the National Coalition Against Legalized Gambling have been successful in mobilizing citizens against gambling. Coalition political director

A MATTER OF PRINCIPLE

A WASTE OF MONEY?

➤ In January 2000, 46 states began receiving initial payments from the $206 billion that tobacco companies will provide over the next 25 years as part of the landmark 1998 Master Settlement Agreement. Florida, Minnesota, Washington, and Mississippi had begun funding antismoking ads, events, Web sites, and other materials. Here's the math: If each state in the Master Settlement Agreement budgets a conservative $20 million, that's $920 million annually. By comparison, tobacco companies spend about $5.6 billion a year on brand marketing.

Tobacco companies also have initiated aggressive prevention programs targeting youth. The Master Settlement Agreement required companies to put a senior vice president in charge of Youth Smoking Prevention activities (without specifying funding). Philip Morris spent $100 million in 2000, mostly on ads, but also on school programs, partnerships with community groups including National 4-H Council, and access-restriction campaigns (including ads reminding parents to watch their own cigarettes). Ads target kids ages 10 to 14 with the tagline, "Think. Don't Smoke."

This begs the question: Are antitobacco campaigns that target kids actually working? So far, the answer is an unequivocal "no." Each year 1 million young people take up smoking, and the figure continues to grow. From a two-year survey of youths across the United States, it was clear that the majority of them underestimated the health risks and addiction possibility associated with smoking. They also had a 75 percent recall of ads featuring smoking.

Several reasons are offered to explain these negative results. First, there is the U.S. Supreme Court ruling made in 2000, that the Food and Drug Administration does not have the power to regulate tobacco products because Congress never gave the agency this mandate. This ruling also ends possible new marketing and advertising restrictions.

A second reason is the inability of antitobacco advertising to connect with young people. For example, the American Legacy Foundation budgets $150–225 million annually to create antitobacco ads targeted at kids. Teen advisors were consulted, and they told Legacy to create ads that slam the tobacco industry. Legacy hired two agencies: Arnold Communications and Crispin Porter & Bogusky. The first ad resembled an acne commercial: Three girls sample a pimple cream. The first two try it, but the third bursts into flames. Four sirens blaze and the following message appears: "Only one product actually kills one-third of the people who use it. Tobacco." Other ads were entitled "Body Bag" and "Lie Detector." The lack of success was explained by Alex Bogusky, a Crespin partner and creative director. "The issue of whether to smoke is way down on the list of priorities for kids. They have violence in schools, sex. We are trying to elevate this issue."

The third reason is the tobacco industry's response to the Master Settlement. Critics argue that the industry has found loopholes. The Massachusetts Department of Public Health, for example, found tobacco ad spending rose $30 million in magazines with 15 percent or more teen readership. As an example of another loophole, music stores advertise concerts that are sponsored by tobacco companies. Tobacco companies contend that licensing their names to nontobacco products simply makes good business sense and isn't intended to encourage smoking.

Ultimately, billions of dollars will be spent on advertising to prevent teen smoking, with little confidence in effective results.

POINT TO PONDER

Is the responsibility placed on the advertising industry to prevent teen smoking reasonable? What else can the industry do?

Sources: Wendy Mellio, "Anti-Tobacco Ads Stir Protests, but Creatures Carry On," *Adweek* (March 6, 2000): 22–23; "Tobacco Ads Still Getting Through to Teens," *Denver Post* (June 12, 2001): 4A; Julie Schmit, "Cigarette Logos Abound Despite Ad Bans," *USA Today* (September 12, 2000): B1, B2; David Gianatasio, "Legacy Ads Up Gross Quotient," *Adweek* (November 26, 2001): 7.

Bernie Horn noted, "We oppose illegal advertising of gambling, which is going on left and right."[20] In fact, advertising of gambling is *not* illegal.

To date there is no evidence that compulsive gamblers are more affected by advertising than other people. Still, the advertising industry should consider the ethical issues, establish standards, and make sure its efforts are socially responsible.

Prescription Drugs In 1997, the FDA loosened its controls on pharmaceutical companies, and as a result, the amount of prescription drug advertising has skyrocketed. While these print and TV ads have proven very successful in terms of increased sales, various consumer groups, government agencies, and insurance companies have been quite critical. In one study, for example, the National Institute for Health Care Management found that direct-to-consumer prescription advertising has led to an increase in requests for costlier drugs, while the less expensive generic drug would be just as effective.[21]

Also, debates have ensued over whether those ads are prodding otherwise healthy people to ask for drugs prematurely, or whether they are helping consumers obtain treatment they might not have known existed.

Subliminal Advertising

Generally, we assume that messages are seen and heard consciously. However, it is possible to communicate symbols that convey meaning but are below the threshold of normal perception. These kinds of messages are called subliminal. A **subliminal message** is transmitted in such a way that the receiver is not consciously aware of receiving it. This usually means that the symbols are too faint or too brief for the consumer to clearly recognize them.

Author Wilson Key maintains that subliminal "embeds" are placed in ads to manipulate purchase behavior, most often through appeals to sexuality. For example, he asserts that 99 percent of ads for alcohol use subliminal embeds that are buried so skillfully that the average person does not consciously notice them unless they are pointed out.[22]

Research shows that subliminal stimuli can cause some types of minor reactions, such as a "like-dislike" response. However, research hasn't proven whether a subliminal message is capable of affecting the public's buying behavior. Physiological limitations make it uncertain as to whether subliminal messages can cause certain behaviors, because many factors besides advertising induce consumers to purchase a product. Most important, consumers normally do not buy products they don't need or can't afford, regardless of whether the advertising message is presented subliminally or directly.

One ad sponsored by the American Association of Advertising Industries (a group of agencies that set voluntary advertising guidelines) represents the industry's viewpoint on the subliminal advertising theory.

During the last presidential campaign, Democrats accused the Republican National Committee of running a subliminal message. In a TV commercial that attacked Al Gore's plan to add prescription drugs to Medicare, the word RATS appeared on the screen for a

The advertising industry considers accusations of subliminal advertising to be both damaging and untrue.

TABLE 2.1	**Ethical Issues Facing Advertisers**
Ethical Issue	**Example**
Puffery	A local retailer claiming it has the best merchandise in town.
Bad taste	An ad for topical medication that shows or describes the affected area in detail.
Stereotyping	Showing a handicapped consumer in desperate need of help.
Advertising to children	Suggesting that wearing a particular brand of basketball shoe makes you more popular.
Controversial products	Tobacco and alcohol ads that appear in magazines read by 17-year-olds.
Subliminal advertising	Embedding an image in an ad for a product so that it isn't noticed on a conscious level.

split second. The Republicans denied the accusation and explained that the word was just part of the word BUREAUCRATS. Even though the FCC concluded the ad was not subliminal, the Republican National Committee pulled the commercial.

Experts in the ad industry contend that it's silly to think such techniques would work. "I'm not saying it might not have been true," says Stephen A. Greyser, Professor of Marketing at Harvard Business School. "But there is no methodically believable research that supports the notion that it works. Besides, advertising wants to impact on people's consciousness, not their unconsciousness."[23]

For a summary of the six key issues in advertising, check out Table 2.1. Next, we turn to the legal and regulatory issues that affect advertising.

ADVERTISING'S LEGAL AND REGULATORY ENVIRONMENT

Few industries have been more heavily regulated than advertising. The next three sections explore federal case law on the First Amendment and privacy, the Federal Trade Commission (the main regulatory body that governs advertising), additional regulatory agencies, and industry self-regulation. Figure 2.1 summarizes all the regulatory factors that affect advertising.

Congress legislates laws while courts interpret those laws in specific situations to create case law. In this section, we examine two pivotal areas of case law: the First Amendment and privacy as they pertain to advertising.

First Amendment Case Law

The most basic federal law that governs advertising is the First Amendment to the U.S. Constitution. The First Amendment states that Congress shall make no law "abridging

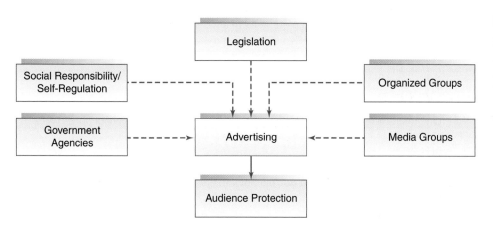

FIGURE 2.1

REGULATORY FACTORS AFFECTING ADVERTISING

As you can see, many factors affect the advertising industry.
Source: Courtesy of the American Advertising Federation.

the freedom of speech, or of the press; or the right of people peaceably to assemble, and to petition the Government for a redress of grievances." How have courts applied the First Amendment to advertising? First Amendment protection extends to **commercial speech**, which is speech that promotes commercial activity. However, that protection is not absolute.

Protection of advertising as commercial speech has varied over the years. In 1980, in conjunction with its ruling on *Central Hudson Gas and Electric v. Public Service Commission of New York*, the Supreme Court established a four part test that determines to what extent the government can restrict advertising. This decision also stipulated the degree to which advertising is considered commercial speech.

There are a number of cases that have attempted to change the common view of advertising as commercial speech. Most notably, the Supreme Court struck down a Massachusetts law that restricted tobacco advertising. The justices ruled that the Massachusetts law violated First Amendment rights, stating that the state did not prove that its regulations were "not more extensive than necessary."[24]

Free speech advocates applauded the decision while critics of tobacco companies lamented. Although no one expects advertising to have the same constitutional protection of free speech that is given to individuals, courts throughout the country are narrowing the gap.

According to the U.S. Supreme Court, freedom of expression must be balanced against competing interests. Essentially, the Supreme Court has ruled that only truthful commercial speech is protected, not misleading or deceptive statements. Because the Supreme Court continues to reinterpret how the First Amendment applies in different cases, advertisers need to keep close track of legal developments. Table 2.2 lists some key First Amendment court decisions that affect advertising.

Two recent cases show how varied First Amendment case law can be. The Supreme Court's 1996 decision in *44 Liquormart, Inc. v. Rhode Island* signaled strong protection for

---

TABLE 2.2	**First Amendment Rulings on Commercial Speech**

Valentine v. Christensen (1942)

First Amendment does not protect purely commercial advertising because that type of advertising does not contribute to decision making in a democracy.

Virginia State Board of Pharmacy v. Virginia Citizens Consumer Council (1976)

States cannot prohibit pharmacists from advertising prices of prescription drugs because the free flow of information is indispensable.

Central Hudson Gas & Electric Corporation v. Public Service Commission of New York (1980)

Public Service Commission's prohibition of promotional advertising by utilities is found to be unconstitutional, placing limitations on government regulation of unlawful, nondeceptive advertising.

Posadas de Puerto Rico Associates v. Tourism Company of Puerto Rico (1986)

Puerto Rican law banned advertising of gambling casinos to residents of Puerto Rico.

Cincinnati v. Discovery Network (1993)

Court ruled that the Cincinnati City Council violated the First Amendment's protection of commercial speech when it banned news racks of advertising brochures from city streets for aesthetic and safety reasons, while permitting newspaper vending machines.

Edenfield v. Fane (1993)

Court ruled that Florida's prohibition of telephone solicitation by accountants was unconstitutional.

44 Liquormart, Inc. v. Rhode Island (1996)

Court ruled that two Rhode Island statutes that banned advertising for alcohol prices were unconstitutional.

Glickman v. Wiliman Bros. (1997)

Court ruled that a mandatory generic advertising program, issued in accord with marketing orders of the Agricultural Marketing Act, did not infringe upon the free speech rights of fruit growers.

companies under the First Amendment. The Court struck down two Rhode Island statutes created to support the state's interest in temperance. Both statutes banned the advertisement on alcohol prices. The first statute prohibited advertising alcohol prices in the state except on signs. The second statute prohibited the publication or broadcast of alcohol price ads. The Supreme Court held that Rhode Island's statutes were unlawful because the ban abridged the First Amendment's guarantee of freedom of speech.

In contrast, a sharply divided (5-4) Supreme Court rejected a First Amendment challenge by California fruit growers who objected to part of a federal agricultural marketing agreement that mandated they spend a certain amount of their federal money on generic product advertising and promotion (*Glickman v. Wiliman Bros. & Elliott, Inc.*). Does this decision diminish the protection of advertising under the First Amendment? Some legal experts contend that the focus on coerced speech rather than commercial speech suggests otherwise.

Changes in who sits on the Supreme Court can also influence the interpretation of First Amendment protection for advertisers. It is important for advertisers to monitor sitting judges and judicial nominees, because should advertising lose its First Amendment coverage, the implications would be enormous.

Privacy Case Law Developments: Online Advertising

With an estimated 100 million American adults online, according to IntelliQuest Information Group, more consumers are questioning whether cybermarketers should be allowed to gather personal information from online users. Many types of businesses share information about consumers/citizens.

During the summer of 2001, U.S. consumers received the first round of privacy notices from their banks, HMOs, and insurers. As a result of the 1999 Gramm-Leach-Bliley Act, companies must now disclose how they're using consumers' personal data. The law's intention is to inform consumers if their personal information is collected or shared, and with whom. The impetus for this concern for privacy has come from the vast amounts of information collected online.

The issue of personal privacy is more complicated than it appears. While people want to protect their privacy, they are also willing to sacrifice some of this privacy if there are benefits to be gained. This was verified by a 2001 poll, commissioned by *American Demographics* magazine and conducted by Market Facts Research. The study found, for example, that although consumers say they hate telemarketing, they are willing to provide personal information if they can enter a contest. Still, consumers don't want companies to collect information or data mine and track their behavior.[25]

ADVERTISING AND THE FEDERAL TRADE COMMISSION

The **Federal Trade Commission (FTC)**, established in 1914 by an act of the U.S. Congress, is the primary agency governing the advertising industry. Its main focus with respect to advertising is to identify and eliminate ads that deceive or mislead the consumer. Some FTC responsibilities are to

- initiate investigations against companies that engage in unfair competition or deceptive practices.
- regulate acts and practices that deceive businesses or consumers and issue cease-and-desist orders where such practices exist. Cease-and-desist orders require that the practice be stopped within 30 days (a cease-and-desist order given to one firm is applicable to all firms in the industry).
- fine people or companies that violate either (1) a trade regulation rule or (2) a cease-and-desist order given to any other firm in the industry.
- fund the participation of consumer groups and other interest groups in rule-making proceedings.[26]

Specifically, the FTC oversees false advertising of such items as foods, drugs, cosmetics, and therapeutic devices. That oversight includes such things as health and weight loss business practices, 900 numbers, telemarketing, and advertising that targets children and the elderly.

TABLE 2.3   **Advertising Legislation**

Pure Food and Drug Act (1906)

Forbids the manufacture, sale, or transport of adulterated or fraudulently labeled foods and drugs in interstate commerce. Supplanted by the Food, Drug and Cosmetic Act of 1938; amended by Food Additives Amendment in 1958 and Kefauver-Harris Amendment in 1962.

Federal Trade Commission Act (1914)

Establishes the commission, a body of specialists with broad powers to investigate and to issue cease-and-desist orders to enforce Section 5, which declares that "unfair methods of competition in commerce are unlawful."

Wheeler-Lea Amendment (1938)

Prohibits unfair and deceptive acts and practices regardless of whether competition is injured; places advertising of foods and drugs under FTC jurisdiction.

Lanham Act (1947)

Provides protection for trademarks (slogans and brand names) from competitors and also encompasses false advertising.

Magnuson-Moss Warranty/FTC Improvement Act (1975)

Authorizes the FTC to determine rules concerning consumer warranties and provides for consumer access to means of redress, such as the "class action" suit. Also expands FTC regulatory powers over unfair or deceptive acts or practices and allows it to require restitution for deceptively written warranties costing the consumer more than $5.

FTC Improvement Act (1980)

Provides the House of Representatives and Senate jointly with veto power over FTC regulation rules. Enacted to limit the FTC's powers to regulate "unfairness" issues in designing trade regulation rules on advertising.

The Telemarketing and Consumer Fraud Act and Abuse Protection Act (1994)

Specifies that telemarketers may not call anyone who requests not to be contacted. Resulted in the Telemarketing Sales Rules.

Table 2.3 lists important advertising legislation, most of which shows the growing authority of the FTC to regulate advertising. However, FTC authority does not necessarily mean stringent oversight. Consider the laissez-faire political climate of the 1980s during the Reagan administration. Appointed FTC personnel did not regulate advertising aggressively unless the regulation had significant economic benefits.

An outcome of the soft FTC years was the development of the National Association of Attorneys General, an organization determined to regulate advertising at the state level. Members of this organization have successfully brought suits in their respective states against such advertising giants as Coca-Cola, Kraft, and Campbell Soup.[27] Most recently, numerous attorneys general have led the way against the tobacco industry and have supported the advertising restrictions discussed earlier.[28]

It appears that new FTC Chairman Tim Muris will continue most of these priorities. In an interview early in his regime, Mr. Muris said he would focus on privacy issues, fraudulent health claims on the Web, and violent movies, video games, and music targeted to kids.

The existence of a regulatory agency such as the FTC influences advertisers' behavior. Although most cases never reach the FTC, advertisers prefer not to risk long legal battles with the agency. Advertisers are also aware that competitors may complain to the FTC about a questionable advertisement. Such a move can cost the offending organization millions of dollars.

Ultimately, advertisers want their customers to trust their products and advertising, so many take precautions to ensure that their messages are not deceptive, misleading, or unreasonable. Let's examine in more detail five areas of FTC regulation that concern advertisers: deception, reasonable basis for making a claim, comparative advertising, endorsements, and demonstrations.

Deception

Deceptive advertising is a major focus of the FTC. Some activities that the commission has identified as deceptive are deceptive pricing, false criticisms of competing products, deceptive guarantees, ambiguous statements, and false testimonials. The current FTC policy on deception contains three basic elements:

1. Where there is representation, omission, or practice, there must be a high probability that it will mislead the consumer.
2. The perspective of the "reasonable consumer" is used to judge deception. The FTC tests reasonableness by looking at whether the consumer's interpretation or reaction to an advertisement is reasonable.
3. The deception must lead to material injury. In other words, the deception must influence consumers' decision making about products and services.[29]

This policy makes deception difficult to prove because the criteria are rather vague and hard to measure. It also creates uncertainty for advertisers who must wait for congressional hearings and court cases to discover what the FTC will permit.

Reasonable Basis for Making a Claim

The advertiser should have a reasonable basis for making a claim about product performance or run the risk of an FTC investigation. For instance, most of the companies that guarantee weight loss, increased muscle definition, or better memory employ difficult criteria with which to prove their claims. Consequently, an advertiser should always have data on file to substantiate any claims it makes in its advertisements. Also, it is best if this research is conducted by an independent research firm.

The FTC determines the reasonableness of claims on a case-by-case basis. In general, the FTC considers these factors:

- *Type and specificity of claim made.* For example, Computer Tutor claims it can teach you the basics of using a computer by simply going through its three-CD set.
- *Type of product.* FedEx promises a certain delivery time, regardless of weather, mechanical breakdown, and so forth. This product has a great many uncontrollable variables, as compared to Heinz Co., which claims its ketchup will be thick.
- *Possible consequences of the false claims.* A Web site that claims it is secure can cause serious damage to its customers if, indeed, it is not.
- *Degree of reliance on the claims by consumers.* Business-to-business customers depend on the many claims made by their vendors. Therefore, if XPEDX (yes, that's how it's spelled), a manufacturer of boxes and other packages, claims in its ad that it can securely deliver any size product, it had better deliver.
- *The type and accessibility of evidence available for making the claim.* The type of evidence could be as simple as testimonials from satisfied customers to as complex as product testing in multiple laboratories. It could be made available through an 800 number request or online.

Comparative Advertising

Advertisers face the common threat that competitors will misrepresent their products, prices, or some other attributes. While no one expects a competitor to be totally objective, there are certain guidelines for protecting advertisers from unfair comparisons. The Lanham Act seeks damages from an advertiser who "misrepresents the nature, characteristics, qualities, or geographic origin in comparative advertising."

Comparative advertising is permitted in the United States, but the ads must compare similar products. Also, companies can't claim that their prices are lower than the competition unless they can prove that the same products are sold at other places for higher prices.

Under the Lanham Act, companies/plaintiffs are required to prove five elements to win a false advertising lawsuit containing a comparative claim. They must prove:

TABLE 2.4   **American Association of Advertising Agencies' Ten Guidelines for Comparative Advertising**

1. The intent and connotation of the ad should be to inform and never to discredit or unfairly attack competitors, competing products or services.
2. When a competitive product is named, it should be one that exists in the marketplace as significant competition.
3. The competition should be fairly and properly identified but never in a manner or tone of voice that degrades the competitive product or service.
4. The advertising should compare related or similar properties or ingredients of the product, dimension to dimension, feature to feature.
5. The identification should be for honest comparison purposes and not simply to upgrade by association.
6. If a competitive test is conducted, it should be done by an objective testing service.
7. In all cases the test should be supportive of all claims made in the advertising that are based on the test.
8. The advertising should never use partial results or stress insignificant differences to cause the consumer to draw an improper conclusion.
9. The property being compared should be significant in terms of value or usefulness of the product to the consumer.
10. Comparisons delivered through the use of testimonials should not imply that the testimonial is more than one individual's, unless that individual represents a sample of the majority viewpoint.

Source: James B. Astrachan, "When to Name a Competitor," *Adweek* (May 23, 1988): 37. Copyright American Association of Advertising Agencies. Reprinted by permission.

1. False statements have been made about either product.
2. The ads actually deceived or had the tendency to deceive a substantial segment of the audience.
3. The deception was "material" or meaningful. In other words, the plaintiff must show that the ad claim is likely to influence purchasing decisions.
4. Falsely advertised goods are sold in interstate commerce.
5. The suing company has been or likely will be injured as a result of the false statements, either by loss of sales or loss of goodwill.

In addition to the Lanham Act, consumers also may rely on state laws governing unfair competition and false ad claims if the consumer is the victim of a false comparative claim. In California, for example, the Business and Professional Code prohibits "unlawful, unfair, or fraudulent business practices" and "unfair, deceptive, untrue, or misleading" advertising.

The American Association of Advertising Agencies has 10 guidelines that advertisers should follow to ensure truthful comparative advertising. These are shown in Table 2.4. An ad for Quantex that provides direct comparisons represents a typical comparative ad in the business-to-business sector.

Endorsements

A popular advertising strategy is the use of a spokesperson who endorses a brand. An **endorsement** or **testimonial** is any advertising message that consumers believe reflects the opinions, beliefs, or experiences of an individual, group, or institution. However, if consumers can reasonably ascertain that a message does not reflect the announcer's opinion, the message isn't an endorsement. For example, using a voice-over of a movie star in a commercial doesn't mean the commercial is an endorsement if the movie star is just narrating the film.

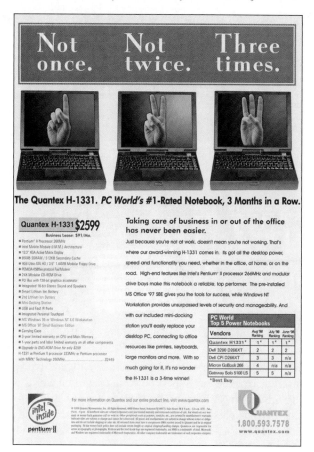

Because many consumers rely on endorsements to make buying decisions, the FTC investigates endorsement advertising. Endorsers must be qualified by experience or training to make judgments and they must actually use the product. If endorsers are comparing competing brands, they must have tried those brands as well. Those who endorse a product improperly may be liable if the FTC determines there is a deception.

Determining whether the endorsement is authentic is not easy. Is tennis player Andre Agassi a regular Coke drinker? Is he qualified to judge the quality of the product? The FTC likely would not pursue this issue unless there is an official complaint from a consumer or competitor. Typically, endorsers must have used the product before they became an endorser.

Product placements have muddied endorsement legal issues. **Product placements** are the use of brand-name items in movies or on TV, and now in novels, sometimes in exchange for a fee paid by the manufacturer to the producer. Is it deceptive if a TV character drinks a certain brand of soft drink or eats Kellogg's cereal, but the celebrity doesn't actually use either brand? Currently, such questions are an ethical issue, not a legal one.

Demonstrations

Product demonstrations in television advertising must not mislead consumers. This mandate is especially difficult for advertisements of food products because such factors as hot studio lights and the length of time needed to shoot the commercial can make the product look unappetizing. For example, because milk looks gray on television, advertisers often substitute a mixture of glue and water. The question is whether the demonstration falsely upgrades the consumers' perception of the advertised brand. The FTC evaluates this kind of deception on a case-by-case basis.

In this ad, basketball star Lisa Leslie endorses Nike sportswear. What legal issues do you think Nike had to consider with this ad?

One technique some advertisers use to sidestep restrictions on demonstrations is to insert disclaimers or "supers," verbal or written words in the ad that indicate exceptions to the advertising claim made. One example is a 30-second spot for Chrysler's Jeep Cherokee that begins with bold shots of the vehicle and music swelling in the background. Suddenly, the message is less clear; for several seconds five different, often lengthy disclaimers flash on the screen in tiny, eye-straining type, including "See dealers for details and guaranteed claim form" and "Deductibles and restrictions apply."[30]

FTC Deceptive and Unfair Advertising Remedies

The common sources of complaints concerning deceptive or unfair advertising practices are competitors, the public, and the FTC's own monitors. If a complaint seems justified, the commission can follow several courses of action: consent decrees, cease-and-desist orders, fines, corrective advertising, substantiation of advertising claims, and consumer redress.

Consent Decrees A **consent decree** is the first step in the regulation process after the FTC determines that an ad is deceptive. The FTC simply notifies the advertiser of its finding and asks the advertiser to sign a consent decree agreeing to stop the deceptive practice. Most advertisers do sign the decree to avoid the bad publicity and the possible $10,000-per-day fine for refusing to do so.

Cease-and-Desist Orders When the advertiser refuses to sign the consent decree and the FTC determines that the deception is substantial, it issues a **cease-and-desist** order. The process leading to the issuance of a cease-and-desist order is similar to a court trial. An administrative law judge presides. FTC staff attorneys represent the commission, and the accused parties are entitled to representation by their lawyers. If the administrative judge decides in favor of the FTC, the judge issues an order requiring the respondents to cease their unlawful practices. The advertiser can appeal the order to the full five-member commission.

Corrective Advertising The FTC requires **corrective advertising** when consumer research determines that an advertising campaign has perpetuated lasting false beliefs. Under this remedy, the FTC orders the offending person or organization to produce messages for consumers that correct the false impressions the ad made. The purpose of correc-

This TV commercial demonstrates the acceleration speed of the Volvo 850 Turbo Sportswagon compared to the BMW 328i. What legal issues do you think company and its agency had to consider with this type of ad?

tive advertising is not to punish an advertiser but to prevent it from continuing to deceive consumers. The FTC may require a firm to run corrective advertising even if the campaign in question has been discontinued.

A landmark corrective advertising case is *Warner-Lambert v. FTC*. According to the FTC, Warner-Lambert's campaign for Listerine mouthwash, which ran for 50 years, had been deceiving customers, leading them to think that Listerine could prevent or reduce the severity of sore throats and colds. The company was ordered to run a corrective advertising campaign, mostly on television, for 16 months at a cost of $10 million. The case is significant for two reasons. First, the Supreme Court gave the FTC the power to apply remedies to both past and ongoing campaigns to curtail future deceptions. Second, the Court rejected the argument that corrective advertising violates the advertiser's First Amendment rights.

Interestingly, after the Warner-Lambert corrective campaign ran its course, 42 percent of Listerine users continued to believe that the mouthwash was being advertised as a remedy for sore throats and colds, and 57 percent of users rated cold and sore throat effectiveness as a key reason for purchasing the brand.[31] These results raised doubts about the effectiveness of corrective advertising and have affected recent court decisions. A 1998 FTC administrative law judge ruled that a decade of Doan's pills advertising, which was deemed misleading, did not require corrective advertising because evidence indicated that such ads are not effective in changing consumer perceptions.

The 1998 decision also prompted the commission (specifically Commissioner Orson Swindle) to publish a statement on the logic of the practice of corrective advertising. In addition to concurring that there is no evidence that corrective advertising works,

---

Practical Tips #2

HOW TO PREVENT LEGAL ACTION

These four tips will help agencies avoid legal pitfalls in advertising:

1. Obtain written permission from the appropriate people early in the creative process if an ad carries the potential to violate copyright or privacy laws.
2. During production, make sure no one hires a person to sound like, look like, or otherwise represent a celebrity.
3. If shooting a commercial, prior to the shoot, get the producers' signed affidavit that demonstrations are not mockups.
4. Have regular seminars with a lawyer to update staff on how to stay within the limits of advertising law.

Commissioner Swindle also noted that the assumption that corrective advertising should run the same length of time as the deceptive ad had run is erroneous.

Consumer Redress The Magnuson-Moss Warranty-FTC Improvement Act of 1975 empowers the FTC to obtain consumer redress when a person or a firm engages in deceptive practices. The commission can order any of the following: cancellation or reformation of contracts, refund of money or return of property, payment of damages, and public notification.

Hold the Advertising Agency Legally Responsible With the resurgence of the FTC has come a new solution for deception within the FTC and in the federal courts: Make the ad agency liable instead of the advertiser. To quote former FTC chairperson Janet Steiger, "An agency that is involved in advertising and promoting a product is not free from responsibility for the content of the claims, whether they are expressed or implied. You will find the commission staff looking more closely at the extent of advertising involvement."[32] Essentially, an agency is liable for deceptive advertising along with the advertiser when the agency is an active participant in the preparation of the ad and knows or has reason to know that it is false or deceptive.

Agencies should heed the FTC's warnings. Several FTC actions and court cases in the early 1990s show that agencies must be prepared to defend their advertising practices. For example, a federal court found that Wilkinson, the maker of the Ultra Glide shaving system, intended to make misleading claims about Gillette and halted the campaign. The court awarded Gillette damages of nearly $1 million, to be paid by Wilkinson, and another $1 million to be paid by Wilkinson's agency, Friedman Benjamin.[33]

ADVERTISING AND OTHER REGULATORY AGENCIES

In addition to the FTC, several other federal agencies regulate advertising. The Food and Drug Administration and the Federal Communications Commission have become dynamic components of the advertising regulatory environment. Let's now examine the importance of these and other key regulatory agencies.

Food and Drug Administration

The **Food and Drug Administration (FDA)** is the regulatory division of the Department of Health and Human Services. It oversees package labeling and ingredient listings for food and drugs. It also determines the safety and purity of foods and cosmetics. Although not directly involved with advertising, the FDA provides advice to the FTC and has a major impact on the overall marketing of food, cosmetics, and drugs, as we saw in the discussion on the FDA's proposed tobacco restrictions.

TABLE 2.5	**Specialized Government Agencies That Affect Advertising**	

Agency	Effect on Advertising
Federal Trade Commission www.ftc.gov	Regulates credit, labeling, packaging, warranties, and advertising.
Food and Drug Administration www.fda.gov	Regulates packaging, labeling, and manufacturing of food and drug products.
Federal Communications Commission www.fcc.gov	Regulates radio and television stations and networks.
U.S. Postal Service www.usps.gov	Controls advertising by monitoring materials sent through the mail.
Bureau of Alcohol, Tobacco, and Firearms www.atf.treas.gov	Division of the U.S. Treasury Department that regulates advertising for alcoholic beverages.
U.S. Patent Office www.uspto.gov	Oversees trademark registration to protect against patent infringement.
Library of Congress www.loc.gov	Provides controls for copyright protection.

Federal Communications Commission

The **Federal Communications Commission (FCC)**, formed in 1934 to protect the public interest in radio and television broadcast communications, can issue and revoke licenses to broadcasting stations. The FCC also has the power to ban messages, including ads, that are deceptive or in poor taste. The agency monitors only advertisements that have been the subject of complaints and works closely with the FTC to eliminate false and deceptive advertising. The FCC takes actions against the media, whereas the FTC is concerned with advertisers and agencies.

Additional Federal Regulatory Agencies

Other federal agencies regulate advertising, although most are limited to a certain type of advertising, product, or medium, as we see in Table 2.5. For example, the Postal Service regulates direct mail and magazine advertising and has control over the areas of obscenity, lotteries, and fraud. Consumers who receive advertisements in the mail that they consider sexually offensive can request that no more mail be delivered from that sender.

The postmaster general also has the power to withhold mail that promotes lotteries. Fraud can include a number of activities that are questionable, such as implausible, get-rich-quick schemes.

The Bureau of Alcohol, Tobacco, and Firearms (ATF) within the Treasury Department regulates deception in advertising and establishes labeling requirements for the liquor industry. This agency's power comes from its authority to issue and revoke annual operating permits for distillers, wine merchants, and brewers. Because there is a danger that public pressure could result in the banning of all advertisements for alcoholic beverages, the liquor industry strives to maintain tight controls on its advertising.

The Patent Office, under the Lanham Trademark Act of 1947, oversees registration of trademarks, which include both brand names and corporate or store names as well as their identifying symbols. This registration process protects unique trademarks from infringement by competitors. Because trademarks are critical communication devices for products and services, they are important in advertising.

A recent trademark issue is protection for uniform resource locators (URLs), which are Internet domain names. Advertisers must remember that URLs have to be registered and protected just like any other trademark. They are issued on a first-come, first-served basis for any domain name not identical to an existing brand name.[34]

Finally, the Library of Congress provides controls for copyright protection. Legal copyrights give creators a monopoly on their creations for a certain time. Advertising is a competitive business in which me-too ads abound. Copyrighting of coined words, phrases, illustrations, characters, and photographs can offer some protection from other advertisers who borrow too heavily from their competitors.

Certain state laws also regulate unfair and deceptive business practices. These laws are important supplements to federal laws because of the sometimes limited resources and jurisdiction of federal legal and regulatory agencies. Because these laws are so numerous and diverse, we cannot begin to examine them in this chapter. Next, we investigate advertising self-regulation and social responsibility.

SOCIAL RESPONSIBILITY AND SELF-REGULATION

Do you think that advertising and advertisers must be governed carefully because without the laws and regulatory agencies most ads would be full of lies? Don't be fooled. Although some advertisers don't act ethically, a great majority of them follow a societal marketing approach. Philip Kotler, Professor of Marketing at Northwestern University, defines the societal marketing concept this way:

> The organization's task is to determine the needs, wants, and interests of target markets and to deliver the desired satisfactions more effectively and efficiently than its competitors in a way that preserves or enhances the consumer's and society's well-being. This requires a careful balance between company profits, consumer-want satisfaction, and public interest.[35]

Admittedly, this is not an easy balance to maintain. Yet advertisers realize that millions of consumers and a host of agencies carefully scrutinize everything they do. Advertisers regulate themselves more stringently than do government agencies.

There are three aspects of social responsibility:

1. Self-discipline: An organization develops, uses, and enforces norms by itself.
2. Pure self-regulation: The industry develops, uses, and enforces norms.
3. Co-opted self-regulation: The industry voluntarily involves nonindustry people in the development, application, and enforcement of norms.[36]

Self-Discipline

Virtually all major advertisers and advertising agencies have in-house ad review procedures. Several U.S. companies (Colgate-Palmolive, General Foods, AT&T) have their own codes of behavior and criteria that determine whether advertisements are acceptable. Companies without such codes tend to have informal criteria that they apply on an ad-by-ad basis. At a minimum, advertisers and agencies should have every element of a proposed ad evaluated by an in-house committee, lawyers, or both.

In the Netherlands, industry members have encouraged the formation of an "ethical office" to oversee all agencies, advertisers, and media. That office is responsible for reviewing advertisements to ensure that they comply with the Dutch Advertising Code and general ethical principles. In Swedish advertising agencies, an executive known as the "responsible editor" is trained and experienced in marketing law; that editor reviews all the advertisements and promotional materials to ensure that they are legally and ethically acceptable. See "The Inside Story" for one executive's viewpoint.

Pure Self-Regulation

In the case of both advertisers and advertising agencies, the most effective attempts at pure self-regulation have come through the Advertising Review Council (ARC) and the Better Business Bureau. In 1971 several professional advertising associations in conjunction with the Council of Better Business Bureaus established the National Advertising

THE INSIDE STORY

ON SOCIALLY RESPONSIBLE COMMUNICATIONS

Bob Witeck   Witeck-Combs Communications

"Since we opened our   in 1993, I have developed strong convictions about the kind of work we can best offer clients. It seems clear to us that a company or organization's brand truly does not go deep enough to reach many stakeholders. Effective branding—alone—also does not imply a socially responsible philosophy or practices.

We also focus on a client's reputation, and the values that an organization or a company communicates—internally and externally. Simply put, if a company's management does not preserve and communicate its values inside the workplace, it can be tougher to earn a solid, lasting reputation in the marketplace. Reputation is often the strongest foundation for a successful brand.

Reputations are built and reinforced in a number of ways. They are based on transparent, consistent strategies and workplace practices that earn public support, consumer loyalty and continued investment. For employers, this also means creating a respectful, diverse and welcoming place to work—including groups that often are stigmatized, such as gays and lesbians, people with disabilities and others.

Companies that consciously instill and communicate their socially responsible actions to their own employees, as well as customers, investors, peers, policy makers and the media, often set the pace for entire industries. For the best in their fields, socially responsible actions also translate into profitability. "

Robert Witeck is CEO and co-founder of Witeck-Combs Communications, with over twenty-five years' professional communications experience in the private sector and as a Senate Press Secretary. Among the firm's clients are American Airlines, the Christopher Reeve Paralysis Foundation, Coors Brewing Company, the Cellular Telecommunications and Internet Association, and the American Association of People with Disabilities. In May 2001, Fortune *magazine included Bob Witeck and his business partner, Wes Combs, as two of the nation's twenty-five most influential openly gay business leaders.*

Review Council, which negotiates voluntary withdrawal of national advertising that professionals consider deceptive. The National Advertising Division (NAD) of the Council of Better Business Bureaus and the National Advertising Review Board (NARB) are the two operating arms of the National Advertising Review Council. None of these are government agencies.

National Advertising Division (NAD) NAD is a full-time agency made up of people from the field of advertising. It evaluates complaints submitted by consumers, consumer groups, industrial organizations, and advertising firms. NAD also does its own industry monitoring. After NAD receives a complaint, it may ask the advertiser in question to substantiate claims made in the advertisement. If such substantiation is deemed inadequate, NAD representatives ask the advertiser to change or withdraw the offending ad. When a satisfactory resolution cannot be found, NAD refers the case to NARB.

National Advertising Review Board (NARB) NARB is a 50-member regulatory group that represents national advertisers, advertising agencies, and other professional fields. When the advertiser appeals a case to NARB, it faces a review panel of five people: three advertisers, one agency person, and one public representative. This NARB panel reviews the complaint and the NAD staff findings and holds hearings to let the advertiser present its case. If the case remains unresolved after the process, NARB can (1) publicly identify the advertiser and the facts about the case and (2) refer the complaint to the appropriate government agency (usually the FTC). Although neither NAD nor NARB has any

FIGURE 2.2

THE NARB APPEAL PROCESS
Consumers or groups submitting a complaint to NAD and NARB go through this process. The ultimate power of NAD and NARB is the threat of passing the claim to the FTC. Usually, cases are settled before that point.

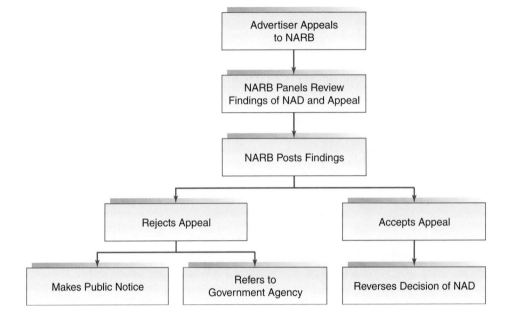

real power other than threatening to invite government intervention, these groups have been effective in controlling cases of deception and misleading advertising. Figure 2.2 summarizes the NARB appeal process.

Local Regulation

At the local level, self-regulation has been supported by the Better Business Bureau (BBB). The BBB (www.bbb.org) functions much like the national regulatory agencies, and also provides local businesses with advice concerning the legal aspects of advertising. Approximately 250 local and national bureaus, made up of advertisers, agencies, and media, have screened hundreds of thousands of advertisements for possible violations of truth and accuracy. Although the BBB has no legal power, it does receive and investigate complaints and maintain files on violators. It also assists local law enforcement officials in prosecuting violators. The ease with which the BBB can be accessed on the Internet has prompted businesses to be more careful about complying with its standards.

Although the Better Business Bureau has no legal power, it does have influence and it does help local law enforcement prosecute businesses that act illegally.

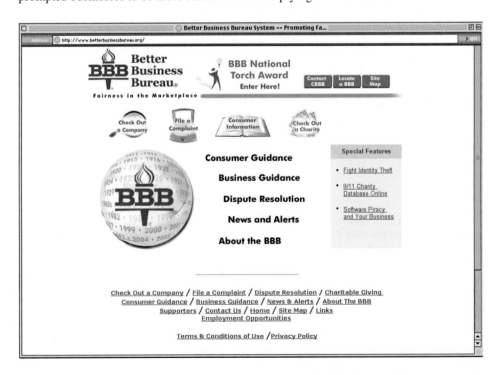

Media Regulation and Advertising

The media attempts to regulate advertising by screening and rejecting ads that violate their standards of truth and good taste. For example, *The Reader's Digest* does not accept tobacco and liquor ads, and many magazines and television stations do not show condom ads. Each individual medium has the discretion to accept or reject a particular ad. In the case of the major television networks, the ARC's advertising standards and guidelines serve as the primary standard.

Advertising, a high-profile industry, will remain extremely susceptible to legislation and the criticisms of the general public. Rather than lament such scrutiny, advertisers would be wise to take the initiative and establish individual ethical standards that anticipate and even go beyond the complaints. Such a proactive stance helps the creative process and avoids the kinds of disasters that result from violating the law or offending members of society.

In addition, as advertisers, agencies, and media become more and more global, it will be imperative that the players understand the ethical standards and laws in which they operate. For example, in Hungary, tobacco ads have been banned since the communist occupation. Advertisers who violate the ethical code of conduct in Brazil can be fined up to $500,000 US or given up to a five-year prison sentence. This punishment would certainly prompt an advertiser to be careful.

IT'S A WRAP
CARING PAYS OFF

A critical issue in advertising is the value of producing socially conscious ads in an economy where consumers are primarily concerned with meeting their own needs and wants. Can an advertiser with limited resources risk producing ads that may not provide additional sales? In the case of the EFFIE-winning CIGNA campaign, it appears that CIGNA has done both. According to Communities Tracking Studies, CIGNA Cares has produced the following results: Brand familiarity among consumers has grown 46 percent, making CIGNA number one in its category; key perceptions have grown between 17 and 70 percent; favorable impressions among consumers are up nearly 75 percent; likelihood to join has increased by 29 percent; and "Benefits Professionals," favorable impressions of CIGNA, have improved from 32 to 40 percent since the campaign began.

Summary

1. **Discuss the social issues advertisers face**. Advertising, a high-profile industry, plays a strong role in society. Ethical questions about advertising revolve around three criteria: advocacy, accuracy, and acquisitiveness. If advertisers fail to act ethically, society usually feels the repercussions. Acting ethically is no easy feat: The issues may be complex, the actions may depend on individual judgment, and they may conflict with business success. Advertising can play a positive social role by promoting and supporting health, education, and welfare issues through such activities as the Connecticut Breast Cancer Awareness campaign.

2. **List the key ethical issues that affect advertising**. The key ethical issues that affect advertising include puffery, taste, stereotyping, communicating with children appropri-ately, promoting controversial products, and subliminal advertising.

3. **Identify the main factors in advertising's legal and regulatory environment**. The main factors in the legal and regulatory environment are the First Amendment and privacy case law, the Federal Trade Commission, additional government regulatory entities including the U.S. Post Office, and the Federal Communications Commission. The industry's self-regulation is another major component.

4. **Outline how federal case law affects advertising**. Federal courts interpret legislation in individual cases, thereby creating case law. Case law interpreting the First Amendment to the U.S. Constitution is the most basic case law that governs advertising. The level of protection the First Amendment

case law offers to advertisers has varied over time, so advertisers must keep abreast of the legal developments to avoid missteps. Case law interpreting consumers' rights to privacy also affects advertisers, particularly online advertisers that collect personal data about consumers.

5. **Summarize how the FTC and other federal agencies govern advertising**. The Federal Trade Commission is the most important government agency affecting advertising. It deals with the following legal issues in advertising: deception, reasonable basis for making a claim, comparative advertising, endorsements, and demonstrations. The FTC can initiate the following remedies for deceptive and unfair advertising: consent decrees, cease-and-desist orders, and corrective advertising. In addition, an ad agency can be held legally

liable if the agency was an active participant in the preparation of the ad and knew or had reason to know that it was false or deceptive. A number of other government agencies influence advertising, including the Food and Drug Administration, the Federal Communications Commission, the U.S. Postal Service, the Bureau of Alcohol, Tobacco, and Firearms, and the Library of Congress.

6. **Debate whether advertising self-regulation fulfills advertisers' responsibility to society**. Advertising engages in self-regulation at various levels: self-discipline, pure self-regulation, co-opted self-regulation, and negotiated self-regulation. Self-regulation is one way for advertisers to act in a socially responsible way. The question remains whether self-regulation fulfills advertising's responsibility to society.

Key Terms

cease-and-desist order, p. 50

commercial speech, p. 44

consent decree, p. 50

corrective advertising,
   p. 50

endorsement, p. 48

Federal Communications
   Commission (FCC), p. 53

Federal Trade Commission
   (FTC), p. 45

Food and Drug Administration
   (FDA), p. 52

indirect advertising, p. 40

product placements, p. 49

puffery, p. 34

social marketing, p. 34

stereotyping, p. 36

subliminal message, p. 42

testimonial, p. 48

Questions

1. Two local agencies are in fierce contention for a major client in Hillsboro, Oregon. The final presentations are three days away when Sue Geners, an account executive for the Adcom Group, learns from her sister-in-law that the creative director for the rival agency has serious personal problems. His son has entered a drug rehabilitation program and his wife has filed for a divorce. Because this information comes from personal sources, Sue knows it's very likely that anyone on the business side of Hillsboro has any knowledge of it. Should she inform Adcom management? If she does, should Adcom warn the prospective client that a key person in the rival agency will be under serious strain for months to come?

2. Sue Geners, our account executive from the preceding question, has a quandary of her own. Adcom keeps very strict hourly records on its accounts for billing and cost accounting purposes. One of Sue's old friends works for an Adcom client that needs some strong promotional strategy. However, the client is very small and cannot afford the hours that Sue would have to charge. Should Sue do the work and charge those hours to one of her larger clients? Should she turn down her friend? What should she do?

3. Zack Wilson is the advertising manager for the campus newspaper. He is looking over a layout for a promotion for a spring break vacation package. The headline says, "Absolutely the Finest Deal Available This Spring—You'll Have the Best Time Ever if You Join Us in Boca." The newspaper has a solid reputation for not running advertising with questionable claims and promises. Should Zack accept or reject this ad?

4. The Dimento Game Company has a new basketball video game. To promote it, "Slammer" Aston, an NBA star, is signed to do the commercial. In it, Aston is shown with the game controls as he speaks these lines: "This is the most challenging court game you've ever tried. It's all here— zones, man-to-man, pick and roll, even the alley-oop. For me, this is the best game off the court." Is Aston's presentation an endorsement? Should the FTC consider a complaint if Dimento uses this strategy?

5. What are the central issues in ethical decision making? Write a short evaluation of a current ad campaign using three ethical criteria.

6. Think of an ad you found deceptive or offensive. What bothered you about the ad? Should the medium have carried it? Who would act more effectively in a case like this: the government or the advertising industry? Explain.

7. Do you think subliminal advertising exists? If so, what do you believe are the risks associated with this technique?

8. A pharmaceutical company has repackaged a previously developed drug that addresses the symptoms of a scientifically questionable disorder affecting approximately 5 percent of women. While few women are affected by the "disorder," the company's advertising strategy is comprehensive, including dozens of television, radio, and magazine ads. As a result, millions of women with symptoms similar to those of the disorder have sought prescriptions for the company's drug. In turn, the company has made billions of dollars. What, if any, are the ethical implications of advertising a remedy to a mass audience when the

affected group is small? Is the company misrepresenting its drug by conducting a "media blitz"? Why or why not?

9. How are ethical decisions about advertising validated? As this chapter discusses, different products offend different people, and context is also relevant. Why have various agencies and laws been created to regulate advertisers? Why haven't advertisers succeeded in self-regulation? Industry regulation?

10. In recent years, the concept of cause marketing has emerged. Companies align their products with a cause like breast cancer or protecting the environment, and in turn, hope to generate more sales as a result. Is this ethical? Why or why not? Are you more likely to buy a product associated with a "good cause"? Why or why not?

Suggested Class Project

Select three print ads that you feel contain one or more of the ethical issues discussed in this chapter. Ask five people (making sure they vary by gender, age, or background) how they feel about the ads. Conduct a short interview with each of your subjects; it would be helpful to have a list of questions prepared. Write a report on their opinions and response to your questionnaire. Don't be afraid to include your own conclusions about the ads. What differences or similarities do you see across the responses?

Suggested Internet Class Project

Check the Web sites of three big-name companies such as:

• Mc Donald's www.mcdonalds.com
• Avon www.avon.com
• Ben & Jerry's www.benjerry.com

Write a two to four page report on their efforts to be socially responsible.

HANDS-ON   Case 2

KEEPING THINGS PRIVATE ON THE WEB

The World Wide Web has virtually joined the entire world into a community of commerce, but with any major advance there are advantages and disadvantages. In the case of the Web, the most serious concern has been the issue of personal privacy. To date, the U.S. government has passed no specific laws defining the criteria for maintaining personal privacy on the Internet, nor provisions for governing privacy on the Internet.

Through the Web, marketers can easily collect personal information, use it themselves, and share (sell) it with other noncompeting marketers. Say, for example, you purchase a fishing rod online and complete the warranty card listing key demographics, along with your hobbies and interests, preferred media, and e-mail address. A file is created through database software with this information, and additional relevant information (purchased from other vendors) is added, so that each time an offer arises that may be of interest to you, the marketer can send you a promotion. Your response can then be stored as a cookie on your Web hard disk and all your future online actions can be tracked over time. Explains the Web site junkbusters.com:

Many organizations use "cookies" to track your every move on their site. A cookie is a unique identifier that a Web server places on your computer: a serial number for you personally that can be used to retrieve your records from their databases. It's usually a string of random-looking letters long enough to be unique. They are kept in a file called cookies or cookies.txt or MagicCookie in your browser directory/folder. They are also known as "persistent cookies" because they may last for years, even if you change ISP or upgrade your browser. http://www.junkbusters.com/ht/en/cookies.html

Many people feel uneasy with this technology, and contend that private citizens should have more control over who gets their information, but much of the concern for privacy abated after

(continued)

September 11, 2001. Terrorism put privacy on the back burner. "The bottom line is that for now, privacy will be a secondary issue to security," says Larry Ponemon, chief executive of the Privacy Council, a Dallas knowledge and technology company. "Because of this disaster, people aren't worrying about giving up too much information as long as a company is going to make the world a safer place." In this case, a company refers to those engaged in legitimate commerce.

While many people are still concerned that this reprioritization will increase the violation of personal privacy through the Internet, there are other people who view it as a blessing. Federal Trade Commission chairman Timothy Muris posits that the focus on anti-terrorism will actually strengthen all legislation that protects personal safety. For example, this new awareness level for personal safety has turned Muris's attention to Web sites that collect data on children without their parents' permission. ∎

IT'S YOUR TURN

1. Do you think self-regulation can be effective in tackling this problem? Should the government regulate marketing practices on the Internet, or should the government trust marketers to regulate themselves?
2. What approach should an advertiser take in respect to Internet privacy?

Sources: Amy Harmon, "Net Privacy at Issue," *Denver Post* (June 4, 1998): 1C, 10C; Dan Soheraga, "The Day the Privacy Died," *Chain Stone Age,* 11 (November 2000): 78; Stephanie Losen and Evan Hansen, "Privacy vs. Safety: Terrorists Threats Shifts Priorities in the Online Rights Debate," *Fortune,* 10 (Winter 2002): 29; Rebecca Gardyn, "Swap Meet," *American Demographics* (June 2001): 51–55.

Notes

1. Barbara Nachman, "Ad Nauseum: 5,000 Commercials Barrage Average Americans Every Day," *Denver Post* (September 25, 2000): 16, 46; Chris Woodyard, "Look Up, Down, All Around—Ads Fill Airports, Planes," *USA Today* (July 10, 2001): 12B.

2. Herbert J. Rotfeld and Kim B. Rotzoll, "Is Advertising Puffery Believed?" *Journal of Advertising* 9(3) (1980): 16–20, 45.

3. Barry R. Shapiro, "Beyond Puffery," *Marketing Management* 4(3) (Winter 1995): 60–62.

4. Suzanne Vranica, "Gruesome Ads Aren't Intended to Hurt," *Wall Street Journal* (May 4, 2000): B14.

5. Bill Abrams, "Poll Suggests TV Advertisers Can't Ignore Matters of Taste," *Wall Street Journal* (July 23, 1981): 25.

6. John Crichton, "Morals and Ethics in Advertising," in *Ethics, Morality and the Media*, Lee Thayer, ed. (New York: Hastings House, 1980): 105–15.

7. Alessandra Galloni, "In a New Global Campaign, Durex Maker Uses Humor to Sell Condoms," *Wall Street Journal* (July 27, 2001): B1; Anita Chang, "Survey: Condom Ads Are OK," *Adweek* (June 25, 2001): 32.

8. Michael J. Etzell and E. Leon Knight Jr., "The Effect of Documented versus Undocumented Advertising Claims," *Journal of Consumer Affairs* 10 (Winter 1976): 233–38.

9. Daniel J. Brett and Joanne Cantor, "The Portrayal of Men and Women in U.S. Television Commercials: A Recent Content Analysis and Trends of 15 Years," *Sex Roles* 18(9/10) (1998): 595–608; Carmela Mazzella, Kevin Durkin, Emma Cerini, and Paul Buralli, "Sex Role Stereotyping in Australian Television Advertising," *Sex Roles* 26(7/8) (1992): 243–58.

10. Erving Goffman, *Gender Advertisements* (Cambridge, MA: Harvard University Press, 1996); John B. Ford and Michael La Tour, "Contemporary Perspectives of Female Role Portrayals in Advertising," *Journal of Current Issues and Research in Advertising* 28(1) (Spring 1996): 81–93.

11. Carol Krol, "Few Direct Efforts Target Hispanics," *Advertising Age* (August 24, 1998): S4, S6.

12. Michelle Wirth Fellman, "Preventing Viagra's Fall," *Marketing News* (August 31, 1998): 1, 8.

13. John J. Burnett, "Gays: Feelings about Advertising and Media Used," *Journal of Advertising Research* (January–February 2000): 75–86.

14. Robert M. Liebert and Joyce Sprafkin, *The Early Window: Effects of Television on Children and Youth* (New York: Pergamon, 1998). See also National Science Foundation, *Research on the Effects of Television Advertising on Children* (1977): 45.

15. "The Positive Case for Marketing Children's Products to Children," comments by the Association of National Advertisers, Inc., American Association of Advertising Agencies, and the American Advertising Federation before the Federal Trade Commission (November 24, 1978).

16. Ira Teinowitz, "Senate Opens Debate on Tobacco Ad Limits," *Advertising Age* (May 18, 1998): 3, 38; Ira Teinowitz, "White House Studies Final Rules on Tobacco Ads," *Advertising Age* (August 19, 1996): 3, 29.

17. Julie Schmit, "Cigarette Logos Abound Despite Ad Bans Abroad," *USA Today* (September 12, 2000): B1–B2.

18. David Leonhardt, "Absolute Folly?" *BusinessWeek* (November 25, 1996): 46; Sally Goll Beatty, "Seagram Baits the Ad Hook for TV," *Wall Street Journal* (September 15, 1997): B10.

19. Chuck Ross and Ira Teinowitz, "Beer Ad Has Wide Underage Reach on MTV," *Advertising Age* (January 6, 1997): 4; Ira Teinowitz, "FTC Governing of Beer Ads Expands to Miller, A-B," *Advertising Age* (April 7, 1997): 1, 50.

20. Nora Fitzgerald, "Roll of the Dice," *Adweek* (February 17, 1997): 21; Ira Teinowitz, "Odds Favor Gaining Ads after Last Court Ruling," *Advertising Age* (March 10, 1997): 16.

21. Bill McInturff, "While Critics May Fret, Public Likes DTC Ads," *Advertising Age* (March 26, 2001): 24; David Goetzi, "Take a Heaping Spoon-ful," *Advertising Age* (November 6, 2000): 32; Angetta McQueen, "Watchdog Blames Ad Spending for High Drug Costs," *Denver Post* (July 11, 2001): 4C.

22. Walter Weir, "Another Look at Subliminal Facts," *Advertising Age* (October 15, 1984): 46.

23. Dave Carpenter, "Hidden Messages are Back in Focus," *Denver Rocky Mountain News* (September 17, 2000): 11G.

24. Robert S. Greenberger, "More Courts are Granting Advertisements First Amendment Protection," *Wall Street Journal* (July 3, 2001): B1–B3.

25. Pamela Paul, "Mixed Signals," *American Demographics* (July 2001): 45–50; Rebecca Gardyn, "Swap Meet," *American Demographics* (July 2001): 51–58; Eve M. Caudill and Patrick E. Murphy, "Consumer Online Privacy: Legal and Ethical Issues," *Journal of Public Policy & Marketing* 19(1) (Spring 2000): 7–19.

26. "Letter to Congress Explaining FTC's New Deception Policy," Advertising Compliance Service (Westport, CT: Meckler Publishing, November 21, 1983) and Ivan Preston, "A Review of the Literature on Advertising Regulation," in *Current Issues and Research in Advertising* (1983), James H. Leigh and Claude L. Martin, eds. (Ann Arbor: University of Michigan Press): 2–37.

27. Steven W. Colford, "FTC Warns Agencies; Eyes Tobacco, Cable," *Advertising Age* (March 12, 1990): 6; Attorney General's Office Investigates Advertising Claims," *Marketing News* (February 29, 1988): 16.

28. David J. Morrow, "Attorneys General Team in Consumer Battle Plan," *Denver Post* (November 1997): 5J.

29. Robert E. Wilkes and James B. Wilcox , "Recent FTC Actions: Implications for the Advertising Strategists," *Journal of Marketing* 38 (January 1974): 55–56.

30. Michael McCartly, "Oops!" *USA Today* (August 28, 2001): 3B.

31. William Wilke, Dennis L. McNeil, and Michael B. Mazis, "Marketing's Scarlet Letter: The Theory and Practice of Corrective Advertising," *Journal of Marketing* (Spring 1984): 26.

32. Stephen P. Durchslag, "Agency Liability Extends to False Advertising Claims," *Promo* (October 1992): 17.

33. Ira Teinowitz, "FTC Faces Test of Ad Powers," *Advertising Age* (March 30, 1998): 26.

34. Robert J. Posch Jr., "Trademark Protection for Internet Domain Names," *Direct Marketing* (July 1998): 63–65.

35. Philip Kotler, *Marketing Management: Analysis, Planning, Implementation, and Control*, 9th ed. (Upper Saddle River, NJ: Prentice Hall, 1997): 28–29.

36. J. J. Boddewyn, "Advertising Self-Regulation: Private Government and Agent of Public Policy," *Journal of Public Policy and Marketing* (January 1985): 129–41.

CHAPTER 3

Advertising and the Marketing Process

CHAPTER OBJECTIVES

When you have completed this chapter, you should be able to

1. Discuss and define marketing and how advertising relates to marketing strategy.
2. Explain the marketing concept.
3. Outline the four tools of marketing and explain advertising's relationship to them.
4. Describe the role of the advertising agency, its organization, and compensation methods.

A Relaunch That Worked

Award: *EFFIE Silver 2001, Financial Services category*

Company: *General Motors, The GM Card*

Agency: *Mullen of Wenham, MA*

Campaign: *"What Are You Charging Toward?"*

One phenomenon the 1990s will be remembered for is the marketing efforts of the credit card industry. Competing on a myriad of factors, such as low introductory interest rates, no annual fees, and reward rebates for amounts purchased, credit card companies spent millions of dollars trying to convince consumers that their offering was best.

However, with the end of the prosperous 1990s came the end of prosperous credit card programs. Many consumers had charged the limit on their credit cards and for various reasons, job loss included, were unable to pay their debts. All in all, the industry was in a serious slump.

The GM Card, a co-branded product from General Motors and Household Credit Services, was one of the credit card superstars of the 1990s. Launched in 1992, it acquired over 1 million card members in its first 30 days, peaking at 12 million by 1996. After those phenomenal years, the card was hit particularly hard by the proliferation of new reward cards, fierce price competition, and a wiser consumer. By 1999, the GM Card found itself with a diminishing membership.

In 1999, GM Card managers began working on a new marketing strategy that would bring their product out of the doldrums. The new card, they said, must retain the primary features that appealed to customers, add a few new bells and whistles, and most importantly, include better financial controls to protect GM Card Inc.

Comfortable with the redesigned card, GM Card marketers decided on summer 2000 as the launch period—just in time for Christmas purchases. The new marketing plan had two primary objectives: (1) to increase brand awareness of the GM Card among bank card and reward users by 10 percent, and (2) acquire 600,000 new customers.

After careful research, GM Card determined that its target audience was consumers who have one or more credit cards, who try to pay off their cards each month, and who view their cards as a financial partner that facilitates financial well-being. Also, because consumers can use the GM Card to purchase GM's cars, the company wanted consumers who had a positive attitude toward American-made cars.

That same research presented some serious obstacles to the success of the GM Card. Most notably, consumers viewed the GM Card reward system, in which they could apply rebates based on their purchases toward a new car, as largely unattainable, and they considered the reward programs of competing cards to be more generous. Instead of avoiding these negative perceptions, GM Card decided to address them directly. The new card was positioned as "the fastest way to save toward a new car or truck of your dreams." The strategy attempted to give consumers a more realistic perspective of what rewards they value.

In addition to a fully integrated advertising campaign, GM Card also employed a direct-mail campaign, a magazine insert that included an application with a return envelope, a new Web site, an e-mail program, and point-of-purchase materials located at GM dealerships. All of these elements were intended to start at the time of the mass media launch.

Clearly, overcoming the barriers cited was difficult. How well did the GM Card campaign do? Check the "It's a Wrap" box at the end of this chapter.

WHAT IS MARKETING?

An advertiser needs an effective campaign to help its new product succeed. However, to succeed a product must offer customers value, a supportive distribution network of retailers, and proper pricing. Because advertising is just one part of the total marketing effort, it's unlikely that an advertising agency could achieve its goals without a thorough understanding of its client's marketing programs.

This chapter explores how marketing influences and shapes advertising. It examines how the relationship between marketing and advertising plays a key role in an integrated marketing communication strategy. It also takes a look at the advertising agency, its variations, and its structures.

The American Marketing Association defines **marketing** as the process of planning and executing the conception, pricing, promotion, and distribution of ideas, goods, and services to create exchanges that satisfy the perceived needs, wants, and objectives of the customer and the organization.[1] Stated simply, marketing is the process of finding, satisfying, and retaining customers while the business meets its goals. Although all marketing focuses on the exchange and the customer, every business must tailor its marketing to fit into its business plan.

An **exchange** is the act of trading a desired product or service for something of value in return. How do marketers prompt the exchange process? They must market effectively from start to finish.

Advertising's Role in the Marketing Plan

Advertising is an integral but relatively small part of the marketing plan. Traditionally, businesses plan their marketing initiatives by examining the **marketing mix**, a blend of activities such as designing the product and its package, pricing the product, distributing

---

TABLE 3.1   Strengths of Advertising as a Marketing Technique

Strengths	Examples
Can reach a mass audience	A commercial on the Super Bowl reaches 150 million consumers.
Introduces products	Windows 98 was simultaneously introduced in multiple world markets.
Explains important changes	MTN Cellular's ads explain changes in its technology.
Reminds and reinforces	Pepsi-Cola has been advertised continuously over the last 50 years.
Persuades	Nike campaigns have helped increase sales by 300% during the last decade.

---

the product so that it is accessible to customers, and promoting or communicating about the product. Marketers use the marketing mix as the means to reach their marketing goals.

The last element of the mix, **marketing communications** (also known as promotion), is an umbrella term for many types of promotional activities: advertising, public relations, sales promotions, personal selling, packaging, point-of-sale, and direct marketing. Advertising is one of several marketing communication techniques.

Advertising, as a marketing communication technique, is capable of reaching a mass audience repeatedly. It also effectively informs customers about new products, explains important changes in existing products, reminds customers to buy, and reinforces past purchases. Finally, advertising can persuade customers to change their attitudes, beliefs, or behavior. Table 3.1 summarizes the strengths of advertising.

Superior advertising cannot save an inferior marketing plan or rescue a bad product—at least not for long—but inferior advertising can destroy an excellent plan or product. The advertising director must thoroughly understand marketing and advertising's role in the marketing plan. The marketing manager, too, must understand the role advertising plays in the marketing effort.

Types of Markets

The word *market* originally meant the place where the exchange between seller and buyer took place. Today we speak of a **market** as either a region where goods are sold and bought or a particular type of buyer.

When marketing strategists speak of markets, they generally refer to groups of people or organizations. As Figure 3.1 shows, the four main types of markets are (1) consumer, (2) business-to-business (industrial), (3) institutional, and (4) reseller. We can further divide each of these markets by size or geography, such as local, regional, national, or international.

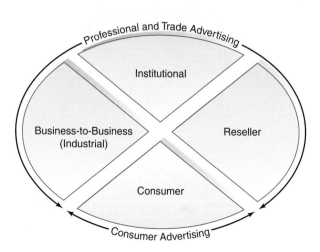

FIGURE 3.1

THE FOUR MAIN TYPES OF MARKETS
The consumer market is only one of four markets.

Consumer Markets Consumer markets consist of people who buy products and services for personal or household use. As a student, you are considered a member of the market for companies that sell jeans, sweatshirts, pizza, textbooks, backpacks, education, and bicycles, along with a multitude of other products. Some ads for Pantene are targeted at upscale consumers between the ages of 16 and 28.

Business-to-Business (Industrial) Markets Business-to-business markets consist of companies that buy products or services to use in their own businesses or in making other products. General Electric, for example, buys computers to use in billing and inventory control, steel and wiring to use in the manufacture of its products, and cleaning supplies to use in maintaining its buildings. Ads in this category usually are heavy on factual content and light on emotion.

Institutional Markets Institutional markets include a wide variety of profit and nonprofit organizations—such as hospitals, government agencies, and schools—that provide goods and services for the benefit of society. Universities, for example, are in the market for furniture, cleaning supplies, computers, office supplies, groceries, audiovisual material, and paper towels and toilet paper, to name a few. Such ads are very similar to business-to-business ads in that they are heavy on copy and light on visuals.

Reseller Markets The reseller market is made up of what we call intermediaries. Resellers are wholesalers, retailers, and distributors who buy finished or semifinished products and resell them for a profit. Microsoft and its retailers are part of the reseller packet. Prestone is a wholesaler that distributes its de-icing fluid and other products to

This ad for Pantene is targeted at consumers age 16 to 28. The consumer market is one of four general markets.

retailers. Companies that sell such products and services as trucks, cartons, and transportation services (airlines, cruise ships, and rental car agencies) consider resellers their market.

Of the four markets, businesses spend the most advertising dollars on consumer markets. They usually advertise to consumers through mass media such as radio, television, newspapers, general consumer magazines, and direct-response advertising media (that is, direct mail and online). Businesses typically reach the other three markets—industrial, international, and reseller—through trade and professional advertising in specialized media such as trade journals, professional magazines, and direct mail.

Approaching the Market

Marketing planners need to develop a strategy for approaching the market. Figure 3.2 shows that the marketer's first step is to assess the needs of the market. Then, because consumers in a market are seldom uniform, planners must decide whether to treat the market as homogeneous (that is, as a single, undifferentiated, large unit) or as heterogeneous (a market composed of separate, smaller groups known as segments). The market segments of potential customers a product provider selects is its target market. Marketers approach their target markets with the competitive strategies of product differentiation and positioning. We discuss these elements next.

Undifferentiated and Segmentation Approaches When planners treat the market as homogeneous, they purposely ignore differences in the market and use one marketing strategy that will appeal to as many people as possible. This market strategy is known as an **undifferentiated or market aggregation strategy**. At one point in its history, Coca-Cola viewed the U.S. market as homogeneous and used general appeals—such as "Coke is it!"—for all consumers. This strategy is risky because it may appeal to no one, or the resources wasted will be greater than the total gain in sales.

Few examples of homogeneous markets exist. Often, companies take an undifferentiated approach because they lack the resources to target different market segments. For certain types of widely consumed items (such as gasoline and basic white bread), however, the undifferentiated market approach makes sense because the potential market is large enough to justify possible wasted resources. At one time, the bottled water industry used this approach. Clearly, that has changed.

Market segmentation is a much more common market approach. It assumes that the best way to sell to the market is to recognize differences and adjust to them accordingly. Marketers divide the entire heterogeneous market into segments that are homogeneous. From these segments, the marketer identifies, evaluates, and selects a **target market**, a group of people with similar needs and characteristics who are most likely to be receptive to the marketer's product. For instance, a retailer such as Computer Shack offers various hardware, software, and support services to select target markets to sell more products to more people more often.

By using a segmentation approach, a company can more precisely match the needs and wants of the customer and generate more sales. That's why soft drink manufacturers such as Coke and Pepsi have moved away from the undifferentiated approach and have introduced diet, caffeine-free, and diet caffeine-free versions of their basic products. This approach also allows a company to target advertising more precisely. As noted in the "A Matter of Practice" box, one segment, kids, are not easy to reach.

In the United States, ethnicity is becoming a major criterion for segmenting markets. According to the Census Bureau, the number of African Americans will increase by 15 percent during the next 20 years; Asian-Americans by almost 68 percent, and Hispanics by about 64 percent; while the Caucasian population will grow by 13 percent. Even so, consumer habits within each ethnic segment will differ, based on factors such as age and income, and in the case of immigrants, how long they have lived in the United States.

A case-in-point is Mazola's campaign to strengthen its status as a premium brand within Asian-American households. The company ran brand print advertisements featuring large photos of the packaging of its corn oil with ad copy in Chinese, and gave out

Step 1

Assess the needs of the market and the company's ability to meet those needs profitably.

Step 2

Choose an undifferentiated, segmentation, or combination strategy.

Step 3

For a segmentation or combination strategy, determine the target market(s) that would be most receptive to the product.

Step 4

Select an approach to each target market through product differentiation and positioning.

Step 5

Take action to approach the target market(s).

FIGURE 3.2

THE PROCESS OF APPROACHING THE MARKET
The marketer cannot proceed until the needs of the target market have been assessed.

A MATTER OF PRACTICE

REACHING KIDS CAN BE TRICKY

▶ Of the $6.5 trillion spent annually by consumers in the United States, some $300 billion is spent by kids under the age of 12. These children are the offspring of the baby boomers, and marketers can expect the effect they have to be similar to the impact their parents had during the 1960s.

The sheer size of the market (some 45 million strong) makes it worth the attention of marketers. Add to that the influence kids have over another enormous market—their parents—and you have a group of consumers with an unprecedented amount of economic clout.

So how can marketers reach this group of powerful consumers? You've got to get inside their heads, relate to their needs, understand how they think, and find out where they spend their time and money and what moves them. Research has found that they are smart, aware, and fair-minded. They like to be entertained in the ads directed at them. They love spoofs and anything that makes them laugh, but not at someone's expense. They don't like ads that make fun of anyone. What they do like is things that are "green." They relate well to causes that help the environment and make the planet better for all people.

Unlike their predecessors, kids aren't as cynical about advertising. This generation is very brand-conscious and loyal—a fact that bodes well for advertisers.

Direct mail can be very successful with this market, but it presents its own challenges. On the plus side, it addresses their fondness for anything personalized for them. It also allows marketers to deliver the free gifts and samples they love. On the negative side, marketers can't purchase lists with the addresses of teens. They have to buy lists of households where kids live and hope the mail reaches them.

Regarding the use of the Internet to market to kids, the numbers aren't quite there yet, but they soon will be. This is a generation that takes the Internet for granted. It has always been a part of their lives and its importance will continue to grow. Currently, 58 percent of U.S. kids are connected online. Further, "online kids" devour more media than their off-line counterparts. Also, kids 11 years old and younger click on screen banner ads more than twice as often as the rest of the population.

One marketing strategy that has been somewhat successful in reaching kids is product placements in schools. After all, it is the easiest place to find kids. For example, companies such as Coke, Pepsi, McDonald's, Pizza Hut, and Nike all have a strong presence in thousands of elementary and junior high schools throughout the United States. But critics of such practices have come down hard, complaining of crass commercialization. Many companies have responded by connecting their products and promotions to educational activities, such as fund-raising, career days, and special speakers or programs.

POINT TO PONDER

If schools benefit from these programs, what harm could they do?

Sources: Steve Jarvis, "Marketing and School Mix Can't be Sold to Some," *Marketing News* (June 10, 2001): 10; Steve Jarvis, "Lesson Plans," *Marketing News* (June 18, 2001): 1, 9; Alstair Ray, "Following School Rules," *Marketing to Kids, Effectiveness and Responsibility* (October 31, 2001): p. 26; "E-Turning to the Classroom," *Newsweek* (September 18, 2000): 74J; Joan Raymond, "Kids Just Wanna Have Fun," *American Demographics* (February 2001): 57–62.

Asian-themed calendars to retailers and related trade associations across the United States. The campaign was particularly effective with Asian-American women from age 32 to 40.[2]

Product Differentiation Regardless of whether a marketer employs an undifferentiated or a segmentation approach, there remains a need to distinguish a brand from that of competitors.

Most markets contain a high level of competition. How does a company compete in a crowded market? It uses **product differentiation**, a competitive marketing strategy designed to create product differences that distinguish the company's product from all others in the eyes of consumers. Those perceived differences may be tangible or intangible. Product differentiation may also exist within segments.

Tangible differences include unique product features, color, size, quality of performance or support services, or available options. Intel has convinced computer buyers that its chip makes computers faster. Price can also be a tangible characteristic. The Swatch watch demonstrates the importance of pricing by offering a fashionable watch at a modest price.

In instances where products really are the same (examples include milk, unleaded gas, and over-the-counter drugs), marketers often promote intangible differences. They create an image that implies difference, although the image may have little to do with the actual product features. Some beer companies, for example, try to suggest status, enjoyment, and masculinity. Coors suggests that the image of the Rocky Mountains makes the beer unique. Amstel suggests that the tradition of the Dutch brewing is special.

Levi Strauss has turned to product differentiation as a market approach. Targeting the youth market for several years, Levi's new theme is "the basics for the new millennium." One of its new styles of jeans has a large watch pocket to hold pagers and other electronic items. Under its youth-oriented Silver Tab brand, Levi's introduced the Mobile Zip-off pant, with legs that unzip to create shorts; and the loose Ripcord pant, which rolls up your legs.[3]

Positioning Determining what place a product should occupy in a given market is called **positioning**. It means a marketer strategically combines the product's tangible and intangible attributes in order to create a relative picture of the product.

Practical Tips #1

POSITIONING GUIDELINES

Marketers can position a product, service, or idea

- by attributes (Pentium III offers 3-dimensional graphics)
- by price (Wal-Mart means value)
- by its ability to surpass the competition (Ford beats Chevy)
- by application (Tylenol Flu is for flu attacks)
- by product user (*TeenPeople* is the favorite magazine of high school students)
- by product class (Carnation Instant Breakfast is a breakfast food)

Wal-Mart, for example, has spent millions of dollars trying to claim the "value" position. Experts would agree it has accomplished this goal.

The role of the advertising strategy is to relate the product's position to the target market. In fact, it represents one of advertising's most critical tasks. An example of a company that had a strong position, but lost it, is McDonald's. Due to increased competition and changes in the food industry, it is no longer the "fast-food" marketer. Instead, McDonald's has spent the last decade repositioning itself. The tactic is to simplify its menu and create a better experience than the one offered by its primary competitors, Burger King and Wendy's. Following trends that are pulling fast-food restaurants toward becoming more homey and relaxed, McDonald's tested new store concepts such as "McDonald's with the Diner Inside" and "McCafe." To help cut service times, the new positioning strategy will split counter services into cashiers and areas where another employee assembles the order. By 2006, McDonald's will add coin changers and double drive-throughs, self-order kiosks, electronic menu boards, and cashless drive-throughs to its restaurants. It will also focus on a national consumer rewards program called "McRewards." With each visit, customers will gain points toward prizes from partners such as Walt Disney and Mattel.[4]

THE MARKETING CONCEPT AND RELATIONSHIP MARKETING

Another element that underlies how marketers approach the market is how they view the role of the customer. Historically, especially when products were scarce because of limited distribution, manufacturers made products and customers were glad to be able to buy them. With the emergence of the Industrial Revolution, there was much more product produced; the job of business was to improve distribution and the role of marketing was to sell. Customers still had little input into the type and design of products they needed. Since the 1950s, competition has grown, along with customer choice. Successful marketers have drawn the conclusion that it is advantageous to include the customer in the product design and development process.

The **marketing concept** suggests that marketing should focus first on the needs and wants of the customer, rather than on finding ways to sell products that may or may not meet customers' needs. A handful of businesses, such as L.L. Bean and United Parcel Services (UPS), adopted this perspective ahead of the pack. However, according to marketing experts like Philip Kotler, most did not embrace the marketing concept until the

1980s. They had to become more marketing-oriented to adapt to changes. Consumers have become more educated and empowered with opinions and dollars. World trade barriers have come down, allowing new competitors and better choices. Creating identical products, although profitable, are no longer acceptable to most consumers.

Today, marketers know that to compete effectively they must focus on customer problems and try to develop products to solve them. The marketing concept suggests two marketing steps. First, determine what the customer needs and wants. Second, develop, manufacture, market, and service goods and services that fill those particular needs and wants.

Once a company adopts the marketing concept, it then develops a strategy to implement it. Integrated marketing has emerged as the strategy with the greatest potential. **Integrated marketing** is a process of understanding the needs of the customer and then responding to those needs through a coordination of the marketing mix (product, price, distribution, and marketing communications) and other functions of the business such as production, research, and finance. The elements of the mix should work together to add value and create a competitive advantage. This integrated approach to marketing influences all marketing decisions, and it is the most effective strategic approach to satisfy the needs, wants, and goals of both the consumer and the advertiser. It means a product such as MasterCard's Business Card is priced correctly; designed in an appealing manner; profitable; well-coordinated with its various financial partners; communicated through relevant, attention-getting advertising; and sent through targeted media.

An integrated marketing approach affects advertising planning and execution. Generally, marketers use advertising to deliver relevant, persuasive information. Through research, the marketer understands how the consumer makes decisions most effectively and satisfactorily and this information is incorporated into the advertising messages to promote a purchase decision. The goal is to create advertising that is honest and useful and that matches the needs of the customer, so that the customer is satisfied with her choices.

This ad for MasterCard's Business Card is just one part of MasterCard's integrated strategy. The other parts of the strategy are pricing, promotion, and distribution.

Along with an integrated perspective has come an extension of the marketing concept of relationship marketing. **Relationship marketing** identifies customers and potential customers and bonds them to the brand through personal attention. Many companies think of sales transactions as isolated events rather than steps in lifelong relationships with customers.[5]

Because many businesses haven't recognized the lifelong value of a customer relationship, some think that a bad experience represents only the loss of a single sale. Experts believe that organizations' relationships with their current customers and other important constituencies intensify overall customer loyalty. Advertising, along with the other communication tools, can play an important role in maintaining relationships.

When advertising is guided by the marketing concept, the central goal—satisfying the customer—helps coordinate advertising with the other marketing functions and increases the likelihood that a particular advertisement will be successful. When a relationship approach is established, this advertising information is even more effective.

THE FOUR TOOLS OF MARKETING

As Figure 3.3 shows, marketers use the four main elements of the marketing mix to achieve their objectives. Communication, which includes advertising, is one of these marketing elements. As indicated, it is just one part of marketing, no more important than product, price, or distribution.

1. **Product**: Includes product design and development, branding, and packaging.
2. **Distribution**: Includes the channels used in moving and storing the product from the manufacturer to the buyer.
3. **Price**: Includes the price at which the product or service is offered for sale and establishes the level of profitability.
4. **Communication**: Includes personal selling, advertising, public relations, sales promotion, direct marketing, point-of-sale, and packaging.

Product

The product is both the object of the advertising and the reason for marketing. Marketing begins by asking a set of questions about the product offering. These questions should always be asked from the consumer's perspective: What product attributes and benefits are important? How is the product perceived relative to competitive offerings? How important is service? How long should the product last? Customers view products as "bundles of satisfaction" rather than just physical things. How do you think customers view the Whitestrips technology advertised by Crest toothpaste?

To give another example, in the United States some car buyers perceive that automobiles made in Germany and Japan offer superior quality, better gas mileage, and less costly service than domestic cars. At the luxury level, cars such as Porsche, BMW, Audi, and Mercedes now offer the status and prestige once associated with Cadillac and Lincoln.

Product	Distribution
• Design and Development • Branding • Packaging • Maintenance	• Distribution Channels • Market Coverage • Storage
Price	**Communication**
• Price Copy • Psychological Pricing • Price Lining • Value Determination	• Personal Selling • Advertising • Sales Promotion • Direct Marketing • Marketing/Public Relations • Point-of-Sale/Packaging

FIGURE 3.3

THE FOUR ELEMENTS OF MARKETING (THE MARKETING MIX)
These four elements, and their related tools, serve as the basics of marketing.

Given that Whitestrips sales were close to $100 million in just its first 6 months on the market, consumers see "whitening" as a product benefit that helps build an attractive smile.

Thus, the intangible, symbolic attributes of foreign-made automobiles provide psychological and social functions for the buyer. Figure 3.4 lists both tangible and intangible product characteristics.

To have a practical effect on customers, managers must translate these product characteristics into concrete attributes with demonstrable benefits—they must develop a message strategy. Consider packaged cookies. The physical ingredients might include sugar, flour, chocolate, and baking powder. The intangible features might be an implied taste and a reputable brand name. However, these characteristics are too far removed from the real attributes or benefits customers perceive. A customer looks for descriptive phrases such as "tastes like homemade" or "a great snack without a lot of fat." These are the real pieces of information the marketer needs to communicate.

Stressing the most important attributes is the key to influencing customer choices and serves as the foundation for most advertising. The ads for All detergent and Famous Amos Cookies emphasize key attributes of their products.

Branding What product name comes to mind when you picture a copy machine? Do you think of a product name when you think of salt? When you think of facial tissues, what product name occurs to you?

The makers of Xerox, Morton's, and Kleenex products have advertised so successfully over the years that their brand names have become synonymous with the products themselves. **Branding** makes a product distinctive in the marketplace, just as your name makes you unique in your community.

A **brand** is a name, term, design, symbol (e.g., package, spokesperson) that identifies the goods, services, institution, or idea sold by a marketer. The **brand name** is the part of

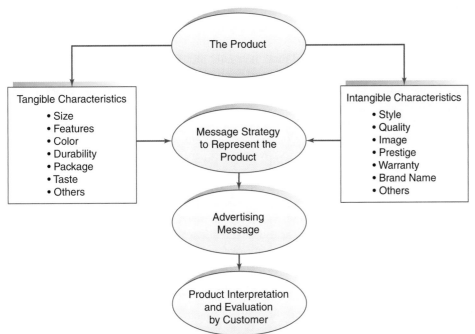

The Product

Tangible Characteristics
- Size
- Features
- Color
- Durability
- Package
- Taste
- Others

Intangible Characteristics
- Style
- Quality
- Image
- Prestige
- Warranty
- Brand Name
- Others

Message Strategy to Represent the Product

Advertising Message

Product Interpretation and Evaluation by Customer

FIGURE 3.4

TANGIBLE AND INTANGIBLE PRODUCT CHARACTERISTICS
Advertisers tell consumers about the tangible and intangible characteristic of a product.

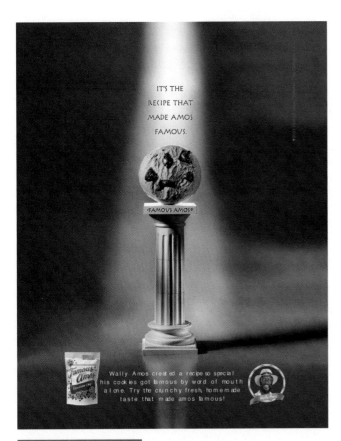

This Famous Amos ad highlights the product's primary attributes. All's message strategy is to play up the product's "safety" benefit—cleans clothes and leaves no harmful chemicals.

The Intel trademark and the "Intel Inside" tagline are legally protected.

a brand that can be spoken, such as words, letters, or numbers. Hershey's is a brand name, as is K2R. The **brand mark**, also known as the logo, is the part of the brand that cannot be spoken. It can be a symbol, picture, design, distinctive lettering, or color combination.

When a brand name or brand mark is legally protected through registration with the Patent and Trademark Office of the Department of Commerce, it becomes a **trademark**. Intel Inside, a trademark has been an important part of Intel's marketing strategy. The worldwide brands with the highest value are shown in Table 3.2.

Coca-Cola is the most recognizable brand in the world. Yet, the success of Pepsi-Co's Pepsi-Cola brand has forced Coca-Cola to increase its global advertising efforts. In mid-2001, Coke executives gave a go-ahead to its advertising department to shoot 50 to 75 new commercials. These commercials, which aired in the company's top global markets, featured so-called "Coke moments," and were built on two existing campaigns: "Bliss comes from within" and "Share something real." The new ads show slice-of-life moments such as college-aged kids throwing parties in the forest or sitting on rooftops to watch the sunrise. In "Spanish Wedding" a beautiful Latin woman dresses for her big day. While soaking in the moment, she motions to a little girl standing nearby holding a can of Coke with a straw in it. The girl serves the Coke. "The bride-to-be takes a dainty sip, but her satisfaction is apparent." The tagline follows: "Life Tastes Good!" Only time will tell whether Coke's global branding strategy will be effective.[6]

The importance of the brand cannot be overstated. When we talk about **brand equity**, we mean the reputation that the name or symbol connotes. It becomes synonymous with the company. Losing brand equity through excessive discounting, substandard products, poor service, or questionable ethical practices has proven disastrous for many companies. Nike's reputation suffered when it was accused of using underage labor in poor working conditions in third-world countries. Ford and Firestone may never recover from the crisis they faced in 2000–2001, when a number of fatal Ford accidents were blamed on Firestone tires.

Packaging The package is another marketing tool. In today's marketing environment, a package is much more than a container; it is the message. When the package works in unison with consumer advertising it catches attention, presents a familiar brand image, and communicates critical information. Many consumers make purchase decisions on the basis of how the product looks on the shelf.

An article in *Advertising Age* explained the importance of the package as a communication medium: "Even if you can't afford a big advertising budget, you've got a fighting chance if your product projects a compelling image from the shelf."[7] The package serves as a critical reminder of the product's important benefits at the moment the consumer is choosing among several competing brands.

If, however, consumers take the product home and find the packaging a formidable obstacle, repeat sales may be lost. Federal safety laws require tamper-proof seals and

TABLE 3.2	**The Top Brands Worldwide**
Rank	**2001 Brand Value $Billions**
1 Coca-Cola	68.94
2 Microsoft	65.07
3 IBM	52.75
4 GE	42.40
5 Nokia	35.04
6 Intel	34.67
7 Disney	32.59
8 Ford	30.09
9 McDonald's	25.29
10 AT&T	22.83

Source: BusinessWeek (August 6, 2001): 60.

THE INSIDE STORY

Branding NFL Sunday Ticket

Andrew Goldberg

Account Executive
Margeotes/Fertitta + Partners LLP

The NFL is one of the strongest brands in the world. So how could one of its premier products, one that clearly is identified with NFL football, have a branding problem? NFL Sunday Ticket did.

To make NFL Sunday Ticket the success it is today, the NFL gave DIRECTV an exclusive contract for distribution in the small satellite dish (DSS) world. Using the NFL as a marketing tool DIRECTTV became the perceived owner/creator of NFL Sunday Ticket. This in turn created a problem that many brands face—lack of ownership of their own product. As NFL Sunday Ticket's ad agency, Margeotes/Fertitta + Partners recognized this problem. Our solution was to adjust the advertising message, as well as delivery.

While keeping in mind that growing the subscription numbers was the main focus of the business, we still needed to deliver a branding message. Recognizing that we had educated the viewers over the past seven years on the details of the service, we switched our focus to the emotional aspect of how fans watch NFL football. Our new strategy focused on indulging in NFL football on Sundays. Using consumers' emotional connection with the NFL, we developed two TV spots, a print ad, and direct-mail pieces (to support subscriptions in a direct-response fashion). All were linked by the same copy and tagline.

"Today, NFL Sunday Ticket is going to give you any game you want.

Today is Sunday.

Today is your day.

(Tag) Have a Nice Day."

For branding and creating NFL ownership, the spots open with the NFL Shield, which then takes the consumer into the lives of NFL fans preparing to watch football all day Sunday. The spots end with the NFL Sunday Ticket logo and the line, "A service of the National Football League."

While the ad is strong, it would not accomplish its goal if it weren't shown in the proper media venues. Working within the limits of a budget, we used air time during the preseason football games on ESPN's family of stations. We have also sponsored a segment of the CNN pregame show on Sundays. This has allowed us to not only seem larger than we are, but it has given us the opportunity to be directly in front of our audience when football is the primary viewing interest of the audience.

This ad contains many elements of price copy, both explicit and psychological.

We have met our objectives of creating a campaign that allows NFL Sunday Ticket to stand on its own as a product of the NFL—not DIRECTTV. At the same time, we have contributed to maintaining the subscription base and working toward increasing it.

Currently an account executive at Margeotes/Fertitta + Partners in New York, Andrew Goldberg graduated from Lehigh University in 1997 with a B.S. in marketing. He has been at Margeotes for four and a half years and has worked on NFL Sunday Ticket, Godiva Chocolatier, Putnam Investments, McGraw-Hill Companies, Hearst Publications, Reckitt-Benchiser products, and more.

Nominated by Professor James Maskulka, Lehigh University.

Celestial Seasonings uses its distinctive packages to send messages to consumers about its marketing position. How do you think the package reinforces the brand image?

child-safety caps on over-the-counter medications, but that makes many of them adult-proof, too. In this instance, the marketer has the problem of making the package safe and risking consumer anger, or reengineering the package. Advertising may play a significant role in informing the consumer about packaging benefits.

In sum, packaging is an important part of the marketing effort. It is a constant communicator and an effective device for carrying advertising messages.

Practical Tips #2

CREATING PACKAGES THAT COMMUNICATE

To make packages that grab attention and send a message, consider these suggestions:

- Make the package colorful and distinctive.
- Use a design that underscores the brand image and sends advertising messages that correspond with mass-media messages.
- Make the package as functional as possible.
- Make sure the product package and the advertising dovetail. How would you react if the advertising for Celestial Seasonings was loud, aggressive, and MTV-like?

Channel of Distribution

It does little good to manufacture a fantastic product that will meet customers' needs unless you have a mechanism for delivering and servicing the product and receiving payment. The people and institutions that move products from producers to customers make up the **channel of distribution**. Resellers, or intermediaries, and primary members of the channel may actually take ownership of the product and participate in the marketing. Wholesalers, retailers, and transporters are also part of the channel. Each member is capable of influencing and delivering advertising messages.

The primary strength of the wholesaler is personal selling. Wholesalers do not advertise often; however, in some instances they use special types of advertising strategies. Regional wholesalers are apt to use direct mail, trade papers, or catalogs. Local wholesalers may use newspapers or local radio. The copy tends to be simple and straightforward, with few pictures or illustrations; the focus is on product, features, and price. Conversely, retailers are quite good at advertising, especially local advertising. Retailers' main concern is that the advertising be directed at *their* customers as opposed to the customers of the manufacturers. (More will be said about retailers in Chapter 17.)

Channels can be direct or indirect. Companies that distribute their products directly, without the use of a reseller, engage in **direct marketing**. Companies such as Lands' End, Spiegel, and Burpee Seeds all use direct-marketing channels. Rather than stores or salespeople, direct marketing relies on advertising media to inform and stimulate customer purchases. Online technology is the newest direct channel. We are all familiar with the tremendous growth in online marketing that has taken place in the last decade. Most businesses now have a Web site and many sell their products through these sites. There has been a proliferation of banner ads on Web sites that move, play music, and are personalized. We cover this topic more in Chapter 14.

Indirect marketing means the product is distributed through a channel structure that includes one or more resellers. A key decision with indirect marketing is whether resellers should participate in advertising. Producers often expect wholesalers and especially retailers to participate in advertising programs. Through **cooperative advertising** allowances, the producers and resellers share the cost of placing the advertisement. This not only saves money (because local advertising rates are less expensive than national rates); it also creates a tie-in with local retailers, who often have a much greater following than the producer's brand does.

Wholesalers and retailers also initiate their own advertising campaigns, which often highlight the items of various manufacturers. Few manufacturers can match the advertising impact of retailers such as Sears, Target, or Federated Stores. Instead, they try to work with those outlets to take advantage of their advertising strength.

Another channel factor that may influence advertising is whether marketers use a pull, push, or combination strategy, as Figure 3.5 shows. A **pull strategy** directs marketing efforts at the consumer and attempts to pull the product through the channel. The process targets consumer demand. There is usually a large emphasis on consumer advertising, along with incentives such as coupons, rebates, free samples, and sweepstakes. Little is expected from resellers other than to stock the product.

In contrast, a **push strategy** directs marketing efforts at resellers, and success depends on the ability of these intermediaries to market the product, which they often do with advertising. Advertising may be targeted first at resellers to gain their acceptance, then at consumers through joint manufacturer-reseller advertising.

Most marketers use a combination strategy of push and pull. A company such as Frito-Lay spends millions of dollars annually on mass-consumer advertising, couponing,

FIGURE 3.5   **PUSH, PULL, AND COMBINATION STRATEGIES**
Advertising and other communication strategies are a major part of both a pull and push strategy.

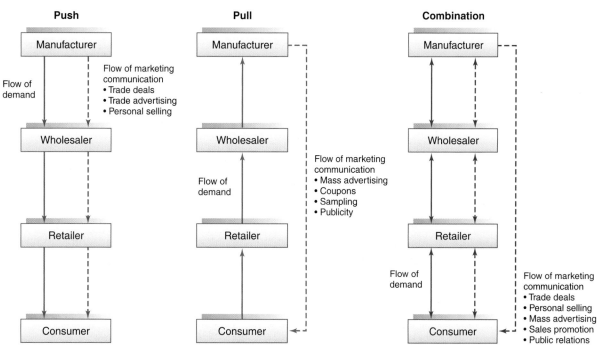

sampling, and so forth (pull), as well as millions more on deals to retailers, including co-op advertising (cost shared), price discounts, and merchandising (push).

A final channel factor influencing advertising is the market coverage desired. Three strategies are possible: exclusive distribution, selective distribution, and intensive distribution. With **exclusive distribution**, only one distributor is allowed to sell the brand in a particular market. Two examples of companies that rely on exclusive distribution are Hart Schafner suits and Ethan Allen furniture. The retailer, who is guaranteed an exclusive market, provides a strong personal-selling effort, effective merchandising, and heavy participation in cooperative (co-op) advertising.

Selective distribution expands the number of outlets but restricts participation to outlets that prove most profitable to the manufacturer. Florsheim Shoes and Timex engage in selective distribution. The role of advertising is quite varied under this arrangement, but normally the manufacturer does some mass advertising and offers co-op possibilities.

Intensive distribution means placing the product in every possible outlet (even vending machines) to attain total market coverage. Manufacturers of soft drinks, candy, and cigarettes use intensive distribution. Marketers can't expect much personal selling from the retailer because these products often require far more maintenance (such as shelving and pricing) than the retailer can provide, so mass advertising is used to create brand awareness and preference.

Market coverage also means the geographic distribution of the product. This distribution may influence both the creative strategy and the media strategy. For example, in the case of creative strategy, an ad for a raincoat distributed only in the Pacific Northwest would require significant differences in copy and illustration than if it were a nationally sold raincoat.

One of the more confusing aspects of the channel of distribution is how "service products" (an intangible) move through the channel, are stored, and so forth. In fact, the channels for a patient moving through hospital admissions or someone obtaining a bank loan are just as real as the channels for tangible products such as automobiles. The channel for services represents contact points that move the consumer to the point of purchase. Wells Fargo Bank advertises that "no customer will wait longer than 5 minutes to receive banking service."

Pricing

The **price** a seller sets for a product is based not only on the cost of making and marketing the product but also on the seller's expected profit level. Certain psychological factors also affect the price. For example, many experts claim that price may suggest quality in the consumer's mind or may equate with the value the consumer places on the product. Ultimately, the price of a product is based on what the market will bear, the competition, the economic well-being of the consumer, the relative value of the product, and the consumer's ability to gauge the value.

With the exception of price information delivered at the point-of-sale, advertising is the primary vehicle for telling the consumer about price and the associated conditions of a particular product. The term **price copy** has been coined to designate advertising copy devoted to this type of information.

A number of pricing strategies influence advertising strategy. For example **customary** or expected **pricing** uses a single, well-known price for a long period of time. Movie theaters and manufacturers of candy use this pricing strategy. Changes in price would be relayed through advertising.

Psychological pricing strategies try to manipulate the customer's judgment. For example, ads showing prestige pricing—in which a high price is set to make the product seem worthy or valuable—would be accompanied by photographs of the "exceptional product" or copy consisting of logical reasons for this high price. Advertisers communicate a dramatic or temporary price reduction through terms such as *sale*, *special*, and *today only*.

Psychological pricing is often used when a marketer is targeting affluent consumers. A case in point is the marketing approach developed by Don Ziccardi, president and CEO of New York ad agency Ziccardi & Partners, and author of a book entitled *Influencing the Affluent: Marketing to the Individual Luxury Consumer in a Volatile Economy*. Ziccardi divides luxury products into four consumer categories: wealthiest of the wealthy, class gone mass, mass gone class, and everyday luxury. Advertising of top-end luxury brands (for example, Bentley and Cartier) targets the "wealthiest of the wealthy."

The second category, "class gone mass," includes those brands that have added an entry-level product that is priced more affordably than their luxury product lines. Rolex did this with its Tudor watch, retailing for about $1,000 compared with the Rolex Submariner, usually priced at $8,050.

Then there are the affordable mass brands that have taken on a patina of class or "mass gone class," such as Banana Republic's upscale yet relatively inexpensive fashions or Pottery Barn's home furnishings.

Finally, a new class of luxury products has emerged, what Ziccardi calls "everyday luxury" items. Starbuck's Caffe Latte or a Bliss Spa massage are examples.[8]

Segmentation studies have a direct bearing on advertising to the affluent. For instance, with luxury goods, there is a high value on print advertising. Additionally, magazines can be better for one category of luxury goods than another: For high-end home furnishings, the title of choice is *Town & Country*. *Town & Country* is also a good place for jewelry, but *Harper's Bazaar* is better for high fashion. One Cartier ad that appeared in *Talk* would probably appeal to the "class gone mass" segment.

Finally, a **price lining** strategy is when a company offers variations of a particular product and prices them accordingly. Sears, for example, offers many of its products on a "good," "better," and "best" basis with prices increasing at each level. Price lining requires that the ad show all the products in the line so the consumer can choose among them.

Advertising should clearly and consistently match the product's pricing strategy.

Marketing Communications

Advertising, personal selling, sales promotion, public relations, direct marketing, point-of-sale, and packaging are the main elements marketers use to reach target markets. These techniques are collectively called marketing communications. It is the fourth element in the marketing mix, and consists of persuasive communication designed to send marketing-related messages to a target audience.

The shift from product-centered to consumer-centered marketing strategies forced businesses to combine activities they had previously handled separately. Author Leo Bogart explains that "when American business was recognized in the postwar years, marketing emerged as a major function" that coordinated individual elements such as product development, sales promotion, merchandising, advertising, and market research.

TABLE 3.3	**Marketing Communications Mix Comparison**		
Marketing Communication Element	**Objectives**	**Customer Contact**	**Time of Response**
Advertising	Attention, attitude change, and behavior change	Indirect	Moderate or short
Personal selling	Sales	Direct	Short
Sales promotion	Sales	Semidirect	Short
Direct marketing	Behavior change	Semidirect	Short
Public relations	Attitude change	Semidirect	Long
Point-of-sale and packaging	Behavior change	Direct	Moderate

Combining these activities produces a coordinate message structure called the **marketing communication mix**.

Implementing the communication mix in a coordinated manner is called **integrated marketing communication (IMC)**. The basic elements of the marketing communication mix—which are listed above—appear in most marketing plans. These elements differ in their objectives, the type of customer contact, and the time element of response, as Table 3.3 shows.

Once again, these categories parallel the effectiveness focus that underlies this text. As noted in Chapter 1, advertising's "objectives" focus on attention, attitude change, and behavior. Advertising also "contacts" the customer indirectly, primarily through mass media, and expects a relatively moderate or short "response time" to the message. Compared to the other marketing communication mix elements, advertising has fairly clear, distinctive traits. Let's examine the elements and how they play into advertising strategy.

Advertising Advertising differs from the other marketing communication elements in several ways. Although advertising has a greater ability to reach a larger number of people simultaneously than do the other elements, it has less ability to prompt an immediate change in consumer behavior, and though not always explicit, the behavior that all advertisers would like to change through their ads is purchase. However, preliminary behavioral changes are more likely, such as inquiry and trial. Furthermore, the contact between the advertiser and the audience is indirect, so it takes a long time to deliver information (in part because most consumer ads have little information), change attitudes, and create a rapport or trust between the two parties.

Personal Selling **Personal selling** is face-to-face contact between the marketer and a prospective customer. Its intent is to create immediate and repeat sales. The different types of personal selling include sales calls at the place of business by a field representative (field sales), assistance at an outlet by a sales clerk (retail selling), and calls by a representative who goes to consumers' homes (door-to-door selling). Personal selling is most important for companies that sell products requiring explanation, demonstration, and service, such as high technology products, homes, and travel.

Sales Promotion **Sales promotion** aims to generate immediate sales for a limited period of time. Simply stated, sales promotion is an extra incentive to buy now—or soon. Price discounts, coupons, product sampling, contests, sweepstakes, and rebates are all sales promotions.

Sales promotions can support advertising campaigns. Advertising and sales promotion can work together to create a synergy in which each makes the other more effective. For example, print ads that carry a coupon such as the one for Stonyfield Farm, are four times as likely to be read.

This ad contains a coupon as a sales promotion element.

Public Relations **Public relations** seeks to enhance the company's image, and includes publicity (placing stories about the company or product in the media), news conferences, company-sponsored events, open houses, plant tours, and donations.

Rather than attempting to sell the product, public relations tries to influence people's attitudes toward the company or product. In most cases, the lag effect associated with public relations is quite long, making any relationship between public relations and sales difficult to measure.

Advertising and public relations can work together. A public relations event or message can serve as part of an advertising campaign. Product publicity can also be used to support an advertising campaign. For example, Kingsford charcoal sponsors a Ribfest cooking contest in Chicago that includes free charcoal for all contestants. This event reinforces the association between Kingford and outdoor activities, which is the goal of Kingford's ad campaign.

Direct Marketing As we said earlier, direct marketing is a communication tool that allows the customer to purchase the product directly, without going through a reseller. Direct marketing is a rapidly changing field and its definition is evolving. However, it does have five basic characteristics: (1) It is interactive, meaning the marketer and customer share information in real time; (2) it provides a mechanism for a customer to respond; (3) it can occur anywhere; (4) it provides a measurable response from the customer; and (5) it requires a database of consumer information.

Direct marketing is the fastest-growing element in the marketing communication mix because it provides consumers with the three things they want most: convenience, efficiency, and compression of decision-making time.[9] When a consumer buys shirts from Lands' End, every step of the process is executed smoothly, from the toll-free conversation

This eye-catching Louisville Slugger display showcases the product and has an area for product literature. What message do you think the display sends to consumers?

with the order taker to prompt delivery of well-made, fully guaranteed shirts, billed to a credit card at a price lower than many retail stores charge.

Unfortunately, not all direct-marketing techniques are viewed as viable product sources for consumers. A great deal is still viewed as junk mail, especially unsolicited material that advertises cheap merchandise or makes hard-to-believe claims.

Messages delivered for direct-marketing products are called **direct-response advertising**. Advertisers design those messages to motivate customers to make some sort of response, either an order or an inquiry. Direct-response advertising is aimed at target groups through means such as direct mail, telemarketing, print, broadcast, catalogs, and point-of-purchase displays.

Point-of-Sale/Packaging Point-of-sale (POS) and packaging attempt to drive sales at the place where the product is sold. The message-delivery capabilities of the package come into play here. POS materials include signs, posters, displays, and other materials designed to influence buying decisions at the point-of-purchase. Depending on the product category, 30 to 70 percent of our purchases are unplanned. The POS marketing material takes advantage of this fact, along with fulfilling other basic communication objectives such as product identification, product information, and product comparisons.

The role advertising plays in this context may vary as well. Often the POS materials are an extension of the ad. Energizer Bunny posters and cut-outs are found in stores that sell Energizer products. These posters match the TV and print ads.

In this section we examined marketing and how advertising supports the marketing function. Next we explore how advertising agencies help businesses combine the marketing and advertising functions.

AD AGENCIES: COMBINING MARKETING AND ADVERTISING

Advertising is the most important tool in the marketing communication mix. This assertion is based on an *Adweek*-sponsored survey of 105 clients in the United States.[10] Over 83 percent of the respondents indicated that advertising was the "most important" tool in their communication mix. Consequently, since there is such a large focus on advertising, companies must decide whether they're going to do the work themselves or hire an agency.

The best advertising agencies create value for their clients. Let's say that an agency clearly interprets what customers want. Then it communicates information about the client's product so meaningfully, so uniquely, and so consistently that customers reward that product with their loyalty. In that case, the agency creates value for its client.

How does each agency add perceived value to the product of its client? By giving a product a personality, by communicating in a manner that shapes basic understanding of the product, by creating an **image** or memorable picture of the product, and by setting the product apart from its competitors.

To do this effectively, communication (not just advertising) must do more than merely inform: It must "tailor the product story to a potential customer."[11] Marketing communications, then, should help consumers convert information into memorable, motivating perceptions that differentiate between brands.

Why Hire an Agency?

Many companies hire agencies to plan and execute their advertising efforts. Why should a company sign a contract with an advertising agency? Hiring an agency has three main benefits: It provides objective advice, experienced staffing, and tailored management of all advertising activities and personnel.

An agency can offer objective advice to its clients because it is not as invested in product development. Also, the client can't hire and fire agency staff. Clients expect an agency to tell them when they are misreading the market or are out of step with consumers, advice that the client's own marketers might be afraid to voice.

A MATTER OF PRINCIPLE

VERIZON HAS IT WORKING

➤ Over the years, the boundaries between different segments of the communications industry have blurred. For advertisers, sorting out this confusion has become a major challenge. One telecommunication giant that appears to be effectively handling this dilemma is Verizon Communications Inc. It was created in July 2000, by the $59 billion merger of GTE Corp. and Bell Atlantic Corp., which had already purchased New York State's local phone company NYNEX. Now Verizon services customers with 260,000 employees and $65 billion in annual revenue.

The intent was to seamlessly create a single brand image. To reach this objective, the ad agencies and media agencies for both companies were consolidated. The $600 million spent on advertising and media in 2001 more than justified the creation of this in-house agency.

Extensive consumer research was conducted to assess perceptions of both brands. Results indicated that both companies were known for their excellent technology and above-industry customer satisfaction scores. In many instances the companies were mirror reflections of one another. The primary issue was creating a brand name that represented these strengths.

Literally thousands of names were proposed and tested. It seemed clear that a single word that represented

technology and innovation would resonate the most with consumers. By combining the word "verity" [quality of being real, accurate, or correct] with the word "horizon" [the range of an individual's knowledge, experience, or interest] they coined a new word, "verizon." The new term tested well with consumers and the ad agency. The latter was particularly pleased that verizon was easy to say and remember and was easily transferred between media. Jane Keeler, senior vice president of brand management and marketing services at Verizon, notes another significant benefit: "The new name allows us to open up the Internet and move into innovative technologies."

Still, there is a bigger challenge—shaping a consistent message about the Verizon brand. Changing an old brand to a new brand is not an easy marketing or advertising task.

POINT TO PONDER

What are the possible risks in giving up two credible brand names and creating a new one?

Source: Tobi Elkin, "Verizon Making the Right Calls in First Year," *Advertising Age* (June 11, 2001): 6.

In addition, an established agency can draw on the collective experience of its staff to put together a professional ad or an ad campaign. Advertising people are experts in their field, whereas few companies are expert advertisers, so they feel less competent to create, approve, and execute advertisements.

Agencies provide the people and the management skills necessary to accomplish the advertising. Creative people who work for advertising agencies may differ from the employees of the client's business. Artists, writers, and television producers might not fit easily into the culture of the corporate environment. Stated work hours, dress codes, and limitations on overtime would be difficult to enforce among the creative people who tend to work in advertising. In addition, pay scales for creative staff may vary widely: A brilliant writer may be paid more than a department head, so there is tremendous value placed on creative individuals. Advertising agencies provide a supportive environment for these people, and can organize their skills, maintain morale, and build spirit more effectively than corporations can.

Why Not Hire an Agency?

Despite the many advantages agencies offer their clients, there are instances when firms are better off doing the work themselves. Some firms have an in-house agency or an advertising department.

An **in-house agency** is a group of advertising specialists that operates its own profit center and handles all the advertising work for its primary client—the company with which it is affiliated. In-house agencies may also handle outside work, particularly for suppliers, vendors, and distributors who work with the company.

Many retailers have in-house agencies (such as Pier 1 and Nieman Marcus) that specialize in retail advertising. Retailers tend to operate with small profit margins and find they can save money by doing their own advertising. Also, retailers must develop and place their ads under extremely tight deadlines. There is seldom time to work with an outside advertising consultant. Also, retailers often receive advertising materials either free or at a reduced cost from manufacturers and trade associations.

Advantages of in-house agencies are: (1) They allow individuals to become technical experts on the product being advertised, (2) the in-house agency works only for the client and gives priority to the client's needs, and (3) minimum staffing is required because all the work is focused on one client.

An **advertising department** is somewhat of a hybrid in that it acts as a facilitator between outside vendors and advertising management. It may contain a handful of client employees who have expertise in all the tools of advertising. So their responsibilities may include selecting all agencies, assigning tasks to these agencies, and doing the same with other communication specialists, such as media providers, event planners, and fulfillment houses. They may also have the responsibility of making sure that the work is done and that objectives are achieved. Advertising departments may also engage in the creative and media-planning/buying tasks. They share several of the advantages and disadvantages of the in-house and external agency.

Types of Agencies

Changes in the business environment prompt changes in the types of ad agencies that flourish. Next, we take a look at the different types of agencies to demonstrate the variety that exists in the advertising agency business today. The top agency brands worldwide are shown in Table 3.4. They are full-service agencies.

Full-Service Agencies In advertising, a **full-service agency** is one that includes the four major staff functions—account management, creative services, media planning and buying, and account planning, which is also known as research. A full-service advertising agency will also have its own accounting department, a traffic department to handle internal tracking on completion of projects, a department for broadcast and print production (usually organized within the creative department), and a human resources department.

Specialized Agencies Many agencies do not follow the traditional full-service agency approach. They either specialize in certain functions (writing copy, producing art, or media buying), audiences (minority, youth), or industries (health care, computers, agriculture, business-to-business communication). In addition, there are specialized agencies in all

TABLE 3.4		World's Top 10 Agency Brands				
Rank					**Worldwide Gross Income**	
2001	**2000**	**Agency**	**Headquarters**		**2001**	**2000**
1	1	Dentsu	Tokyo		$2,078.1	$2,432.0
2	2	McCann-Erickson Worldwide	New York		1,857.9	1,824.9
3	3	BBDO Worldwide	New York		1,611.7	1,534.0
4	4	J. Walter Thompson Co.	New York		1,536.1	1,489.1
5	5	Euro RSCG Worldwide	New York		1,441.2	1,430.1
6	6	Grey Worldwide	New York		1,321.0	1,369.8
7	7	DDB Worldwide Communications	New York		1,214.6	1,176.9
8	8	Ogilvy & Mather Worldwide	New York		1,135.4	1,109.4
9	10	Leo Burnett Worldwide	Chicago		1,072.3	1,029.3
10	9	Publicis Worldwide	Paris		1,066.0	1,040.9

Notes: Figures are in millions of U.S. dollars. Worldwide agency brands are defined as international networks associated with the agency and the agency's U.S. brand. Specialty units (direct marketing, sales promotion, research, etc.) and independent subsidiaries are excluded at both the U.S. and international level.

Sources: Advertising Age (April 23, 2001): S10; *Adage Global,* accessed June, 17, 2002, www.adageglobal.com/cgi-bin/pages.pl?link=514.

marketing communications areas, such as direct marketing, sales promotion, public relations, events and sports marketing, and packaging and point-of-sale. There are also one-client agencies such as the Focus agency in Dallas that serves only GTE.

Recall from Chapter 1 that there are in-house agencies and freelancers (vendors). Here we discuss industry-focused agencies, minority agencies (agencies focused on a specialized market segment), creative boutiques, media-buying services, and virtual agencies, all of which are specialized.

Industry-Focused Agencies Numerous agencies concentrate on certain fields or industries, such as agriculture, medicine and pharmaceuticals, health care, and computers. These agencies handle a variety of clients from within that field, so they are able to apply their particular expertise in those areas, making them essentially full service.

Minority Agencies Agencies that focus on an ethnic group, or minority agencies, grew substantially in the 1980s as marketers realized that African Americans and Hispanics, the two largest minorities, had preferences and buying patterns that differed from those of the general market. These agencies are organized in much the same way as full-service agencies, but they specialize in reaching and communicating with their particular markets.

Creative Boutiques Creative boutiques are ad agencies, usually small (two or three people to a dozen or more), that concentrate entirely on preparing the creative execution of client marketing communications. The focus of the organization is entirely on the idea, the creative product. A creative boutique will have one or more writers or artists on staff. There is no staff for media, research, or strategic planning. Typically, these agencies can prepare advertising to run in print media, outdoors, and on radio and television. Creative boutiques usually serve companies but are sometimes retained by advertising agencies when they are overloaded with work.

Media-Buying Services Media-buying services specialize in the purchase of media for clients. They are in high demand for many reasons (see Figure 3.6), but three reasons standout. First, media has become more complex as the number of choices grows—think of the proliferation of new cable channels, magazines, and radio stations. Second, the cost of maintaining a competent media department has escalated. Third, media-buying services often buy media at a low cost because they can group several clients' purchases together to develop substantial buying power. Although media-buying services seldom can beat the top 25 ad agencies in buying clout, they usually do better than small and medium-sized agencies. For these reasons, some small and medium-sized agencies rely heavily on media-buying services.

Virtual Agencies A recent phenomenon is the agency that operates as a group of freelancers and is paid accordingly. This type of agency does not use conventional office space. Chiat/Day pioneered an approach called "team workroom," or a virtual office. In a virtual agency like Chiat/Day, staff members do not have fixed offices; they work at home, in their cars, or at their clients' offices. Modern technology allows team members to work in environments other than a conventional office.

Better Strategy/Approach	34%
Higher Expertise/Better Resources	19%
Better Access to Information	7%
Buying Clout	3%
Independent of Full-Service Agency	3%
Miscellaneous Answers	18%
No Answer	29%

FIGURE 3.6

WHAT ADVANTAGES DOES YOUR MEDIA SERVICE PROVIDE VERSUS A FULL-SERVICE AGENCY?
Media buying services are in high demand because the world of media has become complex.
Source: Jack Feuer, "What Clients Think about Media," *Adweek* (June 4, 2001): 41.

How Agencies Are Organized

If the agency is large enough, it usually has a chief executive officer, perhaps one or two vice presidents, and several different functional areas. Next, we concentrate on five of those areas: account management, creative development and production, media planning and buying, account planning and research, and internal services.

Account Management The **account management** department acts a liaison between the client and the agency. It ensures that the agency will focus its resources on the client's needs. It develops its own point of view, which the account manager presents to the client. It is also responsible for interpreting the client's marketing strategy for the rest of the agency. Once the client (or the client and the agency together) establishes the general guidelines for a campaign and perhaps even one advertisement, the account management department supervises the day-to-day development within these guidelines.

Account management in a major agency typically has four levels: management representative or supervisor, account supervisor, account executive, and assistant account executives. Sometimes a fifth level may exist, the account director, who is above the account supervisor. A smaller agency will combine some of these levels.

The *management supervisor* reports to the agency's upper management. This supervisor provides leadership on strategic issues, looks for new business opportunities, helps guide growth and development within the account team, keeps agency management informed, and ensures that the agency is making a profit on the account.

The *account supervisor* usually is the key executive working on the client's business and the primary liaison between the client and the agency. This person directs the preparation of strategic plans, assigns task priorities, reviews and approves all recommendations before they are taken to the client, supervises the presentation of annual plans and other major recommendations to the client, and ensures that the agency adheres to deadlines and schedules.

The *account executive* is responsible for day-to-day activities. This person keeps the agency team on schedule and delivers the services promised to the client. The account executive also sees that all assignments are within budget, maintains the cooperating records of the account, prepares status and progress reports, supervises the production of materials, and secures legal or network approval of all advertising before production begins.

Creative Development and Production The creative members of the agency are the creative directors, creative department managers, copywriters, art directors, and producers. In addition to these positions, the broadcast production department and the art studio are two other areas where creative personnel can apply their skills.

Generally, the creative department has people that create and people that inspire. One is the master creator who conceives, writes, and produces innovative advertising. A staff is often built around this person. The second type is the coach, who delegates assignments, works with the staff to find an idea, and then molds, improves, nurtures, and inspires the staff. Coaches are also called creative group heads or associate creative directors.

A *creative group* includes people who write (*copywriters*), people who design ideas for print ads or television commercials (*art directors*), and people who convert these ideas into television or radio commercials (*producers*). Many agencies will employ an art director and a copywriter who work well together, and build a support group around them.

Media Planning and Buying Agencies that don't rely on outside media specialists will have a media department that recommends to the client or another department/level the most efficient means of delivering the message to the target audience. That department has three functions: planning, buying, and research. Figure 3.7 illustrates the roles that media planning and buying play. These media experts may represent one-half of the physical space occupied by an ad agency. Because media is so complex, it is not unusual for some individuals to become experts in planning, others in buying, and still others in doing research about trends and examining characteristics of consumers using different media.

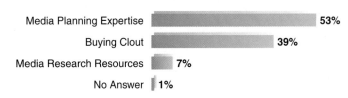

FIGURE 3.7

WHICH AREA OF MEDIA IS MOST CRITICAL TO THE SUCCESS OF YOUR ADVERTISING?
A good media department has planning expertise, buying clout, and ample marketing research.
Source: Jack Feuer, "What Clients Think about Media," *Adweek* (June 4, 2001): 40.

Account Planning and Research Full-service agencies usually have a separate department specifically devoted to account planning or research. Today the emphasis in agency research is on developing an advertising message that focuses on the consumer's perspective and relationship with the brand. An account planning department gathers all available intelligence on the market and consumers. Account planners act as strategic specialists who prepare comprehensive recommendations about the consumer's wants, needs, and relationship to the client's brand, and how the advertising should work to satisfy those elements.

Most major agencies conduct research to make the advertising more focused and appropriate to the target audience. They also purchase research from companies that specialize in this area. The leading research firms work on projects for both clients and agencies.

Internal Services The departments that serve the operations within the agency are called **internal service departments**. These include the traffic department, print production, financial services, and human resources or personnel.

The *traffic department* is responsible for internal control and tracking of projects to meet deadlines. The account executive works closely with the assigned traffic coordinator or traffic manager to review deadlines and monitor progress. The traffic department is the lifeblood of the agency, and its personnel keep track of everything that is happening there.

Taking a layout, a visual, and a page of copy and turning them into a four-color magazine page or a full-page newspaper advertisement is the work of the *print production department*. Thanks to versatile computer graphic software, much of this work is now done the computer.

Whether it is large or small, the agency must send its invoices out and pay its bills on time, control its costs, ensure that expenses incurred on behalf of a client are properly invoiced to that client, meet its payroll, pay its taxes, and make a profit within the budget.

An operation of any size requires keeping personnel files and records, and the larger the agency the more likely it is to have a professional human resources staff.

With the increasing demand for integrated marketing communication programs, agencies have been adding internal departments that provide the specialized functions they regularly use. An agency may include its own public relations, sales promotion, direct marketing, and event marketing departments. An agency handling a major car account, for example, may have a separate department to produce that account's advertising materials and to work with dealer groups.

How Agencies Make Money

Compensation is a critical factor in agency–client relationships. Agencies derive their revenues and profits from two main sources: commissions and fees.

A **commission** is the amount an ad agency charges the client as a percentage of the media cost. For example, if the $85,000 cost of media to the agency has a 15 percent commission allowance, the agency adds $12,750 to the $85,000 when billing the client.

An alternative form of compensation is the **fee** system. This is comparable to the means by which advertisers pay their lawyers and accountants. The client and agency agree on an hourly fee or rate. This fee can vary by department or it could be a flat hourly fee for all work regardless of the salary level of the person doing the work. Charges are also included for out-of-pocket expenses, travel, and other standard items. All charges are billed to the client, and no commission is added to the media cost.

Figure 3.8 shows the use of commission and fees as compensation for U.S. ad agencies. Ultimately, the primary benefit of hiring an ad agency is that it can implement the creative vision of the client, and help it to reach its advertising goals. Each agency tends to have its own style for

These three advertisements show how three different ad agencies interpreted the message for each of the armed forces.

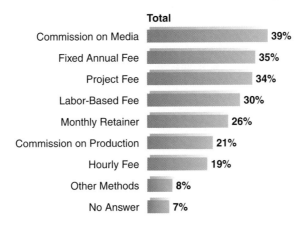

Total

Commission on Media	39%
Fixed Annual Fee	35%
Project Fee	34%
Labor-Based Fee	30%
Monthly Retainer	26%
Commission on Production	21%
Hourly Fee	19%
Other Methods	8%
No Answer	7%

FIGURE 3.8

HOW DO YOU CURRENTLY COMPENSATE THE VARIOUS TYPES OF AGENCIES YOU UTILIZE? NOTE: RESPONDENTS CAN HAVE MORE THAN ONE ANSWER
Agencies derive their revenues from two main sources: Commission and fees.
Source: Jack Feuer, "What Clients Think about Media," *Adweek* (June 4, 2001): 42.

which it is known. Note the ads of three different agencies for the three branches of the U.S. military. Do you perceive a difference in style? Which do you think would be most effective?

The Effect of Technological Changes on Agencies

Few industries have been more affected by technology than the advertising industry. This evolution of technology began in the 1950s, when TV created a visual medium for advertisers to reach the mass audience. In the 1970s, cable TV allowed for targeting of messages to niche audiences, through technologies such as local ad insertion. Digital camera development in the 1980s introduced new graphics and editing capabilities; and the mass adoption of the Internet in the 1990s, which many in advertising say is the most profound technological development of all, provided global audiences to advertisers, allowing them to track virtually all online activities.

But all this has come with a price. With so much technology to choose from, ad executives say there can be a loss of human connection in the process, and overautomation that can limit creativity in the ad business. In some agencies those with creative expertise are separated from those with technical expertise, resulting in the problem that too many people are working on the project.

However, despite the potential downfalls of technology, most people in the industry feel that overall, technology is a good thing for the ad business and it has brought employees powerful new ways to create work for and collaborate with clients. In the case of the Web, for example, agencies can communicate in a much more intelligent manner; they know much more about consumers and what they want, they can tailor their messages much more carefully, and the same information can be used to hone all media planning and buying.

Regardless of what tools are used, the challenge for advertisers and agencies in the future will be to balance advances in technology with the core of the ad business—achieving objectives.

IT'S A WRAP
A CARD THAT DID VERY WELL

Throughout this chapter we have focused on the interaction between the marketing effort of an organization and the advertising campaign that supports it. These two business functions are quite interdependent and weaknesses in one will produce weaknesses in the other. This relationship was clearly illustrated in the GM Card campaign that introduced this chapter. GM Card was faced with a challenge that many businesses never have to deal with. It changed its product and totally repositioned itself. Consequently, GM Card created an entirely original marketing communication strategy, which delivered the key messages at the most opportune times.

The results were impressive. Awareness scores, which were targeted at 10 percent, reached 26 percent after just 30 days; with current cardholders this figure exceeds 53 percent. As to the second goal, acquisition of new accounts, the 600,000 figure was exceeded by 30 percent by the end of the year.

Summary

1. **Discuss and define marketing and how advertising relates to marketing strategy**. Marketing consists of business activities that direct the exchange of goods and services between producers and consumers. Understanding how marketing works and the role advertising plays within the marketing strategy is essential for successful advertising. The success of marketing depends on whether a business can create a competitive advantage that results in an exchange. An exchange usually takes place within four types of markets: (1) consumer, (2) business-to-business (industrial), (3) institutional, and (4) reseller. Advertising aids the exchange by providing information, by changing attitudes, or by persuading consumers.

2. **Explain the marketing concept**. The marketing concept focuses on the needs of the consumer rather than the predetermined goals of the marketer.

3. **Outline the four tools of marketing and explain advertising's relationship to them**. The marketing mix identifies the most effective combination of the four main marketing functions: product, price, distribution, and marketing communications. The product consists of a bundle of tangible and intangible components that satisfies the needs of the customer. Marketers strive to implement a branding strategy that makes the product distinctive in the marketplace. An effective package not only holds the product but is an important communication device.

A channel of distribution is the basic mechanism for delivering the product to the consumer, receiving payment, and servicing the product. The two main types of channel institutions are wholesalers and retailers, each of which uses advertising in a unique manner. Several other channel-related factors influence advertising: Is the channel direct or or indirect? Is a push or pull strategy being followed? Is the market coverage exclusive, selective, or intensive?

Price includes the cost, profit, and value expectations. Factors that influence advertising include the need for price copy, the customary or expected price, psychological pricing, and price lining. Marketing communications includes advertising, sales promotion, public relations, personal selling, point-of-sale/packaging, and direct marketing. Together these are called the marketing communication mix. Each element of the marketing communication mix contributes to the ability of the company to communicate in a special way.

4. **Describe the role of the advertising agency, its organization, and its compensation methods**. An advertising agency provides an advertiser with the necessary creative skills and an objective perspective. Agency organization structures range from full service to boutique and specialty agencies. The majority of agencies are paid based on a fee structure, although many still work on a commission basis.

Key Terms

account management, p. 86
advertising department, p. 84
brand, p. 72
brand equity, p. 74
brand mark, p. 74
brand name, p. 72
branding, p. 72
channel of distribution, p. 76
commission, p. 87
cooperative advertising, p. 77
customary pricing, p. 78
direct marketing, p. 77
direct-response advertising, p. 82

exchange, p. 64
exclusive distribution, p. 78
fee, p. 87
full-service agency, p. 84
image, p. 82
indirect marketing, p. 77
in-house agency, p. 83
integrated marketing, p. 70
integrated marketing communication (IMC), p. 80
intensive distribution, p. 78
internal service departments, p. 87
market, p. 65

market segmentation, p. 67
marketing, p. 64
marketing communication mix, p. 80
marketing communications, p. 65
marketing concept, p. 69
marketing mix, p. 64
media-buying services, p. 85
personal selling, p. 80
positioning, p. 69
price, p. 78
price copy, p. 78
price lining, p. 79

product differentiation, p. 68
psychological pricing, p. 78
public relations, p. 81
pull strategy, p. 77
push strategy, p. 77
relationship marketing, p. 71
sales promotion, p. 80
selective distribution, p. 78
target market, p. 67
trademark, p. 74
undifferentiated or market aggregation strategy, p. 67

Questions

1. Find examples of three advertisements that demonstrate the marketing concept. What elements of these ads reflect this approach?

2. Imagine you are starting a company to manufacture fudge. Consider the following decisions:
   a. Describe the marketing mix you think would be most effective for this company.
   b. Describe the marketing communication mix you would recommend for this company.

c. How would you determine the advertising budget for your new fudge company?

d. Develop a brand image for your fudge.

3. Professor Baker tells her advertising class that advertising's relationship to marketing is like the tip of an iceberg. As the class looks puzzled, she explains that most (80 percent) of the iceberg cannot be seen. "It's the same with the consumer's perception of how much of marketing is advertising-related," Baker explains. What is Baker trying to illustrate with the iceberg analogy?

4. With the introduction of the new Beetle, Volkswagen took a big gamble that nostalgia could create a market for this product. What factors would VW have to consider to reduce this risk? How important do you think advertising was in this effort?

5. This chapter stressed integration of advertising with other components of the marketing mix. If you were in marketing management for Kellogg cereals, how would you see advertising supporting product, price, and place? Could advertising improve each of these functions for Kellogg? Explain your answer.

6. Angie Todd, an account assistant at a local advertising agency, is upset at the comments a marketing consultant is making during a media reception. The consultant is telling listeners that consumer advertising has lost its edge and does not have credibility. He claims consumers pay no attention to glitter or glitz (advertising); they just want a deal on price. "I'll bet none of you can name even two consumer products with ad campaigns last year that made any difference to the target consumer," he challenged. If you were Angie, how would you respond?

7. Julio Bashore has asserted that his current ad agency is doing little, other than handling media and taking commissions. Establish a checklist of activities that he could use to evaluate his agency's current or potential services.

8. You are the director of an advertising firm hired by a consumer-products company to create an ad campaign for the company's new product. In the process of your work, you determine that the company's marketing plan is poorly developed and the product is not well designed. How do you handle the situation? Do you approach the company's marketing department? Do you try to overlook the problems and create an advertising strategy anyway? If you decide to proceed and the advertising strategy fails, how do you protect your firm's reputation?

9. How do advertisers determine the best marketing strategy—segmented, undifferentiated, or combination—for a given product? What must they consider in determining the marketing communication mix? How is the target market figured into the approach? Can you think of any examples of products where the marketing strategy was miscalculated? How is positioning, as discussed in this chapter, impacted?

10. As this chapter states, Coca-Cola is the most recognizable brand in the world. How did the company achieve this? What has the company done in its marketing mix in terms of product, price, distribution, and marketing communications that has created such tremendous brand equity and loyalty? How has advertising aided in building the brand? You might want to visit Coca-Cola's Web site for help: www.coca-cola.com

Suggested Class Project

Interview the manager of a large retail outlet store in your area, such as Target, Kmart, or Wal-Mart. Assess how the retailer uses various elements of the marketing communication mix. Study a few diverse products, such as food items, blue jeans, and small appliances. You might even talk to the automotive service department. Write a report, making conclusions about how advertising comes into play.

Suggested Internet Class Project

Assess the Web sites of three ad agencies (two U.S. and one international). What differences in offerings do you observe? (See Table 3.4 for some agency names. Do a search for their home pages on a search engine such as Yahoo!)

Hallmark BUILD•A•CAMPAIGN *Projects*

Please review the Hallmark Case Appendix at the end of the text before responding to these questions.

1. What various methods did Capitol Advertising use to segment the market for Hallmark?

2. Develop a positioning statement for a local Hallmark Gold Crown Store that leverages Hallmark's positioning as indicated in the Hallmark Case Appendix. Visit a local Gold Crown Store to see if any of these positioning elements are evident.

Notes

1. "AMA Board Approves New Marketing Definition," *Marketing News* (March 1, 1985): 1.

2. John Palmer, "Orient Expressions," *Promo* (July 2001): 23–26.

3. Louise Lee, "Can Levi's Be Cool Again?" *BusinessWeek* (March 13, 2000): 144, 148; Alize Z. Cuneo, "Levi's Makes Move to Drop All the Hype and Push Products," *Advertising Age* (April 17, 2000): 4, 69.

4. Kate MacArthur, "McDonald's Flips Business Strategy," *Advertising Age* (April 2, 2001): 1, 36.

5. Steve Jarvis, "Marketing Relations," *Marketing News* (October 22, 2001): 4, 6.

6. Hillary Chura and Richard Linnett, "Coca-Cola Readies Global Assault," *Advertising Age* (April 2, 2001): 1, 34.

7. Jonathan Asher, "Make the most of package design updates," *Marketing News* (September 18, 2000): 13.

8. Jack Feuer, "What Clients Think about Media," *Adweek* (June 4, 2001): 38–42.

9. James Rosenfield, "The Devil's Dictionary of Marketing," *Direct Marketing* (September 2001): 57–59.

10. Jack Feuer, "What Clients Think about Media," *Adweek* (June 4, 2001): 38–42.

11. Leo Bogart, *Strategy in Advertising*, 2d ed. (Lincolnwood, IL: NTC Business Books, 1990): 3.

PART I ADVERTISING FOUNDATIONS AND ENVIRONMENT

A Company's Social Responsibility

With the invention of the chicken sandwich, S. Truett Cathy founded Chick-fil-A with the vision that his company would be a leader in the quick-serve restaurant industry. While he continues to attain multiple successes year after year with his quality products, employees, and customer service, Truett would also tell people that he has attained success in other areas as well.

Truett's strongest passion is the Chick-fil-A Corporate Purpose, which is "to glorify God by being a faithful steward of all that is entrusted to us. To have a positive influence on all who come in contact with Chick-fil-A." This statement is part of the social responsibility of the company.

While those are pretty big words by which to pattern one's life, Truett Cathy sets a faithful example of how it can be done—not just for himself, but for the rest of the company as well.

Take, for instance, the fact that Chick-fil-A always has been and always will be closed on Sundays. Some argue that Chick-fil-A misses too much in sales by closing the stores one day each week. Truett believes that he gains more by allowing his employees a day of worship or time with family.

Another example of the Corporate Purpose put into action is team-member scholarships. Any team member at a Chick-fil-A unit who meets the set criteria is eligible for a $1,000 scholarship that applies toward the expenses of his or her education.

Also through a WinShape Homes program, Truett helps foster neglected children and "shape them into winners." He receives great satisfaction from making a difference in others' lives.

The Chick-fil-A definition of social responsibility is a little different from those of other companies, where people may speak about a purpose and vision. At Chick-fil-A, they strive to live the words through their actions.

QUESTIONS

1. As a consumer, how do you feel about the socially responsible policies followed by Chick-fil-A?
2. What are the long-term benefits derived by employing such a strategy?

STAYED AT A
HOLIDAY INN EXPRESS
LAST NIGHT.

DIDN'T.

Stay Smart

Holiday Inn
EXPRESS

CHAPTER

The Consumer Audience

4

CHAPTER OBJECTIVES

When you have completed this chapter, you should be able to

1. Define consumer behavior and describe its relationship to advertising.

2. Explain which societal and cultural factors affect advertising and consumers.

3. Identify and describe psychological influences on consumers.

4. Summarize the purchase decision-making process.

"Where You Stay Does Matter"

Award: *EFFIE Gold 2001, Travel/Tourism/Destination category*

Company: *Bass Hotels*

Agency: *Fallon Worldwide*

Campaign: *"Stay Smart"*

You've seen the commercial. The rock band Kiss runs off a raucous stage to their back room. Their gleeful manager, tinted shades popping off his face, exclaims, "That was possibly the finest rock and roll show I have ever seen! I SMELL WORLD TOUR!"

But as the performers take off their wigs and makeup, the manager despairs, "You're not Gene. You're not Paul. You guys aren't Kiss!"

"No," says Gene.

Paul says, "But we did stay at a Holiday Inn Express last night."

Before commercials such as this one or the ad shown here in which an express guest is so empowered he can take on a bull, you had probably heard of Holiday Inn, but had you ever heard of Holiday Inn Express? Didn't think so, and that was the problem facing Express's owners, Bass Hotels & Resorts, Inc. The company needed to break into the hotel industry's already booming "limited-service segment." Limited service means that some services, such as room service and restaurants, are not provided. The company had to establish its name, establish it fast, and establish it on a limited budget.

Enter advertising agency Fallon Worldwide. Bass contacted Fallon in 1997 and the two companies came up with three goals for a new campaign:

1. **Generate awareness of Express as a competitor among limited-service hotel brands.** The company needed to distinguish Express from its parent Holiday Inn in the minds of consumers. "Express"

would have to become a unique and recognized brand name, not only in the limited-service hotel category, but also in pop culture.

2. **Define a clear, compelling market position for the brand.** Bass wanted Express to become not only a player, but also a leader in the limited-service hotel category.

3. **Drive business and increase revenue.**

Now that the goals were set, Fallon's mission was to carve out a target audience from the consumer audience—the topic of this chapter. Wanting to capture both the business travel market and the leisure travel market, Fallon determined that men aged 24 to 54 were the primary target because the research had shown they travel for both reasons. The research had also shown that they feel best about a purchase when they believe they received a great value for their money. Said Fallon: "These men value pragmatism and practicality. When they don't pay more than they need to, they feel smart."

The agency's idea was to turn this feeling of empowerment into an ad campaign—you feel good when you stay at a Holiday Inn Express because you get everything you need and you don't pay for services that you don't need. You feel so smart, in fact, you could take on a bull, impersonate Kiss and fool millions, or, as depicted in another ad, you could imitate a hazardous materials lab worker.

How did Fallon execute the ad campaign? They decided to buy time on television sports channels, such as ESPN, because they were a favorite of men in the target group and because they were not cluttered with competitors' ads. The problem was that Express couldn't afford to place ads all week on these channels for very long, so the Express ads ran on Sunday and Monday nights. Fallon's research had shown that the target group were most likely at home and, not traveling on those nights.

The agency also used postcards and posters to advertise the Express brand and its "Stay Smart" message. The posters where displayed in the hotels. The postcards were placed in the rooms. In addition, the company turned its in-room magazine, *Navigator*, into a resource for savvy travel information and tips on general interest topics.

How effective was the Holiday Inn Express campaign? We can tell you that it won an EFFIE gold award in the travel/tourism/destination category in 2001, but to find out why, read this chapter and the "It's a Wrap" box on page 118.

CONSUMER BEHAVIOR

To create ads that work, advertisers must understand how consumers behave and they must be sensitive to their needs. Part of what made the Holiday Inn Express campaign so successful was Fallon's knowledge of the target market—what men aged 25 to 54 enjoy, how they spend their time, and what makes them feel good about making a purchase. In this chapter, we examine consumer behavior and the social, cultural, and psychological factors that influence it. The study of consumer behavior helps advertisers to design effective campaigns.

The implicit goal of advertising is to persuade the consumer to do something, often to purchase a product. To achieve this goal, advertisers must first understand their audience. They must learn about consumers' ways of thinking, the factors that motivate them, and the environment in which they live.

This task is complicated by several factors. First, the elements advertisers must consider are in constant flux. Valid information about consumers today is often invalid tomorrow.

Second, consumers are affected by many internal and external influences, internal meaning things within themselves and external meaning things outside themselves. The breadth of these influences means advertisers must draw from fields such as psychology, anthropology, and sociology to understand their audience.

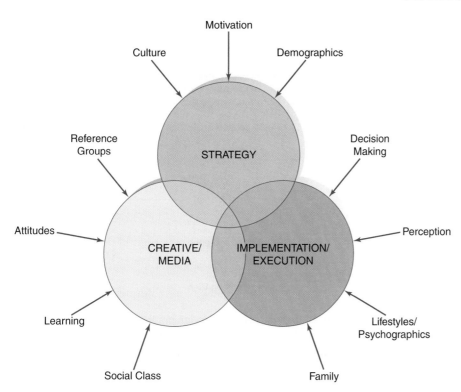

FIGURE 4.1
**THE RELATIONSHIP BETWEEN
EFFECTIVE ADVERTISING AND
CONSUMER BEHAVIOR**
There are many influences on
consumer behavior and on the three-
part process of effective advertising.

Third, every pattern of human behavior has exceptions. Advertisers should prepare for these exceptions but stay focused on the overall pattern. For example, most people are tolerant of ads containing sexual innuendo, yet there are still people who find such ads offensive; so advertisers should create ads with these differences in mind.

Fourth, as businesses move into foreign markets, finding general patterns of consumer behavior becomes more difficult because each culture has its own values, beliefs, and patterns of conduct.

In addition, advertisers need to consider these human behaviors in light of our role as consumers. **Consumer behavior** describes how individuals or groups select, purchase, use, or dispose of products as well as the needs that motivate these behaviors.

Figure 4.1 shows the influences on consumer behavior and the three-part process of effective advertising. These behavioral influences can enter anywhere in the advertising process. For example, a commercial for Kellogg's Rice Krispies Treats attempted to gain the attention of teenagers (demographics), present the product as fun (perceptions), and change their attitudes to create behavior (purchase). Supportive research indicates that most teenagers enjoy off-the-wall humor, especially when it features adults. The commercial showed how a subway rider tried to prevent himself from falling when the train stopped by using a Rice Krispies Treat as part of the handhold. Unfortunately, the treat was so sticky that when the train braked the next time, the man fell but his arm stayed attached to the handhold, thanks to the Rice Krispies Treat.

The Consumer Audience

Consumers are people who buy or use products to satisfy needs and wants. There are two types of consumers: those who shop for and purchase the product and those who actually use the product. This distinction is important because the two groups can have different needs and wants. In the case of children's cereals, for example, parents (the purchasers) often look for nutritional value and a decent price. In contrast, children (the users) look for a sweet taste and a package with a prize inside or a game on the outside. Have you ever noticed that many cereals are advertised as both fun and low in sugar?

FIGURE **4.2**

THE CONSUMER DECISION PROCESS OF THE TARGET MARKET
Advertisers study the influences on consumer behavior and how they play into consumers' decision making.

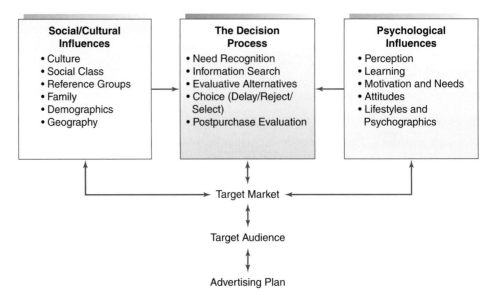

FIGURE **4.2**

THE CONSUMER DECISION PROCESS OF THE TARGET MARKET
Advertisers study the influences on consumer behavior and how they play into consumers' decision making.

Companies that want to understand how consumers think and make decisions about products conduct sophisticated consumer behavior research, to identify their consumers, why they buy, what they buy, and how they buy.

Figure 4.2 is a general model of consumer behavior. It is also a visual roadmap for this chapter. We first explore the target market and then examine social, cultural, and psychological influences on consumer behavior. We close by investigating the decision process.

The Target Market

Targeting helps organizations design specific marketing strategies to match their markets' needs and wants more effectively. In developing a focus for its advertising, the marketer must identify a particular target. Target markets then become **target audiences**, those individuals, groups, or organizations who will receive advertising messages. Not all target markets are target audiences. A business marketer, such as Cisco Systems, has many target markets, but not all of them receive advertising messages. Some appeals will be made in other forms of marketing, such as personal selling and trade deals.

Ultimately, the advertising team tries to understand how and why members of the target audiences think, feel, and behave as they do, and identify the influences affecting these elements. We examine some of these influences next.

CULTURAL AND SOCIAL INFLUENCES ON CONSUMERS

Many factors affect your responses to an advertising message. The culture and the society in which you were raised affect your values and opinions. Likewise, you are a product of the family in which you were raised, and many of your habits and biases developed in the family environment.

These forces on your behavior are **cultural and social influences**. They fall into six major areas: (1) culture, (2) social class, (3) reference groups, (4) family, (5) demographics, and (6) geography.

Culture

Culture is made up of tangible items (art, literature, buildings, furniture, clothing, and music) and intangible concepts (history, knowledge, laws, morals, and customs) that together define a group of people or a way of life. Culture is learned and passed on from one generation to the next, and the boundaries each culture establishes for behavior are called **norms**. Norms are simply rules that we learn through social interaction that specify or prohibit certain behaviors.

The source of norms is our **values**. One example of a value is personal security. Norms that reflect this value range from bars on the windows and double-locked doors in

Brooklyn, New York, to unlocked cars and homes in Eau Claire, Wisconsin. Values are few in number; they are hard to change, they are not tied to specific objects or situations, they are internal, and they guide behavior.

Researchers have attempted to identify core values that could characterize an entire culture. One simplified list consists of nine core values:

1. A sense of belonging
2. Excitement
3. Fun and enjoyment
4. Warm relationships
5. Self-fulfillment
6. Respect from others
7. A sense of accomplishment
8. Security
9. Self respect[1]

Advertisers often refer to core values when selecting their primary appeals. Because values are so closely tied to human behavior and so difficult to change, private research firms try to monitor values and look for groupings of values and behavior patterns. For instance, the importance of sending all children to college is emphasized in America. Conversely, in a country such as Portugal, the custom is to send sons to college before sending daughters. So ads for colleges in America feature both men and women while similar ads in Portugal mostly feature men.

Culture directly influences buying behavior. For example, the busy working mother of today is not as devoted to meal preparation and household cleaning as was the full-time homemaker of the past. Food marketers have changed their promotional strategies to reach those women, and we now see more advertising for fast foods, convenience foods, restaurants, take-home meals, and "meal" home delivery. In addition to food preparation, there are other ways a mom can show her devotion to her family. Even NicoDerm created an ad which targets the mom who shows her devotion to her family by quitting smoking.

In respect to actual growth, few cultures are more important to U.S. marketing than the Hispanic culture. By 2005, Hispanics will make up 13.3 percent or (38.2 million) of the total U.S. population, up from 11.7 percent in 1999. HomeScan, a research firm that investigates household trends, recently compiled a report on a sample of Hispanic households living in Los Angeles. Their findings indicate that Hispanics spend more per shopping trip than non-Hispanics. HomeScan also found that store signage and product labels in Spanish promoted stronger brand loyalty with Hispanics. Companies such as Amoco and Procter & Gamble are taking note of this by advertising in Spanish to reach the Hispanic target audience in the United States.[2]

How does culture affect you as a consumer? Can you think of any cultural factors that influence your behavior? How about patriotism and sacrificing for the good of others? Can you see yourself signing up for the Peace Corps? How about materialism? How do you feel about acquiring possessions and making money?

Answers to questions such as these would be valuable to many advertisers, especially to those marketing products that correlate with cultural factors. Continuing our example, Hispanics tend to have a higher level of patriotism, believe in cash rather than credit cards, and are willing to spend more money on their kids compared to their Anglo-Saxon counterparts.

Sometimes, a culture can be further broken down into smaller groups called subcultures. Hispanics living in Southern California, Texas, Miami, and New York City can be quite different, and they are subcultures of the overall Hispanic culture.

Subcultures can be geographic regions or shared human characteristics such as age, values, or ethnic background. In the United States there are many different subcultures: teenagers, college students, retirees, southerners, Texans, athletes, musicians, and working single mothers, to name a few.

What subcultures do you belong to? Look at your activities. Do you do anything on a regular basis that might identify you as a member of a distinctive subculture? How about going to church or temple? Snowboarding? Rock climbing? Belonging to the Sierra Club? A book club? All of these subcultures become target markets to advertisers.

This ad for Tide exhibits the effective targeting of the Hispanic culture. *Trans:* The salsa is something you dance, not what you wear.

Social Class

Another influence you experience as a consumer is **social class**, the position you and your family occupy within your society. Social class is determined by such factors as income, wealth, education, occupation, family prestige, value of home, and neighborhood. Every society has a social class structure. In more rigid societies, such as those of India or Brazil, people have a difficult time moving out of the class into which they were born. In the United States, although people may move into social classes that differ from their families', the country still has a prominent class system consisting of upper, middle, and lower classes.

Marketers assume that people in one class buy different goods from different outlets and for different reasons than people in other classes. In the United States, people in the upper class purchase a larger percentage of their products through the Internet, spend more per item, and buy more items that are considered luxury goods. A much smaller percentage of people in the lower classes own computers and they tend to use bricks-and-mortar retail outlets almost exclusively.[3] Advertisers can get a feel for the social class of a target market by using marketing research or available census data. This information can help them to create ads that appeal to those social classes and select the appropriate media for the various classes.

In what class do you see yourself? Does social class affect what you buy and how you respond to advertising? Do you know people who belong to a different social class? Do they buy different products from what you buy? Do they look at products differently in terms of price or quality? For media giant ESPN, social class has been a very useful basis for creative design. People who enjoy its off-the-wall TV commercials tend to be in the middle social class—the same class that Holiday Inn Express targets.

Reference Groups

A **reference group** is a collection of people who are used as a guide for behavior in specific situations. General examples of reference groups are political parties, religious groups, racial or ethnic organizations, clubs based on hobbies, and informal affiliations such as fellow workers or students. A reference group is based on behavioral information, while social class is based on general demographics.

For consumers, reference groups have three functions: (1) they provide information, (2) they serve as a means of comparison, and (3) they offer guidance. In respect to providing information, most of us would agree that members of our own reference groups—students, employees, friends—provide most of the information we use on a daily basis. Your

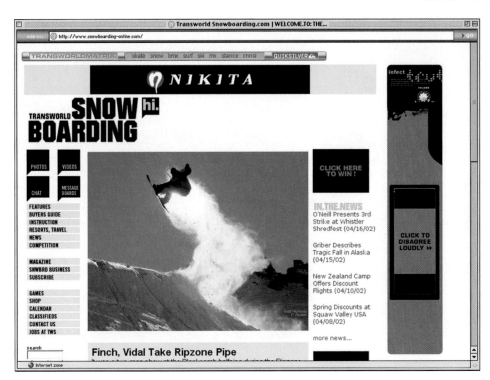

student reference group may tell you what course to take, whether you need to study for an exam, or the availability of a part-time job. That same student reference group will help you assess how you're doing in school academically or socially. When you begin your job search, such comparisons will become even more important. Should your job plight become critical, reference group members may offer you helpful advice.

This same reference group interaction can also apply to a person's role as consumer. Sometimes the group customs require the purchase or use of certain products, such as uniforms, safety equipment, or computer software. The reference group members may be so similar to you that you believe any product or service the group members use is right for you. Ads that feature typical users in fun or pleasant surroundings are using a reference group strategy. You also may be attracted to a particular reference group and want to be like the members of that group out of respect or admiration. Advertisers use celebrity endorsements to tap into this device. The Web site for snowboarding (www.snowboarding-online.com) targets a specific set of reference groups—the young, and those who are outdoor-oriented. Ads focus on action shots featuring similarly dressed young people.

Think about all the groups you belong to, both formal and informal. Why do you belong to these groups? How do other members influence you or keep you informed? Have you ever bought anything specifically because a group you belonged to required it?

Family

The family is the most important reference group because of its longevity and intensity. Other reference groups such as peers, co-workers, and neighbors tend to change as we age and switch occupations or residencies. According to the U.S. Census, a **family** consists of two or more people who are related by blood, marriage, or adoption, and live in the same household. A **household** differs from a family in that it consists of all those who occupy a dwelling whether they are related or not.

Your family is critical to how you develop as an individual. It provides two kinds of resources for members: *economic* resources (money and possessions) and *emotional* resources (such as empathy, love, and companionship). The family is also responsible for raising and training children and establishing a lifestyle for family members. Your **lifestyle** is how you spend your time and money and the kinds of activities you value.

Advertisers need to understand the structure and workings of the family to communicate effectively. For example, the U.S. family structure is changing because of an increase

Sony tries to portray families in a realistic way. Do you think the ad would offend people who have an idealistic image of the family?

in divorces, later marriages, one-partner and two-family households, and other family systems. The household, once largely disregarded, has recently emerged as a viable family structure. The 2000 Census shows that more than 27 million Americans live by themselves, about one-fourth of all households, nearly 10 percent of the population. For the first time, one-person households outnumber married couples with children.[4] This reflects a growing trend in America over the past 30 years to marry later in life, divorce, or never get married at all.

Marketers and their advertisers have been right on top of this familial trend. Banks have created special mortgages, builders are providing homes and apartments to meet the needs of the single, auto manufacturers have brought back versions of the sports car, and food marketers have introduced "single" portions. Their advertisers have used this information to match copy, settings, and appeals to the single consumer.

Advertisers study family purchase and consumption patterns. They have found that parents screen and evaluate product information; and children strongly influence which product or brand is purchased, although they are not necessarily the actual decision makers. Companies such as Sony attempt to portray the family in a realistic manner, including the positives and the negatives. In a Handycam ad, Sony advertises that the product offers something for every type of family.

How has your family influenced you in your choice of schooling, lifestyle, and the way you spend your time and money? Now think about your best friend. Are the two of you different in ways that can be traced to family differences? Would advertising for a product such as an automobile influence you differently because of your family?

Demographics

Demographics is next in our study of the cultural and social influences on consumers. **Demographics** are the statistical, personal, social, and economic characteristics of a population, including age, gender, education, income, occupation, race, and family size. The study of how these characteristics influence your behavior as an individual consumer is called **demography**. These characteristics serve as the basis for most advertising strategies and knowing them assists advertisers in message design and media selection for the target market. On August 8, 2001, at 10:46 A.M. (MST), the U.S. population was 284,852,064 and the world population was 6,154,546,700. As numbers, these stats don't mean much to us, but they do tell us a great deal when we break them down into numbers the advertising strategist needs: age, gender, education, occupation, income, and race/ethnicity.

Age	Radio	TV	Cable	Magazines	Newspapers	Online
18–24	16%	11%	13%	17%	7%	13%
25–34	23	18	20	21	13	23
35–44	25	19	22	23	21	28
45–54	17	16	17	18	21	22
55–64	9	13	12	10	15	9
65–plus	10	24	15	10	23	5

FIGURE 4.3 MEDIA USAGE BY AGE

Overall usage patterns for each medium vary by demographic age group. This table shows the percentage of persons in each age group who are heavy users of the individual media. For instance, 16 percent of heavy radio listeners are in the 18- to 24-year-old age bracket.

Source: Reprinted with permission from the February 26, 2001, issue of Advertising Age. ©, Crain Communications Inc. 2001.

Age People in different stages of life have different needs. An advertising message must be geared to the target audience's age group and should be delivered through a medium that members of that group use. How old are you? What products did you use five or ten years ago that you don't use now? Look ahead 10 years. What products might you be interested in buying then? What products do your parents buy that you don't? Do you read different publications and watch different programs than your parents do? If you were in the market for a car, would you look at the same features your parents look at?

The age distribution in the United States has a bearing on a number of advertising decisions. The "Baby Boomers" (born between 1946 and 1964) and their children, the "Echo Boomers" (born between 1980 and 1996) represent the two largest age categories in sheer numbers. The former are finalizing their careers and are headed for retirement; they are concerned with their physical, emotional, and financial well-being. Thanks to the growth of cable channels, segmented print media, and the Internet, baby boomers can be easily reached with targeted messages. As noted in Figure 4.3, as baby boomers age, TV and newspapers become the predominant media.

The echo boomers are very involved with completing their education and beginning their careers and families. This makes them prime target markets for technology, travel, cars, and furniture. The predominant media that advertisers use to reach this market is the

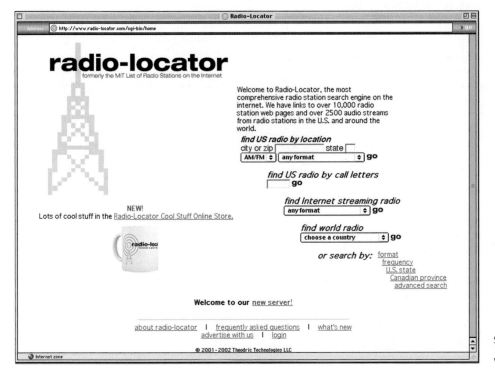

The Radio-Locator search engine is very popular with Echo-Boomers.

Internet, radio, and magazines that can be delivered via the Internet. Radio-Locator is a search engine that is popular with echo boomers. It has helped to enlarge the radio listening audience by funneling consumers to stations of their liking all over the country.

Gender Gender is an obvious basis for differences in marketing and advertising. The gender breakdown in the 2000 Census was 48.9 percent male, 51.1 percent female. When we talk about gender differences, we consider both primary and secondary differences. *Primary* gender differences are physical traits that are inherent in males or females, such as a woman's ability to bear children. *Secondary* gender traits tend to be associated with one sex more than the other. Wearing perfume and shaving legs are secondary traits associated with women.

The primary gender traits of men and women create demands for products and services directly associated with a person's sex. In the past there were many taboos about marketing such products. For example, markets of tampons and sanitary pads were once restricted to advertising in media and retail outlets devoted strictly to women. Condoms, purchased almost exclusively by men, were behind the counter (or perhaps under-the-counter items). These barriers have all but vanished—and products that are primarily male or female are marketed in similar ways and in comparable media.

Many consumers consider certain brands to be masculine or feminine. It is unlikely that men would use a brand of cologne called "White Shoulders" (which is a perfume for women). The Gillette Company found that the majority of women would not purchase Gillette razor blades, so they introduced brands exclusively for women, such as the Sensor and SensorExcel for Women and Daisy disposable razors.

Marketers who want to sell products formerly associated with one sex to both sexes often find it necessary to offer "his and her" brands or even different product names for the same basic goods. What products do you buy that are unisex? What products do you use that are specifically targeted to your sex?

In the last decade gay and lesbian consumers have become target markets. This segment has important implications for advertisers. Because some heterosexuals are still

Subaru targets gay consumers both directly through its own car ads, and as a co-sponsor for Visa's Rainbow Card.

offended by the gay lifestyle, advertisers must determine the best way to target these consumers. Companies that already advertise in gay media include Sony, Apple, Banana Republic, American Express, Hiram Walker & Sons, Miller Brewing, Coors, Subaru of America, and Visa, to name a few. Gay media, such as GLINN GayDish TV network, *Freshmen,* and *Digital Gay World,* all target the gay consumer group and most viewers/ subscribers are gay.

Many of these companies have opted to play it relatively safe and produce two different campaigns, one for the homosexual consumer and one for the heterosexual consumer, placing the former's ad messages primarily in overtly gay media. For these companies, the challenge is to create ads that are an accurate portrayal of the gay lifestyle.

Other companies that target the homosexual consumer group have decided to run the same ad campaign in both straight and gay media. For a company like furniture retailer IKEA, the risks are great. If its ads are obviously gay in content or visually, they might lose the heterosexual market. In one example, IKEA features a male couple shopping for a dining room table together. The two middle-aged guys, who finish each other's sentences, say "A leaf means commitment." At the end, one says, "We've got another leaf waiting when we really start getting along" perhaps implying having children.

Whether an advertiser takes the safe path or the one with more risk, reaching the gay consumer with effective messaging is not easy. It is particularly important to make sure that the portrayal of the gay consumer is authentic and that the problems addressed are real.

Education The level of education attained by consumers is also an influence on the advertising strategy. According to the 2000 census (Figure 4.4) statistics show U.S. males attain higher levels of education than U.S. females. Also, income corresponds with gender, regardless of level of education. As far as race, generally white U.S. consumers attain higher levels of education than Blacks and Hispanics.

For advertisers purposes, education tends to correlate with the type of medium consumers prefer, as well as the specific elements or programs within a medium. Consumers with lower education are higher users of television, especially cable. Consumers with higher education prefer print media, the Internet, and selected radio and cable stations.

Likewise, education dictates the copy written, level of difficulty, and complexity of relationships. Examine ads in *Fortune* or *Forbes* and you will find different words, art, and products than you will in *People* or tabloid publications. Advertisers don't make value judgments about these statistics. They're objective is to match advertising messages to the characteristics of their target markets.

FIGURE 4.4 **EDUCATED AMERICANS**

According to the 2000 Census, Americans are better educated than they were in 1940. Also, as the level of education rises, so does salary.
Source: U.S. Census Bureau, 2000.

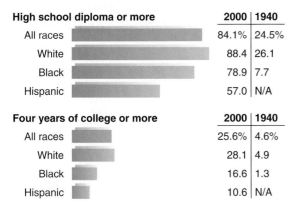

High school diploma or more	2000	1940
All races	84.1%	24.5%
White	88.4	26.1
Black	78.9	7.7
Hispanic	57.0	N/A

Four years of college or more	2000	1940
All races	25.6%	4.6%
White	28.1	4.9
Black	16.6	1.3
Hispanic	10.6	N/A

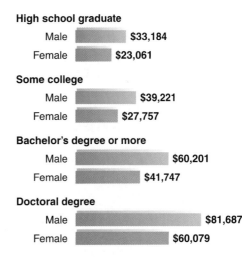

High school graduate
Male $33,184
Female $23,061

Some college
Male $39,221
Female $27,757

Bachelor's degree or more
Male $60,201
Female $41,747

Doctoral degree
Male $81,687
Female $60,079

FIGURE 4.5

HOW MANY HOURS A WEEK DO YOU WORK AT YOUR CURRENT JOB?
It appears that making more money means working longer hours.
Source: "Going for That Gold Watch," *ADWEEK,* October 9, 2000, p. 35.

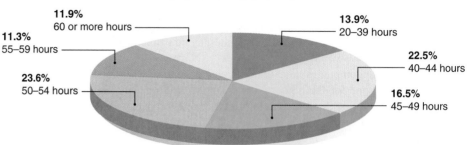

Among college-educated employees making $50,000-plus

11.9% 60 or more hours

11.3% 55–59 hours

23.6% 50–54 hours

13.9% 20–39 hours

22.5% 40–44 hours

16.5% 45–49 hours

Occupation Most people identify themselves by what they do. Even non-wage earners such as homemakers and students identify themselves in this way. In the United States there has been a gradual movement from blue-collar occupations to white-collar occupations during the last three decades. There have also been shifts within white-collar work from sales to other areas, such as professional specialty, technical, and administrative positions.

The number of service-related jobs is expected to increase, especially in the health care, education, and legal and business service sectors. Much of this transition is a direct result of advanced computer technologies, which have eliminated many labor-intensive, blue-collar occupations. Still, as always, the income earned increases with the hours worked (see Figure 4.5). This shift has affected advertising in a number of ways: Today, advertisements seldom portray blue-collar jobs, and ad copy tends to be more technical.

Income You are meaningful to a marketer only if you have the resources to buy the product advertised, either with cash or through credit. Figure 4.6 shows the median household incomes in the United States for the 2000 Census. Advertisers track trends in income, especially **discretionary income**, which is the amount of money available to a household after taxes and basic necessities such as food and shelter are paid for. Some industries, such as movie theaters, travel, jewelry, and fashion, would be out of business if people didn't have discretionary income.

Income may be the most often-used demographic indicator for many advertisers. Affordability correlates strongly with income: If a marketer knows that an annual income of $125,000 is needed to purchase a BMW, that is important information. It suggests that the setting of the ad should be upscale (country club, executive office tower), and the media employed should match the reading habits of the income group (*Fortune, Money, Wall Street Journal, Town & Country*).

Race and Ethnicity Our earlier discussion pointed out that race and ethnicity are two of the factors that contribute to the definition of a culture or subculture. Race and ethnicity can also be important stand-alone demographic variables, quite useful to the advertiser.

The 2000 U.S. Census provided these statistics on American race and ethnicity demographics:

Race and Ethnicity	% of Population[*]
White	79.2
Black or African American	12.4
American Indian/Alaskan	.2
Asian	.4
Native Hawaiian	.001
Hispanic or Latino	12.3
Other	.01

[*]Note that the percentages add up to more than 100 percent. This is due to the continuing difficulty the Census Bureau is having in capturing all the elements of race. Simply, some respondents check more than one category. Although the situation is closer to resolution, there are still potential problems with the validity of the data.

So, how does the advertiser use information on race and ethnicity? If we look at the African American population for an example, certain additional U.S. demographic information might prove useful to the advertiser:

- The African American population, with a median age of 30, is five years younger than the U.S. population, on average.
- The African American population is expected to grow more than twice as fast as the Caucasian population between 1995 and 2020, reaching 45 million.
- In 1998, 55 percent of African Americans lived in the South, yet the cities with the highest African American population are not in the South.
- In 2000, there were 8.7 million African American households, nearly half of them married.[5]

For Merrill Lynch, all this information, plus its own proprietary information, helped to design an advertising campaign targeting affluent African Americans. The company identified two clear priorities: the need for more community involvement from companies African Americans do business with and for more education about financial services. Working with marketing consultant Stedman Graham & Partners, a unit of the advertising agency True North Communications, Merrill Lynch developed a series of financial education programs for affluent African Americans in Chicago. Merrill Lynch hosted three seminars—one targeted to small-business owners, another for individual investors, and the third designed for clergy and nonprofit organizations.[6] Over 1,300 African Americans participated in the three seminars and Merrill Lynch acquired over $200,000 in new business.

Geographic Location

The area in which a target market lives correlates with several demographic characteristics and is important to advertisers. Marketers study the sales patterns of different parts of the country because people residing in different regions need certain products. For example, someone living in the Midwest or the Northeast is more likely to purchase products for removing snow and ice than a Floridian would. Differences also exist between urban areas and suburban or rural areas. Swimming pools that sell well in a residential suburban neighborhood would not be in demand in an urban neighborhood filled with apartment buildings. To plan advertising, marketers must predict geographic trends and understand how those trends can affect their marketing.

PSYCHOLOGICAL INFLUENCES ON CONSUMERS

We have analyzed cultural and social influences on consumer behavior. Now let's look at the internal elements that make you an individual. The elements that shape your inner self are your psychological makeup. Although hundreds of different elements are encompassed under the term *psychological,* the elements with the most relevance to advertising are perception, learning, motives, attitudes, and lifestyles.

Perception

Each day we are bombarded with stimuli—faces, conversations, buildings, advertisements, news announcements—yet we actually notice only a small fraction. Why? The answer is perception. **Perception** is the process by which we receive information through our five senses and assign meaning to it.

Perceptions are shaped by three sets of influences:

1. The physical characteristics of the stimuli
2. The relationships of the stimuli to their surroundings
3. The person's state of mind

The median household income – meaning half earn more, half earn less – rose to $42,148 in 2000 from $40,816 in 1999. Median incomes for various groups:

Household types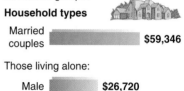

Married couples $59,346

Those living alone:

Male $26,720
Female $18,163

Number of persons in household:

$21,467 (1) $44,526 (2) $54,199 (3) $61,852 (4)

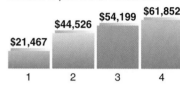

Race, ethnicity

$44,226 (Non-Hispanic white) $30,439 (Black) $51,205 (Asian/Pacific Islander) $33,447 (Hispanic)

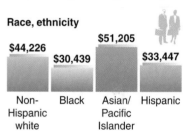

Geography

Northeast $45,106
Midwest $44,646
South $38,410
West $44,744
Outside metro areas $32,837

Age

25–34 $44,473
35–44 $53,240
45–54 $58,218
55–64 $44,992
65 or older $23,048

FIGURE 4.6

DEMOGRAPHIC MEDIANS OF HOUSEHOLD INCOME
Because income corresponds with purchase capability, it is an important demographic for advertisers to understand and track.
Source: U.S. Census Bureau, 2000.

The third influence, the person's state of mind, makes perception a personal trait. Each person perceives a stimulus within her own frame of reference. The sheer number of stimuli to which we are exposed further complicates the perception process. Some of these stimuli are perceived completely, some partially, some correctly, and some incorrectly. Ultimately, we select some stimuli and ignore others because we cannot be conscious of all incoming information at one time.

We engage in perceptional screening at two levels: internal and external. The internal screening process occurs for physical or physiological reasons. For instance, a person with poor eyesight does not understand an ad because the type is too small to read. We also internally screen because our feelings, interests, or experiences cause us to filter out any ads that we don't like or agree with. For example, someone with an aversion to sexual overtones may screen out such ads. External screening takes place because we just can't perceive all the cues we are exposed to daily. Indeed, very few highway billboards grab our attention.

Although perceptual screening is a common psychological concept, another version of it is particularly germane to advertising: selective perception. The process of screening out information that does not interest us and retaining information that does is called **selective perception**. Think about the drive or walk to school every day. How many stimuli do you perceive? You may perceive traffic signals, what's going on near you, other traffic, and pedestrians crossing in front of you, but you may not perceive all the signs you pass, the address numbers on the buildings, or the people behind you. This is selective perception.

This same process occurs when we watch television or read a magazine. It also occurs when we look at an ad and perceive only the headline, photograph, or famous spokesperson. Think back to the ad that highlighted the opening story for this chapter. What do you remember about it?

In addition to our tendency to select stimuli that are of interest to us, we also perceive stimuli in a manner that coincides with our reality. That is, your world includes your own set of experiences, values, beliefs, biases, and attitudes. It is virtually impossible to separate these inherent factors from the way you perceive. For example, we naturally tend to seek out messages that are pleasant or sympathetic with our views and avoid those that are painful or threatening. This is called **selective exposure**.

Similarly, when we are exposed to a message that conflicts with what we believe, we engage in **selective distortion**. For example, a sales person may inform a consumer that a car does not have good gas mileage. Because the consumer has a strong desire to purchase the car because of the heated leather seats and side air bags, she is likely to distort that negative point in order to conclude that the car is a good buy.

Advertisers are interested in these selective processes because they affect whether consumers will perceive an ad and, if so, whether they will remember it. Our attitudes toward the person, situation, and idea in an advertisement also strongly influence selective perception. We will remember details about the message, such as product features and brand name, when perception is intense. An ad for the Kindred Spirits pet memorial program of the Humane Society of the United States produces strong reactions from consumers who perceive their pets as integral parts of the family.

Our responses to stimuli have a direct bearing on advertising. A large part of what the brain processes is lost after only an instant. Even when we try to retain information, we are unable to save a lot of it. **Selective retention** describes the process we go through in trying to save information for future use. Advertising can aid this process by using repetition, vivid images, easily remembered brand or product names, jingles, high-profile spokespeople, music, and so forth.

Another possible response to selective perception is a feeling of dissatisfaction or doubt. Seldom does a purchased product deliver all positive results. According to the theory of **cognitive dissonance**, we tend to compensate or justify the small or large discrepancies between what we actually received and what we perceived we would receive. Research on this phenomenon has shown that people engage in a variety of activities to reduce cognitive dissonance. Most notably, they seek out information that supports their decisions and they ignore and distort information that does not. Advertising can play a central role in reducing dissonance. For example, appliance makers anticipate where dissonance is likely to occur and

This ad catches the attention of pet lovers—an example of selective perception.

provide supportive information. IBM uses testimonials by satisfied customers, and restaurants include discount coupons in their print ads so customers feel they receive a better value.

The next time you watch television, study yourself as you view the ads. What do you select to pay attention to? Why? When do you tune out? Why? Did you find yourself disagreeing with a message or arguing with it? Can you see how your own selection processes influence your attention and response to advertising?

For the advertiser, selective perception and all its subcategories represent a formidable challenge. TV advertisers, for example, note that viewers tend to shift their perceptions as soon as the commercials start. They may even leave the room, change the channel, zap the commercial, converse with a family member, or continue to read a book. That's why the first five seconds of a commercial are so critical in capturing the attention (perception) of the viewer. Using a celebrity spokesperson, a cute puppy or kitten, a startling question, or a half-naked actress are all attempts to hold perception. Even the massive number of ads found in a typical magazine or newspaper represents a significant perceptual challenge. How many ads do you notice?

Learning

Perception leads to learning; that is, we cannot learn something unless we have accurately perceived the information and attached some meaning to it. Learning is often an unconscious activity; consumers usually don't know when it's happening. If advertisers understand how consumers learn, they can design ads that make it simple for consumers to learn the ad's key elements, such as brand name, product features, and price. They can also tap into the different attitudes, beliefs, preferences, values, and standards that affect learning and purchase behavior.

One Shell Oil ad taps into attitudes of concern for children in an attempt to teach a safety lesson. Giving credit to Shell for concern for safety may encourage consumer purchase.

Various theories have been proposed to explain different aspects of learning. Typically, experts rely on two approaches to understanding the learning process. The first focuses on *cognitive* or mental processes; the second focuses on *behavioral conditioning*.

Shell Oil is attempting to teach consumers about an issue that should be of concern to them.

Cognitive learning theorists stress the importance of perception, problem solving, and insight. They characterize people as problem solvers who go through a complex set of mental process to analyze information. Advertisers that adopt the cognitive learning approach try to provide information that will help a consumer's decision-making process.

The second school of theorists argues that people learn behavior by experiencing connections between stimuli and responses through classic or instrumental conditioning. Essentially, *classical conditioning* pairs one stimulus with another that already elicits a given response. It is often associated with the experiments of Ivan Pavlov, in which a dog was trained to salivate at the sound of a bell by associating that bell with food.

Instrumental or *operant* conditioning is the voluntary occurrence of behaviors that are then rewarded, punished, or ignored. The theory assumes that people engage in a trial-and-error process that identifies which of their behaviors result in a favorable response and which do not. The person's reward is instrumental in this behavioral learning process. Advertisers that adopt this view of learning tend to emphasize that their brand provides greater rewards than other brands. For example, a print ad for a local restaurant that carries a 50 percent off coupon is engaging in operant conditioning.

When we repeat a process many times and continue to be satisfied with the outcome, we develop a habit. A **habit** means we learned something so well, it has become second nature. A habit is a decision-making shortcut: We save time and effort because we do not evaluate information about alternative choices. In addition, purchasing by habit reduces risk. Buying the same brand time and again reduces the risk of product failure and financial loss. Obviously, advertisers would like consumers to be habitual users of their products. Achieving that goal requires a powerful message backed by a superior product. For example, Coca-Cola reinforces its local consumers through very positive, entertaining messages.

Once a habit is formed, advertising should reinforce that habit through reminder messages, messages of appreciation, and actual rewards such as coupons, premiums, and rebates. Breaking the consumer's habit is difficult. Attacking a well-entrenched competitor may only make consumers defensive and reinforce their habit. Offering the consumer new, relevant information about your product or your competition is one approach. Providing an extra incentive to change, such as coupons or free samples, has also proven effective. Certainly, consumers who are price-sensitive tend to habitually purchase items of lowest cost. These deal-prone people have a habit that is difficult to break.

Advertisers use a number of techniques to improve learning. Music and jingles improve learning because they intensify the repetition; creating positive associations with a brand name enhances learning; testimonials by well-liked celebrities and scenes of attractive people in attractive settings can also intensify positive associations. An ad may use humor because it gives the audience some reward for paying attention. One Fox Sports ad created a positive association with a product by using humor.

Motivation and Needs

We all have a level of personal motivation. A **motive** is an internal force that stimulates you to behave in a particular manner. This driving force is produced by the release of tension that is caused by an unfulfilled need. People strive both consciously and subconsciously to reduce the tension. At any given point you are probably affected by a number of different motives, some of which may be contradictory, and some motives are stronger at certain times: Your motivation to buy a new suit will be much higher if you have several job interviews scheduled for the next week.

What are your buying motives? Think back over all your purchases during the past week. Did you have a reason for buying those products that you might tell an interviewer, but also a hidden reason that you will keep to yourself? Understanding buying motives is crucial to advertisers because the advertising message and the timing of the ad should coincide with the consumer's motivation priorities.

Needs are one set of factors that influence whether we are motivated and how that motivation is manifested. Needs are the basic forces that motivate us to do something. Each person has his own set of unique needs; some are innate, others are acquired. Innate needs are physiological and include the need for water, food, air, shelter, and sex. Because satisfying these needs is necessary to maintaining life, they are also called primary needs. In the case of the needs pyramid developed by psychologist Abraham Maslow (see Figure 4.7), these are called physiological needs, spilling over into safety needs.

Acquired needs are those we learn in response to our culture and environment. These may include needs for esteem, prestige, affection, power, and learning. Because acquired needs are not necessary to your physical survival, they are considered secondary needs. Maslow called them social, egoistic, and self-actualization. Advertisers try to assess which needs are most important to consumers at any given time. However, no category of needs consistently takes precedence over the others. Since the events of 9/11, safety and security have become overriding needs, especially in the United States. Eventually, the anxiety level will decline and other needs will take priority, although a heightened level of general anxiety will permeate our thinking for a long time. Recall how, following 9/11, all the airlines ran ads to encourage customers to fly again, based on improved security efforts; and companies selling security devices had a field day, including handgun manufacturers. As noted in one American Express ad, advertising provided many opportunities to give money to survivors' families.

Advertisers must also be aware of changing needs trends. Using the security example again, imagine how consumers' needs have changed. You can identify, on one hand, a certain group of people who are so frightened that they never leave home, and on the other hand, there are people who have not changed their behavior at all. In between are those who are installing security systems, not flying (or only flying charters), buying guard dogs, buying automatic weapons, and so forth.

Another change within a need category is how we increase our desire for things, or what Maslow might consider social and egoistic needs. A book researching consumer spending, entitled *Affluenza,* shows our growing dysfunctional habit of acquiring stuff in the United States. Although the book provides hundreds of examples, the most telling one was this: The average square footage of a home in 1955 is the size of the average garage in 2000. Advertisers must be careful not to take advantage of the excessive need to acquire.[7] This is illustrated in the "A Matter of Principle" box on Buzz Marketing (p. 113).

Humor is an effective device for enhancing memory retention: This commercial for Fox Sports uses humor to create a strong memory of the Fox Sports brand.

FIGURE 4.7

MASLOW'S HIERARCHY OF NEEDS
Maslow's hierarchy of needs
pyramid is a popular representation
of how we should look at human
needs.
Source: From *Motivation and
Personality* by Abraham H. Maslow.
Copyright © 1970 by Abraham H.
Maslow. Copyright 1954, 1987 by
Harper & Row Publishers, Inc.
Reprinted by permission of Addison-
Wesley Educational Publishers Inc.

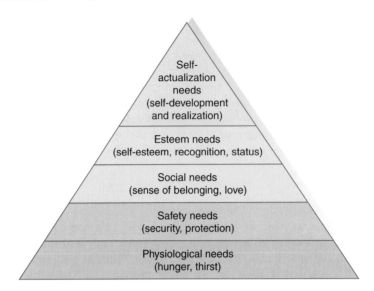

Attitudes

An **attitude** is a learned predisposition, a feeling that you hold toward an object, a person, or an idea that leads to a particular behavior. Attitudes tend to be resistant to change. You can hold an attitude for months or even years.

Because attitudes are learned, we can change them, or replace them with new ones. Attitudes also vary in direction and strength; that is, an attitude can be positive or negative, reflecting like or dislike, or it can be neutral.

Attitudes are important to advertisers because they influence how consumers evaluate products, institutions, retail stores, and advertising. A strong positive attitude toward pet care may be turned into a preference for a certain brand of pet food because it emphasizes health maintenance and products that cost more because they are superior quality. Similarly, a consumer may possess a strong positive attitude toward FAO Schwartz and will purchase products there regardless of the brand. Some consumers distrust advertising per se and this negative attitude translates into a boycott on brands that advertise.

Amazingly, we typically hold few strong attitudes, positive or negative. Strong emotional, social, and political attitudes are most common: witness how less than 30 percent of the U.S. population votes for our president. The general apathy that U.S. citizens had been feeling toward patriotism changed dramatically on 9/11. Several companies made the mistake of underestimating the strong negative attitudes most citizens had about supporting revenge toward the Taliban and ran no ads touting that point of view. Other companies appeared to take advantage of this event and were judged insincere by much of the public. Still others, such as Visa, appeared to hit the U.S. attitude just right by focusing on the tragedy of the event along with the need for targeted retribution.

Ultimately, attitudes are a reflection of our values. Marketers conduct opinion studies and attitude surveys to assess the relationship between attitude and values within a target market. Thus, if an upscale, four-star restaurant in downtown Seattle discovers through attitude surveys that consumers living in a suburb targeted for a second location are opposed to paying its $100+ for a meal per person, several questions arise. Is the owner willing to change the menu? If not, what kind of copy should ads for this new location contain? Would couponing be appropriate? What about other promotions, such as Early Bird specials, senior discounts, and continuity programs? What type of media should the advertiser use? TV commercials may denote lower quality, while magazines aimed at the affluent may equate with quality and fine dining. Remember, strong attitudes are hard to change. Once people are convinced that the restaurant is "overpriced" and "not worth the money," strong negative word of mouth will likely put the restaurant on the edge of collapse.

A MATTER OF PRINCIPLE

BUZZ MARKETING: TREAT OR TRICK?

➤ Throughout this chapter, we've been asking what motivates a consumer to make a purchase. Companies spend millions of dollars on this very question. They make a great effort to hit us with ads in every nook and cranny of our lives; but perhaps all they have to do is a little buzz marketing—that is, spread some free (well, almost free) word of mouth about their products.

Buzz marketing is a relatively new selling technique. Basically, marketers hope to generate artificially what occurs naturally when the public takes to a product. Perhaps you can recall the buzz for *Harry Potter* or *The Blair Witch Project.* In both cases, the public embraced the products so strongly that they practically sold themselves.

Companies looking to create buzz will pay real customers to use and promote their products. For example, Hasbro Games has made little salespeople out of hundreds of fourth and fifth graders, paying them to play Hasbro POX electronic games with their friends. Indeed, the toys and games product segment is one of 10 that are ripe for buzz marketing techniques, according to "The Anatomy of Buzz," by Emmanuel Rosen. The other nine are: automotive, consumer electronics, high-tech, entertainment, fashion, health care, publishing, travel, and consumer packaged goods.

Sounds harmless so far, right? Well, buzz marketing is creating a little buzz of its own. Not all companies are so forthcoming about their buzz marketing practices. IBM ran into some trouble when it printed hearts, penguins, and peace signs on San Francisco and Chicago sidewalks to promote its new Linux software. Not only was the printing illegal; consumers were angered when they learned that IBM had committed so subversive a tactic. Some companies even infiltrate chat rooms to plant some buzz about their products. Such practices, if discovered, can do more harm than good to the company.

Still, the biggest companies today, including Ford and Procter & Gamble, are getting on the buzz bandwagon, if only to find a fresh approach to reaching an increasingly cynical-about-advertising public. What do you think? Is buzz marketing a treat for the marketer looking to get the consumer to make a purchase, or is it a trick?

POINT TO PONDER
Is buzz marketing ethical?

***

Sources: Gerry Khemouch and Jeff Green, "Buzz Marketing," *BusinessWeek,* July 30, 2001, pp. 50–56. www.emanuel-rosen.com

Combining All the Personal Factors: Psychographics

Researchers in marketing have combined demographics and psychological variables into a concept called **psychographics**. Advertisers have been heavy users of psychographics because of its versatility and ability to create fairly complex consumer groupings. For instance, there are libraries of psychographic measures that are available to the public or can be purchased from research firms that develop them; or, a company and its advertising agency can create its own set of psychographic measures to fit its particular product. These psychographic measures can then be applied to a company's product (describe customers who are heavy users of blended coffee), its advertising message (describe customers who prefer comparison ads), or its media choices (describe customers who are heavy users of the Internet).

The travel destination industry uses psychographics to distinguish visitor segments. Check Disney ads and you will notice some ads targeting traditional families (small, medium, large), other adult visitors (vacationers and businesses), and still other foreign visitors (Canadians, Mexicans, Europeans, and Far Easterners).

Over the years there have been several extensions made to the psychographic library. One such extension is called lifestyle analysis. Essentially, **lifestyle analysis** looks at the ways people allocate time, energy, and money. Marketers conduct this research to measure and compare people's activities, interests, and opinions; in other words, what intrigues or fascinates them, and what they believe or assume about the world around them. Lifestyle analysis tends to exclude demographic traits. Thus, a marketer such as Wilson Sporting Goods might like to know more about men who play amateur softball, with a focus on the heavy user who plays two or more games a week. A lifestyle survey could then be administered to this segment in order to identify other characteristics that would aid in product development and advertising planning. Suppose we discovered that the majority of the men in this category exhibited the following lifestyle characteristics: play other amateur sports, value the family, engage in social drinking, hold mostly liberal attitudes, eat out with the family at least once each week, and attend church/synagogue regularly. This information would help us select media as well as write copy that would appeal to this segment.

There are research firms that have taken lifestyle factors one step further by creating lifestyle profiles that collectively reflect a whole culture. One example is the work of SRI International and their Values and Lifestyle System (VALS). The original VALS conceptual model categorized people according to their values and then identified various consumer behaviors that go with these values. The original VALS model was then able to group consumers according to shared values. Advertisers could correlate these VALS groups with their clients' products, and use this information to design ads and select media. Eventually, SRI discovered that the relationship between values and purchase was not very strong. They developed VALS 2, which groups values and other psychological traits.

As we see in Figure 4.8 the system, VALS 2, arranges psychographic groups in a rectangle. They are stacked vertically by resources and horizontally by self-orientation (principle, status, or action oriented). Resources include income, education, self-confidence, health, eagerness to buy, and energy level.

FIGURE 4.8

THE VALS™ NETWORK
VALS 2 is a psychographic model. Advertisers use it when designing targeted advertisements.

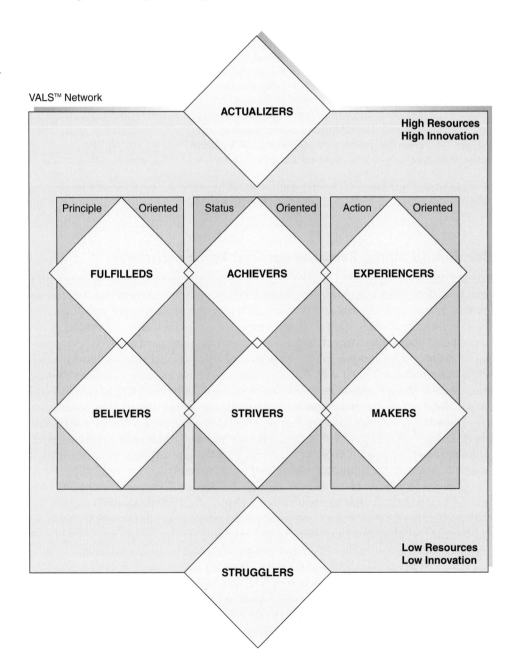

THE INSIDE STORY

THE GRAND MYTH OF EARLY ADOPTION

Cheri L. Anderson

Principal Consultant,
SRI Consulting

One of the leaders in the area of consumer research is SRI Consulting, which created the well-known VALS segmentation system. Cheri Anderson describes one of the lessons she's learned working with the VALS data.

"Our most creative research assignments come from clients who want to preview the future today. These clients want to know what innovative products to put on the shelf in the future and who is most likely to be the early adopters of their innovative products.

At SRI, we use the VALS psychographic segmentation system to identify consumers most likely to be early adopters in the client's category. In addition, VALS is used as a framework to do primary research on the lifestyle and psychological characteristics of early adopters. Our findings show that early adopters

- Are people involved in unusual activities and whose level of activity will disproportionately affect the behaviors of others
- Have many weak social contacts
- Are masters of their own universes
- Are high media users
- Have a more complex history of personal and sexual relationships

Although there are similarities among early adopters, our VALS research found some important differences. Contrary to popular belief, there is no one innovator or early adopter group. Early adopters are in very different strata and roles in society and cannot be identified by demographics alone.

Using VALS, we have identified three early adopter groups with different psychological characteristics. The "digerati" early adopters seek novelty, are attracted to risk, and tend to be more fashion conscious. They have a desire for emotional and physical excitement, all the way to the extreme. The "ego-oriented" early adopters desire leadership and enhanced personal productivity. These consumers have a need to feel superior within their peer groups. The "sage-tronic" early adopters are intense information-seekers and global in perspective. They have a deep need to know and are expertise focused.

We pursue research on early adopters (and other programs of research) with the objective of using psychographics to understand *why* consumers do what they do. By understanding what motivates and de-motivates different early adopter groups, we can help our clients identify targets and steer their brands for successful market entry."

Before joining SRI Consulting's Values and Lifestyles Program, Cheri Anderson was a strategic planner at DDB Needham Worldwide. She earned her doctorate in mass communication/consumer behavior from the University of Minnesota, Twin Cities.

Nominated by Professor Bill Wells, University of Minnesota.

A person's position along the resource and self-orientation axes determines which of eight classifications she falls into: Actualizers, Fulfilleds, Achievers, Experiencers, Believers, Strivers, Makers, or Strugglers. Members of each group hold different values and maintain different lifestyles. Actualizers, for instance have the highest resources, including income, self-esteem, and energy. Actualizers are difficult to categorize by self-orientation because their high resources allow them the freedom to express many facets of their personalities. Image is important to them. Because of their wide range of interests and openness to change, actualizers' purchases are directed at the finer things in life.[8] Obviously, knowing the psychographic orientation of consumers is a valuable asset to an advertiser in deciding to whom the messages should be targeted.

Also on the horizon is iVALS, a project that focuses on the attitudes, preferences, and behaviors of online service and Internet users. Early results of iVALS reinforce the idea of a dual-tiered society, but one based on knowledge, not income. In general people who are out of the information highway loop are excluded more because of their limited education than because of their lower income. Education is the critical factor in who participates in the Internet and to what degree.

VALS is only one of the most highly regarded psychographic models; there are many others. One model that exposes a real difference is Yankelovich Partners Inc.'s Monitor MindBase.™ MindBase™ segments consumers by values, attitudes, and mind-sets, rather than by geography, demographics, consumption patterns, and brand preferences. In essence, the program sets the ambitious goal of uncovering the underlying psychology of consumer behavior on an individual level, in an actionable, date-compatible format. It does this investigation by segmenting consumers into categories with varying degrees of materialism, ambition, orientation to family life, cynicism, openness to technology, and a host of other elements.[9]

Understanding these mind-set segments can be helpful in crafting advertising, direct mail, and other targeted marketing material. For example, a cross-selling opportunity for a financial services product can be improved by understanding the type of message that will grab each recipient.

THE DECISION PROCESS

Advertisers use the information we have explored in this chapter to understand how consumers decide to buy a product. Although every consumer makes different decisions, evidence suggests that most people follow a similar decision process. First, we examine two types of decision processes: low involvement and high involvement. Then we examine the steps of the decision process: need recognition, information search, evaluation of alternatives, purchase decision, and postpurchase evaluation.

Low- and High-Involvement Decision Processes

For the most part, consumers expend a great deal of effort on expensive, personal, or emotion-laden products (such as automobiles, medical care, clothes, and vacations). For the inexpensive, less exciting products that are purchased regularly, such as milk, gum, or soda, consumers tend to put little thought or effort into the decisions. The former example is called a complex, **high-involvement decision process**, while the latter is a simple, **low-involvement decision process**. Figure 4.9 shows both decision processes.

FIGURE 4.9

THE LOW- AND HIGH-INVOLVEMENT DECISION PROCESS
Both high- and low-involvement decision making are part of every consumer's need-satisfying process.

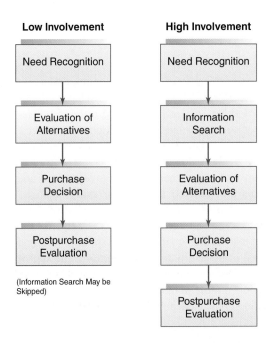

Low Involvement

Need Recognition

Evaluation of Alternatives

Purchase Decision

Postpurchase Evaluation

(Information Search May be Skipped)

High Involvement

Need Recognition

Information Search

Evaluation of Alternatives

Purchase Decision

Postpurchase Evaluation

A MATTER OF PRINCIPLE

WIRELESS: THE MANY-EDGED SWORD

➤ The evolution of wireless technology has a profound impact on advertising. First, wireless, which includes cell phones, PADs, computers, and games, acts as a new medium for delivering a variety of advertising formats. Second, wireless influences how consumers shop and make decisions. Through wireless, consumers can gather product information while they stand in front of the item of interest. They can make comparisons, check features, and list prices. Third, the expectations of consumers will change with the growth of wireless, especially in the realm of product information. Consequently, advertisers may view wireless and mass advertising as two related sources of information for consumers. Advertisers must be careful that these two information sources complement one another and don't duplicate or contradict.

For these reasons, the amount of research on the use of wireless by consumers has grown dramatically. Since wireless is truly a global technology, most of these studies have taken this perspective. In one global study, for instance, respondents indicated difficulty in learning how to use the wireless, as well as a concern that the social value of wireless technology is not stressed enough.

In a much larger international study, Context-Based Research Group surveyed 180 participants in nine major cities in the United States, China, Japan, Sweden, France, and England. The research had three objectives: (1) to assess the expectations of wireless users, (2) to explain how wireless use has changed behavior among certain segments, and (3) to analyze how wireless is advertised and communicated in the media. All of these goals provide important information for advertisers interested in wireless technology.

The outcomes provided salient insights. Most notably, wireless does appear to be a global phenomenon in that current marketing and product design did not differ across nations. Likewise, most respondents indicated that assistance to adequately learn to use wireless is insufficient. Moreover, the fact that manufacturers have designed the product with business users in mind has contributed to the confusion on the part of consumers. Clearly, those who have not adopted wireless are not inspired by the marketing efforts of manufacturers, especially their advertising.

Adding to the problem is the fact that new wireless technologies are being introduced daily—even more confusing choices for the consumer. For example, a key development that should hit the market in 2003 will be handhelds that are built to be disposable and are, by definition, prepaid units. As the desire for mobile service moves downward on the socioeconomic ladder, and the pool of consumers without some form of cellular subscription dwindles, it's logical to expect that prepaid wireless cards services will grow. Also, as wireless penetration increases, some businesses, like the payphone industry, will disappear. Free long distance is also a distinct possibility.

POINT TO PONDER

Can you think of direct impacts the wireless industry has on how consumers make choices?

Sources: "Ethnographic Study Examines Consumers' Wireless Use," *Direct Marketing* (March 2001): 20; Sherie R. Curry, "Wireless Trend Taking Hold," *Advertising Age* (June 25, 2001): 52; "Census Bureau Releases E-Commerce Report," *Direct Marketing* (May 2001): 7.

Steps in the Decision Process

The process consumers go through in making a purchase varies between low-involvement and high-involvement. The generally recognized stages for both are highlighted in Figure 4.9. The stages are (1) need recognition, (2) information search, (3) evaluation of alternatives, (4) purchase decision, and (5) postpurchase evaluation.

The first stage, *need recognition,* occurs when the consumer recognizes a need for a product. This need can vary in terms of seriousness or importance. The goal of advertising at this stage is to activate or stimulate this need. The "A Matter of Principle" box discusses some of consumers' needs related to wireless technology.

The second stage is *information search.* This search can be casual (reading ads and articles that happen to catch your attention) or formal (searching for information in publications such as *Consumer Reports*). Another type of informal search is recalling information you've already seen. Advertising helps the search process by providing information.

The third stage is *evaluation of alternatives.* In this stage, consumers compare various products and features and reduce the list of options to a manageable number. They select certain features that are important and use them to judge alternatives. Advertising is important in this evaluation process because it helps sort out products on the basis of tangible and intangible features.

The fourth stage is the *purchase decision.* This stage is often a two-part decision. Usually, we select the brand first and then select the outlet from which to buy it. Sometimes we select the outlet first. Is this product available at a grocery store, a discount store, a hardware store, a boutique, a department store, or a specialty store? In-store promotions such as packaging, point-of-purchase displays, price reductions, banners and signs, and coupon displays affect these choices.

The last step in the process is the point where we begin to reconsider and justify our purchase to ourselves. As soon as we purchase a product, particularly a major one, we begin our *postpurchase evaluation.* Is the product what we expected? Is its performance satisfactory? This experience determines whether we will keep the product, return it, or refuse to buy the product again. This process may be skipped in a low-involvement decision.

Even before you open the package or use the product, you may experience doubt or worry about the wisdom of the purchase. This doubt is called postpurchase cognitive dissonance. Many consumers continue to read information even after the purchase, to justify the decision to themselves. Advertising, such as copy on package inserts, helps reduce the dissonance by pointing out key features or how many product users are satisfied.

In this chapter we identified several key audience traits and behaviors that are relevant to advertisers. Keep in mind that we haven't examined all possible traits and behaviors. Furthermore, those who work on the design and implementation of an advertisement may interpret these traits differently. The key to successful advertising, then, is staying sensitive to the consumer. If all advertisers know about their audience is what the computer printout tells them, they are unlikely to be effective communicators.

IT'S A WRAP
A SEGMENT THAT RESPONDED

Throughout this chapter we have emphasized the importance of understanding the audiences. Fallon's campaign for Holiday Inn Express paid off in a big way. Let's look at the three goals it had and how the campaign performed on those goals.

1. **Generate awareness of Express as a competitor among limited-service hotel brands.**

   By 2001, Express's brand awareness had increased 27 points while competitors' brand awareness rates had barely increased. Unaided awareness [no hints provided] tripled while unaided awareness for the competitors' brands declined. In addition, Express advertising awareness doubled while competitors' performance was flat. In terms of brand awareness, Express moved from last place to first place in the limited-service hotel category.

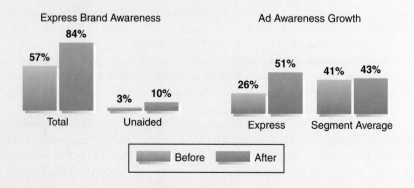

The campaign slogan, "No, but I did stay at a Holiday Inn Express last night," has entered pop culture, as the company had hoped. It made its way into political cartoons—even Al Gore used the slogan in one of his campaign speeches. Pop culture mentions netted 11.6 million incremental media impressions [unpaid media responses] for Express in one year alone, including an ESPN Sports Center commentator's quip: Utah Jazz fans are thinking, "Is he (Jason Kidd) the best point guard ever?" and Kidd's like, "No, but I did stay at a Holiday Inn Express last night."

2. **Define a clear, compelling market position for the brand. Become not just a player but also a leader in the limited-service hotel category.**

   According to Millward Brown's Ad Tracker, a consumer rated Holiday Inn Express first in the surveys' qualitative measures: "brand I trust," "good hotel for business travelers," "good value for the money." Consumers also reported that they stayed at the hotel more times in the past year than in any other hotel.

3. **Drive business and increase revenue.**

   According to growth measure RevPAR—revenue per available room—Express had outpaced the entire limited-service segment with a 20 percent increase in the three years since its campaign started [1997–2000]. When occupancy rates increase, hotels can raise their daily rates for rooms, so their revenue per available room increases as well. According to Fallon: Express achieved "billion dollar revenue" status in year two of the "Stay Smart" campaign—up 55 percent from campaign start and more than a year ahead of our three-year goal.

Knowing the consumer audience was key to the campaign's success. As we saw in this chapter, advertisers are constantly competing for their target market's attention. To stand out and be noticed, Fallon made sure the Express campaign was funny and relevant to men aged 25 to 54.

Summary

1. **Define consumer behavior and describe its relationship to advertising.** Consumer behavior is the process by which individuals or groups select, purchase, use, or dispose of products to satisfy needs and desires. For advertising to attract and communicate with audiences in a way that achieves this goal, advertisers must first understand their audiences. This understanding includes defining the target market and studying its decision process.

2. **Explain which societal and cultural factors affect advertising and consumers.** The social and cultural influences on consumers include society and subcultures, social class, reference groups, age, gender, family status, education, occupation, income, and race.

3. **Identify and describe psychological influences on consumers.** Psychological influences on consumers include perception, learning, motivation, attitudes, personality, psychographics, and lifestyles. Advertisers identify audiences in terms of demographics and psychographics. Demographic profiles of consumers include information on population size, age, gender, education, family situation, occupation, income, and race. Psychographic profiles include information on attitudes, lifestyles, buying behavior, and decision processes.

4. **Summarize the decision-making process of purchase decisions.** The decision process involves five stages: need recognition, information search, evaluation of alternatives, purchase decision, and postpurchase evaluation.

Key Terms

attitude, p. 112
cognitive dissonance, p. 108
consumer behavior, p. 97
cultural and social influences, p. 98
demographics, p. 102
demography, p. 102
discretionary income, p. 106

family, p. 101
habit, p. 110
high-involvement decision process, p. 116
household, p. 101
lifestyle, p. 101
lifestyle analysis, p. 113
low-involvement decision process, p. 116

motive, p. 111
needs, p. 111
norms, p. 98
perception, p. 107
psychographics, p. 113
reference group, p. 100
selective distortion, p. 108
selective exposure, p. 108
selective perception, p. 108

selective retention, p. 108
social class, p. 100
target audiences, p. 98
values, p. 98

Questions

1. How should advertisers adjust their approaches to elderly consumers?

2. Choose four VALS 2 categories and find one or more print advertisements that appear to be targeted to people in each category. Explain why you think the ad addresses that audience.

3. What are the stages of consumer decision process? Give examples of how advertising can influence each stage. Find an ad that addresses the concern of consumers in each stage.

4. Sean McDonnell is the creative director for Chatham-Boothe, an advertising agency that has just signed a contract with Trans-Central Airlines (TCA). TCA has a solid portfolio of consumer research and has offered to let the agency use it. McDonnell needs to decide whether demographic, psychographic, or attitude/motive studies are best for developing a creative profile of the TCA target audience. If the choice were yours, on which body of research would you base a creative strategy? Explore the strengths and weaknesses of each.

5. Consider the social-class segments discussed in this chapter. Select the two class segments that would be most receptive to these product-marketing situations:

   a. Full line of frozen family-style meals (for microwaving) that feature superior nutritional balances.

   b. Dairy product company (milk, cheese, ice cream) offering an exclusive packaging design that uses fully degradable containers.

6. If the age structure of the U.S. population shifts as forecasted over the next 20 years, what impact will these changes have on our current advertising practices (creative influences and media selection)?

7. Avon Products has established an admirable reputation for residence-to-residence personal selling. Now the corporation has seriously modified its marketing approach. For instance, it has a Web site and has opened a retail store and spa on Madison Avenue. What changes in consumer lifestyles have prompted Avon's shift? How can Avon change with the times without giving up its personal selling approach?

8. Increasingly, minorities are exercising their purchasing power. As this chapter discusses, the percentage of Hispanics in the U.S. population is growing. How do advertisers determine what core values characterize a given ethnic group? Do the same psychological influences apply to all ethnic groups? How about social and cultural influences?

9. How do advertisers influence consumer perceptions? Tobacco companies have been intensely scrutinized for their practices. What are these companies doing to change consumers' perceptions of them? Can you think of other examples where a company has had to change consumers' perception of either the company itself or a product?

10. Looking at the VALS model, do you believe that the categories are mutually exclusive? Can consumers be classified in multiple categories? Why or why not? In what category would you be classified? Why? Is the category an accurate representation of your lifestyle? Your purchasing behavior?

Suggested Class Project

Visit one or more stores that sell stereo systems. Report on the sales techniques used (check on advertising, point-of-purchase displays, store design, and so forth). What beliefs concerning consumer behavior appear to underlie these strategies?

Suggested Internet Class Project

Go to the Web site Roper Starch Research [www.roperstarch.com]. Track down a set of secondary data results. Indicate how you would use this information to design an ad for a local furniture store.
[Access code provided in instructor's manual]

Hallmark BUILD·A·CAMPAIGN Projects

Please review the Hallmark Case Appendix at the end of the text before responding to these questions.

1. Divide the class into small groups. Each group should assess how Capitol Advertising used the Brand Insistence Pyramid to explain consumer behavior and the validity of the model.

2. What consumer behaviors must a Hallmark Gold Crown store alter to benefit from the brand insistence campaign developed for Hallmark? Develop a written strategy for changing two of these behaviors.

HANDS-ON

NIKE HOPES WOMEN WILL JUST DO IT ONLINE

For advertisers, keeping up with the growth of the Internet and its issues is becoming a guessing game at best. Companies that specialize in this task, such as Forester Research and Jupiter Communications/Media Metrix, report that 50 percent of the American population now has access to the Internet. The greatest growth is occurring with women, minorities, and families with low incomes.

For e-tailers, the increase in women online is good news, since they are the primary buyers of products sold online. "Women are a very, very important economic force," notes Candice Carpenter, chairperson and CEO of iVillage.com. "Whoever captures their online hearts and minds early on will have a significant advantage over time."

One company that is attempting to attract women online is Nike. Having failed with its early Web site efforts, Nike hired the Interactive Division of advertising and PR firm Cole & Weber (C&W) to assist in the development of a new Web site targeted at women. C&W began its research with a series of in-depth focus groups of six to seven women per session. Participants were active working women, age 21 to 34, who were also peer influencers and had purchased sports equipment or clothing at least three times during the past year.

The information gathered from the focus groups was subjected to a variety of research techniques that sought to identify key words mentioned by participants, frequency of key words or concepts, and emotions associated with those words and concepts.

Although there were many specific findings, the ones most germane to the new Web site design were these: The women said that

- Being active is something you are, not something you do.
- They want information "that inspires and motivates."
- They are looking for new ideas to inspire their lives.
- They like to wear clothes "that are flexible and that they can wear from one activity to another without changing."
- They like to shop and make purchases online.

Nike took these findings and created nikegoddess. com—a site it hoped would convince women that Nike wasn't just about men. Nike also hoped the women would make purchases from the site, which is a part of its overall Web site: niketown.nike.com. ■

IT'S YOUR TURN

1. Click on the nikegoddess.com site and assess how the site satisfies all of the research findings.
2. How does the site "speak" to women? What effect do you think Nike expects to have by naming the site "nikegoddess"?

Source: Kelee Harris, "Nikegoddess.com At a Hit," *Sporting Goods Business* (June 11, 2001): 12.

Notes

1. Wagner A. Kamakura and Jose Alfonso Mazzon, "Value Segmentation: A Model for the Measurement of Values and Value Systems," *Journal of Consumer Research* (September 1991): 208–218.

2. Mary Sutler and Laurel Wentz, "U.S. Conexiones," *Advertising Age* (July 16, 2001): 14.

3. Joan Raymond, "For Richer, For Poorer," *American Demographics* (July 2000): 59–64.

4. John Fetto, "One Size Doesn't Fit All:" Today's Working Mother's Defy the Label "Soccer Mom," *American Demographics* (May 2000): 44–45.

5. Joan Davis, "Blacks in Black and White," *PROMO* (August 2000): 37.

6. Jennifer Lach, "The Color of Money," *American Demographics* (February 2000): 59–60.

7. John De Graaf, David Wann, and Thomas H. Naylor, *Affluenza* (San Francisco: Barrett-Keehler Publishers, 2001).

8. Rebecca Purto Heath, "The Frontier of Psychographics," *American Demographics* (July 1996): 38–43.

9. David Lipke, "Head Trips," *American Demographics* (October 2000): 38–40.

CHAPTER 5

Account Planning and Research

CHAPTER OBJECTIVES

When you have completed this chapter, you should be able to

1. Discuss the value of marketing research.
2. Describe the differences between strategic research and evaluative research.
3. Identify the factors that affect message development research.
4. Summarize key evaluative research objectives and methods.
5. Outline advertising research challenges.

Repairing a Broken Marriage

Award: *EFFIE Silver 2001, Transportation category*

Company: *Delta Airlines*

Agency: *Leo Burnett*

Campaign: *"The Passenger's Airline"*

Try to remember the last time you flew on a commercial airline. How long did it take to check in, go through security, and get to the gate? Was there a comfortable place to sit when you arrived at the gate? Were you able to hear all P.A. announcements? Did you board on time and, more importantly, leave the gate on time? How was your experience once in the air? Were the flight attendants polite? Were the seats comfortable? Now, the biggies. Did you arrive at your destination on time? Was your luggage all there and not damaged or lost?

All these questions represent contact points between the airline and its customers. The answers build the nature of a relationship. Yet, if you're a typical airline customer, you probably have more "no" than "yes" answers. In fact, in a survey conducted by New York–based research company Brand Keys (done prior to September 11, 2001) 165 adults were asked to rate five major carriers to compile a Customer Loyalty Index. Overall, Delta ranked best among airlines, but no brand came even close to meeting these customers' comfort expectations. Factors that the respondents considered most important included—in order of importance—safety, in-flight comfort, airline experience, and booking and boarding efficiency.

All five airlines rated the same on safety. But, Robert Passikoff, president of Brand Keys, contends that differentiation is still possible: "Airlines won't attract loyal customers with trifles like scented soap in bathrooms barely roomy enough for a

Schnauzer. And nobody will fly in their super-comfy armchairs with built-in 250-channel entertainment if they fear the plane may smash into a mountain."

Delta Airlines, building on these research findings, developed an advertising campaign that attempted to mend the broken relationship between it and its customers, specifically New York customers. Delta's own research revealed a general level of distrust and dissatisfaction with all airlines by the general public. This cynicism had spilled over into consumers' view of Delta Airlines.

Delta's research on competitors showed that the market leader, American Airlines, was promising more comfortable seating. Continental Airlines was continuing a New York–specific version of its "Work Hard, Fly Right" campaign. United, an aggressive competitor, was focusing its ad campaign on its breadth of schedule.

Research also showed that in markets where there is no "hub carrier," as is the case in New York City, focus on the brand through advertising can affect customer preferences. Moreover, despite the fact that Delta's strength lies in its strong family of products concentrated in New York (Delta Shuttle, Delta Connection, Delta Business Elite, Delta Express, Delta Mainline), it still was unable to establish a clear brand position.

So, how do you communicate with an audience that no longer trusts you and has quit listening? Delta's ad management decided that this process of reconciliation would take time and that it would be best to target one customer group rather than all. Delta decided to target the frequent business traveler (six-plus trips per year, age 25 to 54, male)—a tough group to win over because they tended to feel airlines didn't deliver on their promises and weren't totally truthful in their advertising. Clearly, familiarity breeds contempt.

To be able to respond to this fact through a creative effort required specialized research. Leo Burnett USA's creative strategy was to establish an image of empathy, where Delta sees the world through the eyes of its passengers. It was critical for Delta to deliver on its promises, but not "overpromise." To cement this concept of empathy, Delta established specific advertising objectives such as: increase consumers' intention to fly Delta and their awareness of the Delta brand, and to create a better understanding of the Delta personality/position in consumers minds.

How effective were these commercials and the "Passenger's Airline" campaign? Check the "It's a Wrap" box at the end of this chapter.

RESEARCH AND ACCOUNT PLANNING: THE QUEST FOR INTELLIGENCE AND INSIGHT

Information comes from two major sources. The first source is informal—it's the experience of the business and personal experience of the advertiser and the advertising agency. In the case of General Motors, for example, Vincent P. Barabba, a former political pollster who ran the U.S. Census under three presidents, directs the research. Because of his experience and insights, along with input from hundreds of staff members and outside consultants, GM marketing research developed a customized model of consumer behavior based on the needs of certain market segments. The GM model is based on a statistical model using car buyers' demographics, attitudes, and desired car features. It serves as input for car design and advertising planning.[1]

The second source of information is formal research, such as surveys, in-depth interviews, observational methods, focus groups (which are like in-depth interviews with a group rather than individuals), and all types of primary and secondary data.

Both sources form **marketing research** which is used to identify consumers needs, develop new products, evaluate pricing levels, assess distribution methods, and help design and test the effectiveness of various marketing communication strategies. A subset of marketing research, known as market research, is research used to gather information about a particular market. Microsoft, for example, studied the children's market thoroughly before it designed and introduced the "XBox" game system. Advertising research is even more specialized in that it focuses on all the elements of advertising, including advertising design, media planning, and evaluation.

Although information plays a big role in every major advertising campaign, it is always assimilated into, combined with, and altered by the professional and personal experiences of those who plan, create, execute, and approve the advertising.

STRATEGIC RESEARCH

As Figure 5.1 shows, advertising research can have different purposes. **Strategic research** is an information-gathering process that enhances the design at a creative strategy level. It covers all the issues that lead to the actual creation of advertising. Think of strategic research as collecting all relevant background information needed to make a decision. You engaged in strategic research when you were looking for an acceptable college to attend, for example.

Evaluative research assesses the effectiveness of your advertising decisions. An advertisement goes through various stages of development and evaluation takes place at each stage. Strategic and evaluative research share some common tools and processes. We highlight the key differences in this chapter.

We begin our discussion with strategic research. Three related components of strategic research are: (1) data collection, (2) organization, and (3) the strategy document.

Data Collection

Strategic research begins with **secondary research**, which is an exploration of all the available published information. When advertising people get new accounts or new assignments, they start by reading all available material on the product, company, industry, and competition: sales reports, annual reports, complaint letters, and trade articles about the industry. What they are looking for is a new insight. That insight might ultimately demand customized research—called **primary research** because it is conducted for the first time.

Secondary Research In an advertising agency the end users of secondary and primary research are the writers, art directors, and producers who create the advertisements and the media planners and buyers who select the media for those advertisements. Many secondary information sources are available to advertisers doing strategic research.

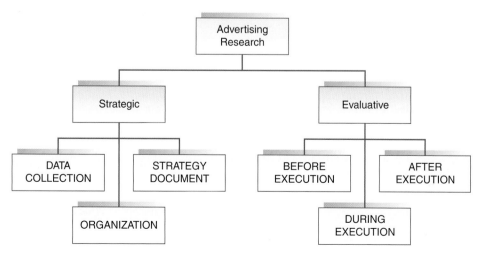

FIGURE 5.1

THE COMPONENTS OF ADVERTISING RESEARCH
Advertising research can be strategic or evaluative.

Government Organizations Governments, through their various departments, provide an astonishing array of statistics that can greatly enhance advertising and marketing decisions. Many of the statistics come from census records on the population's size, geographic distribution, age, income, occupation, education, and ethnicity.

Demographic information of this kind is fundamental to decision making about advertising targets and market segmentation. An advertiser cannot aim its advertising at a target audience without knowing that audience's size and major dimensions. Figure 5.2 lists some government reports that help advertisers make better decisions.

Trade Associations Many industries support trade associations (such as professional organizations whose members all work in the same field) that gather and distribute information of interest to association members. For instance, the American Association of Advertising Agencies (AAAA) issues reports that help ad agencies monitor their own performance and keep tabs on competitors. The Radio Advertising Bureau publishes *Radio Facts*, an overview of the commercial U.S. radio industry, and the Account Planning Group conducts seminars and training sessions for account planners.

Secondary Research Suppliers Because of the overwhelming amount of information available through secondary research, firms called **secondary research suppliers** gather and organize information around specific topic areas for other interested parties. Key secondary research suppliers are FIND/SVP, Off-the-Shelf Publications, Inc., Dialog Information Services, Inc., Lexis-Nexis, Dow Jones News/Retrieval, and Market Analysis Information Database, Inc.

Secondary Information on the Internet For any given company, you're bound to find a Web site where you can learn about the company's history and philosophy of doing business, check out its complete product line, and discover who runs the company. Several sites offer credible information for account planners or others involved in market research. However, it is unlikely that all the needed information will be found on these sites.

Primary Research Research firms that specialize in interviewing, observing, recording, and analyzing the behavior of those who purchase or influence the purchase of a particular good or service are called **primary research suppliers**. The primary research sup-

FIGURE 5.2

A SAMPLE OF GOVERNMENT REPORTS THAT INTEREST ADVERTISERS

An advertiser may find Government Reports to be an invaluable source of research information.

United States

Survey of Current Business: Basic operational statistics on U.S. business. (Bureau of Economic Analysis of the U.S. Department of Commerce)

Requirements of Laws and Regulations Enforced by the U.S. Food and Drug Administration: Laws and regulations affecting food and beverage advertising. (U.S. Department of Health and Human Services, Food and Drug Administration)

Children's Information Processing of Television Advertising: How children react to television commercials. (National Technical Information Services, U.S. Department of Commerce)

Canada

Statistical Profile of Canadian Communities. (Office of the Chief Statistician of Canada)

The Economy in Detail. (Statistics Canada)

Canadian Social Trends. (Statistics Canada)

European Union

Shopping around Europe: European Economic Area. (European Union Eurostat Memo)

Key Data on Relations between the EU and Asian ASEM Countries. (European Union Eurostat Memo)

More Babies Born in the EU. (European Union Eurostat Memo)

Practical Tips # 1

WEB SITES FOR ADVERTISING RESEARCH

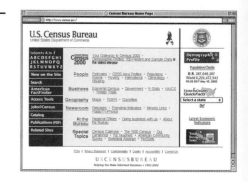

Here's a sampling of Web sites that contain information useful to advertisers:

- Advertising Law (www.webcom.com/-lewrose/home/html): a clearinghouse for articles, regulations, and cases on issues such as testimonials, advertising products that don't exist, and privacy.
- Business Wire (www.businesswire.com): an electronic distributor of press releases and business news.
- Census Bureau (www.census.gov): contains the U.S. Census database, press releases, a population clock, and clips from its radio broadcasts.
- Hoover's Online (www.hoovers.com): a database of detailed profiles for publicly traded companies.
- Marketplace (www.mktplace.com): a clearinghouse of marketing news and information for more than a thousand industries.

Source: A. Jerome Jewler and Bonnie L. Drewniany, *Creative Strategy in Advertising,* 6th ed. (Belmont, CA: Wadsworth, 1998): pp. 69–72.

plier industry is extremely diverse. The companies range from A.C. Nielsen, which employs more than 45,000 workers in the United States alone, to several thousand entrepreneurs who conduct focus groups, individual interviews, prepare reports, and provide advice on specific advertising and marketing problems.

Many advertising agencies subscribe to very large-scale surveys conducted by the Simmons Market Research Bureau (SMRB) or by Mediamark Research, Inc. (MRI). These two organizations survey large samples of American consumers (approximately 30,000 for each survey) and ask questions about the consumption, possession, or use of a wide range of products, services, and media. The products and services covered in the MRI survey range from toothbrushes and dental floss to diet colas, camping equipment, and theme parks.

Strictly speaking, both SMRB and MRI are secondary data sources: Their materials are intended primarily for use in media planning. However, because these surveys are so comprehensive, they can be mined for unique consumer information, which makes them primary sources. Through a computer program called Golddigger, for example, an MRI subscriber can select a consumer target and ask the computer to find all other products and services and all the media that members of the target segment use.

The resulting profile provides a vivid and detailed description of the target as a person—just the information agency creatives need to help them envision their audiences.

Figure 5.3 (on page 128) shows a sample MRI report of the types of programs adults aged 18 to 34 watch. The report breaks down the 18–34 market into four market segments based on size of household and age of children, if any.

Organization

To understand how to use the information in Figure 5.3, the advertiser would start with column A, which indicates the total number of people (in thousands) in that category. Column A totals the percentages vertically. Column C totals all the responses across age categories and Column D indicates the relative size of the group in that cell, with 100 being the base index. So if we look at the "Golf" program type and look at the "Respondent 18-34 and Married, Youngest Child < 6," there are 324,000 people in this cross-category; they represent 1.8 percent of the total across programs, 6.3 percent across age/family categories, and an index of 64 indicates it is well below the norm. Mediamark Research, Inc. could combine information from other reports with Figure 5.3 if an advertiser desires it.

In the 1950s, major advertising agencies featured large, well-funded, highly professional research departments. Some large advertisers still have in-house research departments. These departments collect and disseminate secondary research data and conduct primary research that ultimately finds its way into advertising. As markets have become

Base: Adults Index	Total U.S. '000	Respondent 18-34 1-Person Household				Respondent 18-34 and Married, no children				Respondent 18-34 and Married, Youngest Child <6				Respondent 18-34 and Married Youngest Child 6+			
		A '000	B % Down	C % Across	D Index	A '000	B % Down	C % Across	D Index	A '000	B % Down	C % Across	D Index	A '000	B % Down	C % Across	D Index
All Adults	184274	5357	100.0	2.9	100	7559	100.0	4.1	100	18041	100.0	9.8	100	4978	100.0	2.7	100
Program-Types: Average Show																	
Adven/Sci Fi/West-Prime	19969	590	11.0	3.0	102	875	11.6	4.4	107	2303	12.8	11.5	118	694	13.9	3.5	129
Auto Racing-Specials	6590	*226	4.2	3.4	118	*242	3.2	3.7	90	634	3.5	9.6	98	*251	5.0	3.8	141
Awards-Specials	16490	397	7.4	2.4	83	514	6.8	3.1	76	1576	8.7	9.6	98	*451	9.1	2.7	101
Baseball Specials	28019	806	15.0	2.9	99	1128	14.9	4.0	98	2671	14.8	9.5	97	*506	10.2	1.8	67
Basketball-Weekend-College	7377	*222	4.1	3.0	104	*244	3.2	3.3	81	531	2.9	7.2	74	*183	3.7	2.5	92
Basketball Specials-College	17096	529	9.9	3.1	106	694	9.2	4.1	99	1459	8.1	8.5	87	*423	8.5	2.5	92
Basketball Specials-Pro.	32470	1057	19.7	3.3	112	1369	18.1	4.2	103	3128	17.3	9.6	98	886	17.8	2.7	101
Bowling-Weekend	16808	312	5.8	1.9	654	744	9.8	4.4	108	1476	8.2	8.8	90	*386	7.8	2.3	85
Comedy/Variety	26254	930	17.4	3.5	122	1150	15.2	4.4	107	3257	18.1	12.4	127	999	20.1	3.8	141
Daytime Dramas	7621	*192	3.6	2.5	87	*287	3.8	3.8	92	845	4.7	11.1	113	*343	6.9	4.5	167
Daytime Game Shows	7747	*97	1.8	1.3	43	*194	2.6	2.5	61	734	4.1	9.5	97	*235	4.7	3.0	112
Documen/Information-Prime	22514	532	9.9	2.4	81	504	6.7	2.2	55	1739	9.6	7.7	79	*454	9.1	2.0	75
Early Morning News	12226	280	5.2	2.3	79	*429	5.7	3.5	86	1065	5.9	8.7	89	*330	6.6	2.7	100
Early Morning Talk/Info/News	14681	258	4.8	1.8	60	580	7.7	4.0	96	1291	7.2	8.8	90	*268	5.4	1.8	68
Early Eve. Netwk News-M-F	25946	596	11.1	2.3	79	836	11.1	3.2	79	1822	10.1	7.0	72	*594	11.9	2.3	85
Early Eve. Netwk News-Wknd	11338	*197	3.7	1.7	60	*208	2.8	1.8	45	795	4.4	7.0	72	*187	3.8	1.6	61
Entertainment Specials	19630	408	7.6	2.1	71	701	9.3	3.6	87	1719	9.5	8.8	89	*494	9.9	2.5	93
Feature Films-Prime	17232	371	6.9	2.2	74	*538	7.1	3.1	76	1209	6.7	7.0	72	*475	9.5	2.8	102
Football Bowl Games-Specials	13322	369	6.9	2.8	95	*381	5.0	2.9	70	1512	8.4	11.3	116	*245	4.9	1.8	68
Football Pro.-Specials	44804	1471	27.5	3.3	113	1766	23.4	3.9	96	4555	25.2	10.2	104	1104	22.2	2.5	91
General Drama-Prime	19880	581	10.8	2.9	101	571	7.6	2.9	70	2095	11.6	10.5	108	*555	11.1	2.8	103
Golf	5161	*102	1.9	2.0	68	*152	2.0	2.9	72	*324	1.8	6.3	64	*15	.3	.3	11
Late Evening Netwk News Wknd	5146	*146	2.7	2.8	98	*114	1.5	2.2	54	*293	1.6	5.7	58	*104	2.1	2.0	75
Late Night Talk/Variety	9590	313	5.8	3.3	112	*297	3.9	3.1	75	1009	5.6	10.5	107	*198	4.0	2.1	76
News-Specials	14508	234	4.4	1.6	55	510	6.7	3.5	86	1297	7.2	8.9	91	*212	4.3	1.5	54
Pageants-Specials	22025	439	8.2	2.0	69	952	12.6	4.3	105	2503	13.9	11.4	116	547	11.0	2.5	92
Police Docudrama	23575	726	13.6	3.1	106	1179	15.6	5.0	122	2309	12.8	9.8	100	731	14.7	3.1	115
Pvt Det/Susp/Myst/Pol.-Prime	28183	673	12.6	2.4	82	763	10.1	2.7	66	1739	9.6	6.2	63	*493	9.9	1.7	65
Situation Comedies-Prime	19097	598	11.2	3.1	108	919	12.2	4.8	117	2737	15.2	14.3	146	688	13.8	3.6	133
Sports Anthologies-Weekend	4847	*218	4.1	4.5	155	*232	3.1	4.8	117	*403	2.2	8.3	85	*108	2.2	2.2	82
Sunday News/Interview	5809	*70	1.3	1.2	41	*116	1.5	2.0	49	*214	1.2	3.7	38	*97	1.9	1.7	62
Syndicated Adult General	10444	*271	5.1	2.6	89	462	6.1	4.4	108	766	4.2	7.3	75	*221	4.4	2.1	78
Tennis	10033	338	6.3	3.4	116	380	5.0	3.8	92	826	4.5	8.2	84	*105	2.1	1.0	39

FIGURE 5.3

SAMPLE OF AN MRI CONSUMER MEDIA REPORT

A report such as this one from Mediamark Research can be a source of primary data.

Source: Mediamark Research, Inc.

FIGURE 5.4

A SAMPLE OF QUESTIONS ANSWERED BY A TYPICAL ADVERTISING AGENCY INFORMATION CENTER
The figures shows typical questions for those who work at an agency library/information center.

What are the trends of the past five years as they relate to diet and salt?

We plan to shoot a commercial in northern Australia. What is the average temperature and rainfall there for mid-July?

What information regarding the Fourth of July is available at the Information Center?

Provide pictures of birds flying in a flock, teens walking on a sandy beach, and a close-up of shells on the beach—right away.

Who are the leading marketers of frozen dinners and entrees? Provide sales and market shares.

How many U.S. families have children under five years old and have household incomes over $25,000?

Are people concerned about cholesterol in pancakes? Are people aware that pancakes have cholesterol?

How big is the foot powder market?

We need pictures of brand characters—the original look and the revised ones. Examples: Betty Crocker, the Campbell Soup children, and the Morton Salt girl.

more fragmented and saturated, and as consumers have become more demanding, an increase in account planning has occurred.

The **account planning process**, developed in England in the 1960s and 1970s, is the process of using research efforts to gain more information about the brand in its marketplace, the consumer's perspective, or both, and to use that research to contribute directly to advertising development. This concept has spread to agencies in Europe, Asia, and the United States. Account planning seems to be here to stay.

Many agencies that are too small to sustain internal account planning departments or that lack the expertise for a certain project rely on outside research suppliers. In some cases, these agency–supplier relationships become so productive that the supplier fulfills most of the roles of an internal research department. Aspen Research, in Boulder, Colorado, has this type of relationship with Karsh & Hagen Advertising.

To aid account planners and the creative advertising staff, many agencies maintain specialized libraries (often called information or intelligence centers) that provide access to dictionaries, encyclopedias, atlases, cookbooks, books of famous quotations, and trade and general newspapers and magazines. As Figure 5.4 shows, the intelligence center staff must be prepared to research a wide spectrum of questions.

A typical advertising campaign might be influenced, directly or indirectly, by information from many sources, including outside research suppliers and the agency's account planning department. Surprisingly, the problem usually is not too little information, but too much. Someone must sift through the **qualitative data**, which provides insight into how consumers behave and why; and the **quantitative data**, which includes numerical data such as exposure to ads, purchases, and other market-related information. This person must also separate the potentially relevant from the irrelevant material and put the findings into a format that decision makers and creatives can use.

In advertising agencies with internal account planning or research departments, the research task usually falls to **account planners**. Account planners are the people responsible for the advertising strategy and its implementation in the creative work. To develop effective strategy, they must thoroughly understand their target audience. The ability to organize huge amounts of information and make that information relevant to the problem at hand is one of the most important skills account planners can have. In agencies without these departments the task of collecting and organizing information usually falls to members of the account management group.

Even in agencies with account planning departments, members of the account management group are likely to be involved in the final decisions about what information will be passed on to those who will create the campaign. Account managers play a major role in every facet of their brand.

The Strategy Document

The outcome of strategic research usually reaches agency creative departments in the form of a strategy document or creative brief. Although the exact form of this document differs

The strategy document outlines the intended target audience. For the Freelander model, Land Rover is targeting the young professional looking for a little adventure in his or her daily drive.

from agency to agency and from advertiser to advertiser, most have six major parts: the marketing objective, the product, the target audience, the promise and support, the brand personality, and the strategy statement.

Marketing Objective The section of the document that presents the marketing objective reviews the competition and establishes a goal for the campaign. It includes past and present sales figures; market shares of the brand and of its major competitors; competitors' advertising and promotional resources, tactics, and practices; and any other information about the brand that may lead to a prediction of early success or risk of failure. Although advertisers and agencies are acutely aware that marketing success depends on many factors other than advertising, advertisers do expect advertising to help them meet their marketing goals. It is important, then, that everyone in the campaign understand exactly what those goals are.

If the advertiser has an unspecified and unreasonable marketing objective and the agency, through ignorance, implicitly agrees to meet that objective, the agency has unknowingly put itself in an extremely vulnerable position. In the strategy document, the marketing objective should be specific; it should be agreed to at the outset.

The Product The product section of the strategy document includes the results of surveys, consumers' perceptions of the brand and its major competitors, and tests of or reactions to the brand's and its competitors' advertisements, promotions, retail displays, and packaging. This section of the strategy document presents all facts, opinions, perceptions, or reactions to the product that might fuel an advertising campaign. Account planners have to learn how consumers think, feel, decide, and act toward their product.

The Target Audience The next section of the document provides a demographic and psychographic description of the campaign's target audience. The demographic data comes from secondary sources or from surveys that reveal the age, income, education, gender, and geographic distribution of the consumers who might be persuaded to adopt the brand. The psychographic information comes from attitude and opinion surveys, individual in-depth interviews, observing audience member behaviors, and focus groups, all of which help paint a portrait of the target as a person. [The Land Rover Freelander ad is an example of an ad targeted at a young, professional audience.]

Both the creative team (which must create communication) and the media planners (who must decide how and when to contact targets most efficiently) need to know as much as they can, in as much depth and detail as possible, about the people they are trying to reach.

Promise and Support Advertising always promises some sort of reward that the customer can obtain by buying or using the advertised product or service. The promise section of the strategy document tells writers and art directors which reward, out of many possibilities, the advertising should promise. The support section of the strategy document indicates the facts about the product or the brand's attributes that are likely to make that promise most acceptable to users. Insights into consumer motivations and purchasing decisions help solve the often difficult puzzle of selecting the most motivating promise and deciding how to support that promise.

Brand Personality Brands, like people, have personalities. When a brand has a winning personality, its advertising should perpetuate and reinforce that personality. When a brand has a less than desirable personality, advertising should work to remedy the problem. Research that asks potential customers what the brand and its competitors would be like if they were people or animals, for example, supplies the information needed to specify the brand's present personality and identifies the kind of improvements needed. For instance, research in the telecommunications industry revealed that consumers viewed MCI as a snake, Sprint as a puma, and AT&T as a lion, that is, sneaky, wiley, and strong, respectively.

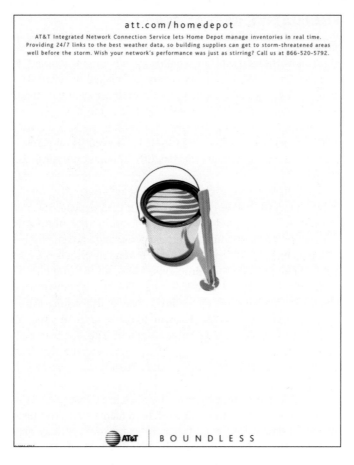

att.com/homedepot

AT&T Integrated Network Connection Service lets Home Depot manage inventories in real time. Providing 24/7 links to the best weather data, so building supplies can get to storm-threatened areas well before the storm. Wish your network's performance was just as stirring? Call us at 866-520-5792.

AT&T | B O U N D L E S S

For brand personality, consumers viewed AT&T as a lion within its industry.

Strategy Statement A strategy document is usually prefaced by a brief strategy statement that distills the document's main points. Following the strategy statement, the document itself presents the highlights of the most relevant research. Figure 5.5 shows a typical strategy statement.

Although formats vary considerably from advertiser to advertiser and from agency to agency, finding a clear and concise way of conveying in writing what is known about the product, the brand, the competitive situation, and the prospective customer is as essential to an advertising campaign as a blueprint is to a construction project.

1. **Marketing Objective**
   Increase consumption of milk by members of the target audience by 10 percent.
2. **The Product**
   Although milk is considered to be among the healthiest beverages, milk drinking drops off sharply in the teenage years. Part of the problem is concern about fat and calories; part has to do with milk's childish and unexciting image. Advertising can have its most direct effect on the image problem.
3. **The Target Audience**
   Males and females 16 to 30 years old. Milk is a beverage they had to drink as children, and although they are still drinking it, they are choosing more often to drink other beverages. Milk has become less relevant to their lifestyle. They believe milk doesn't go as well with foods they like, such as pizza, Mexican, and Oriental dishes. Females in particular are concerned about the calories and fat in milk. Other beverages, such as soft drinks, are of greater interest to this group. Soft drinks are an exciting, versatile, and socially acceptable alternative to milk, which is pratical, unexciting, and conservative.
4. **Promise and Support**
   Today's milk can help you become the attractive, fun, dynamic person you may want to be (promise). Milk has the nutrition your body needs to look and feel terrific. Today's most attractive and dynamic people drink milk. Ice-cold milk tastes great (support).
5. **Brand Personality**
   Personality now: childish, practical, conservative. Needed personality: exuberant, comtemporary, young adult.

FIGURE 5.5

A STRATEGY STATEMENT FOR MILK
This statement prefaces the more lengthy and detailed strategy document.

The average 30-second commercial costs about $200,000 to make.

EVALUATIVE RESEARCH

Now that we've learned about strategic research, let's investigate the research testing techniques advertisers use to see whether the advertising worked. **Evaluative research** is used to make final go/no-go decisions about finished or nearly finished ads, as distinguished from strategic research, which is used to understand the strengths and weaknesses of different strategies and different versions of a concept or approach.

Marketers also use evaluative research to assess the ad during the actual execution as well as to assess to what extent the ad achieved its objective, after it runs. This research identifies and implements various effectiveness measures, such as those introduced in Chapter 1.

Advertisers who use evaluative research hope that it will provide a valid measure of effectiveness so that they can see whether their decisions were the best ones available. The problem is that no one has developed a surefire test of effectiveness, for several reasons. First, there are many truths in numbers. Second, advertising is one part of the overall marketing campaign, so the ability to determine its effects on sales (what many clients try to do) is limited by causality problems. Third, advertising has many purposes, so evaluative tools must be focused on measuring what the ad developers are trying to accomplish. Finally, evaluative research methods change all the time. Advertisers need to stay current and open-minded about the best way to measure an ad's success.

Why worry about evaluative research? The stakes in making an advertising misstep are high. By the time an average 30-second commercial is ready for national television, it has cost about $200,000. If it is run nationally, its sponsor invests several million dollars in airtime.

Ideally, the results of evaluative research should be available before large sums of money are invested in finished work or in media buys. Test results may even be useful after an advertisement has been placed. Sales may fall, or they may not increase as rapidly as expected. Is the advertising at fault? Would sales be better if the advertisers were "working harder?" Advertisers may want to test their advertising at several different times.

Evaluative research suppliers are listed in the American Marketing Association's *International Directory of Marketing Research Companies and Services*. Most major advertisers have a favorite supplier and a favorite research method. Table 5.1 lists well-known evaluative research suppliers. This list is not exhaustive. Many other research companies offer some form of evaluative testing, including qualitative in-depth interviews and brand tracking. The question is, which (if any) of the evaluative research methods really work?

We now discuss several evaluative research techniques that account planners use in creating the ad—before execution. Next we discuss techniques employed during execution. Finally, we discuss evaluation techniques account planners use after execution—when most evaluative research takes place.

Before Execution

There are a variety of evaluation techniques that are used in conjunction with the actual creation of the ad. These techniques are attempts to connect with general components of an effective ad and the stated objectives for that particular ad.

Message Development Research Although facts play an important role in many advertising campaigns, they are always filtered through and evaluated against a system of ideas, experiences, prejudices, memories of past successes and failures, hierarchical relationships, and tastes and preferences within the advertiser's own company and within the advertising agency. Decisions as to what facts find their way into advertisements are never cut and dried. Research is needed to develop messages.

Furthermore, as writers and art directors begin working on a specific creative project, they almost always conduct at least some informal research of their own. They may talk to friends, or even strangers, who might be in the target audience. They may visit retail stores, talk to salespeople, and watch people buy. They may visit the information center, browse

THE INSIDE STORY

RESEARCH IS MUCH MORE THAN NUMBERS

Sally Reinman Worldwide Market Planner,
Saatchi & Saatchi

The stereotypical notion of advertising research as a job restricted only to surveys, number-crunching activities, and focus groups is fading. Sally Reinman, Worldwide Market Planner, Saatchi & Saatchi, discusses some dynamic changes in advertising research.

"Although the title of Worldwide Market Planner sounds broad, it accurately reflects the current role of research and account planning in international advertising agencies. Research in advertising still relies on traditional tools such as secondary data, surveys, and theater tests. However, research processes are more varied and exciting than ever before. Examples include asking consumers to draw pictures, create collages, and produce home videos to show how they use a product.

As consumers around the world become more informed and more demanding, advertisers that target different cultures need to find the "commonalities" (or common ground) among consumer groups from these cultures. Research for Toyota's sports-utility vehicle (SUV), the RAV 4, showed that consumers in all the targeted countries had three common desires: They wanted an SUV to have style, safety, and economy.

To find these commonalities, I work with experts to learn the cultural meaning of codes and symbols that people use to communicate. The experts I work with include cultural and cognitive anthropologists, psychologists, interior decorators, and Indian storytellers. Anyone who can help me understand consumers and the consumer decision-making process is fair game.

For example, one client, who was responsible for introducing the 1997 James Bond movie "Tomorrow Never Dies," asked us to find the common elements of the target audience. The existing audience consisted mainly of older male baby boomers. To get a new slant on James Bond that appealed to a new generation we contacted a hedonologist

(a person who studies language, codes, and symbols) to interpret the James Bond books and movies. This process told us what James Bond stood for so that our client could decide what would and would not reach our target audience effectively. We knew people liked the element of fantasy but not Bond's demeaning attitude toward women. Based on the research findings, a woman became Bond's boss in the new movie and dialogue was changed to suit audience attitudes.

I interpret experts' insights and findings for the creative team so they can incorporate the information to improve the creative process. If advertisers speak to customers more effectively, they are more likely to see customers respond to the brand positively. In the case of the Bond movie, advertising media was selected and the movie trailers focused on fantasy and escapism—the elements the target audience enjoyed.

I love the job. It requires a sincere interest in people and a burning curiosity about what makes them tick. To be perfectly honest, I believe these attributes are more important in this job than your major or your grade-point average. I invite you to consider the world of market planning. "

Ms. Reinman was trained as a biochemist, and received a Ph.D. in 1980. During her postdoctoral studies in Paris at a nuclear lab, she discovered how solitary the work was and switched careers to teach English to French students at Berlitz. A student who owned a Paris ad agency contracted her to translate a Yankelovich Research report into French. After more work in advertising research, Ms. Reinman took some research coursework at UCLA. She worked at a research company for several years, and then at advertising firms Hill/Holiday and J. Walter Thompson/L.A., before joining Saatchi & Saatchi Advertising in 1991.

through reference books, and borrow subject and picture files. They will look at previous advertising (especially the competition's) to see what others have done, and in their hearts they will become absolutely convinced that they are able to create something better than, and different from, anything that has been done before. This informal, personal research has a powerful influence on what happens later in the advertising process.

Strategic research and message development research work hand in hand. The advertiser starts by developing alternative message ideas or creative concepts. The team responsible for evaluative research then determines which creative concept is best. Anyone engaged in the creative process can request this type of feedback. It may be as simple as speaking with others assigned to the project, or as complex as a focus group.

TABLE 5.1   Major Suppliers of Evaluative Research

Suppliers	Medium	Methods
ASI Market Research, Inc., New York, NY	Television, print	Recall, persuasion
Bruzzone Research Co., Alameda, CA	Television	Recognition
Burke Marketing Research, Cincinnati, OH	Television, print	Recall, persuasion, in-market sales
Communications Workshop, Inc., Chicago, IL	Television, print, radio	Communication test
Diagnostic Research, Inc., New York, NY	Television, print, radio	Communication test
Gallup and Robinson, Inc., Princeton, NJ	Television, print	Recall, persuasion
Hall & Partners, Ltd., London and New York	Television, print, radio, interactive	Brand tracking
Information Resources, Inc., Chicago, IL	Television	In-market sales

Feedback may occur several times during the creative process, but eventually the ad will reach a somewhat finished stage called comprehensive (comps), or the story board stage where the ad has its final artwork and copy. It is at this point that feedback is sought from members of the target audience. The evaluative process has become more structured, follows a set procedure, and must respond to certain considerations. These considerations are discussed next.

Methods of Contact There are a variety of ways to contact consumers when conducting message evaluation research. The contact can be in person, by telephone, by mail, or through the Internet. In a personal interview the researcher asks questions to the consumer directly. These interviews are often conducted in malls and downtown areas, where there are lots of people. With telephone contacts the consumer is provided a copy of the test ad and is asked several questions about the ad via a phone call. Mail contacts are similar but in this method the test ad is mailed to the consumer along with a set of questions, which the consumer is expected to return promptly. Contacts through the Internet require access to the consumers in order to deliver the test ad. Concurrently, consumers are sent a set of questions about the ad, which they can return electronically.

Survey Research Several types of quantitative research methods are important in marketing and advertising. Most useful in conducting message evaluation research is survey research. **Survey research** uses structured interviews to ask large numbers of people the same question. The questions can deal with personal characteristics, such as age, income, behavior, or attitudes. The people can be from an entire group, or population, or they can be a representative sample of a much larger group. Sampling uses a smaller number of people to represent the entire population.

Survey Research can be conducted in public places, such as a supermarket or over the telephone.

Observation Research Like anthropologists, observation researchers study consumers where they live, work, and play. Basically, they've elevated people-watching to a science. Direct observation takes researchers into natural settings where they record the behavior of consumers. Many research firms use video and disposable cameras to record consumers' behavior at home (with consumer consent), in stores, or wherever people use their products.

A pioneering study of the direct observation technique concluded that direct observation has the advantage of revealing what people actually do, as distinguished from what people say [they do]. It can yield the correct answer when faulty memory, desire to impress the interviewer, or simple inattention to details would cause an interview answer to be wrong. The biggest drawback to direct observation is that it shows what is happening, but not why. Therefore, the results of direct observation often are combined with the results of personal interviews to provide a more complete and more understandable picture of attitudes, motives, and behavior.[2] More is said about observational research in the "A Matter of Practice" box.

Cognitive Psychology and the Use of Metaphor Some researchers believe that consumers' wants and needs are so deeply embedded in their brains that language becomes an insufficient communication tool, so researchers turn to metaphor. Cognitive psychologists have learned that human beings think in images, not words. But most research uses words to ask questions and obtain answers.

To overcome this hindrance, some researchers, such as Harvard Business School professor Jerry Zaltman, try to uncover mental processes that guide consumer behavior through pictures. In a study on women's hosiery for DuPont, Zaltman selected 20 women and asked, "What are your thoughts and feelings about buying and wearing pantyhose?" To answer the question, the women were asked to collect pictures and photos from magazines and other sources.

One woman had an image of fence posts encased in plastic wrap and a photo of a vase of flowers. Other images included steel bands strangling trees, two African masks hanging on a bare wall, and a luxury car. Later, the subjects discussed the images with a trained interviewer and created collages, with the help of a graphic designer.

A MATTER OF PRACTICE

AN ANTHROPOLOGIST'S GOLDMINE

➤ Undoubtedly the most difficult task a marketing researcher faces is getting a consumer to tell the truth. Employing the adage "a picture is worth a thousand words," researchers are now watching consumers very closely. The kind of research we're talking about here is called observational or ethnographic research.

The case of Best Western International provides an example. In the spring of 2000, the company paid 25 couples who were over age 55 to tape themselves on their travels across the United States. The purpose of the research was twofold.

First, it wanted to learn how seniors decide when and where to stop for the night. Second, based on this information, the company wanted to determine whether it should increase its 10 percent senior discount. The tapes certainly were revealing. Seniors who talked the hotel clerk into a better deal didn't need the lower price to afford the room;

they just liked making the deal. Best Western marketers concluded that increasing the senior discount was not a good idea. Today, virtually all major agencies offer their clients the opportunity to conduct ethnographic research. In fact, at Aurett, Free & Gensberg, 9 out of 15 large clients have opted for the service. "And ethnography is the intimate connection to the consumer," says Bill Abrams, founder of Housecalls, a New York consultancy that worked on the Best Western effort.

POINT TO PONDER

How would you use ethnographic research to create an ad?

Sources: Gerry Khermouch, "Consumers in the Mist," *BusinessWeek* (February 26, 2001): 92–93; Alison Stein Wellner, "Research on a Shoestring," *American Demographics* (April 2001): 38–39.

Zaltman discovered that women hate wearing pantyhose (hence, the steel bands) but they also have positive reasons for wearing them. The flower vase represented how the product made the women feel thin and tall. The luxury car symbolized feelings of elegance. The findings altered the advertising strategy to include both images of competent career women and images of sexiness and allure.[3]

Communication Assessment These are one-on-one interviews, usually conducted in shopping malls that supply central interviewing facilities. Interviewers recruit shoppers to fill out questionnaires on their age, sex, income, and product usage. They are asked to participate in a "study of consumers' opinion," and sometimes receive a small fee for their cooperation.

A popular communication test is the anteroom trailer method. Researchers setup a mobile home or recreational vehicle near a shopping center and invite people into the trailer with some incentive for participating. They enter a comfortable room that contains easy chairs, magazines, and a television set showing a prerecorded program. Test commercials are interspersed throughout the program. After the commercials air, the subjects researchers interview and ascertain the effectiveness of each commercial based on the subjects' responses.

Content Analysis of Competing Ads In preparation for a new campaign, agency researchers or account executives often conduct systematic audits of competitors' advertisements. These audits might include only informal summaries of the slogans, appeals, and images used most often, or they might include more formal and systematic tabulation of competitors' approaches and strategies. The basic question always is, "What are competitors doing and how can we do it better?" By disclosing competitors' strategies and tactics, analysis of the content of competitive advertisements provides clues to how competitors are thinking, and suggests ways to develop new and more effective campaigns to argue against and possibly even overcome their efforts.

Readability Tests An ad must be readable before it is set in final form. The length of the words and sentences and the impersonality of the writing are some of the elements that influence readability. Short words and short sentences make for easier reading.

The Flesch formula, developed by Dr. Rudolph Flesch, is a widely accepted technique for measuring readability: The formula uses four elements as they appear in 100-word writing samples:

> Average sentence length
> Average number of syllables
> Percentage of personal words
> Percentage of personal sentences

Flesch contends that "fairly easy" sentences average 14 words in length and have 139 syllables per 100 words. The Flesch formula cannot be used for radio and television writing because a good announcer can make difficult copy sound very simple. The ad for Neutrogena is considered very readable.[4]

Test Marketing A **test market** might be used to test some elements of an ad or a media mix in two or more potential markets. The test markets should be representative of the target market. Some cities, such as Buffalo, Indianapolis, and San Antonio, are considered excellent test markets because their demographic and socioeconomic profiles are very broad. That is, they have virtually all income, race, ethnic, and education categories represented within the city. In a typical test market, one or more of the test cities serve as controls while the others are the test. In the control markets the researcher can either (a) run no advertising or (b) continue to run the old ad. The new ad is used in the test cities. Before, during, and after the advertising is run, sales results in the test cities are compared by checking inventories in selected stores.

This ad for Neutrogena's Pore Refining® Mask has a high level of readability due to its simple words, white space, and lay out.

In addition, test markets can measure communication variables such as recall, awareness, and correct message interpretation. Kraft Foods conducted a rather sophisticated market test. It tested two versions of a cross-promotion print ad. One version contained the headline "Super Choices Sweepstake" and the other, "The More Super Choices Coupons You Redeem, the More Chances You Have of Winning." Coupon redemption was used as the performance measure.[5] The second headline won, because the words were more relevant to the consumer.

Physiological Measures Over the years, advertisers have experimented with assessing people's physical reactions to ad concepts before the ad is run. Of the many techniques tried, five are worthy of special note:

1. **Eye movement tracking**. Participants are asked to look at a print ad or television commercial while a sensor aims a beam of infrared light at their eyes. A portion of the light reflected by the cornea is detected by the same sensor, which electronically measures the angle between the beam reflected by the cornea and the center of the eye's pupil. This information can be processed to show the exact spot in the ad or on the television screen where the eye is focused, indicating what the participant is looking at and for how long.
2. **The pupillometer**. This device measures pupil size when a person is exposed to a visual stimulus such as an ad or a package. The assumption is that pupil size increases with interest.
3. **The psychogalvanometer**. This device is part of the lie detector apparatus. Two zinc electrodes are attached to the subject, one on the palm of the hand and the other on the forearm. When the subject is exposed to an ad, emitted perspiration on the palm results in lower electrical resistance, which is recorded on a revolving drum. This suggests an emotional response has occurred.

4. **The tachistoscope**. This device controls exposure to a print message so that different parts of the ad can be shown without revealing the other parts. That way, the tester can tell at what point each part is perceived. Advertisers can thus find out how long it takes respondents to get the intended point of an illustration or headline.
5. **The EEG**. Through the use of the electroencephalograph (EEG), data can be collected from several locations on the skull. Several electrical frequencies at each location are checked up to 1,000 times per second. By measuring the electrical activity in various parts of the brain, this technique can tell the researcher when the subject is resting or when there is attention to a stimulus.[6]

These physiological tests suffer from several limitations. First, because respondents may feel threatened by these devices, the validity of the results is questionable. Second, there is a great deal of uncertainty as to what this machinery actually measures. Increased perspiration may provide a measure of emotional arousal, but is it a meaningful sign of advertising effectiveness?

During Execution: Concurrent Testing

Concurrent testing takes place while the advertising is actually being run. There are three primary techniques: coincidental surveys, attitude tests, and tracking studies. The first two techniques assess communication effectiveness. Tracking studies evaluate actual behavior.

Coincidental Surveys This technique is most often used with broadcast media. Random calls are made to individuals in the target market. By discovering what stations or shows people are seeing or hearing, the advertiser can determine whether the target audience is getting the message and, if so, what information or meaning the audience members receive. This technique can be useful in identifying basic problems. For example, several years ago Pepsi discovered that the use of Madonna as a spokesperson was a terrible mistake.

Attitude Tests In Chapter 4 we discussed the relationship between an attitude—an enduring favorable or unfavorable disposition toward a person, thing, idea, or situation—and consumer behavior. The attitude measurement techniques for print and broadcast are virtually identical. Researchers survey individuals who were exposed to the ad, asking questions about the spokesperson, the tone of the ad, its wording, and so forth. Results that show strong negative attitude scores may prompt the advertiser to pull an ad immediately.[7]

Attitudinal tests are considered more valuable than survey opinions because they uncover a direct emotional reaction. People seem to have opinions about a great many things but hold strong attitudes about relatively few. There is also the assumption that a favorable attitude indicates that the person is more likely to purchase a brand than if she has an unfavorable attitude.

Tracking Studies Studies that follow the purchase activity of a specific consumer or group of consumers over a specified period of time are **market tracking studies**. These studies combine conventional marketing research data with information on marketing communication spending. Compared with other tests, tracking studies provide fuller integration of data and a more complete view of the market.

Researchers use market tracking for both concurrent testing and posttesting. It may serve two basic objectives: (1) to show how the marketer's product sales or market share compares with the competition, at a point in time after implementing some marketing communication; and (2) for reassessment, that is, to help the marketer understand how the market responds to changes he made in the marketing communication strategy.

Tracking studies evaluate copy and media and changes in sales. Higher sales for one strategy, compared with those produced by an alternative strategy, implies that the former strategy is better. Tracking studies have had an impact on many decisions, ranging from pulling advertising to changing copy to altering a campaign strategy.

Because spending information enters the analysis, much of the focus of tracking studies is on the target market, the selection of media vehicles, the schedule, the marketing communication mix, and the media mix.

Account planners use several methods to collect tracking data: wave analysis, consumer diaries, pantry checks, and single-source tracking.[8]

Wave Analysis Wave analysis looks at a series of interviews during a campaign. The tracking begins with a set of questions asked of a random sample of consumers on a predetermined date. The first questions usually qualify the person as someone who remembers hearing or seeing the ad. Once the person is qualified, the researcher asks a series of follow-up questions. The answers serve as a benchmark for acceptability and allow adjustments in the message content, media choice, and timing. Perhaps two months later, the researcher makes another series of random calls and asks the same questions. The second wave is compared with the first. The periodic questioning may continue until management is satisfied with the ad's market penetration.

Consumer Diaries Sometimes advertisers ask a group of representative consumers to keep a diary during a campaign. The advertiser asks the consumers to record activities such as brands purchased, brands used for various activities, brand switches, media usage, exposure to competitive promotions, and use of coupons. The advertiser can then review these diaries and determine factors such as whether the message is reaching the right target audience and if the audience is responding to the message as intended. Although the technique is limited by the amount and accuracy of the information obtained, it can serve as an early warning system. One common unfavorable finding from consumer diaries is the indication that no attitude or behavioral change occurred because of exposure to the campaign.

Pantry Checks The pantry check provides much of the same information as the diary method but requires little from the consumer. A researcher goes to homes in the target market and asks what brands or products they have purchased or used recently. In one variation of this procedure, the researcher counts the products or brands currently stocked by the consumer. The consumer may also be asked to keep empty packages, which the researcher then collects and tallies. The purpose is to correlate product use with the introduction and completion of the campaign.

Single-Source Tracking Thanks to scanners, combined with computer technology and data and the use of electronic media, researchers are closer to showing a causal relationship between advertising and sales. To set up a single-source tracking system, researchers first recruit people living in a particular market to join a consumer panel. The system has four elements:

1. Participants receive a card (with an identification number) that they give to the checkout clerk each time they make a purchase in a supermarket. Scanners identify the person and record his purchases so researchers know who he is and what he buys.
2. The participants (who are all cable subscribers) are split into matched groups, with each group receiving a different version of a television ad. Electronic test market services transmit the appropriate commercial to the appropriate home so the advertiser knows which household sees which commercial.
3. Meters record participants television viewing. Researchers can then tell whether members saw the commercial, when they saw it, and how many times they saw it.
4. The advertiser controls all the print advertising, coupon distribution, and other marketing communication activities that the participants see. Researchers therefore know what influences a household's decision to buy or not to buy.

The possibilities for isolating single variables in electronic test markets are almost limitless. Researchers can increase the frequency of advertising or try a different media schedule. They can see whether an ad emphasizing product convenience will stimulate sales to two-career families. They can try an ad that plays up the product's fiber or vitamin content or compare the effectiveness of a two-for-one promotion and a cents-off coupon.

There are three major, electronically based single-source services: Arbitron's Scan America, Nielsen's Scan Track, and Information Resources' Info-Scan. In early tests Arbitron reported that Scan America improved the efficiency of advertising (in terms of reaching the client's target audience) by an average of 43 percent.[9]

Critics contend that current single-source data systems are just fancy versions of the old paper-and-pencil diary and provide little insight into which elements in the marketing communication mix are making a difference and why the consumer reacts in a particular manner to particular cues.

After Execution

Most evaluative research occurs after the ad has run because businesses are most concerned with the bottom line. Was the return on the ad sufficient? Unfortunately, if the various measures indicate that the advertiser has not achieved its objectives, there's not much the advertiser can do to rectify this situation after the fact. Now let's look at the evaluative research techniques that account planners use: memory tests, persuasion tests, direct response counts, frame-by-frame tests, in-market tests, and brand tracking.

Memory Tests Memory tests are based on the assumption that an advertisement leaves a mental residue with the person who has been exposed to it. One way to measure an advertisement's effectiveness, then, is to contact consumers and find out what they remember about it. Memory tests fall into two major groups: recall tests and recognition tests.

Choose Wisely...

The quality of your decisions depends on the quality of your research. **Hauser & Associates, Inc.** is a full-service marketing research firm that delivers actionable consumer information to help build your business. To meet this goal, we apply creative project design, provide insightful analysis and utilize appropriate leading edge technology.

Whether your strategic marketing needs are domestic or international, Hauser & Associates, Inc. provdides the insight you need to make optimal business decisions.

Hauser & Associates, Inc.

The Consumer Insight Company

For more information visit us at *www.hauserandassociates.com* or call us at 201.599.9559

Hauser & Associates, Inc., is capable of doing all the strategic research discussed.

Recall Tests The company most commonly associated with day-after recall tests is Burke Marketing Services. Gallup & Robinson's In-View Service is another recall test company. In a traditional **recall test**, a finished commercial is run on network television within a regular prime-time program. The next evening, interviewers in three or four cities make thousands of random phone calls until they have contacted about 200 people who were watching the program at the exact time the commercial appeared. The interviewer then asks a series of questions:

- Do you remember seeing a commercial for any charcoal briquettes?
- (If no) Do you remember seeing a commercial for Kingsford Charcoal briquettes? (Memory prompt)
- (If yes to either of the above) What did the commercial say about the product? What did the commercial show? What did the commercial look like? What ideas were brought out?

The first type of question is called unaided recall because the particular brand is not mentioned. The second question is an example of aided recall, in which the specific brand name is mentioned. The answers to the third set of questions are written down verbatim. The test requires that the respondent link a specific brand name, or at least a specific product category, to a specific commercial. If the commercial fails to establish a tight connection between the brand name and the selling message, the commercial will not get a high recall score.

Researchers analyze recall test results by examining the verbatim responses (what was said word for word), to determine how many viewers remembered something specific about the ad. If an answer indicates that the viewer was merely guessing, or remembering other advertising, that viewer is not counted toward the recall score.

Researchers also use recall tests to evaluate magazine advertisements. Respondents who have read the magazine go through a deck of cards containing brand names. If the respondent says, "Yes, I remember having seen an advertisement for that brand," the interviewer asks the interviewee to describe everything she can remember about the ad. As in a television recall test, researchers take down answers verbatim and study them later to determine how many respondents remembered the specific advertisement.

Because recall tests are widely used, research companies that conduct them have accumulated norms—records of results that serve the same purpose as batting averages. Norms allow the advertiser to tell whether a particular advertisement is above or below the average for the brand or its product category. Without norms the advertiser would not know whether a score of 23, for example, is good or bad. Like students, commercials are graded with reference to others in the category being tested.

Recall tests are expensive. On average, television recall tests cost $9,000 to $17,000 per commercial; print recall tests cost $7,000 to $13,000 per ad. These costs limit the number of advertisements that an advertiser can afford to test.

Since recall tests are costly, if their validity is unknown, why do so many advertisers use them? One reason is that recall is a fairly reliable measure of something, and many advertisers believe—despite evidence to the contrary—that recall must be related to effectiveness. It just seems logical that a well-remembered advertisement will, on average, be more effective than an advertisement that leaves no impression in the viewer's mind.

Recognition Tests Another way to measure memory is to show the advertisement to people and ask them whether they remember having seen it before. This kind of test is generally called a **recognition test**. Researchers first used recognition tests to evaluate print advertising. One of the earliest recognition tests is named after its inventor, Daniel Starch.

Persuasion Tests Another evaluative research technique to use after execution is a persuasion test. The basic format for a **persuasion test**, or attitude change test, is this: consumers are first asked how likely they are to buy a specific brand. Next they are exposed to an advertisement for that brand. After exposure, researchers again ask them what they intend to purchase. The researcher analyzes the results to determine whether intention to buy has increased as a result of exposure to the advertisement.

Research companies that conduct persuasion tests often invite consumers to a theater to see a "preview of a new television show." They use this pretense because they do not want respondents to pay undue attention to advertising before coming to the testing session and they want to minimize artificial attention to the commercials once the testing session has begun.

Before the audience members see the program, they fill out a questionnaire that asks about their preferences for various brands. They then watch a television program, complete with commercials, after which they answer questions about their reactions to the entertainment. Then they respond to the brand preference questions again.

Like recall tests, persuasion tests come in several different versions. In one variation researchers telephone people at home and ask them to watch a program at a certain time. During the course of the recruitment interview they are asked about their brand preferences. After the program has been telecast, the researchers contact them again and ask them about their brand preferences once more.

Assessing Persuasion Tests Like most testing techniques, persuasion tests have several problems. In particular, there are problems with audience composition, the environment, brand familiarity, and cost.

The validity of a persuasion test depends in part on whether participants in the experiment represent a good sample of the prospects the advertiser is trying to reach. A dog food advertiser, for example, would not be interested in responses from people who do not own dogs. Unless the audience has been specially recruited to contain only dog owners, many of the responses in a typical persuasion test audience will come from people who are not really interested in the product.

Because respondents are in a strange environment and because they may feel that they themselves are being tested, they are likely to be more alert, attentive, and critical than they would be at home. The characteristics of the theater environment may produce artificially high levels of attention and may exaggerate rational rather than emotional responses.

When the advertisement being tested is for a well-known brand, the amount of change that one exposure to one commercial creates is almost always very small. Small changes tend to be unreliable. The advertiser cannot tell whether small differences are real or due to some random combination of factors that accidentally affected the results.

Cost of Persuasion Tests Persuasion tests are unusually expensive. A typical persuasion test costs between $11,000 and $15,000, and if the researcher must make special efforts to recruit a hard-to-find sample, the cost can go much higher. One justification for this large expenditure is that persuasion test suppliers typically provide recall scores and attitude scores, along with persuasion scores, when reporting their findings. Another justification is that persuasion is a key objective for many advertisers, so even a rough estimate of persuasive power is useful.

Direct-Response Counts **Direct-response counts** are ads that contain elements that can be returned. Some television commercials request direct response via a toll-free number. Some print ads request direct response via a toll-free number, a coupon, a Web site, or an offer embedded in the body copy. Responses to these requests provide direct measures of effectiveness. Instead of depending on memory or persuasion or some other indirect and possibly misleading indication of effectiveness, the advertiser simply counts the number of viewers or readers who request more information or buy the product. (See the Arm & Hammer Ad.)

Compared with recall tests and persuasion tests, this type of evaluative research has few reliability or validity problems.

Frame-by-Frame Tests While a television commercial unfolds, viewers' responses to the commercial change as they view each part of it. Researchers have tried to track those

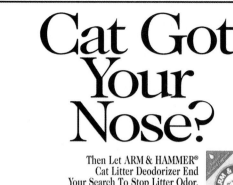

changes in several different ways. In one form of **frame-by-frame test**, viewers turn a dial or press numbers on an electronic keypad to indicate their moment-to-moment reactions to what they are seeing on the screen. That procedure produces a trace—a continuous record of ups and downs. When the trace is correlated with the commercial frame by frame, it provides a record of which parts of the commercial increased attention (or liking, or whatever is being measured) and which parts reduced it.

One of the best-known frame-by-frame tests is VIEWFACTS' PEAC test (Figure 5.6), in which people in a minitheater setting press buttons on handheld keypads to indicate how much they like or dislike what they are seeing on a television screen. The test commercial is embedded in a series of commercials and respondents indicate their reactions to each one. As the test participants are reacting, a computer collects and averages the responses and translates them into a continuous trace line keyed to the commercial's scenes.

In another form of frame-by-frame test, viewers wear tiny electrodes that measure the electrical conductivity of the skin. As various parts of the commercial provoke an emotional reaction, electrical conductivity changes produce an "emotional response" trace line. Unlike the PEAC test, which produces a voluntary measure of liking, an electrical conductivity test measures involuntary emotional reactions. It combines the advantage of frame-by-frame analysis with the advantages of involuntary emotional response.

Frame-by-frame tests bring something to advertising research that other methods do not. They provide an opportunity to look inside a commercial, and they offer clues as to what scenes produce a certain kind of response.

In-Market Tests Tests that evaluate advertisements by measuring their influence on sales are known as **in-market tests**. In view of the various research challenges, a sales impact measurement might appear to be the only measurement an advertiser should accept. However, the practical difficulties of conducting in-market tests are so great that advertisers seldom use full-scale in-market tests to evaluate individual ads.

One problem is that sales are produced by a tightly interwoven set of factors, including economic conditions, competitive strategies, and the effectiveness of marketing activities, including advertising. Within that complicated set of interrelationships, the effect of any single advertisement is extremely difficult to detect. Even with the benefit of a carefully designed, large-scale (and therefore costly and time-consuming) experiment, the effect of a single advertisement may be impossible to determine.

Another reason that in-market tests are not popular is that by the time sales figures become available, most of the important investments have been made: The advertiser has

FIGURE 5.6

THE PEAC TEST

The PEAC test allows consumers to evaluate commercials in a theater setting.

usually paid final production and media costs. For purposes of evaluating an advertisement, in-market test results become available very late in the game.

Substitutes for In-Market Tests Some of the problems of in-market tests can be avoided by using simulated test markets. In a simulated test market the research company exposes respondents to advertising and then asks them to choose among competing brands. Later the researchers contact respondents who have used the advertiser's brand to ask whether they would purchase the same brand again. The two numbers produced by that pair of interviews are trial (the proportion of test participants who chose to try the brand after seeing an advertisement for it), and repeat (the proportion of participants who, having tried the product, chose to purchase the same brand again).

Single-source data tests are another major substitute for a full in-market test. Both are conducted after the ad campaign is introduced. The difference is in the scope and amount of control. Single-source tests are much smaller in scope and have more controls. Unlike the in-market tests where the research cannot detect whether a particular ad produced a given sale, single-source research companies arrange to control the television signal of a community's households.

The company divides the households into equivalent matched groups. It then sends advertisements to one group but not to the other and collects exact records of what every household purchases. This information is collected through the scanners found at the supermarket cash register. Each household is assigned a code number so that it can be matched with the ad treatment it received. Because advertising is the only manipulated variable, the method permits an unambiguous reading of cause and effect. The data collected in this way are known as single-source data because exposure records and purchasing records come from the same source.

Single-source data can produce exceptionally dependable results. Real advertisements are received under natural conditions in the home and the resulting purchases are actual purchases made by consumers. The method is very expensive, however: $200,000 to $300,00 per test. Furthermore, the method usually requires more than six months to produce usable results. Because of the time and expense, single-source data tests are not acceptable for routine testing of individual ads.

Brand Tracking Brand tracking is a relatively new kind of advertising research. Mike Hall, CEO of Hall & Partners, has pioneered a type of brand tracking, highlighted in Figure 5.7. The underlying assumption of this type of research is that with fragmented media and an abundance of high-quality products, tracking the brand is more important than tracking the ad. The relationship with the customer is built in large part on the brand's values rather than the product's attributes. Instead of arguing that a product works better, advertisers show consumers that their brand means more.[10] The thinking is that advertising and other marketing communications should involve customers in the brand's values so they're more favorably disposed toward it.

Although brand tracking is an excellent method for assessing whether the advertiser is meeting its goals, it is a costly, complex process. Some practitioners also fear that it diminishes the importance of advertising by focusing on consumers' response to the brand, not ads.

Implications of Evaluative Research

All the tests of effectiveness we explored in this section have their strengths and weaknesses, as we see in Table 5.2. None are totally accurate, and none can take into account the irrational behavior and responses of the consumer. One wonders whether these measures accurately link the advertiser's goals to ad effectiveness. Figure 5.8 (on page 146) shows how users link evaluative research advertising to effectiveness measures. Ultimately, advertising must address three issues:

- What is the proper research process in advertising?
- What can we realistically expect from ad agencies?
- Can we improve measures of effectiveness?

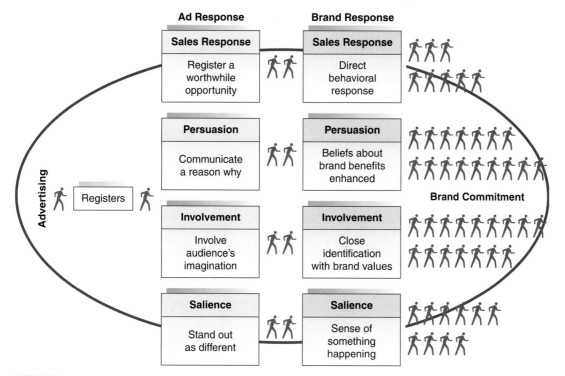

FIGURE 5.7

HALL & PARTNERS' BRAND-TRACKING FRAMEWORK
This research assumes that tracking the brand is more important than tracking the ad.

TABLE 5.2	**Strengths and Weaknesses of Evaluative Measures**	
Evaluative Measure	**Strengths**	**Weaknesses**
Memory test		
Recall tests	Well-established norms that provide high reliability	Low validity as an indicator of sales
Recognition tests	Speed, low cost, and high reliability	Low validity as an indicator of sales
Persuasion tests	Speed and moderate reliability	Problems, related to audience composition, the environment, brand familiarity, and relatively high cost
Direct-response tests	Few reliability or validity problems	High cost
Frame-by-frame tests	High validity	Low reliability, high cost
In-market tests	Relevant results	Low validity
Brand tracking	Relevant results that link to advertiser's purposes; Brand is a better representation of product than advertising	High cost, complex process diminishes the importance of the ad

FIGURE 5.8

EVALUATIVE MEASURES OF ADVERTISING EFFECTIVENESS
Advertisers have a choice of effectiveness research techniques depending on the advertising objectives.

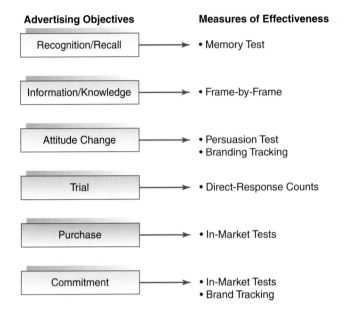

RESEARCH CHALLENGES

Account planners and researchers face four key challenges: globalization, new media technology, virtual research, and embedded research. We examine each challenge briefly in the following sections.

Globalization

Advertisers are becoming increasingly more global. Multinational advertisers and their marketing communication agencies are expanding all over the world. Expansion into Western Europe, South America, and much of the Pacific Rim is virtually complete. In-depth understanding of the economic and cultural conditions, government regulations, and communications media of each country is more important than ever before. Developing research methods aimed at solving global problems would establish a new and important advertising research tradition.

The key issues that global researchers face include how to manage and communicate global brands in different local regions and how to shift from studying differences to finding similarities around the world.

Practical Tips #2

WHEN IN ROME

To conduct global research, keep in mind some basic issues.[11]

- Prepare by analyzing the culture. Culture affects everything from the language used in an interview question to the location of the research site. For example, offering money to focus group participants is considered rude in Latin American countries, while it is standard U.S. practice.
- Make sure you overcome the language barriers. Some researchers suggest having surveys and interview questions translated by someone in the host country to get the subtleties of the language and its idioms correct.
- Consider nonverbal techniques to avoid language problems. These might include building collages and drawing images that represent feelings about the brand.

New Media Technology

The expansion from three on-air television networks to a plethora of cable channels changed television programming, television program audiences, and television advertising throughout the United States. The merger of the telephone, the TV, and the home computer will also change advertising. Changes in media technology will alter the meaning and consequences of almost all of our most familiar research constructs: involvement, brand equity, attitude toward the ad, emotional processing, and cognitive processing, to name a few. Advertising research today focuses largely on full-page print ads and 30-second television commercials. As technology changes in the media unfold, the old evaluative measures will become increasingly invalid.

Because of this media fragmentation, researchers and account planners must help to develop message strategies that enable media planners to reach consumers most effectively. How do consumers live their lives? When are they susceptible to the message?

Virtual Research

Measuring the effectiveness of ads through interactive media is a challenge. Numerous companies provide information about Internet use, but some sources are more valid than others. Some companies use true random surveying to generate figures. Other companies depend on information provided voluntarily by Internet users or industry sources (which often have a vested interest in promoting good news). Those who want to plan or evaluate Internet ads must stay abreast of the latest developments in research on this interactive medium because the methods are still in their infancy.[12]

Another aspect of **virtual research** that provides a challenge is the use of online media to gather research. The low cost and quick speed of gathering research data online has made the Internet a popular survey tool with companies. Online surveys must be designed to accommodate the medium: They must be short and simple. However, the responses can be tallied immediately by a computer and don't require transcription, as phone surveys do.

Multimedia research also allows automated testing of concepts, storyboards, and designs in multiple markets. That's a lot simpler and cheaper than having staff develop actual prototypes or multiple sets of storyboards.

However, people interact with computers differently than they do with actual products and ads, so using the computer and the Internet to do research is not a panacea. In addition, the Internet is difficult to regulate, so less experienced or less scrupulous organizations may offer services that are poorly executed. Advertisers, researchers, and account planners must understand the advantages and disadvantages of this form of research to use it wisely and ethically.

Embedded Research

The development of **embedded research** is related to online research. In this case, the research methods are embedded directly into real purchase and use situations, so that the consumer is a recipient and direct beneficiary of the information. Manufacturers, retailers, and information intermediaries also benefit from this information in numerous ways, but they don't design or control the research in the traditional way.

Applications of embedded research are varied and still evolving. Most common is to use this method for product reviews, where customers enter the Web site and select from an array of product categories they would like to know about. The opinions of reviewers can be accessed with a click.

It is up to the user to sort, codify, and evaluate them. Reviews come from other customers, who report their own experience with the product on an open-ended basis, following no particular format or style. Participation is completely voluntary; the "sample" of consumers who provide reviews is not selected or controlled in any way. Quality control can be built into the process through ratings of the usefulness of opinions offered. Most importantly, the context is the buying process rather than a traditional research process.

A second application is called **collaborative filtering**. In this case customers at a Web site can see product recommendations based on predictive models that classify them with others who have similar profiles of attitude or behavior. If similar customers tended to purchase product X then the Web site recommends this product is under the theory that customers who haven't yet tried it would also find it appealing. Customers freely offer information about their attitudes and behavior. They receive recommendations in exchange. Providers receive qualified customers for marketing opportunities.

Another application of embedded research is called **attribute trade-offs**. Here a Web site asks customers to provide quantitative ratings of their preferences for specific attributes, including brand, price, and features. From evaluation ratings of attribute and product profiles the Web site can generate a list of the most preferred products for that individual. In addition, the site can identify specific retailers that offer the product at a particular price. These could be off-line or online retailers.[13]

IT'S A WRAP
DELTA FLIES HIGHER

The discussion in this chapter focused on two elements related to advertising. First, the rudiments of conducting strategic and evaluative research. Second, how these facets of research are applicable to the advertising plan and the various measures of effectiveness.

Having accomplished these two objectives, we can now go back to the Delta Airlines campaign that introduced this chapter. It seems apparent that Delta conducted the research necessary to create an effective campaign. For the most part, its evaluative measurers of effectiveness concentrated on results prior to actual sales. For example, when Delta assessed whether potential customers would consider Delta as a flying alternative, there was a 23 percent increase, compared to a year earlier with the goal being 20 percent. More importantly, this category did not increase with all competitors. A second measure was "involvement by the target audience." This measure increased by 10 points, achieving the desired results. Finally, Delta wanted to increase the extent to which customers understood the new position of empathy and trust. There were significant positive changes in all the measures related to these concepts. Ultimately, however, sales declined during the period this campaign ran, but the decline was far less than that experienced by Delta's competitors.

Summary

1. **Discuss the value of marketing research.** Information and insight are the basic ingredients used to develop plans for advertisements and media purchases. A critical part of advertising information comes from the personal and professional experiences of the people responsible for developing and evaluating advertising. Another part of this information comes from formal research. In the development of any campaign these two information sources interact in complex ways. Government departments, trade associations, secondary research suppliers, primary research suppliers, the research departments of advertisers, and the account planning groups of advertising agencies provide formal research.

2. **Describe the differences between strategic research and evaluative research.** Both strategic and evaluative

research are valuable to the marketer and the advertiser. The former is used to identify important advertising-related factors deemed useful in the creative process. The latter is used to assess whether the various advertising objectives have been achieved. In the development of an advertising campaign, the problem is seldom too little information, but too much. Someone must identify, collect, and organize the most useful information and present it in a useful form. That task usually falls to the members of the advertising agency account planning group, or, in the absence of a planning department, to the account management group.

3. **Identify the factors that affect message development research.** The most important research information usually

goes into a strategy document that is a rough plan for the campaign. The difficult decisions about what information should go into the strategy document and how that information should be interpreted call for judgments on the part of the advertiser and its agency. Within the agency, these judgments involve all those responsible for making sure that the communication works, and these judgments are never cut and dried.

4. **Summarize key evaluative research objectives and methods.** This type of research includes memory tests, persuasion tests, and communications tests, which include physiological tests, frame-by-frame tests, in-market tests, single-source tests, and brand tracking. Advertisers rarely trust their agencies to evaluate the effectiveness of the work they created, so they usually turn to outside research firms.

5. **Outline advertising research challenges.** Four key advertising challenges are: globalization, new media technology, interactive research, and embedded research.

Key Terms

account planner, p. 129	frame-by-frame test, p. 143	primary research suppliers, p. 126	secondary research suppliers, p. 126
account planning process, p. 129	in-market tests, p. 143	qualitative data, p. 129	single-source data tests, p. 144
attribute trade-offs, p. 148	market tracking studies, p. 138	quantitative data, p. 129	strategic research, p. 125
collaborative filtering, p. 147		recall test, p. 141	survey research, p. 134
direct-response counts, p. 142	marketing research, p. 124	recognition test, p. 141	test market, p. 136
embedded research, p. 147	persuasion test, p. 141	secondary research, p. 125	virtual research, p. 147
evaluative research, p. 132	primary research, p. 125		

Questions

1. Every year Copper Mountain must decide how much emphasis to put on front-range day skiers, skiers from the Denver market who stay overnight, and skiers from outside Copper Mountain's geographic area. What research information would help Copper Mountain's managers make those decisions? Where would they get that information?

2. Suppose you are developing a research program for a new bookstore serving your college or university. What kind of exploratory research would you recommend? Would you propose both qualitative and quantitative studies? Why or why not? What specific steps would you take?

3. The research director for Angelis Advertising always introduces her department's service to new agency clients by comparing research to a roadmap. What do maps and research studies have in common? How does the analogy of a map reveal the limitations of research for resolving an advertising problem?

4. Judging from the chapter discussions, would you expect the following databases to be developed from primary or secondary resources?
   a. National television ratings
   b. Consumer brand's ad awareness scores
   c. Household penetration levels for VCRs

5. Research professionals recommend using focus groups to help develop a campaign strategy or theme, but many are opposed to using focus groups to choose finished ads for the campaign. Is this advice self-contradictory? Why or why not?

6. A new radio station is moving into your community. Management is not sure how to position the station in this market and has asked you to develop a study to help them make this decision.
   a. What key research questions must be asked?
   b. Outline a research program to answer those questions that uses as many of the research methods discussed in this chapter as you can incorporate.

7. In the course of diagnostic research you are conducting, a few focus-group respondents contradict an opinion based on years of professional and personal experience. Suppose your client's top management also has the respondents' opinion. If you are a researcher, what do you do? Suppose the creative director of your agency holds that opinion. What do you do?

8. This chapter discusses the idea of international research suppliers. Do you think companies need both domestic and international research suppliers? Why or why not? What do marketers and advertisers need to consider when selling a product to different countries? What role does research play in this process?

9. In the dot-com craze of the late 1990s, new Internet companies emerged almost daily. What types of strategic or evaluative research do you think many of these companies conducted, if any? Do you believe research would have helped any of these companies make decisions that might have helped them survive the dot-com crash? Why or why not? What particular decision might have been considered?

10. You are an account planner with a large advertising firm. Much of the research you use is purchased from an outside supplier. Recently, you've begun to question the validity of some of the information the supplier is providing. What do you do? What sort of qualitative and quantitative information do you look for to support your suspicion?

Suggested Class Project

Run a focus group. Brainstorm to come up with something the class would like to advertise, such as new audio equipment. Divide into researchers and the consumer group (you can run two groups and trade roles, if you'd like). Meet to decide on questions and format. Make assignments for note taking, facilitating, and collecting and organizing feedback. Write a one- to two-page report on the process and the group's findings.

Suggested Internet Class Project

Assume you are working for Gerber Baby Foods. Your assignment is to identify the relevant trends that are forecasted for U.S. birth rates between 2003 and 2010. Identify Internet sources that would provide that information. Select one and write a 1-page report on the trends you find.

Hallmark Build•a•Campaign Projects

Please review the Hallmark Case Appendix at the end of the text before responding to these questions.

1. Meet in small groups to discuss the marketing research questions that Capitol Advertising needed to ask to estimate the number of consumers at each level of the Brand Insistence Pyramid. The group should develop a set of questions to provide this information.

2. What types of marketing research might Hallmark Gold Crown stores conduct to learn how to convince consumers to buy from them rather than from more convenient drug or grocery stores? Develop a research tool and see what you can learn about consumer behavior at a local Gold Crown Store. Write a report.

HANDS-ON   Case 5

RESEARCHING THE HOG

Everything appeared to be going well for Harley-Davidson. Sales have steadily increased every year since 1985. New models, such as the Electra Glide, Sportster®, and the Fat Boy are selling faster than hotcakes through their network of 1,300 dealers across the world. Even the Hog's bad biker image has gone by the wayside.

Despite all of this good news, the company faces an aging market. As people age, especially people over age 55, they are less likely to replace their existing Hog or take up the hobby. The median age of a Harley buyer was 46 in 2001, up from 37 in 1990. Moreover, because the current motorcycle market is growing so rapidly, and Harley has limited production capacity, Harley look-a-likes from competitors such as Honda, Yamaha, Suzuki, and Kawasaki are gradually taking some of the market share.

Harley had to take a close look at current customers and potential customers, through a more formalized research process. While the old research process of talking to the more than 4,000 employees who own a Hog, or going to rallies to talk to owners, were quite effective in the past, a new system was needed. The research question was straightforward: Is there a general appeal that would speak to current owners and also resonate with younger, potential owners.

A two-stage research process was employed. Stage one involved some very unusual focus groups. Each focus group included current Harley owners, potential owners, and owners of competing bikes. Participants were provided with old magazines, paste, and construction paper and were asked to create a collage that expressed their feelings about Harley-Davidson. Expert judges evaluated the collages and three common themes emerged: enjoyment, the great outdoors, and freedom.

In stage two, a survey was mailed to more than 16,000 owners, potential owners, and owners of other bikes. Questions included standard demographics, psychographics, behavioral variables, and several original questions based on the information derived from the focus groups. The response rate was 30 percent, quite high for a questionnaire offering no incentive.

The data was submitted to a statistical technique that clusters respondents by similarity in answers and/or characteristics. Seven clusters or segments resulted: (1) The Adventure-Loving Traditionalist, (2) the Sensitive Pragmatist, (3) the Stylish Status Seeker, (4) the Laid-Back Camper, (5) the Classy Capitalist, (6) the Cool-Headed Loner, and (7) the Cocky Misfit. In addition, the final customer groups were measured in respect to their loyalty to Harley-Davidson. In some cases, scores were in the 90-plus category.

Ultimately, these research findings proved useful in a number of strategic aspects of marketing, especially advertising. Rather than being overly concerned with existing customers, who were clearly committed to the brand, Harley was able to target the 24- to 45-year-old age group. In this case, good research produced real strategic benefits. ■

IT'S YOUR TURN

1. What major research questions did Harley-Davidson address?
2. How could the answers to the survey questions help create better advertising?

Sources: Betsy Spethmann, "Happy Birthday to Us," *Promo* (April 1998): 37–42; Jonathan Fahey, "Love Into Money," *Forbes* (January 7, 2002): 60–65; Ted Shelsby, "Harley Sales Go Hog Wild," *Baltimore Sun* (November 25, 2001): 1C; Rob Griffin, "Harley-Davidson Continues to Set Standard for Motorcycle Enthusiasts," *Sunday Business* (London) (November 11, 2001): 18.

Notes

1. Daniel McGinn, "Divide and Conquer," *Newsweek* (December 1, 1997): 50–51.

2. Roy S. Johnson, "Banking on Urban America," *Fortune* (March 2, 1998): 129–132.

3. Jim Kirk, "Ad Agencies Rise to United's Challenge," *Chicago Tribune* (June 15, 1997): 1B.

4. Rudolph Flesch, *The Art of Readable Writing* (New York: Harper & Row, 1974).

5. Julie Liessee, "KGF Taps Data to Target Consumers," *Advertising Age* (October 8, 1990): 3, 38.

6. Michael L. Rothschild, Esther Thorson, Judith E. Hirsch, Robert Goldstein, and Byron Reeves, "EEG Activity and the Processing of Television Commercials," *Communication Research* (April 1986): 14–21.

7. Don E. Schultz, *Strategic Advertising Campaigns*, 3rd ed. (Lincoln, IL: NTC Business Books, 1990): p. 550.

8. James F. Donius, "Market Tracking: A Strategic Reassessment and Planning Tool," *Journal of Advertising Research* (February/March 1985): 15–19.

9. Lawrence N. Gold, "TV Ad Testing Enters New Generation," *Marketing News* (October 23, 1989): 2.

10. Mike Hall, "How Advertising Works," paper for the 1998 ATG Conference: 6.

11. Jan Larson, "It's a Small World After All," *Marketing Tools* (September 1997).

12. Paula Kephart, "Virtual Testing," *Marketing Tools* (June 1998).

13. Gordon A. Wyner, "Life (on the Internet) Imitates Research," *Marketing Research* (Summer 2000): 38–39.

God bless
business travel.

Häagen-Dazs
Butter Pecan

Häagen-Dazs
Too much pleasure?

♥2000 HDIP, Inc.

haagen-dazs.com

CHAPTER

How Advertising Works

6

Passion on a Spoon

Award: *EFFIE Silver 2001, Snacks/Desserts category*

Company: *Häagen-Dazs Ice Cream*

Agency: *Wolf New York*

Campaign: *"Too Much Pleasure?"*

Have you ever felt guilty about digging into a bowl of rich, creamy ice cream? If so, an EFFIE award–winning campaign for super premium Häagen-Dazs may make you feel better. Created by New York's Wolf Group, the campaign was designed to help the brand face the most competitive selling season ever in the summer of 2000 when Godiva, Starbucks, and Dryer's/Edy's "Dreamery" were all entering Häagen-Dazs's premium market with new offerings.

The Wolf creative team knew from research that even though the brand's image was seen as aloof, cold, and corporate, the eating experience was much richer. The language for the new campaign idea came from the brand's most devoted users, who said, "Häagen-Dazs is a joy, a spiritual thing. It's a wonderful downfall. And, if it wasn't so bad, it wouldn't be so good. Eaten as it is, straight from the pint, places you in a blissful world all your own." As another consumer said, "When I enjoy Häagen-Dazs, I experience such passion, I surrender to it body and soul."

The core essence of this brand is not just the premium brand image or the variety of flavors, but rather the experience of eating it, an experience captured in the campaign's slogan, "Too Much Pleasure?" Who else but Häagen-Dazs could offer such complete surrender to an eating experience? Who else could so convincingly promise "passion on a spoon"?

The idea behind the pleasure theme is that it's okay for you to take some time out to indulge yourself in this little pleasure. In one ad, a man longingly opens a pint of ice cream, with the headline, "Thank God she's late." Mike Rogers, Wolf agency president and creative director, explained that "with pleasure, there's a little bit of guilt or sinfulness" and these perfectly normal feelings are something we all share.

By unleashing the power of the experience, the campaign not only won an EFFIE award; it also proved to be highly effective in increasing brand awareness and positive product perceptions, as well as increasing the volume of brand sales in this highly competitive category. In the end, it helped to secure Häagen-Dazs's position as the leader in the super premium ice cream category.

To better understand the effectiveness of this campaign, let's consider some ideas about how advertising works. You will find out more about Häagen-Dazs's campaign in the "It's a Wrap" box at the end of this chapter.

Sources: The 2001 EFFIE Awards brief provided by Häagen-Dazs (www.haagendazs.com) and the Wolf Group (www.wolfgroup.com); Simon Butler, "The Pleasure Principle," *Adweek Midwest* (July 24, 2000): 48.

THE EFFECTIVENESS OF ADVERTISING

USA Today conducts an annual poll on which TV commercials are the most popular among its readers. For years, those clever Energizer bunny commercials topped the field in the poll. They started off like commercials for other products—but then the Energizer bunny crossed the screen, catching viewers by surprise. The campaign slogan was "It keeps going and going and going. . . ." The commercials won a number of advertising awards, but which company made the Energizer battery? (See www.Energizer.com/bunny/.)

Most people weren't quite sure. So when they got to the store, they bought the brand leader—Gillette's Duracell, instead of the Eveready Energizer. In other words, the Energizer bunny commercials did little to influence the actual sales of Eveready batteries, even though they had high levels of awareness and were well liked. Energizer has taken steps to correct this. Newer commercials have more brand tie-ins to Energizer and Eveready, and more importantly, you see the bunny on the battery's packaging and on store displays.

So are these creative commercials effective if they fail to sell the product? It might have been because people didn't quite understand that the commercials were advertising the Energizer battery rather than the Duracell. Most people are paying only a limited amount of attention to a TV commercial or print ad, so the ad may create little impact if the message is complicated or the brand links are unclear, even though it's well remembered and well liked.

That's the point of this chapter. How do we decide if an advertisement—or other marketing communication message—is effective? What are these messages designed to accomplish and how do they work to create impact?

When we say that advertisements (or other promotional messages) are designed to accomplish something, we are referring to their objectives. Setting objectives is an important part of an advertisement's strategy and meeting those objectives is the primary way effectiveness is determined. But before we can discuss objectives, we need to first understand how advertising works—all the various kinds of effects it can have on an audience and all the different results it can achieve. This is what is called the "impact" of a message.

How much **impact** can advertising actually have on its audience? Consider a survey reported in the industry magazine *Adweek*:[1] The survey found that when consumers were asked what prompts them to try new food products, coupons were the most effective and advertising was eighth. This suggests that price promotions are more effective, at least for trial, than advertising. Although only 13 percent of the respondents confessed that advertising is "very influential" to their own food purchases, nearly half (48 percent) believed it is very persuasive in motivating other people. In other words, people think it has impact, but they feel that they themselves are immune to the impact.[2]

In addition to such effects as motivation and persuasion leading to trial, another objective of advertising is to provide information about a product. However, Regis

The Florida's Natural® advertising campaign was effective because it has a strong visual appeal.

McKenna, author of *Relationship Marketing*, believes that advertising's effectiveness is limited in this area because it doesn't provide an opportunity for questions and feedback.[3] In McKenna's viewpoint, to be effective, ads should open up a dialogue with the consumer. That's not a common view of the role of advertising, however. Most advertisers and their agency partners are more concerned with whether ads have an impact on immediate sales rather than whether they create long-term "soft" effects, such as brand awareness and perceptions of a brand's image.

To answer the sales question, for example, Syracuse University Professor John Philip Jones analyzed hundreds of ads using single-source data (information about media use and products purchased by a single household). In his book on this research, *When Ads Work*, Jones concludes that the strongest ad campaigns can triple sales, whereas the weakest can contribute to sales falling by more than 50 percent.[4] According to Jones, effective ads have three qualities: "One, the ad itself has to be attractive enough for consumers to look at, it has to have likability; two, all effective advertising is totally visual in its communication impact; and three, you must have more than warm, fuzzy images."[5] Results like Jones's suggest that ads can be effective, but if they are not correctly designed they may just as easily fail. The Florida's Natural campaign, in fact, met all three of Jones's requirements—it's likable, it's visual, and the visuals have strong emotional appeal.

In this introduction to advertising and its impact, we've talked about advertising's role in creating such effects—the impact of the message on the audience—as influencing, informing, motivating, and persuading, as well as creating trial, sales, brand awareness, and a likable brand image in consumers' minds. That's not a complete list of all the things an advertisement can accomplish, but it gives you an idea of why it is important to understand the logic behind how advertising works, so you know what is achievable with an advertising message.

HOW COMMUNICATION WORKS

Advertising is, first of all, a form of communication. In a sense, it is a conversation with a consumer about a product. It gets attention, provides information and a little bit of entertainment, and tries to create some kind of response, such as a sale. The legendary David Ogilvy, founder of the advertising agency that bears his name, explained his view of an advertisement:

> I always pretend that I'm sitting beside a woman at a dinner party, and she asks me for advice about which product she should buy. So then I write down what I would say to her. I give her the facts, facts, facts. I try to make it interesting, fascinating, if possible, and personal—I don't write to the crowd. I try to write from one human being to another. . . . And I try not to bore the poor woman to death, and I try to make it as real and personal as possible.[6]

Most advertising, however, is not as personal as a conversation because it relies on mass communication, which is more indirect—and complex—than a simple conversation. (Note that other forms of marketing communication, such as personal selling and telemarketing, for example, do deliver the personal contact of a conversation.)

Mass communication is usually thought of as a process; a process depicted in a communication model that outlines the important players and steps (see Figure 6.1a). It begins with a source (S), a sender who encodes a message (M)—puts it in words and pictures. The model explains how communication works: The message is presented through channels of communication (C), such as a newspaper, radio, or TV. The message is

---

FIGURE 6.1

Mass communication (a) is a one-way process—the message moves from the source to the receiver. Interactive communication (b) is a conversation—the source and receiver change positions as the message bounces back and forth between them.

A Basic Communication Model

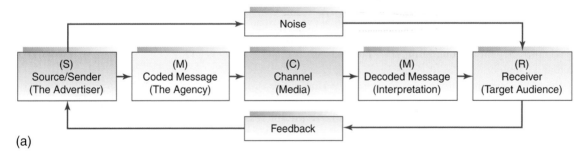

(a)

An Interactive Communication Model

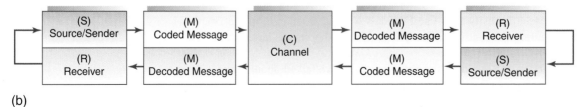

(b)

decoded, or interpreted, by the receiver (R), who in advertising is a member of the target audience. Feedback is obtained by monitoring the response of the receiver to the message. This process is sometimes referred to as the SMCR model of communication.

Mass communication is a one-way process with the message depicted as moving from the source to the receiver. However, interactive communication—the personal conversation Ogilvy wanted to emulate—is a form of two-way communication. Figure 6.1b illustrates the difference between one-way and two-way communication, in which the source and receiver change positions as the message bounces back and forth between them. This is a model of how a conversation works. It suggests that if advertisers want to address the limitations noted by McKenna, they need to learn to listen to, as well as send, messages to customers. That's done partly by using more interactive forms of marketing communication (personal selling, telemarketing, online marketing). Advertising can also achieve more interactivity, by providing such response devices as toll-free numbers and e-mail addresses to open opportunities for dialogue.

How Advertising Communication Works

This basic SMCR communication process is the foundation for a model of the advertising process, which Figure 6.2 depicts. It begins with the source, or advertiser and its agency, and what they hope to accomplish with the message—the objectives. In a campaign from Iceland, for example, the government's objective was to increase the participation of women in Icelandic politics. The message, which was encoded by the HÉR & NÚ agency of Reykjavik, Iceland, was a series of humorous photos that used political leaders in gender-reversed situations. (To read more about the story of this campaign, see "The Inside Story.")

Advertisers usually deliver their messages through a variety of tools, which we call a **media mix**. Surrounding and affecting the message and media mix is noise, which comes from both internal and external factors—internal meaning internal to the consumer and external meaning in the environment. Next is message reception and response, where the message is decoded. This step is so complicated that it needs its own model. This section on reception will close with a discussion of the feedback step.

FIGURE 6.2

The Model of Advertising Communication Is Based on the SMCR Process.

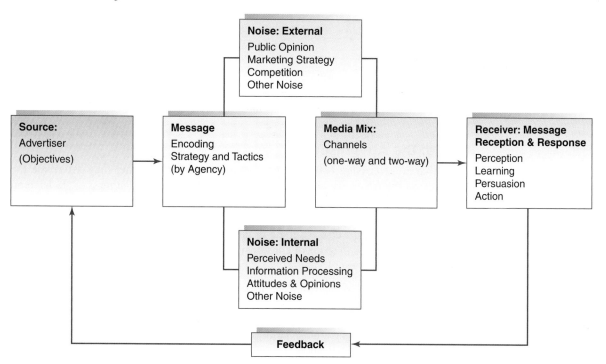

THE INSIDE STORY

"Cabinet Appointed Committee to Increase Women's Role in Icelandic Politics"

Ingvi Logason   Principal, HÉR & NÚ Advertising, Reykjavik, Iceland

Imagine seeing George W. Bush trying on women's shoes, Colin Powell pregnant, and Gale Norton standing in front of a urinal. That was the American equivalent of a big idea for a client I worked with early in my career.

Political and social advertising is one type of advertising that's usually not covered deeply in classrooms. Early in my career I got to work on this kind of an account, a newly established, government-funded committee aimed at increasing women's participation in politics. The main idea was to level the playing field in Icelandic politics—to get more women involved in politics, to increase the public's confidence in women as political figures, and to create more talk about women in politics.

With a tight budget we needed a strong creative strategy and execution. So we sat down and took a regular "what's-in-it-for-me" business approach to showing "consumers" what they would gain from proportional representation of women in politics. We did a SWOT analysis (strengths, weaknesses, opportunities, and threats) and set down communication strategies, objectives, and tactics just like we would for any consumer good.

We knew that all the leaders of the various political parties in Iceland were behind the project, which allowed us to maximize awareness and create talk among key decision makers within certain target groups.

Our strategy was to portray the chairperson of each political party in a gender-reversed situation (for humor and attention) with strong headlines that would encourage discussions of the topic, rather than steering opinions toward a certain candidate.

The copy was exceptionally well written. With a textbook attribute–benefit approach to the body text we explained how two heads work better than one, how using 100 percent of Iceland's talent rather than just 50 percent will yield more profit for the nation as a whole, and so forth.

We limited the campaign to one-page newspaper ads to keep media costs down while maintaining high coverage (the combination of two Icelandic newspapers gave us a 90 percent reach for our target group). This strategy accomplished many objectives:

1. By featuring the chairperson of each political party we influenced their followers.
2. The ads made the chairpersons responsible for increased participation among women within their own political parties.
3. We created extremely high awareness by showing well-known persons in unusual gender-reversed situations–with copy that enticed you to read on.
4. Light humor made sure the ads were informative and intriguing, never condescending or lecturing.
5. With the unusual approach we created ads that assisted and strengthened the public relations part of the campaign and created interest on behalf of the media.

Source: The Advertiser

The source in advertising is the advertiser and its agency. Together they determine the objectives for the advertisement in terms of the effects they want the message to have on the consumer. The source's objectives in advertising are focused on the receiver's response. It is that response that is measured to determine if the message met its objectives and was effective. That's also the logic of **customer-focused marketing** where all communication is evaluated in terms of consumer response.

Objectives So how do advertisers and their agencies evaluate the impact of advertising? Management guru Peter Drucker put it best. He said, "Performance is everything. It's the way you look at your grades. Ultimately, it doesn't matter how creative the ad is; it's not how beautiful it looks; or how funny; or whether or not it wins an award. It is simply results. Does the communication deliver the desired results? Does it meet its objectives? If not, it has failed."

The results were fantastic: Because of its news interest, the newspaper, radio, and TV coverage was five times what was scheduled through the advertising. BBC 1 in the United Kingdom aired a prime-time show about the campaign, as well as women's roles in European politics. The icing on the cake was the results of the elections four months later: 33 percent increase in female candidates, 38 percent more women in government, and three more women ministers (making it five of eleven).

A principal in his own agency, Ingvi Logason graduated with a degree in advertising from Western Florida University.

Nominated by Professor Tom Groth, Western Florida University.

The "Women in Politics" campaign from Iceland featured party leaders in gender-reversal situations, to impress its message on party members in humorous ways.

More often than not, the objective of advertising is to increase sales. However, a big debate in advertising management is the question of just how much advertising contributes to sales. Increasing sales is an important behavioral objective—getting consumers to buy the product—but many other marketing factors affect sales, so it is sometimes difficult to prove that advertising was the cause of a sales increase. However, other marketing communication tools, such as direct marketing, do have a connection between the message and the sales, which means it is considered to be the most accountable form of marketing communication.

There are other communication effects that may also be important and may lead directly or indirectly to sales. These other effects are drivers of sales and may be a better indicator of the effectiveness of the message than sales (remember there are other marketing factors besides advertising that impact on sales). These communication drivers were depicted in the Effectiveness Model in Chapter 1, which is revisited here in Figure 6.3. These categories of effects—perception, learning, persuasion, and behavior—are sometimes more directly traceable to an advertising message than sales.

FIGURE 6.3

A MODEL OF KEY EFFECTS
These key effects may lead to sales.

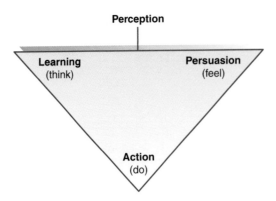

And even if the objective is action, it may not always be sales. In the case of the Häagen-Dazs ads, the objective was to get people to eat more ice cream, which, of course, would eventually lead to more sales. In the women in politics campaign, the objectives were to get more women to become candidates and then to get more votes for their candidacies.

The objectives represent what the advertiser hopes to accomplish, but they are stated in terms of effects on the consumer. In other words, objectives represent a set of dual processes—what the source wants to accomplish with a message and how the receivers respond to a message. This source–receiver relationship is illustrated in Figure 6.4, which shows how various source objectives are evaluated in terms of different types of consumer responses.

FIGURE 6.4

THE DUAL PROCESS OF EFFECTIVENESS
Advertisers look for certain responses to see if their managers are reaching their objectives.

Source Objectives	Receiver's Response
Perception	
Create exposure, awareness	→ Register, perceive, aware, recognize
Gain attention	→ Attend, concentrate, focus
Create engagement; hold attention	→ Interest
Create memorability	→ Recall, remind
Education	
Impart knowledge, information	→ Learn, understand
Link to category	→ Define product
Establish brand cues	→ Link brand with image, position, personality
Differentiate	→ Distinguish, compare, evaluate
Associate	→ Link to lifestyle and other brand values
Persuasion	
Attitudes and opinions	→ Form, change attitudes and opinions
Create consideration	→ Prefer; intend to buy
Create conviction; credibility	→ Believe; commit
Touch emotions	→ Feel (like, hate, fear, anger, laugh, etc.)
Behavior	
Encourage trial	→ Try, sample
Increase sales	→ Buy
Repeat sales; loyalty	→ Buy again
Increase usage	→ Use more, use more often
Encourage other behaviors, actions	→ Visit, enter, send back, place order, redeem coupon, phone, click

Source Credibility Another source-related factor that affects effectiveness is **source crediblity**. This is an important principle in persuasion—you believe messages you hear from some people more than from others because they are simply more credible. That's why doctors and authority figures are used in ads. However, people perceive an advertisement as biased because it is produced and paid for by a company. A news report, however, is trustworthy because people presume it has been through an objective editorial review. So a public relations news release that becomes a mass-media story has more credibility than an ad. But further, you're more likely to believe a story from someone you know than from an article in the press. That's why word of mouth is such a powerfully persuasive form of communication—even more persuasive than a mass-media story.

It's all about trust, and that can affect the channel as well as the source. For example, newspapers are generally thought by the public to have more credibility than TV. The Internet, however, has a serious problem with trust as users generally do not know the source of the information they receive online and whether it is accurate and reliable. A story in *pr reporter* found that 70 percent of the people interviewed in a survey did not trust the information they got online.[7]

Noise: External and Internal

Surrounding the SMCR process is noise, which can hinder the communication of the message. Any factor that interferes with or distorts the delivery of the advertising message to the target audience is called **noise**. For example, if the sender of the message is tired and garbles the message, that's noise. Likewise, if the receiver can't clearly hear or see the message because of a distraction, that's also noise.

External Environment Essentially, the external factors affecting the advertising process are the marketing strategy and other marketing communication by competitors, as well as general patterns of consumer use and public opinion.

General consumer trends, such as an interest in healthy foods and exercise, affect marketing strategies. And external events, such as the World Trade Center terrorist attacks, can have massive impact on consumers and industries. The airline and travel industries were devastated after September 11, 2001. Even in the area of social marketing, there are considerations that affect advertising plans, such as the government's desire to increase the number of politically active women in Iceland. Undoubtedly, this affected the campaigns of men who were running for office.

We examined marketing strategy and its influences on the advertising process in Chapter 3. Recall that marketing elements such as the product, price, and distribution have a direct bearing on whether advertising is able to achieve its objectives. For example, if there is a distribution failure and the product isn't in the store, then advertising can't help the product sell. Likewise, if there is a product design problem or if the pricing strategy is unrealistic, then the advertising will be ineffective. Competitors are also manipulating their own marketing mix of product design, pricing, distribution, and marketing communication, which further complicates an advertiser's planning.

How do such external factors affect advertising? In the aftermath of 9/11, for example, movies and advertising that had anything to do with bombings, airplane crashes, or terrorist threats were immediately shelved. The auto industry responded with campaigns promoting zero percent financing in an attempt to link up with President Bush's drive to keep the economy going. GM used the campaign slogan "Keep America Rolling" to tie in with President Bush's effort to encourage people to buy. United Airlines, one of the airlines whose planes were used in the attack, responded quickly with a series of TV ads that featured interviews of United employees renewing their commitment to service. On the one hand, these companies were praised for returning to business as usual; on the other hand, some people criticized both United and the carmakers' efforts as taking advantage of a national tragedy.

There are different types of noise in advertising's external environment. The interference can be technical, such as an unreadable newspaper ad. Noise can also occur in the consumer's environment, as when he or she sees a TV ad in a noisy room. The most common and serious type of external noise in advertising is **clutter**, which means the audience sees an excessive number of commercial messages. Our environment is full of promotional messages that get in

GM used a zero percent financing plan to sell cars after the September 11th terrorist attacks.

the way of an advertiser's intended message. The average American sees an estimated 3,000 advertisements a day. And they are seeing them in increasingly odd places—on stickers on apples and bananas, on sidewalks and rooftops, in the sand at the beach, in full-color, full-sound videos at the ATM, and PC commercials that transfer onto screensavers for computers and personal digital assistants, like Palm Pilot.

Clutter is frustrating for advertisers and agencies (not to mention consumers). The greater the number of ads, the less people pay attention to them. As Jonathan Weber, editor of *The Industry Standard*, explains: "More media choices are making audiences more fragmented, and more advertising is making people numb."[8] When ad industry people use the term *breakthrough advertising*, they mean advertising that is so visible that it breaks through the clutter.

Carfax, an online service that provides histories of used cars, has its own clutter-busting technique. The company places a small ad right in or near the used car classified ads in newspapers. In other words, the idea is to make the ad a part of the consumer's search by placing it in a spot with minimal clutter where the consumer is already focused on the search.

Internal Factors The internal environment includes those personal factors that affect the reception of an advertisement, such as the target audience's needs, purchase history, information-processing abilities, and level of avoidance of advertising in general.

- *Perceived Needs.* Consumers are willing to act to satisfy needs that they recognize. Advertisers use three strategies to stimulate these perceived needs: Create an unknown or unrecognized need (difficult to do), reawaken a need, or offer a solution to a known need (most common approach). The "Women in Politics" campaign attempted to create a need for female candidates, as well as voters' support for them.
- *The Customer's History and Attitudes.* We know that customers who already use a product tend to note and respond more favorably to ads for that product. In contrast, consumers who are loyal to another brand are less likely to pay attention to advertising for a different brand.[9] Advertisers use reminder ads to maintain consumers' awareness of the brand and comparative ads to encourage others to switch.
- *Information Processing.* Short attention spans and low levels of concentration affect the way we process advertising information. The approach we take to make sense of information is not always predictable or thorough. Consider that most people reading a newspaper browse, scan, jump back and forth, and find snippets of useful information in both editorial material and advertisements. When they lose interest, they move on to their own thoughts or some other distraction. Much depends on how relevant the advertising makes the information to the consumer.

One in 10 used cars has a costly, hidden problem.

And someone may be selling it today.

CARFAX
VEHICLE HISTORY REPORTS

A **R.L.** *Company*

We'll give you the real history of any used car. Ask your dealer for a Carfax Vehicle History Report™ or visit
carfax.com

© 2000 Carfax, Inc. *Based on an analysis of vehicles checked by consumers at carfax.com

In contrast to the humor in the TV commercials, the Carfax print ad was more focused on delivering information.

All kinds of creative new media are being used to get people's attention, but they also add to the clutter of endless promotional messages everywhere you go.

- ***Avoidance.*** Advertisers face an increasingly cynical generation of new consumers who are skeptical of sales messages from big corporations. Advertisers compete fiercely for the attention of people who are disinterested, distrustful, and distracted. Research also suggests that some consumers hold a negative attitude toward advertising in general and are unlikely to consider it a viable source of information or entertainment.[10] For example, disabled consumers distrust advertising and are far more likely to use personal information sources, such as friends.[11] This is because few ads speak to the particular needs and wants of the disabled. Advertisers try to deliver their messages through people and sources that have credibility with these audiences.

Message and Media-Mix Factors

The message and media sections in Figure 6.2 are discussed in more detail in the chapters to come—the media mix is the focus of Part III, and the message is the focus of Part IV. Briefly, then, the process of creating an advertising message begins with an analysis of the marketing and advertising strategy and the target audience (as discussed here in Part II) to craft a message strategy. To execute the strategy, the creative team designs the actual ads and produces them.

In terms of the media mix, the ability of a particular advertising message to reach a target audience depends on the effectiveness of the media plan. The media plan outlines the media choices (the media mix) that have the best chance of delivering the advertising message to the right target audience at the right time and place. Advertisers may require a different media mix to reach different target audiences. For example, HBO might use a prime-time commercial about its service when it wants to attract new users. However, when HBO wants to prompt these potential new customers to subscribe to its service, it often uses a direct-mail campaign. Although, a television commercial is good at delivering information to a large number of viewers, direct-mail advertising to a smaller number of serious prospects is better at stimulating a response.

MESSAGE RECEPTION AND RESPONSE

The last two steps in the advertising communication model presented in Figure 6.2 are the receiver's message reception and response, and feedback.[12] The success of an advertisement depends on the target audience receiving and processing it as accurately and completely as the advertiser intended. Figure 6.5 is a model of how this reception process works. It is based on the discussion in Chapter 1 of the four categories of effects—perception, persuasion, learning, and behavior.

So how does advertising work to create a response? This question doesn't have a simple answer, mostly because no two people respond to an advertisement in exactly the same way. Advertising may, however, communicate messages in a number of ways and cause different types of simultaneous responses. For example, at the moment you understand an ad's copy (the learning effect), you may also form an opinion of the advertised product (the persuasion effect).

We will first discuss how advertising meets the challenge of perception. Then we will look at the two responses that typically happen simultaneously: the learning, or cognitive, response and the persuasion (emotion and feeling) response. Finally, we will consider the behavior, or action, response. These three effects are commonly referred to as "Think/Feel/Do" and reflect some pioneering work on planning advertising objectives at the Foot, Cone and Belding (FCB) advertising agency in the 1970s and 1980s. As you can see in Figure 6.5, the think, feel, do model inside the triangle represents how an audience responds to an advertising message once it has been perceived.[13]

Perception: Breaking Through

Perception is when a person notices something, the message has registered; it has broken through the consumer's disinterest and made an impression. As we've said, one of the biggest challenges for advertisers is to get consumers to notice their messages. This is harder than it seems. How many ads did you notice in today's newspaper? On the way to school? On the way to work? Not only do consumers miss most of the messages directed at them, but other messages continuously compete for their attention. The outdoor ad for the Los Angeles Fire Department has stopping power because it is unexpected. Ads have a better chance of being perceived if they're intrusive and original. To understand how this perceptual process works, we look at the steps of exposure, attention, awareness, and interest. These are the communication drivers that we measure in order to track how well the perception process is working.

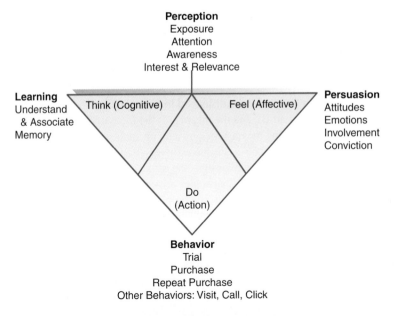

FIGURE 6.5

MESSAGE RECEPTION AND RESPONSE
Even though no two people respond to an advertisement in exactly the same way, there are three general responses ads elicit once perceived.

TH OF JULY.

THERE'S NOTHING COOL ABOUT FIREWORKS.
L.A. CITY FIRE DEPT.

This billboard for the Los Angeles Fire Department is likely to be perceived and get the attention of most people passing it because of its powerful visual pun.

Exposure: Making Contact The first step in perception is exposure. For the advertiser, exposure is mainly a media-buying task. First, the advertiser has to place the message in a medium that the target audience listens to, sees, reads, or watches. Educated, older consumers watch the History Channel, so if those consumers are your target, that's a sound medium for your ad. Exposure is the first and minimum requirement of perception. If your target never sees or hears the advertisement, or if your target skips the page or changes the channel, then no matter how great the message is, it will not be effective.

Attention: Creating Stopping Power Once the audience has been exposed to the message, the next step is to get and keep their attention, which leads to a state of awareness. Attention means that the mind is engaged; it is focusing on something. A trigger, something that catches the target's interest, arouses attention. It can be something in the message or something within the readers or viewers that makes them lock onto a particular message. In print it may be a sale price in large type, a startling illustration, or a strong headline. On television the trigger may be sound effects, music, an action-oriented or visually interesting scene, or a captivating idea. Snickers gets young male sports enthusiasts' attention through humor and celebrity athletes.

Special promotions such as events and all the hoopla surrounding them offer great opportunities for attention-getting impact. Inflatable characters, such as the huge lobster on top of a truck for Red Lobster, are used, because they have such high stopping power. (See www.redlobster.com.)

Clawde, Red Lobster's crustacean cruiser, tours the country and makes appearances at events that offer an opportunity for brand visibility.

A new battleground for attention is the desktop—computer desktop, that is. A number of e-companies, such as Real Networks and EntryPoint, have developed desktop assistants—toolbars or little windows that sit on the computer screen—that offer one-click access to personal files or favorite Web sites. On these desktop assistants, the advertiser pays for the space on the toolbars. So while computer users are surfing the Web or composing notes, advertisers hope to divert their attention to an ad on the toolbar.

The advertising message can and must compete with other messages in the same medium. Within a news medium, the advertising has to be able to compete with the intrinsically interesting nature of the news. In an entertainment medium such as television, the advertising has to compete with the entertainment values of movies and shows. Radio is almost always a background medium, so advertisers compete for the attention of listeners who are driving, mowing the lawn, cleaning the house, or doing some other activity. Outdoor advertising is directed toward an audience whose attention, by definition, is directed elsewhere. Not only does outdoor advertising have to compete for attention, it also has to be able to win out over distractions such as other signs along the road, the car radio, and conversation among passengers.

If the objective is simply a brand or product reminder, then the attention level doesn't need to be as high as it does when the objective calls for the understanding of a copy point. A poor return on attention, or ROA (similar to ROI or return on investment), is what some

A MATTER OF PRACTICE

UNCOVERING THE REAL HISTORY OF A USED CAR

➤ It's the age-old problem when you buy a used car—do you trust the salesperson? Do you actually believe that old line that the car's previous owner was an old woman who only drove it to church on Sundays? Overcoming these negative perceptions is a challenge for the used car industry. So use a Vehicle History Report. What's that? By Carfax. Who's that?

Even though Carfax has been providing information about used cars to car dealers nationwide for more than 14 years, few consumers knew about the product or recognized the company name. The Carfax hard-hitting campaign created by the Martin Agency of Richmond, Virginia, won first place in the John Caples International Awards, as well as an EFFIE award. The campaign took direct aim at this lack of awareness and the negative perceptions of the used-car buying experience.

Considering that 43 million used cars are bought and sold annually, there's a big market for such a service. Carfax uses 450 data sources, such as motor vehicle departments and accident reports.

The campaign's slogan told the Carfax story: "With Carfax, you'll know the real history on any used car." The campaign plays off the basic human emotion of fear, says Hal Tench, the campaign's creative director. "When you buy a used car," he explains, "you are scared to death. Rather than dialing up fear in a haunting way, we tried to lighten it up and make it acceptable."

The campaign used a series of simple but humorous commercials that show all the crazy things that owners do to their cars. They highlight the trust problem—maybe that dear old grandma hit the garage or the tree every time she got

behind the wheel. Maybe a wild man drove it backwards to roll back the odometer. There's even a commercial where the man in the passenger seat of a pickup whines, "You don't pay attention to what I say." When you see the driver, it's a dog, and he isn't listening because he's chasing a flock of ducks through a pond with the truck.

In addition to the commercials, the campaign also used small black and white ads placed in the used-car classified ads in local newspapers. These ads, which are right under the noses of prospective buyers, reminded them that "One in ten cars has a costly hidden problem. And someone may be selling it today." So, the company is selling security—to make sure you're not the poor sucker who buys the lemon.

Overall, the campaign was very effective proving that security sells in the used-automotive market. The campaign drew in numbers that surpassed awareness, visitor, and sales projections.

POINT TO PONDER

The Carfax ads were designed to get attention and overcome negative impressions. Explain how they worked to accomplish those objectives.

Sources: 2001 EFFIES Brief provided by Carfax (www.carfax.com) and the Martin Agency (www.martinagency.com); Theresa Howard, "Cautious Used Car Buyers Trust Carfax," *USA Today* (August 20, 2001): 5; "XXIII John Caples International Awards Winners," *Direct Marketing* (April 2001): 26; EFFIE Awards, www.effie.org/award_winners

Internet marketers criticize when viewers click on a Web site and find nothing there that gets their attention.[14] This could be because of poor design but it could also be because the information that is there is boring. In such a situation, attention is obtained by providing relevance, interesting information, and personal involvement.

Awareness: Making an Impression Once a message has been perceived and has caught the attention of consumers, their perceptual process moves to the next step, which is awareness of the brand message. **Awareness** means that the message has made an impression on the consumer, and the consumer can identify the advertiser. When you ask someone what comes to mind when he thinks of soap, and he responds "Ivory," then that brand has *top-of-mind awareness* for that person.

Although awareness of the advertising comes first, that is not the ultimate objective. As far as the advertiser is concerned, the ultimate objective is awareness of the brand, not the advertisement. Being aware means that the receiver of the message has an impression of something. Sometimes we refer to this as a perception. For example, the "Women in Politics" ads were trying to overcome the perception that politics in Iceland is mostly for men. Perceptions can be negative and overturning those negative perceptions also can be an objective of an advertising campaign, as the "A Matter of Practice" box illustrates.

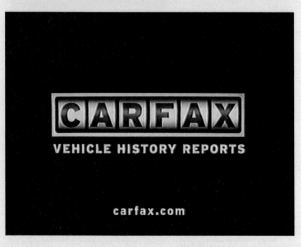

Awareness can evolve through public opinion, just as consumer trends catch the attention of the public. One product that has had a huge launch into the market is the push scooter, which achieved a high level of awareness without doing much advertising. Awareness of the Razor scooter soared, for example, because it was used by popular teenagers who influenced other teens' buying patterns. This trendiness sold the product. Later entries, like Huffy, have had to use carefully developed marketing and advertising plans to build awareness in this market. Huffy launched its Micro plush scooter in 2000 with a $3 million print campaign that paired its scooters with its extreme sport bicycles.

Interest and Relevance: Creating Pulling Power After awareness, the next step in the perception process is interest. **Interest** provides the pulling power of an advertisement; it keeps people tuned in to the message. One of the most important drivers of interest is personal relevance.

People are interested in many things. You might be interested in the product advertised or in some element in the ad itself—the model or the star, the promise made in the headline or by the announcer, or an unusual graphic. Different topics, product categories, and specific products have varying levels of built-in interest. Some products are just inherently more interesting than others. Food and vacations are more interesting to most people than are toilet brushes.

People will pay attention to advertising only if it's relevant to them. They make a deal with the advertiser: "Make it worth my time and I'll pay attention to your message as long as it doesn't bore me." Say you are planning a trip. A message that applies to travel has personal relevance to you. Most people also resonate to general human-interest topics that strike some universal chord, such as babies, kittens, puppies, tragedies, and success stories.

One goal of public relations or publicity campaigns is to create **buzz**, which, as was discussed in Chapter 5, means people are interested enough in something—a celebrity, a new product like the Razor—to talk about it among themselves. That was one of the primary objectives of the "Women in Politics" campaign. The message designers knew they had to get opinion leaders talking about the campaign for its message to have impact.

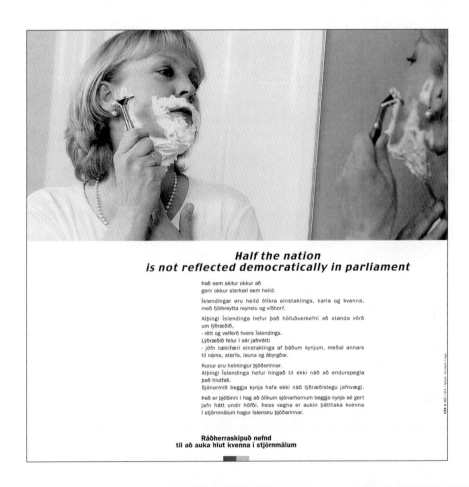

The "Women in Politics" campaign from Iceland used some interesting visuals to deliver its message about gender roles in politics.

Interest is a momentary thing; it dies easily as attention shifts. A major advertising challenge is to maintain interest until the point of the message is reached. In Web advertising, designers work to create "stickiness" for their sites, which means people will stay on the site and navigate through its pages. For Web marketers, attracting people to a site is one thing but keeping them is a different type of problem. Table 6.1 is a list of the "stickiest" sites from *Brandweek*.

Learning: Making It Clear

The second major category of effects is learning, which we introduced in Chapter 4 as a factor in consumer behavior. We discuss it here because it is also an important factor in how people receive advertising messages. There are two types of learning that are particularly important to advertising: cognitive learning, which refers to understanding, and classical conditioning, which explains how association works.

Cognitive Learning: Creating Understanding When we say **cognitive learning**, we mean that most advertisers want people to know something new after they have read, watched, or heard the message. Some campaigns' objectives are to specifically increase understanding. For example, city leaders and educators in Santa Ana, California, wanted to encourage reading and promote literacy among their diverse residents, which included a number of immigrants who lack fluency in English. The objective of the educational campaign was for residents to understand that reading is the basis of all learning and, further, that learning leads to academic success and greater earning power.

In the case of new products, advertisers try to get consumers to understand how to recognize and use the product. For an existing product, learning about new features or benefits may be the goal for the consumer, as well as the advertiser. The Carfax campaign, for example, told why its service was necessary ("One in 10 cars has a costly, hidden problem") and how to use it ("Ask your dealer for a Carfax Vehicle History Report™, or visit carfax.com").

Understanding is a conscious mental effort to make sense of information. Although perception can be a passive process, understanding demands an active response from consumers. First, we find ourselves interested, then we learn something about the subject of our interest, and then we file it away in our memories. That series of steps is also called cognition, or a cognitive response to information. Even though the "Women in Politics" campaign was designed to get attention with unexpected and funny visuals, the ads still told a story that demanded understanding. They wanted people to understand that using 100 percent of Iceland's talent would profit the country as a whole, more than using 50 percent.

Understanding is particularly important for ads that present a lot of information (brand, price, size, how the product works, when and where to use it). When product differences exist between competitive products, the features and how they translate into selling points are also important pieces of information. Informational advertising, advertising that contains a large amount of product information, requires clear and relevant explanation. Consumers have little patience for ads that are confusing, vague, or unfocused. The reader or viewer must be able to follow the logic, make choices, compare points of view, comprehend reasons and arguments, synthesize and organize facts, and, in general, make "cognitive" sense of things.

Conditioned Learning: Creating Associations Another way to learn something is to make a connection in your mind. The process of making connections and linking ideas, called **association**, is particularly important to how advertising works.[15] When you associate two concepts (fall and football, or Coca-Cola and refreshment, for example) you have learned something.

Advertisements use association to try to get consumers to link the product with something they aspire to, respect, value, or appreciate, such as a personality or type of person, a pleasant experience or situation, or a specific lifestyle. A Polo/Ralph Lauren ad uses a photo of the company president himself in a heavy knit sweater with an American flag design to associate his upscale clothing and home products with patriotism, following the World Trade Center attacks. The hope is that consumers who value this patriotic response will buy Ralph Lauren's products.

Association is at the heart of **conditional learning**. In classical conditioning, repeated exposure to a stimulus leads to a reward until people learn to connect that stimulus with the

TABLE 6.1	**Sticking around Web Sites**
Automotive	carpoint.msn.com
	kbb.com
	autotrader.com
	cars.com
	autoweb.com
Shopping	amazon.com
	eBay.com
	barnesandnoble.com
	priceline.com
	cdnow.com
Travel	mapquest.com
	maps.yahoo.com
	travelocity.com
	expedia.com
	travel.yahoo.com
Entertainment	disneygo.com
	windowsmedia.com
	uproar.com
	ticketmaster.com
	webshots.com
Financial	Finance.yahoo.com
	marketwatch.com
	moneycentral.msn.com
	etrade.com
	quicken.com

Adapted from "Sticking Around," *Brandweek's IQ Interactive Report*, June 15, 2000, p. IQ66.

The humorous ads designed for the "Women in Politics" campaign in Iceland also had an educational message as they created "buzz" about the idea of supporting more women candidates.

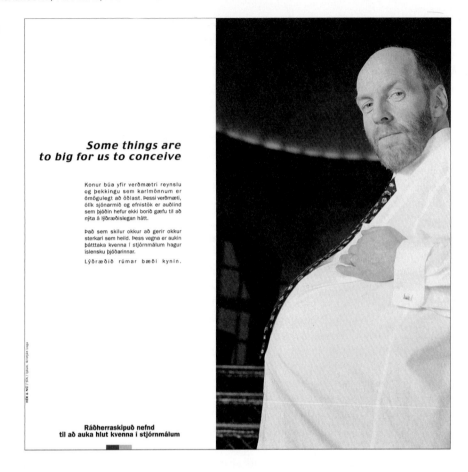

reward. The famous Pavlovian example is the dog that learns to salivate at the sound of a bell, after a researcher has repeatedly paired the sight of the food with the sound of the bell. The dog has learned, through conditioning, that the bell is associated with food. By repeating certain visuals as cues, teenagers having fun is associated with Mountain Dew and protecting a baby is associated with Michelin tires. Mountain Dew then offers a fun time as its reward and Michelin offers a reward of protection for a precious cargo.

Memorability: Locking Power Ads that work effectively, such as the funny Icelandic politics commercials, are not only engaging, they also have **locking power**—that is, they lock their messages into the mind once they have been learned. If consumers can't remember seeing the ad, or if they can remember the ad but not the brand, as in the Energizer bunny example, then as far as the advertiser is concerned, they might as well not have seen it. So advertisers study how our memories work, to understand how better to anchor their messages in the minds of their target audiences.

Our memories are like filing cabinets. We watch a commercial, retain the parts that interest us, and then find a category in our mental filing cabinet where we can store that fragment of information. Suppose we see a commercial for a soft drink and unconsciously extract certain information from it. We may then file it away as a fragment that contains a brand label and a situation with people drinking a soft drink. The fragment, incidentally, may not look much like the original information we saw or heard because our minds will change it to fit our own concerns, preoccupations, and preconceptions.

A week later you may not remember where or even if you have a fragment labeled "soft drink" filed away because most of us have messy mental filing systems. However, the information may resurface when a cue triggers the memory. Maybe you remember a party planned for the weekend and that reminds you about the soft drink. A cue pulls fragments out of the file so that they become topmost in our minds.

Advertising focuses on two types of memory: recognition and recall. **Recognition** means that a person can remember having seen something before. In the period before the dot-com crash in 2000 and 2001, one of the main objectives of new startup Web companies was to build name, or brand, recognition. All these companies were new so they spent a tremendous amount of money, including expensive Super Bowl ads, to create some minimal brand name recognition. Some experts say these extravagant expenditures, which could have been as high as $7 to $10 billion in 2000, may have contributed to the crash.[16]

It is more difficult for an advertiser to get consumers to recall something in an ad than it is to get consumers to recognize something they have seen in an ad. With recall you not only remember having seen something before, but you also can remember the information in the message. You can either remember it all by yourself, called **unaided recall**, or you can remember it after seeing a cue, which is called **aided recall**. Unaided recall is harder to achieve than aided recall and both are harder to produce than recognition.

Persuasion: Changing Attitudes

In addition to providing information and creating associations, advertisements can use **persuasion** to encourage people to believe or feel something—the next category of message responses in Figure 6.5. A persuasive message tries to establish, reinforce, or change an attitude, touch an emotion, or anchor a conviction firmly in the potential customer's belief structure.

Arguments, the reasons behind a statement or claim, are particularly important in persuasive communication. Argument in this sense is not disagreement, but a line of reasoning in which one point follows from another, leading to a logical conclusion. Ads often focus on logic and proof when trying to persuade us to buy a product. Other motivations, such as saving money or getting a good deal, are addressed by sales promotion and advertising that focuses on sale prices. The Häagen-Dazs ads gave consumers permission to indulge, thus arguing against the guilt people might feel about eating the rich ice cream and, in this case, not sharing it.

Attitudes and Opinions: Affecting Beliefs Every person has unique attitudes and opinions based on individual experiences. Attitudes are underlying beliefs; opinions are the expression of these attitudes. Advertising that seeks to persuade us by addressing our attitudes usually attempts to accomplish one of three things:

- Establish a new opinion where none has existed before
- Reinforce an existing opinion
- Change an existing opinion

Advertisers know that consumers establish opinions of new products. Consumers modify or confirm their opinions about the product as they use it. No matter how strong the advertising, a bad experience with a product negates all the positive attitudes the advertising message implanted. To win back customers, advertisers have to work harder to change their attitudes toward the product. They do this by offering samples that persuade people to try again and by using celebrities and experts whose opinions people trust to convince them to give the product another try.

Preference for a brand, which advertisers evaluate through "intend-to-buy" responses, is an attitude that advertisers try to elicit from consumers because preference leads to loyalty. Preference means that someone who has received a promotional message wants to try or buy the product. To encourage consumers to prefer its products, Waldenbooks launched a Web site for "preferred readers" (www.preferredreader.com). One of the longest-running retail reward or loyalty programs with a membership in the millions, the site allows users to sign up for e-mail so they can receive advance notice of special in-store promotions and book releases.

One technique that advertisers use to intensify preference is to associate a product with aspirations using campaign ideas that resonate with people's self-identity, which is particularly important for campaigns directed at ethnic groups. For example, Coca-Cola has reached African American audiences by featuring yet-undiscovered black musical artists such as Tyrese and Ja Rule before they hit the big time. Marketing consultant Chris Rooney explains that by leveraging aspirational marketing with an ethnic twist, companies can create strong brand preferences.[17]

Emotions: Affecting Feelings Influencing attitudes and opinions is not the only means of persuasion. Emotions persuade, too. How someone feels about the product, service, brand, or company, whether they like it, may be just as important as what that person knows about it. These feelings may be buried deep beneath the logical reasons people give for making a purchase. The Häagen-Dazs campaign played on our emotions by telling us it's okay to enjoy pleasure and indulge in ice cream.

Advertisers that touch people's emotions with their messages have greater success in getting consumers to remember that message. Telephone and greeting-card companies have succeeded with emotional campaigns because they are selling sentiment—warm feelings, love, missing someone, nostalgia. Insurance companies sell their products using fear or pride in careful planning. Sex is used to sell perfume and cosmetics and, sometimes, inappropriately to sell unrelated products such as auto parts. Even drug manufacturers are moving away from narrow, scientific product claims. Viagra, for example, broke the mold for prescription drugs by making its ads emotionally engaging.

Involvement: Creating Engagement People can become emotionally involved in a message, which is a common persuasion device. **Involvement** is the intensity of the consumer's engagement with a message, the brand (you may be more engaged in buying certain brands, such as clothes, than others), or the medium (television is thought to be more engaging than newspapers).

Getting people involved in completing a message or participating in its development is another way advertisers engage consumers. Advertisers do this by asking questions, sparking curiosity, or using ambiguity to tease people into filling in the blanks in an interesting message with their own personal interpretations. Compelling readers or viewers to get involved in developing the message creates more personal impact through a psychological principle called **closure**. For example, the "Bud" . . . "Weis" . . . "Er" frog croaks demanded that the audience put the sounds together to get closure by creating the familiar brand name.

Sometimes the involvement is physical, as in a taste test in a grocery store or sampling as part of event marketing. Such promotional tools are particularly good at intensifying feelings of engagement through participation. Both techniques were used in the Häagen-Dazs campaign to involve people with the brand and create buzz. For example, samples of the ice cream were offered at several events hosted by epicurean magazines.

The concept of involvement is the foundation for a common theory of persuasion that says people process information differently for products and messages that involve (or don't involve) them.[18] You may have heard the phrases **low involvement** and **high involvement** used to refer to products, purchasing situations, and advertisements. High involvement means that a product (or information about it) is important and personally relevant. Low involvement means that the product or information is perceived as unimportant. The level of involvement determines how much or whether a consumer needs to learn and understand something about a product.

Typically, people in a high-involvement situation—such as purchasing a new car, home, or vacation—will be searching for information and evaluating it critically, a state of mind referred to as **central processing**. Advertising for high-involvement products usually provides a lot of information about the product. In contrast, we make low-involvement purchases, such as chewing gum, toothpaste, and paper towels, without much searching and with little effort to think critically about the decision. Advertising for this type of product often focuses on catchy slogans, brand reminder cues, celebrities, or distinctive graphic imagery. In contrast to central processing, this is referred to as **peripheral processing** because the decision factors are not particularly related to the product or its selling points—it's like buying wine because you like the label design.

Conviction: Creating Certainty The result of persuasion, particularly persuasion through central processing, is conviction. A **conviction** is a particularly strong belief, such as that which drives national allegiance and religious fervor. Attitudes, reasons, logic, and emotion are all part of the persuasive package that leads to belief. We believe something about every product we purchase; if we didn't, we wouldn't buy it. We believe it is good for us, will make us look better or live better, will make us healthier—or simply that it will satisfy our needs and desires. Even low-involvement products such as chewing gum entail some beliefs on our part, perhaps that this gum will taste better, freshen breath, or do less damage to teeth than other brands. When you believe such an idea strongly enough, then you tend to buy the same brand of gum over and over.

The award-winning Carfax campaign, for example, tried to change consumers' negative beliefs about buying used cars and convince consumers that there is a way to get reliable information about the history of a used car. If the message worked, then consumers would become convinced that, with the help of Carfax, they can make a sound decision in a risky area.

For many people, seeing is believing, so a product demonstration tends to remove doubt and increase consumer belief and conviction in the sales message. For example, in order to convince consumers of the water-saving innovations of its Neptune washer and dryer, Maytag replaced all the washers in a Boston apartment building with the Neptune model. The company then monitored the building's water savings in this metro area, which is recognized as having the highest water costs in the nation. The results of the demonstration proved its advertising claim that the new Neptune design saved water, which led to a convincing competitive advantage.

Believability is an extremely important concept in advertising and other forms of marketing communication. Do consumers believe the advertising claims? Do spokespeople, particularly authority figures, have credibility? Because consumers say they do not believe advertising claims, another tool used in an IMC campaign to build conviction is public relations. Because of the credibility of news stories, publicity can provide important support to an advertising message, so a news story about the Neptune water-saving demonstration would have more believability than an ad by the company.

Action: Motivating Behavior

The fourth category of response to advertising depicted in Figure 6.5 is action. Advertisers hope that their advertising will lead to some behavior, such as trying, sampling, or buying a product, which could lead to increased sales. The first step is trial, which permits a consumer to experience the brand and decide if it's worth a purchase or repurchase. Although it is often difficult to prove that the advertising led to an increase in sales (because there are other marketing and situational factors that might have contributed to the increase), most advertisers still hope to see that result. The objectives for the EFFIE-winning Lake Wales Florida orange juice campaign, which is featured in the "A Matter of Principle" box, were focused primarily on sales.

One strategy for increasing sales is to increase the usage level by giving people reasons for buying more than they normally would. The outcome of the Häagen-Dazs campaign was just that—an increase in sales because more people found more reasons to buy, and eat, the ice cream. In addition to purchase, an advertisement may also focus on increasing usage, such as the Campbell's Soup recipe ads in women's magazines that show homemakers new ways to use soup, thereby increasing the amount of soup they use.

There are other behaviors that might be the subject of advertising objectives. For example, ads may try to get people to send back cards, redeem coupons, enter contests, visit showrooms, take a test ride, phone the company, or visit the company's Web site. These are all behaviors that indicate a response to an advertising message, a response that may lead to purchase. In some cases, such as the "Drug-free America" campaign and anti-teen smoking campaigns, the ads may be designed to stop or prevent a behavior.

Ultimately, most marketers strive to get customers to repurchase their products regularly. The goal is to build strong brand loyalty, which is best measured by repeat behavior (note Figure 6.5 again). Customers become loyal to companies and brands that are known for their product quality, innovative initiatives, and market leadership. But hard-won loyalty can disappear in a blink when disaster strikes. For example, in 1997, UPS employees went on strike. The strike caused an almost immediate drop in customer loyalty. Both UPS's reputation within the financial community and its credit rating suffered. Some experts believe the company lost 5 to 20 percent of its business that it will never recover. Its campaign to restore its brand and reputation has cost millions of dollars.[19]

Web-based promotion is another tool that advertisers believe can nurture brand loyalty, particularly with high-involvement products such as cosmetics or music. The trick, they say, is to entertain customers on their web site while informing them about the brand or product. For example, to promote a new line of Physique hair care products, Procter & Gamble's Physique advertisements sent consumers to Physique.com to learn about the product, get

A MATTER OF PRINCIPLE

IT'S NATURAL IN FLORIDA

➤ Lake Wales is a real place in Florida and the people featured in the Lake Wales ads for Florida's Natural® brand orange juice are real, too—not actors, but growers. The ads' stars are members of a co-op that makes up the company behind the Florida's Natural brand of orange juice. And they care a lot about how their oranges are used to make juice—not concentrate—but real orange juice.

That's the logic behind the strategy Atlanta's West-Wayne agency used that led to an EFFIE-winning campaign, which was designed to increase sales of the brand as well as increase the brand's share of the orange juice market. The co-op was up against some big brand names, such as Tropicana® and Minute Maid®, and the effort was complicated by a flat orange juice market.

The core message was that the growers own the land, they own the trees, and they own the company. It is their level of involvement in the juice-making process that suggests they know the perfect time to pick the fruit. The WestWayne creative team believed that this was a message that the target audience—women who care about purchasing quality products for their families—would appreciate.

To express the idea of pride and care, the campaign created a sense of place, the hometown of Lake Wales, Florida, with its small-town values, pace, and way of life. The campaign featured its residents and local sites in the commercials. The message is conveyed with a line in the commercial saying that the growers "take all the time we need to make our juice just right."

But it's not all just homey images; there is also a touch of humor implied in the unwritten rules that the growers have concerning their groves, such as "always brake for alligators."

The "Lake Wales" campaign was effective and delivered results in excess of 200 percent in three key measurements: cases sold, market share, and volume growth. The cases sold increased by 230 percent; the share of market figure increased by 200 percent; and the volume growth—in comparison with the not-from-concentrate (NFC) category growth—was 201 percent. So, the brand actually grew more than the NFC market segment.

The local hometown theme was successful in illustrating the point-of-difference in Florida's Natural juice. The pride and care of the co-op owners contributed to sales results that were double those of the campaign's objectives.

POINT TO PONDER

This campaign for Florida's Natural® orange juice won an EFFIE award for its effectiveness. Explain how the ads work and why they are considered effective.

Source: Adapted from the 2001 EFFIE Brief provided by Florida's Natural Growers and WestWayne, Inc.

free samples, and locate retailers who carry it. But the important loyalty factor was moving more than 600,000 of the 5 million visitors to the site during the product launch to spend nine minutes on the site per visit, an indication that they were highly involved with the brand.[20]

Feedback

In addition to the various types of responses to a message, there are other forms of feedback that are used to determine if the advertising is effective. Feedback to an advertisement, because it is primarily one-way communication, is often delayed or incomplete. This is the problem Regis McKenna referred to when he said that ads should open a dialogue with consumers.

Consequently, there is a need for more structured research efforts to determine if the message truly achieved its objectives. Objectives are meaningless if they are not measurable as stated. Evaluative research, as you read in Chapter 5, measures the effectiveness of the advertising.

HOW BRANDS WORK

Brand personalities and brand images create a feeling of familiarity with a known product. Because the brand is familiar, consumers feel comfortable or even pleased to buy it again. **Branding**, the process of creating a unique identity for a product, is the secret behind the phenomenal success of Levi's and Coke over the years. The jeans maker and soft-drink producer have familiar and comfortable images, and consumers know from experience that they offer dependable quality at a reasonable price. Branding creates memorability, but it also establishes preferences, habits, and loyalties. In short, it encourages a relationship between a brand and its user.

The secret ingredient in branding is trust. A brand promises that the product will deliver the same satisfactory performance as it has in the past. In that sense, as Jacques Chevron, a brand consultant, explains, "the brand is a covenant with the consumer, a promise that the brand and the products it names will conform to the expectations that have been created over time."

Branding is particularly important for parity products, those for which there are few if any major differences in features. Salt is an example of a parity product. The products are undifferentiated in the marketplace, but through the development of a brand image, they are differentiated in the minds of their users. What image comes to mind when you think of Morton Salt? What enhances the difference between one type of salt and another is advertising. Advertising can establish a personality for the product. Personality is important both in positioning a brand and in developing a brand image.

Salt is a product that requires a brand image to add perceived value and develop a relationship with the consumer.

Brand Image

Northwestern University Professor Sid Levy coined the term "brand image" for a *Harvard Business Review* article in 1955. The article defined it as "the sets of ideas, feelings and attitudes that consumers have about brands." It is an image in customers' minds that reflects what they think and feel about a product—how they value it. Brand personality—the idea that a product takes on familiar human characteristics, such as friendliness, trustworthiness, or snobbery—is an important part of an image. Levy and his colleagues at the SRI research center in Chicago found that a product's personality could be just as important as performance or price.

A brand, then, has both physical and psychological dimensions. The physical dimension consists of the attributes, ingredients, and design of the product itself, as well as the design of the package or logo: the letters, shapes, art, and colors that advertisers use to define the graphics of the image. In contrast, the psychological side includes the emotions, beliefs, values, and personalities that people ascribe to the product. For example, when we talk about the brand image of Hershey's, we are talking about the chocolate itself (the physical side), and also about the distinctive brown package, the lettering of the name, as well as the multitude of impressions and values (the psychological side) conveyed by its slogan "the all-American candy bar."

The tools used to transform products and lock brands into memory include distinctive names, slogans, graphics, and characters (such as the Maytag repairman or the Pillsbury Doughboy). All these tools, which are elements in brand advertising, convey subtle yet complex meanings about the products' values and benefits, in addition to serving as identity cues.

Brand Relationships

Advertisers also try to establish their brands as having special relationships with customers and other key stakeholders. McKenna asks, "What is a brand but a special relationship?"[21] People have unique relationships with the brands they buy and use regularly and this is what makes them brand loyal. The richness of the brand image determines the quality of the relationship and the emotional connections that link a customer to a brand. An example of a brand relationship is the bond that Apple (computers) has established with its customers. The slogan, "The computer for the rest of us," contributes to an extreme level of loyalty on the part of Macintosh users. The company's advertising focuses on the computer's creative applications as well as its colorful design. The image of this brand—not to mention the quality of the product—has created strong emotional bonds in a high-tech category that seldom comes across as such in computer advertising.

A brand is also a promise. Because it seeks to establish a familiar image, a brand creates an expectation level based on familiarity, consistency, and predictability. Green Giant, for example, built its franchise on the personality of the friendly giant who watches over his valley and makes sure that Green Giant vegetables are fresh, tasty, and nutritious. The name "Green Giant" on the package means there are no unexpected and unwanted surprises when you buy a Green Giant product. This accumulated reservoir of goodwill and good impressions is called **brand equity**, which we talk about next.

Brand Equity

Branding can transform a product and make it more valuable because of the respect that has been created for the brand name. In that sense, branding has a financial impact that can show up on a company's balance sheet. Successful brands can be bought and sold based on the value of their brand equity.

In 1988, when U.K.-based GrandMet acquired Pillsbury, it was estimated that 88 percent of the $1 billion it paid consisted of "goodwill," which is how accountants assess the intangible value of brands, most of which is built up through the brand's advertising. More recently, Volkswagon paid $780 million for the assets of Rolls Royce, but BMW bought the Rolls Royce trademark for $65 million. Many analysts believe BMW got the better deal.

Researchers can now decipher not only how much a brand's image is worth, but also how much the value of the brand affects other marketing considerations such as pricing. If the brand's appeal goes up, the company can raise the price. Harley-Davidson, which has one of the world's strongest brand images, prices its motorcycles at around $18,000. Its Japanese competitors run about $6,000, which gives Harley a triple-the-price bonus because of the power of its brand.

IT'S A WRAP

INFORM OR ENTERTAIN?

The debate about effectiveness tends to center on the how ads move people to make purchase decisions—whether the ads should be primarily hard sell with an emphasis on facts and offers or whether they should entertain in order to engage people's emotions and interests.

The debate arises from a basic disagreement about what the role of advertising is, says Bob Kuperman, president and CEO of TBWA Chiat/Day North America, a shop passionately on the side of creative ads that move people emotionally. As Kuperman sees it, one side says you must sell, and that you do that by giving consumers just the facts; as the other side holds that you have to build an emotional bond between consumers and brands that goes beyond product attributes.

Some ads, like those for Häagen-Dazs or the Icelandic "Women in Politics" campaign, deliver consumer responses by entertaining their audiences. However, that's not the only route to persuasion. A person preparing a grocery list is not very interested in clever supermarket advertising; she simply wants to know which products are on sale. Although both approaches can be effective, a campaign can also deliver information and entertain, as the Florida's Natural and Carfax campaigns demonstrated.

The EFFIE award–winning campaign for Häagen-Dazs was clearly designed to build an emotional bond between the ice cream and its customers. The objective of the campaign was to protect the brand from competitive inroads; however, the results were far more dramatic. Sales grew by 20 percent and brand awareness grew from 57 percent to 82 percent after the campaign. Growth of the brand's awareness outpaced all its competitors during the same time frame.

The perception of the brand also improved. Despite a shift from advertising focused on product features to a user-focused campaign, the brand's intrinsic attributes (smooth, rich, creamy) also became a more important part of the Häagen-Dazs brand image. In other words, the target audience not only took ownership of the brand experience; it also better understood the characteristics of premium ice cream and made that association with the Häagen-Dazs brand.

What made this Häagen-Dazs campaign so effective? The results indicated that it worked on both levels—it was emotionally engaging and yet it also strengthened the brand's associations with the attributes of premium ice cream. It more than met its objectives by unleashing the power of the brand experience and by involving its customers in an emotionally engaging way. But advertising can only meet its objectives if its creators understand how it works—or doesn't work—in various situations with various types of audiences.

Summary

1. **What are the components of a basic communication model and how does it differ from an interactive model of communication?** A basic communication model identifies the primary roles in a communication situation—source, message, channel, noise, receiver, and feedback or response. The interactive communication situation identifies similar roles; however, the process of communication goes back and forth with the source and receiver changing roles. The source may send a message to a receiver who then becomes a source when that person sends a message back to the original source, who is now the receiver.

2. **Explain how the advertising communication model works.** Similar to a basic communication model—source, message, channel, noise, receiver, and feedback or response—the advertising communication model begins with an advertiser (the source) who, with the agency, sets the objectives. Then there are the message and media factors whose planning is surrounded by external and internal factors. The message reception step is a complex process based on the kinds of effects that advertising creates in the receiver or target audi-ence. The last step in the message reception process is the response step, which can take a variety of different forms.

3. **Outline the Message Reception and Response process.** The message reception process begins with perception and then moves through the think, feel, do categories of effects. Each of these four main categories of effects has specific types of responses associated with it. The responses that lead to percep-tion include exposure, attention, interest, and memory. There are two types of learning effects: understanding, or cognitive learning, and images and associations, or conditioned learning. Persuasion is concerned with attitudes, emotions, involvement, and conviction. Finally, the behavioral response is driven by trial, purchase, repeat purchase, and other actions.

4. **Summarize the key factors in brand communication.** Brand communication focuses on brand image, which is a mental image in the minds of consumers that reflects what they think about a brand; brand relationships, which are the ways in which people connect emotionally with a brand; and brand equity, which is the value that a brand adds to a product.

Key Terms

aided recall, p. 171
association, p. 169
awareness, p. 167
brand equity, p. 176
branding, p. 175
buzz, p. 168
central processing, p. 172
closure, p. 172

clutter, p. 161
cognitive learning, p. 169
conditional learning, p. 169
conviction, p. 172
customer-focused marketing, p. 158
high involvement, p. 172
impact, p. 154

interest, p. 168
involvement, p. 172
locking power, p. 170
low involvement, p. 172
media mix, p. 157
noise, p. 161
peripheral processing, p. 172

persuasion, p. 171
recognition, p. 170
source credibility, p. 161
unaided recall, p. 171
understanding, p. 169

Questions

1. Explain the basic communication process outlined the SMCR model and differentiate it from the interactive communication process. Why is it important for advertisers to understand how the interactive communication model works?

2. What is noise and how does it affect advertising?

3. What are the four categories of effects that drive the message reception and response process?

4. What is breakthrough advertising? Give an example and explain how it works.

5. This chapter identifies four major categories of responses. Find an ad that you think is effective and explain how it works, analyzing the way it cultivates responses in these four categories.

6. What do you think makes an effective ad? One that creates an emotional bond with consumers or one that is designed to inform about the product's unique benefit? Or do you have another definition and explanation?

7. Explain the difference between brand image, brand relationships, and brand equity.

8. Uma Proctor is a planner in an agency that handles a liquid detergent brand that competes with Lever's Wisk. Suma is reviewing a history of the Wisk theme, "Ring around the Collar." It is one of the longest-running themes on television, and Wisk's sales share indicates that it has been successful. What is confusing Uma is that the Wisk history includes numerous consumer surveys that show consumers find "ring around the collar" to be a boring, silly, and altogether an irritating advertising theme. Can you explain why Wisk is such a popular brand even though its advertising campaign has been so disliked?

Suggested Class Project

From current magazines, identify five advertisements that have exceptionally high stopping power, five that have exceptionally high pulling power, and five that have exceptionally high locking power. Which of these advertisements are mainly information and which are mainly emotional and focused on feelings? How do the informational advertisements differ from the emotional advertisements in their strategy and design?

Suggested Internet Class Project

Organize the class into five teams and refer to the "sticky" Web sites listed in Table 6.1 (p. 169). Each team should take one of the five categories of Web sites. Check out those sites that don't require you to subscribe and analyze them in terms of the four categories of effectiveness: perception, learning, persuasion, and behavior. Can you determine from this analysis why these sites are "sticky" Web sites? Which one does your team rate as the most effective? Why?

Hallmark BUILD·A·CAMPAIGN Projects

Please review the Hallmark Case Appendix at the end of the text before responding to these questions.

1. Explain how altering the Hallmark slogan from "When You Care Enough to Send the Very Best . . ." to "When You Care Enough to Send the Very Best . . . *Send a Hallmark*" helps to accomplish the goal of brand insistence. Are there any negative effects this tactic might have?

2. How might a Hallmark Gold Crown Store establish customer loyalty for the local store by building on the brand insistence campaign for Hallmark? Explain your ideas in writing, to be used as part of the campaign plan you will be developing.

HANDS-ON

Case 6

A LITTLE STOPPING POWER

How did the stodgy John Hancock company turn around its image and who's to blame?

For over a century, the company favored modest promotions that didn't even live up to the flair of its corporate namesake, well-known for his prominent signature on the Declaration of Independence. Today, the thirteenth-largest insurer with $61 billion in assets is easily recognized by award-winning ads produced by the Hill Holliday agency of Boston.

Who's to blame is David D'Alessandro, a gutsy guy who recently became chairman of John Hancock's Financial Services. D'Alessandro, who entered the company as vice president of corporate communication in 1984, knew that the key to building a new image and increasing sales would be in creating lasting impressions and attracting new segments. (The company's existing segment was older, affluent consumers.) His leadership did just that. He replaced the old warm, fuzzy ads based on traditional father/son scenes with edgy straight talk about finances, contemporary family realities, and death.

Outperforming stagnant rivals, John Hancock sales surged 17 percent in 1985, the first year of the first-ever TV campaign—"Real Life, Real Answers." Since then the "slice-of-life" scenes have become more emotion-laden and contentious. Issues such as single parenting, deadbeat dads, and lesbian adoption have especially connected with women and minority groups.

D'Alessandro continues to push the envelope and hold his own against conservatives who object to the company's advertising campaigns. He's not afraid of bold moves. In a public relations stand, D'Alessandro pulled John Hancock from the Olympic Committee when the bribery scandal broke. Copying Lee Iacocca and John F. Weld, he, too, wrote a book—*Brand Warfare: 10 Rules for Building the Killer Brand.* Like these creative men, he uses publishing to boast about personal skills while promoting the company. Where will he go from here? ■

IT'S YOUR TURN

1. What are the other creative advertising strategies Hancock could use? Do you think an in-your-face campaign works? Why or why not?

Sources: Christopher Helman, "Stand-up Brand," *Forbes* (July 9, 2001): 127; Peter Mawn, "Hancock Studies Use of Banks by Consumers," *National Underwriter* (November 13, 2000): 7, 13; Barbara Lippert, "All Too Real," *Adweek* (November 5, 2001): 20.

Notes

1. "Strongly Influenced by Ads?" *Adweek* (November 13, 1995): 23.

2. Ibid.

3. Regis McKenna, *Relationship Marketing* (Cambridge, MA: Perscus Books, 1993).

4. John Philip Jones, *When Ads Work: Proof That Advertising Triggers Sales* (New York: Lexington Books, 1995).

5. Kevin Sullivan, "A U.S. $10 million Study is Underway to Find Out What Makes an Ad Effective," *Singapore Business Times* (July 5, 1996): 3.

6. Ennis Higgins, "Conversations with David Ogilvy," in *The Art of Writing Advertising* (Chicago: Advertising Publications, 1965).

7. "Internet Users Satisfied, but Seek More Accountability," *pr reporter* (August 20, 2001): 3.

8. Jonathan Weber, "The Advertising Slump," *The Industry Standard* (March 19, 2001): 7.

9. John Tierney, "Why Negative Ads Are Good for Democracy," *New York Times* (November 3, 1996): 52.

10. Stephen J. Hoch and Young-Won Ha, "Consumer Learning and the Ambiguity of Product Experience," *Journal of Consumer Research* (September 1986): 221–233.

11. John J. Burnett, "What Services Marketers Need to Know about the Mobility-Disabled Consumer," *Journal of Services Marketing* 10(3) (1996): 2–20.

12. Adapted from Sandra E. Moriarty, "Beyond the Hierarchy of Effects: A Conceptual Model," in *Current Issue and Research in Advertising* 1 (1983): 45–56.

13. Richard Vaughan, "How Advertising Works: A Planning Model," *Journal of Advertising Research* 26(1) (February–March 1986): 57–66.

14. David Kiley and Gerry Khermouch, "Going Internet for the Brand Makeovers," *Brandweek's Superbrands* (June 19, 2000): 27–31.

15. Ivan Preston, "The Association Model of the Advertising Communication Process," *Journal of Advertising* 11(2) (1982): 3–15; Leonard Reid and Herbert Rotfield, "Toward an Associative Model of Advertising Creative Thinking," *Journal of Advertising* 5(4) (1976): 24–29.

16. John Bissell, "Brand Name Recognition, but No Brand," *Brandweek* (May 8, 2000): 29.

17. Chris Rooney, "Ethnic Marketing: It's the Aspiration, Stupid," *Brandweek* (September 11, 2000): 44.

18. Richard Petty and John Cacioppo, "The Effects of Involvement on Responses to Argument Quantity and Quality: Central and Peripheral Routes to Persuasion," *Journal of Personality and Social Psychology* 46(1) (1984): 69–81.

19. Prema Nakra, "Corporate Reputation Management: 'CRM' with a Strategic Twist?" *Public Relations Quarterly* (Summer 2000): 35–42.

20. David Kiley and Gerry Khermouch, "Going Internet for the Brand Makeover," *Brandweek's Superbrands* (June 19, 2000): 27–31.

21. Regis McKenna, *Relationship Marketing* (Reading, MA: Addison-Wesley, 1991).

CHAPTER 7

Advertising Planning and Strategy

CHAPTER OBJECTIVES

When you have completed this chapter, you should be able to

1. Explain how advertising strategy and planning lead to more effective advertising.
2. Identify the key elements of a marketing plan.
3. Outline what an advertising plan is and list its key elements, including its relationship to the marketing plan.
4. Describe the main parts of a creative platform and types of copy strategy.

SignBoy a Hole in One?

Award: *EFFIE Gold 2001, Leisure Products category*

Company: *FootJoy golf shoes*

Agency: *Arnold Communication Worldwide*

Campaign: *FootJoy "SignBoy"*

If you're like most Americans, your closet probably contains more recreation shoes than dress shoes. This has been a trend since the 1980s, initiated by companies such as Nike and Adidas. We have become a society of shoe specialization, especially as far as our recreation is concerned: shoes for walking, others for running, and still others for other sports.

FootJoy has been making top-of-the-line golf shoes since 1946, and was the market leader until 1998, when the company's market share dropped by 2 percent and new competitors were introducing golf shoes with new designs and technology. The move from metal to plastic cleats was a big change in the industry, too. Nike was a particularly strong new competitor, supported by a huge marketing budget and the endorsement of Tiger Woods. Nike's brand of golf shoes was positioned as cool and stylish, while the FootJoy brand remained a golf shoe your father or mother would wear.

The challenge seemed clear. FootJoy had to retain its position as the shoe of choice for the world's best golfers, while creating a new image of being young, cool, and with it. If it could match the Nike image and offer a superior product, it could increase sales and regain market share.

In partnership with Arnold Communication Worldwide, FootJoy created the SignBoy character to present the FootJoy message in an entertaining and intelligent manner. SignBoy became the spokesperson across all FootJoy's media. SignBoy was a jovial looking man dressed as a caddy, the premise was to represent him as a golf expert and supportive companion who was with the FootJoy customer as he played a round of golf. The SignBoy campaign was a huge success for FootJoy, as we explain in the "It's a Wrap" section at the end of this chapter.

ADVERTISING PLANNING AND STRATEGY

As we'll see in this chapter, FootJoy had to use both the art and the science of advertising to develop a distinct brand image. The art comes from writing, designing, and producing exciting messages; the science comes from strategic thinking. Advertising is a disciplined art. Applying that discipline to make advertising work is the focus of this chapter, in which we discuss strategy, planning, and the creation of marketing and advertising plans.

Figure 7.1 shows a simplified process of how strategic planning connects at each level of an organization. It begins at the corporate level, extends to the functional level, and ends with advertising. The functional level of a business is the department level (marketing, finance, human resources, production). Marketing tactics include advertising, as well as product development, pricing, and distribution.

STRATEGIC PLANNING

Advertisers don't create messages by relying on whimsy or a sudden flash of inspiration. They formulate messages to achieve specific objectives and then develop strategies to achieve those objectives. The planning process is the means advertisers use to accomplish these two activities.

FIGURE 7.1

STRATEGIC PLANNING FROM TOP TO BOTTOM
Strategic planning reaches all levels of an organization, from the corporate level to tactical daily operations.

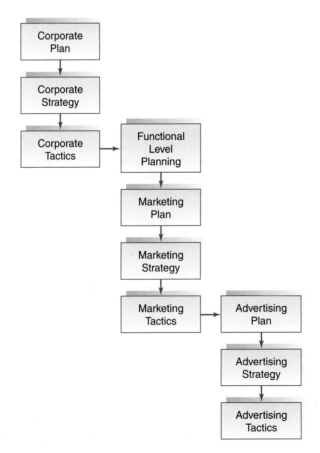

Strategic Planning: Making Intelligent Decisions

Strategic planning is the process of determining **objectives** (what you want to accomplish), deciding on **strategies** (how to accomplish the objectives), and implementing the **tactics** (which make the plan come to life). This process occurs within a specified timeframe. Marketing and advertising strategies are chosen from an array of possible alternatives. Intelligent decision making means weighing these alternatives and choosing the best approach. Often there is no completely right way, but there may be a best way to accomplish the objectives.

Even those experienced in advertising sometimes have a hard time telling the difference between an objective and a strategy. Both are important to successful marketing and advertising plans; they are related to each other, but they are also different and serve different purposes. An objective is a goal to be accomplished (the destination). A strategy is the means by which the objective is accomplished (the route to the destination).

For example, if the objective is to reinforce brand loyalty for the product, advertisers could use any number of strategies. Suppose an advertiser wants to create brand loyalty by emphasizing how the brand delivers more of a certain benefit than competing brands (objective). The company could compare the brand to its leading competitor through demonstrations, testimonials, and emotional or funny stories, or a straightforward, fact-based sales approach. (But, we haven't set levels yet, have we?)

An example of a company that effectively brought all these elements together is Rockport, which has been making comfortable shoes since 1971. Its objective was to reach baby-boomer men and displace their preference for sneakers. The real challenge emerged: to reinvent comfort itself and modernize the brand. After doing research on existing customers, the company concluded that Rockport users are actively seeking comfort on every level: physical, emotional, and spiritual. The core Rockport strategy emphasized the need for comfort by challenging the consumer: If you compromise your comfort, you compromise yourself.

In developing Rockport's advertising, the creatives arrived at a highly original perspective on the strategy. They wanted the advertising to challenge consumers by featuring

This ad for Rockport's shoes used consumer insights and focused on comfort, a key attribute that loyal users should respond to.

people who are truly comfortable with themselves, hoping that might make the viewer uncomfortable. To do this, they invented a rallying cry: "Uncompromise." They launched an integrated marketing communication plan featuring print and TV advertising that used the umbrella theme of "Be comfortable, uncompromise. Start with your feet."[1] Rockport shoes were offered as the comfort solution.

The Business Plan

While we're exploring the advertising planning process, let's look at the business plan and also review the marketing plan (which we examined in Chapter 3) to assess how they relate to the advertising plan.

Strategic planning usually is a three-tiered process. It starts with the **business strategic plan**, then moves to functional plans such as a **marketing plan** or a financial plan, and ends with specific plans for each subfunction. A marketing plan is a document that proposes strategies for using the marketing mix to achieve marketing objectives. For marketing, then, the business might have specific plans for advertising or product development. Naturally, each plan depends on the plan that precedes it.

Typically, the business plan covers a specific division of the company or a strategic business unit (SBU). These divisions or SBUs share a common set of problems and factors. Figure 7.2 depicts a widely used framework for the strategic planning process that starts with a *business mission statement*. Such a statement supports the corporate values and includes the broad goals and policies of the business unit. It might answer questions such as these: Does the business unit want to pursue long-term growth, short-term profits, or technological leadership? How does it value its customers, its employees, or its stockholders? Tom's of Maine states its mission clearly on its Web site.

The business unit next examines its external and internal environment. It engages in a **SWOT analysis**. That is, it evaluates the internal and external Strengths, Weaknesses, Opportunities, and Threats inherent in that business.

The *strengths* of a business are its positive traits, conditions, and good situations. For instance, possessing a large percentage of the market, being in a growth industry, or having a solid financial standing are all strengths.

The *weaknesses* of a business are traits, conditions, and situations that are perceived as negatives. Losing market share, belonging to a dying industry, and not being able to attract venture capital are all weaknesses.

An *opportunity* is an area in which the company could develop an advantage over its competition. In the high-tech telecommunications industry, TCI and AT&T merged to combine their technological resources. This move gave them an edge over their rival Sprint. Often, one company's weakness is another company's opportunity.

A *threat* is a trend or development in the environment that will erode business unless the company takes action. Competition is a common threat. U.S. automakers have long been threatened by Japanese imports. Some U.S. manufacturers have responded by acquiring or being acquired by foreign companies. Mercedes-Benz's acquisition of

FIGURE 7.2   THE BUSINESS STRATEGIC PLANNING PROCESS

For most organizations, strategic planning starts by formulating a business mission statement.

Source: Philip Kotler, *Marketing Management*, 10th ed. (Upper Saddle River, NJ: Prentice Hall, 2000): 76.

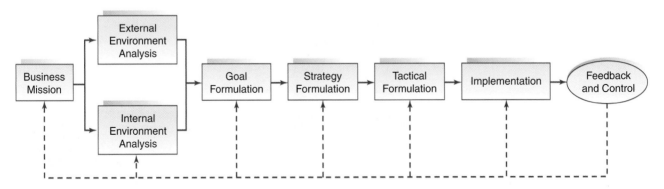

Chrysler is one example (now Daimler Chrysler). One way to respond to a competitor's threat is to meet it directly. A competitor's strengths may be your threat.

As an example of how this works, say we're marketers doing a SWOT analysis for Coca-Cola. Assume that the strength of Cola-Cola is its powerful worldwide brand identity. Its greatest weakness is its high turnover of top management and as a result, its lack of a clear company vision. A primary threat is the high number of new competitors emerging worldwide. What might an opportunity be? Coca-Cola has saturated most of its primary markets and has its best opportunities in buying specialty beverage companies and introducing the Coke brand into new markets. "The brand asset is the single largest asset that differentiates Coca-Cola from its competitors," noted Clivie Chajet, chairman at the Chajet Consultancy in New York, a corporate identity consultant. "There is not a substantial difference between Coca-Cola and Pepsi-Cola except in the brand image."[2]

After the business managers have defined the mission and examined the external and internal environment, they can develop specific objectives and goals for the planning period. Most businesses pursue multiple goals at the same time, such as a 10 percent sales growth, a higher return on investment, better quality, stronger brand image, and market share improvement.

Then the business plan outlines specific strategies that relate to each goal. For example, many corporations throughout the late 1980s and early 1990s viewed running the business at a low cost as the best strategy regardless of the goal. CEOs were selected on the basis of their reputation for ruthless cost cutting. Sunbeam CEO Al Dunlap (known as "Chainsaw Al"), who downsized Sunbeam by 30 percent, is a prime example of a leader who used cost cutting as a one-size-fits-all strategy. Sunbeam's workforce, net profits, and sales growth were harmed as a result. The strategy must match the business mission and its goals. Other companies, such as Microsoft, believe that technological innovation is the best means for supporting a business mission of innovation, regardless of the costs. Still other companies, such as ConAgra, maker of Healthy Choice, use a strategy of focusing on one segment of the market (the health conscious) to achieve sales growth.

Once the business develops its key strategies for attaining its goals, it must work out supporting programs, also known as tactics, for carrying out these strategies. Let's say that a business decides its strategy is to become a leader in software technology. Its tactics might include strengthening its research and development department, gathering intelligence on the newest technologies that might affect the business, and so forth.

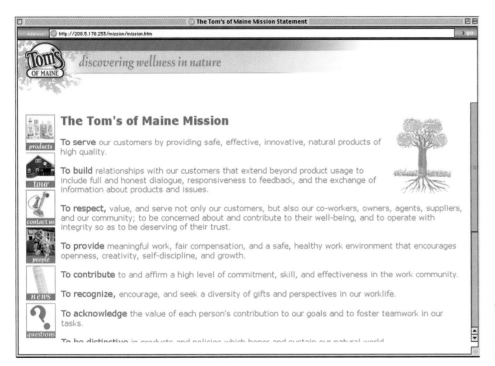

This mission statement for Tom's of Maine helps its managers develop specific business objectives and goals.

Even the best plans run the risk of failure if there is poor implementation. Although some businesses have wonderful planners, they simply cannot handle the hundreds of decisions that are required to implement the plan. Assuming that the new plan is implemented, the business needs to track the results and monitor late developments in the environment. Depending on these findings, the company must determine what, if any, adjustments are necessary.

A case in point is the situation Volkswagen found itself in at the end of 2000. Despite an award-winning ad campaign (remember Chapter 1?) and increased sales, several of Volkswagen's financial indicators were out of whack. In particular, earnings before taxes were forecasted to be 6.5 percent, but turned out to be 3.5 percent.

After careful investigation the problem turned out to be labor. About half of VW's 325,000-person labor force was in Germany. These plants produced about 40 vehicles per employee annually, while those in Spain produced 79 vehicles per employee. Consequently, VW's average profit per car was $373, well below Renault's $571 and Ford Motor's $974.[3] VW had to make adjustments.

Referring again to Figure 7.1, we now move on to the marketing planning process.

THE MARKETING PLAN

A marketing plan analyzes the marketing situation, identifies the problems, outlines the marketing opportunities, sets the objectives, and proposes strategies and tactics to solve these problems and meet objectives. A marketing plan is developed and evaluated annually, although sections dealing with long-term goals might operate for a number of years. Some companies are finding that the marketplace changes so rapidly that plans have to be updated more frequently than once a year, so they opt for shorter revision time frames.

To a large extent, the marketing plan parallels the business strategic plan and contains many of the same components, as we see in Figure 7.3. For advertising managers, the most important part of the marketing plan is the marketing strategy. It links the overall strategic business plan with specific marketing programs, including advertising. Also, the marketing plan is able to draw on research that the business plan supplies. As a result, the marketing plan begins with a statement of objectives and assesses the external and internal environments on an as-needed basis. In the sections that follow, we explore each step in the marketing plan development process.

Selecting Marketing Objectives

The marketing planning process begins with a selection of marketing objectives. The objectives may refer to a percentage of market share, unit sales, store traffic, or profit. In some companies, the marketing planning process generates the company's corporate objectives; in others, the company's overall corporate objectives determine the marketing objectives. In most successful companies, corporate objectives and marketing objectives influence each other.

FIGURE 7.3 STEPS IN THE MARKETING PLAN

The marketing plan parallels the business strategic plan and contains many of the same steps.

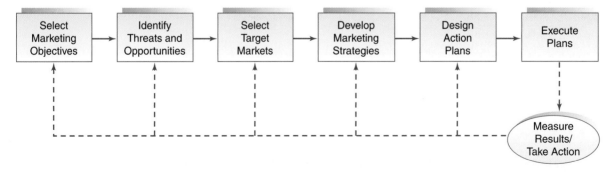

Selecting Marketing Opportunities

Guided by the objectives, as well as research, the marketer must then identify and evaluate opportunities. Finding a cure for cancer, for example, is a market opportunity for hundreds of pharmaceutical and research firms. Customers' complaints or suggestions sometimes identify opportunities. In the case of high-tech companies, opportunities are often little more than a new product looking for a market. It took the marketing people at 3M more than four years to find a profitable use for the adhesive that led to Post-It Notes. In any case, companies must have a mechanism for collecting information, examining trends, and assessing possible opportunities.

Conducting a SWOT analysis is also a part of the marketing plan. Some of the results will repeat or overlap the SWOT for the total organization; others will be unique to the marketing plan. If we look at a fictitious manufacturing company that produces inexpensive tableware, such as plates, bowls, cups, and so forth, the corporate SWOT reveals that the company has significant strengths in raw material costs and reputation for quality; weaknesses in respect to distribution costs, level of competition, and cash flow. Opportunities exist in purchasing two smaller competitors, and the threat of consumer cutbacks in purchasing its products is quite real. Some of these factors are also marketing-related. Reputation for quality, distribution costs, high level of competition, and consumer spending cutbacks might all be part of the marketing SWOT. In addition, the marketing SWOT would include the following: higher-than-industry profit margins, unique product designs, limited access to retail outlets, no Web site, direct distribution, and limited consumer information.

Selecting Target Markets

As we know from Chapter 4, a market segment is a group of consumers having one or more similar characteristics. The dog food market, for example, is segmented according to age of the dog, its weight, breed, and its activity level. Dog-owning consumers make choices among brands in these three or four segments. A company such as GlaxoSmithKline selects market segments that it can best serve from a competitive point of view. The segments it selects are the target market.

Developing Marketing Strategies

An important part of marketing planning is identifying key strategic decisions that will give the firm a competitive advantage in the marketplace and achieve stated objectives. Strategy selection begins with several assumptions that marketers must make about the market. In the case of our tableware marketer, an assumption can be made that the targeted consumer segment does value high quality in inexpensive tableware, and that the best way to communicate and demonstrate value in this product category is through appropriate distribution methods. Retail outlets such as Pier 1 and Williams-Sonoma would be better choices than Kmart or Target. These assumptions determine the relative emphasis given to each of the marketing mix elements and lead to the next stage of the planning process. Product quality and selective distribution will be the focus in our example.

To develop specific action plans or tactics, each element of the marketing strategy must be dissected. Here, marketers specify tactics for each aspect of the marketing mix. Simply using different combinations of these mix variables makes dramatic differences in marketing action programs. Our example company stresses product manufacturing design and selective distribution. It could just as easily focus on discount pricing and mass advertising. The goal is to design a marketing mix that will appeal to the target market and prove profitable, given the limitations imposed by available resources and the requirements of the marketing strategy. Of course, developing strategies for overseas markets introduces unique limitations and challenges. The "A Matter of Practice" box discusses the state of advertising in Nigeria.

Executing Plans

Implementing the typical marketing plan requires a great number of decisions. Making sure that the product reaches the warehouse at the right time, that ads run on schedule, and that salespeople receive the right support material are just a few of the details marketers must

A MATTER OF PRACTICE

ADVERTISING IN NIGERIA

➤ Much of what we know about advertising has evolved from economically powerful and strong countries, especially the United States. There are other countries that offer important insights. One such country is Nigeria, a third-world economy.

Located on the west coast of Africa, Nigeria is comparable in size to the state of Texas, with a population estimated at 120 million, the largest in Africa. About 57 percent of people over 15 years of age are literate compared to 87 percent in the United States. It is estimated that there are about half a million telephones in Nigeria compared to 380 million in the United States. There are more than 350 recognized tribal groups with almost the same number of languages and dialects. Nigeria is dominated by two monotheisms (Islam, Christianity) and native faiths; about 48 percent of the population is Muslim.

Advertising has a long history in Nigeria. Its first newspaper, established in 1859, obtained some of its revenue from advertising. Since then, advertising has remained a permanent feature in private and government-owned print and broadcast media. As the only outlet with country-wide scope, the government-owned Federal Radio Corporation of Nigeria and National Television Authority are the only sources of national broadcast advertising. Most other state- and privately-owned stations do not have networks and are incapable of covering the entire nation, which means advertising tends to be tightly controlled and regional in nature.

Advertising remains a source of revenue for government-owned media and existing private broadcast stations. Advertisements are aired in blocks in and between programs and there may be from 10 to 60 spots. There is no standard rate schedule; negotiation is a big part of the Nigerian culture.

The largest proportion of advertising and program sponsorships in Nigeria is provided by the subsidiaries of transnational corporations (Nestle, Unilever, PepsiCo, Coca-Cola, and Toyota). Other advertisers and sponsors include indigenous manufacturers, distributors, banks, and breweries.

As the medium of the masses, radio advertising remains most important, but television advertising represents the most expensive medium.

Technology is moving the Nigerian advertising industry from the manual to the computerized age. The industry is also making strong strides in Internet advertising. Almost 100 percent of the members of the Association of Advertising Practitioners of Nigeria, a professional advertising body, are computerized and 50 percent of them are on the Internet. Internet advertising is growing, but can only be accessed by the rich since very few Nigerian households have home computers. It is unlikely, therefore, that Web-based advertising will ever reach the level of penetration reported in the United States.

An analysis of the cultural values in Nigerian mass-media ads found that family and savings represented the most common values, with gift giving, collectivism, wisdom, security and investment, good health, honesty, love, and endurance as runners-up.

POINT TO PONDER

Given the unique cultural elements found in Nigeria, would the typical U.S.-type advertising plan work?

Sources: J. Ajayi, "Challenges of Advertising in Nigeria, by Practitioner," *Vanguard* (March 10, 2000): 18–23; C. Amuzo, "Advertising Industry Is in a State of Stagnation," *Vanguard* (October 11, 1999): 36–40; R. Ilori, "Why Nigerians Suffer," *Post Express Wired* (August 28, 1998): 81–86.

---

track day by day, or even minute by minute. Poor execution has been the downfall of many excellent marketing plans. A case in point is Stouffer Foods Corporation's Right Course frozen dinner entrees. Relying heavily on its reputation for high quality, Stouffer decided to introduce upscale, ethnic offerings such as Chicken with Peanut Sauce and Fiesta Beef with Corn Pasta. Its rationale was the growing popularity of ethnic foods along with the need for convenience. It sounded like a natural move. The company made these choices without any input from retailers. In addition, the advertising campaign didn't appear until four weeks after the products hit the stores. Needless to say, the products did not sell well.

Evaluating Plans

Every marketing plan includes an evaluation component that compares actual performance with planned performance. In most modern businesses, technology allows access to several comparison indicators, such as sales that management can monitor over any time interval they choose. Usually, an annual review is a minimum. In addition to collecting performance data, managers must assess why particular results have occurred. Finally, if the marketer determines that the gap between objectives and performance is significant enough, corrective action must be taken. For example, if our tableware marketer increased sales by 3 percent rather than the targeted 5 percent, it must determine why it failed.

THE ADVERTISING PLAN

Advertising planning must dovetail with marketing planning. A firm may operate with an annual advertising plan. In addition to or instead of an annual advertising plan, a firm may develop a campaign plan that is more tightly focused on solving a particular marketing communication problem. Finally, a company may put together a copy strategy for an individual ad that runs independently of a campaign. The advertising plan and the campaign plan are similar in outline and structure. These plans are the responsibility of the account manager.

An **advertising plan** matches the right audience to the right message and presents it in the right medium to reach that audience. Three elements summarize the heart of the advertising plan:

- *Targeting the audience.* Whom are you trying to reach?
- *Message strategy.* What do you say to them?
- *Media strategy.* When and where will you reach them?

The same elements that guide the development of an advertising plan are similar in some ways to those that guide the development of a marketing plan. Both include a situation analysis, although in the case of an advertising plan the focus tends to be specific to defining the advertising problem and identifying advertising opportunities. Likewise, the key planning decisions concentrate on advertising-related issues. Three strategic elements support the planning decisions—the creative strategy, the media strategy, and other communication strategies. Implementation, tactics, evaluation, and budget conclude the advertising plan (see Table 7.1).

TABLE 7.1 Typical Advertising Campaign Plan Outline

I. Introduction
II. Situation analysis
- The advertising problem
- Advertising opportunities
III. Key planning decisions
- Advertising objectives
- Target audience
- Competitive product advantage
- Product image and personality
- Product position
IV. Implementation/Tactics
V. Evaluation
VI. Budget
VII. The creative strategy
VIII. The media strategy
IX. Other communication tools
- Sales promotion
- Public relations
- Direct marketing
- Personal selling
- Sponsorships, merchandising, packaging, point-of-purchase

Introduction

Not everyone needs to read the entire advertising plan, so the introduction should provide an executive summary or overview of the plan. The former highlights the key elements of the plan in a page or less. The overview is more detailed, outlining the plan and the important ideas of each part in a page or two.

Situation Analysis

The first step in developing an advertising plan, just as in a marketing plan, is not planning but backgrounding, researching, and reviewing the current state of the business that is relevant to the brand's advertising. This section details the search for and analysis of important information and trends affecting the marketplace, the competition, consumer behavior, the company itself, and the product or brand. The key word in the title of this section is **analysis**, and that means making sense of all the data collected and figuring out what the information means for the future success of the brand. Despite everyone's best efforts, there will always be factors that are overlooked or misanalyzed.

Once again the business goes through the process of conducting a SWOT analysis at the advertising level. Advertisers, and ad agencies especially, develop their own customized process to assess a client's strengths, weaknesses, opportunities, and threats. For example, the challenge is to enable the advertising strategy to address the outcome of the analysis.

One way to analyze the market situation is in terms of the communication problems that affect the successful marketing of a product and the opportunities the advertising can create or exploit. Analyzing the situation and identifying the problem that can be solved with an advertising message are at the heart of strategic planning.

For example, DDB Needham searches for "Barriers to Purchase."[4] These barriers are reasons why people do not buy any or enough of a product. The American Dairy Association asked DDB Needham to find out why cheese consumption was declining. A study identified the major barriers to consumption and directed the agency toward the one barrier that was most easily correctable through advertising: the absence of simple cheese recipes for homemakers. As you can see here, the American Dairy Association's Web site (ilovecheese.com) offers many such recipes.

DDB Needham agency found that a "barrier to purchase" cheese was the lack of good recipe ideas using cheese products. The American Dairy Association responded by getting more recipes out there through advertising.

Flowers Direct is a long-distance floral delivery service that competes with FTD and 1-800-Flowers, both of which, research discovered, had a major weakness that Flowers Direct could exploit. Flowers Direct connects the customer with a florist in the area where the flowers will be delivered, rather than having customers place the order with their own neighborhood florist. The advertising challenge was to explain this problem to the consumer and then capitalize on Flowers Direct's opportunity to create a competitive advantage.

Advertising can solve only message-related problems such as image, attitude, perception, and knowledge of information. It cannot solve problems related to the price of the product, availability, or quality. However, a message can speak to the perception that the price is too high. It can portray a product with limited distribution as exclusive. In other words, advertising can affect the way consumers perceive price, availability, and quality.

Advertising Planning Decisions

Following along with Table 7.1, several decisions are crucial to developing an advertising plan: how to set objectives, identify the target audience, create a competitive advantage, establish a brand image and brand personality, and position a product.

Advertising Objectives We cannot overstate the importance of delineating specific advertising objectives. Every advertising campaign, and the ads in it, must be guided by specific, clear objectives. Advertising objectives are derived from the marketing objectives along with the results of the marketing and advertising SWOT analysis. Basically, the overriding advertising objective should be an increase in the sale of the product or service. This contribution may be minor or it may be the main cause for purchase. Given the huge amounts of money spent on advertising, it is important for advertisers to know what to expect from a campaign or an ad. Recall from Figure 1.2 in Chapter 1 (page 8), that advertising objectives fall into four general categories; perception, learning, persuasion, and behavior. Determining which of these alternatives, or combination of alternatives, is most appropriate for a particular ad or campaign is difficult. While the experience of the account manager is often helpful, it is hardly ever sufficient.

Fortunately, there are several models account managers can employ to derive advertising objectives. All these models assume that consumers go through a series of steps when exposed to a cue. For example, the classic AIDA model describes the effect of advertising on consumers, starting with *attention*, then moving to *interest*, then *desire*, and finally *action*. A variation of the model developed by advertising researcher Russell Colley, called the DAGMAR model (defining advertising goals for measured advertising results) begins with *awareness*, moves to *comprehension*, then *conviction*, and ends with *action*.

DAGMAR works like this: If you have skin allergies and Procter & Gamble advertises a new detergent for people with sensitive skin, the ad will probably catch your attention—you are aware of a possible desire for the product. If you are the person who buys detergent for your household, then you many find yourself interested in the idea of this new formulation—you have comprehended its value and are convinced it's worth considering. You may want to try it, so when you receive a coupon in the mail, you may respond by picking up a trial package when you are at the store; you are spurred to action, the primary objective.

As Figure 7.4 demonstrates, simpler objectives, such as awareness, are easy to create and get high levels of response. However, a lot of people may be aware of the product, but far fewer will actually try it. The **Hierarchy-of-Effects** model illustrates the relative impact of these various objectives with the simplest but broadest impact at the bottom and the most complex but smaller impact at the top.[5]

The goal of the FootJoy campaign was to give the FootJoy brand a more contemporary personality to attract younger golfers, while continuing to strengthen FootJoy's

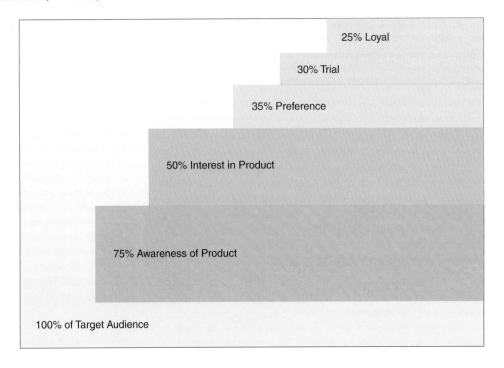

FIGURE 7.4

SETTING OBJECTIVES USING A HIERARCHY-OF-EFFECTS MODEL
The higher advertisers go on the Hierarchy, the more difficult the desired response.

position as the category leader among the best golfers. Its specific objectives were: (1) increase sales by a minimum of 5 percent, (2) increase overall market share by a minimum of 2 points, (3) increase FootJoy's share among young golfers, and (4) maintain FootJoy's dominant share among single-digit handicappers. Do you think the ads helped accomplish those goals?

The goal of the FootJoy SignBoy campaign was to attract younger golfers. Would these ads accomplish that goal?

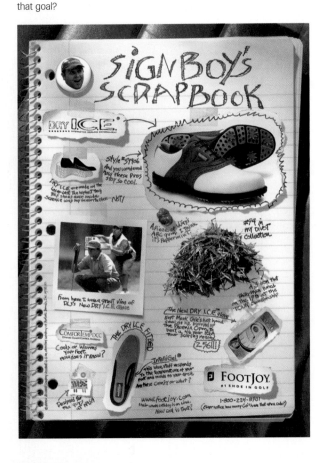

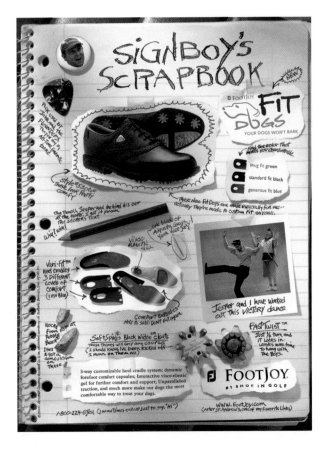

Targeting the Audience To differentiate between the marketing plan and the advertising plan, substitute the term "audience" for the term "market." As explained in Chapter 3, market and audience may contain exactly the same people, or there may be no overlap whatsoever. Essentially, target markets are consumers you hope will buy your product. **Target audiences** are consumers you want to receive your marketing message. The latter may not be actual users or purchasers, but they influence that decision.

On the advertising plan, advertising planners usually describe the target audiences in respect to their demographics. Because these demographics often overlap, the process of describing an audience narrows the targeting. For example, the plan might use descriptors such as "women aged 25 to 35" and "suburban mall shoppers." These two categories overlap because a certain percentage of women aged 25 to 35 are also in the suburban mall category. Each time you add a descriptor, the target audience gets smaller because the group is defined more tightly. This kind of analysis lets the advertising planner zero in on the most responsive audience. Figure 7.5 illustrates how these descriptors pinpoint a target audience. In this case, the target audience is males, 18 to 24 years old, urban dwellers, and professionals. Demographic descriptions are particularly important to media planners who are comparing the characteristics of the targeted audience with the characteristics of the viewers, listeners, or readers of a particular medium.

Advertisers also create **profiles** of target audiences that include demographics, personality descriptors, and lifestyle traits. The intent is to make that "typical" person as real as possible for the creative people, who then try to write believable messages that will appeal to this person. For this reason, advertising planners usually redefine the target as a profile of a typical product user. Copywriters then associate that general profile with someone they know so they can write creative messages more easily and believably. The FootJoy campaign was targeted at a distinct audience of golfers who play at least eight or more rounds of golf per year. This core golfer audience has an average age of 44, income of $65,000+, and averages almost 35 rounds per year. The younger half of this golf population (18–39) was targeted because it represents 45 percent of the total golf audience, and it is the strongest supporter of Nike and Adidas brands.

Product Features and Competitive Advantage Another section in the key decisions part of the advertising plan is to analyze the product in comparison to competing products. **Feature analysis** is one way marketers structure this analysis (see Table 7.2). First, they make a chart of their product and competitors' products, listing each product's relevant features. For example, taste is important for sodas, horsepower and mileage are important for cars, and trendiness is important for fashion watches.

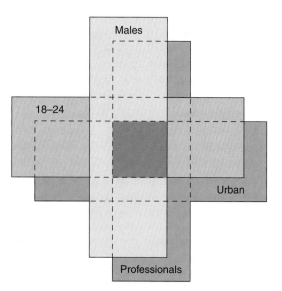

FIGURE 7.5

Targeting entails the use of overlapping descriptors to identify the most receptive audience.

TABLE 7.2	**Feature Analysis**				
Feature	**Importance to Prospect**	**Product Performance**			
		Yours	*X*	*Y*	*Z*
Price	1	+	−	−	+
Quality	4	−	+	−	+
Style	2	+	−	+	−
Availability	3	−	+	−	−
Durability	5	−	+	+	+

Next, they evaluate how important each feature is to the target audience (based on primary research) and how well the products perform on that feature. Competitive advantage lies where the product has a strong feature that is important to the target and the competition has a weaker one. So the product in Table 7.2 would compete well in the tableware example introduced earlier.

Brand Personality Given all the information gathered so far, the account planner is now ready to create two related advertising elements: the brand personality and the brand position. Both are most relevant to advertising because they are based on perceptions and image rather than concrete facts.

Creating a brand personality for a potato might sound like an impossible challenge, but that actually has been accomplished in the case of Idaho Potatoes. The Idaho Potato Commission, a small state agency, has been so successful in this effort that studies show that over 82 percent of all Americans recognize and prefer an Idaho potato to all others, a higher rating than Florida citrus fruits or Washington apples. Has this success led consumers to confuse a russet potato grown anywhere with a genuine Idaho potato? No; studies show that most Americans know that an Idaho potato can be grown only in the state of Idaho. This awareness is due to a concerted campaign by the Idaho Potato commission that registered "Idaho" as a federal trademark and educated the public about the unique qualities of Idaho potatoes. The campaign also taught consumers to look for the "Grown in Idaho" seal so that they could be certain they were purchasing genuine Idaho potatoes.[6]

The Idaho Potato Commission has successfully built a personality for the unique Idaho potato. This personality, along with the position for the Idaho potato, can now serve as the core foundation for all future advertising.

Positioning Strategies A company's position is the first thing that comes to mind when you hear a company's name. Volvo owns the safety position, while ESPN owns the sports information position. Because of its off the wall advertising, ESPN also owns the fun position among sports broadcasters.

Positioning strategy descriptions usually have a prominent role in the advertising plan. **Positioning** goes beyond the brand personality in that it incorporates many marketing tools. Which, when combined, produce a unique perception in the mind of the consumer. An ad for Timberland, for example, might be just one element contributing to its position. The ad might focus on the rugged individualism associated with the Timberland brand. However, the ad's placement in *Sports Illustrated*, along with its placement in the Timberland retail outlets and the merchandising used in those stores, also contribute to its position.

Implementation

The next section of an advertising plan details the campaign's specific tactics, along with delineating the schedule and the person(s) responsible for implementing these tactics.

Executing the advertising plan is undoubtedly the most difficult part of the plan. As the old adage goes, "Success is in the details," and there are thousands of details in a typical advertising plan. Missing even one deadline (they are very short in advertising) might mean scrapping an entire campaign. Larger ad agencies often have "traffic" people who make sure that everything is done as the plan describes.

The GE Exchange ad looks pretty straightforward, but there are were hundreds of tactical decisions that had to be implemented before it appeared in *Fortune* magazine.

Evaluation

Evaluation is based on how well the advertising plan meets its objectives. As discussed in Chapter 5, a variety of research techniques are available to evaluate effectiveness. Recall that evaluation can be done before, during, or after a campaign. When we think about evaluation at this point in the advertising plan, we are evaluating after the fact. Essentially, the following question is addressed: Now that the campaign has run for a prescribed period of time, how well did we achieve our stated objectives? At the end of this chapter, in the "It's a Wrap" section, we will answer that question for FootJoy.

The Advertising Budget

Determining the total appropriation allocated to advertising is not an easy task, nor is it always done at the end of the advertising plan. Often a dollar amount, say $370,000, is budgeted for advertising during the budget planning process (just before the end of the fiscal year). The amount could be totally arbitrary, based on the opinion of the marketing vice president or the amount the advertising manager was able to beg, borrow, or steal.

In addition, dollar allocation usually is a political process. Companies led by financial types are unlikely to give much money to advertising and will require the advertising manager to justify every penny. Companies led by marketing or advertising types are likely to be generous to advertising and will view the cost as a long-term investment.

Although the appropriation and budgeting process relies on numerical information, the process is more art than science. It is often based on educated guesses, tradition, or the

THE INSIDE STORY
CREATIVITY AND CHANGE

Carol Fletcher

Vice President; Strategy Director
Storcom Worldwide

Life in an advertising agency is not as tidy as I'd imagined while in college. Clients do not always have clearly defined objectives or ideal budgets. Further complicating things is that advertising today goes well beyond traditional definitions of the discipline. To succeed in this world, I've learned that you need two key things: creativity and an appetite for change.

CREATIVITY

Creativity doesn't stop and start with art directors and copywriters. Everyone on the team needs to come up with new ideas and approaches that positively impact the client's business. Great researchers and planners are designing more effective ways to gather insights about consumers. Top-notch media strategists are building more innovative communication plans that get the brand in front of the right consumers, using the right context to make the message work harder.

Being creative means changing your perspective—looking at the problem from every possible angle. Being creative means asking yourself "How can we?" instead of "Can we?" Being creative also means constantly exploring—experimenting with new technologies, discovering new ways to use traditional options, anticipating new trends.

APPETITE FOR CHANGE

The advertising world has exploded with options over the past 20 years. Advertising is no longer just a 30-second TV ad on the three networks. Today there are millions of advertising options—from product placement, to eggshells, to satellite radio. Consumers are changing too. They are more fickle; they spread their viewing over more places—sometimes simultaneously! They're more skeptical, more hurried, and will generally find a way to avoid ad messages that bore them or waste their time. Advertisers need to be on their toes to infiltrate those screens.

Today's leading companies are not afraid to go beyond the expected and the traditional. For some, that means experimenting with new technologies that deliver finer targeted messages. Others are exploring new venues that better link the brand with the creative concept and the target's interests.

A creative team has the potential to drive change. A team that is not afraid of change has the potential to create new ideas. Those are advertising principles and practices that spell success!

Carol Fletcher is Vice President; Strategy Director at Starcom Worldwide. In her 12-year tenure, she's enjoyed working with a diverse group of clients including Allstate, Pillsbury, Altoids, Kraft, Hallmark, and many others. She graduated with a B.S. in Mass Communication from Middle Tennessee State University in 1988 and from the University of Illinois in 1989 with an M.S. in Advertising.

Nominated by Professor Edd Applegate, Middle Tennessee State University.

financial condition of the company. It is also in constant flux; that is, if a campaign seems to be working, it is easy to get additional dollars. The opposite is also true: If the company has a financial downturn, advertising will probably take the hit.

The budget is a critical part of planning an advertising campaign. A $50,000 budget will only stretch so far and probably will not be enough to cover the costs of television advertising in most markets. The budget also determines how many targets and multiple campaign plans a company or brand can support. McDonald's, for instance, can support multiple campaigns.

Certain types of advertisers'—industrial and business-to-business, for example—typically operate on smaller advertising budgets than consumer packaged-goods companies. Their media choices and narrow targeting strategies reduce their budgets so these companies often rely more on direct mail, trade publications, and telemarketing for their advertising.

The big budgeting question at the marketing-mix and marketing communication-mix level is: How much should we spend? Let's examine five common budgeting methods to help answer that question.

Historical Method Historical information is the source for this common budgeting method. A budget may simply be based on last year's budget, with a percentage increase for inflation or some other marketplace factor. Say Morris Hardware spent $12,000 on advertising last year. It will spend $12,000 + 5 percent ($12,600) this year. This method, though easy to calculate, has little to do with reaching advertising objectives.

Objective-Task Method: Bottom-Up The **objective-task method** is also a common method for determining the budget. This method looks at the objectives for each activity and determines the cost of accomplishing each objective: What will it cost to make 50 percent of the people in the market aware of this product? How many people do we have to reach and how many times? What would be the necessary media levels and expenses? This method's advantage is that it develops the budget from the ground up so that objectives are the starting point. Conversely, its results are only as good as the stated objectives and the dollar amounts assigned to each objective.

Percentage-of-Sales Method The **percentage-of-sales method** compares the total sales with the total advertising (or marketing communication) budget during the previous year or the average of several years to compute a percentage. This technique can also be used across an industry to compare the expenditures of different product categories on advertising.

For example, if a company had sales figures of $5 million last year and an advertising budget of $1 million, then the *ratio* of advertising to sales would be 20 percent. If the marketing manager predicts *sales* of $6 million for next year, then the ad budget would be $1.2 million. How can we calculate the percentage of sales and apply it to a budget? Follow these two steps:

$$\text{Step 1: } \frac{\text{past advertising dollars}}{\text{past sales}} = \% \text{ of sales}$$

Step 2: % of sales X next year's sales forecast = new advertising budget

This method has two advantages. It is simple to use and expenditures are directly related to funds available or solid projections. However, it has several limitations. It assumes that advertising is a result of sales rather than the cause of sales. Also, this method does not include the possibility of diminishing returns, meaning that after a certain point additional dollars may generate fewer and fewer sales. In short, using the percentage-of-sales method may mean underspending when the sales opportunities are high and overspending when the potential is low.

Competitive Methods Budgeting often considers the competitive situation and uses competitors' budgets as benchmarks. Competitive parity budgeting relates the amount invested in advertising to the product's share of market. To understand this method, you need to understand the share-of-mind concept. This concept suggests that the advertiser's share-of-advertising voice—that is, the advertiser's media presence—affects the share of attention the brand will receive, and that, in turn, affects the market share the brand can obtain. Here's a depiction of these relationships:

Share of   Share of   Market
media voice = consumer mind = share

Keep in mind that the relationships depicted here are only a guide for budgeting. The actual relationship between share-of-media voice (an indication of advertising expenditures) and share of mind or share of market depends to a great extent on factors such as the creativity of the message and the amount of clutter in the marketplace. A simple increase in the share of voice does not guarantee an equal increase in share of market.

All You Can Afford When a company allocates whatever is left over to advertising, it is using the "all you can afford" budgeting method. It's really not a method, but rather a philosophy about advertising. Companies using this approach don't value advertising as a strategic imperative. However, as unsophisticated as this approach appears, it might prove effective if allocations made to the other business functions do well. For example, a company that allocates a large amount of its budget to research and has a superior product may find the amount spent on advertising fairly irrelevant.

While all these budgeting techniques have their proponents, the discussion in the "A Matter of Principle" box discusses a more optimum approach to advertising budgeting practices.

A MATTER OF PRACTICE
SHOW ME THE MONEY

➤ The financial and employee resources needed to accomplish advertising goals declined dramatically during 2001, and especially after 9/11. Most agencies have engaged in serious downsizing due to reductions in client expenditures on advertising. There is also the fact that advertisers have increased their expectations. Ads are expected to reach goals and provide a targeted rate of return, just like an investment in a new manufacturing plan, equipment, or a salesperson.

For many advertisers, an agency requesting $6 million for three 30-second spots on the Super Bowl is unacceptable without measurable payoffs. The rationale for doling out advertising money must change.

Don Schultz, Professor of Integrated Marketing Communication at Northwestern University, advocates changing the advertising budgeting process. Essentially, he posits that budgeting to meet the marketing needs in most businesses is designed to meet the internal needs of the organization, not the requirements of customers. The needs/wants of the customer is always a good starting point, regardless of the marketing decision. Basing dollar allocation from the company's perspective means that a company will start with next year's sales forecast, say $5 million, and dole out money to all the business functions based on some proportion of the $5 million.

Depending on the business and the value it places on advertising, the share advertising receives could range from quite large down to inconsequential. However, if actual sales are lower than expected, say $4 million, the functional budgets are reduced accordingly. If advertising were to receive 5 percent of sales, its allocation would now be reduced from $250,000 to $200,000. This reduction would be made regard-less of the fact that additional advertising may be the necessary decision to spike sales.

Schultz advocates two major changes in traditional budgeting. First, he argues that all objective-setting should start with the customer, and the particular changes you wish to effect. Do you want them to buy more? Buy differently? Buy for different reasons? Based on the specific objectives, you would then determine how much money is needed to accomplish each one. You next allocate these dollars to the various business functions, including advertising, based on how they each contribute to goal attainment. The company calculates a Return-on-Investment (ROI) for the final budget.

If the company does employ this fundamental approach toward budget determination, then Schultz posits a second step. The organization must view advertising dollars as variable costs rather than fixed costs. Setting a $5 million budget for advertising means that under a fixed cost perspective, $5 million is all that's available for advertising, regardless of changes in the marketplace.

Viewing advertising dollars as a variable cost means that the amount will change, tied directly to how close it is performing relative to the corporate target ROI. If advertising exceeds the ROI it should be allocated additional dollars. If it is below the ROI, its budget should be reduced.

POINT TO PONDER
What problems would you anticipate in implementing this new budgeting perspective? Are they insurmountable?

Sources: Don E. Schultz, "How to Generate an Unlimited IMC Budget," *The Marketing News* (July 22, 1999): 7; Don E. Schultz, "Why Investing in Brands Is so Difficult," *The Marketing News* (July 31, 2000): 8; Don E. Schultz, "Make Communications Worth the Profit," *The Marketing News* (January 15, 2001): 13.

The Creative Strategy

So far we've investigated advertising planning in terms of an annual plan or a campaign plan, but planning occurs at the level of individual ads, too. Advertisers may develop a message strategy for an individual advertisement. The document that sets out the message strategy may go by various names—*creative* or *copy platform, creative work plan,* or *creative blueprint.* A **creative platform** is a guide to those developing the advertisement. It ensures that everyone is working with the same understanding of the message strategy.

Most creative platforms combine the basic advertising decisions—problems, objectives, and target markets—with the critical elements of the sales message strategy, which include the selling premise and details about how the idea will be executed.

The Media Strategy

The media strategy section of the advertising plan details all the elements that are part of planning, buying, and evaluating the advertising media selected. Media strategy planning takes place in conjunction with creative strategy. In the case of FootJoy, it focused on media that targeted core and avid golfers. Those media vehicles that reached the top of the pyramid of influence were consumer golf publications, Network TV golf broadcasts, the Golf Channel, and golf-related Web sites.

Selecting Other Communication Tools

Advertising works in concert with the other marketing communication tools. Most of these tools are part of either sales promotion, public relations, or personal selling. For instance, we know that a print ad containing a coupon is far more effective than the same ad without a coupon. Add an 800 number and effectiveness increases even more.

The FootJoy campaign contained one collateral element. There was a point-of-purchase sweepstakes promotion. It provided golfers with a chance to play a round of golf with David Duval.

IT'S A WRAP
FOOTJOY WINS!

The strategy decisions—analyzing the marketplace, setting objectives, targeting the right audience, creating a brand personality, creating a position, implementing, evaluating, and budgeting—are at the heart of the creative process in advertising. Once these decisions are in place, the advertising team can develop the creative plan that determines what the message will say. Even then, success is not guaranteed.

The SignBoy campaign proved to be the most successful campaign in FootJoy's history. Overall sales increased by 5.7 percent; market share increased from 46.2 percent in 1998 to 57.7 percent in 2000, and FootJoy's New Shoe use among golfers under 30 increased 10.2 percent in 1999, while Nike dropped 3.3 percent in the same year.

Summary

1. **Explain how advertising strategy and planning lead to more effective advertising**. Advertising messages are formulated to accomplish specific objectives. Strategic planning ensures that the ads are developed to achieve these objectives. Strategic planning is the process of determining objectives, deciding on strategies, and implementing tactics. Planning is usually a three-tiered operation containing interrelated operations: the business strategic plan, functional plans, and advertising plans. The business plan relates to a particular company division or strategic business unit. It

begins with the mission statement and is followed by an analysis of the external and internal environment, goal formulation, strategy formulation, and program formulation.

2. **Identify the key elements of a marketing plan**. A marketing plan (functional level) proposes strategies for using the various elements of the marketing mix to achieve marketing objectives. It parallels the business plan. Its parts include selection of marketing objectives, identification of threats and opportunities, selection of target markets, development of marketing strategies, design of action plans, and evaluation of results.

3. **Outline what an advertising plan is and list its key elements, including its relationship to the marketing plan**.

An advertising plan matches the right audience to the right message and presents the message in the right medium to reach the audience. A typical advertising plan includes the following components: situation analysis (problems and opportunities), key strategic decisions (objectives, target audience, competitive advantage, product image, product position), the creative plan, the media plan, the promotion plan, implementation and evaluation, and budgeting.

4. **Describe the main parts of a creative platform and types of copy strategy**. The creative plan includes copy strategies that are used for individual ads. Message strategies determine what is going to be said about the product and how. This is reflected by the selling premise (sales logic).

Key Terms

advertising plan, p. 189
analysis, p. 190
business strategic plan, p. 184
creative platform, p. 198
feature analysis, p. 193

Hierarchy-of-Effects, p. 191
marketing plan, p. 184
objective, p. 183
objective-task method, p. 197

percentage-of-sales method, p. 197
positioning, p. 194
profiles, p. 193
strategic planning, p. 183

strategies, p. 183
SWOT analysis, p. 184
tactics, p. 183
target audience, p. 193

Questions

1. What do advertisers mean by strategy? What are the key considerations in an advertising strategy?

2. Think of a product you purchased recently. How was it advertised? Which strategies can you discern in the advertising? Did the advertising help to convince you to purchase the product? Why or why not?

3. Day-Flo products sold 400,000 units in 2001. The total category sales (all competitors) for 2001 were 3.5 million units. What was Day-Flo's share of sales in 2001? In 2003, Day-Flo's objective is to increase unit sales by 15 percent; projections for total category sales are estimated at 10 percent. If these projections prove to be correct, what will Day-Flo's share of the market be at the end of 2003?

4. Advertising strategies are particularly sensitive to marketers who follow benefit segmentation targeting. If you were marketing a new line of denim jeans for women, what are some of the logical benefit segments that consumer research would identify? How would advertising creative strategy shift according to segment priorities? Be as specific as possible.

5. The following is a brief excerpt from Luna Pizza's situation analysis for 2002. Luna is a regional producer of frozen pizza. Its only major competitor is Brutus Bros. Estimate the year 2003 advertising budgets for Luna under each of the following circumstances:

    a. Luna follows a historical method by spending 40 cents per unit sold in advertising, with a 5 percent increase for inflation.

    b. Luna follows a fixed percentage of projected sales method, using 7 percent.

    c. Luna follows a share-of-voice method. Brutus is expected to use 6 percent of sales for its advertising budget in 2003.

	Actual Last Year	Estimates Next Year
Units sold	120,000	185,000
$ Sales	420,000	580,000
Brutus $ Sales	630,000	830,000

6. A key to marketing advertising strategy is the ability to convert attributes into customer-oriented benefits. Look at these attributes for an automobile of the future and change them to benefit statements.

    a. The V car's computer-directed braking system senses the exact pedal pressure needed for every road surface condition.

    b. The V has a special battery with a separate section that is insulated against temperature extremes.

    c. The V has a programmed memory for the driver's seat that automatically positions height, distance from pedals, and steering wheel for each user.

7. Using resources such as the *Wall Street Journal* online, find an example of a company whose strategy matches its mission and goals. What leads you to believe its strategy matches its mission and goals? Next, find an example of a company whose strategy does not seem to match its mission and goals. What leads you to believe its strategy does not

match its mission and goals? Support your arguments with points from this chapter.

8. As this chapter discusses, target audiences are initially described in terms of their demographics, then "profiled" according to personality and lifestyle. Find examples of three products that are targeted to you. Using points from this chapter, discuss what strategies the companies are using

to target their products to you. What is successful and why? What is not successful and why?

9. Advertising can solve only message-related problems such as image, attitude, perception, and knowledge of information. In what ways does advertising solve these problems? What is the impact on consumers? On the company's strategy? On the advertising budget?

Suggested Class Project

With some classmates, select two print ads, one for a consumer product and one for a business-to-business product. Working from the ads, determine the selling premise, the product position, the product image, the competitive advantage, and the specific target audience. What were the objectives? Were they achieved? Determine where the strategy was clear and where it was unclear.

Suggested Internet Class Project

Examine The Following Web Sites; (suv.ford.ru/hondasuv.com) (cadillacsuv. com). Based on what you find on these sites, compare the positioning strategies for their top-of-the-line SUV models.

Hallmark BUILD•A•CAMPAIGN Projects

Please review the Hallmark Case Appendix at the end of the text before responding to these questions.

1. Using the Hallmark case as a model, meet in small groups to explore how marketing, media, communication, and creative objectives work together to provide the path for developing the advertising campaign.

2. Visit a Hallmark Gold Crown store in your area. Develop two marketing and two communication objectives for the store you visited. Provide a clear rationale for setting these objectives. Now suggest the best advertising budget–setting method for accomplishing these objectives for the store you visited.

Notes

1. "Comfort Zone," *Adweek* (Special Planning Section) (July 3, 1998): 31.

2. Allison Fass, "Online Archive for Coke Advertising," www.nytime.com, December 10, 2001.

3. Christopher Watts, "VW Misses Its Mark," *Forbes* (February 19, 2001): 78–79.

4. Russell Colley, *Defining Advertising Goals for Measured Advertising Results* (New York: Association of National Advertisers, 1961).

5. Michael L. Ray, "Communication and the Hierarchy of Effects," in *New Models for Mass Communication Research*, P. Clarke, ed. (Beverly Hills, CA: Sage, 1973), 147–175.

6. Robert C. Lavidge and Gary A. Steiner, "A Model for Predictive Measurements of Advertising Effectiveness," *Journal of Marketing* (October 1961): 59–62.

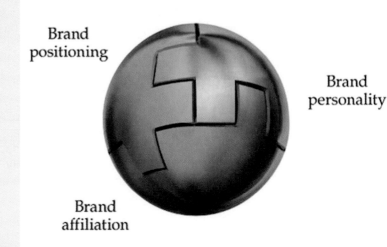

Brand positioning

Brand personality

Brand affiliation

There are three key components to building a powerful brand—positioning, personality, and affiliation.

BUILDING THE CHICK-FIL-A BRAND

Building the Chick-fil-A brand is top priority for both Chick-fil-A and its advertising agency, the Richards Group. In their opinion, of all the things Chick-fil-A owns, nothing is as important as its brand. Its brand is its future, and great brands have the potential to continue forever.

At the Richards Group, they define a brand as a promise. It is a promise that is made to consumers through everything they can observe, like logos, the color of a package, signage, the store appearance, and the employees. The list goes on and on.

To fully understand a client's brand, the Richards Group uses a discipline they have developed, called Spherical branding. This is a process they go through with the client. The first step is to accurately identify the client's business. The next step is to identify three branding strategies: brand positioning, brand personality, and brand affiliation. These strategies work together to form a brand.

The development of a brand positioning strategy is not done by mere consensus. It requires thorough data analysis and primary research. It must define the target audience, a competitive frame of reference, and the most meaningful point-of-difference for the brand. Here is an example:

Chick-fil-A Brand Positioning: **To choosy people in a hurry**,

↑

(target audience)

Chick-fil-A is the premium **fast-food restaurant** brand

↑

(frame of reference)

that **consistently serves America's best-loved chicken sandwiches.**

↑

(point-of-difference)

Next is the task of identifying the brand personality. What are the human traits your brand portrays to the consumer? To illustrate:

Chick-fill-A Personality: Caring, genuine, clean-cut, dependable, and unexpectedly fun.

The final branding strategy is brand affiliation. In essence, brand affiliation answers the question, "How are other people going to perceive me as a result of using this brand?"

Chick-fil-A Brand Affiliation: Chick-fil-A customers don't mind paying a little more because it's worth it. They appreciate a nicer, better experience. They like associating with a company that has good values.

These three strategies affect the mind (positioning), heart (personality), and ego (affiliation) of the consumer. All three strategies are necessary for consumers to build conviction for a brand.

Spherical branding provides everyone in the company, no matter what the department, a framework for developing consistent communication to the consumer. After all, it's not just the marketing and advertising departments that are responsible for communicating to consumers and building the brand.

IT'S YOUR TURN

1. Do you agree that the brand is most important? Why or why not?
2. How can the brand be the responsibility of every person working for the organization?

i-Zone pocket camera and sticky film from Polaroid.

i-zone.com

Polaroid
i-zone

CHAPTER

8

Media Planning and Buying

CHAPTER OBJECTIVES

When you have completed this chapter, you should be able to

1. Explain how media planning fits into the advertising process.
2. Outline how media planners set media objectives.
3. Describe how media planners develop media strategies.
4. Explain the functions and special skills of media buyers.
5. Summarize the process of staging a media plan.

Polaroid Pictures You Everywhere

Award: *EFFIE Gold 2001, Consumer Electronics category*

Company: *Polaroid I-Zone Camera*

Agency: *Sterling Group; Goodby, Silverstein and Partners; Ideo*

Campaign: *"Where Will You Stick Yours"*

When Polaroid cameras came on the scene years ago, everyone loved them. They provided instant gratification—just shoot and watch the photograph develop. While the traditional 600 series instant camera remains the company's cornerstone, Polaroid made a decision that it needed to target new users and introduce new products if it was going to grow. The company had to make several key decisions about its marketing and advertising strategies.

Polaroid's first decision was to target Generation Y (age 21 and under) and provide a new image-creation technology. The strategy began in Japan in late 1997 with a low-cost plastic camera called Xiao (Mandarin for "small"). Selling for an equivalent $20, the camera was an instant hit with females age 12 to 26. Still, research indicated that the current version of the camera was not ready for a global market. Most notably, it could shoot in focus at only 2.5 feet. By early 1998, Polaroid had enlisted Sterling Group, New York, to work on packaging and identity; Goodby, Silverstein and Partners, San Francisco, for ads; and Ideo, Palo Alto, California, for industrial design.

The engineers at Ideo started the design of a new product. The result was a pocket-sized camera called the I-Zone that takes instant photo-booth sized pictures that you can stick anywhere—on phones, t-shirts, and so on. It cost $17.99, and comes in four funky colors.

Polaroid's biggest challenge was reaching the targeted teenagers (primarily girls) at the optimal time. The company knew that teenagers used a host of electronic devices, including cell phones, pagers, and e-mail. These devices satisfied the teens' needs for independence and social interaction. Now the question was how to tell these teenagers that the I-Zone fit into their world.

The initial media strategy was both formal and informal. It was also quite systematic. Initially, five TV spots were produced. The formal strategy was to use e-mails, instant messaging, and Web advertising before the TV campaign hit. The TV campaign was a series of 30-second spots on programs with a high teen viewership such as *Dawson's Creek* and *Sabrina the Teenage Witch*. Complementing the broadcast TV, the company used Channel One television to reach teens at school.

As part of its informal media strategy, Polaroid courted teen celebrity endorsements before the I-Zone was released by sending complimentary cameras to Christina Aguilera, Britney Spears, the stars of Fox's *Beverly Hills 90210*, and the Backstreet Boys. Polaroid also sponsored the Backstreet Boys' 1999 tour, Britney Spears' 2000 tour, and a mall tour with Nobody's Angel—all of this to get cameras into the hands of teenage girls while providing a link between product and stars.

How well did the campaign work? Check the "It's a Wrap" at the end of this chapter.

MEDIA PLANNING AND BUYING

As Polaroid knows, media planning is a problem-solving process. The problem: How can media choices help meet marketing objectives? The ultimate goal is to reach the target audience in the best possible way, and contribute to sales and profitability.

In this chapter, we examine the media planning and buying functions, where they fit in the advertising process, and how media planners set objectives and develop media strategies. We then explore the skills media planners need and explain how one company staged a media plan. (We discuss specific types of media in Chapters 9 and 10.)

A word of caution: Some media terminology (and there's lots of it) is confusing to people outside the advertising business. If you plan to be involved in marketing for any business, no matter what its size, familiarity with the terms is important. We also do some calculations. Try not to get bogged down. Media specialists generally do the number crunching. However, to read, understand, and evaluate a media plan, you need to know what the numbers in the plan actually mean.

Media planning is the process of determining how to use time and space to achieve advertising objectives. One of those objectives is always to place the advertising message before a target audience. A **medium** is a single form of communication (television, billboards, online media). Combining media (using TV, radio, and magazines) is a **media mix**. A **media vehicle** is a single program, magazine, or radio station. Although these terms have specific meanings, people in the advertising industry typically use the term *media* in most situations.[1] For simplicity's sake, we use that term, too.

Media planning demands the biggest portion of the advertiser's budget (cost for space and time). To see where media buying and planning fit into the advertising process, look at Figure 8.1. Even though we examine media planning before creative planning, they are parallel processes that constantly influence one another. Think back to Chapter 5. Ideally, the insights culled from the strategic research influence the creative and media plans for all aspects of marketing communication, not just advertising, so that the marketing communications work in concert.

The process presented in Figure 8.1 would make you think that media planning is systematic and complex. But in fact, a media plan may be quite simple and somewhat haphazard. A psychotherapist operating out of her home may purchase a small Yellow Pages ad, along with a much smaller ad in the local newspaper, when her finances permit. That's it—say $590 per year on media. Even a small sporting goods store may focus on a somewhat larger directory ad, along with a print ad placed biweekly in the local newspaper. The latter is likely paid for by the various manufacturers whose brands he carries. Total media cost, say $2,850 per year.

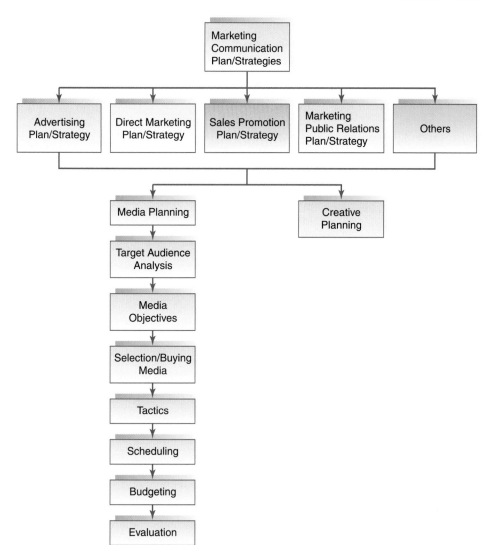

FIGURE 8.1

THE MEDIA PLANNING PROCESS
Media planning and creative planning go on simultaneously. They are parallel processes and influence one another.

Regardless of whether a company is spending a few hundred dollars on one medium or millions of dollars on thousands of media alternatives, the goal is still the same: to reach the right people, at the right time, with the right message. The same principles of media planning apply.

MEDIA: STILL BIG BUSINESS

Advertising and especially media are directly affected by the economy. Good economic times have produced tremendous spending in many media categories, while bad times have put individual mediums out of business. Consequently, projections about media spending must be flexible enough to deal with economic unknowns as well as other uncontrolled negative factors. In this case we mean the events of 9/11, which not only created tremendous pain and anguish for thousands of people but also exacerbated an economic downturn that had already gained momentum before the tragedy. As noted earlier, the advertising industry was particularly hard hit in 2001, with a severe decline in billing, most of which was related directly to media, and which experts estimate was 30 percent or more.

Consequently, the figures displayed in Figure 8.2 have little validity in projecting a trend, positive or negative. No one knows for sure what these numbers will look like for 2001 and beyond. Most likely they will be substantially lower. Still, $243.6 billion suggests media spending is still a big business.

	100 Leading National Advertisers Advertising expenditures*			Medium as % of total		All U.S. advertising spending Advertising expenditures*			Medium as % of total		Coen's U.S. totals**	
Medium	2000	1999	% chg	2000	1999	2000	1999	% chg	2000	1999	2000	1999
Magazine	$7,039	$6,720	4.7	8.4	8.7	$16,697	$14,672	13.8	6.9	6.6	*$17,285*	*$15,707*
Sunday magazine	357	323	10.6	0.4	0.4	1,110	1,006	10.3	0.5	0.5	*NA*	*NA*
Newspaper	5,883	5,679	3.6	7.1	7.3	18,817	17,797	5.7	7.7	8.0	*41,821*	*40,290*
National newspaper	1,093	979	11.6	1.3	1.3	3,785	3,320	14.0	1.6	1.5	*7,229*	*6,358*
Outdoor	508	481	5.4	0.6	0.6	2,391	1,989	20.2	1.0	0.9	*5,176*	*4,780*
Network TV	14,407	13,240	8.8	17.3	17.1	18,417	16,354	12.6	7.6	7.4	*15,888*	*13,961*
Spot TV	6,982	6,255	11.6	8.4	8.1	17,107	15,115	13.2	7.0	6.8	*25,806*	*23,180*
Syndicated TV	2,247	2,219	1.3	2.7	2.9	2,804	2,650	5.8	1.2	1.2	*3,108*	*2,870*
Cable TV networks	5,231	4,713	11.0	6.3	6.1	9,506	8,181	16.2	3.9	3.7	*14,429*	*12,570*
Network radio	343	160	114.3	0.4	0.2	871	417	108.7	0.4	0.2	*18,515*	*16,531*
National spot radio	942	826	14.0	1.1	1.1	2,672	2,349	13.8	1.1	1.1	*780*	*684*
Internet	350	379	−7.7	0.4	0.5	4,333	2,832	53.0	1.8	1.3	*4,333*	*2,832*
Yellow Pages	101	115	−12.4	0.1	0.1	13,228	12,652	4.6	5.4	5.7	*13,228*	*12,652*
Measured media	45,481	42,090	8.1	54.5	54.3	111,739	99,335	12.5	45.9	44.7	*167,598*	*152,415*
Unmeasured spending estimates	37,904	35,374	7.2	45.5	45.7	*131,941*	*122,973*	7.3	54.1	55.3	*76,082*	*69,893*
Total U.S. advertising	83,385	77,464	7.6	100.0	100.0	*243,680*	*222,308*	9.6	100.0	100.0	*243,680*	*222,308*

Notes: Dollars are in millions. *Measured media for 100 Leaders and all advertisers from Taylor Nelson Sofres' CMR, except Yellow Pages for the 100 Leaders, from Yellow Pages Publishers Association. **Figures extrapolated from Robert J. Coen's media analysis at Universal McCann (AA, June 2001) are shown in italic for comparison. In the Coen figures shown, spot radio, spot TV and cable TV include national and local spot buys; magazine includes business publications. For definitions and more information see methodology below.

FIGURE 8.2 DOMESTIC ADVERTISING SPENDING BY MEDIUM

Even though advertisers might use these statistics to plan their media spending, they shy away from relying on them too heavily, as advertising spending tends to be affected by economic shifts.

Source: "Leading National Advertisers," *Advertising Age* (September 24, 2001): 12.

Media Consolidation: A New Perspective

The media planning field has undergone a metamorphosis because of the proliferation of new media such as electronic billboards, the Internet, and interactive media. Media department employees who once worked silently behind the scenes are now in the forefront, directing marketing strategy.

Traditionally, media planning was essentially based on a client's media strategy. The ad agency was responsible for developing the media plan, which was usually devised jointly by the agency's media department, the account and creative teams, and the marketer's brand management group. Once the plan was formed, a media buying unit, sometimes attached to the ad agency, executed it.

Today an advertising client is just as likely to outsource media planning to an agency as it is to develop its own plan. Because of these shifts, the line between media planning and media buying has become hazy.

Consolidation is taking place within the media agency industry. During the 2000–2001 period, at least a dozen major mergers took place. The largest was the creation of Magna Global, the first worldwide negotiation company, with initial total billing of over $40 billion. The primary reason for consolidation is that it not only creates definite cost savings, but it also provides more opportunity to negotiate better prices when buying media.

The Aperture Concept in Media Planning

Each prospective customer for a product or service has an ideal time and place at which she can be reached with an advertising message. This point can be when the consumer is in

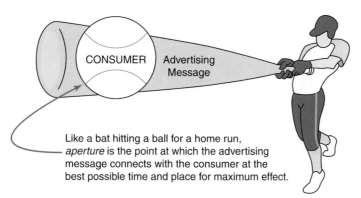

FIGURE 8.3

THE CONCEPT OF APERTURE IN MEDIA PLANNING
Advertising should expose the consumer to the product when interest and attention are high.

Like a bat hitting a ball for a home run, *aperture* is the point at which the advertising message connects with the consumer at the best possible time and place for maximum effect.

the "search corridor"—the purchasing mode—or it can occur when the consumer is seeking more information before entering the corridor. The goal of the media planner is to expose the target audience to the advertiser's message at these critical points.

This ideal point is called an **aperture**. The most effective advertisement should expose the consumer to the product when interest and attention are high. As Figure 8.3 demonstrates, aperture can be thought of as the home-run swing in baseball: The ball meets the bat at the right spot and at the precise instant for maximum effect.

Locating the aperture opportunity is a major responsibility of the media planner. The planner must study the marketing position of the advertiser to determine which media opportunities will do the best job. Finding aperture opportunity is a complex, difficult assignment. Success depends on accurate marketing research, appreciation of the message concept, and a sensitive understanding of the channels of mass communication.

Media Planning Information Sources

Some people believe that media planners are the hub in the advertising wheel, the central point where all campaign elements (that is, the spokes of the wheel) are joined. This belief may stem from the sheer volume of data and information that media planners must gather, sort, and analyze before media decision making can begin. Figure 8.4 illustrates the wide range of media information sources.

In many ad agencies, account planners collect, gather, and analyze some of this market and creative information, especially if it relates to the target audience, message design, or brand image. The bases for the information selection process are the media objectives that start the media plan.

SETTING MEDIA OBJECTIVES

Each media plan has a series of objectives that support some basic goals that can be met only if the advertiser implements a strategic plan of action. The basic goals that direct media strategy typically focus on whom to advertise to, which geographic areas to cover,

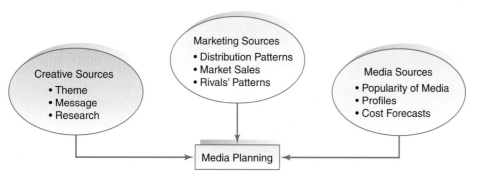

FIGURE 8.4

SOURCES OF INFORMATION IN MEDIA PLANNING
Media planners look for data from many sources, including creative, marketing, and media sources.

when to advertise, what the duration of the campaign should be, and what the size or length of the ad should be. However, they're still directly connected to the overall advertising objectives.[2]

Finding Target Audiences in Media Opportunities

Two major challenges face media planners: (1) Assessing the media for target audience opportunities; and (2) discrepancies between the language of internal strategic research and external media research and the lack of reliable audience research for new media.

Company research can provide profiles of the firm's valued customers and prospects; these profiles often contain descriptions of people's interests, activities, and attitudinal concerns—in all, a valuable insight into the company's target audience. The problem for media planners is that these profiles are not used by the mass media in describing their audiences. This discrepancy forces planners to translate the company's marketing research language into the language of mass-media information sources—no small task.

Suppose you work for Biofoam, a small firm that sells biodegradable packing material to consumers and businesses. You want to look for prospects with strong ecological feelings, but mass media doesn't profile audiences based on ecological concerns. With no media measurement of this attitude, you must find another indicator of environmental concerns. Instead, you look for media that tends to be read or viewed by people with environmental concerns. You must assume that such media attracts certain people.

Another challenge is the lack of reliable audience research on new media. New traditional media (that is, magazines or cable networks that have just recently been introduced) must wait some time before research companies can supply audience estimates. For innovative media such as store-based advertising, special event promotions, and online media, the existing research firms do not have measurements available that are comparable to those for traditional media. Although these opportunities have marketing value, it is hard to judge their impact without research.

Sales Geography

Although companies may distribute goods and services in many cities and states, sales are seldom consistent across all areas, no matter how popular the brand. Sales differences affect which markets the advertiser runs the campaign in and how many dollars are allocated to each geographic region. For the media planner a system of evaluation is needed to distribute the advertising dollars accurately. Billboards are inexpensive and serve as an excellent reminder vehicle, especially if located on the correct streets and highways.[3]

Timing

When is the best time to place the message before the target audience? The concept of aperture suggests that advertising is most effective when people are most receptive to the product information. Exposing consumers to the ad at that time is more easily said than done. Media planners might have to juggle a number of variables to make correct timing decisions; how often the product is bought, whether it is used more in some months than in others, and how heavily it is advertised by competitors from month to month. Each combination of influence makes the timing strategy unique to each company and brand. Timing decisions relate to factors such as seasonality, holidays, days of the week, and time of day.

Duration: How Long to Advertise?

For how many weeks of the sales year should the advertising run? If there is a need to cover most of the weeks, the advertising will be spread rather thin. If the amount of time to cover is limited, advertising can be concentrated more heavily. The selection of duration depends on a number of factors, including schedule and the advertising budget, consumer use cycles, and competitive strategies. Let's look at those factors now.

THE INSIDE STORY

NATIONAL VERSUS LOCAL ADVERTISING

Heather Beck   Media Coordinator
Stern Advertising, Cleveland

The difference between local advertising and national advertising may seem obvious, but it is probably more complex than you think. National advertising is more than just nationally recognized brands on TV, and local advertising is more than just a small "mom and pop" business placing ads in the town newspaper. Several factors are considered in deciding whether to use local or national vehicles, and it is important to know these differences, especially when it comes to budgeting.

Although a small company conducting business in one local area would not likely advertise nationally, many national brands advertise at the local level. Retailers are the most common example. A well-known chain may place national advertising to promote its brand and then complement those efforts with local advertising to promote a specific store or product. For example, a national department store's commercial will air on television, promoting the store name as well as the store's brand names. Then you may see an ad in the local Sunday paper announcing a sale on those brands at the nearest store. Don't think, however, that all national ads are on TV and that all local ads are in local newspapers. Many companies prefer to complement their advertising in the same medium and at the same time. For example, many times an advertiser, such as an automobile company, may run a commercial on TV, featuring its product and its current incentive program. Within the same television program, you may see a spot showcasing the local dealership where that

car can be purchased. This reinforces the advertising of the brand by showing the product and then letting the consumer know where to get it.

Another difference between local and national advertising is cost. Newspapers, for example, have separate rates for national advertisers and local, or retail, advertisers. It is necessary to distinguish this difference when you work in media and are purchasing advertising space for your client. The newspaper may automatically charge the national rate for a nationally known brand, but as long as the local store is mentioned in a *locator*, the ad will qualify as a local retail ad, saving the advertiser a substantial amount of money. This is called co-op advertising—when the corporation and the local retailer share the cost of advertising.

Again, many factors influence whether advertising will be on a local or national level. Details concerning the client, the market, the medium, and the ad itself will require careful consideration when making this determination.

Heather Beck is a media coordinator with Stern Advertising, a Cleveland-based agency with a few satellite offices in Buffalo, Pittsburgh, and smaller cities throughout Ohio. The agency is a member of the Integer Group, an Omnicom Company. Heather's primary account is Pearle Vision.

Nominated by Professor Edd Applegate, Middle Tennessee State University.

Schedule and the Advertising Budget If advertising allocations were unlimited, most companies would advertise every day. Not even the largest advertisers are in this position, so advertisers must rely on shorter schedules with stronger levels of advertising.

Consumer Use Cycles Continuity should match consumer use cycles (the time between purchase and repurchase), especially for products and services that demand high usage rates, such as soft drinks, toothpaste, candy and gum, fast-food restaurants, and movies. The advertiser views these cycles as chances to gain or lose customers. For example, movie marketers do most of their newspaper advertising on the weekends, when most people go to movies.

Competitive Advertising In crowded product categories (household products, food, and durable goods) few advertisers are willing to ignore competitors' advertising activity. In such situations media planners make scheduling decisions based on the amount of competitive traffic. The objective is to find media where the advertiser's voice is not drowned out by competitors' voices. This concept, often called **share of voice** (percentage of total advertising messages in a medium used by one advertiser), might mean scheduling to avoid the heavy clutter of competing advertising.

DEVELOPING MEDIA STRATEGIES

To achieve the key plan objectives of who (target), where (location), when (time frame), how long (duration), and what (the size of the ad), media planners use a selection process of choosing the best alternatives and methods to satisfy the plan's needs. In all cases, the final media strategy must meet the advertising objectives. This section discusses some common strategies that companies use to meet advertising objectives: target audience, geographic, timing and duration, and size and length strategies.

Target Audience Strategies: New Technology of Measurement

Media planners are limited by mass-media audience research. However, future developments may help them overcome this limitation so that they can better execute their target audience strategies.

Retail Scanners Many retail outlets, but especially supermarkets, use electronic scanners at the checkout. When you shop at your local Safeway, each product you buy has an electronic bar code that contains the name of the product and its price. The regional Safeway system may decide to establish a consumer panel so it can track sales among various consumer groups. You would be asked to join the panel, which might contain hundreds of other customers, and would complete a fairly extensive questionnaire, and be assigned an ID number. You might receive a premium or a discount on purchases for your participation. Each time you make a purchase, you also submit your ID number. Therefore, if Safeway runs a two-page newspaper ad, it can track actual sales to determine to what extent the ad worked. Various manufacturers who sell products to Safeway can do the same kind of testing. Your panel questionnaire will also contain a list of media that you use; so media can also be evaluated.

Database Developments Software technology has revolutionized the old-fashioned customer list. Businesses can now store an individual name, address, age, income, and other information in a database. A database is a list of people and their various charac-

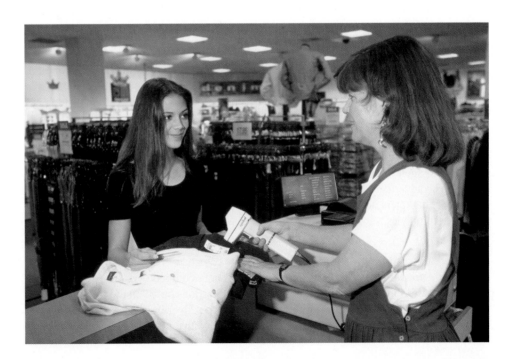

Many retail outlets use electronic scanners to track sales among consumer groups.

teristics, gathered with or without their knowledge and stored electronically. Every time you buy a product, fill out a warranty card, apply for a credit card, or enroll at a university, it is possible that this information will be added to your file. Businesses can store customers' media preferences regarding what they watch, hear, and read. Imagine how much information your cable or satellite system has on your viewing preferences. This information can then be employed to create a match between target audience and media.

Marketing Mix Modeling **Marketing mix modeling** is a technique that enables marketers to determine the precise impact of the media plan on product sales. There are many mix modeling software programs available to advertisers today. The development of this technology began in the packaged goods sector as a result of the supermarket scanner systems. It is now part of virtually all product categories.

An example of one model came about through the partnering of McCann-Erickson Worldwide, New York and Media Plan, a leading developer of media planning software and systems. They created a media allocation software system code named MediaFX. The system can create an unlimited number of media combinations and then simulate the sales produced by each. The media planner can then make intelligent decisions, given factors such as budget, timing, and so forth.

Internet Audience Measurement When compared to most other media, the advantages of the Internet as a potential advertising vehicle are tremendous, with rapid, near instantaneous feedback and results chief among them. Rather than wait weeks or months to measure the success of an advertising campaign, marketers can instead run tests online, measure meaningful results within days, and quickly invest in the best performers with minimal switching costs. However, the measures of effectiveness used to evaluate off-line campaigns don't seem to transfer well to the online world.[4]

The biggest issue with measuring audience on the Internet has been the lack of standardization of the measurement tools. CASIE (a joint project of the Association of National Advertisers, Inc., and the American Association of Advertising Agencies, with the support of the Advertising Research Foundation [ARF]), created the Guiding Principles of Interactive Media Audience Measurement in 1996. This working paper focuses on supplying guidelines for providing quality audience measurement of interactive media. (See www.ciadvertising.org/studies/student for a complete report.)

Having the ability to quantitatively measure audience is particularly important to media buyers, who need to plan their buys based on the reported numbers. These buyers want to be able to show what the "click through or page view or total traffic" means to them and their clients. It would also be meaningful for advertisers or media buyers to obtain similar information from comparable sites so that they could see if they were getting a fair deal. This information about audience measurement is good for companies who want to structure their advertising rates according to the activity on their Web sites. Accurate audience measurement also helps advertisers show their clients the effectiveness of their ads.[5]

Geographic Strategies: Allocating Media Weight

Most national or regional marketers divide their market geographically. A company such as E & J Gallo Winery, for instance, divides the United States and Canada into six regional markets. The amount of sales produced in each geographic market will often vary, and marketers try to match advertising investment with the amount of forecasted sales. The formula planners use to allocate advertising dollars may rely on any or all of the following market statistics: target population, distribution of product, strength of brand, media costs, and company sales results (forecasts).

Planners typically don't make heavy allocations in weak sales areas unless strong marketing signals indicate significant growth potential. Conversely, strong sales markets may not receive proportional increases in advertising unless clear evidence suggests that company

FIGURE 8.5

THE CONTINUITY TACTICS OF
PULSING AND FLIGHTING
Pulsing continuity strategies means
ads run all the time, sometimes more
often than not. A flighting continuity
strategy means ads alternate between
running intensely for a period and
then not at all for a period.

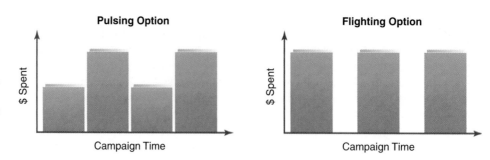

sales can go much higher with greater advertising investment. Successful allocation strategy entails the combined efforts of the media planner and marketing (sales) management.

Timing and Duration Strategies

When to advertise can be based on seasons, months, or parts of the day or week, but it all fits within the aperture concept. The strategy for meeting time and duration objectives involves a balance between the available advertising dollars and the length of the campaign. A **continuity** strategy spreads the advertising continuously and evenly over the length of the campaign. Planners who cannot afford or do not want continuous scheduling have two other methods to consider: pulse patterns and flight patterns, as shown in Figure 8.5.

An alternative to continuous advertising, known as **pulsing**, is designed to intensify advertising before an open aperture and then to reduce advertising to much lower levels until the aperture opens again. The pulse pattern has peaks and valleys.

Fast-food companies such as McDonald's and Burger King use pulsing patterns. Although the competition for daily customers demands continuous advertising, they will greatly intensify activity to accommodate special events such as new menu items, merchandise premiums, and contests. Pulsed schedules cover most of the year, but still provide periodic intensity.

The **flighting** strategy is the most severe type of continuity adjustment. It is characterized by alternating periods of intense advertising activity and periods of no advertising (hiatus). This on-and-off schedule allows for a longer campaign without making the advertising schedule too light. The hope in using nonadvertising periods is that the consumers will remember the brand and its advertising for some time after the ads have stopped.

Figure 8.6 illustrates this awareness change. The jagged line represents the rise and fall of consumer awareness of the brand. If the flight strategy works, there will be a **carryover effect** of past advertising that means consumers will remember the product until the next advertising period begins. The advertiser will then have fewer worries about low share-of-voice conditions.

Size and Length Strategies

Effectiveness of a media plan also involves determining the size or length of a particular message, in print or broadcast media, respectively. Although researchers have studied this area a great deal, data on which size or length is most effective are inconclusive.

FIGURE 8.6

CONSUMER AWARENESS LEVELS
(RED LINE) IN A FLIGHTING
STRATEGY
By using a flighting strategy,
advertisers hope that there will be a
carry-over effect, meaning
consumers will remember the
product during advertising
downtimes.

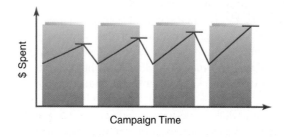

We do know that simply doubling the size of an ad does not double its effectiveness. Although a larger promotion creates a higher level of attraction and greater opportunity for creative impact, the extent of this effect is still undetermined. Equivocal results have been reported for print media of various sizes and for television and radio commercials of various lengths. Depending on what advertisers have to say and how well they can say it, a 30-second commercial may do the job much better than a 60-second commercial.

The size or length chosen should relate to the advertising objectives. If the objective is to educate the target audience through a great deal of technical information, a full-page ad or a 60-second spot might be necessary. However, a 10-second spot might be sufficient to create name recognition.

Positioning research is only slightly more enlightening. In general, some evidence suggests that within a print medium the inside cover and first few pages get a slightly better readership, placement of compatible stories adjacent to an ad may enhance its effect, and having many competing ads on the same page detracts from its effectiveness. Findings related to broadcast and interactive media are almost nonexistent.

Simply getting ready to select specific media is an arduous task that takes many hours. Although it would certainly be tempting to skip all this preparatory work and select the obvious magazines or TV programs, mistakes are costly. Assuming that Hispanics listen to a local Hispanic radio station, for example, may seem correct until you look at the research and discover that non-Hispanic college students make up a large portion of the audience. Make one error in judgment in this initial investigation and it can have a domino effect for the entire media plan. In many cases, finding the optimum aperture point for a particular target audience is like finding a needle in a haystack. Media planning is extremely complicated.

MEDIA SELECTION PROCEDURES

Setting objectives and recommending strategies help to focus the media plan, but planners must consider three other factors to select the specific advertising media for the message. These factors are: the number of different people exposed to the message (reach), the degree of exposure repetition (frequency), and the efficiency (cost per thousand or CPM) of the selected media vehicles. We investigate each of these factors of media planning in the sections that follow, but first we look at basic methods planners use to measure media impact.

Audience Measures Used in Media Planning

In the same way that a carpenter uses feet and inches and a printer uses points and picas, the media planner uses specific measurements to evaluate a media plan: gross impressions and gross rating points. Even though a carpenter is building your home, it would still be important for you to understand the jargon so that you could discuss the project in an intelligent manner. Likewise, everyone working on an ad should understand the language of the media planner.

Gross Impressions An *impression* is one person's opportunity to be exposed to a program, newspaper, magazine, or outdoor location anywhere there is an ad. Impressions are a measure of the size of the audience either for one media (one announcement or one insertion) or for a combination of vehicles as estimated by media research.

If the *David Letterman Show* has an audience of 100,000 viewers, then each time the advertiser buys time on that program to advertise a product, the value in impressions is 100,000. If the advertiser used an announcement (usually a 30-second commercial) in each of four consecutive broadcasts, the total viewer impressions would be 100,000 times 4, or 400,000. In practice, media planners use **gross impressions** as a primary measure. Gross impressions are the sum of the audiences of all the media vehicles used during a certain span of time—when multiple vehicles are used. The summary figure is called "gross" because the planner has made no attempt to calculate how many different people were in the audience.

TABLE 8.1 Total Target Impressions Calculation

Media Vehicle	Target Impressions	Number of Messages	Total Target Impressions
Jeopardy	3,270,000	4	13,080,000
People Magazine	8,620,000	2	17,240,000
USA Today	1,700,000	2	3,400,000
			33,720,000

To get the sum of gross impressions, the media planner finds the audience figure for each vehicle used, multiplies that figure by the number of times the vehicle was used, and adds the vehicle figures. Table 8.1 provides an example of how gross impressions would be calculated, assuming an ad was run four times on *Jeopardy*, in two issues of *People*, and two issues of *USA Today*.

Gross Rating Points Gross impression figures become very large and difficult to remember. The gross rating (percentage of exposure) is an easier measurement to work with because it converts the raw figure to a percentage. The sum of the total exposure potential expressed as a percentage of the audience population is called **gross rating points (GRPs)**. GRPs are calculated by dividing the total number of impressions by the size of the audience and multiplying by 100.

To demonstrate GRP calculations, let's revisit our David Letterman example. Letterman had 100,000 viewer impressions. Suppose there were a total of 500,000 possible viewers (total number of households with televisions, whether the sets are on or off) at that hour. The 100,000 viewers watching Letterman out of the possible 500,000 would represent 20 percent of viewers, or a 20.0 rating. The gross rating point total on four telecasts would be 80 (20 rating × 4 telecasts).

Total rating values are calculated just as total impressions are. Planners can use the sum of rating points to calculate the total of gross rating points for any schedule, whether actual or proposed. In Table 8.2 the impressions schedule is changed to gross rating points.

How are GRPs used by media planners? Is 36.2, as noted in Table 8.2, a good number? The answer is, we're not sure. Based on experience, intelligent guessing, and software, planners have a general idea of how many GRPs are necessary to effectively impact a particular market. So, for example, it might take 4,800 GRPs per month to be sufficient for San Diego, 1,200 GRPs per month for Richmond, Virginia, and 300 GRPs per month in Paducah, Kentucky.

Reach and Media Planning

An important aspect of an advertising campaign is how many different members of the target audience can be exposed to the message in a particular time frame. Different, or unduplicated, audiences are those that have at least one chance for message exposure. Most

TABLE 8.2 National Target Audience Gross Rating Points, September 2001

Media Vehicle	Target Rating	Number of Messages	Total GRPs
Jeopardy	3.5	4	14.0
People Magazine	9.1	2	18.2
USA Today	2.0	2	4.0
			36.2

TABLE 8.3	Viewing Homes/Week for David Letterman				
Home	**Week 1**	**Week 2**	**Week 3**	**Week 4**	**Total Viewers**
1	TV	–	TV	TV	3
2	–	TV	–	TV	2
3	TV	–	–	–	1
4	–	TV	–	–	1
5	–	TV	TV	TV	3
6	–	–	–	–	0
7	–	–	–	TV	1
8	TV	TV	TV	–	3
9	TV	–	TV	–	2
10	–	–	–	–	0
Viewing/week	4	4	4	4	16

advertisers realize that a campaign's success is due in part to its ability to reach as many people as possible.

Reach is the percentage of the target population exposed at least once to the advertiser's message during a specific time frame. The media planner calculates the reach of a media schedule according to research estimates that forecast the unduplicated audience. Planners measure most mass media this way, although for some media the estimate is only a statistical probability. This means the reach is not based on actual data but is calculated from the laws of chance. Reach can be calculated only when the planner has access to media audience research or projections from statistical models. It is not arbitrary guesswork.

To see how the reach calculation could work in television, we use a simplified scenario. Our fictional television market of Hometown, U.S.A., has only 10 television households. Table 8.3 is a television survey that shows home viewing for the *David Letterman Show*. The viewing survey is for four weeks, during which the commercial ran once each week.

Each week four homes viewed the *David Letterman Show*. Because there are 10 homes in Hometown, the average program rating per week was 4 of 10, or 40 percent. To be counted as "reached," the household only has to view one episode, and 8 of the 10 homes did that during the week. The reach is 8 of 10, or 80 percent.

Frequency and Media Planning

Equally as important as the percentage of people exposed (reach) is the number of times they are exposed. This rate of exposure is called **frequency**. While the reach estimate is based on only a single exposure, frequency estimates the number of times the exposure is expected to happen.

To measure the frequency of a schedule, planners use two methods: a shorthand summary called **average frequency** and the **preferred frequency** method, which shows the percentage of audience reached at each level of repetition (exposed once, twice, and so on). Reach and frequency measures are the basis for most media planning and are terms familiar to everyone who works in advertising.

Average Frequency To figure the average frequency, you need only two numbers: the gross rating points (GRPs) of a schedule and the reach estimate. (Media planners can also calculate the average frequency from the gross impressions and the unduplicated impressions if ratings are not available.) Table 8.4 shows readership measures needed to plan the purchase of space in three magazines, including rating and impression values.

The schedule involves three magazines: *Today's Happiness, News Round-Up,* and *Fast-Paced Life.* Each magazine is listed by its total readership, readers expressed as a percentage (rating), and the number of unduplicated readers (those who do not read either of the other two magazines). Note the formula calculations at the bottom of the table.

TABLE 8.4	**Average Frequency Calculation Magazine Schedule (One Insertion Each)**

Magazine	Reader/Issue	Rating (GRP)	Unduplicated Readers = Reach
Today's Happiness	50,000	50.0	30,000
News Round-Up	40,000	40.0	15,000
Fast-Paced Life	18,000	18.0	11,000
Totals	108,000	108.0	56,000

Target population: 100,000 [100,000 represents the total target audience]

Total gross impressions: 108,000

Gross rating points: 108.0

Unduplicated readers: 56,000

Reach: 56.0 (56,000/100,000)

Average frequency: 1.9 issues seen (108,000/56,000 = 1.9) or (108 GRP/56 Reach = 1.9)

$$\text{Average frequency} = \frac{\text{Gross rating points}}{\text{Reach (\%)}}$$

or

$$\text{Average frequency} = \frac{\text{Gross audience impressions}}{\text{Unduplicated impressions}}$$

Frequency Distribution Average frequency can give the planner a distorted idea of the plan's performance. Suppose you had a schedule that meant that the ad could be seen a maximum of 20 times. If we figured the average from one person who saw 18 and another who saw 2 exposures, the average would be 10. But 10 exposures aren't close to the experience of either audience member. Most planners who consider frequency tend to calculate **frequency distribution** whenever possible. The distribution shows the number of target audience members.

Table 8.5 spotlights the importance of frequency distribution for a schedule of three news magazines: *Time, Newsweek*, and *U.S. News & World Report*. Each publication is to receive two ad insertions for a total of six advertising placements. The minimum exposure would be one insertion, and the maximum would be six.

The planner who evaluates this distribution might consider changing this schedule for two reasons: (1) 44 percent of the target audience would not be exposed, and (2) only 22.5 percent would read more than half the scheduled issues (that is, four, five, or six issues). The frequency distribution method is more revealing, and thus more valuable, than the average frequency

TABLE 8.5	**Magazine Frequency Distribution Table Based on Three Magazines, Two Issues Each**

Issues Read	Readers	Target Population (%)
0	44,000	44.0
1	7,000	7.0
2	6,500	6.5
3	20,000	20.0
4	10,600	10.6
5	8,200	8.2
6	3,700	3.7
Totals	100,000	100.0

56,000 read at least one issue. Reach = 56.0

method of reporting repetition. However, frequency distribution data are expensive to obtain because they're derived from special research tabulations and sophisticated math models.

Combining Reach and Frequency Goals

As we have just seen, the reach of an audience alone is not a sufficient measure of an advertising schedule's strength. Because of the proliferation of information and clutter, many media planners believe there should be a threshold, or minimum frequency level, before they consider an audience segment to have been exposed to the advertising message. So for people to be considered part of the reached audience, they must have been exposed more than once. This theory essentially combines the reach and the frequency elements into one factor known as **effective frequency**.

What is this minimum threshold? There is no single standard in media planning today, and it is doubtful there will ever be one. Some observers say that two or three is the minimum, but to prove an ideal level, we must know the aperture, message content, consumer interest, and competitors' advertising.

Even without all the answers, planners can use their knowledge and experience to determine a probable range of effective frequency. Many planners believe that effective frequency is the key planning dimension.

Cost Efficiency as a Planning Dimension

Advertisers don't always evaluate the media plan in terms of audience impressions. Sometimes the decision comes down to cold, hard cash. Cost may determine the number of messages that can be placed and in which media or media vehicles they are placed.

Given cost constraints, media planners usually select the media that will expose the largest target audience for the lowest possible cost. The key to this notion is the target audience. After all, the advertiser wants prospects and not just readers, viewers, or listeners. Therefore, advertisers should compare the cost of each proposed media vehicle with the medium's ability to deliver the target audience. The cheapest medium may not deliver the target audience, so the selection process is a balancing act.

The process of measuring the target audience size against the cost of that audience is called *efficiency*—or more popularly, **cost per thousand (CPM)** and **cost per rating (CPR)**. Typically, media specialists make these calculations and provide them to the account executive or the advertiser. Nonetheless, anyone working in advertising should understand the CPM variables and calculation process.

Cost Per Thousand It is best to use CPM analysis to compare vehicles within one medium (one magazine with another or one television program with another). It is also important to base it only on the portion of the audience that has the target characteristics, such as women between the ages of 25 and 34. To calculate the CPM you need only two figures: the costs of the unit (say time on TV or space in a magazine) and the estimated target audience. We divide the cost of the unit by the target audience's gross impressions to determine the advertising dollars needed to expose 1,000 members (because cost per thousand) of the target.

$$\text{CPM} = \frac{\text{Cost of message unit}}{\text{Gross impressions}} \times 1,000$$

How to Calculate CPMs Here are two examples that show how to calculate CPM:

- **Magazines**. An issue of *You* magazine has 10,460,000 readers who could be considered a target audience. The advertising unit is a four-color page and its rate is $42,000. The CPM is

$$\text{CPM} = \frac{\text{Cost of page or fractional page unit} \times 1,000}{\text{Target audience readers}}$$

$$= \frac{\$42,000 \times 1,000}{10,460,000} = \$4.02$$

- **Television**. The show *Inside Gossip* has 92,000 target viewers. The cost of a 30-second announcement during the show is $850.

$$\text{CPM} = \frac{\$850 \times 1{,}000}{92{,}000} = \$9.24$$

Cost per Rating Some planners prefer to compare media on the basis of rating points (ratings) instead of impressions. The calculation is parallel to CPM with one exception: The denominator is the rating percentage rather than the total impressions.

$$\text{CPR} = \frac{\text{Cost of message unit}}{\text{Program or issue rating}}$$

(Note: Because CPR is not calculated on a per-thousand basis, we do not multiply by 1,000.) If the target audience rating for the program *Inside Gossip* was 12.0 and the cost was still $850, the CPR would be 850/12, or $70.83.

Although both efficiency calculations are used, planners favor the CPR because of its simplicity. Both the CPM and the CPR are relative values. The absolute numbers mean very little unless there are similar values to compare. A planner would not know whether *Newsweek*'s CPM of $27.89 for the target audience was good or bad unless she had comparable figures for *Time* and *U.S. News & World Report*.

Although we can use these efficiency analyses across media (comparing one medium to another), such comparisons should be made carefully. When comparing the CPMs for radio and television, for example, we are comparing very different audience experiences, and if the experience is totally different, it is difficult to say that one medium is more efficient than the other. CPM and CPR are more valid when used to compare alternatives within a medium.

Selecting and Buying Acceptable Media

Success in media planning depends on more than knowledge of the audience size, reach, and cost per thousand. Success also depends on some intangibles that can influence the target consumer's reception of the advertising message. To many readers, viewers, or listeners, advertising is intrusive. Because audiences only tolerate advertising (with the exception of shopping ads in newspapers), planners should find the medium that consumers believe suits the message most effectively.

Media buyers need to be consulted as early as possible in the marketing plan. The planning stage is the time to explain to advertisers who have their hearts set on a certain medium that it isn't feasible given their budget or product. It's also the time to plan for other marketing communication methods and merchandising. An experienced media buyer knows what it takes to make an impact and the equation involves more than a certain number of gross rating points. How and where messages are placed is just as critical as the overall media mix.

The media planners, along with their experience and knowledge, play a pivotal role in making integrated marketing communication work. They know, for example, whether a particular magazine is capable of delivering a coupon, or which network news show should be targeted for a publicity story, or whether direct mail can deliver a sample for a new product introduction. They also know which media mix is best at delivering a consistent message to a particular target audience.

In previous sections we examined where media planning fits in the advertising process, and media planning objectives, strategies, and selection procedures. Now we turn to media buying functions and special skills.

MEDIA BUYING FUNCTIONS

A media buyer has distinct responsibilities (outlined in Figure 8.7) and must have specific skills to implement these duties. In this section, we examine the most important buyer

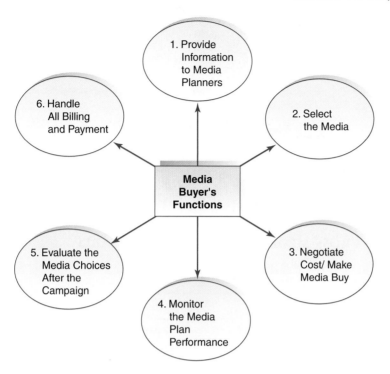

FIGURE 8.7

THE SIX MAIN FUNCTIONS
OF A MEDIA BUYER
Media buyers have six main
responsibilities.

functions: providing information to media planners, selecting the media, negotiating costs, monitoring the media choices, evaluating the media choices after the campaign, and handling billing and payment.

Providing Inside Information to the Media Planner

Media buyers are close enough to day-to-day changes in media popularity and pricing to be a constant source of inside information to media planners. For example, a newspaper buyer discovers that a key newspaper's delivery staff is going on strike; a radio time buyer learns that a top disk jockey is leaving a radio station; or a magazine buyer's source reveals that the new editor of a publication is going to change the editorial focus dramatically. All of these things can influence the strategy and tactics of current and future advertising plans.

Selecting Media Vehicles

One essential part of buying is choosing the best media vehicles to fit the target audience's aperture (the time and place at which the audience is most receptive to the message). The media planner lays out the direction, but the buyer is responsible for choosing the specific vehicles.

Armed with the media plan directives, the buyer seeks answers to a number of difficult questions: Does the vehicle have the right audience profile? Will the program's current popularity increase, stabilize, or decline? How well does the magazine's editorial format fit the brand? Does the radio station's choice of music offer the correct atmosphere for the creative theme? How well does the newspaper's circulation pattern fit the advertiser's distribution? The answers to those questions bear directly on the campaign's success. For instance, *Alternative Press Magazine* clearly matches Generation X. As indicated in the "A Matter of Practice" box, instant messaging is a medium teens find attractive.

Negotiating Media Prices/Authorizing the Buys

Aside from finding the aperture of target audiences, nothing is considered more crucial in media buying than securing the lowest possible price for placements. Time and space charges make up the largest portion of the advertising budget, so there is continuing pressure to keep costs as low as possible. To accomplish this, buyers operate in a world of negotiation.

This announcement demonstrates the importance of consultants as cross-media experts in advertising.

Buying is a complicated and tedious process. The American Association of Advertising Agencies (AAAA) lists no less than 21 elements in the authorization for a media buy.

Monitoring Vehicle Performance

In an ideal world every vehicle on the campaign schedule would perform at or above expectations. Likewise, every advertisement, commercial, and posting would run exactly as planned. In reality, underperformance and schedule problems are facts of life. The buyer's response to these problems must be swift and decisive. Poorly performing vehicles must be replaced or costs must be modified. Production and schedule difficulties must be rectified. Delayed response could hurt the brand's sales.

Postcampaign Analysis

Once a campaign is completed, the planner's duty is to compare the plan's expectations and forecasts with what actually happened. Did the plan actually achieve GRP, reach, frequency, and CPM objectives? Did the newspaper and magazine placements run in the positions expected? Such analysis is instrumental in providing the guidance for future media plans.

Billing and Payment

Bills from the various mediums come in continuously. Ultimately, it is the responsibility of the advertiser to make these payments. However, the agency may be contractually obligated to pay the initial invoice; or, because of various negotiations between the agency and selected mediums, it may be advantageous for the agency to make the payment and then bill the client. Keeping track of the invoices and paying the bills is the responsibility of the media planner in conjunction with the accounting department.

These six tasks are the highlights of media buying. For a better understanding of buying operations, however, we need to look at some of these duties in closer detail.

A MATTER OF PRACTICE
IN A SPLIT SECOND

➤ New forms of communication technology seem to be emerging faster than we can keep track of them. Speaking of fast, about 75 million people worldwide now have access to instant messaging (IM). If you're not familiar with instant messaging, it's kind of a hybrid of e-mail and an old-fashioned telephone party line. It allows people to communicate very quickly, especially teenagers.

Given the potential of this emerging technology, it was inevitable that someone would create a marketing opportunity. A New York–based software company called Active Buddy, has taken this concept in an interesting direction. Clients hire Active Buddy to create custom bots, or intelligent agents. Simply, this software connects instant messaging (IM) users to various types of data. Simultaneously, the IM user receives the information in either the form of an electronically produced voice or through the bot's IM dialogue box. It's possible for the database to deliver a client's marketing message or the advertisement (go online at www.activebuddy.com to demo the system).

The amazing thing about this technology is the manner in which it stimulates strong word-of-mouth messaging. Combined with more traditional media, this combination of print and broadcast offers an opportunity to create an integrated media strategy that speaks to multiple audiences.

Instant messaging is clearly a rapidly growing medium. And with as many as 150 million potential IM users projected by 2004, others are going to catch on too. In fact, a competitor called FaceTime has recently popped up, offering customer-service bots for high-profile clients such as Alaska Airlines, Dell, and FAO Schwartz.

POINT TO PONDER

Do you think this concept will have any appeal for adults?

Sources: Cathleen Moore, "Wireless Collaboration Deepens Value," *InfoWorld* (December 10, 2001): 38; Stephanie Sandborn, "Coming Together," *InfoWorld* (December 10, 2001): 36–37; James Kobielus, "Simple, but More Complex," *Network World* (October 8, 2001): 51.

MEDIA BUYERS' ABILITY TO NEGOTIATE

Buyers' knowledge and expert preparation are tested when they represent clients in the media marketplace. It is here that execution of the plan takes place. The key questions are whether the desired vehicles can be located and whether a satisfactory schedule can be negotiated and maintained.

Just as a labor union negotiates with management for pay raises, security, and work conditions, so does a media buyer pursue special advantages for clients. For instance, Liz Workman, European vice president and regional media director for Leo Burnett, London, negotiated a deal for client United Distillers in Scotland. "We went to the big media owners and told them how much we were spending with them across 15 markets in Europe. I told them we deserved a discount." After some intense wrangling, she got it. Here are some key negotiation areas.

Vehicle Performance

Selection through negotiation is especially important when the medium offers many options and when the buyers might need to use forecasted audience levels. One good example is network television.

Nighttime programming is particularly fluid or changeable. Because of the money at risk, networks are very quick to rearrange programs, to cancel them and replace them with new ones, and to make other sorts of shifts. Buyers of time in network television are usually faced with selecting programs that are new, are not new but have been scheduled on a different night, or have new lead-in programs. Under these conditions, little, if anything, stays the same. Selection must be made with little or no guarantee of audience popularity. Buyers deal with these uncertainties through careful research on the type of program (action, situation comedy), the rating history of the time slot, the audience flow patterns of competing programs, and other factors.

Unit Costs

Getting a low price has always been a goal for media buyers, but today it is mandatory. Every medium has a published rate card. Rather than simply accepting these stated rates, many media buyers engage in **open pricing**, in which each buyer or buying group negotiates a separate price. The buyer must understand the balance or trade-off between price received and audience objectives before pursuing open pricing. For example, a media buyer might be able to get a lower price for 30 commercials on ESPN, but part of the deal is that half the spots are scheduled with programs that don't reach the primary target audience.

Preferred Positions

Media buyers must bargain for **preferred positions**: the spots in print media such as magazines that offer readership advantages. Imagine the value a food advertiser would gain from having its message located in a special recipe section that the homemaker can detach from the magazines for permanent use. How many additional exposures might that ad get? An ideal position in newspapers might be in the food section. With so many competing voices, buyers are anxious to find the most widely read sections.

Because they are so visible, preferred positions often carry a premium surcharge, usually 10 to 15 percent above standard space rates. In these days of searching for the lowest possible media prices, buyers are not hesitant about requesting that such charges be waived. Buyers will offer publications a higher number of ad placements if the special positions are guaranteed without extra cost.

Extra Support Offers

With the current trend toward strong emphasis on other forms of marketing communication in addition to advertising, buyers often demand additional assistance from the media besides space and time. These activities, sometimes called *value-added* services, can take any number of forms, including contests, special events, merchandising space at stores, displays, and trade-directed newsletters. The "extra" depends on what facilities each media vehicle has and how hard the buyer can bargain with the money available.

Some media companies actively solicit marketers' budgets by integrating multimedia activities. That is, they will not only provide pages in their magazines, but they will also provide buys in related media. Advertisers who favor integrated marketing communication programs give these plans serious consideration. The ad for Meredith Company promotes a number of its available media service options.

CHANGES IN MEDIA BUYING

Physically, buying media has gone through a technical revolution during the last 25 years. If you were a media buyer in 1975 you would have to place individual orders, probably by phone, for each medium ordered. Then, in the 1980s consolidators (media buying services) came on the scene; they would place the individual orders for the buyer, based on a summary order. These buying services could also be contracted by the advertiser, who could bypass the agency's media operations. In the late 1980s the various mediums gained access to the computer, and buyers could check prices and place orders electronically. Today, the media buying process has moved online.

The following topics have created dramatic changes in the media buying process.

Media Buying Services

Many agencies and advertisers employ media buying services whose sole responsibility is the purchase of media. Such media buyers are in regular contact with the media suppliers with whom they do business on behalf of the client/agency. During the course of the numerous media buyer–seller transactions, the buyer acquires a familiarity with market-

A WORLD OF MEREDITH MERCHANDISING/SALES SUPPORT OPPORTUNITIES

We can also help create a customized merchandising/sales support program that maximizes the effectiveness of your advertising with your sales staff, distributors and dealers. Some of the many possibilities:

▲ Producing special videos for promotional use.
▲ Using consumer direct mail lists (35 million names in all) for specialized direct marketing.
▲ Creating special publications to maintain contact with your customers or with your distribution network.
▲ Using Meredith books as consumer premiums or in sales incentive programs.
▲ Conducting quantitative or attitudinal marketing research.
▲ Using our real estate network to reach homebuyers.

These and other programs can be used individually or in combination.

This company offers a wide variety of media choices to advertisers and agencies.

place events. Such familiarity can assist the media planner in forecasting media price changes. Media buyers are expected to maintain good media supplier relations to facilitate this flow of information. Media planners should make it a point to maintain close communications with the media buyers so as to tap this source of media cost information. Note the Web site for Saveontv.com as an example of a media buying service. However, given the uncertain economy and the need for agencies to increase revenue, media buying services are no longer an alternative for many media buyers.

Faced with competition from media buying services, the large agencies have set up or bought up buying services themselves to compete with the independents and go after outside business. Some agencies use their own buying services as a substitute for their media departments. Others use them only to place orders but retain the media planning functions.

Small and medium-sized agencies have increasingly closed down their media departments. They may still have a media director who performs a planning and coordinating function, but their accounts work directly with buying services, including both the independents and those owned by the super agencies. Typically, the client determines the budget for a product brand. The agency recommends an overall media strategy, and the buying service plans and negotiates the specifics of the media schedule.

While buying services traditionally touted their ability to bargain down rates, they now claim that they select media using highly sophisticated skills. They've developed "optimization models" that stress "accountability" and performance rather than cost efficiency. A number of specialized media research companies offer software programs (such as Optimizer and Midas) that combine audience and cost information to compare different media schedules. All this has led to more reliance on research. As indicated in the "A Matter of Principle" box on page 227, controversy has emerged.

Saveontv.com is an example of a media buying service on the Internet.

Online Media Buying

In late 2000, General Motors and several other major corporations changed the way they purchase media. Buying media through the Internet has become part of GMTradeExchange. com, the business-to-business Web site GM set up for its vendors to buy and sell their goods and services.

A comparable system to GM's has been set up by over 50 consumer-goods companies, including Procter & Gamble, Coca-Cola, and Unilever. The Internet technology allows them to buy billions of dollars in advertising.

Some experienced media buyers would argue that bypassing the representatives of the various mediums and ordering online is not necessarily a good thing. While it does provide convenience and speed, it does not include the one-on-one interaction between the buyer and the seller. Such interaction often provided personal insights and suggestions by the latter that may have contributed to a better media buy.

Global Media Buying

The definition of global media buying varies widely, but everyone agrees that few marketers are doing it yet. However, many are thinking about it, especially computer and other information technology companies that are being pursued by everyone from CNN International to International Data Group. For some media planners, a schedule on CNN International counts as a global media buy. To others, a truly global media deal should not just encompass space, but should give the marketer favored status with a media outlet. It should be a true partnership between media and marketer.[6]

Today, the growth area is media buys across a single region. But as media becomes more global, some marketers are beginning to make the leap between regions. About 60 percent of ad buys on CNN International are regional and 40 percent are global, including campaigns by Eastman Kodak Co. and IBM Corp.

In Europe, the rise of buying "centrals" came about with the emergence of the European Union and the continuing globalization of trade and advertising. Buying centrals are media organizations that buy across several European countries. Their growth also began with the development of commercial broadcasting and the expansion of media choices.

A MATTER OF PRINCIPLE

UNBUNDLING MEDIA

➤ Although it appears that most of the recent conflict between media agency departments and media buying services has been about their own well-being, with little concern for the client, that seems to be changing. Recently, some clients have taken the initiative and created their own media buying structure.

No company better exemplifies this approach to media than General Motors Corp., the largest advertiser in the United States. GM made a crucial decision in 2001. It turned over all its media planning responsibilities to Bcom 3's Starcom Media Vest Group, which then created GM Planworks expressly to handle the $2.9 billion account. Gaining even more control over the media planning process, General Motors designed a unique compensation program for GM Planworks. Essentially, it paid a fee based on the number of people and amount of time they worked on the account, plus an appropriate profit margin. This did away with the traditional 15 percent commission.

Because of its enormous spending power, General Motors gave increased credibility to the strategy of separating media buying from the brand advertising agency. Advocates of this strategy say that there are clear cost savings as well as other benefits. But concerned brand advertising agency executives contend that media planning and buying have traditionally been their profit center. There is also the criticism that in an era of integration, this separation of the creative from the media is a destructive strategy. Rather, creative people should be aligned with those in media.

If advertisers such as General Motors insist on this strategy, it is unlikely that the trend will reverse itself, regardless of the movement toward integration.

POINT TO PONDER

Do you agree that media and creative should not be separated?

Sources: Laurie Freeman, "Taking Apart Media," *Agency* 11(1) (Winter 2001); 20–25; Wayne Freedman, "Cross-Media Ad Deals Lose Some Luster," *Advertising Age* (February 26, 2001): S-10.

These firms have flourished in an environment of flexible and negotiated rates, low inflation, and a broken up advertising market. The buying centrals weakened the ties between media and advertisers and eroded fixed advertising rates and media revenues because each buy was an attempt by the buyer to get a lower rate.

The buying centrals have nearly three-fourths of the media market in France, nine-tenths in Spain, and about two-fifths in Britain, Holland, Italy, and Scandinavia.

Maintaining Plan Performance

A media buyer's responsibility to a campaign does not end with the signing of space and time contracts. Buys are made in advance, based on *forecasted* audience levels. What if vehicles under perform? What happens if unforeseen events affect scheduling? What if newspapers go on strike, magazines fold, or a television show is canceled? Buyers must fix these problems.

Monitoring Audience Research When campaigns begin, the forecasts in the media plan are checked against each performance. Whenever possible, buyers check each incoming research report to determine whether the vehicle is performing as promised.

Change is the foundation of broadcast buying. Forecasting future popularity or target audience interest is risky. Once the schedule is running, buyers make every attempt to get current audience research. It is the only way to ensure that schedules are performing according to forecast.

Newspaper and magazine readership reports are produced less often than broadcast ratings, but print buyers are still concerned about changes in circulation. If a circulation audit shows a drop, it may indicate serious readership problems. Buyers also check the publication issues to verify whether advertisements have been placed correctly.

Major users of outdoor advertising understand that it is necessary to check sign and billboard positions. They must check the condition of the ad, the presence of obstructions (buildings or trees), lighting, and any other factor that would reduce the expected audience exposure.

Scheduling and Technical Problems Temporary snags in scheduling and in the reproduction of the advertising message usually are unavoidable. Buyers must be alert for missed positions or errors in handling the message presentation and ensure that the advertiser is compensated appropriately when they occur. Most adjustments involve free replacement positions or refunds. A policy of compensating for such errors is called "making good on the contract." The units of compensation are known as **makegoods**. Here are some examples.

- **Program preemptions**. Special programs or news events often interrupt regular programming. When this happens, the commercial scheduled is also interrupted. Program preemptions occur nationally and locally. In the case of long-term interruptions (for example, congressional hearings or war coverage), buyers may have difficulty finding suitable replacements before the schedule ends.
- **Missed closings**. Magazines and newspapers have clearly set production deadlines, called **closings**, for each issue. Sometimes the advertising materials do not arrive in time. If the publication is responsible, it will make the same sort of restitution. If the fault lies with the client or the agency, there is no restitution by the publication.
- **Technical problems**. Technical difficulties are responsible for numerous goofs, glitches, and foul-ups that haunt the advertiser's schedule. In one extreme case, the buyer for a new consumer brand learned that someone at the television station had inserted a "super" (an optical phrase superimposed on the film or tape) informing viewers that the product was available in only two small area towns. In truth, those towns accounted for less than 10 percent of the brand's distribution. The damage was serious, and the station did more than make good. It settled out of court.

Most technical problems are not quite so disastrous. Bleedthroughs and out-of-register colors for newspapers, torn billboard posters, broken film, and tapes out of alignment are more typical of the problems that plague media schedulers.

STAGING A MEDIA PLAN

To control the flow of information and to ensure that each media component makes a logical contribution to strategy, the planner uses a media plan. The plan is a written document that summarizes the recommended objectives, strategies, and tactics pertinent to the placement of a company's advertising messages. Plans do not have a universal form, but there is a common (and logical) pattern to the decision stages. To illustrate a style of presentation in a real-life setting, we use an actual media plan (excerpted with disguised numbers) from Pizza Hut's national media plan for 2000.

Typical media plans begin with the general questions and work down to the more specific ones. Similarly, they begin with the most important decisions and work down to those of lesser priority. Let's briefly explore each stage in this planning process.

Background and Situation Analysis

The background and situation analysis is the marketing perspective we discussed at the beginning of the chapter. Pizza Hut's overview discusses media options and opportunities to narrowly target consumers using niche channels and programs. It also describes the target audiences, their psychographics, and the best way to reach these audiences. The overview is shown in Figure 8.8.

Media Objectives and Aperture Opportunities

A **media objective** is a goal or task the plan should accomplish. Objectives are relevant to the brand's strategy, are detailed, measurable, and have a realistic time frame. The objec-

Background/Situation Analysis

The turn of the century is seeing an explosion of media choices for consumers, from increased networks and cable channels to the Internet. On the positive side, Pizza Hut can now narrowly target its consumers using these niche channels and programs. The Pizza Hut 2000 strategy defines occasion-based marketing opportunities and the challenges realized through media ownership consolidation.

Occasion-Based Marketing

Research shows that Pizza Hut is a strong brand with the 40-plus age group, who make "food-focused" dinner decisions. The groups where Pizza Hut has not maximized its share of occasions are the Echo Boomers and Generation X groups, age 20 to 40, who make decisions based on functional needs. These needs are reflected predominantly by "Pressure Cooker" and "Hanging Out" occasions.

- "Pressure Cooker" occasions are driven by impulse orders, dominated by moms who are looking for a dinner solution that appeals to kids (cheese pizza) with a good price point. They make dinner decisions between 4 and 8 P.M., with 56 percent of decisions made within one hour of dinner. Solutions to this dilemma should be presented during dinnertime broadcast TV and family-focused cable. Because Mom is also found in her car coming home from work, going to soccer practice or piano lessons, or running other errands, radio can put Pizza Hut in her mind at the right time.

- The "Hanging Out" occasion skews heavily toward the 18 to 24 age group, who think of eating pizza as part of a social occasion. High-profile programming such as late-night television, MTV, ESPN, and Sports capture the heart of the need-state. Alternative rock and young country radio stations are also important pieces of the media makeup of these young adults.

- Finally, prime will continue to be a key component of any media buy. It's still the most effective opportunity for building each quickly and it addresses the "Crave" occasion, the core of the existing Pizza Hut business.

FIGURE 8.8

PIZZA HUT MEDIA PLAN OVERVIEW
Pizza Hut's Background/Situation analysis sees media ownership consolidation as a road to marketing opportunities.

tives should be limited to goals that media can accomplish, as Figure 8.9 illustrates. The figure shows that the objectives concentrate on brand awareness, reaching the target audience, and integrating national and local media plans.

Some media plans discuss aperture opportunities. Pizza Hut's Media Plan Objectives spotlight research findings about aperture that shaped its media plan, as we see in Figure 8.10. Other aperture opportunities include the following:

- Launches that will build broad reach for new products and big events using a strategy of 8–0 percent reach with a frequency of four times per week.
- Using national media covering the NFL and the NCAA, which ensures that male targets are reached.
- A balanced delivery between adults aged 18 to 35 and 35 to 49 through focus on network broadcast media and programs that target the echo boomers (children of baby boomers).

Establish a Pizza Hut Presence
- Maintain Top-of-Mind Awareness

Create Highly Visible Launch Platforms
- Build Broad Research for New Products/Big Events

Reach Heavy Pizza Users Target
- Ensure Important Male Targets Are Reached
- Balance 18–34 and 35–49 Demographic Deliveries

Integrate National and Local Media Plans
- Provide Option Windows to Address Local Needs

FIGURE 8.9

PIZZA HUT NATIONAL MEDIA OBJECTIVES
Pizza Hut's media plan objectives concentrate on brand awareness, reaching the target audience, and integrating national and local media plans.

FIGURE 8.10

PIZZA HUT MEDIA PLAN SPECIFICS
Research findings are a part of Pizza Hut's media plan specifics.

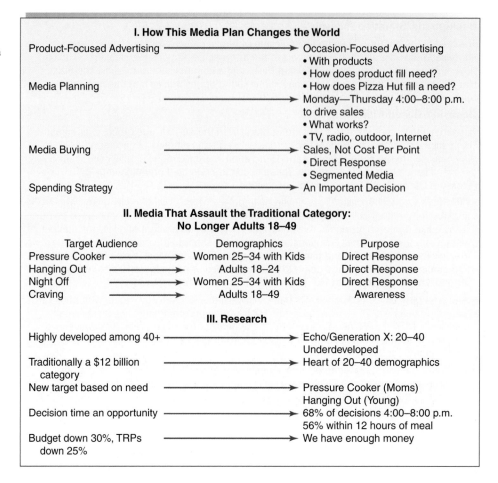

I. How This Media Plan Changes the World

Product-Focused Advertising ⟶ Occasion-Focused Advertising
- With products
- How does product fill need?

Media Planning
- How does Pizza Hut fill a need?
⟶ Monday—Thursday 4:00–8:00 p.m. to drive sales
- What works?
- TV, radio, outdoor, Internet

Media Buying ⟶ Sales, Not Cost Per Point
- Direct Response
- Segmented Media

Spending Strategy ⟶ An Important Decision

II. Media That Assault the Traditional Category: No Longer Adults 18–49

Target Audience		Demographics	Purpose
Pressure Cooker	⟶	Women 25–34 with Kids	Direct Response
Hanging Out	⟶	Adults 18–24	Direct Response
Night Off	⟶	Women 25–34 with Kids	Direct Response
Craving	⟶	Adults 18–49	Awareness

III. Research

Highly developed among 40+ ⟶ Echo/Generation X: 20–40 Underdeveloped

Traditionally a $12 billion category ⟶ Heart of 20–40 demographics

New target based on need ⟶ Pressure Cooker (Moms) Hanging Out (Young)

Decision time an opportunity ⟶ 68% of decisions 4:00–8:00 p.m. 56% within 12 hours of meal

Budget down 30%, TRPs down 25% ⟶ We have enough money

Strategy: Selection of Media

This section of the media plan explains why a single medium or set of media is appropriate for the campaign objectives.

Because planning typically occurs months before the campaign actually begins, some detail is omitted. For the television portion of the Pizza Hut campaign, shown in Figure 8.11, the planner cannot be assured of program availability or specific pricing in television except for major events such as an NFL Pregame Super Bowl sponsorship. As a result, the strategies deal with specifics where possible and omit detail when the specific media vehicle hasn't been identified. For simplicity's sake, we show excerpts from the TV and Internet media strategies and omit the print and co-op radio strategies with local franchisees.

The Flow Chart: Scheduling and Budgeting Allocation

Figure 8.12 on page 232 illustrates most of the media recommendations. It uses graphics to show the month-by-month placement of messages, detail the anticipated impact through forecasted levels of GRPs, and illustrate how the campaign budget is allocated by medium and by month. In a concise fashion, the flow chart is the blueprint of the media plan.

I. National TV Media Strategy

A. Establish a Pizza Hut Presence
- Own the SCAA: Basketball 15 Weeks
- Own Fox NFL: Pregame Sponsorship 20 Weeks
- ESPN and Fox Cable Sports: Sports Show Feature 32 Weeks
- Cable Stretch: Own Tuesday Night Pizza Occasions 32 Weeks

Enhancement
- CBS NFL Pregame Sponsorship 10 Weeks
  - Shared with KFC, but *locks out* Domino's!

B. Create Highly Visible Launch Platforms for *Big New Yorker* and *Star Wars* Event
- Roadblocks
- Network Strips
- Highly Visible Programming
- 1 Week Reach 80% with a 4 Frequency

Enhancement
- Leverage Tricon Partners Inventory to Achieve These Goals for Star Wars

C. Reach Heavy Pizza User Target
- Continue Leveraging Sports to Ensure Male/Female Balance and Target Key Pizza Consumption Occasions

Enhancement
- Target Echo Boomers/Genration X to Balance 18–24 and 25–34 with 35–49
  - Increased mix of Fox and Warner Brothers
  - Cable focus on USA, TNT, F/X, E!, and Comedy Central

D. Integrate National and Local Media Plans
- Provide Local Option Windows
- When on Air Nationally Have Sufficient Prime/Sports/Cable So That Co-ops Do Not Have to Buy Premium Programming

II. The Brave New World: Internet

America's Online: 70.5 Million Adults
USA Today, August 27, 2000

ESPNet SportsZone: A Toe In the Water
- 300 Million E-mailed Coupons
- Special Coupon Offer Just for Internet?

Pizza Hut Must Become More Active
- Using Our Website
- Investments That Facilitate Internet Ordering
- Advertising More Effectively

FIGURE 8.11

PIZZA HUT TV AND INTERNET MEDIA STRATEGIES
Here Pizza Hut lays out how it plans to advertise on TV and Internet mediums.

The media plan is a recommendation that the advertiser must approve before any further steps are taken. In fact, planning is only the first stage in advertising media operations. Once the plan directions are set, media buyers convert objectives and strategies into tactical decisions. They select, negotiate, and contract for the time and space in media. In the next two chapters we explore types of media, which provide insight into the seller's side of the media business.

1999 PLANNING TEMPLATE

	Period 1	Period 2	Period 3	Period 4	Period 5	Period 6	Period 7	Period 8	Period 9	Period 10	Period 11	Period 12	Period 13	
	De / January	February	March	April	May	June	July	August	September	October	November	December	December	
National Topic		Big NY	Big NY	TBD		Star Wars	Star Wars		Big NY		TBD	TBD		
NETWORK														
Product :30;:15		630	475	440		530	420		445		600	425		3,965
Promo :30 Only	160				30			25		85			35	335
Kids 6–11 (A18–49 20 index)				500		600				500				320 / 4,620
SPOT TV														
Product	800	600	400	400	700	600	500	700	400	700	400	400		6,600
TOTAL TV	960	1230	875	940	730	1202	968	725	845	885	1000	825	35	11,220
SPOT RADIO		400	400		300			300		300			300	2,000

Key Events: Xmas, Bowl Gms, NFL POs, Sup Bowl, Fnl 4, Estr Chmp, AA, Mem Day, Jul 4th, Lbr Day, Hwe, Tks gvn, Xmas

FIGURE 8.12 EXCERPT FROM PIZZA HUT BROADCAST MEDIA PLAN BLUEPRINT
Pizza Huts' media planning template maps out month-by-month placement of ads, as well as their expected gross rating points.

IT'S A WRAP
THE PICTURE SEEMS CLEAR

Getting the message to the right person at the right time is what media planning is all about. Accomplishing this objective is complex and difficult. Thousands of decisions become part of the process. This was no less true for Polaroid and its I-Zone Camera.

Recall that the product launched in 1999–2000, and was targeted at teens, primarily girls. The media strategy was focused on TV spots and various online delivery mechanisms. Overall, the initial campaign was highly successful, selling 1.49 million I-Zone cameras and 3.1 million I-Zone films the first year. It became America's best-selling camera and had built a 7.9 percent market share with the nearest competitor having a 3.8 percent share. Most importantly, 83 percent of sales were among females 13 to 17 years old.

However, Polaroid soon learned that it had chosen a target market that has a short attention span. Since the end of 2000, the I-Zone camera has gone through many extensions and changes to keep the brand experience fresh. Finally, the company has also had to constantly review and change its media strategies to make sure it is effectively and efficiently reaching its teen target.

Summary

1. **Explain how media planning fits into the advertising process**. Media planning is part of the advertising process. It requires marketing intelligence to choose the time, placement, cost, and specific choice of advertising measures. Planners rely on market, consumer, and media information to develop the media plan. Media planning runs parallel to the creative message design process. The media plan should coordinate all the elements of the marketing communication mix. The media planner's goal is to identify and exploit the aperture, the time and place at which the customer's purchase interest is the highest.

2. **Outline how media planners set media objectives**. Media planning objectives are directed by a series of key questions including who (target), where (location), when (time frame), and how long (duration). Cost is also a key factor.

3. **Describe how media planners develop media strategies**. The selection of media for the campaign is based on a number of factors, including target size (impressions/reach), repeated exposure opportunities (message frequency), cost efficiency (CPM and CPR), and important qualitative features such as content moods and other compatible message environments.

4. **Explain the functions and special skills of media buyers**. Media buyers must be able to provide inside information to the media planner. They must also be able to select media vehicles, as well as negotiate media prices. Finally, they monitor media performance and conduct post campaign analyses.

5. **Summarize the process of staging a media plan**. Media-related decisions are presented in a systematically organized document called a media plan. Plans are driven by the media goals to be accomplished and the strategies and tactics needed to achieve each goal. To stage a media plan, most planners provide a plan overview, media objectives, media plan specifics and strategies, and a flow chart of the planning process.

Key Terms

aperture, p. 209
average frequency, p. 217
carryover effect, p. 214
closing, p. 228
continuity, p. 214
cost per rating, p. 219
cost per thousand, p. 219

effective frequency, p. 219
flighting, p. 214
frequency, p. 217
frequency distribution, p. 218
gross impressions, p. 215
gross rating points, p. 216
makegoods, p. 228

marketing mix modeling, p. 213
media mix, p. 206
media objective, p. 228
media planning, p. 206
media vehicle, p. 206
medium, p. 206
open pricing, p. 224

preferred frequency, p. 217
preferred positions, p. 224
program preemptions, p. 228
pulsing, p. 214
reach, p. 217
share of voice, p. 211

Questions

1. Why is the media planning function considered the bridge between sales marketing and the creative function of advertising?

2. Allan Johnson is a graduating senior from a journalism program. He is seeking some career advice from one of his professors. Allan has an interest in advertising, and wants to know what an advertising and journalism major with a business minor in marketing has prepared him for. In addition to account management positions, the professor urges Allan to consider media planning as a logical entry-level position. Why does the professor advise this? Why is marketing study so important for media planners?

3. Susan Ellet has just begun a new job as senior media planner for a new automobile model from General Motors. The planning sequence will begin in four months, and Susan's media director asks her what data and information she needs for her preparation. What sources should Susan request? How will she use each of these sources in the planning function?

4. If the marketing management of McDonald's restaurants asked you to analyze the aperture opportunity for its breakfast entrees, what kind of analysis would you present to management?

5. The Pioneer account has accepted your recommendation for 10 one-page insertions (10 issues) in a magazine known as the *Illustrated Press*. The magazine reaches an estimated 3 million target readers per month, or a 10 percent rating issue. The cost per page of the publication is $20,000. What is the total GRP delivered by this schedule? What are the CPR and the CPM?

6. If you were doing a frequency analysis composed of two magazines, a radio network schedule, and a national newspaper, would you rather use the average frequency procedure or a frequency distribution analysis? Explain your choice.

7. Explain why media planners try to balance reach, frequency, and continuity of proposed media schedules. What considerations go into this decision?

8. Explain the differences between media planning and media buying.

9. Your client is a major distributor of movie videotapes. Its early media plan for magazines has been settled and you are in negotiation when you learn that a top publishing company is about to launch a new magazine dedicated to movie fans and video collectors. Although the editorial direction is perfect, there is no valid way to predict how the magazine will be accepted by the public. Worse, there won't be solid research on readership for at least a year. The sales representative offers a low charter page rate if the advertiser agrees to appear in each of the first year's 12 issues. To use it you will have to remove one of the established magazines from your list. Is the risk worthwhile? Should you bother the client with this information, considering that the plan is already set? Make some recommendations.

10. Now assume the same facts as in question 9, but the new magazine is delivered over the Internet. (The Internet budget has also been planned for.) Do you have any different recommendations? Explain your reasoning.

Suggested Class Project

In performing an aperture analysis, consider the following products: video games (Nintendo, for instance), men's cologne (such as Davidoff's "Cool Water"), computer software (such as Lotus), and athletic shoes for aerobics (Reebok, for example). For each of these products, find the answers to these questions:

1. Which media should be used to maximize aperture leverage?
2. How does aperture work in each of your recommendations?
3. Explain how the timing and duration of the advertising improve the aperture opportunity.

Suggested Internet Class Project

Go to www.overture.com. Indicate how you would use the information provided by this site in developing your media plan for a new reality TV show. Focus on the Internet as a primary medium. Write a one- to two-page report.

Hallmark BUILD•A•CAMPAIGN*Projects*

Please review the Hallmark Case Appendix at the end of the text before responding to these questions.

1. Meet in small groups to discuss how Capitol Advertising used its media plan to enhance the creative efforts to build brand insistence for Hallmark.

2. Visit your local Gold Crown store and draft a media plan that would take advantage of the most appropriate local media. Specify the scheduling and the size/length decisions for the various media types.

HANDS-ON   Case 8

PIZZA HUT GAINS AN EDGE

The fast-food segment of the restaurant industry is intensely competitive when it comes to food quality, price, service, convenience, location, and concept. Fast-food restaurants compete with other restaurants in their segments (McDonald's competes with Wendy's) and with restaurants in other segments (for instance, Quizno's sandwich shops competes with Pizza Hut for consumers looking for a quick meal).

Given the intense competition of this segment, fast-food restaurants rely on product innovations to increase consumer interest and broaden appeal. Pizza Hut's product innovations include stuffed-crust pizza, Bigfoot, Sicilian Pizza, The Edge, and most recently, the P'Zone. Brand awareness is a key part of Pizza Hut's media plan objectives. The company uses promotions and sampling to generate trial and remind old customers about the brand. A Pizza Hut spokesperson stated, "We believe that sampling is critical to driving trial and getting people who may have walked away from our franchise."

Product innovations and promotions are important, but they are unlikely to be effective if consumers do not know about them. As a result, Pizza Hut develops integrated media plans that support its promotions and new product introductions. For example, in early 2000, Pizza Hut decided to sample its "totally new pizzas" to one of every 100 U.S. households. Although some of the sampling techniques were unconventional (helicopters and Hummers were used to deliver pizzas), traditional media played an important role in the promotion's success:

- The effort was accompanied by a massive TV campaign from BBDO Worldwide.
- Local print media was used for ads that delivered coupons.
- Pizza Hut (with the help of TLPartnership, Dallas) negotiated with radio stations in each market to forego traditional Pizza Hut radio spots in favor of more promotional coverage. Stations gave away Pizza Hut coupons during call-in contests and provided live coverage of sampling events.

Media support for brand and promotional advertising is essential. Pizza Hut and its main competitor, Domino's, make a significant investment in advertising media. While hamburger and chicken fast-food restaurants obtain the vast majority of their revenues from dine-in customers, pizza restaurants derive a significant portion of their revenues from take-out and delivery orders. Consumers need a quick, easy way to contact pizza restaurants. In response, advertisers make certain that appropriate print and broadcast ads contain a local telephone number and that they incorporate the Yellow Pages into their overall media plan. (The Yellow Pages are Pizza Hut's and Domino's second-largest media expenditure.)

Broadcast and print advertisements inform consumers of current happenings and foster a desire for the product, and the Yellow Pages provide the means to obtain the product once the consumer decides to act. About one out of every three pizza purchasers turns to the Yellow Pages before buying a pizza. As a result, the *Pizza* heading is referenced over 470 million times a year, making it the fifth most heavily used heading in the Yellow Pages. After years of flat-to-declining sales and revenues, Pizza Hut says it is growing twice as fast as the industry.

IT'S YOUR TURN

Pizza Hut and Domino's allocate their media budgets in nearly identical ways. Assume these tables are a representation of how these two fast-food giants might spend their advertising dollars in a given year.

1. What are the advantages of allocating your budget similarly to your competitors? What are the disadvantages?
2. What recommendations for Pizza Hut advertising would you make with regards to timing and duration strategies, reach, and frequency?
3. Imagine that Pizza Hut wants to decrease its budget by $10 million. Which of the following options would you recommend?
   - Decrease television advertising by $10 million.
   - Decrease radio and television advertising by $5 million each.
   - Decrease Yellow Pages advertising by $8 million and decrease radio advertising by $2 million.

Explain and defend your recommendation. ■

2000 Media Allocation: Actual Dollars by Advertising Media (in Thousands)

	Total	Magazines	Newspapers	Outdoor	Television	Radio	Yellow Pages
Pizza Hut	$181,943.8	$0.0	$126.4	$301.6	$165,535.8	$5,980.0	$10,000.0
Domino's	120,969.6	0.0	457.1	232.8	108,516.6	5,262.6	6,500.5

2000 Media Allocation: Percentage of Total Allocation by Advertising Media

	Total	Magazines	Newspapers	Outdoor	Television	Radio	Yellow Pages
Pizza Hut	$181,943.8	0.0%	0.07%	0.16%	91.0%	3.3%	5.5%
Domino's	120,976.1	0.0	0.03	0.19	90.0	4.4	5.4

2000 Media Allocation: Percentage of Total Television Allocation by Television Type

	Total	Network	Spot	Syndicated	Cable
Pizza Hut	$165,535.8	57.44%	32.64%	0.63%	9.29%
Domino's	108,516.96	48.90	34.50	0.53	16.07

Notes

1. Joe Mandese, "Media Buying & Planning," *Advertising Age* (August 3, 1998): S1, S18.

2. Bob Donath, "Match Your Media Choice and Ad Copy Objectives," *Marketing News* (June 8, 1998): 6; Jay Klitsch, "Making Your Message Hit Home: Some Basics to Consider When Selecting Media," *Direct Marketing* (June 1998): 33, 42; Melinda Ligos, "The Right Fit," *Sales & Marketing Management* (July 1997): 18.

3. Joe Mandese, "Markets Want to Justify Plan Strategy," *Advertising Age* (August 3, 1998): S2, S15.

4. Lisa Napoli, "You Say 'Page View,' I Say 'Visit': How to Count Web Traffic," *New York Times* (August 26, 1998): retrieved online at www.nytimes.com/library/tech/98/08/cyber/articles/226traffic.

5. Denman Mahoney, "Measuring the Web," *Agency* (Winter 1998): 48–52.

6. Laurel Wentz and Juliana Koranteng, "Global Media," *Ad Age International* (February 9, 1998): 15–17.

CHAPTER 9

Print Media

CHAPTER OBJECTIVES

When you have completed this chapter, you should be able to

1. Describe the newspaper medium and identify its strengths and weaknesses.
2. Identify the key factors that advertisers should know to make effective decisions about the magazine medium.
3. Explain what out-of-home media are and discuss factors that advertisers should consider for making out-of-home media decisions.
4. Describe directories and analyze the factors that advertisers use to make decisions about this medium.
5. Discuss the factors that contribute to an effective print media strategy.

"Harvard of Leadership"

Award: *EFFIE Gold 2001, Recruitment category*

Company: *United States Marine Corps*

Agency: *J. Walter Thompson, U.S.A.*

Campaign: *"Harvard of Leadership"*

Maybe you've seen those old John Wayne movies featuring the brave U.S. Marines attacking various Pacific islands. In 2001–2002, we saw members of the Marine Corps and Special Forces attacking the Taliban and terrorist camps. Inspired by these events, enlistments in all the military branches have been right at their target levels, but that trend might reverse should the fighting stop and the economy recover.

Just two years prior, the U.S. Marine Corps had been struggling to find recruits. You might recall that 1999 was a very good year for most of us. College enrollments were up over 14 million, those seeking employment found jobs, and college grads were courted through high salaries, signing bonuses, and other perks. No one was interested in joining the military, especially the Marines. In fact, fewer young Americans signed up for the Marines officer program in 1999 than any other year since the advent of the volunteer military.

The challenge for the Marine Corps and J. Walter Thompson, their agency of record, was quite daunting. Somehow they had to reposition the Marines Officer Program with a new caliber of Marine, without lowering the traditionally high standards. And, they were to accomplish this with a smaller recruiting force, the smallest marketing budget of all the military services, and a mandate to attract a higher percentage of minority officers.

The strategy group at J. Walter Thompson decided that part of their repositioning of the Marines Corps Officers Program School was to let prospective Marines know that a career as a Marine officer was not a second-rate career. The idea was to attract recruits to the Marine Corps Officer Program by advertising its exclusive and proprietary means to success. Enlisted Marines make up about 80% of the Corps and do not require a college education. Officers, however, are the leaders of the Corps and not only require a college education, but must pass rigorous mental skills tests. Marine Corps officers are the elite of the elite. And so the strategy of the campaign was coined the "Harvard of Leadership."

The Marines outlined its creative approach in four areas: "(1) Establish military officer service, in general, as a management track and a worthwhile use of a college degree; (2) acknowledge and exploit the difference between Marine officer service and a typical corporate job; (3) differentiate the Marine Corps Officer Program from its competition; and (4) leverage the overarching Marine Corps brand." Moreover, the campaign stressed that becoming a leader in the Marines offered advantages no corporate leadership position would provide.

The media strategy was targeted at college freshmen and sophomores, on college campuses. Because of a limited media budget of $2.5 million, the focus was on 28 college campuses, employing a variety of print media—the subject of this chapter. The campaign included college newspapers, in-school postings, direct mail, permissive e-mail, an officer Web site, campus posters, Hotstamps postcards, and a variety of collateral materials to match the individual college programs. It was all rolled out at the beginning of 2000.

How did the campaign work? Check the "It's a Wrap" section at the end of this chapter to find out.

Source: 2000 EFFIEs Brief submission from U.S. Marine Corps.

PRINT MEDIA

Print media are media that deliver messages one topic at a time and one thought at a time. In contrast, television and electronic media use a simultaneous approach, delivering a great deal of information quickly, using sound, motion, and text. Advertising revenues of the combined print categories are significantly larger than those of the combined broadcast categories.

Because the print message format is fairly traditional and is more concrete to readers, people tend to trust print more than broadcast and absorb it more carefully. For example, those wishing to capture a college-age audience may be inclined to advertise in *U*, or one of the other popular college newspapers or magazines. This is not to discount the value of broadcast media, especially the Internet. But using print in this example points to certain advantages, such as providing more detailed information, a longer time the information is available, and the assurance that the information is unlikely to change.

Although we will be discussing the advantages and disadvantages of the various print media throughout the rest of this chapter, print media have several general benefits that have strategic implications. For instance, if your target audience is clearly defined, print may be the best option. Or, if your product does not have to be demonstrated, but requires space for identification, print alternatives would make strategic sense. Finally, print is an excellent medium for carrying supplemental elements, such as coupons, samples, and access to contact information that may lead to action.

As you read this chapter and the next it will become evident that the distinctions between print and broadcast media are more and more blurred. Still, matching the right media mix with the creative strategy is only possible if the advertising manager has a clear understanding of specific media.

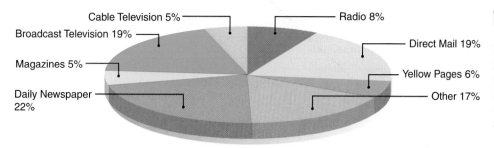

FIGURE 9.1

U.S. ADVERTISING EXPENDITURES
Newspapers still account for the greatest percentage of ad dollars spent, despite the growth of other media.
Source: Newspaper Association of America.

NEWSPAPERS

As indicated in Figure 9.1, newspapers represent the largest medium in respect to total advertising billing. It has been this way for several decades, despite the growth in competing media, especially television.

The high cost of responding to competition combined with the increased costs of newspaper production have resulted in a general consolidation in the newspaper industry. This consolidation has helped the industry implement new technologies and delivery mechanisms. Some technology advances include the introduction of computerized type, online circulation information systems, electronic libraries, and database publishing. The emergence of the Internet as a mechanism for delivering a newspaper, or part of a newspaper, has had a tremendous impact on the newspaper industry. Virtually every major newspaper and many medium-sized newspapers are now online.

The industry has also tried to match the market selectivity advantages of magazines and radio as well as the total market coverage of TV. **Market selectivity** means that the medium can target specific consumer groups well. Examples of market selectivity are special interest newspapers and free-standing inserts.

The *Wall Street Journal* and *The Financial Times* are considered specialty newspapers because they concentrate on financial business information. A *free-standing insert* is the set of advertisements and special magazines such as *Parade* that are inserted into the middle of your newspaper. Advertisers can place free-standing inserts in certain newspapers that are delivered to certain neighborhoods, or even certain people. The *Houston Post* does this for retailers such as Arby's and Kohl's by distributing a Spanish-language insert to neighborhoods where Spanish is the dominant language.

What have these changes meant for newspapers? The declines in daily readership are tapering off and Sunday readership is high. Newspapers have learned that Sunday morning is one of the few times when they have their audience almost entirely to themselves. People aren't usually watching television then. Table 9.1's circulation numbers for the top 10 U.S. newspapers shows how the Sunday circulation numbers exceed the weekly numbers by a significant amount and shows the changes in circulation over a 1-year period.

The Structure of Newspapers

Newspapers can be classified by three factors: frequency of publication (daily, weekly, and so on), size, and circulation. Each factor helps the media planner to better fit newspapers into the overall media mix.

Frequency of Publication Most newspapers are published either daily or weekly. About 1,530 dailies and 8,000 weeklies currently exist in the United States. Daily newspapers usually are found in cities and larger towns, and have morning editions, evening editions, or all-day editions. Daily papers printed in the morning deliver a complete record of the previous day's events, including detailed reports on local and national news, and on business, financial, and sports events.

Evening papers follow up the news of the day and provide early reports of the events of the following day. Evening papers tend to depend more on entertainment and information features than do morning papers. The *San Francisco Examiner* is an example of a daily evening paper.

TABLE 9.1 Top Newspapers in Circulation

Top newspapers by circulation

Figures for the six months ending March 31, 2001, compared with the same period last year. Rank is based on Monday–Friday circulation. When papers report separate circulations for some weekdays, the number used is the weighted average. In some cases, Sunday papers have different names.

Rank	Newspaper	Circulation	% of Change	Sunday Circulation	% of Change
1	*Wall Street Journal*	1,819,528	0.4	NA	NA
2	*USA Today*	1,769,650	0.7	2,184,359	1.2
3	*New York Times*	1,159,954	0.9	1,698,281	0.4
4	*Los Angeles Times*	1,058,494	−4.8	1,391,343	0.5
5	*Washington Post*	802,594	−1.2	1,070,809	−1.5
6	*New York Daily News*	716,095	−2.0	821,080	0.1
7	*Chicago Tribune*	621,870	−1.9	1,001,662	−2.4
8	*Newsday*	576,692	0.2	663,220	0.2
9	*Houston Chronicle*	545,066	−1.5	737,626	−1.4
10	*San Francisco Chronicle*	527,466	13.4	540,074	−5.4

Source: Advertising Age, May 31, 2001.

Approximately 30 percent of the dailies and a few of the weeklies also publish a Sunday edition. The *Chicago Sun-Times* is a daily paper that publishes both a morning and a Sunday edition. Sunday newspapers are usually much thicker and contain a great deal of news, advertising, and special features.

Weekly papers appear in towns, suburbs, and smaller cities where the volume of hard news and advertising is insufficient to support a daily newspaper. These papers emphasize the news of a restricted area; they report local news in depth but tend to ignore national news, sports, and similar subjects. National advertisers often shun weeklies because they are high in cost, they duplicate the circulation of daily or Sunday papers, and they create an administrative headache because ads must be placed separately for each newspaper. *Beverly Review* is an example of a weekly circulated in a Chicago neighborhood.

For a media planner, matching the timing of the advertising message with the aperture of the target audience is crucial; so, knowing that your target audience reads the Sunday edition twice as much as the daily edition suggests the best placement.

Size Newspapers typically are available in two sizes. The first, called the **tabloid**, consists of five or six columns, each of which is about 2 inches wide and has a length of approximately 14 inches. The *Chicago Sun-Times* uses this size, as does the *New York Daily News*, the *National Enquirer*, and *The Star*. The standard size, or **broadsheet** newspaper, is twice as large as the tabloid size, usually eight columns wide and 300 lines deep, or 22 inches deep by 14 inches wide. More than 90 percent of all newspapers, including the *New York Times* and the *Los Angeles Times* use standard size.

Newspaper formats are not fixed and frozen. The success of *USA Today* indicates that newspapers can and will adjust to changing consumer tastes. *USA Today* stories are brief and breezy, dressed up with splashy graphics and full color in every section, and they include an array of charts and graphs to simplify the day's events for readers. The *Newsday* ad is an example of a newspaper with a novel format, influenced by the success of *USA Today* and designed to attract young readers.

Apart from the size and publishing schedule of a newspaper, advertisers pay close attention to newspapers' required advertisement format. Until the 1980s national advertisers shied away from using newspapers because each paper had its own size guidelines

for ads, making it impossible to prepare one ad that would fit every newspaper. In the early 1980s, however, the American Newspaper Publishers Association and the Newspaper Advertising Bureau introduced the Standard Advertising Unit (SAU) system to solve this problem.

The latest version of the SAU, shown in Figure 9.2, made it possible for newspapers to offer advertisers a great deal of choice within a standard format. An advertiser can select one of the 56 standard ad sizes and be assured that its ad will work in every newspaper in the country.

Circulation For the most part, newspapers are a mass medium, attempting to reach either a regional or a national audience. The word **circulation** refers to the number of copies a newspaper sells. A few newspapers have a national circulation, such as the *London Times* and *USA Today*. A far greater number have only regional circulation. Some newspapers try to reach certain target audiences in other ways. Most common among these are newspapers directed at specific ethnic or foreign-language groups, such as *El Nuevo Herald*, a Spanish daily published in Miami. Over 200 newspapers in the United States are aimed primarily at African Americans. In New York City alone, there are Chinese, Spanish, Russian, Yiddish, German, and Vietnamese newspapers.

AT&T uses newspapers targeted to African American, Asian, and Hispanic audiences to tout local corporate events. Honda, Canon, and Ricoh advertise in Japanese papers, such as the *Yomiuri Shimbun* (see ad). Carnation and GTE run ads in Hispanic papers in California and other regions. As is the case with mainstream newspapers, most advertisers are local retailers, especially ethnic restaurants, travel agents, banks, and stores.[1]

Special newspapers also exist for special interest groups, religious denominations, political affiliations, labor unions, and professional and fraternal organizations. For example, *Stars & Stripes* is the newspaper read by millions of military personnel.

El Nuevo Herald is one example of a successful newspaper targeted at a specific ethnic group, in this case the Spanish-speaking consumer.

Depth In Inches	1 col. 2-1/16"	2 col. 4-1/4"	3 col. 6-7/16"	4 col. 8-5/8"	5 col. 10-13/16"	6 col. 13"
			13"			
FD	1 × FD	2 × FD	3 × FD	4 × FD	5 × FD	6 × FD
18%	1 × 18	2 × 18	3 × 18	4 × 18	5 × 18	6 × 18
15.75"	1 × 15.75	2 × 15.75	3 × 15.75	4 × 15.75	5 × 15.75	
14"	1 × 14	2 × 14	3 × 14	4 × 14	5 × 14	6 × 14
13"	1 × 13	2 × 13	3 × 13	4 × 13	5 × 13	
10.5"	1 × 10.5	2 × 10.5	3 × 10.5	4 × 10.5	5 × 10.5	6 × 10.5
7"	1 × 7	2 × 7	3 × 7	4 × 7	5 × 7	6 × 7
5.25"	1 × 5.25	2 × 5.25	3 × 5.25	4 × 5.25		
3.5"	1 × 3.5	2 × 3.5				
3"	1 × 3	2 × 3				
2"	1 × 2	2 × 2				
1.5"	1 × 1.5					
1"	1 × 1					

1 Column 2-1/16"
2 Columns 4-1/4"
3 Columns 6-7/16"
4 Columns 8-5/8"
5 Columns 10-13/16"
6 Columns 13"

Double Truck 26-3/4"
There are four suggested double-truck sizes:
13 × FD 13 × 18 13 × 14 13 × 10.5
*FD (full depth): Can be 21" or deeper.
Depths for each broadsheet newspaper are indicated in the Standard Rate and Data Service (SRDA). All broadsheet newspapers can accept 21" ads, and may float them if their depth is greater than 21".

Tabloids: Size 5 × 14 is a full page tabloid for long-cut-off papers. Mid cut-off papers can handle this size with minimal reduction. The N size measuring 9-3/8 × 14 represents the full-page size—the size for tabloids such as the *New York Daily News* and *Newsday* and other short cut-off newspapers. The five 13-inch-deep sizes are for tabloids printed on 55-inch wide presses such as the *Philadelphia News*. See individual SRDS listings for tabloid sections of broadcast newspapers.

FIGURE 9.2   THE EXPANDED STANDARD ADVERTISING UNIT SYSTEM
The expanded Standard Advertising Unit system offers a greater number of choices within a standard format.
Source: Guide to Quality Newspaper Reproduction, joint publication of the American Newspaper Publishers Association and Newspaper Advertising Bureau, 1986.

By subscribing to auditing and research firms, newspapers gather valuable objective data about readership. This ad demonstrates a Japanese newspaper using such information to attract advertisers.

Newspaper Readers

Newspaper readers encompass all income brackets, educational levels, age groups, and ethnic backgrounds. They live in cities, suburbs, towns, resorts, and rural areas. By all demographic standards, the newspaper is a solid mass-market medium, representing about 68 percent of the adult population.[2] Frequent readers of daily newspapers tend to be the most regular readers of the Sunday paper. Nearly half of all adults receive home delivery of a Sunday or weekend newspaper: delivery levels are highest in medium-sized cities and lowest in rural locations and the largest in metropolitan areas.

Historically, newspaper reading tends to be lowest among people in their late teens and early twenties. "Then it always bumps back up as people reach 30 and settle into homes and need access to the kind of information that newspapers provide," says Frederick Toccills, director of new media and products with *Newsday*.[3] Experts are concerned that the proliferation of new media information sources may mean that the latest generation of young adults won't follow this trend. Figure 9.3 shows more information about newspaper readership.

Measuring the Newspaper Audience

Newspapers need to measure their audiences to assess their performance and spot growth opportunities. They also use the measurements to attract advertisers who want to reach their readers. Newspapers obtain objective measures of newspaper readership by subscribing to one or both of the following auditing companies:

- **The Auditing Bureau of Circulations (ABC).** The ABC is an independent auditing group that represents advertisers, agencies, and publishers. This group verifies statements about newspaper circulation statistics and provides a detailed analysis of the newspaper by state, town, and county. ABC members include only paid-circulation

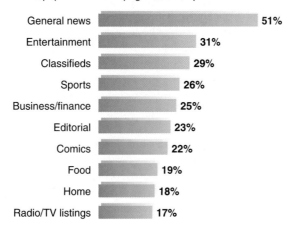

Like most adults, baby boomers (ages 35-54) read newspapers selectively. Only 21% of those surveyed read every section of the newspaper. Section or page readership:

General news 51%
Entertainment 31%
Classifieds 29%
Sports 26%
Business/finance 25%
Editorial 23%
Comics 22%
Food 19%
Home 18%
Radio/TV listings 17%

FIGURE 9.3

NEWSPAPER READERSHIP SELECTIVE
Newspaper readership tends to be selective, with a greater percentage reading specific sections rather than the whole paper.

newspapers and magazines. Note that the ABC's activities have nothing to do with setting the rates a newspaper charges its advertisers.

Newspapers that do not belong to an auditing organization such as the ABC must provide prospective advertisers with either a publisher's statement or Post Office Statement. The former is a sworn affidavit and the latter is an annual statement the publisher files with the U.S. Post Office.

- **Simmons-Scarborough**. Simmons-Scarborough Syndicated Research Associates provides a syndicated newspaper readership study that annually measures readership profiles in approximately 70 of the nation's largest cities. The study covers readership of a single issue and the estimated unduplicated readers for a series of issues. Simmons-Scarborough is the only consistent measurement of popular audiences in individual markets.

Once again, this type of information facilitates the media planner's ability to match a certain newspaper with the target audience. It also helps in the calculation of effective reach, a concept we discussed in Chapter 8.

Advertising in Newspaper Markets

Let's now explore the three general types of newspaper advertising: classified, display, and supplements.

Classified The first type of advertising found in newspapers is **classified advertising**. Classified ads generally consist of all types of commercial messages arranged according to their interest to readers, such as "Help Wanted," "Real Estate for Sale," and "Cars for Sale." Classified ads represent approximately 40 percent of total newspaper advertising revenue.

Many analysts say that classified advertising will move from print to online media, and that classified spending will shrink considerably by 2005. Jupiter Research (www. Jup.com) has stated, "newspapers will lose $4.1 billion in traditional classifieds, or 14.9 percent of what the market would be without the existence of online classifieds."[4]

Although most advertisers use classifieds to sell their business or hire new employees, these trends in newspaper classifieds are useful to the media planner in anticipating ad rate changes or space availability.[5]

Display The dominant form of newspaper advertising is **display advertising**. Display ads can be any size and can be placed anywhere in the newspaper except the editorial page. Display advertising is further divided into two subcategories: local (retail) and national (general). National and international businesses, organizations, and celebrities use national display advertising to maintain brand recognition or to supplement the efforts of local retailers or other promotional efforts. Local businesses, organizations, or individuals that use local display advertising pay a lower, local rate.

Newspapers justify the higher cost for national advertising in several ways. First, they contend that national advertisers request more assistance, especially with special promotions, such as coupons and free-standing inserts. Second, they argue that national advertisers are less reliable than local advertisers, often placing no ads for weeks or months at a time. Finally, newspapers believe that the national advertiser is unlikely to change the number of ads placed in a given newspaper regardless of whether the rates go up or down.

Some newspapers discount for frequency or as an incentive to attract certain categories of advertising. To retain current profitable customers, some newspapers offer hybrid rates to regular national advertisers (such as airlines, car rental companies, and hotels) that are lower than the national rate but higher than the local rate.

One alternative that allows the national advertiser to pay the local rate is cooperative (co-op) advertising with a local retailer. **Co-op advertising** is an arrangement between the advertiser and the retailer whereby both parties share the cost of placing the ad. The two parties negotiate their exact shares.

A newer system designed to avoid the rate differential is known as **one-order, one-bill**. Essentially, media companies buy newspaper advertising space for many national advertisers. The one-order, one-bill company handles all rate negotiation and billing. Because the company has so many advertising clients, it has buying power that allows it to offer lower rates for newspaper ad space. The client advertisers not only benefit from lower rates, but they also do not have to deal with the hassle of billing. In the past, national advertisers buying space from 150 newspapers would receive as many as 150 pieces of paper using 150 different accounting methods.[6]

The two major one-order, one-bill companies are Media Passage and Publicitas/Globe Media. However, newspapers can set up networks, too. Newspapers from three states worked together to form a one-order, one-bill network tailored and priced to appeal to the national automobile dealer associations. The network is designed to cover an association's trading area so it does not include unwanted circulation.[7]

Supplements Newspaper supplements can carry both national and local advertising. **Supplements** are syndicated (an independent publisher that sells its publications to newspapers throughout a country) or local full-color advertising inserts that appear throughout the week and especially in the Sunday edition of newspapers. One popular type is the magazine supplement, which can be both syndicated and local.

Independent publishers create and distribute syndicated supplements to newspapers throughout the country. The logo for the publisher and the local paper appear on the masthead (the top of the page). The best-known syndicated supplements are *Parade* and *USA Weekend*. Either one newspaper or a group of newspapers in the same area produce local supplements. Whether syndicated or locally edited, magazine supplements resemble magazines more than newspapers in content and format.

Another type of newspaper supplement is the **free-standing insert advertisement (FSIA)**, or loose insert. These preprinted advertisements range in size from a single page to over 30 pages and may be in black-and-white or full color. This material is printed elsewhere and then delivered to the newspaper. Newspapers charge the advertiser a fee for inserting the material plus a special rate for carrying the ad in a particular issue. This form of newspaper advertising is growing in popularity with retail advertisers for two reasons: (1) It allows greater control over the reproduction quality of the advertisement, and (2) the multipage FSIA is an excellent coupon carrier. Newspapers are not necessarily happy about the growth of free-standing inserts because they make less revenue from this form of advertising.[8]

The Advantages of Newspapers

The newspaper medium has numerous advantages, which is why newspapers are still the number-one medium in respect to ad billings.

- **Range of market coverage**. Advertisers can reach local or regional markets, special interest groups, and racial and ethnic groups in a cost-efficient manner.
- **Comparison shopping**. Consumers use newspapers for comparison shopping, so they are especially useful for advertisers that have products with an obvious competitive advantage.
- **Positive consumer attitudes**. Readers generally perceive newspapers, including the advertisements, to be current and credible information sources. Because consumers can control when and how they read the paper of their choice, they view newspaper ads positively.
- **Flexibility**. Newspapers offer geographic flexibility: Advertisers can choose to advertise in some markets and not in others. Newspapers also offer production flexibility. Unusual ad sizes, full-color ads, free-standing inserts, different prices in different areas, sample products, and supplements are all newspaper advertising options.
- **Interaction of national and local**. Newspapers provide a bridge between the national advertiser and the local retailer. A local retailer can easily tie in with a national campaign by using a similar advertisement in the local daily. In addition, quick-action programs, such as sales and coupons, are implemented easily through local newspapers.

The Disadvantages of Newspapers

Like every other advertising medium, newspapers also have disadvantages. The most problematic issues in newspaper advertising include:

- **Short life span**. People tend to read newspapers quickly and only once. The average life span of a daily newspaper is only 24 hours, so the life span of the ad is limited.
- **Clutter**. Most newspapers are cluttered with ads, particularly on supermarket advertising days and on Sundays, when information overload reduces the effect of any single advertisement. Even supplemental inserts are now so thick that they represent additional newspaper clutter.
- **Limited coverage of certain groups**. Although newspapers have wide market coverage, certain market groups are not frequent readers. For example, newspapers traditionally have not reached a large part of the under-20 age group. The same is true of the elderly and those speaking a foreign language who do not live in a large city. Newspapers often cannot provide total market coverage for national advertisers because of cost and the fact that there are few national newspapers.
- **Product criteria**. Newspapers suffer the same limitations shared by all print media. Certain products should not be advertised in newspapers, such as those that require demonstration. Also, products that consumers do not expect to find advertised in newspapers, such as professional services (doctors, lawyers) and tradespeople (plumbers, electricians), might easily be overlooked.
- **Poor reproduction**. Despite the introduction of new production technology, with the exception of special printing techniques and preprinted inserts, the reproduction quality of newspapers is poor, especially for color advertisements, compared to magazines, brochures, and direct mail. In addition, the speed necessary to compose a daily newspaper prevents the detailed preparation and care in production that is possible with weekly or monthly publications.
- **Inability to keep up with urban sprawl**. The tremendous growth of urban areas has made it difficult for newspapers to provide one of their primary benefits— on-time delivery.

Online newspapers are proliferating but are not expected to replace traditional newspapers any time soon.

Changes in the Newspaper Industry

As a whole, the newspaper industry has wrapped its arms around emerging technology, and this adoption has not been restricted to conventional Internet sites. Stories are now being distributed through Web-enabled phones, pagers, e-mail, and Palms.[9] A busy executive is now able to download stories from the *Wall Street Journal* and the *New York Times* via SkyTel, any time and anywhere. Companies such as Audible Inc. even provide audio digests of the papers. Files can be downloaded from its Web site Audible.com and played on carry-along CD players. Experts in the newspaper industry expect these new delivery systems to be profitable soon.[10]

Newspapers are by no means obsolete. The traditional benefits to an advertiser are obvious, but today's customers expect more. Whether the industry as a whole can deliver on these expectations remains to be seen, but there is potential for positive change. Now let's look at magazines.[11]

MAGAZINES

The earliest American magazines were local journals of political opinion. Most were monthly and did not circulate far beyond their geographic origins.

Since that time, magazines have come and gone. All have been aimed at specific audiences; most sell advertising and are published monthly.[12] New magazine launches peaked in 1989, a year in which publishers introduced 605 titles. In the 1990s the number of new magazines dropped to about 550 per year.[13] Historically, over half of all new titles fail. Despite the high risks associated with the magazine business, new ones do continue to emerge, especially those that target growing market segments such as teenagers.

Within this changing environment, publishers are investing more money than ever in existing titles to hold on to market share. The magazine industry recognizes that it has entered the age of skimming, a time when readers acquire 80 percent of their information from the story titles, subheadings, captions, and pictures rather than from the editorial content. Individual magazines have become bigger and brighter. Heavy paper stock, lush photographs, and sophisticated graphics create beautiful, eye-catching editorial environments that entice both readers and advertisers.

TABLE 9.2   **Top 25 Consumer Magazines by Paid Circulation**

Top paid circulation magazines for the second half of 2001 compared to the second half of 2000. The results also demonstrate the effect 9/11 had on the industry as interest in newsweeklies climbed.

Rank 2001	Rank 2000	Publication	Circulation	% in Chg
1	1	Modern Maturity	17,780,127	−15.2
2	2	Reader's Digest	12,565,779	−0.0
3	3	TV Guide	9,097,762	−8.6
4	4	National Geographic	7,664,658	−2.1
5	5	Better Homes & Gardens	7,601,377	−0.2
6	6	Family Circle	4,712,548	−5.8
7	7	Good Housekeeping	4,527,447	−0.7
8	8	Woman's Day	4,257,742	0.3
9	10	Time	4,189,981	3.3
10	9	Ladies' Home Journal	4,100,675	0.0
11	12	People Weekly	3,723,848	4.8
12	11	Rosie (formerly McCall's)	3,613,055	−9.8
13	16	Newsweek	3,308,912	5.2
14	13	Home & Away	3,307,217	1.2
15	15	Sports Illustrated	3,206,098	0.0
16	14	Playboy	3,157,540	−1.7
17	17	Prevention	3,121,340	3.8
18	20	Cosmopolitan	2,759,448	6.4
19	21	Guideposts	2,743,726	5.9
20	18	Via Magazine	2,642,929	0.5
21	19	The American Legion Magazine	2,624,754	0.9
22	23	Maxim	2,553,895	3.9
23	22	Southern Living	2,549,601	0.5
24	28	O, The Oprah Magazine	2,530,712	17.0
25	24	Martha Stewart Living	2,437,970	0.1

Source: Advertising Age, February 19, 2001 and February 25, 2002; based on Audit Bureau of Circulation figures; ABC also audits nonpaid circulation.

Upscale magazines seem to have an edge over mass-consumer magazines in attracting advertisers. Upscale advertisers tend to turn to the image advertising that upscale magazines provide. For example, magazines such as *Gourmet, Architectural Digest*, and *Conde Nast Traveler* have increased their ad pages in the last 10 years.[14] Steve Forbes, president and CEO of *Forbes* magazine, attributes this increase to the addition of more companies such as Cadillac, Jaguar, and Lear Jets appealing to the wealthier consumer segment.

The number-one magazine in terms of paid circulation is *Modern Maturity* with a paid 2001 circulation of almost 18 million, followed by *Reader's Digest* at 12.5 million (see Table 9.2).

Types of Magazines

Advertisers that want to place their ads to target specific audiences use many types of magazine classifications when planning and buying print media and when creating print ads. As we see next, they classify magazines according to audience, geographic coverage, demographics, editorial diversity, physical characteristics, and distribution and circulation.

Audience The three main types of audiences that magazines target are consumer, business, and farm audiences. Consumer magazines, directed at consumers who buy products

Advertisers look at the audience, geographic coverage, demographics, and editorial diversity of magazines as criteria for advertising feasibility.

for personal consumption, are distributed through the mail, newsstands, or stores. Examples are *Reader's Digest, Lear's, Time*, and *People*. Business magazines target business readers; they include the following types:

- **Trade papers** aimed at retailers, wholesalers, and other distributors. *Chain Store Age* is an example.
- **Industrial magazines** aimed at manufacturers. One example is *Concrete Construction.*
- **Professional magazines** aimed at physicians, lawyers, and other professionals. *National Law Review* targets lawyers, for instance.

Business magazines are also classified as vertical or horizontal publications. A **vertical publication** presents stories and information about an entire industry. *Women's Wear Daily*, for example, discusses the production, marketing, and distribution of women's fashions. A **horizontal publication** deals with a business function that cuts across industries, such as *Direct Marketing*.[15]

Farm magazines, the third audience category, targets farmers and those engaged in farm-related activities. *Peanut Farmer* is an example of a farm magazine. This category is mostly traditional, since this group has certainly declined in the last five decades.

Geography Magazines generally cover certain sections or regions of the country. The area covered may be as small as a city (*Los Angeles Magazine* and *Boston Magazine*) or as large as several contiguous states (the southwestern edition of *Southern Living Magazine*). Geographic editions help encourage local retail support by listing the names of local distributors in the advertisements. Most national magazines also offer a zone edition that will carry different ads, and perhaps different stories, depending on the region of the country.

Demographics Demographic editions group subscribers according to age, income, occupation, and other classifications. *McCall's* for example, publishes a special "ZIP" edition for upper-income homes that is sent to subscribers who live in a specific Zip code. A Zip code presumably tells something about the people living in an area. They typically share common demographic traits, such as income. *Newsweek* offers a college edition and

Time sends special editions to students, business executives, doctors, and business managers. Advertisers who describe their target audience by their demographics can more effectively select magazines.

Editorial Content Various magazines emphasize certain types of editorial content. The most widely used categories are general editorial (*Reader's Digest*), women's service (*Family Circle*), shelter (*House Beautiful*), business (*Forbes*), and special interest (*Ski*). Categories often correspond to audience characteristics, which prompt selection of specific magazines by consumers.

Physical Characteristics Media planners and buyers need to know the physical characteristics of a magazine because ads containing various elements of words and pictures require a different amount of space. The most common magazine page sizes are 8½ × 11 inches and 6 × 9 inches. Note the V8 ad found in *Reader's Digest* is a 6 × 9-inch ad and allows for fewer visuals and little copy.

Distribution and Circulation Media planners and buyers also pay attention to the way a magazine is distributed to its audience so they can assess circulation potential. These delivery methods help determine whether the correct audiences will be reached. **Traditional delivery** is done through newsstand purchases or home delivery via the U.S. Postal Service. **Nontraditional delivery** methods include hanging bagged copies on doorknobs, delivery inserted in newspapers (such as *Parade* magazine), delivery through professionals (doctors' and dentists' offices), direct delivery (company magazines or those found on airplanes), and electronic delivery. Nontraditional delivery is normally provided free of charge and is referred to as *controlled circulation* (magazine is distributed to specific audiences).

Magazine Readers and Their Measurement

For the media planner and buyer it is most critical to know if there are unique characteristics associated with magazine readers and, if so, whether there is a way to verify these facts. We do know, for instance, that 92 percent of all American adults read at least one magazine per month, and 80 percent of these readers consider magazine advertising "helpful as a buying guide." In general, people pay more attention to magazine advertising than to television advertising.[16]

There are several companies that attempt to verify the paid circulation of magazines, along with demographic and psychographic characteristics of specific readers. Media planners and buyers rely heavily on this information when making choices.

Magazine rates are based on the number of readers, which correlates with the circulation that a publisher promises to provide, or the guaranteed circulation. Magazine circulation is the number of copies of an issue sold, not the readership of the publication. A single copy of a magazine might be read by one person or by several people, depending on its content. As with newspapers, the ABC is responsible for verifying circulation numbers. The ABC audits subscriptions as well as newsstand sales and also checks the number of delinquent subscribers and rates of renewal.

The *Simmons Market Research Bureau* (SMRB) goes one step further by relating readership patterns to purchasing habits. The bureau provides data on who reads which magazines and which products these readers buy and consume. Most advertisers and agencies depend greatly on SMRB estimates of magazine audiences. Other research companies such as Starch, Gallup, and Robinson provide comparable information about magazine audience size and behavior.

MediaMark is a company that provides a service called MRI, which measures readership for most popular national and regional magazines (along with other media). Reports are issued to subscribers twice a year and cover readership by demographics, psychographics, and product use.

Advertising in Magazines

Magazines are a valuable medium for reaching many demographic groups. By their nature, magazines must fill a niche with unique editorial content to satisfy specific groups of readers. In deciding in which magazines to place ads, advertisers need to examine certain factors such as technology and format.

Technology New technologies have enabled magazines to distinguish themselves from one another. For example, selective binding and ink-jet imaging allow publishers to construct and personalize issues for individual subscribers. Selective binding combines information on sub-

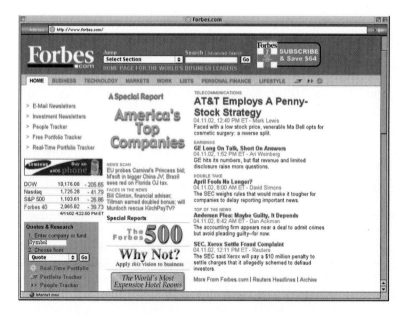

This screen shot for Forbes.com may represent the future of magazines–electronic delivery.

scribers kept in a database with a computer program to produce magazines that include special sections for subscribers based on their demographic profiles. Ink-jet imaging allows a magazine such as *U.S. News & World Report* to personalize its renewal form so that each issue contains a renewal card already filled out with the subscriber's name, address, and so on. Personalized messages can be printed directly on run-of-book ads (the technology that is used for the entire magazine) or on inserts (e.g., "Mr. Jones—check our new mutual fund today").

Many magazines also use desktop publishing technology. This method, when combined with satellite transmission, allows magazines to close pages just hours before press time so that advertisers can drop up-to-the-minute information in their ads. Sophisticated database management has also improved the advertising effectiveness of magazines. This technology lets publishers combine the information available from subscriber lists with other public and private lists to create complete consumer profiles for advertisers. This process has come under close scrutiny with the public's increasing concern for personal privacy.

Format Although the format may vary from magazine to magazine, all magazines share some format characteristics. For example, the front cover of a magazine is called its first cover page. The inside of the front cover is called the second cover page, the inside of the back cover the third cover page, and the back cover the fourth cover page.

Normally, the largest unit of ad space that magazines sell is the double-page spread, in which two pages face each other. A double-page ad design must bridge or jump the gutter (the white space between the pages running along the inside edge of the page), meaning that no headline words run through the gutter and that all body text is on one side or the other. A page without outside margins, in which the color extends to the edge of the page, is called a bleed page (see the *Wall Street Journal* ad).

Magazines can sometimes offer more than two connected pages (four is the most common number). This is called a gatefold. Armstrong Floors used a five-sided gatefold in the inside front cover of *Better Homes & Gardens* for several years. The use of multiple pages that provide photo essays is really an extension of the gatefold concept.

A *bleed* page has no outside margins, as exemplified by this ad for the *Wall Street Journal*.

Photo essays also are becoming more common in magazines such as *Fortune* and *BusinessWeek*; these magazines may present a 20-page ad for a business in a foreign country. Finally, a single page or double page can be broken into a variety of units called fractional page space (for example, vertical half-page, horizontal half-page, half-page double spread, and checkerboard in which ads are located on double-page upper left, lower right, on both pages).

These various formats are employed in media planning. Most magazines have a great deal of clutter, so cutting through this clutter through size or novelty is a common strategy. Being on a cover cuts down on the clutter but requires a premium price, often two or three times more than a full page inside the magazine. Employing a vertical or horizontal half-page may be effective in attracting the attention of readers.

The Advantages of Magazines

The benefits of magazine advertising include the ability to reach specialized audiences, audience receptivity, a long life span, format, visual quality, and the distribution of sales promotion devices.

- **Target audiences**. The ability of magazines such as *Men's Health, Fast Company*, and *Sassy* to reach specialized audiences is a primary advantage of magazines. For example, *B-to-B* would be very effective in reaching people interested in business-to-business Internet marketing.
- **Audience receptivity**. Magazines have a high level of audience receptivity. The editorial environment of a magazine lends authority and credibility to the advertising. Many magazines claim that advertising in their publication gives a product prestige. Clearly, an ad in *Fortune* would impress business audiences, just as an ad in *Spin* would impress teenagers.
- **Long life span**. Magazines have the longest life span of all the media. Some magazines, such as *National Geographic* and *Consumer Reports*, are used as ongoing references and might never be discarded. (Other publications, such as *TV Guide*, are used frequently during a given period of time.) In addition, magazines have high reach potential because they are passed along to family, friends, customers, and colleagues.
- **Format**. People also tend to read magazines at a slow rate, typically over a couple of days, so they offer an opportunity to use detailed copy. The magazine format also allows creative advertising variety through multiple pages, inserts, and other features.
- **Visual quality**. The visual quality of magazines tends to be excellent because they are printed on high-quality paper that provides superior photo reproduction in both black-and-white and color. This production quality often reflects the editorial content.
- **Sales promotions**. Advertisers can distribute various sales promotion devices, such as coupons, product samples, and information cards through magazines. A 1987 U.S. Post Office ruling allowed magazines to carry loose editorial and advertising supplements as part of the publication if the magazine is enclosed in an envelope or wrapper.[17]

All of these advantages are demonstrated in the "A Matter of Principle" box.

The Disadvantages of Magazines

Magazines are limited by certain factors. The most prominent disadvantages are limited flexibility, lack of immediacy, high cost, and difficult distribution.

- **Limited flexibility**. Although magazines offer advertisers many benefits, long lead time and limited flexibility are drawbacks. Ads must be submitted well in advance of the publication date. In some instances advertisers must have camera-ready full-color advertisements at the printer more than two months before the cover date of a monthly publication. As noted earlier, magazines that have adopted desktop publishing and satellite transmission can allow advertisers to submit ads just hours before press time. Magazines also limit the choices for ad locations. Prime locations, such as the back cover or inside front cover, may be sold months in advance.
- **Lack of immediacy**. Some readers do not look at an issue of a magazine until long after it comes to them, so the ad may take a long time to have an effect on the reader.

A MATTER OF PRINCIPLE

DEM BONES

➤ One of the most difficult challenges faced by advertisers over the years has been persuading people to think about things they don't want to think about or do things they don't want to do. Preventive health care has been particularly ineffective. Despite the fact that health-related companies have spent millions of dollars, too many people still smoke, eat poorly, and refuse to get annual checkups.

When Merck Pharmaceutical introduced Fosomax in 1999, it came face-to-face with this historical dilemma. Fosomax is a prescription drug that treats osteoporosis, the most undiagnosed bone disease that attacks women age 60 and older. The Merck marketing team viewed the challenge as a two-step operation. First, they had to convince women of 50-plus that screening for osteoporosis was a worthwhile activity. Second, they had to introduce Fosomax as the best treatment for osteoporosis.

Foote, Cone & Belding (FCB) was hired as the agency of record and was given an initial budget of $7 million from Merck. After extensive research, the situation was cogently expressed by Ellen Oppenheim, senior vice president/media director at FCB, "Women don't think they're old, so if you tell them they have to do something because they're aging and there are no obvious symptoms, it's hard to motivate them to want to do something. The marketing challenge then was to get women to take action against osteoporosis, and from a media point of view we had to tell a compelling story in print."

Print was selected over broadcast because it could more effectively tell a complex story in a sensitive tone. Also, because of the many legal requirements associated with advertising prescription drugs, print is almost mandatory.

The FCB team in New York spearheaded the print campaign which included full-page ads in 37 magazines, including *TV Guide, Parade*, and *Biography*. The launch coincided with National Osteoporosis Month.

Guided by the two objectives mentioned above, the ads were unbranded in that the focus was on educating the reader about the disease itself. Information was provided about bone density tests, along with the kinds of doctors who administer them. The elegant black-and-white portraits of various women provided a sensitive touch. Another clever element was added to the campaign. FCB negotiated with several publications to give them a free one-third page. Readers could clip this extra third-of-a-page and use it as a reminder for their annual mammogram, Pap smear, and of course, bone density test. The results were immediate: From April to November 1999 bone density testing increased significantly among the targeted population.

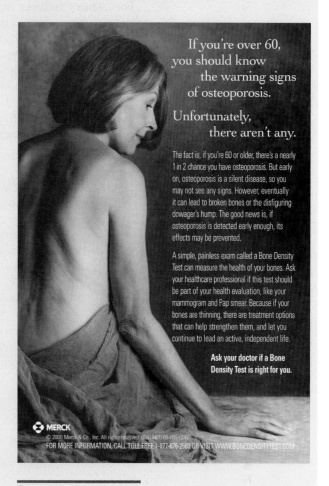

If you're over 60, you should know the warning signs of osteoporosis.

Unfortunately, there aren't any.

The fact is, if you're 60 or older, there's a nearly 1 in 2 chance you have osteoporosis. But early on, osteoporosis is a silent disease, so you may not see any signs. However, eventually it can lead to broken bones or the disfiguring dowager's hump. The good news is, if osteoporosis is detected early enough, its effects may be prevented.

A simple, painless exam called a Bone Density Test can measure the health of your bones. Ask your healthcare professional if this test should be part of your health evaluation, like your mammogram and Pap smear. Because if your bones are thinning, there are treatment options that can help strengthen them, and let you continue to lead an active, independent life.

Ask your doctor if a Bone Density Test is right for you.

◆ MERCK
© 2000 Merck & Co., Inc. All rights reserved. 004194(1)-09-FOS-CON
FOR MORE INFORMATION, CALL TOLL FREE 1-877-676-2663 OR VISIT WWW.BONEDENSITYTEST.COM

This ad from Merck attempts to present a subject (osteoporosis) with sensitivity.

FCB claims that much of the reason for the success of this campaign was its avoidance of the obvious print vehicles. Research on the 50-plus lifestyle revealed a list of magazines much broader than expected. For example, bird watching came up as a prominent activity, suggesting that the Fosomax campaign would be a good fit for magazines such as *Audobon, National Geographic*, and *Travel Holiday*.

POINT TO PONDER

What other types of creative approaches do you think would work in the Fosomax print campaign?

Source: Lisa Granastein, "Foote, Cone & Belding," *Mediaweek* (June 19, 2000): 22–25.

Even if you might keep a *National Geographic* for many years, advertisers hope you will read it immediately.

- **High cost**. The third disadvantage of magazine advertising is its high cost. In 2001 the cost for a full-page, four-color ad in *Newsweek's* top 20 markets edition was $38,500. For a general audience magazine such as *Newsweek*, advertising rates are quite high, and magazines of this type do not compare favorably with other media. However, magazines with carefully segmented audiences, such as *Byte*, can be cost-efficient because they reach a tightly targeted audience.
- **Distribution**. The final disadvantage of magazines is their limited distribution. With the exception of magazines such as *Woman's Day* and *People*, which are distributed on newsstands throughout the United States, many of the 2,500 different magazines that exist typically are not distributed to a broad spectrum of potential audience members. Media decision makers should understand the pros and cons of magazines so they can compare this medium to other media types and choose the best one for their situation.

Changes in the Magazine Industry: Online Technology

As with newspapers, emerging technology—particularly online technology—is changing the magazine industry. How much the industry will change is still in question. For example, *Salon* is a virtual magazine distributed only on the Internet. These virtual magazines do not rely on paper or postage, and have no length limitations. But however exciting the words, however beautiful the layout, critics contend that online magazines may never overcome "the bathroom factor."[18] There are also questions by circulation experts who doubt Internet subscription sales will be large enough to supplement more traditional methods.

An interesting irony about magazines going into the Web has been the reversal of that pattern since the semidemise of the dot-coms in 2000–2001. Not long ago the Internet was supposed to ruin print media. However, at least seven Web sites have created a print magazine in recent months, including Nerve.com, Space.com, and the travel site Expedia.

Magazines and newspapers have existed for several years in their current format because they provide interesting writing that's portable. The Web is most certainly not that yet, which begs the question: Will people really want their newspapers and magazines online after the novelty has worn off?[19]

The life or death, prosperity or difficulty of any communication vehicle is based on its ability to produce an acceptable cost-benefit relationship. The question is not the inherent superiority of the Internet over traditional print. The question is which works better as part of an intelligently developed media strategy.

OUT-OF-HOME ADVERTISING

Not long ago, a media planner would base a schedule around newspaper, radio, television, and outdoor advertising. The outdoor portion was easy: There were 8- and 30-sheet posters and painted bulletins. Not so anymore. Even the name of the medium has changed. No longer called outdoor advertising, it is now **out-of-home advertising**, and it includes everything from billboards to hot-air balloons.

When you think of billboards you may visualize giant posters or painted bulletins. But out-of-home advertising also includes ads on buses, walls, telephone kiosks, semi-trucks, taxi signs, transit and rail platforms, airport and bus terminal displays, bus shelter displays, bus benches, shopping mall displays, grocery store carts, public restroom walls, skywriting, in-store clocks, and aisle displays. And don't forget blimps and airplanes towing messages over Yankee Stadium.

Out-of-home advertising also has taken giant steps to target specific people with specific messages at a time when they are most susceptible. A sign at the telephone kiosk reminds you to call for reservations at your favorite restaurant; a sign on the rail platform suggests that you enjoy a candy bar while riding the train; and a bus card reminds you to listen to the news on a particular radio station.

Out-of-home advertising grew during the 1990s. Today total spending on outdoor media is estimated to be over $5 billion. A major shift has been from predominantly national advertisers to local companies and national companies with a local message.[20]

Outdoor Advertising

There are two kinds of billboards: poster panels and painted bulletins.

Posters are created by designers (provided by the advertiser or agency), printed, and shipped to an outdoor advertising company. They are then pre-pasted and applied in sections to the poster panel's face on location, much like applying wallpaper. The advertiser can print and distribute thousands of copies around the country or the world.

Designers can add **extensions** to the painted billboards to expand the scale and break away from the limits of the long rectangle. The extensions are limited to 5 feet, 6 inches at the top and 2 feet at the sides and bottom. These embellishments are sometimes called **cutouts** because they present an irregular shape. The board for the Workers Compensation Fund is an example.

The other kind of billboard is the **painted bulletin**. Painted bulletins differ from posters in that they are normally created on site and are not restricted to billboards as the attachment. They can be painted on the sides of buildings (see the *Armageddon* bulletin), on roofs, and even natural structures, such as the side of a mountain. They can also be painted in a studio on fiberboard, disassembled, and reassembled on-site.

An advertiser would use a billboard for two primary reasons. First, it would supplement a mass-media strategy by providing reminders to the target audience. Microsoft would use billboards to keep the Windows XP product in front of drivers as they go to and from their offices. A second use for billboards is to act as primary medium when the board is in close proximity to the product. Most common are billboards directing travelers to hotels, restaurants, resorts, and gas stations.

Because of the very short time consumers are normally exposed to a billboard (i.e., 3 to 5 seconds), the message must be short and the visual must have stopping power. No

The Workers Compensation Fund uses billboard extensions for greater visual impact.

Painted bulletins can be used for even more dramatic effect, as in this promotion for the movie *Armageddon*, which caused rubbernecking among L.A. commuters.

more than 8 to 10 words is the norm. The Chick-fil-A billboard featuring two cows asking us to "Eat mor chikin" meets all these criteria.

Buying Outdoor Space

The outdoor advertising industry has increased its professional standards and become more competitive with other media. The industry uses a system based on gross rating points (GRPs). The GRP system provides a standard unit for space sales based on a quantifiable number of exposures. An exposure occurs when a person sees the outdoor advertising message. This is typically based on a traffic count, that is, the number of vehicles passing a particular location during a specified period of time. If an advertiser purchases 100 GRPs daily, the basic standard unit is the number of poster boards in each marketing that will expose the message to 100 percent of the market population every day. If three posters in a community of 100,000 people achieve a daily exposure to 75,000 people, the result is 75 GRPs. Conversely, in a small town with a population of 1,200 and one main street, two boards may produce 100 GRPs.

Advertisers can purchase any number of units (75, 50, or 25 GRPs daily are common quantities). The number of boards required for 100 GRPs varies from city to city. Boards are usually rented for 30-day periods, with longer periods possible. Painted bulletins are bought on an individual basis, usually for one, two, or three years.

The Audience As one would expect, accurately measuring the mobile audience for outdoor advertising is tough. Media that cannot verify their audience size or composition usually have a slim chance of being selected by advertisers. In the case of outdoor advertising, this assessment process is still under revision. Currently, however, the audience-reach frequency of outdoor advertising is reported nationally by Simmons Market Research Bureau (SMRB) and locally by Audience Measurement by Market of Outdoor (AMMO). It all begins with a series of local market surveys, called calibration surveys, that the outdoor industry conducts periodically in specific U.S. markets. The surveys aim (1) to measure respondents' actual frequencies of exposure and (2) to relate these frequencies to respondents' demographic characteristics and travel behavior.[21]

Frequency of exposure to a 100-GRP advertisement in a week is measured by the map recall method, in which the respondent recalls each trip out of home in the past seven days and physically draws his or her travel route on a separate map for each trip. In the home office, a transparent sheet is laid over each map, showing the location of panels in a 100 GRP ad, and trained office coders tally the number of exposures (if any) for each respondent trip. Although a bit more complicated, this information is sampled and verified by SMRB at the national level and by AMMO at the local level. Some flaws in this methodology are being rectified. One of the problems is accounting for all the people and all possible travel patterns.

Advantages of Outdoor Advertising Although it is rare for a media strategy to be built around outdoor advertising, it does offer several advantages. Most notably, it is a high-impact medium offering larger-than-life visuals, on a hard-to-ignore structure. It can also serve as a constant reminder and can reinforce a creative concept employed in other media. Finally, it is the least expensive of all major media, especially in light of its long life.

Disadvantages of Outdoor Advertising As previously noted, because consumers pass outdoor boards very quickly and are often distracted, the message must be brief and simple. Historically, many people have been critical of outdoor advertising because it creates visual pollution. Further, boards are often vandalized. Several states, such as Oregon and Hawaii, have banned billboards, while other states have restricted locations.

Transit Advertising

Transit advertising is mainly an urban advertising form that uses vehicles such as buses and taxis to carry messages that can circulate through the community. Many semitrailer trucks carry graphics to identify the company that owns them. Some of these graphics are striking, such as the designs on the sides of the Mayflower moving trucks. In addition to this corporate identification, the sides of trucks may be rented out for more general advertising messages.

Transit advertising also includes the posters seen in bus shelters and train, airport, and subway stations. Most of these posters must be designed for quick impressions, although posters on subway platforms or bus shelters are often studied by people who are waiting, so they can present a more involved or complicated message than a billboard.

Transit advertising is reminder advertising; it is a high-frequency medium that lets advertisers get their names in front of a local audience at critical times such as rush hour and drive time. Companies around the world are using or otherwise profiting from this type of advertising. Polo Jeans is a global media company that specializes in carrying ads on various transit modes.[22]

The Transit Audience There are two types of transit advertising: interior and exterior. **Interior transit advertising** is seen by people riding inside buses, subway cars, and some taxis. **Exterior transit advertising** is mounted on the sides, rear, and tops of these vehicles, so pedestrians and people in nearby cars see it.

Transit messages can be targeted to specific audiences if the vehicles follow a regular route. Buses that are assigned to a university route will expose a higher proportion of college students, while buses that go to and from a shopping mall will expose a higher population of shoppers.

Related Locations Special structures called **kiosks** are designed for public posting of notices and advertisements. Some of these locations are places where people walk by; others are places where people wait. The location has a lot to do with the design of the message. Some out-of-home media serve the same function as the kiosk, such as the ad-carrying bus shelter and the sign subway riders encounter coming up the exit stairs.

Companies all over the world are using transit advertising to promote their products.

Transit media, in all their various forms, offer the same advantages and disadvantages as outdoor media. The strategic rationale is much the same as well. Used primarily as a reminder or supplement to other media, it would be a minor part of the media mix unless the product and the ad are in close proximity. Also, transit media do not have the size advantage of outdoor media but the consumer has more time to view the message.[23]

DIRECTORIES

Directories are books that list the names of people or companies, their phone numbers, and their addresses. In addition to this information, many directories publish advertising from marketers that want to reach the people who use the directory. The most common directories are those that a community's local phone service produces. The listings and ads in the Yellow Pages are a major advertising vehicle, particularly for local retailers. National advertisers such as Pizza Hut also use them extensively. In fact, the Yellow Pages is Pizza Hut's second largest media expenditure after TV. A single line for each Pizza Hut store is considered a unique ad.

But that is just the beginning of the directory business. An estimated 7,500 directories exist that cover all types of professional areas and interest groups. For example, the *Standard Directory of Advertisers and Advertising Agencies* (known as the Red Books) not only lists advertisers and agencies; it also accepts advertising targeted at those who use the directory. *The Creative Black Book* also takes ads for photographers, illustrators, typographers, and art suppliers.[24]

The ads in trade and professional directories usually are more detailed than those in consumer directories because they address specific professional concerns, such as qualifications and scope of services provided. Trade directories also use supplemental media such as inserts and tipped-in cards (glued into the spine) that can be detached and filed.

Directories fall into several categories. *Area-wide* or *overlay* directories combine areas covered by multiple directories into one large directory area. There is an area-wide directory for the Seattle/Spokane area. These directories usually correspond to sales territories or some other criteria found to be useful. *Suburban* or *neighborhood* directories serve a smaller, more localized portion of an area that a larger directory covers. Advertising in a suburban or a neighborhood directory allows advertisers to target specific geographic markets. *Special interest* or *niche* directories are demographically targeted to reach specific consumer markets. Examples include Hispanic directories, women's directories, and university directories. *Business-to-Business* directories are targeted to the purchasing needs of business customers. These directories have unique heading structures and are distributed only to businesses.

Most of the directories can be transformed into an electronic version, accessible through the Internet. Electronic directories provide convenience and speed to customers who have the right technology. The dominant directory is the Yellow Pages, which can be either an area-wide or a neighborhood directory, as well as electronic.

Yellow Pages

The Yellow Pages directory lists all local and regional businesses that have a telephone number. In addition to the phone number listing, retailers can buy display space and run a larger ad. The industry's core advertisers are service providers (restaurants, travel agents, beauty parlors, and florists, for example). For some small businesses, the Yellow Pages are the only medium of advertising, because it's where customers find out about them and it's affordable.

Yellow Pages advertising is described as **directional advertising** because it tells people where to go to get the product or service they want. The key difference between directional advertising and brand-image advertising is this: Directory advertising reaches prospects, people who already know they have a need for the product or service. If you are going to move across town and you want to rent a truck, you will consult the Yellow Pages. Directory advertising is the main medium that prospects consult once they have decided to buy something they need or want. This is illustrated in the "A Matter of Practice" box.

Because AT&T never copyrighted the name "Yellow Pages," any publisher can use it. In many cities, there are competing directories giving advertisers a choice and an opportunity to target their messages. (In fact, there are so many competing directories in some areas that publishers of Yellow Pages advertise their directories to build customer loyalty.) Directory advertisements are designed differently from other ads. The Yellow Pages, as we've said, are consulted by consumers who are interested in buying something. They know what they want; they just don't know where to go to find it. Almost 90 percent of those who consult the Yellow Pages follow up with some kind of action. Because a Yellow Pages ad is the last step in the search for a product or service by a committed consumer, the ads are not intrusive. Consequently, Yellow Pages users spend more per year than most advertisers' average customers do.[25]

Creating ads for the Yellow Pages follows guidelines similar to those for advertising in any medium. You start with the identification of the target audience(s), along with a description of their needs and wants. This is followed by a delineation of the goals of the ad. The creative process, including the message, the benefits, and the tone of the ad, must be developed next. Most Yellow Pages ads are quite factual, showing name of business, service offered, address, telephone/fax numbers, and hours of operation. However, if it's possible to tie into an existing tagline or an image from a broadcast or print ad, that would be appropriate. Since the Yellow Pages are filled with ads, the level of clutter is quite high. Finding that breakthrough concept is really the key. Finally, driven by the budget and competition, decisions about ad size, use of color, and listings in several sections of the directory must all be made.

The Yellow Pages industry has made many changes to become a more viable media alternative. For example, audiotext combined with Yellow Pages is now available in approximately 175 cities in the United States and Canada. After referring to the appropriate section of the Yellow Pages directory, the consumer dials an access number and a code for the individual advertiser and listens to a message about business hours, special services, special promotions, or other helpful information.[26]

The Talking Yellow Pages also offers news, sports, weather, and financial information. Yellow Pages publishers have also begun offering a variety of merchandising services. Many carry coupon pages and samples. Telephone subscribers in Orange County, California, received with their Yellow Pages a 16-page set of discount coupons for Pizza Hut pizza, Reese's Pieces, Peter Pan peanut butter, and other food and nonfood items.

Strengths of Directories

Like all the mediums we have discussed so far, directories offer certain advantages to advertisers. Most prominent is the fact that directories are a shopping medium, meaning that consumers initiate the search process when they have a need or want. If done correctly, therefore, a directory ad can be a very effective selling tool. Directories are inexpensive and provide a Return-on-Investment of 1:15; every dollar spent on a directory ad produces $15 in revenue. Directories also offer a great deal of flexibility in respect to size, colors, and formats. Finally, directories have a long life.

A MATTER OF PRACTICE

THE VALUE OF THE YELLOW PAGES

➤ For many advertisers, the Yellow Pages represents the most effective medium in achieving their objectives. In fact, consumers refer to Yellow Page ads more than any other ad when they have a personal need or want. It is the number-one shopping medium.

Simmons' National Consumer Survey collects data on events in people's lives and how often they consult the Yellow Pages. The table below shows the increase in Yellow Pages usage for those who have experienced major events in the year (2000) or who anticipate an event in the year 2001, compared with those who experienced or anticipated no major events.

The table shows that major life events lead people to consult the Yellow Pages, on average, 56 percent more often than those who do not experience or anticipate such events. Further investigation of the Simmons data indicates that about 80 percent of Yellow Pages personal use is by people who have either experienced major life events in the past year or expect to experience such events in the next 12 months.

This information is useful to advertisers in several ways. Most notably, if you are an advertiser who sells products directly related to these life events, placing your ad in the Yellow Pages is clearly advantageous. This is why doctors and lawyers advertise extensively in the Yellow Pages.

If an advertiser can find consumer groups that tend to experience several of these life events, it can also tap into other information known about this group. Baby boomers, a consumer group discussed in Chapter 4, represent an example: Baby boomers are just beginning to enter the "later stages" of the family cycle with children moving out, graduating from school, and getting married. Many baby boomers also see retirement looming. These events are associated with higher-than-normal use of the Yellow Pages (about 35% higher) and suggest opportunities for Yellow Pages advertisers as baby boomers enter their fifties and sixties.

Drivers of Yellow Pages Personal Usage

Event Experienced/ Anticipated	% of Pop.	YP Usage Increase[*]
Youngest daughter getting married	2.2%	78%
Making last home mortgage payment	3.1%	73%
Getting married	6.1%	71%
Youngest child graduating college	2.2%	69%
Oldest child entering school	3.2%	66%
Youngest child getting married	2.0%	62%
Losing job—laid off/out of business	4.8%	61%
Buying first home	7.6%	61%
Getting separated/divorced	2.8%	59%
Child will be born	3.7%	58%
Collect from pension/savings/ stock plan	6.7%	51%
Youngest child leaving home	3.2%	47%
Retiring/early retirement	8.1%	46%
Job change—lower level/pay	3.1%	59%
Job change—something different	11.1%	45%
Job change—same level/pay	5.7%	44%
Job change—better job	19.1%	41%

[*]Usage increase compared with those that experienced no events and did not anticipate any events in the next 12 months.

Source: Simmons National Consumer Survey.

POINT TO PONDER

What other segments would be heavy Yellow Pages users?

Source: CACTUS/MARKETING COMMUNICATION, August 27, 2001. Study conducted for Yellow Pages Professional Association and permission provided by YPPA.

Weaknesses of Directories

The primary weakness of directories is extreme clutter. Literally hundreds of look-alike ads are listed on a single page, often forcing advertisers to purchase larger ads they cannot afford. Ads cannot be changed for several months, meaning that if a business changes location or phone number, its ad may be wasted. Finally, there are consumers, such as non-English speakers or the illiterate, who cannot easily use directories.

PRINT MEDIA STRATEGY

Now that we have explored the main types of print media and their strengths and weaknesses, we can determine how to use these media effectively. Understanding the strengths

TABLE 9.3   **When to Use Print**

Use Newspapers If	Use Magazines If	Use Out-of-Home If	Use Directories If
You are a local business	You have a well-defined target audience	You are a local business that wants to sell	You are a local business or can serve local customers
You want extensive market coverage	You want to reinforce or remind the audience	You are a regional or national business that wants to remind or reinforce	You want to create action
You sell a product that is consumed in a predictable manner	You have a product that does not have to be demonstrated, but must be shown accurately and beautifully	You have a product requiring little information and little demonstration	You want to allow comparisons or provide basic inquiry and purchase information
You do not need to demonstrate the product	You need to relate moderate to extensive product information	You have a small to moderate budget	You have a small to moderate budget
You have a moderate to large budget	You have a moderate to large budget		

and weaknesses of the media options is the first step. Advertisers should always ask their media planner the cost of each medium, its ability to meet their advertising objectives, its ability to accommodate the style of message, and how targeted the audience is. Table 9.3 provides guidelines for print media decision makers.

In addition to the strengths and weaknesses, advertisers must concentrate on three overriding issues to develop a sound media strategy: integration, culture, and technology.

Aim for an **integrated media strategy**. Integration means that advertisers understand which media fit particular advertising needs, which media are complementary, and which detract from each other. An example is the Sears "Umpteen Appliances" campaign. The plan called for the initial use of mass-reach weekly magazines such as *People* and *Time* to launch the campaign. In the third month, monthly print publications such as *Better Homes & Gardens* and *Country Living* were added to the schedule. In the fourth month, television kicked in. Continuity through the print advertising and reinforcement with broadcast reached a broad adult audience of homeowners and helped Sears make target consumers aware of the 1-800-4-REPAIR number. Advertisers also need to think about how media interact with the other elements of the marketing and communication strategy.

Plan a print media strategy that matches the **culture** of the market segments. Advertisers, print media buyers, and media planners must create print ads that match the values of the culture in which they appear and adhere to the laws and mores of a particular medium. In Denmark, for instance, headlines that contain superlatives are frowned upon and print ads cannot carry coupons, because the public is offended by both techniques.

Carefully consider the effects of emerging technology. Technology has injected uncertainty into the future of print media. Will traditional hard-copy versions of print media still exist in 10 years? Or will *Time*, the *New York Times*, and the local directory all be online? Moving too soon into the **interactive technology** options may alienate current readers and add to media costs. Moving too late may mean that ads aren't reaching the selected target audience as effectively as competitors' ads. In either case, interactive technology may create a form of print media that is similar to broadcast, and its advantages and disadvantages may change dramatically.

THE INSIDE STORY

Jane Dennison-Bauer

In the years I've been in the Yellow Pages industry I've been responsible for many interesting projects. One of the projects I am most proud of is the effectiveness of color in Yellow Pages advertising.

Now it may seem funny to study color in advertising, but if you think about the Yellow Pages most people think of black-and-white informational ads, not slick, colorful ads like you see in magazines. So several years ago I was asked to help reposition color ads in the market place.

I decided to let the users of Yellow Pages give me information about how color ads, in general, are perceived and what the perception is of color ads in the Yellow Pages. I also wanted to find out how color ads were positioned to advertisers by the sales force. A major market research project to understand the present positioning and market dynamics was commissioned.

I found that color ads in Yellow Pages were positioned by the sales organizations as a way to "capture attention," and color ads "popped" off the page. The sales organizations, unfortunately, believed that the more color ads there are on a page the less effective the ads become. So as the amount of color ads increased the sales organizations would sell less.

One-on-one interviews with users showed that indeed color captured attention. During the interviews the participants were asked to choose a company to do business with in headings with a mix of color and noncolor ads. The color ads were viewed first and the participants spent more time looking at the color ads.

When questioned about what the participants' perceptions of advertisers that use color were, they indicated businesses with color ads have been in business longer, are more trustworthy, and provide quality service. These findings were confirmed in a unique quantitative study (*Quirk's Market Research Review*, May 1999).

What I found to be the most enlightening is that the effectiveness of color ads does not diminish as their number increases. Of course, this makes sense; look at all the beautiful color ads in magazines . . . the effectiveness of magazine ads doesn't decrease because they are all in color.

Now I had the positioning. For the advertisers, color gives them a way to communicate key messages more effectively, such as trustworthiness, quality service, and they have been in business longer. I equipped the sales organization with the key messages and the fact that increased color penetration does not equate to less effective ads.

What are the results? The repositioning has produced increased penetration and revenue for color. In addition, we are now targeting advertisers that use creative ads in other media to encourage them to keep the same look and message in the Yellow Pages. There is no better way to continue the advertising message developed for magazines, outdoor media, television, and newspapers than to include the same ad and message in the Yellow Pages!

Jane Dennison-Bauer graduated in 1979 from Virginia Tech with a Bachelor of Science degree, and in 1983 received a Masters of Business Administration in Marketing from the University of Denver. She worked for Qwest (formerly US West) for 15 years in various positions, including Director of Strategy, Director of Market Research, and General Manager of the audio services division. For the past three years, Ms. Dennison-Bauer has been Vice-President of Marketing and Business Development for the Yellow Pages Publishers Association. She is now a partner in CRM associates, a marketing consulting firm based in Boulder, Colorado.

IT'S A WRAP

SEMPER FI

As we have examined print media as a message delivery mechanism, it should be clear that the various print alternatives each have their advantages and disadvantages. For the U.S. Marine Corps, changing its position in the minds of potential officers was a tremendous challenge. Rejecting the traditional broadcast medium, with its ability to show action, was risky. Yet this print strategy proved to be a huge success. The number of leads generated by the campaign exceeded the goal by 285 percent. The direct-mail campaign exceeded goals by 33 percent, and the overall response rate was an incredible 8 percent, with 2 percent being the industry norm. Finally, applications by minorities exceeded goals by 9 percent.

The USMC's decision to pursue a print strategy over a broadcast strategy proved a great success—overall response rate was 8 percent, with 2 percent being the industry norm.

Summary

1. **Describe the newspaper medium and identify its strengths and weaknesses.** Newspapers, still the leading local medium, face tough competition from broadcast and direct-mail media and are diminishing in number. The structure of newspapers is determined by frequency of publication, size, and circulation. Newspapers reach all income brackets, educational levels, age groups, and ethnic backgrounds. Readership varies by gender, age, and interests. Newspapers measure their audience through two independent agencies: the Audit Bureau of Circulations (ABC) and Simmons-Scarborough. The three general types of news-

paper advertising are classified, display, and supplement. The greatest advantage in newspapers is extensive market coverage. The biggest disadvantages are a short life span, clutter, and poor reproduction.

2. **Identify the key factors that advertisers should know to make effective decisions about the magazine medium.** Magazines have the greatest ability to reach preselected or tightly targeted audiences. This selectivity is exhibited through the elaborate structure found in the industry. The disadvantages of this medium include limited flexibility, high costs, and difficult distribution. Magazines are categorized

by audience, geography, demographics, and editorial content. Almost all adults read at least one magazine per month. The magazine industry measures its audience through such companies as the ABC, Simmons Marketing Research Bureau (SMRB), and MediaMark.

3. **Explain what out-of-home media are and discuss factors that advertisers should consider for making out-of-home media decisions.** Out-of-home advertising delivers messages to moving audiences using quick-impact techniques such as strong graphics and short, catchy phrases. Out-of-home advertising is any form of advertising that consumers encounter outside their homes. This type of medium includes billboards, transit advertising, and kiosks. Posters, the oldest form of advertising, focus on a visual message. Billboards, including painted buildings, are the largest advertising medium. National billboards are distributed as preprinted posters; local billboards are original, hand-painted art. Interior transit messages are placed on **car cards**; exterior transit messages are seen at a glance. Out-of-home advertising has visual impact and the ability to reach local audiences.

4. **Describe directories and analyze the factors that advertisers use to make decisions about this medium.** Directories, such as the Yellow Pages, are the most universal advertising medium. Yellow Pages ads focus on the service offered or the store personality. Its strengths are its flexibility, ability to sell, low cost, and long life. Its weaknesses are perceptions of clutter, lack of message permanence, lack of creative message options, and limited accessibility.

5. **Discuss the factors that contribute to an effective print media strategy.** Advertisers and media planners and buyers should be able to assess the relative strengths and weaknesses of different types of print media to make effective print media choices. They should consider cost, advertising goals, how targeted the audience is, the amount of information the message requires, and the advertising goals (to sell, to remind, to build awareness). They should also develop an integrated media strategy, one that fits the culture of the market segment, and one that considers the effects of emerging technology.

Key Terms

broadsheet, p. 240
car cards, p. 264
circulation, p. 241
classified advertising, p. 243
co-op advertising, p. 244
culture, p. 261
cutouts, p. 255
directional advertising, p. 259

display advertising, p. 243
extensions, p. 255
exterior transit advertising, p. 257
free-standing insert advertisement, p. 244
horizontal publication, p. 248
integrated media strategy, p. 261

interactive technology, p. 261
interior transit advertising, p. 257
kiosks, p. 257
market selectivity, p. 239
nontraditional delivery, p. 249
one-order, one-bill, p. 244
out-of-home advertising, p. 254
painted bulletin, p. 255

poster (panels), p. 255
supplements, p. 244
tabloid, p. 240
traditional delivery, p. 249
vertical publication, p. 248

Questions

1. Discuss the various characteristics of newspaper readers. What are the implications for an advertiser considering newspapers?

2. You are the head media planner for a small chain of upscale furniture outlets in a top-50 market that concentrates most of its advertising in the Sunday supplement of the local newspaper. The client also schedules display ads in the daily editions for special sales. Six months ago a new, high-style metropolitan magazine approached you about advertising for your client. You deferred a decision by saying you'd see what reader acceptance would be. Now the magazine has shown some steady increases (its circulation is now about one-quarter of the newspapers'). If you were to include the magazine on the ad schedule, you'd have to reduce the newspaper media somewhat. What would be your recommendation to the furniture store?

3. Many magazines have editorial environments that are well suited to certain products and services (home services, entertainment, sports, recreation, and financial magazines).

Compatibility between the advertising and the reader's editorial interest is a plus. However, editorial compatibility will attract your competitors' ads, too. Would the prospect of having a number of competitors' ads in an issue where your ad appeared cause you to consider less compatible publications? Explain your reasons.

4. Discuss the advantages and disadvantages of advertising in newspapers and magazines, from the viewpoint of the advertising director for GE small appliances.

5. Petra Wilcox, a display ad salesperson for the *Daily Globe*, thought she had heard all the possible excuses for not buying newspaper space until she called on the manager of a compact-disc store that sold new and used discs. "I heard about newspaper reader studies that prove how wrong the audience is for me. Readership is too adult—mostly above 35 years of age," he said. "And besides, readers of newspapers are families with higher incomes—the wrong market for our used disc business," he continued. If the *Globe* is a typical metropolitan daily, could the store manager be cor-

rect? In any event, how should Wilcox try to counter the manager's views?

6. A terrific debate is going on in Professor Morrison's retail advertising class. The question is, "Why do national advertisers refuse to seriously consider newspapers in media plans?" The advertising manager for a home-products company argues that despite newspapers' creative limitations, more firms would buy newspaper space if the medium did not practice rate discrimination against national companies. The sales manager for a small chain of newspapers admits the price difference, but says it is justified by the extra attention and the commissions (sales rep and agency) newspapers have to pay for each national order. The sales manager also claims the price issue is a "smokescreen" for advertisers to hide their continuing "love affair" with television. Which position would you accept? Is price difference an issue large enough to restrict marketers' interest? How does cooperative advertising figure into the debate?

7. Out-of-home advertising is described as having quick impact. What does that mean? How would it affect your decision to use this medium if you were trying to advertise a home health product designed for checking the blood sugar levels of people with diabetes?

8. You are constantly exposed to poster advertising all over your campus. If you had authority over all poster advertising, what would you do to improve the effectiveness of poster advertising on campus?

9. Since his freshman year in college, Phil Dawson, an advertising major, has waited tables at Alfredo's, a small family-operated restaurant featuring excellent food and an intimate atmosphere. A Yellow Pages representative approaches the owner to run a display ad. The owner asks Phil for advice on whether such an ad would help, and if so, what the ad should look like. What should Phil recommend?

10. You're the owner of a medium-sized appliance repair service firm in Chicago. You can repair all types of appliances, offer 24-hour service, and have highly trained professionals on your staff. The Sears "Umpteen Appliances" ad campaign is cutting into your business. You decide it's time to advertise. What print options should you consider and why? (Assume your budget isn't as large as Sears', but it's larger than those of most local repair shops.)

Suggested Class Project

Contact a medium to large newspaper, magazine, and outdoor or directory advertising business. Think of yourself as a potential advertiser. What do you need to know? Collect all the relevant information on services provided to advertisers. Ask as many questions as you need to. Compare the types of information and services available. Was the customer service helpful? Is this the right media choice for your company? Analyze the results in a brief report; begin by stating your product and your advertising goals, then state what you might or might not accomplish by advertising in the publication. Make a decision.

Suggested Internet Class Project

Collect Web site versions of three online newspapers or magazines. Write a 1-2 page report on how these vehicles could be better advertising mechanisms.

Hallmark BUILD•A•CAMPAIGN Projects

Please review the Hallmark Case Appendix at the end of the text before responding to these questions.

1. Meet in small groups to discuss why you believe Capitol Advertising elected not to use newspapers as a medium to help build brand insistence.

2. What print media should your local Gold Crown store rely on as its principal print medium? Why? Revisit the media plan you developed in Chapter 8 and provide specific details about your plan for your local Gold Crown store.

HANDS-ON
Case 9

DODGE GOES NASCAR

There was a time when Dodge cars were the big winners in NASCAR events. But the 1970s and 1980s were not kind to Chrysler Motors and its Dodge division, and in 1981 a decision was made not to participate in NASCAR. Then in October 2000, Chrysler top management decided that there were good reasons to reenter the fray of racing. Most notably, the popularity of NASCAR and the Winston Cup circuit had skyrocketed during the 1990s. Also, Chrysler engineers had designed a turbo-charged vehicle that could compete with the current racing teams.

With only 250 days until the 2000 Daytona 500, the creative team at Chrysler's media agency, PentaCom, had the task of producing a campaign that would not only announce the reentry of Dodge cars into the circuit, but also position Dodge properly.

Initial research conducted by PentaCom showed that two consumer groups were particularly excited about Dodge's return to NASCAR racing: NASCAR enthusiasts and current Dodge owners.

The team of 25 started with a "teaser" campaign asking readers to guess the name of the driver of the first Dodge factory team. Over 60,000 people responded to the message delivered through magazine ads, newsletters, and the NASCAR and ESPN Web sites (Bill Elliott was the correct answer).

The next phase of the campaign used a very unusual ploy. If you've ever attended a Winston Cup race or viewed one on television, you know that the race cars and the track are covered with ads. Dodge decided that an integrated sponsorship would be more effective than covering the car with ads. They signed on over 50 co-sponsors to leverage their marketing message. General Mills agreed to put a die-cast car from the Dodge race team in a window on the front of 14 million cereal boxes. Bill Elliott was also on the front of 3.5 million Wheaties boxes. In turn, these cereals added a new level of excitement to their products.

The final phase of the campaign occurred just a few days before the race. In addition to print ads appearing in magazines such as *Sports Illustrated* and *Field & Stream*, and newspapers such as *USA Today*, PentaCom also created an eight-page insert featuring the new Dodge team and placed it in several car-buff magazines. Finally, a 64-page custom-published booklet was attached (polybagged) to the March issue of *Automobile*. By all standards, the campaign was a total success, creating a 78 percent level of awareness and an increase in positive attitude scores of nearly 30 percent. ■

IT'S YOUR TURN

1. What other print media alternatives could Dodge have used?

Sources: Jeff Green, "Dodge May Return to Winston Cup," *Brandweek* (August 25, 1999): 4; Eric Schmukler, "Best Campaign Spending Between $10 Million–$25 Million: PentaCom," *Brandweek* (June 18, 2001): SR6–SR8.

Notes

1. Christine Larson, "Ethnic Issues," *Adweek* (May 6, 1991): N3.

2. Kim Long, *The American Forecaster Almanac*, 1993 Business Edition.

3. Rebecca Pirto Heath, "In So Many Words," *American Demographics* (March 1997): 39–45.

4. Charles Pappas and Nancy C. Webster, "Classified Slide," *Advertising Age* (May 8, 2000): S8.

5. Beth Snyder, "Specter of Online Classifieds Spurs Papers to Experiment," *Advertising Age* (April 20, 1998): 516, 518.

6. Alice Z. Cuneo, "Drumming Up Demand for One Order/One Bill," *Advertising Age* (April 24, 1995): S4.

7. Laurie Freeman, "A Tweak Here, Twist There for 1-Order-1 Bill Systems," *Advertising Age* (April 20, 1998): 510, 518.

8. Warren Berger, "What Have You Done for Me Lately?" *Adweek* (April 23, 1990): 13.

9. Jane Hodges, "Newspapers Plug Along in Quest for Web Answers," *Advertising Age* (April 29, 1996): S6; Dana Blankenhorn, "Online Newspapers Create Niche Content Sites," *Advertising Age* (July 27, 1998): S4.

10. Lori Lefeure, "Waiting for the Web," *Brandweek* (October 22, 2001): SR22.

11. Christy Fisher, "Newspapers of the Future Look to Go High-Tech as Experiments Abound," *Advertising Age* (October 5, 1992): S3; "Back Page," *Adweek* (April 20, 1998): 26.

12. John McDonough, "In Step with History," *Advertising Age* (May 24, 1989): 23.

13. Laura Loro, "Heavy Hitters Gamble on Launches," *Advertising Age* (October 19, 1992): S13.

14. Jon Berry, "Trade Magazines," *Adweek Supplement* (September 1, 1989): 196.

15. MediaMark Research, Inc., *Doublebase 1988 Study*, 19.

16. "Study of Media Involvement," *Audits & Surveys* (March 1988).

17. DDB Needham, *Media Trends* (1987): 55.

18. Anne Marie Kerwin, "Magazines Blast Study Showing Reader Falloff," *Advertising Age* (March 8, 1999): 13, 55.

19. Elizabeth H. Weise, "On-Line Magazines: Will Readers Still Want Them after the Novelty Wears Off," *The Marketing News* (January 29, 1996): 1, 14.

20. Cara Beardi, "From Elevators to Gas Stations, Ads Multiplying," *Advertising Age* (November 13, 2000): 40, 42.

21. Amanda Beeler, "Outdoor Ad Group Adopts Global Stance," *Advertising Age* (May 29, 2000): 36.

22. Bruce Horovitz, "Ahh, the Surf, the Surf … and Tons of Ads," *USA Today* (May 24, 2001): 33

23. Rebecca Gardyn, "Moving Targets," *American Demographics* (October 2000): 32–34.

24. Rachel Emma Silverman, "Despite Net's Growth, Print Yellow Pages are Profitable," *The Wall Street Journal* (May 22, 2000): B16.

25. Eugenia C. Daniels, "Critical Shift in Direction," *Advertising Age* (February 14, 2000): S12.

26. Karen V. Fernandez and Dennis L. Rosen, "The Effectiveness of Information and Color in Yellow Pages Advertising," *Journal of Advertising* (29, Summer, 2000): 59–73.

CHAPTER 10

Broadcast and Interactive Online Media

CHAPTER OBJECTIVES

When you have completed this chapter, you should be able to

1. Discuss the structure of television, how it is organized, its use as an advertising medium, the TV audience, and the advantages and disadvantages of TV advertising.

2. Discuss the structure of radio, how it is organized, its use as an advertising medium, its audience, and the advantages and disadvantages of radio advertising.

3. Discuss interactive media, how it is structured and organized, its use as an advertising medium, its audience, and the advantages and disadvantages of interactive advertising.

A Drugstore Goes Online

Award: *2000 EFFIE Bronze, Health Care category*

Company: *drugstore.com*

Agency: *Fallon McElligott*

Campaign: *"A Very Healthy Way to Shop"™*

Although drugstore.com™ was the first Internet drugstore, introduced in 1999, it has since faced ferocious competition from a variety of dot-coms looking to hit it big offering drugs via the Internet. With most of them stocking many of the same products, it became clear that drugstore retailing was becoming a high-cost, inventory management nightmare, and that drugstore.com would have to become an expert in customer service and same-day delivery if it was going to survive.

Based on initial research, drugstore.com, targeted head-of-household women, known as gatekeepers because they make most purchase decisions for the entire family. Also, unlike men, women actually enjoy shopping for drugstore products, but they hate the long lines and the medical environment. So drugstore.com positioned itself as a comfortable way for women to buy pharmaceuticals online. This positioning approach was based on research that indicated that women prefer not to make multiple trips to the drugstore. A second round of research showed that this need to limit shopping trips was very much tied to their greater concern for saving time.

On the basis of the two rounds of research, Fallon McElligott, the agency of record, designed a campaign around the tagline "A very healthy way to shop."™ The agency positioned drugstore.com as a premier online shopping alternative, less taxing and more convenient than driving to a drugstore.

The campaign broke in eight top Internet markets including New York, Chicago, and San Francisco in conjunction with the Academy Awards telecast in March 2000. The first 30-second spot featured a woman who runs her entire life while relaxing in her bathtub. Ads that followed during the next four months showed a series of vignettes highlighting how a woman can solve her problems as well as those of others by using drugstore.com.

These spots also had a secondary purpose. Customers and potential customers were not quite sure what drugstore.com did and how it worked. Drugstore.com management thought that the slice-of-life vignettes would indirectly provide this information as well as support the positioning strategy. The ads showed what products drugstore.com carried. How the company delivered them and the reliability of product quality were demonstrated in a variety of creative ways.

How did drugstore.com's new campaign do? Check the "It's a Wrap" section at the end of this chapter.

BROADCAST MEDIA

Broadcast media, which transmit sounds or images electronically, include radio, television, and interactive (i.e., internet-based) media. Broadcast media messages differ from print advertising messages in large part because broadcast engages more than the sense of sight with its combination of movement, imagery, and sound. Also, print is a medium bound by space; broadcast media are transient and bound by time. Broadcast media messages may affect the viewer's emotions for a few seconds and then disappear. Interactive media, the newest member of the broadcast category, bridge print and broadcast because newspapers, magazines, and other print mechanisms can be delivered online. Interactive media deliver messages to audiences electronically, so they more closely fit the broadcast description.

In this chapter, we investigate television, radio, and interactive media. We explore the uses, structure, audiences, and the advantages and disadvantages of each medium. This information allows advertisers to evaluate media plans and assess which media options support their advertising goals most effectively.

THE STRUCTURE OF THE TELEVISION INDUSTRY

Advances in technology have expanded the number of television options advertisers can use to deliver their messages to audiences. In this section we examine these key types of television systems: wired and unwired network, public, cable and subscription, local, specialty, syndicated, and interactive. Figure 10.1 shows these options.

Networks

A **network** exists whenever two or more stations are able to broadcast the same program that originates from a single source. Networks can be over-the-air or cable. The FCC (Federal Communications Commission) defines a network as a program service with 15 or more hours per day of prime-time (8–11 P.M.) programming.

Currently, there are four national, over-the-air television networks in the United States: the American Broadcasting Company (ABC), the Columbia Broadcasting System (CBS), the National Broadcasting Company (NBC), and Fox Broadcasting. WB and UPN are cable-delivered networks. ABC, CBS, and NBC own 15 regional stations. The remaining 600 regional stations are privately owned **affiliates** (each network has about 150 affiliates).

An affiliate station signs a contract with the national network (ABC, CBS, NBC, or Fox) agreeing to carry network-originated programming during a certain part of its sched-

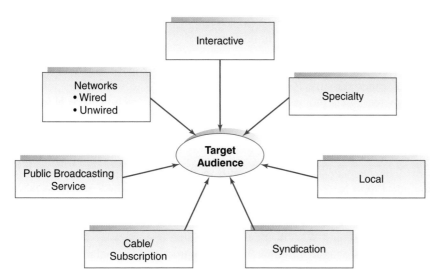

FIGURE 10.1
THE STRUCTURE OF THE TV INDUSTRY
Advances in technology have expanded the number of television options advertisers can use to deliver their messages to audiences.

ule. For example, WDIV-TV is NBC's Detroit affiliate. The major networks originate their own programs and are compensated at a rate of 30 percent of the fee charged for programs in a local market. That is, 30 percent of the advertising revenue generated by affiliates through their charges to regional/local advertisers goes to major networks.

In turn, affiliates receive a percentage of the advertising revenue (12 to 25 percent) paid to the national network and can sell some advertising time during network programs and between programs. This advertising is the primary source of affiliate revenues.

In over-the-air network scheduling the advertiser contracts with a national or a regional network to show commercials on a number of affiliated stations. Sometimes an advertiser purchases only a portion of the network coverage, known as a *regional leg*. This type of purchase is common with sports programming, where different games are shown in different parts of the country.

Public Television

Although many people still consider public television to be commercial-free, in 1984 the FCC liberalized its rules and allowed the 341 (349 in 2002) PBS stations some leeway in airing certain messages. The FCC says messages should not make a call to action (ask for sale) or make price or quality comparisons. Public television had requested the right to advertise to compensate for a 30 percent cutback in federal funding and to compete more effectively with cable television.

PBS is an attractive medium for advertisers because it reaches affluent, educated households, minority market segments, and lower-income consumers. It also attracts households with children. In addition, PBS still has a refined image, and PBS advertisers are viewed as good corporate citizens.

Current FCC guidelines allow ads to appear on public television only during the local 2.5 minute program breaks. Each station maintains its own acceptability guidelines. Some PBS stations accept the same ads that appear on paid programming. However, most PBS spots are created specifically for public stations.

Some PBS stations will not accept any commercial corporate advertising, but do accept noncommercial ads that are "value neutral"—in other words, ads that make no attempt to sell a product or service.

Cable and Subscription Television

The initial purpose of **cable television** was to improve reception in certain areas of the country, particularly mountainous regions and large cities. However, cable systems have grown rapidly because they provide programming options. Currently, two out of three homes subscribe to cable through traditional coaxial cable delivery systems (a line from the post to your home). Cable has 43 percent of total viewing time, compared to 28 percent for network, 15 percent for affiliates, and 14 percent for local programming viewing times.

Some cable stations develop and air their own programs in addition to programs initiated by other stations. Pay programming, available to subscribers for an additional monthly fee, offers movies, specials, and sports under such plans as Home Box Office, Showtime, and The Movie Channel. Pay networks do not currently sell advertising time.

Who Provides Cable Programs? About 8 percent of cable programming comes from independent cable networks and from independent superstations. These networks include Cable News Network (CNN), the Disney Channel, the Entertainment and Sports Programming Network (ESPN), and a group of independent superstations whose programs are carried by satellite to cable operators (for example, WTBS-Atlanta, WGN-Chicago, and WWOR-New York). Cable operators are creating more original programs; for instance, Lifetime for Women produces original movies and series, such as *Any Day Now*, and USA Network has several original series, including *La Femme Nikita* and *The Pretender*.

Cable Scheduling The two categories of cable scheduling are network and local. **Network cable** scheduling runs commercials across the entire subscriber group simultaneously. With **local cable** scheduling, advertisers can show their commercials to highly restricted geographic audiences through **interconnects**, a special cable technology that allows local or regional advertisers to run their commercials in small geographic areas through the interconnection of a number of cable systems. Interconnections offer small advertisers an affordable way to reach certain local audiences through television.

Local Television

Local television stations are affiliated with a network and carry both network programming and their own programs. Costs for local advertising vary, depending on the size of the market and the demand for the programs carried. For example, KHIO in Houston charges local advertisers $1,950 for a 30-second spot during prime time of a network program. This same time slot may cost $15 in a small town.

The local television market is substantially more varied than the national market. Most advertisers for the local market are local retailers, primarily department stores or discount stores, financial institutions, automobile dealers, restaurants, and supermarkets. Advertisers buy time on a station-by-station basis. Although this arrangement makes sense for a local retailer, it is not an efficient strategy for a national or regional advertiser, who would have to deal individually with a large number of stations.

Specialty Television

Several alternative program delivery systems try to reach certain audiences with a television message more effectively or efficiently than network, cable, or local television. For example, the FCC licensed low-power television (LPTV) to provide programming outlets to minorities and communities that are underserved by full-power stations. LPTV stations have signals that cover a radius of 15 miles. (Full-power stations reach viewers in a 70-mile radius.) Homes pull in LPTV signals through special antennas and LPTV carries advertising for local retailers and businesses.

Multipoint distribution systems (MDS) and subscription television (STV) both deliver limited programming without the cost of cable installation. Hotels and restaurants use MDS to provide guests with movies and other entertainment. STV offers one-channel capabilities of pay cable programming transmitted to individual homes through a **signal** decoder. Although specialty systems can carry ads, they are a minor delivery system. Viewers on average get very few of their ads on the former.

Television Syndication

Although originally intended to fill the void between network shows, the growth of independent TV and cable stations has fueled the **syndication** boom. Syndicated shows are television programs purchased by local stations to fill time in open hours. Today both networks and independents have been forced to bid on these shows, called strips (like a comic strip, a syndicated strip is a show that appears Monday through Friday at the same time) to fill the day's many open hours. Syndicated programming is off-network or first-run. Off-network syndication includes reruns of network shows, like *M*A*S*H, The Bob Newhart Show, Star Trek, ER,* and *Seinfeld.* The FCC imposes several restrictions for a show to be labeled off-network. Most important, a network show must have run 88 episodes before it can be syndicated. Why 88? It's an arbitrary number.

    Seinfeld went into syndication in 1998. Each episode was sold for $6 million, meaning that the 160 episodes will generate nearly $1 billion, $50 million of which goes directly to Jerry Seinfeld as producer. *Everybody Loves Raymond* went into syndication during the summer of 2001, and has been a huge success.[1]

    Sometimes network shows that did not meet the minimal number of episodes, such as *Too Close For Comfort, It's A Living,* and *Rescue 911,* are purchased by syndication distributors, such as Starcom Worldwide or Viacom, from the networks and moved into syndication even as the shows' owners continue to produce new episodes. This process is called *first-run syndication.* Such shows are now produced by the shows' owners strictly for syndication. Syndicates also produce their own original shows; examples include *Baywatch* and *Highlander.*

Interactive Television

After several false starts, interactive television has finally come of age. An interactive TV set is basically a television with computer capabilities. With some systems it is possible to

"Everybody Loves Raymond" went into off-network syndication in the summer of 2001. That means local TV stations can purchase the program.

do everything you can do online, except that the monitor is either the TV screen or a picture-in-picture configuration that lets you watch one or more television programs while surfing the Internet.

There are three types of *interactivity*. The first type is video-on-demand (VOD), where viewers control what and when they watch. Pay-per-view (PPV) is a limited version of VOD that allows viewers to choose programs at predetermined two-hour intervals.

The second type of interactivity is a system that stores information at the television set and allows viewers to choose programs with a set-top box in the home, in much the same way VCRs function.

The third type of interactivity is the *simulcast*, which transmits digital information in conjunction with an actual broadcast. Simulcast viewers can take part in programming. By punching in their choices on a keypad, viewers can second-guess NFL quarterbacks or order more information during a documentary.

Although interactive television development was initially slow, it appears to be taking off, thanks to **broadband**. Simply defined, broadband has more capacity to send data and images into a home or business through a cable television wire than the much smaller capacity of a traditional telephone wire or television antenna system.

Time Warner took the plunge into interactive television in 2000. It provided 5,000 homes in Oahu, Hawaii, with video-on-demand. By the fall of 2001, the Ocean Cable system had over 30,000 subscribers, who each paid $52/month. While the current system provides movies-on-demand, program blocking, and banner ads, there is the promise that features such as high-speed Web browsing, e-mail, and digital storage are on the horizon.[2]

The new medium's big advantage is that it is two-way. Audience measurement can be based on a census, not a sample. And programs that require viewers to log in can contain highly targeted messages, since the sender will know the recipient. A sponsor could theoretically "buy" a specific audience.

Changes in Broadcast Television

The structure of the television industry has undergone several changes over the past 20 years. First, cable is quite firmly entrenched worldwide and is still growing. Furthermore, evidence suggests that recent mergers and acquisitions will change cable from a fragmented to a consolidated sector of the TV industry.

Second, the telecommunication industry and the cable industry are battling over who will control digital TV technology. Digitization (the transfer of analog pictures, text, and video into a series of ones and zeros) will allow information to flow into households just as electricity does today. As a result, tomorrow's viewers will see only what they want to see. Switching channels will be a thing of the past because TVs will be programmed to send only programs preselected by the viewer.

The question then becomes which medium (telephone or cable) is better able to deliver this new technology. The better alternative appears to be coaxial cable, already used by cable television providers. Coaxial cable can carry much more data than the copper wire used in most telephone systems.

Legislation has encouraged this battle. In 1992 the FCC abolished a ruling restricting telephone companies from carrying other types of signals. In 1996 the Telecommunications Act passed, which essentially allowed all communication companies to engage in all aspects of business, meaning that someday there may be little distinction between telephone, cable, and networks.

Various factors have contributed to the decline in network TV's viewership, including the spread of the direct-broadcasting satellite business and the growth of the Fox Television Broadcasting Network and other upstarts. However, the cable industry has been most responsible for the decrease in network shares of TV audiences.

The implications of these changes for the advertising strategist are significant. Most notably, the advantage of traditional network television to deliver a message to a mass audience is quickly disappearing. Instead, television is becoming an increasingly fragmented medium, which means that reaching a domestic or international mass audience will require

DVR technology poses a challenge for advertisers since it enables consumers to bypass commercials.

hundreds of different station buys. However, if the advertiser has a well-defined target audience, television will be cost-effective. Some experts predict that this fragmentation may reduce the emphasis of image advertising and increase the use of informational ads.

Another new technology that is expected to have a profound effect on television is the digital video recorders (DVRs) produced by Replay TV and TiVo in 1999. DVRs allow users to select shows from the TV log, click the record button once to record the one show, click twice to record the whole series; and later on you look at which shows have been captured, and select one. Here's the rub for advertisers: the owner need not fast-forward through a commercial; the owner can program out commercials. Advertisers are alarmed over the technology, as are television executives. It calls into question audience measurement numbers—if 20 percent of the audience is recording West Wing on Wednesday night only to watch it Saturday morning commercial-free, then is the Wednesday night measurement accurate? It also raises the issue of how advertisers should respond. Should they seek legislation to block such technology? After all, ads are what keep television (relatively) free. Or should they seek new ways to send messages? Indeed, Coca-Cola has created ads that appear on screen when a DVR user pauses a program for a few minutes.

Perhaps advertisers have a little more time to prepare. Even though DVR technology was forecasted to reach 800,000 households by 2000, and 3.6 million by 2001, the actual number was less than 350,000. Still, the technology appears here to stay, with Forrester Research predicting as many as 50 million American households could have the technology by 2007.[3]

TELEVISION ADVERTISING

Like television programming, television ads can be aired through a number of different arrangements. Television advertisers can run their commercials through over-the-air network scheduling, local scheduling, or cable scheduling.

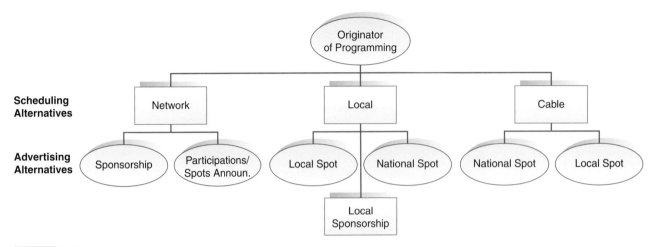

FIGURE 10.2   THE TELEVISION ADVERTISERS' MEDIA CHOICES

Television ads can be aired through a number of different arrangements. The forms they take depend on whether
a network, local, or cable schedule is used.

Forms of Television Advertising

The actual form of a television commercial depends on whether a network, local, or cable schedule is used, as we see in Figure 10.2. Networks allow *sponsorships, participations,* or *spot announcements* through their affiliates. In turn, local affiliates allow *local sponsorships, spot announcements,* and *national spots.* Cable systems allow *system* (national) *spots* and *local spots.* Finally, interactive television allows *(national) spots* and *local spots.*

Sponsorships In **sponsorships**, which characterized most early television advertising, the advertiser assumes the total financial responsibility for producing the program and providing the accompanying commercials. Examples of early sponsored programs are *Bonanza* (sponsored by Chevrolet), *The Hallmark Hall of Fame,* and *The Kraft Music Hour.*

Sponsorship has a powerful effect on the viewing public, especially because the advertiser can control the content and quality of the program as well as the placement and length of commercials. However, the costs of producing and sponsoring a 30- or 60-minute program make this option too expensive for most advertisers. Several advertisers can produce a program jointly as an alternative to single sponsorship. This plan is quite common with sporting events, where each sponsor receives a 15-minute segment.

A local advertiser can also offer a sponsorship or a shared sponsorship. For instance, a local bank might sponsor a high school football game and preempt national programming.

Participations Sponsorships represent less than 10 percent of network advertising. The rest is sold as **participations**, where advertisers pay for 10, 15, 20, 30, or 60 seconds of commercial time during one or more programs. The advertiser can buy any time that is available. This approach not only reduces the risks and costs associated with sponsorships but also provides a great deal more flexibility in market coverage, target audiences, scheduling, and budgeting. Participations do not create the same high impact as sponsorships, however, and the advertiser does not have any control over the content of the program. Finally, the "time avails" (available time slots) for the most popular programs are often bought up by the largest advertisers, leaving fewer good time slots for the small advertisers.

Spot Announcements The third form a television commercial can take is the **spot announcement**. (Note that the word "spot" is also used in conjunction with a timeframe, such as a 30-second spot, but don't confuse these spots with spot announcements.) Spot announcements appear in the breaks between programs, which local affiliates sell to adver-

TABLE 10.1	**Standard Television Dayparts**
Early morning	M-F 7:00 A.M. - 9:00 A.M.
Daytime	M-F 9:00 A.M. - 4:30 P.M.
Early fringe	M-F 4:30 P.M. - 7:30 P.M.
Prime access	M-F 7:30 P.M. - 8:00 P.M.
Prime time	M-S 8:00 P.M. - 11:00 P.M.
	Su 7:00 P.M. - 11:00 P.M.
Late news	M-Su 11:00 P.M. - 11:30 P.M.
Late night	M-Su 11:30 P.M. - 1:00 A.M.
Saturday morning	Sa 8:00 A.M. - 1:00 P.M.
Weekend afternoon	Sa-Su 1:00 P.M. - 7:00 P.M.

Note: All times are Eastern Standard Time (EST).

tisers who want to show their ads locally. Commercials of 10, 20, 30, and 60 seconds are sold on a station-by-station basis to local, regional, and national advertisers. However, local buyers dominate spot television.

The breaks between programs are not always the best time slots for advertisers because there is a great deal of clutter from competing commercials, station breaks, public service announcements, and other distractions. Program breaks also tend to be the time when viewers take a break from their television sets.

The price of a spot or set of spots is based on the rating of the program and the daypart during which the commercial is shown. Table 10.1 shows the Television Standard Dayparts. Figure 10.3 displays the cost of a 30-second spot for network programs for fall 2001. Can you guess which show took top dollar?

THE TELEVISION AUDIENCE

Television has become a mainstay of American society, with 98 percent of American households having one or more television sets. A great number of advertisers consider television their primary medium. Can television deliver a target audience to advertisers effectively? What do we really know about how audiences watch television? Is it a background distraction? Do we switch from channel to channel without watching any single show? Or do we carefully and intelligently select what we watch on television?

In 1961, Newton Minnow, then chairman of the FCC, wrote a book that called television a "vast wasteland." In a recent issue of *USA Today,* a story contrasted TV audiences of 1961 and 2001 (see Figure 10.4 on page 279), so it was natural to interview Mr. Minnow again. He notes that today's TV is "a toxic waste dump," and the only way the offerings will improve is if the government intervenes.[4]

Measuring the Television Audience

Many of us have had our favorite television show taken off the air because of "poor ratings." Although we may have had some idea of how these ratings were derived, the "Nielsen family" (i.e., individual households from which viewership data is collected) and the rating process remains a mystery to most people.

Actually, rating the number of people who view television programs is a simple process. Several independent rating firms periodically sample a portion of the television viewing audience, assess the size and characteristics of the audiences watching specific shows, and then make these data available, for a fee, to advertisers and ad agencies, who use them in their media planning. Currently, A. C. Nielsen dominates this industry and provides the most commonly used measure of national and local television audiences.

FIGURE 10.3

FALL 2001 NETWORK TV PRICE ESTIMATES

The cost of 30-second spots on the prime-time schedule.

Fall 2001 Network TV Price Estimates

Sun. 7 p.m. (ET) — 8 p.m. — 9 p.m. — 10 p.m.

ABC	Wonderful World of Disney $117,200		Alias $173,800	The Practice $263,800
CBS	60 Minutes $118,600	The Education of Max Bickford $148,400	CBS Sunday Night Movie $105,400	
NBC	Dateline NBC $65,200	The Weakest Link $118,200	Law & Order: Criminal Intent $167,600	UC: Undercover $104,400
FOX	Futurama $132,000 / King of the Hill $173,200	Simpsons $249,400 / Malcom/Middle $254,400	The X-Files $238,600	No Fox programming
WB	Lost in the USA $34,000	Steve Harvey $45,600 / Men, Women/Dogs $51,000	Nikki $41,800 / Off Centre $41,800	No WB programming

Mon. 8 p.m. — 9 p.m. — 10 p.m.

ABC	Who Wants to Be a Millionaire $115,600	Monday Night Football $330,200	
CBS	King of Queens $185,800 / Yes, Dear $165,800	Raymond $305,600 / Becker $191,200	Family Law $152,800
NBC	The Weakest Link $123,600	Third Watch $134,000	Crossing Jordan $115,000
FOX	Boston Public $233,200	Ally McBeal $289,800	No Fox programming
UPN	The Hughleys $33,700 / One on One $27,500	The Parkers $36,500 / Girlfriends $32,800	No UPN programming
WB	7th Heaven $92,400	Angel $68,400	No WB programming

Tue. 8 p.m. — 9 p.m. — 10 p.m.

ABC	Dharma & Greg $166,400 / What About Joan $201,000	Bob Patterson $177,600 / Spin City $199,600	Philly $146,400
CBS	JAG $132,600	The Guardian $98,200	Judging Amy $137,200
NBC	Emeril $93,400 / Three Sisters $92,800	Frasier $248,400 / Scrubs $213,000	Dateline NBC $113,600
FOX	That 70s Show $210,400 / Undeclared $155,800	24 $155,800	No Fox programming
UPN	Buffy the Vampire Slayer $62,000	Roswell $42,600	No UPN programming
WB	Gilmore Girls $82,000	Smallville $89,600	No WB programming

Wed. 8 p.m. — 9 p.m. — 10 p.m.

ABC	My Wife and Kids $164,600 / The Dad $131,200	Drew Carey $234,000 / The Job $172,000	20/20 $147,000
CBS	60 Minutes II $97,600	The Amazing Race $129,200	Wolf Lake $96,400
NBC	Ed $123,000	The West Wing $268,200	Law & Order $248,400
FOX	Comedy Wheel $152,200 / Grounded for Life $141,800	Titus $143,400 / Bernie Mac Show $128,600	No Fox programming
UPN	Enterprise $81,800	Special Unit 2 $25,630	No UPN programming
WB	Dawson s Creek $104,600	Felicity $77,800	No WB programming

Thur. 8 p.m. — 9 p.m. — 10 p.m.

ABC	Who s Line? $93,400 / Who s Line? $93,400	Who Wants to Be a Millionaire $107,800	PrimeTime Thursday $102,800
CBS	Survivor $445,000	CSI: Crime Sceen Investigation $242,400	The Agency $111,400
NBC	Friends $353,600 / Inside Schwartz $238,800	Will & Grace $321,200 / Just Shoot Me $286,400	ER $425,400
FOX	Family Guy $65,000 / The Tick $69,200	Temptation Island $175,000	No Fox programming
UPN	WWF Smackdown! $29,500		No UPN programming
WB	Popstars 2 $43,250 / Elimidate Deluxe $28,000	Charmed $71,000	No WB programming

Fri. 8 p.m. — 9 p.m. — 10 p.m.

ABC	The Mole II $127,200	Thieves $127,200	Once and Again $185,600
CBS	The Ellen Show $94,600 / Danny $82,600	That s Life $71,800	48 Hours $79,800
NBC	Providence $117,000	Dateline NBC $88,800	Law & Order: Special Victims Unit $116,800
FOX	Dark Angel $118,600	Pasadena $105,000	No Fox programming
UPN	UPN Friday Movie $13,300		No UPN programming
WB	Sabrina $53,000 / Maybe It's Me $51,200	Reba $41,800 / Raising Dad $39,800	No WB programming

Sat. 8 p.m. — 9 p.m. — 10 p.m.

ABC	ABC Big Picture Show $77,400		
CBS	Touched By An Angel $75,400	Citizen Baines $68,400	The District $98,200
NBC	NBC Saturday Night Movie $70,000		
FOX	Cops $84,200	America s Most Wanted $87,800	No Fox programming

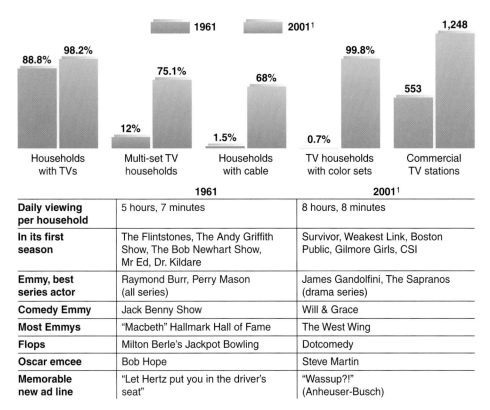

	1961	2001¹
Daily viewing per household	5 hours, 7 minutes	8 hours, 8 minutes
In its first season	The Flintstones, The Andy Griffith Show, The Bob Newhart Show, Mr Ed, Dr. Kildare	Survivor, Weakest Link, Boston Public, Gilmore Girls, CSI
Emmy, best series actor	Raymond Burr, Perry Mason (all series)	James Gandolfini, The Sopranos (drama series)
Comedy Emmy	Jack Benny Show	Will & Grace
Most Emmys	"Macbeth" Hallmark Hall of Fame	The West Wing
Flops	Milton Berle's Jackpot Bowling	Dotcomedy
Oscar emcee	Bob Hope	Steve Martin
Memorable new ad line	"Let Hertz put you in the driver's seat"	"Wassup?!" (Anheuser-Busch)

¹ Or most recent available

FIGURE 10.4

TV THEN AND NOW
With 98.2% of American households owning at least one television set, advertisers can be sure their commercials reach any area of the country.
Source: TV facts. The TV Guide Book of Lists, Television & Cable Factbook. Nielsen Media Research.

Nielsen Indexes Nielsen measures television audiences at two levels: network (Nielsen Television Index, NTI) and spot (Nielsen Station Index, NSI). Nielsen uses two measuring devices for local measurement, one of which is the Nielsen Storage Instantaneous Audiometer, or audiometer for short. This instrument records when the TV set is used and which station it is tuned to, but it cannot identify who is watching the program. The second measurement device is the viewing diary, which provides data on who is watching which shows. Diaries are mailed each week during survey months to sample homes in each of the 211 television markets, amounting to approximately 1 million diaries returned per year.

People Meters Nielsen began to measure not only what is being watched but who is watching which shows nationally in 1987. It replaced its audiometer and supplemented the diary system with 5,000 *people meters,* which record what television shows are being watched, the number of households that are watching, and which family members are viewing. The recording is done automatically; household members indicate their presence simply by pressing a button.

Customers have long bristled about Nielsen's shortcomings, from its methodology to its pricing. Now, digital television presents a new ratings challenge to Nielsen. Current meters measure only the channel a television is tuned to, but digital TV can transmit several signals through a single channel, so existing meters won't be able to measure accurately who is watching what. Nielsen has spent almost $30 million developing a new digital meter but concedes that there is no guarantee that it will be adopted by the various networks.[5]

ClusterPLUS Nielsen now provides data for the 47 ClusterPLUS geodemographic groupings developed by Donnelly Marketing Information Services. **Geodemographic clusters** are distinct types of neighborhoods. Each of the nation's 250,000 census block groups is assigned to one of 47 cluster groups based on its demographic and socioeconomic makeup. Cluster 1, the Established Wealthy, is composed of the most elite, affluent neighborhoods, like Greenwich, Connecticut, and Beverly Hills, California. Residents of Cluster 47, Lowest-Income Black Female-Headed Families, live in poverty-stricken areas such as the South Bronx or Watts.

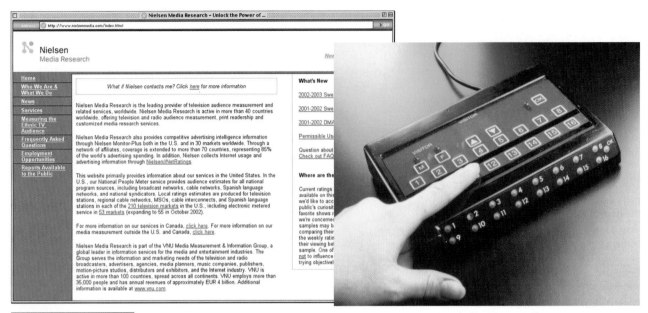

Nielsen measures television audiences with its "people meters" and viewing diaries. To keep up with new technology, it is currently testing a metering system capable of identifying analog and digital transmission.

One packaged-goods manufacturer used the ClusterPLUS Nielsen connection to market an ingredient used in baking cakes and cookies. The goal was to buy television commercials only for programs whose audience has a large proportion of consumers who regularly bake from scratch. By merging the 10 highest-ranking clusters that fit the audience profile into one target group, the packaged-goods marketer got a detailed look at the product's best prospects. The advertiser decided to zero in on older, rural, and blue-collar viewers in the South and Midwest.[6]

Target TV: A New Challenger Many organizations in the media industry have long resented the lock Nielsen has on the TV audience measurement system. Several challengers have come and gone. A recent contender that may have a chance is Target TV, a company that places specially equipped digital e-top boxes in viewer homes. Unlike Nielsen, which only collects viewing data, Target TV will try to produce extra revenue by providing interactive advertising, home shopping, surveys, and games. It still has to work out some problems, such as sample validity problems (noncable viewers are not included) and a description of the viewers is incomplete.

BUYING TIME ON TV

When buying time on network television, the three most common alternatives are: upfront, scatter, or opportunistic. In the case of the upfront, the television buy is for all four quarters for the upcoming year. The Upfront Market occurs in the spring for the television season that begins in September. Buying large amounts of media time guarantees the media buyer a lower cost and the assurance that it will have access to the network TV schedule. Scatter buying is the purchase of time inventory within a specific quarter before that quarter begins. The media buyer has a better handle on price and may have a seasonal product that requires a one- or two-quarter media buy. However, the buyer takes the risk that the most preferred times may be gone. If the media buyer wishes to buy network TV time at the last minute it makes an opportunistic buy. The choices may be limited but the price might be greatly discounted, since the networks may be wanting to dispose of surplus inventory.

ADVANTAGES OF TELEVISION

Television has three key advantages. First, its influence on consumers' taste and perceptions is pervasive. Second, it can reach a large audience in a cost-efficient manner. Third, its sound and moving images create a strong impact.

Cost-Efficiency

Many advertisers view television as the most cost-effective way to deliver a commercial message because it has such a wide reach. Millions of people watch some TV regularly. Not only does television reach a large percentage of the population, but it also reaches people that print media misses. NBC's *Today* show averages approximately $45,000 for a 30-second spot, and the household cost per thousand (CPM) is $3.62. This mass coverage is extremely cost-efficient. Reaching the same number of people with a $60,000 ad in *Time* magazine would have a CPM of $11.85. For an advertiser attempting to reach an undifferentiated market, a 30-second spot on a top-rated show may cost a penny or less for each person reached.

Impact

Television makes a strong impact. The interaction of sight, sound, color, motion, and drama creates a level of consumer involvement that often approximates the shopping experience itself. It can make mundane products appear important, exciting, and interesting. It can also create a positive association with the sponsor if the advertisement is likable. Certainly, this has been the case for Pepsi's commercials featuring Britney Spears. It is also the case with Nutri-Grain bars (see the "A Matter of Practice" box).

A MATTER OF PRACTICE

HUMOR CAN APPLY ANYWHERE

➤ Writing a humorous print ad is difficult at best.

Converting that humorous concept into a TV commercial, while efficient, does not always work. This was the challenge facing Kellogg's Nutri-Grain bar and its agency Leo Burnett.

The essence of the initial print campaign was cogently expressed by Anne Patanelea, creative director and copywriter on the campaign: "We looked at what people grabbed on the run and it was pretty much bad food. . . . We wanted to remind people that [a Nutri-Grain bar] was a smart choice." The target audience was upper-income women on the go; a group that Kellogg had never gone after before. The new tagline, "Respect yourself in the morning," would have the humorous double meaning that these women should understand. Extending this tagline to a creative concept showed young women "on the go" with doughnuts on their derrieres. The ads ran in magazines, on trains and buses, benches/bus stops, and outside pastry shops. Tests showed that the print ads seemed to be working and it was time to create a TV version.

The creative team went with a very subtle approach with no dialogue. People are shown on a subway, all eating pastries. The joke isn't revealed until a woman exits the subway with two cinnamon buns attached to her rear.

A voiceover says, "If this is what you sometimes eat for breakfast, remember you are what you eat." A visual of the Nutri-Grain bar along with the tagline complete the spot.

POINT TO PONDER

Is there a chance this creative concept will overshadow the name of the product?

Source: Aaron Baar, "Wake-up Call," *Adweek* (August 6, 2001): 19.

DISADVANTAGES OF TELEVISION

Despite the effectiveness of television advertising, it has four problems: expense, clutter, nonselective targeting, and inflexibility.

Expense

The most serious limitation of television advertising is the extremely high cost of producing and running commercials. Although the cost per person reached is low, the absolute cost can be restrictive, especially for small and even midsized companies. Production costs include filming the commercial (several thousand to several hundred thousand dollars) and paying the talent—writers, directors, and actors. For celebrities such as Jerry Seinfeld, Candice Bergen, and Michael Jordan, the price tag can be millions of dollars.

The prices charged for network time simply result from supply and demand. Programs that draw the largest audiences—that supply the greatest number of viewers—can charge—demand—more for their advertising space. A 30-second prime-time spot averages about $185,000. Special shows, such as the Super Bowl, World Series, or Academy Awards, charge much more. Table 10.2 shows the ad rates for the top TV shows from 1970 to 2001. Some experts comment that television advertising is very cheap if you can afford it.

Clutter

Television suffers from commercial clutter. In the past, the National Association of Broadcasters (NAB) restricted the allowable commercial time per hour to approximately six minutes. In 1982 the Justice Department overturned this restriction. Although there are nonrestrictions, the networks continue to honor the NAB guidelines. This could change as revenue needs increase. If the number of 30-second commercials, station break announcements, credits, and public service announcements increases, the visibility and persuasiveness of television advertising would diminish.

TABLE 10.2	**Time Is Money: The Top Shows by Ad Rates**
2001	**$/:30**
ER	$425,400
Friends	$353,600
1998	**$/:30**
Seinfeld	$575,000
ER	$560,000
1992	**$/:30**
Murphy Brown	$310,000
Roseanne	$290,000
1987	**$/:30**
Cosby Show	$369,500
Cheers	$307,000
1980	**$/:30**
M*A*S*H	$150,000
Dallas	$145,000
1972	**$/:30**
Bonanza	$26,000
Peyton Place	$ 2,750

Sources: Joe Mandese, "The Buying and Selling," *Advertising Age* (Spring 1995): 20; "Top 10 Shows by Ad Rates," *Advertising Age* (September 15, 1997): S2.

Nonselective Audience

Although the networks attempt to profile viewers, their demographic and psychographic descriptions are quite general, offering the advertiser little assurance that appropriate people are viewing the message. Television advertising includes a great deal of waste coverage: communication directed at an unresponsive (and often uninterested) audience that may not fit the advertiser's target market characteristics.

Inflexibility

Television also suffers from inflexibility in scheduling. Most network television is bought in the spring and early summer for the next fall season. If an advertiser is unable to make this up-front buy, only limited time-slot alternatives remain available. Also, it is difficult to make last-minute adjustments in copy and visuals. Production of a TV commercial may take days or weeks, and is changed reluctantly.

Cable television is much more targeted than network and spot television and so it has far less waste. However, cable cannot cover a mass audience and probably is more cluttered than network TV.

Television may offer the benefits of sight and sound, many advertisers (especially local ones) want to target audiences more specifically than the TV medium can. In addition, consumers may find television commercials too intrusive. In the case of these instances, radio offers a reliable medium.

THE STRUCTURE OF THE RADIO INDUSTRY

Radio became the first broadcast medium just after World War I; it grew in popularity during the 1920s and 1930s, and became the primary source of entertainment during the Great Depression. It maintained this number-one spot until the late 1940s and early 1950s when television emerged. The basic structure of radio is shown in Figure 10.5

Radio stations are AM or FM. The strength of an AM signal depends on the power the FCC grants the station. Stations with a broadcast range of approximately 2.5 miles are considered local stations. Regional stations may cover an entire state or several states. The most powerful stations are called "clean channel" stations. An FM station typically sends a signal that travels 50 miles. The tonal quality of an FM signal is superior to that of AM. For an advertiser, knowing the advantages and disadvantages of AM and FM radio would assist in better targeting as well as determining the technical quality desired for the transmission of the radio commercial.

Cable radio was launched in 1990. This technology uses cable television receivers to deliver static-free music via wires plugged into cable subscribers' stereos. The thinking behind cable radio is that cable television needs new revenue and consumers are fed up with commercials on radio. The service typically is commercial-free and costs $7 to $12

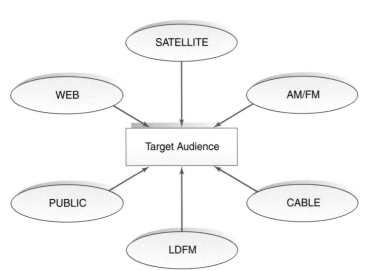

FIGURE 10.5

THE STRUCTURE OF RADIO
As seen here, the structure of the radio industry has expanded to include cable, public, Web, and satellite radio.

per month. An example of cable radio is Digital Music Express, which offers CD-quality sound in 30 music formats (rock, classical, etc.) around the clock.

LPFM

If you're a college student, you probably have a low-power FM (LPFM) station on your campus. These nonprofit, noncommercial stations serve a small market, with a reach of three to five miles. Although the FCC has not allowed these stations to carry advertising, many have positioned themselves in case this ruling is changed. Advertising would provide revenue to the stations and local advertisers would enjoy a new, likely affordable outlet. Often, these stations provide usual programming unavailable through other radio venues.[7]

Public Radio

Public radio is very much like its television counterpart and must abide by the same rules and regulations. But while public television is losing market share to the many new cable competitors, public radio is growing relative to its competitors. Public radio audience size increased by nearly 60 percent during the 1990s. Likewise, corporate underwriting (sponsorship) has increased since public radio is one of the few mediums that can deliver the well-educated, affluent consumer. "It's a desirable audience that's difficult to find in a lot of commercial broadcasting," says James Harman, manager of corporate giving for General Electric, which underwrites *Marketplace,* a PBS show that discusses business trends and issues.[8]

Web Radio

Web radio provides audio streaming through a Web site. Radio station operators from giant clear channel communications down to smaller station groups such as Buckley Broadcasting and Emmis Communications all provide radio programming through the Web. There are many unresolved technical and legal issues surrounding Web radio, and its future remains uncertain.

Still, Web radio does offer thousands of highly diverse radio shows. Moreover, Web-based radio could offer advertisers spots that run only in certain parts of a city, something impossible with broadcast radio. Such localization would open up new opportunities for smaller advertisers and help them handle their budgets more efficiently.

Satellite Radio

The newest rage in radio technology is satellite radio. It can deliver your favorite radio stations, regardless of where you are in the continental United States. New York City–based Sirius Satellite Radio and Washington, D.C.–based XM Satellite Radio will introduce their systems in 2002. For $12.95 a month, the system allows you to access 100 stations. A few car manufacturers offered three-band radios (AM/FM/SAT) in several of their high-end 2002 models. The retailers Circuit City, the WIZ, and others have agreed to market satellite-compatible car radios.[9]

RADIO ADVERTISING

Radio advertising is available on national networks and in local markets. We will now examine network, syndicate, and spot radio.

Network Radio

Network radio is a group of local affiliates connected to one or more national networks through telephone wires and satellites. Complete market coverage combined with high-quality programming has increased the popularity of network radio. In the 1980s network radio went through a period of consolidation that produced four major radio networks: Westwood One, CBS, ABC, and Unistar. Today, more than 20 national radio networks program concerts, talk shows, sports events, and dramas. Satellite transmission has produced important technological improvements.

Many advertisers view network radio as a viable national advertising medium, especially for advertisers of food, automobiles, and over-the-counter drugs. The growth of network radio has contributed to the increase in syndicated radio, creating more advertising opportunities for companies eager to reach new markets. In fact, syndication and network radio have practically become interchangeable terms.

Syndicated Radio

Syndication has benefited network radio because it offers advertisers a variety of high-quality, specialized programs. Both networks and private firms offer syndication.

Syndicated radio is somewhat different from sydication in television. Primarily, radio syndication mostly involves programs that are created for syndication. So there may be a local talk show, such as Rush Limbaugh, who became so popular that it was "taken into syndication." Here we're not talking about reruns of Seinfeld, but original radio programming playing on a large number of affiliate stations.

Spot Radio

In **spot radio advertising** an advertiser places an advertisement with an individual station rather than through a network. Although networks provide prerecorded national advertisements, they also allow local affiliates open time to sell spot advertisements. Spot radio advertising is nearly 80 percent of all radio advertising. Its popularity results from the flexibility it offers the advertiser. With over 8,000 stations available, messages can be tailored for particular audiences. In large cities such as New York, Chicago, and Los Angeles, 40 or more radio stations are available. Local stations also offer flexibility through their willingness to run unusual ads, allow last-minute changes, and negotiate rates. Buying spot radio and coping with its nonstandardized rate structures can be very cumbersome, however.

Radio advertising revenue is divided into three categories: network, spot, and local. Network revenues are by far the smallest category, accounting for approximately 5 percent of total radio revenues. Local advertising revenues account for 90 percent, and national spot advertising makes up the remaining 5 percent.

THE RADIO AUDIENCE

Radio is a highly segmented medium. Program formats offered in a typical market include hard rock, gospel, country and western, top-40 hits, and advice, from car repair to finances to dating. Virtually every household in the United States (99 percent) has a radio (527 million radios in total, with an average 5.6 per household).[10]

Market researcher Michael Hedges separates radio listeners into four segments: station fans, radio fans, music fans, and news fans. Station fans make up the largest segment of radio listeners, at 46 percent. They have a clear preference for one or two stations and spend up to 8 hours or more each day listening to their favorites. Most station fans are women between the ages of 25 and 44. Radio fans represent 34 percent of the population. They may listen to four or five different stations per week, and they show no preference for one particular station. Most are under 35 years of age, although many women aged 55 and older are radio fans.

Only 11 percent of the population are music fans: people who listen exclusively for the music being played. Men between the ages of 25 and 45 are most likely to be music fans, although many elderly adults fit into the profile. Finally, a percentage of radio listeners choose their stations based on a need for news and information. They have one or two favorite stations, listen in short segments, and are almost exclusively aged 35 or older.[11]

Experts contend that much of the future of radio depends on kids and teens. Recent research has provided some findings that bode well for radio. For example, in a study conducted by Arbitron Research, the results indicated that "90 percent of 6- to 11-year-olds tuned into their favorite radio stations eight to nine hours each week." Moreover, kids are loyal to both stations and formats.[12]

Arbitron is one of several major audience-rating services in the advertising industry. It estimates the size of radio audience for over 250 U.S. markets.

Measuring the Radio Audience

Advertisers considering radio are most concerned with the number of people listening to a particular station at a given time. The radio industry and independent research firms provide several measures for advertisers, including coverage and circulation.

The most basic measure is the station's coverage. This is simply the number of homes in a geographic area that are able to pick up the station clearly, whether those homes are acutally tuned in or not. A better measure is circulation, which measures the number of homes acutally tuned in to the particular station. Factors such as competing programs, the types of programs, and the time of day or night influence the circulation figure.

Arbitron Several major audience-rating services operate in the advertising industry. One, the Arbitron Ratings Company, estimates the size of radio audience for over 250 markets in the United States. Arbitron uses a seven-day self-administered diary that the person returns to Arbitron at the end of the week. Editors check that each diary has entries for every day and that the postmark shows the diary wasn't mailed before the week was over.

RADAR A second audience-rating service is Radio's All-Dimension Audience Research (RADAR). This company (owned by Arbitron) deals with both local and network radio. For RADAR, Statistical Research calls 12,000 respondents for seven consecutive days and asks about network radio listening done the day before. The company contacts respondents before beginning data collection, asking them to pay close attention to their listening habits. Final reports are based on data collected over 48 weeks.

BUYING TIME ON RADIO

Radio time is bought as either network or spot. As noted, network radio programming for sales includes news, music, sports, and drama. Costs are relatively low, averaging approximately $3,600 for a 30-second announcement. Time is purchased the same way as network television. There is an up-front market and the advertiser is contractually obligated for a specified number of commercials over a designated period of time.

Spot radio reflects a much wider range of programming formats, and consequently, a much wider range of rates. Because these programs are strongly targeted, the efficiency of the dollars spent tends to be very high. One difference in purchasing spot radio is that the quality of the audience information is often questionable.

ADVANTAGES AND DISADVANTAGES OF RADIO

Radio is not for every advertiser, and it is important to understand its advantages and disadvantages.

Advantages of Radio

Radio has five key advantages for advertisers. Let's look at each briefly.

- *Target audiences.* The most important advantage radio offers is its ability to reach specific audiences through specialized programming. In addition, radio can be adapted for different parts of the country and can reach people at different times of the day. For example, radio is the ideal means of reaching people driving to and from work. Known as drive time, these radio time slots provide the best audience for many advertisers. Pizza Hut, for instance, reached out to its target audience of women making dinner choices by using radio during the 4:00–7:00 P.M. time slot.
- *Flexibility.* Radio offers advertisers flexibility. Of all the media, radio has the shortest closing period: Copy can be submitted up to airtime. This flexibility allows advertisers to adjust to local market conditions, current news events, and even the weather. For example, a local hardware store can quickly implement a snow-shovel promotion the morning after a snowstorm. Radio's flexibility is also evident in its willingness to participate in promotional tie-ins such as store openings, races, and so on.
- *Affordability.* Radio may be the least expensive of all media. And because airtime costs are low, extensive repetition is possible. In addition, the costs of producing a radio commercial can be low, particularly if a local station announcer reads the message. Radio's low cost and high reach of selected target groups make it an excellent supporting medium. In fact, the most appropriate role for most radio advertising is a supportive one. Columbia Bank used local radio to support its print ad campaign and give the bank a strong presence. Its radio spot is shown in Figure 10.6.

FIGURE 10.6
COLUMBIA BANK "NEVER MIND"
RADIO SCRIPT

COLUMBIA BANK
60 second radio: "Nevermind"

Banker: (uninterested, agitated, "nasally," sighs throughout)

Effective May 1, the following charges apply for all automated banking services: $3.50 per call for general account information in excess of 10 per statement period. $1.00 for each employee assisted call for general account information in excess of four per statement period. If you request general information on more than one account during the same phone call, each account will be charged as stated above. if you should actually like to see a real, live human being . . . well, nevermind, you couldn't *possibly* have enough money for that.

Announcer:

If this sounds like your bank, maybe it's time you switched to ours, *Columbia Bank.* And though we have all the modern conveniences, we still believe in meeting your needs *in person. Banking is what banking was,* at Columbia Bank, Member FDIC.

- *Mental imagery.* Radio allows the listener to imagine. Radio uses words, sound effects, music, and tonality to enable listeners to create their own pictures. For this reason, radio is sometimes called the theater of the mind.
- *High level of acceptance.* The final advantage is radio's high acceptance at the local level. Partly because of its passive nature (background sound), radio normally is not perceived as an irritant. People have their favorite radio stations and radio personalities, which they listen to regularly. Messages delivered by these stations and personalities are likely to be accepted and retained.

Disadvantages of Radio

Radio is not without its drawbacks. Here are five key disadvantages:

- *Listener inattentiveness.* Because radio is strictly a listening medium, radio messages are fleeting, and listeners may miss or forget commercials. Many people think of radio as pleasant background and do not listen to it carefully.
- *Lack of visuals.* Being restricted to using sound can hamper a person's creativity. Developing radio ads that encourage the listener to see the product is a difficult challenge, and clearly, products that must be demonstrated or seen to be appreciated are inappropriate for radio advertising. Experts believe that humor, music, and sound effects may be the most effective way to create visualization.
- *Clutter.* The number of radio stations has increased, and so has the heavy repetition of some ads. The result is tremendous clutter in radio advertising.
- *Scheduling and buying difficulties.* Scheduling and buying radio time can be cumbersome. Advertisers seeking to reach a wide audience often need to buy time on several stations, complicating scheduling and ad evaluation. The bookkeeping involved in checking nonstandardized rates, approving bills for payment, and billing clients can be a staggering task. Fortunately, computers and large-station representatives have helped to ease much of this burden.
- *Lack of control.* A large percentage of radio is talk shows, and most of radio's recent growth has come through talk shows. There is always the risk that a radio personality will say something that offends the audience, which would in turn hurt the audience's perception of an advertiser's product.

MAKING RADIO MEDIA CHOICES

We have seen that radio is highly targeted and inexpensive. Although radio may not be a primary medium for most businesses, it does have excellent reminder and reinforcement capability. To maximize the impact of a radio spot, timing is critical. Restaurants run spots before meals; auto dealerships run spots on Friday and Saturday, when people are free to visit showrooms; jewelry stores run them before Christmas, Valentine's Day, and Mother's Day. For a company like Pizza Hut, radio buys at the local level supplement national television and cable. Radio acts as a reminder, with 30-second spots concentrated from 11:00 A.M. to noon and 4:00 to 7:00 P.M. The messages focus on the location of local Pizza Hut restaurants and any special promotions.

For nearly half a century, radio and television represented the broadcast category. In the last 5 to 10 years the world of interactive media has emerged, changing the face of advertising.

INTERNET MEDIA

On September 6, 2001, the U.S. Census Bureau reported that 50.1 percent of U.S. households owned a computer and 42 percent went on the Internet at least once a day. Although these data are impressive, the Internet is still a long way from the penetration levels of newspapers, TV, and radio. The Internet is an impressive technology and will clearly change some of the ways we do advertising, but it is just one choice in the media mix.

Practical Tips #1

SOME INTERNET BUZZWORDS

The Internet has its own buzzwords that advertisers need to know when making decisions about interactive media. Here are some key advertising terms:

- *Button ads.* Squarish ads that are usually at the bottom of a Web page and contain only a corporate name or brand.
- *Click-through.* How often a viewer responds to an ad by clicking on it; also known as the click rate.
- *Cookies.* Information stored on a viewer's Web browser to help identify that particular person to the Web provider—or at least that particular browser—the next time that viewer visits a particular site.
- *Cost per click.* The rate charges to advertisers if the user responds to a displayed ad.
- *Cost per lead/sale.* The rate charged to advertisers if the viewer responds with personal information.
- *Impressions.* The total number of times an ad is displayed on a Web page; impressions aren't the same as hits, which count the number of times each page or element in a page is retrieved.
- *Sponsorships, or co-branded ads.* These ads try to integrate companies' brands and products with the editorial content on targeted Web sites.
- *Ad views.* The number of times an ad banner is downloaded.
- *Banner.* A type of ad on a Web site that is hot-linked to the advertiser's site.
- *Interstitial.* An advertisement that appears in a window on your screen while you are waiting for the Web page to load.
- *Rich media.* Special effects technology applied to Internet ads (such as streaming video, audio, and so on).

TYPES OF INTERNET ADVERTISING

What kinds of Internet advertising are available today? The industry is moving so quickly that by the time you read this passage, other categories may replace or supplement those we discuss here. Essentially, Internet advertising can be delivered in the following formats.

World Wide Web Home Page

The **Web page** for Sears delivers basic information about the sponsor, and also carries advertising and other sales messages. In addition, the B2B Web page can carry the same or supplementary information used by the field sales forces—for example, product categories, price sheets, and promotions. Finally, the Web page can identify retailers and other product providers that can prove useful to the consumer.

Banners

IBM introduced banner ads in 1994. While very popular when they first appeared, the overall click-through rate has dropped to 0.3 percent. **Banner ads** are easy to create and are usually placed on a Web site featuring complementary products. For example, Visa has a banner ad on the Yahoo! Web site so people will be reminded to use their Visa when purchasing through Yahoo!

Creating a banner ad simply by trimming down a print ad does not seem to work on the Internet. New technologies—including plug-ins, Java script, and media streaming—provide an interactive component. A recent study by Greg Interactive, New York, and ASI Interactive Research found that the click-through rate nearly doubles when an interactive element is added to a banner ad.

E-Mail

Today's improved databases allow marketers to reach target prospects with unsolicited e-mail. In fact, the response rate for an unsolicited e-mail campaign is 5 to 15 times higher than for a banner ad campaign. Unfortunately for e-mail advertisers, generally, people

do not welcome unsolicited e-mail, also known as *spam*. Permission marketing attempts to address this criticism by asking potential consumers for their permission to send them e-mail. Willing customers provide their e-mail address when they enter a sweepstake, fill out a product warranty card, or fill out an information card at a trade show.

Skyscrapers

The extra-long, skinny ads running down the right or left side of a Web site are called skyscrapers. The financial site CBSMarketWatch.com, for instance, regularly runs this kind of ad. Response rates for skyscrapers, which began to be used aggressively by more companies in 2000, can be 10 times higher than traditional banner ads.

Minisites, Pop-Ups, and Superstitials

Pop-up ads burst open on the computer screen, and companies like Volvo and GlaxoSmith-Kline (for its Oxy acne medicine) dish up games and product information.

Through these ads, minisites allow advertisers to market without sending people away from the site they're visiting. The General Motors minisite will appear on the Shell Oil site, and the consumer can access and enlarge them later.

Both types of advertising get a higher click rate—around 5 percent of the people who see the sites click on them, estimates portal About.com. Still, such sites can be intrusive and annoying.

Superstitials, unveiled by online marketer Unicast in April 1999, are thought of as "the Internet's commercial," designed to work like TV ads. When you go from one page on a Web site to another, a 20-second animation appears in a window. These ads now run on more than 350 Web sites. About 85 percent of the superstitial advertisers are traditional—that is, they are not dot-com companies.

B2B Networks

Thanks to a new sector of the online advertising market—business-to-business (B2B) ad networks—getting the word out now means deciding which small-business segment an advertiser would like to target with its next campaign. B2B ad networks, the oldest of which (B2B Works) appeared in early 2000, link together B2B Web sites vertically (through an industry) and horizontally (across a mass market). These networks produce something akin to a custom directory of B2B Web sites for each advertiser, helping the

THE INSIDE STORY
HOW USERS EXPERIENCE BRANDS ON THE WEB

Harley Manning, Research Director, Site Design and
Development Forrester Research

When it comes to interactive media, usability goals are business goals. Hard-to-use Web sites frustrate customers, forfeit revenue, and erode brands.

Since January 2000, Forrester Research has graded the user experience at more than 170 Web sites belonging to the global 2,500 FIRMS (Web sites belonging to the largest 2,500 companies in the world). We define "user experience" as the total interaction visitors have with a Web site, including their satisfaction with content, function, and interface.

As part of the review process, analysts give sites pass/fail grades on 25 different criteria. The criteria are adapted from a combination of consumer research and software evaluation techniques such as trying to complete a specific task, or conducting searches for known content.

Overall, sites fared poorly. On a scale ranging from −50 (25 critical failures) to +50 (25 exemplary passes), the average score was −3.9. The top site scored 23 out of 50, but even it suffered from poor legibility and incomplete information.

Every review uncovered a range of problems. The worst sites were those that lacked both content *and* function. Others provided value but embarrassed themselves with broken links and search engines that mostly retrieved "page not found" messages.

How could a poor Web site hurt a brand? Because the Web is active—not passive—customers use it in much the same way they use products. According to a 1985 study done for the White House Office of Consumer Affairs, people who have a bad experience with a product typically tell nine others. If a person finds a Web site to be frustrating and annoying, the person will have a negative experience with that brand—and then tell nine friends about it.

In going from a passive medium like television to an interactive medium like the World Wide Web, designers need to provide a satisfying user experience. To do this, Forrester recommends that they borrow methodologies from software development practice. They should start by defining all target user groups, which is the kind of segmentation that any good marketer knows how to do. From there, they can specifically identify the goals and needs of each group. It is these goals and needs that must drive site design. In this way, site attributes such as speed, reliability, and value can also become attributes of the brand.

Leading the Site Design and Development group at Forrester Research, Harley Manning's work focuses on design, production, and content management strategies for INTERACTIVE media. Harley came to Forrester after 18 years of designing and building interactive services for Dow Jones, AT&T, MCI, Prodigy, and Sears. He was recently awarded a patent for a software tool used to build and maintain knowledge bases. He received a Master of Science degree in Advertising from the University of Illinois, Urbana, in 1977.

Nominated by Kim Rotzell, Dean, University of Illinois College of Communication.

advertiser target a precise business audience with the right message. The networks then track the response to ads on different Web sites and adjust the campaign as appropriate.

ONLINE ADVERTISING EFFECTIVENESS

Two primary questions arise with Internet advertising: Is it effective? And How do we measure effectiveness? Many critics contend that Internet advertising is simply not effective. As we noted earlier, the response to a typical banner ad is less than .5 percent. So why isn't the Internet effective? Advertisers may not yet have created ads that take advantage of the unique characteristics of the Internet. Many advertisers simply transpose print ads onto the Net. But then creating more dynamic ads through pop-up ads, for instance, appears to irritate more than sell. So, if both traditional ads and more active ads don't work, what's the next move? Millions of dollars are being spent by Internet advertisers to learn how to be more creative, more relevant, and more targeted.

The second primary question on Internet advertising focuses on the industry's inability to develop a system that accurately measures effectiveness. There are measures that assess the effectiveness of the Web site as a whole. Consider hits (the number of times a particular site is visited), viewers (the number of viewers to a site), unique visitors (the number of different viewers during a particular time period), and page views (the number of times viewers view a page). These measures track a consumer through a Web site, but they offer no insights as to motivation.

There are two methods for measuring consumer response to Internet advertising: clicks, click-through (the number of people who click on a banner ad), and the click-through rate (the rate of click-through from an ad to a page on that advertiser's Web site). Both these measures are considered insufficient by many Internet advertisers and a host of private research providers have emerged. For example, Denver-based Match Logic identifies for its clients what viewers do next after not clicking on a banner ad.

Buying Time/Space on the Internet

Advertising on the Internet has elements of both broadcast and print media. Consequently, the process for buying time/space on the Internet is a bit unsettled. To date, it is treated as a print ad, and CPM, along with the size of the ad, are the primary criteria for the setting price.

Advantages of Internet Advertising

One reason why Internet advertising is growing in popularity is that it offers distinct advantages over other media alternatives. Most notably, advertisers can customize their message over the Internet. Thanks to database marketing, an advertiser can input key demographic and behavioral variables, making the consumer feel like the ad is just for him. Check out classmates.com for an example. Ads appearing on a particular page are for products that would appeal to that age group. Someone who graduated from high school in 1960 would see banner ads for investments that facilitate early retirement.

These same databases can be merged so that the Internet advertiser knows a great deal about the habits of the consumer. Travel behavior, media usage, and credit card usage can all combine for a fairly comprehensive profile. Advertisers may combine databases to develop fairly comprehensive profiles. Consider how an advertiser might tailor a message to people if it knew their travel behavior, media preferences, and credit card usage.

For the B2B advertiser, the Internet advertising process can provide excellent sales leads or actual sales. Users of the Silicon Graphic Web site, for example, can access over 100 product catalogs, request a call from a salesperson, or actually purchase software.

The Internet can level the playing field for small and medium-sized companies that compete against larger organizations. The cost of creating a Web site, a set of ads, and a database is affordable for virtually every marketer.

Disadvantages of Internet Advertising

Internet advertising is still in its infancy, and it may have more disadvantages than advantages. Undoubtedly, the most serious drawback is the inability of strategic and creative experts to consistently produce effective ads and to measure their effectiveness.

Consider, too, that clutter is just as much a problem with the Internet as it is in other mediums. In fact, because multiple ads may appear on the same screen—many moving or popping up—the clutter may be even worse.

BROADCAST AND INTERACTIVE MEDIA STRATEGIES

When using a broadcast medium, advertisers should ask about its cost, its ability to meet their advertising objectives, its ability to accommodate the style of message, and how targeted the audience is. In general, broadcast media offer a higher level of consumer involvement compared to print but do not allow as much information. The potential of

| TABLE 10.3 | **Rating of Media: A Strategic Approach** |

Medium	Absolute Cost	CPM	Targeting	Primary Objective	Clutter	Message	Flexibility
Newspapers	High	Moderate	Moderate	Info/sales	High	Moderate length	Good
Magazines	High	Low	High	Recall/sales	Very high	Moderate length	High
Television Network	Very high	Moderate	Low	Recall/reminder	High	Short length	Fair
Cable Television	Moderate	Moderate	High	Info/reminder	Moderate	Short length	Good
Network Radio	High	High	Low	Recall/reminder	Low	Short length	Low
Local Radio	Moderate	Low	High	Info/reminder	High	Short length	Good
Directories	Moderate	Low	High	Info/sales	High	Moderate length	Good
Out-of-Home	Moderate	Low	Low	Reminder	High	Short length	Good
Interactive	High	Moderate	Moderate	Info/sales	High	Moderate length	Good
Specialty	Low	Low	Moderate	Reminder	Moderate	Moderate length	High

interactive media is that they may combine the advantages of broadcast and print (the ability to inform).

Table 10.3 tallies the characteristics of the media we explored in chapters 9 and 10. This chart is useful for media planners who are trying to create the best media strategy for their message.

There have been many changes in media since 2001. The D-Map described in the "A Matter of Principle" box helps advertisers assess the effectiveness of various interactive media.

A MATTER OF PRINCIPLE

FORECASTING NEW MEDIA

➤ Accurately forecasting the emergence of new media and its impact on media planning has become a full-time job for a handful of media experts and others. Their hypothesis: "The growth of new media spreads through a population much the same way a disease would."

This isn't actually a new hypothesis in marketing. Several years ago the Theory of Adoption and Diffusion was introduced into the consumer behavior literature, to explain how and why consumers adopt new products. Still, the use of the spread of disease as an analogy to the spread of new media wasn't entirely accurate.

A project was initiated in 2001, by strategic planning executives from leading technology, media, and advertising companies. They, along with the Advertising Research Foundation, worked on D-Map—a project based on the principle that like infectious diseases, new media spread through the population in waves. The key is to identify the variables that are most important in predicting how quickly new media spread.

Possible variables include "assumptions about new technology development, the regulatory landscape, consumer demand for a particular new media product, as well as the potential consumer penetration." A beta test of the new software was scheduled in mid-2002.

It is hoped that the finished product will become the industry standard. Jon Swallen, project director and senior vice president of media knowledge at Interpublics Universal McCann, expressed the wishes of the team as follows: "What we expect to get out of this project is a tool for more reliable and more credible projections for the rollout and adoption of different kinds of consumer technologies." He notes that the main reason why past models have not worked is because they were developed by consultants working for companies that had a vested interest in the results. The cross-section of media experts, academicians, and independent mathematicians should mean that D-Map is less tainted.

POINT TO PONDER

Does the fact that the selection of the variables is still done by people make the D-Map subjective?

Source: Joe Mandese, "Creating a New Media Model," *American Demographics* (January 2002): 31.

IT'S A WRAP
DRUGSTORE.COM ADS A BALM FOR WOMEN

Throughout this chapter we have described the benefits and problems attached to the three primary broadcast media: television, radio, and the Internet. One of the most prominent drawbacks is the actual cost of producing and sending broadcast advertising. In the case of drugstore.com™, they spent far less on this campaign compared to what their competitors spent in advertising in 2000. Yet, their objectives were quite ambitious and readily met.

In the case of each goal, drugstore.com reached or exceeded its goals. In fact, the majority of the goals were reached within six months. With the help of the campaign, drugstore.com increased brand awareness in the various target markets and average weekly visits to the site increased from the previous year. The most satisfying surprise was the leap in the number of consumers who perceived the site as a convenient place to shop for their drugstore items.

Summary

1. **Discuss television structure and advertising, the TV audience, and the advantages and disadvantages of television advertising.** Advertisers can use network, public, cable, subscription, local, and specialty television. Network television is still the dominant form, although cable television has become entrenched. Television commercials can be sponsorships, participations, or spot announcements. Audimeters and diaries at the local level and people meters at the national level measure the television audience. Television offers advertisers cost efficiency, impact, and influence. However, TV is expensive, cluttered, and inflexible. The advantages and disadvantages of TV may change as the industry becomes more fragmented.

2. **Describe radio structure and advertising, its audiences, and the advantages and disadvantages of radio advertising.** Radio advertising can be delivered via networks, through syndication, and through spots. A station's coverage or circulation measures radio audience. The advantages of radio include its specialized programming, speed and flexibility, low cost, the use of mental imagery, and high levels of acceptance. Its disadvantages include audience inattentiveness, lack of visuals, clutter, and scheduling and buying difficulties.

3. **Discuss interactive media, its structure, its audience, and the advantages and disadvantages of interactive media advertising.** Interactive advertising is effective in reaching well-defined target audiences receptive to this technology. The key advantage is the ability of the consumer to interact with the banner ad. However, this type of advertising is expensive and still reaches only a small market.

Key Terms

affiliates, p. 270
banner ad, p. 289
broadband, p. 274
broadcast media, p. 270
cable television, p. 271

frequency, p. 295
geodemographic clusters, p. 279
interconnects, p. 272
local cable, p. 272
network, p. 270

network radio, p. 284
network cable, p. 272
participations, p. 276
signal, p. 272
sponsorship, p. 276

spot announcement, p. 276
spot radio advertising, p. 285
syndication, p. 273
Web page, p. 289

Questions

1. What are the major differences between broadcast and print media? How are the two media similar?

2. Describe television syndication. Contrast off-network syndication with first-run syndication. What is barter syndication? How does syndication affect the advertiser?

3. What primary advantages and disadvantages does cable television offer to advertisers? How do interconnects affect the decision to advertise on cable?

4. You are a major agency media director who has just finished a presentation to a prospective client in convenience food

marketing. During the Q and A period a client representative says: "We know that network television viewers' loyalty is nothing like it was 10 or even 5 years ago because so many people now turn to cable and VCRs. There are smaller audiences per program each year, yet television-time costs continue to rise. Do you still believe we should consider commercial television as a primary medium for our company's advertising?" How would you answer?

5. Local market radio audiences are measured primarily by the diary (Arbitron) and the telephone interview (Birch). If you, as a media sales director for a radio station, had to choose one service to measure station popularity, which one would you subscribe to? Assume that the services cost roughly the same.

6. Message clutter affects both radio and television advertising. Advertisers fear that audiences react to long commercial groupings by using the remote control for the television set or the tuner on the radio to steer to a different channel. Some have proposed that advertisers should absorb higher time costs to reduce the **frequency** and length of commercial interruptions. Others argue that broadcasting should reduce the number of commercials sold and also reduce program advertising even if it means less profit for broadcasters. Which of these remedies would be better?

7. One interesting way to combine the assets of radio and television is to use the soundtrack of a television commercial for a radio ad. Why would an advertiser consider this creative strategy? What limitations would you mention?

8. With the growth of cable television channels and the continued strength of network television, how do media planners choose the television stations on which they advertise? What is an appropriate mix of cable and network advertising?

9. You are the media planner for a cosmetics company introducing a new line of makeup for teenage girls. Your research indicates that television advertising will be an effective medium for creating awareness about your new product line. How do you design a television advertising strategy that will reach your target market successfully? What stations do you choose? Why? What programs and times do you choose? Why? Do you consider syndicated television? Why or why not? What advertising forms do you use and why?

10. As many Internet companies fold, what is the impact on using the Internet for advertising? How can Internet sites entice companies to advertise on them? What competitive advantage, if any, does Internet advertising provide? How can media planners understand and measure the effectiveness of advertising on the Internet?

Suggested Class Project

Each student should make a chart for five radio stations. List the type of station (easy listening, top 40, classical, and so on), the products commonly advertised, and the probable target markets for these products. Note the time of the day these products are advertised. Now put all of the products in a hat and have everyone draw one out. Each student is now responsible for the media planning of his or her product. Each one needs to allocate a budget of $2,500 among the five stations for a week's worth of programming. Assume 30 seconds of air time costs $250. Draw up a media plan.

Suggested Internet Class Project

Examine the various ads found on www.nike.com, www.IBM.com, and www.Sears.com. Which ads did you find most appealing? Engaging? Motivating? Write a one- to two-page report on your assessment.

Hallmark BUILD•A•CAMPAIGN *Projects*

Please review the Hallmark Case Appendix at the end of the text before responding to these questions.

1. Meet in small groups to discuss how Capitol Advertising used television and radio to take advantage of each medium's key benefits and how it might have improved those uses.

2. Given the various advantages and disadvantages of television, radio, and interactive media, which of the three would best serve the needs of your local Gold Crown store? Why?

Notes

1. Wayne Friedman, "Syndie Stuck in a Rut," *Advertising Age* (January 21, 2002): S5, S9.

2. Tobi Elkin, "What's Ahead on the Net," *Advertising Age* (January 14, 2002): 54, 57.

3. Amy Harmon, "Digital Video Recorders Give Advertisers Pause," *New York Times* (May 23, 2002): A1; Jeff Howe, "Ready for Prime Time," www.adweek.com (September 10, 2001): 10-12.

4. Newton Minnow, "Television More Vast Than Ever, Turns Toxic," *USA Today* (Wednesday, May 9, 2001): 15A.

5. Richard Sikes, "Will the Nielsen Spin-Off Be a Hit?" *BusinessWeek* (July 20, 1998): 66-67.

6. Jonathan Marks, "ClusterPLUS Nielsen Equals Efficient Marketing," *American Demographics* (September 1991): 16.

7. Steve Jarius, "Marketing Issues Raised by LPFM Stations," *Marketing News* (August 28, 2000): 7.

8. Leigh Gallagher, "Prairie Home Commercial," *Forbes* (August 6, 2001): 54-55.

9. Beth Snyder, "Rolling Stone Radio Seeks New Revenue, Expands Mage Brand," *Advertising Age* (November 2, 1998): 40.

10. Joan Raymond, "Radio-Active," *American Demographics* (October 2000): 28-29.

11. Leslie Whitaker, "Behind the Music," *American Demographics* (April 2001): 31-32.

12. "Radio Days," *American Demographics* (November 1988): 18.

PART-ENDING CASE

PART III
ADVERTISING MEDIA

8 Media Planning
  and Buying

9 Print Media

10 Broadcast and Interactive
   Online Media

LOSE THAT BURGER BELLY

Chick-fil-A

A Company's Media Plan

Chick-fil-A is not your "typical" quick-serve restaurant chain, and nowhere is it more evident than in its media plans. So how is it different? Chick-fil-A is dramatically outspent by its competition, which allows the competition to buy more media. Second, a majority of Chick-fil-A competitors use broadcast media as their primary vehicle. Chick-fil-A focuses its media dollars on outdoor advertising. Third, the competitors buy national advertising to promote their brands and sell products. Conversely, Chick-fil-A spends its dollars at the local level where it knows it can have an impact. Besides, a national media campaign for a chain located predominantly in the southern part of the country would be a waste. Finally, Chick-fil-A customizes each plan by market where its competitors have more of a one-size-fits-all approach.

The company's planning process is probably similar to its competition's process, however. It sets media objectives and develops strategies. It reviews and analyzes media opportunities within each individual market. What may be a breakthrough idea in one market might fall short in another. Again, Chick-fil-A customizes its media mix based on the needs and competitive factors in each market. It completes and reviews preliminary plans and after several discussions and revisions, a media plan is finally approved.

A typical media plan for a larger Chick-fil-A market might include 50 percent outdoor, 20 percent radio, 20 percent TV, and 10 percent local marketing. However, there are several Chick-fil-A markets whose media plan might include 70 percent outdoor and 30 percent local marketing. Chick-fil-A is patient in its approach to media planning and buying. [If a market has not reached a 30 showing (daily TRPs) delivered by an outdoor board, which is the medium of choice for a campaign, media planners are strongly encouraged to wait until it does before moving dollars into radio.]

Chick-fil-A uses radio primarily to drive traffic during key promotional periods. Local Area Marketing Directors for Chick-fil-A use the radio buys as an opportunity to receive value-added promotions, which provide additional exposure for a Chick-fil-A brand. Television is the place where everyone wants to be, but, again, Chick-fil-A is patient and waits for markets to mature to the point where a consistent TV schedule is cost-effective.

IT'S YOUR TURN

1. What are the problems with Chick-fil-A using a media strategy based primarily on secondary media?

2. What role does competition play in designing this media strategy?

CHAPTER

11

The Creative Side of Advertising

CHAPTER OBJECTIVES

When you have completed this chapter, you should be able to

1. Define creative advertising and explain how it leads to a Big Idea.
2. Describe the characteristics of creative people and their creative process.
3. Identify key elements in creative strategy.
4. Outline the key parts of a creative brief.
5. Explain how creative advertising relates to advertising effectiveness.

Everything You Need

Award: *EFFIE Gold, Automotive category*

Company: *Nissan North America*

Agency: *TBWA/Chiat Day*

Campaign: *"Nissan Xterra Launch Campaign"*

The EFFIE award–winning Xterra Launch ads, using the tagline "Everything you need. Nothing you don't," demonstrated that this rugged, no-nonsense SUV is built for the true outdoor enthusiast. Images of mud-drenched mountain bikers, outrageous skiers and snowboarders, and extreme surfers and kayakers fill the screen. The "Xtreme" theme, which was created by California-based TBWA/Chiat Day, is mirrored in the Lenny Kravitz Grammy-winning hit, "Fly Away"—a Generation X anthem.

Xterra's strategy was not to be all things to all people, but rather to be everything to just a few, attracting an all-new buyer. Directed at active, outdoorsy types between the ages of 25 and 35, the campaign used highly targeted media. To speak to that target, the ads focused on extreme athletes doing their things and outdoor adventurers getting as far from civilization as possible. The voice-over on the TV spots said: "Choose your sick days wisely."

The car has more to offer than a clever advertising campaign, however. Nissan, which has been hurt for years by bland designs dictated from Japan in the 1990s, and falling sales, has gotten an image boost from the innovative design of the Xterra.

The prelaunch campaign started nearly a year before the Xterra went on sale. Teaser print ads directed prospects to the Web site, a toll-free phone number, or business reply cards. Before the car was in the showrooms, Nissan had collected 65,000 names from people who wanted more information about the new SUV.

Prospects then got a series of direct mailings to maintain their interest. One offered a free vehicle accessory to consumers who put down deposits before a certain date. TV teaser spots featured Jerry Hirshberg, Nissan's design chief, who had just started as the brand's pitchman.

The campaign did more than just build an image for the Xterra. Ads also promoted such features as an aluminum roof rack, internal bike rack, first-aid kit, and water-resistant seats. In keeping with the tagline, they also celebrated the Xterra's lack of certain features, such as leather seats and wood trim. Hirshberg says the ads "reek of authenticity"; they also reek of testosterone and sweat. Almost all of the images are males involved in rugged activities.

Just how effective was this campaign? You'll see in the "It's a Wrap" box at the end of this chapter.

Adapted from: Mark Rechtin, "Have Product, Will Advertise," *Automotive News* (June 7, 1999): 4; "Nissan's Ads Hawk Cool Lifestyle and Cars," *USA Today* (October 25, 1999): 5B; James Zoltak, "Nissan 'Driven' to Extreme Sequel," *Adweek* (June 7, 1999): 6; Jean Halliday, "Xterra: Gary Van Houten," *Advertising Age* (June 26, 2000): S2.

Creative ideas, such as the award-winning Xterra campaign, aren't limited to advertising. People such as Henry Ford, the father of the Model T; Steven Jobs, the co-founder of Apple Computer; and Lucille Ball of *I Love Lucy* fame are highly creative. They are idea people, creative problem solvers, and highly original thinkers. Creative people are found in business, science, engineering, advertising, and many other fields. But in advertising, creativity is both a job description and a goal.

In this chapter we'll investigate how some ad agencies define creative advertising, the different approaches advertising people use to stay creative, characteristics of creative people, the creative concept, and the process of creative thinking and creative strategy. In the end, though, all advertisers use creativity to lead to a more effective advertisement, one that delivers on its objectives.

WHAT IS CREATIVE ADVERTISING?

What's it like to work on the creative side of advertising? Derek Clark, a copywriter at Detroit's Campbell-Ewald agency, described it this way:

> In the real world, just when you think you've approached a campaign from every possible angle, your creative director will ask you to try again. It's usually when you think you're at the end of your rope that the best ideas are born. This is the never-ending cycle of the creative process at an ad agency. It'll push you to new creative heights or to an early retirement in your own personal padded room.[1]

So what leads people like Clark to spend endless days and sleepless nights searching for that great idea? What is the "never-ending cycle of the creative process" in advertising?

In their book *Creative Strategy in Advertising*, Jewler and Drewniany say that an ad "needs to contain a persuasive message that convinces people to take action." To be creative, however, they suggest that an ad "must make a relevant connection with its audience and present a selling idea in an unexpected way."[2]

According to the DDB Needham agency, an ad is relevant, original (in an unexpected way in Jewler and Drewniany's definition), and has impact—which is referred to metaphorically as ROI.[3] These three characteristics help to explain what makes ideas creative in advertising. In DDB Needham's philosophy they also describe what makes an ad effective.

Advertising tries to deliver the right message to the right person at the right time. That's what DDB Needham means by relevance. In effective persuasion, ideas have to mean something to the target audience. No matter how much the creative people or the

relevance + originality + impact = ROI

The Nissan Xterra ad campaign is an effective advertisement because it has impact. The campaign equated extreme sports with an SUV designed for extreme driving conditions.

client or the account executive may like an idea, if it doesn't communicate the right message or the right product personality to the right audience, then it is not effective.

An advertising idea is considered creative when it is novel, fresh, unexpected, and unusual. That's what DDB Needham means by originality. Original means one of a kind. Any idea can seem creative to you if you have never thought of it before, but the essence of a creative idea is that no one else has thought of it either. In classes on creative thinking, a teacher will typically ask students to come up with ideas about, for example, what you can build with ten bricks. Some ideas—such as build a wall—will appear on many people's lists. Those are obvious and expected ideas; the original ideas are those that only one person thinks of.

In an industry that prides itself on creativity, *copycat advertising*—that is, using an idea that someone else has originated—is a concern. Advertising expert John Eighmy estimates that about 50 percent of the advertising in the United States falls into this category.[4] Despite claims of unoriginal ads, those in the ad business believe ads have gotten more, not less, creative. A recent study found that the overwhelming majority of top-level creative people believe that advertising is more creative now than when they entered the business.[5]

To be effective, the ideas must also have, as DDB Needham says, impact. Many advertisements just wash over the audience. An idea with impact helps people see themselves or the world in a new way, as the Xterra campaign demonstrated by equating extreme sports with a car designed for extreme driving conditions. A commercial with impact has the stopping power that comes from an intriguing idea, something you have never thought about before.

The Big Idea

So originality that is relevant creates impact. But how does originality work? Let's look first at the Big Idea. According to advertising legend James Webb Young, a founder of the Young & Rubicam agency, an idea is a new combination of thoughts. In his classic book on creative thinking, Young claims that "the ability to make new combinations is heightened by an

What the best dressed desks
will be wearing this season.

Elegance meets convenience with our Designer dispensers.

Post-it® Brand
Notes
www.Post-it.com

New ideas are important in advertising but they are valued in other areas such as product design, as this ad for 3M Post-it® Notes illustrates.

ability to see relationships."[6] An idea, then, is a thought that comes from placing two previously unrelated concepts together. The ad for Post-it Notes shows this process. The juxtaposition of fashion and desk accessories creates a new way of looking at things. It makes the familiar strange and the strange familiar.

Behind every effective advertisement is a **Big Idea**, a **creative concept** that implements the advertising strategy so that the message is attention-getting and memorable. In a campaign, which is a series of advertisements, a Big Idea serves as an umbrella theme. In the award-winning California Milk Board campaign "Got Milk?" the Big Idea is that people drink milk with certain foods such as cookies. If milk is unavailable to drink with those foods, they are—to say the least—frustrated.

In a study of award winners of the One Show, which is a premier creative award program in advertising, Lisa Duke found that these professionals who were winners define a creative concept in terms of four characteristics:[7]

1. Focus: The professionals used the terms "single-minded" and "main idea" to describe creative concepts that were narrowly focused.
2. Uniqueness: An approach that "no one has ever seen before" is another characteristic of the creative concept.
3. Generativeness: A good creative concept "has legs,"—that is, it can extend beyond the initial execution into related ideas to permit the development and evolution of a campaign.
4. Truth/Honesty: Good creative concepts find "some truth about the product," an authenticity and relevance to the product and the audience.

The Creative Leap

A Big Idea that expresses an original advertising thought involves a mind-shift. Instead of seeing the obvious, a creative idea looks at something in a different way, from a different angle, such as in an ad for British Airways that associates an airplane lounge with a green oasis in the middle of a desert. The "Practical Tips" box provides some advice for creating original ideas.

Finding the brilliant creative concept entails what advertising giant Otto Kleppner called "the creative leap,"[8]—a process of jumping from the strategy statement to an original idea that conveys the strategy in an interesting way. Since the creative leap means moving from the safety of a predictable strategy statement to an unusual idea that hasn't been tried before, this leap is often referred to as the creative risk: If it hasn't been tried before, then it's a gamble. All creative ideas in advertising involve this element of risk, and that's why copy-testing is used to test the idea before it runs, to try to determine if it works.

What stimulates a creative leap? A common technique advertisers use to force the leap is to make an unusual association. For example, Michelin's tire advertising is driven by the strategic idea that the tire is durable and dependable, language which would make a pretty boring ad. The creative idea, however, comes to life in the long-running campaign that shows a baby sitting in a tire. The visual is reinforced by the slogan, "Because so much is riding on your tires." The creative concept, then, "leaps" from the idea of a durable tire to the idea of protecting your family, particularly precious members like tiny children, by surrounding them with the dependability of a Michelin tire.

The idea that some moments, such as eating cupcakes and cookies, require a glass of milk is the creative concept, the Big Idea, behind the award-winning "Got Milk?" campaign.

Practical Tips #1

TIPS FOR CREATING ORIGINAL IDEAS

To create an original and expected idea, use the following techniques:

- **An unexpected twist.** An ad for Amazon.com used the headline, "460 books for Marxists. Including 33 on Groucho."
- **An unexpected association.** An ad for Compaq used a visual of a chained butterfly to illustrate the lack of freedom in competitors' computer workstations.
- **Catchy phrasing.** Isuzu used "The 205 Horsepower Primal Scream" for its Rodeo headline.
- **A play on words.** Under the headline "Happy Camper," an ad for cheese showed a picture of a packed sports utility vehicle with a huge wedge of cheese lashed to the rooftop.
- **Analogy and metaphor.** Harley-Davidson compared the legendary sound of its motorcycles to the taste of a thick, juicy steak.
- **Familiar and strange.** Put the familiar in an unexpected situation: UPS showed a tiny model of its familiar brown truck moving through a computer cord.

To prevent unoriginal ideas, avoid the following:

- **The common.** Avoid the obvious or the predictable, such as a picture of a Cadillac on Wall Street or in front of a mansion.
- **The look-alike.** Avoid copycat advertising that uses somebody else's great idea.
- **Clichés.** They may have been great ideas the first time they were used, but phrases such as "the road to success" or "the fast track" become trite when overused.
- **The tasteless.** In an attempt to be cute, a Subaru ad used the headline, "Put it where the sun don't shine."

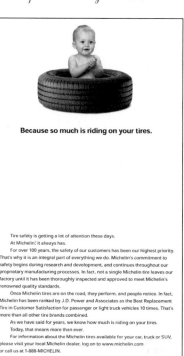

Because so much is riding on your tires.

Tire safety is getting a lot of attention these days.

At Michelin, it always has.

For over 100 years, the safety of our customers has been our highest priority. That's why it is an integral part of everything we do. Michelin's commitment to safety begins during research and development, and continues throughout our proprietary manufacturing processes. In fact, not a single Michelin tire leaves our factory until it has been thoroughly inspected and approved to meet Michelin's renowned quality standards.

Once Michelin tires are on the road, they perform, and people notice. In fact, Michelin has been ranked by J.D. Power and Associates as the Best Replacement Tire in Customer Satisfaction for passenger or light truck vehicles 10 times. That's more than all other tire brands combined.

As we have said for years, we know how much is riding on your tires.

Today, that means more than ever.

For information about the Michelin tires available for your car, truck or SUV, please visit your local Michelin dealer, log on to www.michelin.com or call us at 1-888-MICHELIN.

MICHELIN

Because so much is riding on your tires.

Michelin's dependability and durability surround a car's precious cargo.

Strategy and Creativity

To be creative, an idea must be both original (different, novel, unexpected) and strategic (right for the product and target). Cleverness is not enough. The Wrigley ad that attempts to promote gum as a substitute for smoking after the airlines instituted nonsmoking flights is an example of a creative idea that is also strategic. It offers a new use for the chewing gum—to help smokers who are flying on a nonsmoking flight.

There is a big difference between the strategic language used in the marketing plan and the language of the creative concept. The use of a street phrase like "whassup" to catch attention of beer drinkers drove a highly successful and EFFIE award–winning advertising campaign for Budweiser. It demonstrates the difference between the formality of strategy statement language and the clever phrase that becomes a cultural catchword. If the Budweiser advertising had relied on the strategy language, which was probably something like—"the beer wants to fuel additional momentum to counter a declining category and further improve young adult brand perception"—those ads would have bored everyone. The difference between the marketing statement and the creative concept—the smartmouth "whassup"—represents the creative leap, which is not merely a step away from marketing language, but miles away.

To come up with the Big Idea, you have to move beyond the safety of the strategy statement and leap into the creative unknown. Advertisers take a risk every time they come up with a new idea—maybe it won't make sense to others, maybe it won't relate to the product, maybe it will even turn people off to the product. Yet those are the risks they must face when they try to find new ideas.

CREATIVE THINKING

So how do you make the creative leap and get creative ideas? Creativity is a special form of problem solving and everyone is born with some talent in that area. In advertising, as in all

CARRY ON LUGGAGE.

WRIGLEY'S SPEARMINT CHEWING GUM

Wrigley's uses an analogy to create a mind-shift that causes readers to think of chewing gum as carry-on luggage for a nonsmoking flight.

The Harley-Davidson ad uses the taste of a steak as a metaphor for the throaty roar of a Harley engine.

areas of business, creativity is not limited to the writers and art directors. Media planners and market researchers are just as creative in searching for new ideas and innovative solutions.

A lot of what happens when you get an idea comes from just letting the mind wander to make unexpected associations and juxtapositions. For example, the Harley-Davidson ad uses the taste of a steak as a metaphor for the sound of a motorcycle. The most common techniques that creative thinkers use to stimulate new ideas are free association, divergent thinking, analogies and metaphors, and right-brain thinking. Let's look at these techniques.

- **Free Association.** Creates the juxtaposition of two seemingly unrelated thoughts. In free association you think of a word and then describe everything that comes into your mind when you imagine that word.
- **Divergent Thinking.** Differs from rational, linear thinking that we use to arrive at the "right" conclusion. Divergent thinking, which is the heart of creative thinking, uses exploration (playfulness) to search for all possible alternatives.[9]
- **Analogies and Metaphors.** Used to see new patterns or relationships. William J. J. Gordon, a researcher who founded the Synectics school of creative thinking, discovered that creative thinkers often expressed new ideas as analogies.[10]
- **Right-brain thinking.** Intuitive, nonverbal, and emotion-based thinking (in contrast to left-brain thinking, which is logical and controls speech and writing). A left-brain dominant person is presumed to be logical, orderly, and verbal. A right-brain dominant person tends to deal in expressive images, emotion, intuition, and complex, interrelated ideas that must be understood as a whole rather than as pieces.[11]

Another technique is *creative aerobics*. Creative aerobics is a thought-starter process that works well in advertising because it uses both the head and the heart, which we refer to in strategy development as rational and emotional appeals. Developed by Linda Conway Correll, a professor at Southeast Missouri State, it is a four-step, idea-generating process, which is explained here in terms of finding a creative idea for selling oranges:[12]

1. **Facts.** The first exercise is left brain and asks you to come up with a list of facts about a product (an orange has seeds, is juicy, has vitamin C).
2. **New names.** In the second exercise you create new "names" for the product (Florida, a vitamin supplement, a kiss of sunshine).
3. **Similarities.** The third exercise looks for similarities between dissimilar objects. (What are the similarities between the new names and the product—for instance, Florida sunshine and oranges both suggest warmth, freshness, sunshine, the fountain of youth.)

4. **New definitions.** The fourth exercise, a cousin of the pun, creates new definitions for product-related nouns. Peel (face peel, peel out), seed (seed money, bird seed), navel/naval (naval academy, contemplating one's navel), pulp (pulp fiction), C/see/si/sea (C the light). Headlines derived from those definitions might be: "Seed money" (the money to purchase oranges), "Contemplating one's navel" (looking at oranges), "Peel out" (when your grocer is out of oranges), "Navel intelligence" (information about an orange), "Pulp fiction" (a story about an orange), "C the light" (the orange is a low-calorie source of vitamin C). These new definitions stimulate the flowering of a new Big Idea.

Creative Roles

So who does this creative thinking? All agencies have copywriters and art directors who are responsible for developing the creative concept and crafting the execution of the advertising idea. They often work in teams, are sometimes hired and fired as a team, and may work together successfully for a number of years. Broadcast producers can also be part of the team for television commercials. The creative director manages the creative process and plays an important role in focusing the strategy of ads and making sure the creative concept is strategically on target.

Because advertising creativity is a product of teamwork, copywriters and art directors must develop teamwork skills,[13] and usually both generate concept, word, and picture ideas. Their writing or design specialties come into play in the execution of the idea. The Big Idea may come to mind as a visual, a phrase, or a thought that uses both visual and verbal expression. If it begins as a phrase, the next step is to try to visualize what the concept looks like; if it begins as an image, the next step is to develop words that express what the visual is saying.

The Creative Person

You probably know people who are just naturally zany, who come up with crazy, off-the-wall ideas. In terms of creativity, these people start off with a little advantage. But that's all it is. And it may be a disadvantage if they can't tame their craziness to fit into a business environment. Creative advertising people may be zany, weird, off-the-wall, and unconventional, but they can't be eccentric. They still must be very centered on creating effective advertising.

Research by the Center for Studies in Creativity and the Creative Education Foundation, both in Buffalo, New York, has found that most people can sharpen their skills and develop their creative potential. First, let's explore what makes a person creative (also see Table 11.1). Then let's see how people develop creative skills.

Although everyone has some problem-solving abilities, certain traits seem to be typical of creative problem solvers. Research indicates that creative people tend to be independent, assertive, self-sufficient, persistent, and self-disciplined, with a high tolerance for ambiguity. They are also risk takers with powerful egos that are internally driven. They don't care much about group standards and opinions and typically have inborn skepticism and strong curiosity. Creative problem solvers are alert, watchful, and observant, and reach conclusions through intuition rather than through logic. They also tend to have a good sense of humor and a mental playfulness that allows them to make novel associations.

Coming up with a great idea is also an emotional high. According to Derek Clark, a copywriter at Detroit's Campbell-Ewald agency, "Creative advertising at the national level has to be one of the biggest emotional rollercoasters in the business world. When it's bad, you feel like fleeing the country. When it's good, there's nothing better. I love it." This type of thinking is showcased in the "A Matter of Practice" box, in which an art director explains his approach to handling products that are sometimes thought to be boring.

The Ability to Visualize Most copywriters have a good visual imagination as well as excellent writing skills. Art directors are able to visualize, but they can also be quite verbal. The heart of the advertising concept team is "writers who doodle and designers who scribble."[14]

TABLE 11.1 Let's Get Personal: The Creative Personality

Leonardo DaVinci, Albert Einstein, and Georgia O'Keefe excelled in different fields, but all three qualify as geniuses.

Do you ever wonder whether you are creative? Does creativity have anything to do with your personality? Your personality is your own distinctive and consistent pattern of how you think, feel, and act.

A current view of creativity suggests that the area of personality most related to creativity is how open you are to new experiences. According to researchers McCrae and Costa,[15] how open you are to new experiences can be measured by survey questions that ask if you agree or disagree with the following statements:

1. "I enjoy working on 'mind-twister'-type puzzles."
2. "Once I find the right way to do something, I stick to it."
3. "As a child I rarely enjoyed games of make-believe."
4. "I enjoy concentrating on a fantasy or daydream and exploring all its possibilities, letting it grow and develop."

If you said "I agree" to 1 and 4, you're thinking like a creative person.

Source: Information provided by Sheri J. Broyles, University of North Texas.

Good copywriters paint pictures with words. They describe what something looks like, sounds like, smells like, and tastes like. They use words to transmit these sensory impressions. Most of the information we accumulate comes through sight, so the ability to manipulate visual images is crucial for good copywriters. In addition to seeing products, people, and scenes in the mind's eye, good copywriters can visualize a mental picture of the finished ad while it is still in the talking, or idea, state.

Openness to New Experiences As we said earlier, one characteristic that identifies creative people is that they are open to new experiences. Sheri Broyles, a professor at the University of North Texas, looked at creative directors in advertising to test that idea.[16] When given the Openness to Experience questionnaire, part of which is shown in Table 11.1, Broyles found that these creative directors were more open than most other people. A second study showed a similar finding with students in a creative advertising class. A comparison between the two studies showed that the advertising students scored higher than the test's established norms and the advertising professionals scored even higher than the students did.

Conceptual Thinking According to Broyles, it's easy to see how people who are open to experience might develop innovative advertisements and commercials because they are more imaginative. Such imagination led to the famous Nike commercial in which Michael Jordan and Larry Bird play an outlandish game of horse—bouncing the ball off ceilings, buildings, billboards, and places that were impossible. Over the course of a lifetime, open-

A MATTER OF PRACTICE
IT DOESN'T HAVE TO BE BORING

➤ Vacuum ovens. Anaerobic chambers. Incubator shakers. Who needs Nike when you can sell sexy products like these? The truth is, you're going to have a few clients with products that aren't as exciting as others. And chances are these products will be in the business-to-business category.

But why let the products appear boring in advertising? I've found with our client, Shel Lab, even though we are selling vacuum ovens, anaerobic chambers, and incubator shakers to biologists and chemists, there is still room for a little humor and good design.

I have to admit, when we first started the project I was not too excited. But after some account planning workshops and a tour of the manufacturing plant, I realized Shel Lab is actually very cool.

The company had a ton of "firsts" in its industry, and the tour revealed how enthusiastic Shel Lab is about its products—or rather, how enthusiastic people at Shel Lab are about their products. Both of those things were very energizing for me creatively.

Maybe too energizing. The first batch of work we produced was shot down; it was outside their comfort zone. We went back and forth a few times and finally they approved our ideas and my copy. For example, for the incubator shaker line we played with the idea of earth shaking. It wasn't pushed as far creatively as I would have liked, but for this category, it was "out there" stuff.

That's when I realized great work is relative. So in the case of Shel Lab, it became a matter of raising the creative bar in the category, rather than trying to raise the creative bar for all categories.

POINT TO PONDER

Are you a creative person? How would you handle rejection of an idea that you thought was creative, but the client disliked?

Source: Karl Schroeder, Copywriter, Coates, Kokes Agency, Portland, Oregon.

ness to experience may give you many more adventures from which to draw. Broyles concludes that those experiences would, in turn, give a novelist more characters to write about, a painter more scenes to paint, and the creative team more angles from which to tackle an advertising problem.

In taking a peek into the minds of those who hire new creative people, Kendrick, Slayden, and Broyles[17] found repeated verbatim comments from creative directors concerning the importance of strategic thinking and Big Ideas. "Emphasize concept," said one creative director. "Teach them to think first and execute later."

The Creative Process

People tend to think of a creative person as someone who sits around waiting for an idea to strike. But only in cartoons do light bulbs truly appear above our heads. In reality, most people who are good at thinking up new ideas will tell you that it is hard work. They read, study, analyze, test and retest, sweat, curse, and worry. Sometimes they give up. The unusual, unexpected, novel idea rarely comes easily—and that's as true in science and medicine as it is in advertising.

Steps and Stages The creative process usually is portrayed as a series of steps. English sociologist Graham Wallas is credited with identifying the steps in the creative process: preparation, incubation, illumination, and verification.[18] Alex Osborn, former head of the BBDO agency and founder of the Creative Education Foundation, suggests a more comprehensive process. His list of seven steps includes a creative process starting with orientation, then moving to preparation, analysis, ideation, incubation, synthesis, and finally ending with evaluation.[19] These various approaches to the creative process share a number of the key steps shown in Figure 11.1.

Many creative people admit that often their ideas just don't work and sometimes the idea they thought was wonderful does not seem so great a day or a week later. Part of evaluation is the personal go/no go decision, either by the creative team or the client. Craig Weatherup, president and CEO of PepsiCo, explained, "You must have a clear vision and have the nerve to

FIGURE 11.1   STAGES IN THE CREATIVE PROCESS

There are many ways to portray the stages in the creative process. Here we show what are generally the key stages.

pull the trigger." BBDO's president Phil Dusenberry says, "On Pepsi, the kill rate is high." He explains, "For every spot we go to the client with, we've probably killed nine other spots."[20] It's not enough to develop a great creative idea, the concept also has to be focused on strategy.

Brainstorming As part of the creative process, some agencies use a thinking technique known as, simply, **brainstorming.** In brainstorming a group of 6 to 10 people work together to come up with ideas. One person's ideas stimulate someone else's, and the combined power of the group associations stimulates far more ideas than any one person could think of alone. The secret to brainstorming is to remain positive and defer judgment. Negative thinking during a brainstorming session can destroy the informal atmosphere necessary to achieve a novel idea.

To force group creativity against a deadline, some agencies have special rooms and processes for brainstorming, with no distractions and interruptions (such as telephones and access to e-mail) and walls that can be covered with sheets of paper on which to write ideas. Some agencies rent a suite in a hotel and send the creative team there to get away and immerse themselves in the problem.

The brainstorming session can take on a life of its own. When the GSDM agency was defending its prized Southwest Airlines account, president Roy Spence ordered a 28-day "war room" death march that had staffers working around the clock, wearing Rambo-style camouflage, and piling all their trash inside the building to keep any outsiders from rummaging around for clues to their pitch.

CREATIVE STRATEGY AND EXECUTIONS

Creating an ad entails deciding first on the message strategy, translating the strategy into a creative concept, and then using that idea as the foundation for one or more executions. In its section on advertising, the *Encyclopedia of Creativity* points out that effective advertising creativity is measured not only by originality, but also by its strategic contributions.[21] Unlike fine art, which celebrates creativity for its own sake, the creators of advertising must merge creativity with advertising and marketing strategy. A message is designed, therefore, to meet both types of requirements—an idea summarized in the phrase "creative strategy."

As we've been telling you in this book, there are a number of award shows that recognize great creative work in advertising. Some of them focus primarily on the creative idea, such as the One Show or the Addy awards; others, however, also look at the advertisement's strategy and effectiveness. The EFFIE award show (EFFIE is short for "effectiveness"), sponsored by the American Marketing Association, is the primary strategy-focused award program, and the one from which we pull a number of winners featured in this book's cases.

People who create advertisements also make a distinction between creative strategy and creative executions. Creative strategy is what the advertisement says and execution is how it is said. This chapter is focused on creative strategy and the two chapters that follow will explore the writing and design dimensions of advertising execution.

What we want to do here is introduce the concepts of creative strategy and creative executions. We will make the basic distinction between emotional and rational strategies, and then we will explain in more detail the logic behind selling strategies.

Advertising award shows, such as the Addy's, celebrate with a banquet and exhibits that display the winning ads to the public.

Creative strategy identifies the general problem and suggests how it can be solved with a message. For example, when the Nissan Xterra was introduced, the TBWA/Chiat Day creative team knew that the car had to be differentiated to enter the highly competitive SUV market. To differentiate the model, the team built an image for Xterra as the car for the Xtreme situation.

In addition to solving a communication problem, there are other basic strategic decisions. To be considered "on strategy," advertisements also have to address the basic marketing and advertising strategies relating to product category, target audience, and product positioning.

Nissan positions the Xterra as the extreme SUV for extreme outings.

Creative Strategy

Creative strategy is the logic behind the message. It is driven by all the marketing and advertising objectives and strategic decisions that were discussed in Chapter 7. As the Xterra campaign demonstrates, creative, or message, strategy is, first of all, a reflection of the product category. Some kinds of products such as clothes, jewelry, and cosmetics are fashion items, and their advertising needs to make a fashion statement.

Some product categories are just naturally difficult to advertise, such as hemorrhoid treatments and feminine hygiene products, and technical products such as Shel Lab's incubator shaker (from the "A Matter of Practice" box). And so creatives must understand the ramifications of the product category, and do a lot of copy-testing.

Other product categories are a particular challenge because they are in competitive markets. Products used in the home (cleansers, light bulbs), for personal care (toothpaste, toilet paper, laxatives, cold remedies), or for sustenance (food of all kinds, including snacks and soft drinks) are in commodity markets where it is difficult to differentiate the products based on product features. In such cases, the creative strategy is designed to build a distinctive brand personality.

In Europe these products are described as *fast-moving consumer goods* (FMCG); in the United States they are called *packaged goods*. Advertising for these products can range from the basic problem solution (ring around the collar, toilet bowl, or sink) to fun (the Pepsi Generation and the Pillsbury Doughboy).

In addition to product category, the creative strategy is also driven by targeting strategies. For the creative person, targeting means being able to identify with the target audience. Creativity in advertising requires empathy and a keen awareness of the audience—how they think and feel, what they value, and what makes them take notice. This ability to identify with the target audience delivers consumer insights that often lead directly to the creative idea. Lisa Fortini-Campbell calls that "hitting the sweet spot," in her book on consumer insights.[22] That's also why account planners are so helpful for the creative team—they have insights into the consumer that lead to great creative strategies. An analysis of the winning ads in the annual *Communication Arts* award show found that agencies using account planners were more successful in winning awards than were other agencies.[23]

Other creative people put themselves in the audience's shoes. The creative people behind the "Got Milk?" campaign, copywriter Harry Cocciolo and art director Sean Ehringer of the Goodby, Silverstein agency, spent a week without milk to identify with their target audience.

Targeting young people (or older people, for that matter) is a particular problem for agencies because of the age difference between those who create ads and those who read them. For youth marketing, advertisers have to understand the sometimes twisted humor and cynicism of the youth market. An example of a successful campaign that spoke to this market is one for Genetic, a brand of high-end skateboarding shoes by the Airwalk company. Chris Hutchison (see "The Inside Story" in Chapter 17) and his creative team at Bulldog Drummond found that skateboarders are a difficult group to connect with, so, as he explains, "your brand has to stand for something strange, sick, or different." Bulldog Drummond's strategy was to use highly visible pro skaters as central figures in the campaigns, depicting them interacting with genetic shoes while undergoing a strange pseudo-medical procedure. Genetic has been an extremely successful brand, and is a great example of youth-oriented "engineered cool." As the genetic campaign showed, positioning, which is how a consumer sees a product relative to its competition, is as important as targeting.

Head and Heart Creative Strategies

In addition to communicating the product category and position to the target audience, effective advertising messages are designed to touch the head or the heart, or both. Remember the discussion in Chapter 6 on the three types of effects: learn and feel and how they connect with the do, or action decision. The learn and feel dimensions are sometimes referred to in message strategy as "hard and soft sell," or as "rational and emotional," equating with what we are calling here the head and heart factors. The decision about which approach to use in an advertising message is a key part of creative strategy.

	Head: Information (Hard Sell)	Heart: Emotion/Feelings (Soft Sell)
Hi	**The "Thinkers"** *Path:* Learn–Feel–Do *Products:* Insurance, cameras, contact lenses, TV *Message Strategy:* Use information, emotion, reasons, news announcements, facts and details, demonstrations	**The "Feelers"** *Path:* Feel–Learn–Do *Products:* Sports cars, eye glasses, perfume, wallpaper & paint *Message Strategy:* Use appeals, entertainment, imagery
Lo	**The "Doers"** *Path:* Do–Learn–Feel *Products:* Insect repellant, shampoo, razors *Message Strategy:* Use incentives such as price deals and coupons, sampling, exhibits, trade shows	**The "Reactors"** *Path:* Do–Feel–Learn *Products:* Fast food, fruit, beverages, women's magazines, snacks *Message Strategy:* Use reminder ads

(left axis label: **INVOLVEMENT**)

FIGURE 11.2

DECISION PATHS AND MESSAGE STRATEGIES
This chart creates four categories of consumer decision makers based on involvement strategies, on the one hand, and head and heart creative strategies on the other hand. This chart sets up four different sets of message strategies and shows some sample products associated with them. Adapted from: Richard A. Vaughn, "How Advertising Works: A Planning Model," *Journal of Advertising Research* 20(5) (October 1980): 27–33.

But deciding between head and heart strategies is just the first step in developing a message. Figure 11.2 illustrates how these two factors relate to involvement and different product categories, as well as the different decision paths discussed in Chapter 6. The Foote, Cone & Belding agency has been a leader in creating strategies that combine logic and emotion with an understanding that some decisions may involve a lot of thought (high involvement), while others are made with little or no thought or even on impulse.[24] Different kinds of messages emerge from an analysis of thinking and feeling for low- and high-involvement products. Figure 11.2 is particularly useful in understanding how these factors relate to each other and how they drive creative strategy. So let's talk a little more about these two basic creative strategies and their objectives.

A **hard sell** is an informational message that is designed to touch the mind and create a response based on logic. The assumption is that the target audience wants information and will make a rational product decision. The approach emphasizes tangible product features and benefits.

A **soft sell** uses emotional appeals or images to create a response based on attitudes, moods, dreams, and feelings. The assumption with soft-sell strategies is that the target audience has little interest in undertaking an information search and will respond more favorably to a message that touches their emotions. A soft sell can be used for hard products. NAPA auto parts ran an emotional ad that showed a dog sitting at a railroad crossing, forcing a truck to brake hard to avoid hitting him as a train bears down on the scene. The slogan puts the heart-stopping visual story into perspective: "NAPA because there are no unimportant parts."

Lectures and Dramas Most advertising messages use a combination of two basic literary techniques to reach the head or the heart of the consumer: *lectures and dramas.*[25] A lecture is a serious, structured instruction given verbally. Lectures are a form of direct address. The speaker presents evidence (broadly speaking) and uses a technique such as an argument to persuade the audience. Assuming they aren't dull, the advantages of lectures are many. They are (relatively speaking) not expensive to produce and are compact and efficient: A lecture can deliver a dozen selling points in seconds, get right to the point, and make the point explicitly.

Drama, however, relies on the viewer to make inferences. Through dramas, advertisers tell stories about their products; the characters speak to each other, not to the audience. Like fairy tales, movies, novels, parables, and myths, advertising dramas are essentially stories about how the world works. Viewers learn from these commercial dramas by inferring lessons from them and by applying those lessons to their everyday lives. When a drama rings true, viewers join in, draw conclusions from it, and apply those conclusions to their lives.

An example of a drama as part of creative strategy comes from Iceland where advertiser Ingvi Logason had a client, Nói-Síríus. After 10 years of successful advertising, Nói-Síríus found that its brand of chocolate Easter eggs had saturated the Icelandic market (it owned 73 percent of it). Logason's team used a head and heart strategy to expand the market by telling parents and grandparents that kids are not satisfied with

Enlarging the market for chocolate Easter eggs made for happy customers and clients. This commercial told parents through drama that once kids have one, they want more and more.

just one chocolate Easter egg—they crave more. Their heart-warming commercial led to a happy client whose sales volume increased by 5 percent for three years running.

Storytelling is the strategy of the Goodby Silverstein agency, which is known for its famous "Got Milk?" and Budweiser lizards campaigns. Co-founder Jeff Goodby explains, "We have the conviction that we're a storytelling place."[26] An example from the high-tech industry is the campaign for Hewlett-Packard with the "HP invent" tagline that told the story of HP's heritage as innovators in engineering.

Transmission and Ritual   There are other techniques advertisers use to formulate strategies. Professor Ron Taylor of the University of Tennessee has developed a model that divides strategies into *transmission* view, which is similar to the more rational "head" strategies, and the *ritual* view, which is similar to the more feeling-based "heart" strategies.[27] He then divides each view into three segments based on various authors' attempts to categorize message strategies: Rational, Acute Need, and Routine on the Transmission side; and Ego, Social, and Sensory on the Ritual side. Finally, he identifies the appropriate message objective for each segment relative to the most typical product categories. Figure 11.3 adapts his model to our creative strategy discussion.

Selling Premises

The sales message, or **selling premise**, states the logic behind the sales offer. A premise is a proposition on which an argument is based or a conclusion is drawn.

A selling premise is either product- or prospect-centered. A product-centered strategy focuses on the product and its features or attributes. A **claim**, for example, is a statement about how the product will perform. Torture tests, comparisons, and before-and-after demonstrations are used to prove the truth of a claim.

Prospect-centered (or consumer-focused) strategies stress the needs and wants of consumers and translate the product's features into benefits that consumers can gain by using the product. The message focuses on the reward to the customer who uses the product.

A rational, prospect-centered selling premise is a **benefit**, which identifies what the product can do for the consumer. Types of benefit statements include **promises** (something that will happen if you use the product) and **reasons why** (statements on why you should use the product). A **unique selling proposition (USP)** is a complex type of benefit strategy, one that identifies something unique about a product that is also important to the consumer. Here is a summary of these rational selling premises.

- **Benefit Strategy.** The promotion emphasizes what the product can do for the user by translating the product feature or attribute into something that benefits the consumer. For example, a GM electric car ad focuses on the product feature (the car doesn't use gas) and translates it into a benefit: lack of noise (no pistons, valves, exhaust).
- **Promise.** A benefit statement looks to the future and predicts that something good will happen if you use the product. For example, Dial soap has promised for decades that if you use Dial, you will feel more confident.
- **Reason Why.** A type of a benefit statement that gives you the reason you should buy something, although the reason sometimes is implied or assumed. The word "because" is the key to a reason-why statement. For example, an Amtrak ad tells you that travel on Amtrak is more comfortable than on a plane because Amtrak is a more civilized, less dehumanizing way to travel.
- **Unique Selling Proposition (USP).** A benefit statement that is both unique to the product and important to the user. The USP is a promise that consumers will get this unique benefit by using this product only. For example, an ad for a camera states, "this camera is the only one that lets you zoom in and out automatically to follow the action."

Emotional appeals can also be seen as prospect-centered strategies in that they highlight the psychological attraction of the product to the target audience through fear, love, pride, status, appetite, sex, guilt, safety, responsibility, nostalgia, convenience, and economy. Entertainment uses drama, humor, and song-and-dance messages to reward the audience with an engaging message.

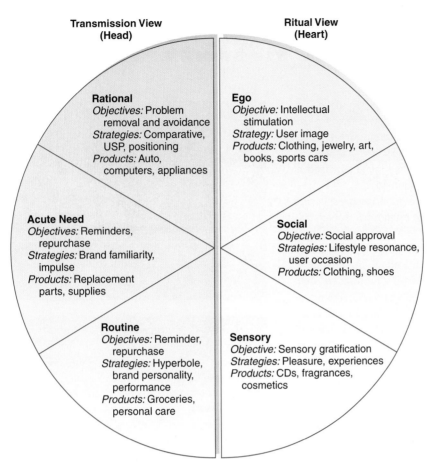

FIGURE 11.3

**THE SIX-SEGMENT STRATEGY
WHEEL**
The wheel divides message strategy
into two general views—the
Transmission view and the Ritual
view. The Transmission view aligns
with head strategies; the Ritual view
aligns with heart strategies.
Source: Adapted from Ronald Taylor,
"A Six-Segment Message Strategy
Wheel," *Journal of Advertising
Research* (November–December
1999): 7–17.

The "A Matter of Principle" box explains the development of a selling premise for the EFFIE award–winning Maytag refrigerator campaign. Maytag's objective was to add a new dimension to the Maytag dependability message conveyed for years through the "The Lonely Repairman" brand character. However, in the Maytag refrigerator campaign, the advertising team knew that gaining consumer attention for a refrigerator ad was a problem, and they also had the problem of explaining the dual cooling feature, which let consumers vary the temperature in different parts of the freezer section. Their "Dual Cool" campaign idea used offbeat presentations to overcome these problems.

An important part of a selling premise is the proof given for the claim or benefit statement. The proof, or substantiation needed to make a claim believable, is called **support**. In some cases this calls for research findings. Most selling premises demand facts, proof, or explanations to support the sales message. To illustrate, suppose Hubba Bubba wanted to support a unique selling proposition that its gum is the only chewing gum that lets you blow great big bubbles that won't stick to your face. The support for that USP could be that Hubba Bubba uses an exclusive nonstick formula.

Structural Analysis

The Leo Burnett agency has developed an approach for analyzing the logic of the creative strategy design. Advertisers use it to keep the message strategy and creative concept working together, as well as the head and the heart appeals. This method, called **structural analysis**, relies on these three steps:

1. Evaluate the power of the narrative or story line (heart).
2. Evaluate the strength of the product claim (head).
3. Consider how well the two aspects are integrated—that is, how the story line brings the claim to life.

A MATTER OF PRINCIPLE
Keeping Your Cool with Dual Cool

➤ Maytag's lonely repairman has made Maytag the leader of dependability in appliances. Unfortunately, customers see no difference in brands in the refrigerator market, so Maytag's dependability image didn't help it beat out the market leader—Sears's Kenmore. Consumers generally believe refrigerators are all just cold closets for food.

John Thomas, Maytag director of advertising, explained this campaign: "We're really trying to extend the dependability message into more product performance."

Despite the many players in the highly competitive refrigerator marketplace, no one manufacturer, including Maytag or Kenmore, had a unique selling proposition. That lack of differentiation creates a problem for refrigerator manufacturers because the refrigerator is the largest and most expensive household appliance category with low turnover. If a refrigerator sale is lost to a competitor, that consumer won't be in the market again for another 15 years.

Maytag's solution: a heavy investment in product development that led to a new two-thermostat design, which lets the consumer vary the temperature in different parts of the freezer. The advertising objective was to differentiate Maytag refrigerators in a category where there had been no perceived differences and create a perception of brand superiority. That was the challenge for Maytag's agency, Chicago-based Leo Burnett, who tackled it in the award-winning "Keep Your Cool" campaign.

The "Keep Your Cool" ads introduced an element of humor to grab attention. In one offbeat spot called "I scream," a mother is shown trying to remove ice cream from a carton taken out of a too-cold freezer. The ice cream with a frozen spoon stuck in it, goes flying around the house and through a window, landing on a plate next to a bewildered-looking toddler. Leo Burnett's associate creative director, Susan Thurber Jones explained that her team had to "create some new excitement for the brand."

Maytag's "I scream" commercial demonstrates in a humorous way what happens when a refrigerator keeps ice cream too cold.

POINT TO PONDER

Explain how Maytag used a creative idea to gain attention for a selling point.

Source: Adapted from the EFFIEs brief provided by Maytag and the Leo Burnett agency.

Burnett creative teams check to see whether the narrative level is so high that it overpowers the claim or whether the claim is strong but there is no memorable story. Ideally, these two elements will be so seamless that it is hard to tell whether the impact occurs because of the power of the story or the strength of the claim. Such an analysis keeps the rational and emotional sides of an advertisement working together.

THE CREATIVE BRIEF

The creative strategy and the key execution details are spelled out in a document called a **creative brief** (also called creative platform, worksheet, or blueprint). The brief is the document prepared by the account manager or the account planner to summarize the basic marketing and advertising strategy. It gives direction to the creative team as they search for a creative concept. The account manager or account planner prepares the brief. As explained in Chapter 5, account planners are particularly useful because of the consumer

---

TABLE 11.2   Creative Strategy Briefs

Young & Rubicam
Key Fact (the key piece of information
  that will be used in the campaign—i.e.,
  a product point of difference, a consumer
  need, etc.)
Consumer Problem the advertising
  will solve
Advertising Objective
Creative Strategy
  Prospect Definition
  Competition
  Consumer Benefit
  Reason Why

Ogilvy & Mather
Product
Key Issue/Problem
The Promise
The Support
Our Competition
Target Consumer: Who are we talking to?
Desired Behavior: What we expect?
Target's Net Impression
Tone and Manner

Leo Burnett
Convince: Target audience—current belief
  re: brand/category
That: Desired belief (benefit)
Because: Focus of sale or proposition
  (key drama)
Support: Reasons why

DDB Needham
Marketing Objective
Advertising Objective
Position
Target
Key Insight
Reward and Support
Execution: Personality or Tone

Tracy-Locke
Target Audience
User Benefits
Reason Why
Brand Character
Focus of Sale
Tone

The Phelps Group
Client/Product
Target: Demographics & Psychographics
Positioning *(In the mind of our client)*
Objectives *(What we want the prospect to do)*
Ad Strategy *(What we are saying)*
Tactical Strategy *(Where/How are we saying it)*
Support

---

insights they bring to the strategy. Planners are the bridge between account service and the client, consumers, and the creative team.[28]

The formats of these briefs vary, but most combine the basic advertising strategy decisions (the problem to be solved, the objectives, the target market, and the positioning strategy) with the critical elements of the message strategy (the selling premise, the creative strategy, and details of the ad's execution). The briefs typically are in outline form, to be filled in by account planners and given to the creative team, as you can see from the examples in Table 11.2. These outlines summarize the information that is contained in the brief.

An example of a completed creative brief comes from an EFFIE-winning campaign designed to sell season tickets for a university football team that rarely wins and whose fans say the team "has little appeal to anyone born after the Truman administration."

A little history: The Minnesota Golden Gophers have not played in the Rose Bowl for 35 years. And the team had six consecutive losing seasons in the 1990s. One season ticket holder complained, "When you look around the stands all you see is a bunch of 50-year-olds and a couple of sections of students. It is like we have lost an entire generation of Gopher football fans." The assistant athletic director admitted that fans had to be 50 years old to have seen a very good Gopher football team.

Even though the Golden Gophers play in the Metrodome, an off-campus, indoor stadium, over the years the stadium has rarely been filled because few fans come to home games. And, during the six losing seasons old traditions linked to better days in Gopher football began to die as losses overshadowed the wins. Minnesota fans who had never experienced Gopher football as a tradition-rich event had no reason to invest in season tickets. Local sportswriter Jim Caple wrote, "There's only one marketing method that will recover the lost generation of Gopher football fans. It's called winning."

It sounds like a pretty hopeless challenge, doesn't it? But the Minneapolis-based Fallon McElligott advertising agency hoped to prove Jim Caple wrong by attracting people to Gopher games even if the team wasn't winning. The "Gopher Talk" creative brief is

---

Gopher Football Creative Brief

Problem To Be Solved?

The Gophers are coming off six consecutive losing seasons. They play in the Metrodome and struggle to draw large groups of students. During the losing seasons, old traditions linked to Gopher Football as a tradition-rich event began to die.

Who Are We Talking To?

Primary Target: *Students*

Many of these students have attended Gopher Athletics and probably even a football game, but for some, interest is still only latent. They have a positive disposition and respect tradition, but don't necessarily see anything attracting them to Gopher football games.

Secondary Target: *Recent Alumni and the Lost Generation of Gopher Fans*

These groups represent the people who have become disillusioned with Gopher football. "The team doesn't win and the games aren't fun anymore." These fans want to support the team, but are waiting for something to change their perceptions.

What We Expect the Advertising to Accomplish?

Compel students to rediscover Gopher Football by demonstrating that everything about Gopher Football (the games, the pregame events, the parties) is an exciting, entertaining and unpredictable source of fun.

Key Idea

On the field or off the field, with Gopher Football, *anything can happen!*

Why Should They Believe This?

- U of M will sponsor events and activities that make the game a three-day event (on-campus treasure hunts, Maroon & Gold nights at local bars, band and Alumni band events, pre-game parties, tailgating parties on Metrodome Plaza).
- With a new coach, the Gophers are committed and could start winning.
- Students and season ticket purchases are the highest since Lou Holtz was coach.

Brand Personality?

Enthusiastic. Unpredictable. Slightly Irreverent.

Executional Considerations

The administration is committed to Coach Mason and his vision for the team. Fortunately, Coach Mason understands that students and their traditions help make games more exciting. The advertising needs to be edgy enough to appeal to students, but cannot be offensive to the general public. "Anything Can Happen" should not be used as a tagline.

FIGURE 11.4   GOPHER FOOTBALL CREATIVE BRIEF

Creative strategy and key execution details are spelled out in a document called the creative brief. Here we see the brief for the Minnesota Golden Gophers football team.

To increase attendance at Minnesota Gopher football games, Fallon-McElligott's "Big Idea" was to create the Marge and Barb characters—two football crazed grandmothers.

shown in Figure 11.4 and explains the strategy behind this EFFIE award–winning campaign. The Big Idea focused on two smart-mouth, football-crazed grandmothers named Marge and Barb who parodied the blue-hair stereotype of the typical Gopher fan.

Message Approaches

Advertisers use a number of common formats sometimes called "formulas," for advertising messages. These formulas are fairly standard ways to present advertising messages, such as straightforward information or problem solution. The creative brief uses them as a way to give direction to the creative team. The formulas also help creatives communicate in a general way the advertisement's approach. It gives them a sense of what the account planner sees as an appropriate way to communicate the message and it becomes a springboard to the creative concept.

In a way these formats are formulaic. Common formats include straightforward messages, demonstrations, comparisons, problem solution, slice of life, spokesperson, and teaser, all of which we summarize here.

- **Straightforward.** A factual or informational message conveys information without any gimmicks, emotions, or special effects. For example, in an ad for www.women.com, the Web site advertises that "It's where today's educated, affluent women are finding in-depth coverage on issues they care about" and that more than two million women visit each month, "the highest composition of professional/managerial women of any network."
- **Demonstration.** Straightforward in tone, the demonstration focuses on how to use the product or what it can do for you. For example, an ad for Kellogg's Special K and Smart Start uses cereal bowls to demonstrate how a daily regimen of healthy cereal would help a dieter lose six pounds.

Kellogg's uses 21 cereal bowls to demonstrate the amount of Special K and Smart Start it would take to help a person lose six pounds in two weeks.

- **Comparison.** A comparison contrasts two or more products and finds that the advertiser's brand is superior. The comparison can be direct, with competitors mentioned, or indirect, with just a reference to "other leading brands." In comparison, as in demonstration, seeing is believing, so conviction is the objective. When people see two products being compared, they are more likely to believe that one is better than the other.
- **Problem Solution/Problem Avoidance.** In a problem solution format, also known as "product-as-hero," the message begins with a problem and the product is the solution. A variation is the problem avoidance message format, in which the product helps avoid a problem. A form of threat appeal, problem avoidance is often used to advertise insurance and personal care products.
- **Slice of Life.** This format is an elaborate version of a problem solution staged in the form of a drama in which "typical people" talk about a common problem and resolve it.
- **Spokespeople/Endorsers.** In this format, the ad uses celebrities we admire, created characters (the Energizer Bunny), experts we respect, or someone "just like us" whose advice we might seek out to speak on behalf of the product to build credibility.
- **Teasers.** Teasers are mystery ads that don't identify the product or don't deliver enough information to make sense.[29] These are often used to launch a new product. The ads run for a while without the product identification and then when curiosity is sufficiently aroused, usually at the point when the product is officially launched, a concluding ad runs with the product identification. Teasers create curiosity and appeal, especially to the anti-hard-sell attitudes of young people.

Message Execution

They are many ways to execute any ad. An **execution** is the form in which the ad's message is presented. Creative teams will spend hours comparing and testing various approaches to arrive at the one version they feel best delivers on the strategy. The execution details are the specifics about how the message will look, read, and sound in its finished form. Although general decisions about how the creative message is to be executed are suggested in a creative brief, as you can see in Table 11.2, the brief also contains entries for such things as tone and attitude, as well as the critical production decisions that make it a distinctive message in its medium—television, radio, newspapers, magazines, and so forth. (We will discuss the production of ads in more detail in the chapters that follow.) These decisions are what make one execution of an ad concept different from another.

Consider how GM used two different executions to create radically different images for two trucks that are built on essentially the same body. The different executions are what communicate the different positions for the two trucks. For the Chevrolet Silverado, GM's "macho" campaign is full of rugged cowboys and steelworkers. For the Pontiac-GMC Sierra truck, a "snob appeal" campaign targets a fussy group of white-collar types. Those ads feature shipyards and hydroelectric dams and the clean-cut men (and women) who run them. Even though both trucks are built on the same platform, the two campaigns target their market segments in ways as different as night and day.[30]

Because ad copy is written as if it were a conversation, it can also be described in terms of tone of voice. Most ads are written as if an anonymous announcer were speaking. Even with anonymity, however, the tone of voice may be identifiable. Some ads are angry, some are pushy, some are friendly. Message tone, like your tone of voice when you speak to someone, reflects the emotion or attitude behind the ad.

Recently, attitude has become a synonym for a style of advertising that is in-your-face, outrageous, or even abrasive. Although most of the 1980s and early 1990s advertising was fairly serious, in the 1990s, attitude began creeping into advertising as a way to reach a younger generation. Finding the right balance is difficult. An ad for Rib Ticklers barbecue sauce has a cynical attitude that is sure to offend animal rights activists and vegetarians. At the same time it speaks to those in the younger generation who are cynical. With a children's choir singing in the background, the commercial begins with an ode to the cow, the chicken, and the lamb. Then a barbecue grill appears silhouetted against a brilliant blue sky and the announcer says, "Let's eat them."

Advertisers use humor as a creative strategy because it is attention-getting and they hope that people will transfer the warm feelings they have as they are being entertained to the product. Humor is hard to handle—some people will love it but others hate it. For a humorous ad to be effective, the selling premise must reinforce the point of the humor. Most advertising experts agree that humor should never be used to poke fun at the product or its users.

We've talked about creative strategy and how it is developed, both in terms of common types of strategies and the process and planning document creative teams use to express their ideas. Now let's consider the types of effects advertising creates and the message strategies that deliver on these objectives.

EFFECTIVE CREATIVITY

Creative people sometimes are more interested in winning awards than in achieving sales objectives. The legendary Bill Bernbach reminds us that effective advertising makes the product—not the author—shine:

> Merely to let your imagination run riot, to dream unrelated dreams, to indulge in graphic acrobatics and verbal gymnastics is not being creative. The creative person has harnessed his imagintion. He has disciplined it so that every thought, every idea, every word he puts down, every line he draws, every light and shadow in every photograph makes more vivid, more believable, more persuasive the product advantage.[31]

As "The Inside Story" explains, the creative idea has to be "on strategy" to be effective. Advertisers must evaluate advertising before they can consider it effective. The most common evaluation approach is to test the ad against its objectives. In Chapters 6 and 7 we described these objectives in terms of the effects the advertising was supposed to achieve. So to analyze effectiveness, we return to these basic categories of effects and the objectives that are tied to them to determine if the creative strategy was effective.

Let's review the four main categories of effects from Chapter 6: perception, learning, persuasion, and behavior. Now we will look at them in terms of message design—how to

THE INSIDE STORY
THE IDEA IS ONLY HALF THE BATTLE

Adam Lowrey   Copywriter,
Rubin Poestaer, Los Angeles

I left school with a diploma and the notion that once I found a job I would spend the next 30 or so years coming up with good ads. That's it. I would sit around thinking of clever visuals and witty headlines, and everything else would just sort of take care of itself.

Not so. I soon found myself saying things like, "Yeah, I know it's not on strategy, but it's pretty funny," and, "What do you mean the client just didn't like it? Don't they have to give us a reason why they didn't like it?" In short, the real world was full of variables I had never anticipated.

My professors had done a fine job of equipping me with the essential skills, but I suppose meeting for an hour and a half every Tuesday and Thursday just wasn't enough time to completely prepare me for the onslaught of advertising.

To produce an ad, my art director and I have to please a lot of people. A creative must learn not only how to create an engaging ad but also how to shepherd that ad through everyone at the agency and everyone associated with the client.

But don't get me wrong. Doing smart, funny, and generally good work is still what it's all about. Just keep in mind that thinking of an idea is only half the battle as well as only half of your job.

Born, bred, and educated in Colorado, I moved to Los Angeles and started working at Rubin three years ago, and have been working late every night since.

Nominated by Professor Brett Robbs, University of Colorado.

do effective advertising. Table 11.3 summarizes some basic strategies. This section will discuss ways to design advertisements that will create these effects.

Ads That Drive Perception

To be effective, advertisements need to get exposure through the media buy. The message, however, needs to get attention and build awareness. Then it needs to get consumers' interest, which it tries to do by being relevant. Then advertisers hope consumers will remember the message. Here are some suggestions on how to do that.

Attention and Awareness Getting consumers' attention requires some kind of stopping power. Ads that stop the scanning are usually high in intrusiveness and originality. That means they sometimes have to do something with the message that demands attention. Intrusiveness is particularly important for products that have a small "share of mind"—those that are not very well known or not very involving or interesting, such as toilet paper, canned vegetables, or motor oil. In many cases there is little difference between competing brands, so the product interest is created solely by the advertising message.

What can you do to create this kind of impact? Many intrusive ads use loud, bold effects to attract viewer attention—they work by shouting. Others use captivating ideas or mesmerizing visuals. In print ads, for instance, research indicates that contrast can attract viewer attention. If every other ad in the medium is big and bold, then try one that is small, quiet, and simple; use a lot of white space. If everything else is tiny and gray (like type), then be big and bold or use color. If everything else is colorful, then use black-and-white.

Creative advertising is interesting because it presents a unique or novel thought. The function of originality is to capture attention. People will notice something that is new, novel, or surprising. Creative advertising breaks through the old patterns of seeing and saying things without being irrelevant or bizarre. The unexpectedness of the new idea creates stopping power.

Advertising agencies go to great lengths to create original advertising. The Young & Rubicam (Y&R) agency pushes its creative people to take more risks to make their ads more distinctive. Such unexpected approaches to mundane products are being used successfully by Y&R to sell things such as toothpaste, coffee, and ice cream. To encourage this kind of

TABLE 11.3	**Creative Strategies**	
Creative Strategy	**Description**	**Uses**
Preemptive	Uses a common attribute or benefit but gets there first; forces competition into me-too positions.	Used in categories with little differentiation or in new product categories.
Unique selling proposition	Uses a distinct difference in attributes that creates a meaningful consumer benefit.	Appropriate in categories with high levels of technological improvement.
Brand image	Uses a claim of superiority or distinction based on extrinsic factors such as psychological differences in the minds of consumers.	Used with homogeneous, low-technology goods with little physical differentiation.
Positioning	Establishes a place in the consumer's mind relative to the competition.	Suited to new entries or small brands that want to challenge the market leaders.
Resonance	Uses situations, lifestyles, and emotions that the target audience can identify with.	Used with highly competitive, nondifferentiated product categories.
Anomalous/affective	Uses an emotional, sometimes even an ambiguous message to break through indifference and charge the product's perception.	Used where competitors are playing it straight.

Source: Adapted from Charles Frazer, "Creative Strategy: A Management Perspective," *Journal of Advertising,* vol. 12: 4 (1983): 36–41.

freewheeling thinking, Y&R set up a program called the Risk Lab that allows copywriters and art directors to have their ideas tested informally by researchers in the early stages of concept development. The director of creative research, Stephanie Kugelman, took the title "Dr. Risk" and moved to the creative floors to work closely with the creative people.

Interest Advertisers trying to develop a message that stimulates interest will speak to the personal interests of their target audience and do something to elicit curiosity. Ads that open with questions or dubious statements are designed to build interest and create curiosity. Teasers also work. Buick used a teaser strategy to announce the new Buick Regal Web site. Getting attention, then, is the stopping power of an advertisement. Keeping attention is the pulling power of an ad: It keeps pulling the reader or viewer through to the end of the message.

Advertisers try to make consumers curious about their products. Whenever you are confronted with something new, there is a period of curiosity, usually accompanied by doubt or some kind of questioning. New information is often greeted by phrases such as "Can you believe it?" This confrontation of curiosity with doubt means you have entered the interested state. You are interested because the message might be personally relevant. Teasers, like the ad for a car's Web site, are also good at building interest.

To maintain interest, advertisers must consider the pulling power of their message. The sequencing of the ad affects its pulling power: Does the copy pull the reader or viewer through to the end? How does the message develop? For example, if we start with a ques-

This teaser ad is for a car's Web site. Its deliberate ambiguity is intended to excite curiosity about the site.

tion, then readers tend to continue through the ad to find the answer. Storytelling is another good technique for holding the audience. Most people want to know how a story ends. Suspense, drama, and narrative are good tools for maintaining interest.

Memorability Advertisers can do several things to ensure the memorability of their messages. One technique is repetition. Psychologists maintain that people need to hear or see something a minimum of three times before it crosses the threshold of perception and enters into memory. Jingles are valuable memorability devices because the music allows the advertiser to repeat a phrase or product name without boring the audience.

The Maytag repairman holds an ice cream cone. This serves as a dominant visual that conveys the essence of the message, which can be remembered easily by the target audience.

Clever phrases are useful not only because they catch attention, but also because they can be repeated to intensify memorability. Advertisements use slogans for brands and campaigns (a series of ads run under an umbrella theme). An example of a slogan is "Get Met. It Pays" (Met Life), or Nike's previous slogan, "Just Do It."

Taglines are used at the end of an ad to summarize the point of the ad's message in a highly memorable way, such as "Nothing outlasts the Energizer. It keeps going and going and going." When a tagline is used consistently on all marketing messages, it becomes a slogan. Both slogans and taglines are written to be highly memorable, often using mnemonic devices (techniques for improving memory) such as rhyme, rhythmic beats, and repeating sounds.

In addition to verbal memory devices, many print and interactive ads and most television commercials feature a key visual. This visual is a vivid image that the advertiser hopes will linger in the viewer's mind. Because television is mainly a visual medium, an effective commercial relies on some dominant scene or action that conveys the essence of the message and can be remembered easily, as in the image of the Maytag repairman with an ice cream cone, from the "Dual Cool" campaign discussed earlier in the "A Matter of Practice" box.

Memorability also depends on the ad's structure. The beginning of an advertising message is the most important part for attracting attention and the end or closing of a message is the most important part for memorability. To help consumers to remember the product name, an advertiser will repeat it at the end of the commercial. Most print ads end with a logo (a distinctive mark that identifies the product or company) or a signature (the name of the company or brand, written in a distinctive type style). Television commercials often conclude with a memorable tagline and superimpose the product name on the last visual, accompanied by the announcer repeating the brand name.

Ads That Deliver Learning

Now let's look at effective creative strategies to get consumers to learn about products. Companies often use news announcements to launch new products, to tout reformulated products, or even let consumers know about new uses for products. The news element, which is usually delivered by publicity stories, is information-focused. An example is the ad for American Airlines that announces its new seating in coach and its promise of more room.

When designing an advertising message for which understanding is an objective, advertisers must present the facts in a way that makes it easy for people to assimilate the information. One technique is to define terms, particularly technical terms, that most people might not understand. Also, think about explaining concepts, ideas, steps, and procedures, which are important pieces of information that help someone better understand a product and how it works. With steps and procedures, it's sometimes useful to provide a chart.

In terms of explaining something, television ads will often use a demonstration. Demonstrations not only add believability; they also teach how to do something or how something works. Companies will also use product comparisons to highlight differences between their products and competing products. Pepsi made major inroads into Coca-Cola's market some years back by using and promoting taste tests in which more people said they preferred the taste of Pepsi over Coca-Cola.

Clarity is also important in creating effective advertising. Ads that don't work (for example, their explanations are unclear or it's hard to follow the logic of the selling premise) are ineffective because they contribute to consumer confusion. An example is the battle between Nike and Oakley Sunglasses. In retaliation against Nike for going into the sunglasses business, Oakley introduced a shoe line in the late 1990s. Soon afterward, an ad war ensued between Nike and Oakley, often leaving the consumer confused about which brand was which.

To creatively communicate its new seating in coach, American Airlines used a visual of the brain and how each hemisphere interpreted the increased room.

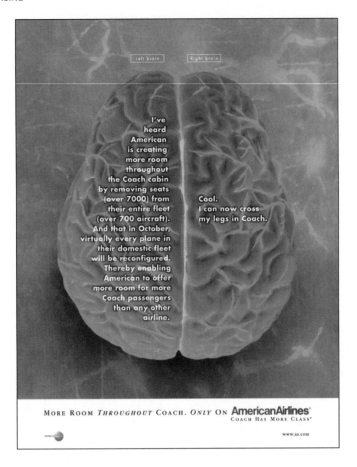

Ads That Are Persuasive

Advertisers also have to use creativity effectively when persuading consumers to consider their products. Persuasion in advertising rests on the psychological appeal of the product to the consumer. An appeal is something that makes the product particularly attractive or interesting, such as security, esteem, fear, sex, and sensory pleasure. Appeals generally pinpoint the anticipated response of the audience to the product and the message.

For example, if the price is emphasized in the ad, then the appeal is value, economy, or savings. If the product saves time or effort, then the appeal is convenience. A message that focuses on a mother or father making something for a child, such as cookies or a rocking chair, might appeal to family love and concern. Advertisers use a status appeal to establish something as a high-quality, expensive product. Appetite appeal using mouth-watering visuals is used in food advertising.

One aim of persuasive advertising is to touch an emotional button—to create positive perceptions of a product or brand. One strategy in this area is the use of entertainment. Advertisers have found that commercials that look like TV shows and provide high entertainment value seem to be better liked by audiences than ads with high levels of information. One format that has become popular is short films called **advertainments** for corporate clients. BMW, Diet Coke, Ford, and Volkswagen are using these advertainments for trade shows and dealer meetings.[32]

Using entertainment to sell is an issue that advertising experts debate because although entertainment may get and keep attention, some people believe that it doesn't sell products very well. The creative directors who participated in the study of creative concepts, however, felt that entertainment, particularly humorous entertainment, was of paramount importance.[33]

Persuasive advertising is also designed to affect attitudes. Strategies that are particularly good at that are testimonials and messages that generate word of mouth about the product. A referral from someone who is not affiliated with the product will have more persuasiveness than an ad. One study about influence "found that an endorsement from, for example, the Pulitzer Committee, *Consumer Reports,* or Oprah can make people who have no opinion of a product suddenly see it in a popular light."[34] That's why Oprah's book club has had such an impact on the sales of popular books and why creative strategy uses testimonials and endorsements where appropriate.

Another challenge to the creative team is to find interesting and original ways to generate word of mouth and get people talking about the product. This is sometimes called "viral marketing,"[35] or buzz, and it takes advantage of the fact that personal communication is generally seen as more persuasive than mass communication.

The end result of persuasion is conviction, which means the consumer is committed to something, prefers it, and probably intends to buy it or respond in some way. Conviction is often built on strong, rational arguments that use such techniques in their creative strategies as test results, before-and-after visuals, testimonials by users, and demonstrations to prove something. The endorsements mentioned earlier are also used to intensify conviction in the target audience.

It's easier to make people aware of a brand than it is to convince them that the brand is better than its competitors. That's why conviction is one of the last steps in the persuasion process and one of the hardest objectives to accomplish with an advertising message.

Ads That Stimulate Action

Even harder than conviction, however, is the accomplishment of a behavioral objective. Sometimes an advertising message can drive people to act by offering something free or at a discounted sales price, as in retail advertising. However, a lot of the strategies advertisers use to encourage behavior come from other marketing communication areas, such as sales promotion. Sampling, coupons, and free gifts are incentives for action. Advertising plays a role in delivering information about these promotions. For example, to increase product use, some advertisers are able to provide information about new uses of their products, such as recipes, which is a favorite technique used by Kraft cheese and Campbell's Soup in their ads.

Ultimately, advertisers want loyal customers. Advertising can foster loyalty, or repeat purchases, in a number of ways. The use of testimonials in advertising is a message strategy designed to reinforce the customer's belief in the product. Likewise, distributing coupons or introducing a continuity program (such as a frequent flyer program) is effective in keeping customers. Simply keeping the brand name in front of customers goes a long way toward reinforcing continued use of that brand by customers who have had a positive brand experience. That's what reminder advertising strategies are designed to do.

Evaluation

The preceding discussion focuses on the objectives of the ad and the effects it is designed to create. To do that, the objectives need to be measurable—which means they can be evaluated to determine the effectiveness of the creative strataegy.

Evaluating the effectiveness of an ad, either in a draft form or after it has been used, is called **copy-testing**. Most copy-testing focuses on recognition (awareness), recall, comprehension, and persuasion (attitude change). Another factor, likability, surfaced as important in a study by the Advertising Research Foundation, which found that liking may be just as important, if not more so, than persuasion and recall in predicting sales response.[36] It opened the door to a broader view of what makes an advertisement effective, and made it possible to better evaluate what the creative dimension—those aspects of the ad that make it likable—really contributes to advertising effectiveness.

Another problem in evaluating the effectiveness of advertising that is truly creative is the risk-averse nature of many large organizations, both agencies and clients. Evaluating a new idea, in particular, is hard because there are no benchmarks. It is much easier to evaluate ideas that have been used before because advertisers can see the effects of the past performance of similar ideas. Consequently, a manager will use a proven formula for an ad, knowing that the approach is safe and the ad probably won't fail, even though it may not be highly successful either. A new approach is always a gamble.

In addition to analyzing the message strategy in terms of the effects it hopes to create, another method is to assess the effectiveness of the ad's creative features. Research firm McCollum Spielman determined the characteristics of effective creative messages based on 25 years of research and 25,000 copy-tests, as Table 11.4 shows.

TABLE 11.4   Twelve Tested Creative Hot Buttons

What makes a creative message effective? Here are the 12 recurring qualities found in the most sales-effective advertising as measured by research firm McCollum Spielman.

1. Brand rewards/benefits are highly visible through demonstration, dramatization, lifestyle, feelings, or analogy.
2. The brand is the major player in the experience (the brand makes the good times better).
3. The link between the brand and execution is clear (the scenario revolves around and highlights the brand).
4. The execution has a focus (there's a limit to how many images and vignettes the consumer can process).
5. Feelings (emotional connectives) are anchored to the needs and aspirations of the targeted consumer.
6. Striking, dramatic imagery is characteristic of many successful executions, enhancing their ability to break out of clutter.
7. An original, creative signature or mystique exists in many of the best commercials to bond the consumer to the brand and give it a unique personality.
8. In food and beverage advertising, high taste appeal is almost always essential.
9. The best creative ideas for mature brands often use fresh new ways of revitalizing the message.
10. Music (memorable, bonded tunes and lyrics) is often a key to successful executions for many brands.
11. When humor is used, it is relevant, with a clear product purpose.
12. When celebrities are used, they are well matched to brands and have credibility as users/endorsers, and their delivery is believably enthusiastic.

Source: McCollum Spielman Worldwide, *Topline* (October 1993): 2, 32.

IT'S A WRAP
"CHOOSE YOUR SICK DAYS WISELY"

Good creative people know that every advertising message competes in a cluttered environment for the attention of a generally indifferent audience. The only way to break through the clutter is to express the selling message in an original, fresh way. In other words, dull advertising can be persuasive, but it will rarely get the attention of the audience. To be effective, breakthrough advertising has to be both persuasive and creative.

The Xterra launch campaign is an example of how breakthrough creativity that speaks to its target in language they understand can deliver sales. Not only was the Xterra launch one of Nissan's greatest success stories in the past decade, it also shook up the entire SUV category. Xterra, the underdog in the category, redefined SUV advertising. And Nissan's share of the SUV market doubled to 8.9 percent after it rolled out the Xterra in 1999. Nissan planned to sell 48,000 units in its launch year but sold nearly 67,000 instead.

And, the new SUV design, as well as the creative strategy of the ads, attracted first-timers to the brand, with 80 percent of early Xterra buyers new to Nissan. Not only that, the popular design brought a "halo effect" to the entire Nissan lineup, boosting Nissan's overall brand awareness. And that's the reason the "Everything You Need. Nothing You Don't" campaign was an EFFIE winner—it built an image for the car and company as it delivered buyers to the showroom.

Summary

1. **Define creative advertising and explain how it leads to the Big Idea.** Creative advertising can be defined in terms of relevance, originality, and impact (ROI). The advertising implements a strategy built on creative concepts that make a creative leap and dramatize the strategy in an attention-getting, memorable way.

2. **Describe the characteristics of creative people and their creative process.** All people are born with creative skills but people who are particularly good on the creative side in advertising are visual thinkers and open to new experiences. The stages in the creative process vary, depending on what source you consult, but generally they are immersion, ideation, brainfog, incubation, illumination, and evaluation.

3. **Identify key elements in creative strategy.** The creative strategy, which is outlined in a creative brief, refers to what the advertisement says and how it is said. Creative strategy

is different for different types of products and can be characterized as head or heart strategies that use lectures or dramas to communicate a selling premise. Execution of the creative strategy is seen in the message format, the ad's tone, and the production decisions.

4. **Outline the key parts of a creative brief.** The creative brief is a document that summarizes the key strategic decisions of, and gives guidance to, the execution of the creative strategy. The brief begins with the basic advertising strategy questions (the problem to be solved, the objectives, the target market, and the positioning strategy) and the critical elements of the message strategy (the selling premise, the creative strategy, and details of the ad's execution).

5. **Explain how creative advertising relates to advertising effectiveness.** Effective advertising addresses the four basic categories of effects: perception, learning, persuasion, and behavior. The evaluation of effectiveness is based on how well the advertising meets its objectives.

Key Terms

advertainment, p. 322	copy-testing, p. 323	promise, p. 312	support, p. 313
benefit, p. 312	creative brief, p. 314	reason why, p. 312	unique selling proposition
Big Idea, p. 302	creative concept, p. 302	selling premise, p. 312	(USP), p. 312
brainstorming, p. 308	execution, p. 317	soft sell, p. 311	
claim, p. 312	hard sell, p. 311	structural analysis, p. 313	

Questions

1. Find the ad in this book that you think is the most creative. Analyze it in terms of the ROI formula for evaluating effective creative advertising.

2. One of the challenges for creative ad designers is to demonstrate a product whose main feature cannot be seen by the consumer. Suppose you are an art director on an account that sells shower and bath mats with a patented system that ensures that the mat will not slide (the mat's underside is covered with tiny suction cups that grip the tub's surface). Brainstorm some ways to demonstrate this feature in a television commercial. Find a way that will satisfy the demands of originality, relevance, and impact.

3. Peter Madison, a sophomore in advertising, is speaking informally with a copywriter from a local advertising agency following the writer's class presentation. Peter states his strong determination to be some sort of creative professional once he gets his degree. "My problem is that I'm a bit shy and reserved. I'm interested in all sorts of stuff, but I'm not really quick in expressing ideas and feelings. I'm not sure my personality is suited for being an advertising creative. How do I know whether I've picked the right career direction?" What advice should the writer give Peter?

4. Some time ago a copywriting analyst warned writers that they should be aware of the "ignorance distance" between the writer and the audience. He meant avoiding copy that is either over the heads of the audience or well below the audience's knowledge of the product. What are the dangers in speaking above the audience's frame of reference? What are the dangers of underestimating the audience's knowledge? Which of the elements discussed in the copywriting section of the chapter would reduce the risk of "ignorance distance?"

5. What are some of the major traits of creative people? Which characteristics of the advertising world do you think enhance creativity? Which discourage it? How do you compare yourself on these traits?

6. Find a newspaper or magazine advertisement that you think is bland and unexciting. Rewrite it, first to demonstrate a hard-sell approach, and then to demonstrate a soft-sell approach.

Suggested Class Project

Divide the class into groups of 8 to 10. Each group should find an area to work apart from the other groups. Here's the problem: Your community wants to encourage people to get out of their cars and use alternative forms of transportation. How many different creative concepts can your team come up with to express that idea in an advertisement? Brainstorm for 15 minutes as a group, accumulating every possible idea regardless of how crazy or dumb it might initially sound. Appoint one member to be the recorder who lists all the ideas as they are mentioned. Then go back through the list as a group and put an asterisk next to the ideas that seem to have the most promise. When all the groups reconvene in class, each recorder should list the group's ideas on the blackboard. Cover the board with all the ideas from all the groups. As a class, pick out the three ideas that seem to have the most potential. Analyze the experience of participating in a brainstorming group and compare the experiences of the different teams.

Suggested Internet Class Project

Consult the BrandEra.com Web site and open up the "Creative" or "Advertising" topics in the Department section. Find an article that discusses the creative strategy behind an ad or campaign. Summarize the discussion and relate it to things you have learned in this chapter about how creative strategies are developed.

Hallmark Build•A•Campaign*Projects*

Please review the Hallmark Case Appendix at the end of the text before responding to these questions.

1. Meet in small groups and examine the key strategic links between Capitol Advertising's research and its creative executions.

2. How can local Gold Crown stores leverage the image developed through Hallmark's creative executions to enhance their own image? Develop a creative brief for your local Hallmark Gold Crown store.

HANDS-ON   Case 11

RELIGION AND ADVERTISING

There was a time when religion and advertising were the ultimate adversaries. During the last decade, however, virtually all religious denominations have experienced declining memberships and the need to engage in marketing, especially advertising, has become apparent. Still, advertisers and their various sponsors have remained sensitive to "using religion as a hook, worried about being insensitive."

One company that has had a long history of effectively producing religious marketing strategy is Gl I Kraft Foods and its coffee brand Maxwell House. For 70 years, Maxwell House has been supporting the biggest Jewish holiday of the year, Passover.

Each March, the company's kosher-certified program runs a gift-with-purchase offer of a Passover Haggadah (a book that tells the story of the holiday in Hebrew and English). About 750,000 copies are distributed annually through a variety of grocery chains. Ads announcing the program are run in Jewish magazines and newspapers. The campaign costs about $6 million.

Maxwell House, as well as other marketers such as Verizon Wireless, engages in sponsoring other special events. For example, in 2002 both companies sponsored the Chabad Centennial Celebration in New York City, an event commemorating the 100th birthday of deceased Rabbi Menachem Schneerson. The producer of the event, Walter Urban, posits that the same marketing tactics used for traditional marketing are employed for religious marketing. The celebration included extensive media coverage (including a global closed-circuit telecast), on-site signage, and sampling at the celebration and at Jewish centers around Manhattan.

There are also instances when the religious community takes the initiative. Beliefnet.com is an ecumenical community site that includes sponsors such as BMG Entertainment and Rodale Press. The site draws over four million visitors and distributes 100 million religion-specific e-mail newsletters each month. The site is a production partner of ABC News and produced the special *In Search of Jesus*. Sponsors pay $5,000 to $400,000 for marketing packages, which include sweepstakes, coupons, and so on. ∎

IT'S YOUR TURN

1. How would the creative process change when targeting the religious consumer?
2. Develop a creative brief for advertising an online religious bookstore named Heavenly Blessings.com

Source: Matthew Kinsman, "Spreading the Word," *Promo* (March 2002): 19–28.

Notes

1. Derek Clark, "The Dark Side of Big Ideas," in Wiliam Wells, John Burnett, and Sandra Moriarty, *Advertising Principles and Practices,* 5th ed. (Upper Saddle River, NJ: Prentice Hall, 2000), 300.

2. A. Jerome Jewler and Bonnie L. Drewniany, *Creative Strategy in Advertising* (Belmont, CA: Wadsworth/ Thomson Learning, 2001), 3.

3. Jerri Moore and William D. Wells, *R.O.I. Guidebook: Planning for Relevance, Originality and Impact in*

Advertising and Other Marketing Communications (New York: DDB Needham, 1991).

4. John Eighmy, *The Creative Work Book* (Iowa City: University of Iowa, 1998), 1.

5. Leonard N. Reid, Karen Whitehill King, and Denise E. DeLorme, "Top-Level Agency Creatives Look at Advertising Creativity Then and Now," *Journal of Advertising* 27(2) (Summer 1998): 1–15.

6. James Webb Young, *A Technique for Producing Ideas,* 3d ed. (Chicago: Crain Books, 1975).

7. Lisa Duke, "Like an Idea, Only Better: How Do Advertising Educators and Practitioners Define and Use the Creative Concept?" *Journal of Advertising Education,* 5(1) (Spring 2001): 11–23.

8. Thomas Russell and Glenn Verrill, *Kleppner's Advertising Procedure,* 14th ed. (Upper Saddle River, NJ: Prentice Hall, 2002), 457.

9. J. P. Guilford, "Traits of Personality," in *Creativity and Its Cultivation,* H. H. Anderson, ed. (New York: Harper, 1959).

10. W. J. J. Gordon, *The Metaphorical Way of Learning and Knowing* (Cambridge, MA: Penguin, 1971).

11. Betty Edwards, *Drawing on the Right Side of the Brain* (Los Angeles: Tarcher, 1979).

12. Linda Conway Correll, "Creative Aerobics: A Technique to Jump-Start Creativity," *Proceedings of the American Academy of Advertising Annual Conference,* Carole M. Macklin, ed. (Richmond, VA: AAA, 1997), 263–64.

13. Brett Robbs and Larry Weisberg, "Identifying Critical Teamwork Tools: One Way to Strike a Balance between Team Training and Course Content," AEJMC Conference, Advertising Division, Baltimore, MD, 1998.

14. Stephen Baker, *A Systematic Approach to Advertising Creativity* (New York: McGraw-Hill, 1979).

15. R. R. McCrae and P. T. Costa Jr., "Openness to Experience," in *Perspectives in Personality,* Vol. 1, R. Hogan and W. H. Jones, eds. (Greenwich, CT: JAI Press), 145–72.

16. Sheri J. Broyles, *The Creative Personality: Exploring Relations of Creativity and Openness to Experience.* Unpublished doctoral dissertation, Southern Methodist University, Dallas, 1995.

17. A. Kendrick, D. Slayden, and S. J. Broyles, "Real Worlds and Ivory Towers: A Survey of Top Creative Directors," *Journalism and Mass Communication Educator* 51(2) (1996a): 63–74; A. Kendrick, D. Slayden, and S. J. Broyles, "The Role of Universities in Preparing Creatives: A Survey of Top U.S. Agency Creative Directors," in *Proceedings of the 1996 Conference of the American Academy of Advertising,* G. B. Wilcox (ed.) (Austin: University of Texas, 1996b): 100–106.

18. Graham Wallas, *The Art of Thought* (New York: Harcourt, Brace, 1926).

19. Alex F. Osborn, *Applied Imagination,* 3d ed. (New York: Scribner's, 1963).

20. Betsy Sharkey, "Super Angst," *Adweek* (January 25, 1993): 24–33.

21. Sandra Moriarty and Brett Robbs, "Advertising," in *The Encyclopedia of Creativity,* Vol. 1 (San Diego, CA: Academic Press, 1999), 23–29.

22. Lisa Fortini-Campbell, *Hitting the Sweet Spot: How Consumer Insights Can Inspire Better Marketing and Advertising* (Chicago: The Copy Workshop, 1992).

23. Kathleen O'Donnell, "Practicing What We Teach: Account Planning from the Inside Out," *Proceedings of the American Academy of Advertising Annual Conference,* Darrel D. Muehling, ed. (Richmond, VA: AAA, 1998): 270–76.

24. Richard Vaughn, "How Advertising Works: A Planning Model," *Journal of Advertising Research* 20(5) (October 1980): 27–33.

25. William Wells, "How Advertising Works," speech to the St. Louis AMA, September 17, 1986.

26. Blair Clarkson, "Got Brand," *The Industry Standard* (March 19, 2001): 80-82.

27. Ronald Taylor, "A Six-Segment Message Strategy Wheel," *Journal of Advertising Research* (November–December, 1999): 7–14.

28. Kathleen O'Donnell, "Practicing What We Teach: Account Planning from the Inside Out."

29. Ellen Nevborne, "Great Ad! What's it For?" *Business Week* (July 20, 1998): 118–19.

30. Sally Beatty, "Two GM Divisions Try to Create Different Images for Their Trucks," *Wall Street Journal* (October 14, 1998): B8.

31. Bill Bernbach, *Bill Bernbach Said* (New York: Doyle Dane Bernbach International, n.d.).

32. Laura Rich, "That's Advertainment," *The Industry Standard* (June 25, 2001): 60–61.

33. Duke, "Like an Idea, Only Better," pp. 11–23.

34. James Surowiecki, "The Power of the Prize," *The New Yorker* (June 18 and 25, 2001): 67.

35. Erin Kelly, "This Is One Virus You Want to Spread," *Fortune* (November 27, 2000): 297–300.

36. Russell I. Haley, "The ARF Copy Research Validity Project," *Journal of Advertising Research* (April–May 1991): 11–32; Cyndee Miller, "Study Says 'Likability' Surfaces as Measure of TV Ad Success," *AMA Newsletter* (January 1, 1991): 6.

His business depends on mail that arrives in seconds. Not days.

The shelf life of information is shrinking. And getting shorter as you read this.

Instantaneous response to customers, vendors and partners is critical. The best way to respond to the pressure of today's deadlines is to put the Internet to work for your business. To do that, you'll need a strategic ally who can help you deploy the technologies and network services your organization needs to survive in these demanding times.

That's where we come in. We're Cisco Systems. Virtually all Internet traffic travels across Cisco equipment. We are uniquely qualified to help you turn the Internet into a change agent for your company. At hyper-speed.

Visit us at www.cisco.com.

Do it now. Seconds count.

CISCO SYSTEMS

EMPOWERING THE
INTERNET GENERATION℠

CHAPTER 12

Copywriting

CHAPTER OBJECTIVES

When you have completed this chapter, you should be able to

1. Identify the good and bad practices in copywriting.
2. Describe the various copy elements of a print ad.
3. Explain the message characteristics and tools of radio advertising.
4. Discuss the major elements of television commercials.
5. Discuss how Web advertising is written.

"Cisco = Internet"

Award: *EFFIE Gold, Corporate Reputations/Image/Identity*

Company: *Cisco Systems*

Agency: *GMO/Hill Holliday*

Campaign: *"Cisco Internet Generation"*

Cisco Systems is today's worldwide leader in networking for the Internet. Before 1998, however, network engineers and information technology buyers may have been the only ones to know that. Cisco pioneered the networking industry by introducing powerful routers and switches. However, when market conditions and technological advances started blurring the lines between the networking and telecommunications industries—and as Cisco gained new competitors five times its size—company leaders wanted to increase the awareness of Cisco among business and technology leaders around the world. Cisco executives soon asked advertising firm GMO/Hill Holliday of San Francisco to create a corporate campaign that would make Cisco synonymous with Internet networking.

Most of Cisco's competitors, such as Lucent and Nortel, were focusing on new technologies and e-business. The Cisco strategy was simpler, and bolder—to own the networking dimension of the Internet and, in so doing, own the Internet. The objective then was to create an enduring link as expressed in this simple positioning formula: "Cisco = Internet."

The strategy in the EFFIE-award-winning campaign was to portray Cisco as not only a global company, but also a human company that provides the assurance of capability without seeming intimidating. The creative team called this campaign, the "Internet Generation," in recognition of its focus on people who rely on the Internet to run their businesses. Business-to-business advertising doesn't tend to be as creative as consumer advertising. However, that doesn't mean that it isn't just as effective, particularly when it speaks to people in an accessible way.

In the Cisco campaign, print ads feature single photographs of people who represent this Internet Generation, combined with copy either about or directed to the featured individual. The copy typically addressed a typical workplace problem or issue that Cisco could help solve. For example, notice the headline in the ad to business decision makers shown here: "His business depends on mail that arrives in seconds. Not days." The body copy follows with, "The shelf life of information is shrinking. And getting shorter as you read this. Instantaneous response to customers, vendors, and partners is critical."

The copy continues to explain how important speed of response is to today's business managers—not the guy in the suit in the corner office but the average guy managing the operations. The copywriting technique that makes this an effective ad lies in its choice of language with phrases like "shelf life," "strategic ally," and "hyper speed." This is copy that successfully targets its audience, catches their attention with ideas they are familiar with and problems they deal with daily. It addresses them in language they use, rather than the stiff language you often find in advertising for high-tech hardware and software.

The "Are You Ready?" television ads tied in with the tone and style of the print ads. In a television spot about networking, images of people from around the world support the narrator's voice saying, "There are over 800,000 job openings for Internet specialists right now. . . . Are you ready?" Another commercial about e-learning features similar global images while the announcer states, "There are over 17 million people receiving an education over the Internet this year. . . . Are you ready?"

The "Internet Generation" campaign for Cisco Systems carved out a position of ownership for Cisco by talking to business people about how Cisco's networking capabilities could help them improve their businesses. And it did so, not by talking technology, but by talking in accessible, human terms about Internet use.

Source: Adapted from the EFFIE brief provided by the GMO/Hill Holliday agency and Cisco Systems.

COPYWRITING: THE LANGUAGE OF ADVERTISING

Words and pictures work together to produce a creative concept. However, the idea behind a creative concept in advertising is usually expressed in some attention-getting and memorable phrase. Finding these "magic words" is the responsibility of copywriters who search for the right words to warm up a mood or soften consumer resistance.

An example of a word-oriented creative concept comes from a long-running NYNEX campaign for its Yellow Pages. The campaign uses a play on words to illustrate some of the headings in its directory. One commercial in the series included three train engineers with overalls, caps, and bandannas sitting in rocking chairs in a parlor and having tea to illustrate the "Civil Engineering" category; furniture doing a striptease with materials flying off it was used to illustrate the "Furniture Stripping" category. A picture of a bull sleeping on its back illustrates the category "Bulldozing."

Although advertising is highly visual, there are five types of advertisements in which words are crucial.

1. If the message is complicated, words can be more specific than visuals and can be read over and over until the meaning is clear.
2. If the ad is for a high-involvement product, meaning the consumer spends a lot of time considering it, then the more information the better, and that means using words.

3. Information that needs definition and explanation, like how a new wireless phone works, is also better delivered through words.
4. If a message tries to convey abstract qualities, such as justice and quality, words tend to communicate these concepts more easily than pictures.
5. Finally, slogans and jingles help lock in key phrases that cue a brand image or remind consumers of a brand feature.

Words are powerful tools in advertising and the person who understands their beauty and power, as well as how best to use them in situations like these is the *copywriter.*

The Copywriter

A person who shapes and sculpts the words in an advertisement is called a **copywriter**. *Copy* is the text of an ad or the words that people say in a commercial. In most agencies, copywriters work in teams with **art directors** who design the way the ad will look. **Creative directors** manage the creative process and oversee the work of the copywriter/art director team.

A successful advertising copywriter is a savvy marketer and a literary master, sometimes described as a "killer poet." Copywriters love words and they search for the clever twist, the pun, the powerful description, the punch, the nuance—for words that whip and batter, plead, sob, cajole, and impress. Copywriters get paid good money for playing very skillful word games. They are experts on words, or, rather, students of them. They know meanings and derivations, as well as the moods and feelings of words and the reverberations and vibrations they create in a reader's mind.

Because of their ear for evocative language, many copywriters have a background in English or literature. In addition to having an ear for the right, or clever phrase, they listen to how people talk and identify the tone of voice that best fits the target audience and advertising need. The secret to the Cisco EFFIE-winning "Internet Generation" campaign was in the language, which the Hill Holliday creative team described as: "Humanity. Not hype, but real people, talking in the vernacular of the target. Everyday discourse, not tech speak."

Versatility is a common trait of copywriters. They can move from toilet paper to Mack trucks and shift their writing style to match the product and the language of their target audience. Copywriters don't have a style of their own because the style they use has to match the message and the product. Except in a few rare cases, advertising writing is anonymous, so people who crave a byline generally would not be happy as copywriters.

Like poets, copywriters spend hours, even days, crafting a paragraph. They write a first draft, revise it, then tighten and shorten it. After many revisions others read the copy and critique it. It then goes back to the writer, who continues to fine-tune it. Copywriters have to have thick skins as there is always someone else reading their work, critiquing it, and making changes. Most often those people are called clients, and they have to be pleased with the copy, even if the copywriter doesn't like the changes. The following discussion of advertising style explains the way copywriters approach the writing of copy for an advertisement.

Advertising Style

In advertising, there is good writing and there is bad writing, just as there is good and bad in every other area of expression. One characteristic of good advertising writing is that it is succinct and single-minded, meaning it has a clear focus and usually tries to convey only one selling point.

Advertising has to win its audience, no small task given that it usually competes with so much noise. For that reason, the copy should be as simple as possible. Simple ads avoid being gimmicky or too cute; they don't try too hard or reach too far to make a point.

Advertising copy is tight. Every word counts because both space and time are expensive. Ineffective words—such as interesting, very, in order to, buy now and save, introducing, nothing less than—waste precious space. Copywriters revise copy a hundred times to make it as concise as possible. The tighter the copy, the easier it is to understand and the greater its impact. The "Practical Tips" feature summarizes some characteristics of effective copy.

Practical Tips

WRITING EFFECTIVE COPY

- *Be succinct.* Use short, familiar words, short sentences, and short paragraphs.
- *Be specific.* Don't waste time on generalities. The more specific the message, the more attention-getting and memorable it is.
- *Get personal.* Directly address your audience whenever possible as "you" and "your," rather than "we" or "they."
- *Keep a single focus.* Deliver a simple message instead of one that makes too many points. Focus on a single idea and support it.
- *Be conversational.* Use the language of everyday conversation. The copy should sound like two friends talking to one another, so don't shy away from incomplete sentences, thought fragments, and contractions.
- *Be original.* To keep your copy forceful and persuasive, avoid stock advertising phrases, strings of superlatives and brag-and-boast statements, and clichés.
- *Use variety.* To add visual appeal in both print and TV ads, avoid long blocks of copy in print ads. Instead, break the copy into short paragraphs with subheads. In TV commercials, break up television monologues with visual changes, such as shots of the product, sound effects, and dialogue. The writer puts these breaks in the script while the art director designs what they will look like.

Tone of Voice To develop the right tone of voice, copywriters write to a typical user. If they know someone who fits that description, then they write to that person as if they were in a conversation. If they don't, then they may go through a photo file, select a picture of the person they think fits the description, and develop a profile of that personality. Copywriters may even hang these pictures above their desks while writing the copy.

An example of how important it is to identify the target and that group's way of speaking comes from the EFFIE-winning "The Good, The Bad, and The Ugly" campaign for AWNY. But it's not just the tone of the words that should match the target audience, the visuals also have to match. The materials in this case are addressed to advertising professionals who create sexist advertising. So the tone of voice represented in the materials used in the call for entries parodies the copy of advertisers who think that they are speaking effectively to their male target audience, although they are actually offending a larger target audience of women who may see the advertising as sexist (see the "A Matter of Practice" box).

A MATTER OF PRACTICE

THE GOOD, THE BAD, AND THE UGLY OF AWARD SHOWS

➤ The Good, the Bad, and the Ugly (GBU) Award Show is sponsored by the Advertising Women of New York (AWNY). Historically an insider "watchdog" event that critiques the portrayal of women in advertising, the award show has called attention to advertising that unnecessarily "showed skin," disparaged women, and used sexist and stereotypical appeals.

In 2000 the GBU committee decided that it wanted to elevate its image and transform itself into a legitimate awards show grounded in creative credibility. Moving away from its "little ole ladies at lunch" image meant targeting the male-dominated group of art directors and copywriters in the advertising community. The strategy was to have a laugh at itself in its call for entries, which was creative enough that it became an EFFIE-award winner.

To create interest and intrigue, the campaign produced a "secret rulebook" as a call for entries, one that used hyperbole, parody, and humor to demonstrate the belittling treatment women sometimes receive in advertisements. Creatives at ad agencies in New York received the illustrated handbook filled with odd "how-to" instructions on marketing to women that used the sexist approaches the GBU had previously debunked.

The tongue-in-cheek call for entries featured the Playboy-esque "silhouette girl" seen on truck mud flaps. The copy included "handy" tips such as, "Only use small, monosyllabic words" and "When using a woman in a lingerie ad, make sure her back is arched into near-contortionist posi-

tions." And to continue the parody, it unfolded into a life-size pin-up, including measurements ("post-rib removal") and turn-ons ("will take credit cards").

The handbook was supported by a PR effort designed to heighten the sense of intrigue and a viral marketing e-mail campaign (one person passes it on to another). Select ad trade media were given exclusive behind-the-scenes "scoops" on the new "mud-flap girl" logo and rulebook. Postcards with the "mud-flap girl" were distributed throughout the New York ad community, as well as art and design schools, clubs, and bars; and exhibits invited submissions and ticket sales.

"We wanted to show people we're not old biddies at a garden party," said Catherine St. Jean, a partner at the Judy Wald agency and one of the co-chairs of the GBU awards. She explained, "We're vital, and we want to make a change." Even in its parody form, the handbook's message about sexist advertising was still hard-hitting.

Fallon New York, whose president, Alison Burns, is another GBU co-chair, and Duffy Design created the campaign and entry brochure. The guide may have confused some, but the laughs generated by the piece also produced a huge increase in the number of entries and award-show attendance. Still, the goal of the piece was to go beyond the laughs to make attendees aware of how there are still sexist portrayals of women in advertising and that sometimes their work may be offensive and they may not realize it.

Source: Adapted from 2001 EFFIE award winners, http://www.effie.org/cat2001.htm; Tim Nudd, "Shop Talk: AWNY Has a Laugh in Its Call for Entries," *Adweek* (July 31, 2000): 21; and the EFFIES brief provided by Fallon New York.

Grammar Copywriters also are attuned to the niceties of grammar, syntax, and spelling, although sometimes they will play with a word or phrase to create an effect, even if it's grammatically incorrect.

An example comes from the elegant Apple Computer campaign by TBWA Chiat/Day for the Macintosh that used the slogan "Think different." The campaign featured pictures of geniuses such as Albert Einstein and Pablo Picasso. The copy should read "Think differently" to be grammatically correct, which caused a bit of an uproar in Apple's school market. In response to the hundreds of letters from schoolteachers and other offended citizens, Apple replied, "differently, being an adverb, would communicate an unintended message. It would tell the reader HOW to think." The company's reply added that in the slogan, the word "different" shouldn't be treated as an adjective, but as a noun, "Because 'different' is not a modifier but a 'thing.'" In other words, "the message of the tagline tells us WHAT TO THINK ABOUT rather than HOW to think." It's a somewhat convoluted explanation but one that had to be made because of the tremendous amount of criticism leveled at the ad.[1]

Adese Formulaic advertising copy is one problem that is so well-known that comedians parody it. This type of formula writing, called **adese**, violates all the guidelines for writing effective copy that we described in the Practical Tips for writing effective copy. Adese is stereotyped ad writing. It is full of clichés, superlatives, stock phrases, and vague generalities. For example, can you hear yourself saying things like this to a friend?: "Now we offer the quality that you've been waiting for—at a price you can afford," and "Buy now and save."

The parody ads used in the AWNY announcement used tongue-in-cheek copy to call attention to the clichéd copy that is sometimes directed to women. For example, one ad about how to convince women to clean a toilet had the following copy:

> When showing a woman cleaning toilets, make sure she has a knock-down, drop-dead, slammin' body. This will ensure that other women believe that toilet bowl scrubbing will give them a killer figure—thereby increasing their overall value as a human being.

Adese is also brag-and-boast copy, which is "we" copy written from the company's point of view with a pompous tone. Research has consistently found that this is the weakest form of ad writing. An example would be: "Brought to you by [company/brand name]. We are the technological leader of the decade."

Consider a print ad by Buick for the Somerset, one of its models. The ad starts with the stock opening, "Introducing Buick on the move." The body copy includes superlatives and generalities such as, "Nothing less than the expression of a new philosophy," "It strikes a new balance between luxury and performance—a balance which has been put to the test," and "Manufactured with a degree of precision that is in itself a breakthrough."

The problem with adese is that it looks and sounds like what everyone thinks advertising should look and sound like—it's clichéd. Because people are so conditioned to screen out advertising, messages that use this predictable style are the ones that are the easiest to ignore. This discussion of advertising style has been fairly general, so now let's look at how copy is written for print and broadcast media.

COPYWRITING FOR PRINT

A print advertisement is created in two pieces: a copy sheet and a layout. We discuss the copy in this chapter and the layout in the next chapter.

Copy Elements

The two categories of copy that print advertising uses are **display copy** and **body copy** (or text). Display copy includes all elements that readers see in their initial scanning. These elements—headlines, subheads, call-outs, taglines, and slogans—usually are set in larger type sizes than body copy and are designed to get attention and to stop the viewer's scanning. Body copy includes the elements that are designed to be read and absorbed, such as the text of the ad message and captions. Table 12.1 summarizes the primary copy elements that are in the copywriter's toolkit.

How to Write Headlines Most experts on print advertising agree that the headline is the most important display element. The headline works with the visual to get attention and communicate the creative concept. This Big Idea usually comes across best through a picture and words working together, as the DuPont ad illustrates. The headline carries the theme ("To Do List for the Planet") and the underline ("Find food that helps prevent osteoporosis") makes the most direct connection with the visual.

The **headline** is a key element in print advertising. It conveys the main message so that people get the point of the ad. It's important for another reason. People who are scanning may read nothing more, so advertisers want to at least register a point with the consumer. The point has to be clear from the headline or the combination of headline and visual. Researchers estimate that only 20 percent of those who read the headline go on to read the body copy.

TABLE 12.1	**The Copywriter's Toolkit**

No one ad uses all of the copy elements; however, they are all used in different ads for different purposes. Here are the most common tools in the copywriter's toolkit:

Cancer Patients Fly Free

Headline: A phrase or a sentence that serves as the opening to the ad. It's usually identified by larger type or a prominent position and its purpose is to catch attention. In the Corporate Angel Network ad, for example, the headline is "Cancer Patients Fly Free."

Overlines and **underlines:** These are phrases or sentences that either lead into the headline or follow up on the thought in the headline. They are usually set in smaller type than the headline. The purpose of the overline is to set the stage, and the purpose of the underline is to elaborate on the idea in the headline and serve as a transition to the body copy.

Body Copy: The text of the ad. It's usually smaller-sized type and written in paragraphs or multiple lines. Its purpose is to explain the idea or selling point.

Subheads: Used in longer copy blocks, subheads begin a new section of the copy. They are usually bold type or larger than the body copy. Their purpose is to make the logic clear to the reader. They are useful for people who scan copy and they help them get a sense of what the copy says. The Corporate Angel Network ad uses subheads.

Call-outs: These are sentences that float around the visual, usually with a line or arrow pointing to some specific element in the visual that they name and explain. For example, Johnson & Johnson once ran an ad that used call-outs as the main pieces of the body copy. The head read: "How to bathe a mommy." Positioned around a picture of a woman are short paragraphs with arrows pointing to various parts of her body. These "call outs" describe the good things the lotion does for feet, hands, makeup removal, moisture absorption, and skin softening.

Captions: A sentence or short piece of copy that explains what you are looking at in a photo or illustration. Captions aren't used very often in advertising because the visuals are assumed to be self-explanatory; however, readership studies have shown that, after the headline, captions have high readership.

Taglines: A short phrase that wraps up the key idea or creative concept that usually appears at the end of the body copy. It often refers back to the headline or opening phrase in a commercial. For example, see the line, "Need a lift? Just give us a call. We'll do the rest," in the Corporate Angel Network ad.

Slogans: A distinctive catch phrase that serves as a motto for a campaign, brand, or company. It is used across a variety of marketing communication messages and over an extended period of time. For example, see "The Miracles of Science" line that serves as a corporate motto for the DuPont company.

Call to Action: This is a line at the end of an ad that encourages people to respond and gives information on how to respond. Both ads—Corporate Angel Network, and DuPont—have response information: either an address, a toll-free phone number, an e-mail or Web address.

Writers cover notepads with hundreds of headlines and spend days worrying about the wording. They have to be catchy phrases, but they also have to convey an idea and attract the right target audience. Tobler chocolates has won EFFIE awards for a number of years for its clever headlines and visuals. For Tobler's Chocolate Orange, the creative concept showed the chocolate ball being smacked against something hard and splitting into slices. The headline was "Whack and Unwrap." The next year the headline was "Smashing

Good Taste" which speaks to the candy's British origins and to the quirky combination of chocolate and orange flavors. The headline and visual also tell consumers how to "open" the orange into slices—by whacking or smashing.

Agencies will copy-test headlines to make sure they can be understood at a glance and that they communicate exactly the right idea. Split-run tests (two versions of the same ad) in direct mail have shown that changing the wording of the headline while keeping all other elements constant can double, triple, or quadruple consumer response. That is why the experts, such as ad legend David Ogilvy, state that the headline is the most important element in the advertisement.[2]

Ogilvy explained why headlines that work can last for so long when he said, "You aren't advertising to a standing army; you are advertising to a moving parade."[3] His point is that an ad headline may wear out with the copywriter, agency, or advertiser and still pull in readers because new people are seeing it and, if the idea is timeless, responding to the pull of the message. Because headlines are so important, some general principles guide their development and explain the particular functions they serve:

- A good headline will attract only those who are prospects—there is no sense in attracting people who are not in the market—by speaking to their interests. An old advertising axiom is, "Use a rifle, not a shotgun." In other words, use the headline to tightly target the right audience.
- The headline must work in combination with the visual to stop and grab the reader's attention. An advertisement by Range Rover shows a photo of the car parked at the edge of a rock ledge in Monument Valley with the headline, "Lots of people use their Range Rovers just to run down to the corner." These elements stop the reader.
- The headline must also identify the product and brand, and start the sale. The selling premise should be evident in the headline. If you have a strong sales point, lead with it and keep the headline single-focused.
- The headline should lead readers into the body copy. For readers to move to the body copy, they have to stop scanning and start concentrating. The fact that the reader needs to change the perceptual mode—the mind-set—is the reason why only 20 percent of scanners become readers.

Headlines can be grouped into two general categories: direct and indirect action. Direct headlines are straightforward and informative, such as when Tylenol uses the headline, "The Power to Stop Pain." It identifies the product category and links the brand with the benefit. Direct headlines are highly targeted, but they may fail to lead the reader into the message if they are not captivating enough.

Types of Direct Action Headlines

- *Assertion.* An assertion is a headline that states a claim or a promise that will motivate someone to try the product.
- *Command.* A command headline politely tells the reader to do something.
- *How-To Heads.* People are rewarded for investigating a product when the message tells them how to use it or how to solve a problem.
- *News Announcements.* News headlines are used with new-product introductions, but also with changes, reformulations, new styles, and new uses. The news value is thought to get attention and motivate people to try the product.

Indirect headlines are not as selective and may not provide as much information, but may be better at drawing the reader into the message.

Types of Indirect Action Headlines

- *Puzzles.* Used strictly for their curiosity and provocative power. Puzzling statements, ambiguity, and questions require the reader to examine the body copy to get the answer or explanation. The intention is to pull readers into the body copy.
- *Associations.* These headlines use image and lifestyle to get attention and build interest.

This ad for Motorola Talk About™ two-way radio ran in *Backpack* magazine and caught the attention of readers by using a great creative concept and headline.

The "Help, I Think I Need A Tourniquet" headline draws us into the Motorola Talk About™ ad. Headlines like this one, which also plays on the sounds of words, are provocative and compel people to read on to find out the point of the message. Sometimes these indirect headlines are called "blind headlines" because they give so little information. A **blind headline** is a gamble. If it is not informative or intriguing enough, the reader may move on without absorbing any product name information, but if it works as an attention getter, it can be very effective.

How to Write Other Display Copy Next to the headline, captions have the second highest readership. Copy-testing data shows that attention is drawn immediately to the captions under the illustrations. In addition to their pulling power, **captions** also serve an information function. Visuals do not always say the same thing to every person; for that reason, most visuals can benefit from some explanation. Captions often explain what's happening in photos, because people may find visuals confusing. Captions also have high readership.

In addition to headlines, copywriters also craft the subheads that continue to help lure the reader into the body copy. Subheads are considered display copy in that they are usually larger and set in different type (bold or italic) than the body copy. **Subheads** are sectional headlines and are also used to break up a mass of "gray" type (or type that tends to blur together when one glances at it) in a large block of copy.

Taglines are short catchy phrases and particularly memorable phrases used at the end of an ad to complete or wrap up the idea. An ad from the Nike women's campaign used the headline "You are a nurturer and a provider. You are beautiful and exotic" set in an elegant script. The tagline on the next page used a rough, hand-drawn, graffiti-like image that said, "You are not falling for any of this."

Slogans, which are repeated from ad to ad as part of a campaign or a long-term brand-identity effort, also may be used as taglines. Copywriters use a number of literary techniques to enhance the memorability of subheads, slogans, and taglines. The most important way to create memorability is through repetition. These are other techniques copywriters use to create catchy slogans:

- *A startling or unexpected phrase.* The NYNEX campaign used the phrase, "If it's out there, it's in here," which is an example of a twist on a common phrase that makes it unexpected.
- *Rhyme, rhythm, alliteration.* Uses repetition of sounds, as in the *Wall Street Journal*'s slogan—"The daily dairy of the American Dream."
- *Parallel construction.* Uses repetition of the structure of a sentence or phrase, as in the army's "Be all that you can be."

As the "A Matter of Practice" story about the Good, Bad, and Ugly awards demonstrated, copywriters need to be sensitive to ethical issues such as gender and ethnic stereotyping when writing these clever phrases. An example of the trouble one can inadvertently stumble into comes from a Nissan Frontier pickup campaign to young Hispanic men.[4] The Hispanic agency that developed the campaign suggested such taglines as "A 3,172-pound can of whoop-ass" and "100% testosterone, 0% estrogen" during the campaign's development. Even though these were only ideas, they were leaked to *USA Today,* which ran a story on the campaign. Nissan and its agency found out quickly that many Hispanic women don't take kindly to such blatant and stereotyped machismo.

How to Write Body Copy The body copy is the text of the ad. It develops the sales message, states the argument, summarizes the proof, and provides explanation. It is the persuasive heart of the message. You excite consumer interest with the display elements, but you win them over with the argument presented in the body copy, assuming the ad uses body copy. And there are instances where the idea is presented primarily in the headline and, perhaps, other display copy such as **call-outs**.

There are as many different kinds of writing styles as there are copywriters and product personalities, but there are also some standard styles:

- *Straightforward.* Factual copy usually written in the words of an anonymous or unacknowledged source.
- *Narrative.* Tells a story in first person or third person.
- *Dialogue.* Lets the reader "listen in" on a conversation.
- *Explanation.* Explains how something works.
- *Translation.* Technical information, such as that written for the high-tech and medical industries, must be defined and translated into understandable language.

The Cisco Systems "Internet Generation" campaign used a straightforward copy approach to address prospects about a technical subject, so you might say that it also used some aspects of a translation approach as well. You can see that in the body copy for the ad that features a woman and her need for instant news.

In her world,

your morning paper

is already 12 hours

out of date.

Wake up.

The Internet is changing the way we work, live, play and learn.

For millions of people, the Internet is their first source of news. Their prime source for product information. The place where they spend billions of dollars.

For your business, the Internet offers enormous potential in terms of communication, commerce and community. For your strategic Internet partner, seek Cisco Systems. Virtually all Internet traffic travels across Cisco equipment.

Visit us at www.cisco.com. And get ahead instead of getting outdated.

CISCO SYSTEMS

EMPOWERING THE INTERNET GENERATION™

©1999 Cisco Systems, Inc. All rights reserved.

This ad for Cisco uses a straightforward copy approach to deliver its message.

Body copy also has to speak to the target audience in an appropriate language style. An ad for Trojan condoms makes a pointed argument on a touchy subject for its young, single-person target audience. Combining headline with body copy, it reads as a dialogue:

> *I didn't use one because I didn't have one with me.*
> *Get Real.*
> *If you don't have a parachute, don't jump, genius.*

Two paragraphs get special attention in body copy: the **lead** and the **close**. The lead, the first paragraph of the body copy, is another point where people test the message to see whether they want to read it. An example comes from Nike's women's campaign. Notice how the first line works to catch the attention of the target audience:

> **A magazine is not a mirror.**
> *Have you ever seen anyone in a magazine who*
> *Seemed even vaguely like you looking back?*
> *(If you have, turn the page.)*
> *Most magazines are made to sell us a fantasy of what we're supposed to be.*
> *They reflect what society deems to be a standard,*
> *However unrealistic or unattainable that standard is.*
> *That doesn't mean you should cancel your subscription.*
> *It means you need to remember*
> *That it's just ink on paper.*
> *And that whatever standards you set for yourself,*
> *For how much you want to weigh,*
> *For how hard you work out,*
> *Or how many times you make it to the gym,*
> *Should be your standards.*
>
> *Not someone else's.*

Closing paragraphs in body copy have several functions. Usually, the last paragraph refers back to the creative concept and wraps up the Big Idea. Direct action messages usually end with a **call to action** with instructions on how to respond. A Schwinn bicycle ad that is headlined "Read poetry. Make peace with all except the motor car," demonstrates a powerful and unexpected ending, one that is targeted to its youthful audience:

> *Schwinns are red, Schwinns are blue.*
> *Schwinns are light and agile too.*
> *Cars suck. The end.*

Print Media Requirements

There are a variety of media in the print category—everything from newspapers and magazines to outdoor boards and product literature. They all use the same copy elements, such as headlines and body copy; however, how these elements are used varies with the medium.

Newspapers Newspaper advertising is one of the few types of advertising that is not considered intrusive. People consult the paper as much to see what is on sale as to find out what is happening in City Hall. For this reason, the copy in newspaper advertisements does not have to work as hard as other kinds of advertising to catch the attention of its audience.

In addition, because the editorial environment of a newspaper generally is serious, newspaper ads don't have to compete as entertainment, as television ads do. As a result, most newspaper advertising copy is straightforward and informative. Local retail advertising announces what merchandise is available, what is on sale, how much it costs, and where you can get it. The writing is brief, usually just identifying the merchandise and giving critical information about styles, sizes, and prices.

Magazines Magazines appear less frequently than newspapers and, therefore, there is time for better quality ad production. That also means more care is taken in the writing and testing of the ad's strategy, copy, and other elements. Consumers may clip and file advertising that ties in with the magazine's special interest as reference information. For this reason, magazine ads often are more informative and carry longer copy than do newspaper ads. Copywriters carefully craft the copy for both aesthetic and functional impact to mirror the higher-quality design and production values that magazines offer. Copywriters also take care to craft clever phrasing for the headlines. The body copy, as in the Nike women's campaign, may read more like poetry.

Directories Publications that provide contact information, such as phone numbers and addresses, often carry display advertising. These ads can be linked to a campaign by using words and pictures that are taken from a print or broadcast ad. For example, the Delta ad, with its "Delta: Fly Easier" art and copy, is taken directly from the EFFIE-winning campaign (described in Chapter 5). The directory ad is leveraging the brand identity being promoted in the bigger campaign to create recognition and familiarity for someone looking up airlines.

In writing a directory ad, copywriters who write ads for the Yellow Pages advise using a headline that focuses on the service or store personality rather than a headline that just states the name of the store. The ad should describe the store or the services it provides, unless the store's name is a descriptive phrase such as "Overnight Auto Service" or "The Computer Exchange."

Sometimes the company name gives no clue to the product, so the advertiser has to use descriptive phrases and a visual to signal the product category. Complicated explanations don't work well in the Yellow Pages either, because there is little space for such explanations. Putting information that is subject to change in an ad can become a problem because the directory is published only once a year.

Brand identification is increased in this Delta directory ad by tying it to the national advertising campaign.

Poster and outdoor ads can attract attention primarily through visuals and creative copy, as demonstrated by these ads for the Coffee Rush chain.

Posters and Outdoor Advertising Posters and outdoor boards are primarily visual, although the words generally try to catch consumers' attention and lock in an idea, registering a message. In these forms, all the copy is display copy. An effective poster, however, is built around a creative concept that marries the words with the visual. For Coffee Rush, Karl Schroeder's agency (see "The Inside Story") created a series of posters to change consumers' perceptions that the shop was merely a drive-through for coffee.

He explains the strategy behind the posters: "The public's perception is that the quality and selection of drinks sold out of a trailer would pale in comparison to Starbucks' menu. So Coffee Rush, although its shops looked much nicer than some of those parking lot sheds, still had to overcome the "cup of joe" perception people have of that kind of coffee joint."

Schroeder's team did this by using posters during the summer to promote a line of cold drinks with captivating names such as Mango Guava and Wild Berry. These posters told newcomers that Coffee Rush sold more than just "a cup of joe." The copy, which had to be simple to be read by people in a car, was designed to tease people into tasting these fun drinks:

> For the Smoothies: "Any more fruit in these smoothies and we'd have to sell them by the pound."
> For the Rush Slush drinks: "Honey, your coffee is melting."

One of the most famous billboard campaigns ever was for a little shaving cream company named Burma Shave. The campaign used a series of roadside signs with catchy little poems, which is a most unlikely format for a highway sign. There were some 600 poems and they worked well for nearly 40 years, from 1925 to 1963, until the national interstate system made the signs obsolete.[5] More recently, Albuquerque used the Burma Shave format to encourage drivers to reduce their speeds through a construction zone, using rhyme. Today, a construction zone is about the only place where traffic moves slowly enough to use a billboard filled with copy.

> *Through this maze of machines and rubble*
> *Driving fast can cause you trouble*
> *Take care and be alert*
> *So no one on this road gets hurt.*

THE INSIDE STORY

MR. YUCK

Karl Schroeder   Copywriter
Coates, Kokes, Portland, Oregon

When is an idea too creative? Hard to say. Consider the following story:

I'm young. I'm a creative. And like any young creative, I want to do bold, conceptual work and build my book. So every time I get a project I look at it as an opportunity to get published in the next award annual. Then I cross my fingers behind my back and say, "I'm doing it all for the client." This mind-set works better for some clients than others.

Coffee Rush happens to be a client that encourages good work. In one sentence, Coffee Rush is a group of small, drive-through coffee shops in Portland that produce drinks at or above the quality of Starbucks. The shops have a personable feel that the large chains lack.

As summer came around, Coffee Rush needed to promote its line of cold drinks, so we created a series of posters for its shop windows that called attention to its summer drinks.

But we wanted to take the idea a step further with a guerrilla warfare–like approach. So we produced stickers that looked very much like Mr. Yuck—you know, the little green anti-poison guy that our parents stuck on harmful substances under the sink. Basically, each hot drink that customers ordered was tagged with one of these stickers that read, "Hot coffee on a hot day? Yuck. Next time try one of our cold summer drinks."

Well, the younger customers loved the stickers. They laughed. They ordered summer drinks. But moms hated the stickers because they didn't want their young kids seeing their mom drinking something marked poison.

So was the campaign a success or failure? Fortunately, the client considered the work a success. Coffee Rush would rather do work that got noticed (positively or negatively) than do work that no one noticed at all. In the end, the client still used the stickers but was more cautious about whose drinks got stickers.

A copywriter in Portland, Oregon, I graduated from the University of Oregon with a degree in Advertising and minors in English and Fine Arts. The Monday following graduation, I started work at Coates, Kokes in Portland, Oregon, as a copywriter. At school I participated in a student-run ad agency for two years as a writer and then as a creative director. I was creative director for our ad team when we took third place in a regional competition. My senior year I competed at the One Show's young creative competition in New York.

Nominated by Professor Charles Frazer, University of Oregon.

The copy on a billboard is minimal. Usually, there is one line that serves as both a headline and some kind of product identification. Often the phrase is a play on words. A series of black-and-white billboards in the Galveston-Houston area, recruiting priests for the Roman Catholic diocese, features a Roman collar with witty wording such as, "Yes, you will combat evil. No, you don't get to wear a cape." Others are more thoughtful, "Help wanted. Inquire within yourself."

The most important characteristic of copywriting for outdoor advertising is brevity. Some experts suggest that copywriters use no more than six to seven words. It must catch attention, but it also must be memorable. For example, a billboard for Orkin pest control showed a package wrapped up with the word Orkin on the tag. The headline read, "A little something for your ant."

Product Literature   Sometimes called **collateral materials** because they are used in support of an advertising campaign, brochures and pamphlets provide details about a product, company, or event. Sometimes they are produced as part of a public relations or sales promotion program; sometimes they are considered advertising's responsibility. Typically, product literature is a heavy copy format, or at least a format that provides room for explanatory details along with visuals; the body copy may dominate the piece.

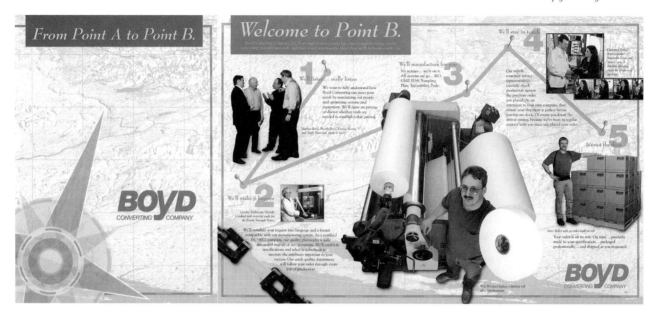

For a pamphlet with folds, a writer must also consider how the message is conveyed as the piece is unfolded. These pieces can range from a simple three-panel flyer to a glitzy full-color brochure.

The Boyd Converting Company brochure, which is a basic 8½ × 11-inch folder, demonstrates how Gargan Communication copywriter Peter Stasiowski (see The Inside Story, Chapter 13) was able to update the manufacturer's marketing materials.[6] After touring projects in production at Boyd's factory, meeting some of the floor staff, and digesting key facts about the company's business, Stasiowski got the idea of creating a "tour guide." The brochure was developed using this analogy to communicate 1) a deliberate step-by-step approach in Boyd's processes and, 2) the empowerment Boyd management bestows on its experienced and friendly staff. Detailed information (which could conceivably require future updating and therefore expensive printing costs) was not included. Inserts were designed to allow Boyd office staff to update and customize such detailed information using office printers. The presentation folder visually and physically ties the elements together.

HOW TO WRITE RADIO COPY

Ads that are broadcast on either radio or television are usually 15, 30, or 60 seconds in length. This short length means the commercials must be simple enough for consumers to grasp, yet intriguing enough to prevent viewers from switching the station. To hold viewer attention, the messages need to be interesting and entertaining.

Characteristics of Radio Advertising

Radio has some unique characteristics that make it a challenging medium for advertisers. The most intimate of all media, radio functions as a good friend, particularly for teenagers, and appeals to their special musical interests. Although radio is pervasive in that it tends to surround many of our activities, it is seldom the listener's center of attention and more usually a background element. Also, because radio is a transitory medium, the ability of the listener to remember facts (such as the name of the advertiser, addresses, and phone numbers) is difficult. These characteristics are typical of radio advertising:

- **_Personal._** Radio advertising has an advantage over print—the ability to use the human voice. The copy for radio ads should use conversational language—as if someone is "talking with" the consumer rather than "selling to" the consumer.

- *Interest-based.* Radio allows for specialized programming to target markets. Listeners mostly tune in to hear music, but talk radio is popular, too. There are shows on health, pets, finance, politics—whatever people are interested in. Copywriters should design commercials to speak to that audience interest; use the appropriate tone of voice. If the station plays heavy metal music, then the style and tone of the commercial might be raucous and spirited.

- *Inattention.* Most people who are listening to the radio are doing something else at the same time, such as jogging or driving. Radio spots must be designed to break through the inattention and capture attention in the first three seconds with sound effects, music, questions, commands, or something unexpected.

- *Retention.* To help the listener remember what you are selling, commercial copy should mention the name of the product emphatically and repeat it. An average of three mentions in a 30-second commercial and five mentions in a 60-second commercial may not be too frequent, as long as the repetition is not done in a forced and/or annoying manner. Copywriters use taglines and other key phrases to lock the product in consumers' memories.

- *Call to action.* The last thing listeners hear is what they tend to remember, so copywriters make sure the product is it. They phrase the Big Idea in a way that serves as a call to action and reminds listeners of the brand name at the close of the commercial. For example, a commercial about the wonderful things that happen when people eat Edy's Grand Ice Cream ends with the line: "It's creamy, it's rich, it's wonderful. It's Edy's Grand Ice Cream."

- *Ephemeral.* A radio message is here one moment and gone the next. You cannot tune in to the middle of an ad and then go back to the headline as you can with print. You cannot reread a radio message. That's why copywriters repeat the key points of brand name and identification information, such as a phone number or Web address.

Conversational Style In addition to being entertaining, another message characteristic of radio is its conversational style. Radio copywriters write in a conversational style using vernacular language. Spoken language is different from written language. We talk in short sentences, often in sentence fragments and run-ons. We seldom use complex sentences in speech. We use contractions that would drive an English teacher crazy. Spoken language is not polished prose.

In advertising, word choice should match the speech of the target audience. Slang can be hard to handle and sound phony, but copy that picks up the nuances of people's speech sounds natural. Each group has its own way of speaking, its own phrasing. Teenagers don't talk like 8-year-olds or 80-year-olds. A good radio copywriter has an ear for the distinctive patterns of speech for the target audience. An example comes from the classic commercial written by Stan Freberg for the Radio Advertising Bureau. Notice how easy it is to hear the announcer's voice and the sound effects as you read through the script.[7]

Freberg:	Okay, people, now when I give the cue, I want the 700-foot mountain of whipped cream to roll into Lake Michigan, which has been drained and filled with hot chocolate. Then the Royal Canadian Air Force will fly overhead towing a ten-ton maraschino cherry which will be dropped into the whipped cream to the cheering of 25,000 extras.
Freberg:	Allright, cue the mountain.
SFX:	(creaks, groans, prolonged splash)
Freberg:	Cue the Air Force.
SFX:	(Propellers roar into and past mike; wing struts whine)
Freberg:	Cue the maraschino cherry.

SFX:	(Screaming, whistling fall, and large plop)
Freberg:	Now—you want to try that on television?
Sponsor:	Wel-l-l—
Freberg:	You see, radio's a very special medium because it stretches the imagination.
Sponsor:	Doesn't television stretch the imagination?
Freberg:	Up to 21 inches—yes.

Courtesy of the Radio Advertising Bureau.

Theater of the Mind For radio commercials that tell a story, radio is a theater of the mind, as Freberg's "Lake Michigan" commercial demonstrated. The story is visualized in the listener's imagination. How the characters look and where the scene is set come from their personal experience. Sometimes radio advertising copywriters imagine they are writing a musical play. This particular play will be performed before an audience whose eyes are closed. The copywriter has all the theatrical tools of voices, sound effects, and music, but no visuals.

Radio urges the copywriter to reach into the depths of imagination to create an idea that rouses the inattentive listener. Remember, radio is visual, or at least it uses imagination to create an image in a listener's mind. The Radio Advertising Bureau has used the slogan "I saw it on the radio" to illustrate the power of imagery. Even though we're talking about imagery, it is still produced by the copywriter's masterful use of the tools of audio—voice, music, and sound effects. Research indicates that the use of imagery in radio advertising leads to high levels of attention and more positive general attitudes toward the ad and its claims.[8]

Radio broadcast specialist Peter Hochstein, of the Ogilvy & Mather agency, recommends that copywriters create vivid images in the minds of listeners, particularly for commercials that tell a story. To meet this challenge, he recommends that they follow these 10 guidelines:[9]

1. **Identify your sound effects.** Tell listeners what they're hearing, and they'll be more likely to hear it.
2. **Use music as a sound effect.**
3. **Build your commercial around a sound.** Use the sound of a crisp new cracker, for example, or thunder to represent the power of a solid bank account.
4. **Give yourself time.** Fight for 60-second spots. It is often impossible to establish your sound effects in 30 seconds and still relate them to product benefits.
5. **Consider using no sound effects.** A distinctive voice or a powerful message straightforwardly spoken can be more effective than noises from the tape library.
6. **Beware of comedy.** It's rare when you can sit down at your computer and match the skill of the best comedians. However, well-written and relevant humor can be a powerful advertising technique.
7. **If you insist on being funny, begin with an outrageous premise.** Lake Michigan will be drained of water and refilled with whipped cream. A man puts on his wife's nightgown at 4 a.m. and goes out to buy *Time* magazine—and the cops catch him.
8. **Keep it simple.** Radio is a wonderful medium for building brand awareness. It's a poor medium for registering long lists of copy points or making complex arguments. What one thing is most important about your product?
9. **Tailor your commercial to time, place, and specific audience.** If it is running in Milwaukee, you can tailor it for Milwaukee. You can talk in the lingo of the people who will be listening and tailor it to the time of day in which your commercial will be broadcast. Talk about breakfast at the breakfast hour or offer a commuter taxi service during rush hour.
10. **Present your commercial to your client on tape, if possible.** Most radio scripts look boring on paper. Acting, timing, vocal quirks, and sound effects make them come alive.

In summary, the key to effective radio advertising stories is to evoke visual images based on what the listener hears. Writers creating ads for radio need to capitalize on its intimacy and ability to reach listeners' imaginations. Successful radio writers and producers have excellent visualization skills and a great theatrical sense.

The Tools of Radio Copywriting

Print copywriters use a variety of tools—headlines, body copy, slogans, and so forth—to write their copy. In radio advertising, the tools are the audio elements that the copywriter uses to craft a commercial, which are voice, music, and sound effects. Audio producers can manipulate these tools to create a variety of effects.

Voice Voice is probably the most important element in radio advertising. Voices are heard in jingles, spoken dialogue, and announcements. Most commercials have an announcer, if not as the central voice, at least at the closing to wrap up the product identification. Dialogue uses character voices to convey an image of the speaker: a child, an old man, an executive, a Little League baseball player, or an opera singer. The absence of pictures demands that the voices the copywriter specifies help listeners "see" the characters in the commercial. The copywriter understands that we imagine people and what they are like based on their voices.

Music Music is an important radio advertising element because it lets consumers sing the selling message. Anything consumers can sing along with makes them remember the message more easily. For that reason, radio copywriters are often very good at writing jingles. They understand the interplay of catchy phrases and "hummable" music that creates little songs that stick in our minds. They may work with a composer who writes the music, but the words in the song are the responsibility of the copywriter.

Music can also be used behind the dialogue to create mood and establish the setting. Any mood, from that of a circus to that of a candle-lit dinner, can be conveyed through music. Similar to movie scriptwriters, radio copywriters have a sense of the imagery of music and the role it plays in creating dramatic effects.

Advertisers can have a piece of music composed for a commercial or can borrow it from a previously recorded song. Numerous music libraries sell stock music that is not copyrighted. The drawback to using stock music is the chance that other ads will use the same music. Jingle houses are companies that specialize in writing and producing commercial music, catchy songs about a product that carry the theme and product identification. A custom-made jingle—one that is created for a single advertiser—can cost $10,000 or more. In contrast, many jingle houses create "syndicated" jingles made up of a piece of music that can be applied to different lyrics and sold to several different advertisers in different markets around the country for as little as $1,000 or $2,000.

Sound Effects The sound of seagulls and the crash of waves, the clicking of typewriter keys, and the cheers of fans at a stadium all create images in our minds and cue the setting, as well as the action. The Freberg commercial shows how **sound effects** are described in a radio script, as well as the importance of these effects in making a commercial attention-getting and memorable. The BellSouth campaign featuring Dixie Carter (see Figure 12.1) used construction sound effects to help identify the setting and move the story along. Sound effects can be original, but more often they are taken from sound effect libraries. As with anything else, restraint is a good rule with sound effects. Use only those you need unless the genuine purpose is to bombard the listener with sounds.

Radio Commercial Planning

Radio commercials are usually written for 30-, 45-, and 60-second timeframes, although 10- and 15-second spots may be used for brand reminders or station identification. As a

WESTWAYNE

BellSouth Advertising & Publishing: 60 Radio
"Landscaping"/The *Real* Yellow Pages® Online

MUSIC:	EXISTING DIXIE THEME
SFX:	LIGHT CONSTRUCTION. HIGH-TECH BEEPING OF COMPUTER KEYBOARD IN BACKGROUND.
DIXIE:	This is Dixie Carter on the Tennessee River and I'm just finishing up my getaway home, with my "hubby," Hal Holbrook.
	He's been in the den all day using The *Real* Yellow Pages Online, researching the best way to landscape. Now that the *Real* Yellow Pages® from BellSouth is on the Internet, you can find anything on your computer. It's SO easy! And accurate. All the information from the book, plus maps and helpful facts on hundreds of subjects so you can do your homework in a hurry!
SFX:	WORKER YELLING: Hey, guys, give me a hand with this sod, will ya?
DIXIE:	Hal's such a sweetie. I don't want to peek and spoil his surprise, but I can't wait to see what he's doing with the lawn!
SFX:	DING DONG.
WORKER:	We're about finished out here, ma'am. Where do you want the flag?
DIXIE:	Flag?
WORKER:	For the *putting green* on the par 3 golf hole your husband is putting in. Haven't you seen it? It's a beauty!!
SECOND WORKER:	Excuse me, ma'am, where sould we park the golf cart?
DIXIE:	(FLABBERGASTED) I think that's a question HAL should answer…
ANNCR:	Use the *Real* Yellow Pages Online from BellSouth at www.yp.bellsouth.com. Is there anything that book can't do?!

FIGURE 12.1   BELLSOUTH "LANDSCAPING" RADIO SCRIPT

rule, you can estimate that two to three words per second is average for a well-paced commercial, which means you can go as high as 90 words in a 30-second, all-copy commercial. If you write longer ones, chances are your speaker will have to rush through the copy with little or no time for the pauses and special inflections that add color and dimension to the spoken word.

Copywriters working on a radio commercial use a standard **script** format to write the copy to certain time blocks—all the words, dialogue, lyrics, sound effects, instructions, and descriptions. The instructions and descriptions are to help the producer tape the commercial so that it sounds exactly as the copywriter imagined. The script format usually has the source of the audio written down the left side, and the content—words an announcer reads, dialogue, and description of the sound effects and music—on the right. The instructions and descriptions, anything that isn't spoken, are in capital letters.

For example, here is a script for the PowerBar energy bar by Black Rocket copywriter, Aaron Stern, from a radio campaign that conveys the bar's benefits in a humorous way.[10] The creative idea is that someone would attempt absurd feats, such as riding a bike 40 miles in freezing temperatures to buy flowers for an angry girlfriend, to demonstrate long-lasting energy during strenuous workouts.

PowerBar Radio "Mattress" :45

Bill: Hello Fredricks, this is Bill.

Tim: Hi Fredricks, I was wondering. . . . Do you have any queen size mattresses in stock?

Bill: Lots of 'em.

Tim: Oh great, okay. Um . . . what do those weigh?

Bill: Oh geez, I don't know. The mattress probably weighs 90 pounds . . . a hundred. I mean I can help you get it out to your truck. Whatdya got?

Tim: Actually, I'm on foot, so I thought I'd carry it.

Bill: Oh—[Bleep!]

Tim: But it's not a problem. I'm gonna eat a PowerBar and it'll give me plenty of energy to get home.

Bill: (LAUGHS) Where do you live?

Tim: Broadway and 65th. The other side of the Park.

Bill: No [bleeping!] chance! Don't even think about walking.

Tim: I'll be fine. The PowerBar will keep me going. I'll just carry the mattress home.

Bill: You're nuts. (TO FRIEND) He's on Broadway and 65th. (TO TIM) You gotta be outta your mind. You'd never make it. You'd collapse.

Tim: Just have the mattress ready. I'll be there in 10 minutes.

Bill: You're nuts. You ain't gonna make it.

Tim: I'll see you there.

Bill: (LAUGHS, AND HANGS UP)

ANNCR: PowerBar energy bars. Balanced nutrition and lasting energy for everyday life . . . and then some. Power on.

HOW TO WRITE TELEVISION COPY

Television is unlike radio or print in many ways, but mostly because it is a medium of moving images. The challenge for the advertiser is to fuse the images with the words to present not only a creative concept, but also a story. One of the strengths of television, then, is its ability to reinforce verbal messages with visuals or reinforce visuals with verbal messages. As Ogilvy's Peter Hochstein explains, "The idea behind a television commercial is unique in advertising. The TV commercial consists of pictures that move to impart facts or evoke emotion, and selling words that are not read but heard. The perfect combination of sight and sound can be an extremely potent selling tool."[11]

The point of audiovisual fusion is that words and pictures must work together or commercials will show one thing and say something else. Researchers have found that people have trouble listening to and watching television commercials at the same time unless the audio and visual messages work together to develop the point. People process television information by rapidly switching back and forth between the visuals and the words. The process works more easily when the words and visuals reinforce one another. A Mountain Dew commercial that worked effectively was a takeoff on a James Bond adventure with 007 in grunge dress on snowboards and mountain bikes. The storyline was reinforced by the Bond-like music and the tagline, "Shaken, not stirred."

Most people pay more attention to television than they do to radio programming. People watching a program they enjoy often are absorbed in it. Their absorption is only slightly less than that experienced by people watching a movie in a darkened theater. Effective television commercials can achieve this level of audience absorption if they are written to maximize the dramatic aspects of moving images and storytelling. Copywriters can minimize viewers' patterns of avoidance by creating commercials that are intriguing or intrusive.

For example, the Best of Show award for a One Show competition (that's one of the creative advertising award shows) showcased a British campaign for Volkswagen that featured a 30-second humorous commercial built around the low price of the VW Polo. Fallon's Bob Barrie, who was president of The One Club (an association for people in the creative side of advertising), explained that it was possibly the quietest, most understated TV spot entered in the show. The idea was simple: A woman sits at her kitchen table. She slowly reads her morning newspaper, hiccuping. Her ailment is relieved by a subtly surprising VW Polo ad with its "surprisingly ordinary" price.[12]

Characteristics of Television Copy

Television is a visual medium, but so are newspapers and magazines. So what makes the difference in impact between television and print visuals? Television copywriters understand that it is the moving image, the action, that makes television so much more mesmerizing than print.

Storytelling is one way that copywriters can present action in a television commercial more powerfully than in other media. Television's ability to touch our emotions, and to show us things—to demonstrate how they look and work—make television advertising highly persuasive. These are just a few of the characteristics of television ads. Here are more.

Characteristic	Message Design
• **Action:** When you watch television you are watching a walking, talking, moving world that gives the illusion of being three-dimensional.	• Good television advertising uses the effect of action and motion to attract attention and sustain interest. Torture tests, steps, and procedures are all actions that are easier to present on TV than in print.
• **Demonstration:** Seeing is believing. Believability and credibility—the essence of persuasion—are high because we believe what we see with our own eyes.	• If you have a strong sales message that lends itself to demonstration, such as "how-to" messages, then television is the ideal medium for that message.
• **Storytelling:** Most of the programming on television is narrative so commercials use storytelling to take advantage of the medium's strengths.	• TV is our society's master storyteller because of its ability to present a plot and the action that leads to a conclusion in which the product plays a major role. TV can dramatize the situation in which a product is used and the type of people using it. Stories can be riveting if they are well told, but they must be imaginative to hold their own against the programming that surrounds them.
• **Emotion:** The ability to touch the feelings of the viewer makes television commercials entertaining, diverting, amusing, and absorbing. Real-life situations with all their humor, anger, fear, pride, jealousy, and love come alive on the screen. Humor, in particular, works well on television.	• Emotional appeals are found in natural situations that everyone can identify with. Hallmark has produced some tear-jerking commercials about the times of our lives that we remember by the cards we receive and save. Kodak and Polaroid have used a similar strategy for precious moments that are remembered in photographs.

The Tools of Television Copywriting

Television copywriters have two primary tools: their audio and visual toolkits. Both words and pictures are designed to create exactly the right impact. For example, a Saatchi & Saatchi creative team once proposed this idea to its Toyota client: "I will always speak my mind. Every day," says a man wearing sunglasses, followed by the campaign's slogan on a black screen, "Toyota. Everyday." The creative director explained there were six months of arguments about the incorrect spelling of "everyday" in the slogan. Grammatically, "everyday" should be two words (except when it's an adjective), but the client chose the one-word "everyday" because it looks friendlier. The creative director explained, "It's more than just a word. It's how the word looks. It's how you deconstruct the message."[13] So choosing words for a commercial takes a lot of thought—as do the other audio and video components of commercials. Let's take a look at those components in more depth.

Video Usually, when we watch a commercial, we are more aware of what we're seeing than anything else. So the creative team makes sure the visuals deliver the Big Idea. Copywriters keep in mind that visuals and motion, the silent speech of film, should convey as much of the message as possible. Likewise, emotion, which is the effect created by storytelling, is expressed convincingly in facial expressions, gestures, and other body language.

Because television is theatrical, many of the copywriter's tools, such as characters, costumes, sets and locations, props, lighting, optical and computerized special effects, and on-screen graphics, are similar to those you would use in a play, television show, or movie. Because of the number of video and audio elements, a television commercial is the most complex of all advertising forms.

An example of an engaging video story comes from London's WCRS agency, which created an Andy award–winning commercial for Land Rover that shows the car being "let free" in a game reserve to go back to nature.[14] Here's how the copy for the commercial reads:

Freeing the Freelander

VIDEO: The commercial opens on a truck hacking its way across the Massai Mara game reserve in Kenya with a huge timber crate loaded on the back of it.

CUT to head ranger driving the truck. He speaks Africaans but his words are subtitled at the bottom of the screen.

RANGER (SUBTITLES): "It's all wrong. The city is no place for them. Stood all day. Crammed up with no space to move around in. They should be out here in these wide-open spaces where they can run free the way they were meant to."

VIDEO: The truck stops and a pair of giraffes peer curiously over at it. Three game wardens shoulder their rifles, lower the truck's tailgate and open the front of the giant crate. They bang on the side of the crate. But whatever is inside seems reluctant to come out. The huge crate starts to vibrate as whatever is inside reacts badly to the rangers' banging.

Then, finally realizing there's a whole new world out there, a Freelander shoots down the truck tailgate ramp and out onto the Savannah, where he's joined by a little friend . . . a 3-door Freelander.

The two meet bumper to bumper. Then the released Freelanders take a last look around at the rangers and the pair tears off over the Savannah, churning up the dust behind them.

CUT back to the rangers. They've stopped to watch the pair from a rocky escarpment overlooking the Savannah. Through a pair of binoculars we see the pair racing to catch up to a herd of Freelanders in the distance.

Happy to see the Freelanders racing around enjoying themselves, the rangers pat each other on the back and climb back on board the truck. As the head ranger drives off he seems almost to wipe a tear from his eyes.

SUPER: Freelander. Made by Land Rover.

The Freelander commercial is creative because of its unexpected comparison of the car to a wild animal being let free in the wilderness. It's an intriguing thought, but it also has strong visual imagery tied to the idea of a wild animal exulting in its freedom. Even though the message is carried in the visuals with very little dialogue, the commercial is still "written," as demonstrated in this script, and the copywriter is responsible for putting the creative team's vision of this commercial on paper so it can be produced as they imagined it.

Audio The three audio elements of television, as in radio, are music, voices, and sound effects, but they are used differently in television commercials because they are connected to a visual image. The copywriter, for example, may have an announcer speak directly to the viewer or engage in a dialogue with another person, who may or may not be on camera. The copywriter has to block out on paper how this "talk" happens, as well as write the words they will say.

A common manipulation of the camera–announcer relationship is the **voice-over**, in which an announcer who is not visible describes some kind of action on the screen. Sometimes a voice is heard off camera, which means it is coming from either side, from behind, or from above. There are people who specialize in voice-overs for both television and radio, called voice-over artists.

A commercial for Geico insurance won a John Caples International award for its engaging use of a voice. The copywriter was responsible for both the words and the way they were delivered. In a spot titled "Collect Call," which was set in a hospital waiting room, a man places a collect call to his parents. To save on the costs of the call, he states as his name:

"Bob Wehadababyitsaboy."

The message is delivered, however, the call is refused. So the next scene shows him trying to cram even more information into his name:

"Bob WehadababyitsaboyeightpoundssevenouncesMomsfine."

The voice-over advises the audience that they don't have to cheat the phone company to save money. A 15-minute call to Geico can save them up to 15 percent on their insurance.

Music is also important in most commercials. Sometimes it is just used as background, other times the song is the focus of the commercial. In the catchy "Da Da Da" commercial by Trio, which won an EFFIE for the VW Golf, the pleasantly monotonous song helped tell the story of two Gen Xers on a Sunday afternoon tooling aimlessly around town in their red VW Golf, but going nowhere in particular, an idea reflected in a minimalist piece of European music, called "Da Da Da." The commercial's creative director, Lance Jensen, was the one who remembered the weird little tune from college. His copywriter colleague, Alan Pafenbach, commented, Lance is "a repository for musical trivia like this." "Da Da Da" perfectly expressed the feeling of doing nothing on a Sunday afternoon but driving aimlessly around town.

In recognition of the role of music in advertising, Universal Music released a CD in 2001 called "As Seen on TV: Songs From Commercials," a collection of tunes that have become popular—or resurrected—thanks to their use in TV commercials. Included among the 20 songs are the "Da Da Da" song, "Mr. Roboto" by Styx, "Right Here, Right Now" by Fatboy Slim, "Lust for Life" by Iggy Pop, and "Got to Give It Up" by Marvin Gaye. All of these songs have been used effectively in a television commercial because they add to the message strategy.

Other TV Tools The audio and video tools must be put into the right setting and surrounded by appropriate props. The right talent must be chosen, and appropriate lighting and pacing are critical. The creative tools examined next are the setting, casting, costumes, props, and lighting—all of which the copywriter must describe in the script.

The setting, or **set**, is where the action takes place. It can be something in the studio, from a simple tabletop to a constructed set that represents a storefront. Commercials shot outside the studio are said to be filmed **on location**, which means the entire crew and cast are transported somewhere away from the studio. The location could be an alley or a garage down the street, or it could be some exotic place such as New Zealand. The location conveys the physical details of a setting in terms of what the setting adds to the ad message.

A television commercial has all the ingredients of a play. For many commercials, the most important element is the people who are called **talent**. Finding the right person for each role is called **casting**. People can be cast as:

- *Announcers* (either onstage or offstage), presenters, introducers
- *Spokespersons* (or "spokesthings"—such as talking butter dishes)
- *Character types* (old woman, baby, skin diver, police officer)
- *Celebrities,* such as Shaquille O'Neill, who came to the NBA with a complete marketing plan in hand outlining his endorsement strategy

Depending on the featured people, costumes and makeup can be an important part of the story. Of course, historical stories need period costumes, but modern scenes may also require special clothing such as ski outfits, swimsuits, or cowboy boots. Makeup may be important if you need to create a skin problem or change a character from young to old. All of these details have to be specified by the copywriter in the script, although makeup artists do the actual work.

The director usually manipulates the lighting, but the copywriter might have to specify special lighting effects in the script. For example, you might read "Low lighting, as in a bar," or "Intense bright light, as though reflected from snow," or "Light flickering on people's faces as if it were reflecting from a television screen."

Copywriters might also have to specify the commercial's **pace**—how fast or slowly the action progresses. Some messages are best developed at a languid pace; others work better when presented at an upbeat and fast pace. The pacing in the "Da Da Da" commercial, unlike many MTV-inspired commercials aimed at a young audience, was slow—a deliberate decision made to emphasize the underoccupied lifestyle of some Gen Xers.

Planning the TV Commercial: Scripts and Storyboards

A print advertisement is created in two pieces: a copy sheet and a layout. Commercials are planned with two similar documents—a script prepared by the copywriter and a storyboard drawn by the art director. Similar to a radio script, a TV script is the written version of the commercial's plan. It contains all the words, dialogue, lyrics (if important to the ad message), instructions, and descriptions of the details we've been discussing—sets, costumes, lighting, and so forth.

The **storyboard**, which is the visual plan or layout of the commercial, shows the number of scenes, the composition of the shots, and the progression of the action. Although there are art directors (and sometimes producers) who design the look and rough out the storyboard, the copywriter does most of the actual writing of the commercial.

For television commercials, the script is written in two columns, with the audio on the right and the video on the left. The BellSouth "Bedroom" script featuring Dixie Carter is an example of a television script, in this case combined with descriptions of key frames from the commercial. The key to the structure of a television script is the relationship between the audio and the video. The video is typed opposite the corresponding audio (see Figure 12.2). Sometimes these audio and visual segments are numbered to correspond to the frames on the storyboard.

Key TV Decisions Copywriters need to answer many questions when planning a television spot. How much product information should there be in the commercial? Should the action be fast or slow? Is it wise to defy tradition and do unusual ads that create controversy? How intrusive should the ad be?

WEST WAYNE

BellSouth Advertising & Publishing: TV
The *Real* Yellow Pages® "Bedroom"

SUPER: Dixie Relaxes in Bedroom.

OPEN ON DIXIE SITTING IN YOGA POSITION ON BED, FULLY CLOTHED.

SHE CONTENTEDLY PATS COVER OF BOOK LYING NEXT TO HER ON BED.

DIXIE IN 2ND YOGA POSITION.

FINGER POINTS TO "DONNA'S GLASS" IN THE BOOK.

DIXIE IN 3RD YOGA POSITION.

FINGER POINTS TO "D.J. SMITH RUGS" IN THE BOOK.

DIXIE IN 4TH YOGA POSITION.

DIXIE HOLDING BOOK.

SFX: (DOORBELL)

CUT BACK TO DIXIE ON BED.

SUPER: Next Living Room.

TITLE: The *Real* Yellow Pages® from BellSouth.

DIXIE: Now that the bedroom's finished, I can finally relax!

Fortunately, with The *Real* Yellow Pages®, I can do all the work on my new living room right from here!

DIXIE: Delivery at twelve. GREAT.

DIXIE: Cobalt blue glasses . . .

DIXIE: . . .lovely!

DIXIE: Carpet? No . . .

DIXIE: A big area rug.

DIXIE: Isn't it amazing how much you can do with this trusty, dependable book?

DIXIE: Except open the door.

FIGURE 12.2 BELLSOUTH "BEDROOM" TV SCRIPT

Every producer and director will respond to these questions differently, depending on personal preferences and advertising objectives. Nevertheless, these general principles as outlined by Jewler in his creative strategy book, are relevant for most effective television commercials:[15]

- Gain the interest of your viewer at the beginning; the first 3 seconds are critical.
- Focus on a key visual, a scene that encapsulates your entire selling message into one neat package.
- Be single-minded. Tell one important story per commercial. Tell it clearly, tell it memorably, and involve your viewer.
- Observe the rules of good editing. Make it easy for the viewer to get into the idea of the commercial.
- Always try to show the product in close-up at the end.

In planning a television commercial, many considerations determine how the commercial is built—its internal logic. Copywriters must plan how long the commercial will be, what shots will appear in each scene, what the key visual will be, and where and how to shoot the commercial. Other key decisions the copywriter has to consider in planning a commercial are the length, number of scenes, and key frames.

The common lengths of commercials are 10, 15, 20, 30, and 60 seconds. The 10-, 15-, and 20-second lengths are used for reminders and product or station identification. The 60-second spot, which is common in radio, has almost disappeared in television because of the increasing cost of air time. The most common length for a TV commercial is 30 seconds. A longer timeframe allows a radio copywriter to create a more well-developed drama or product explanation than is possible in television.

A commercial is planned in scenes—
segments of action that occur in a
single location as seen here in the
EFFIE winning Southwestern Bell
"Squirrels" commercial. The
commercial demonstrated the need
for additional phone lines.

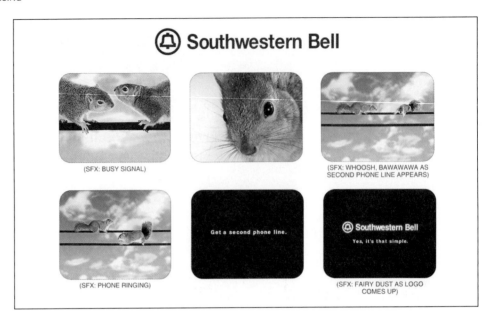

A commercial is planned in scenes—segments of action that occur in a single location. Within a scene there may be several shots from different angles. A 30-second commercial usually is planned with four to six scenes, but a fast-paced commercial may have many more.

Because television is a visual medium, the message is often developed from a key visual that contains the heart of the concept, as Jewler mentioned in his list of tips. A key frame is that visual that sticks in the mind and becomes the image that viewers remember when they think about the commercial.

Alternative concepts are also tested as key visuals in the development of the idea for the commercial. For each idea, a card with the key visual drawn on it is given to a respondent, along with a paragraph that describes the concept and how it will be played out in the commercial.

WRITING FOR THE WEB

As we all know, the last 10 years or so have brought a new frontier for advertising—the Web. This new medium is more interactive than any other mass medium—not only does the viewer initiate the contact; viewers can send an e-mail on many if not most Web sites (see the "Quote Quilt" ad). This makes Web advertising more like two-way communication, and that's one of its primary strengths and a major point of difference from other advertising forms.

So not only is the Web copywriter challenged to attract people to the site, but also to manage a dialogue-based communication experience. Web advertisers have to listen and respond, as well as target messages to audiences. That's a major shift in how Web marketing communicators think about advertising.

Take a surf and you'll see there's a variety of types of marketing communication formats available on the Web; everything from hot buttons and banners that flash a quick message to home pages with extensive information and corporate sites that track orders and provide internal communication systems for employees. It's all marketing communication, but it doesn't all look like traditional advertising.

In this complicated, fast-moving medium, there aren't a lot of rules. For banners and other formats that look like advertising and seek to attract someone to a company's Web site, verbosity is a killer. In that situation, no one wants to read a lot of type online. However, the Web is an information medium and users come to it, in some

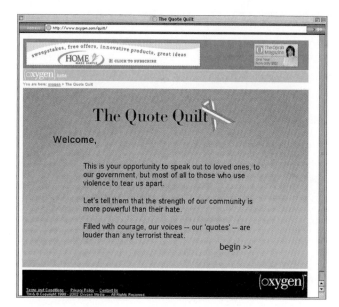

The Web encourages interactivity as this site demonstrates in its invitation for people to respond to the aftermath of the September 11 terrorist attack.

cases, for extensive reference information—formats that look a lot like catalogues, or even encyclopedias.

The challenge for Web advertisers, then, is to understand the user's situation and design messages that fit the user's needs. That means Web copywriters have to be able to write everything from catchy phrases for banners to copy that works like traditional advertisements, or brochures, or catalogues. And, all the time they have to remember that one of the strengths of Web communication is that Web users write back. So let's look at some of the tricks used in Web copywriting, particularly for banners and Web advertisements.

Banners

The most common form of online advertising, **banner ads** are usually small box ads containing text, images, and perhaps animation. Banners in this extremely small format have to be creative to stand out amidst the clutter on a typical Web page and, similar to outdoor advertising, they have to grab the surfer's attention with few words. Effective banners must arouse the interest of the viewer, who is often browsing through other information on the computer screen. The key to stopping surfers is vivid graphics and clever phrases. In general, the copywriter has these strategies for grabbing the surfer.[16]

The copywriter must think about:

1. Offering a deal that promises a discount or a freebie as a prize.
2. Using an involvement device such as a challenge or contest.
3. Changing the offer frequently, perhaps even daily. One of the reasons people surf the net is to find out what's happening now. Good ads exploit "nowness" and "newsiness."
4. Keeping the writing succinct because most surfers have short attention spans and get bored easily.
5. Focusing surfers' attention by asking provocative questions or offering knowledge they can use.
6. Finding ways to use the advertisement to solicit information and opinions from users as part of your research. Reward surfers for sharing their opinions with you by offering them three free days of a daily horoscope or something else they might find fun or captivating.

Sometimes banners provide brand reminder information only, like a billboard, but they usually also invite viewers to "click" on the banner to link to an ad or the advertiser's home page. A major reason for using banners is to lure viewers from other

A MATTER OF PRINCIPLE

THE OCEAN SPEAKS

▶ The scuba diving industry wanted to revive interest in the sport of scuba, both with current divers and potential newcomers. Chris Hutchinson, of San Diego's Bulldog Drummond agency, explained how this striking campaign came together. The objective was to build a relationship with diving and move people from print to the company's Web site.

He explains, "So we created a campaign in the literal voice of the ocean. The Ocean irreverently compares itself to the dull world up above, and invites people to come down for a visit. Instead of using traditional beauty shots of scuba diving, we commissioned surreal organic underwater scenes. The ads were recently featured in *Archive*. The creative idea is that the ocean not only has a personality, it speaks in the body copy."

First read the copy from these ads, then consider how that style of writing has been transferred to the Web site.

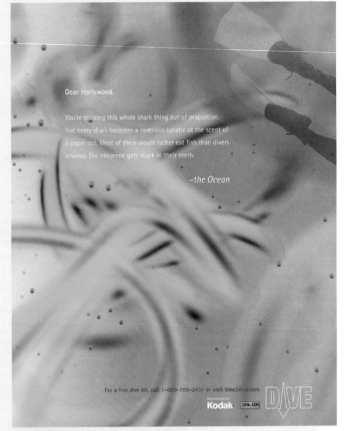

> ### Dear Hollywood,
> *You're blowing this whole shark thing out of proportion.*
> *Not every shark becomes a ravenous lunatic at the scent of a paper cut.*
> *Most of them would rather eat fish than divers anyway. The neoprene gets stuck in their teeth.*
>
> —*the Ocean*

> ### Excuse me Mr. Jobs.
> *This whole iMac thing—distinctly shell-like.*
> *I think you ripped those colors from me too.*
> *Let's give credit where credit is due, huh?*
>
> —*the Ocean*

The ocean also speaks on the Web site (time2dive. com). Once on the home page, visitors identify themselves as either new divers or experienced divers. Each page has its own message from the ocean at the top, followed by a sign-up sheet. This is from the new diver page:

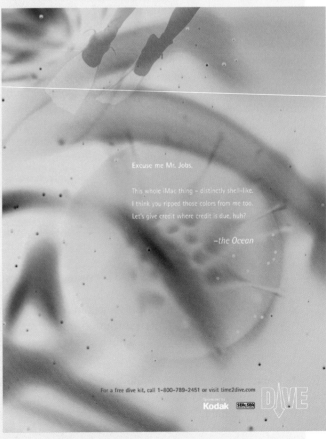

> ### About this weekend.
> *I have 15,000 unidentified species down here all waiting to be classified.*
> *But if you have to help somebody move or something, I'll understand.*
>
> —*the Ocean*

And this is from the old timers' page:

> ### Haven't seen you in a while. So what's up?
> *It's come to my attention that you haven't been diving in what, 6 months?*
> *Did I do something wrong? Was it that rip tide when you were body surfing? Lighten up.*
>
> —*the Ocean*

Source: Material contributed by Chris Hutchinson, art director for San Diego–based Bulldog Drummond. He and his work were nominated for this feature by Professor Charles Frazer, University of Oregon.

sites to the advertiser's Web site. The effectiveness of such efforts is monitored by the number of "click-throughs," which is considered a measure of the pulling power of the banner.

Banners should be entertaining in order to attract attention. Their creators do this by using multimedia effects such as animation and sound, interactivity, emotional appeals, color, and provocative headlines. One mistake copywriters sometimes make, however, is to forget to include the company name or brand in the banner or ad. Surfers should be able to tell immediately what product or brand the banner is advertising.

A study of the most effective banner ads found that although they satisfy the need for entertainment, information, and context (a link to a product), they seldom provide economic appeals. In other words, most banners were deficient in offering promotional incentives, such as prizes or gifts for clicking through to the sponsor's Web site.[17] These standard promotional techniques also are useful in Web advertising to drive action.

Web Ads

Similar to traditional advertising, Web ads are designed to create awareness and interest in a product and build a brand image. Their effectiveness is compounded by the problem that they have to be accessed from somewhere else, like a banner ad or an ad in a magazine. The banner, for example, gets the surfer's attention, which then turns to interest when the surfer clicks through to the ad (or Web site). Therefore, these ads aren't focused as much on attracting attention as they are on maintaining interest.

In terms of creating interest, good copywriting works well in any medium. One print ad campaign that has effectively moved from print to a Web page is featured in the "A Matter of Principle" box. This is an example of how traditional advertising writing techniques continue to work effectively on the Web.

Other Web Formats

Many marketers are experimenting with new forms of Web advertising such as games, pop-up windows, daughter windows, and side frames. For example, one Procter & Gamble site supports the Scope "Send-a-Kiss" campaign, where visitors can send an electronic kiss to the special people in their lives. The site is customized for special holidays such as Valentine's Day and Mother's Day. P&G has found that of those who visit the site, 20 percent actually send e-mail kisses to Mom on Mother's Day.

Ultimately, these marketers want Web ads that are totally interactive. An Internet approach that uses broadcast media as a model may be the answer. They want to make Internet advertising better than television advertising—all the visual impact of traditional broadcast with the additional value of interactivity.

Oxygen.com is an integrated media company offering entertainment and information for women. Founded by Oprah Winfrey and others, it includes a 24-hour cable television network and an interactive Web site. But the most innovative product is "Deep Creek," a popular online soap opera. Part of the draw of the cyber series is that viewers can log on to www.oxygen.com/deepcreek, watch the latest episode, and vote for what they want to happen next.

Interactive participation attracts both viewers and advertisers to Deep Creek, an online soap opera at Oxygen.com.

Because of the show's massive popularity, Oxygen also sponsored the online soap's first contest, "The Deep Creek Celebrity Cameo Sweepstakes," in which viewers guessed the identity of a mysterious celebrity appearing in the soap. The winner of the promotion was animated into a "webisode" of Deep Creek. What was the advertising angle? Banners surround the entertainment site for everything from Ameritrade and Shop@aol.com, to the official Madonna Web site, so it is fast becoming an effective vehicle for other sponsors' ads.

The creative team comes up with the ideas for such Web formats and it's up to the copywriter to put the idea in words and explain how the user's experience with this Web site will work.

IT'S A WRAP
CISCO SYSTEMS AND THE INTERNET GENERATION

This chapter started with a story about Cisco Systems and its 1998 "Internet Generation" campaign that used non-technical language to talk to business managers about networking systems. The effective campaign exceeded many of its objectives:

1. Unaided brand awareness of Cisco increased 80 percent from the previous year; these results gave Cisco a brand awareness level that was 80 percent higher than two strong competitors, Lucent and Nortel.
2. Unaided ad awareness was up 91 percent from the previous year. Although Cisco competitors spent more on advertising, awareness of Cisco ads was 81 percent higher than that of Lucent's or Nortel's.
3. The "Internet Generation" campaign successfully established Cisco as the Internet company. This relationship was measured in two ways:
   • When asked what companies come to mind as having the greatest influence on the future of the Internet, the number of times Cisco was named increased by 101 percent.
   • When asked which company is leading the Internet revolution, Cisco was named six times more frequently than Sun, and ten times more than Nortel or Lucent.

The Internet Generation campaign was an EFFIE award–winner because it not only achieved its objectives, but it also made the Internet synonymous with Cisco for an increasingly important target audience. The campaign helped business managers understand that the Internet is the ultimate global network and, more importantly from a campaign perspective, that Cisco builds and delivers the ultimate systems that make this network run worldwide.

Summary

1. **Identify the good and bad practices in copywriting.**
   Words and pictures work together to shape a creative concept; however, it is the clever phrases and "magic words" crafted by copywriters that make ideas understandable and memorable. Copywriters who have an ear for language match the tone of the writing to the target audience. Good copy is succinct and single-minded. Copy that is less effective uses adese to imitate the stereotyped style of advertising.

2. **Describe the various copy elements of a print ad.** The key elements of a print ad include the headlines and body copy. Headlines target the prospect, draw the reader's attention, identify the product, start the sale, and lure the reader into the body copy. Body copy provides persuasive details, such as support for claims, as well as proof and reasons why.

3. **Explain the message characteristics and tools of radio advertising.** Radio commercials are personal and play to

consumers' interests. However, radio is primarily a background medium. Special techniques, such as repetition, are used to enhance retention. The three audio tools are voice, music, and sound effects.

4. **Discuss the major elements of television commercials.** The elements of TV commercials include audio and video tools. Television commercials can be characterized as using action, emotion, and demonstration to create messages that are intriguing as well as intrusive.

5. **Discuss how Web advertising is written.** Web advertising is interactive and involving. Web advertising has primarily focused on banners, although advertisers are using new forms that look more like magazine or television ads. Banners, and other forms of Web advertising, have to stand out amidst the clutter on a typical Web page, stop the surfing, and arouse the interest of the viewer.

Key Terms

Questions

1. Creative directors say the copy and art must work together to create a concept. Of all the ads in this chapter, which ones do you believe demonstrate that principle? Explain what the words contribute and how they work with the visual.

2. There are a number of principles discussed in the section on headlines. Find an ad that you think is particularly effective. Analyze how the headline works in terms of these headline principles.

3. One principle of print copywriting is that the headline catches the reader's eye, but the body copy wins the reader's heart. Find an ad that demonstrates that principle and explain how it works.

4. What are the major characteristics of radio ads?

5. What are the roles of voice, music, and sound effects in radio advertisements?

6. Professor Strong has set up a debate between the advertising sales director of the campus newspaper and the manager of the campus radio station, which is a commercial operation. During the discussion the newspaper representative says that most radio commercials sound like newspaper ads, but are harder to follow. The radio manager responds by claiming that radio creativity works with "the theater of the mind," and is more engaging than newspaper ads. Explain what these media selling points mean. Would you rather write for, or sell ads for, newspaper or radio?

7. Jingles are a popular creative form in radio advertising. Even so, there are probably more jingles that you don't want to hear again than ones that you do. Identify one jingle that you really dislike and another one that you like. Write an analysis of why these jingles either don't work or do work effectively for you.

8. What are the major characteristics of TV ads?

9. What are the roles of audio and visual elements in TV ads? What other elements must a copywriter consider in planning a TV commercial?

10. A principle of TV message design is that television is primarily a visual medium. However, very few television commercials are designed without a vocal element (actors or announcers). Even the many commercials that visually demonstrate products in action use an off-screen voice to provide information. Why is there a need to use a voice in a television commercial?

Suggested Class Project

Select a product that is advertised exclusively through print using a long-copy format. Examples might be business-to-business and industrial products, over-the-counter drugs, and some car and appliance ads. Now write a 30-second radio and a 30-second TV spot for that product. Present your work to the class along with an analysis of how the message design changed when you moved from print to radio and then to TV.

Internet Project

Surf the Web and find one banner ad that you think works to drive click throughs and one that doesn't. Print them out, then write an analysis that compares the two banner ads and explains why you think one is effective and the other is not.

Hallmark BUILD•A•CAMPAIGN *Projects*

Please review the Hallmark Case Appendix at the end of the text before responding to these questions.

1. Meet in small groups to discuss how Capitol Advertising used print media to achieve its brand insistence goals.

2. Should your local Hallmark store use print media? If so, develop a proposal for a print creative strategy and include two sample print ads for a magazine, newspaper, directory, or out-of-home ad.

HANDS-ON

SLICING AND DICING THE MARKET

Thomas Burke, president of Saatchi & Saatchi's infomercial division, calls infomercials "the most powerful form of advertising ever created." Infomercials are a form of paid television programming in which a particular product is demonstrated, explained, and offered for sale. Advertisers produce infomercials and pay cable and satellite systems and local television channels to air them.

Philips Electronics of Sweden broke ground with an infomercial that helped launch its $700 CD-i multimedia player in the United States. Microsoft, Sears, AT&T, and Apple Computer have also used infomercials, as have companies in Japan, Singapore, China, Indonesia, and other Asian countries.

Even though worldwide sales revenue from infomercials run in the billions, the infomercial industry has suffered a decline as media rates have risen and viewership has fallen. One reason for viewer decline is the drop in demand for fitness products that were sold effectively through infomercials. Still, the use of infomercials is increasing in product categories such as beauty, self-improvement, housewares, golf, and diet products.

Why do advertisers believe infomercials are powerful? Unlike regular commercials that are sandwiched between programming, viewers consciously choose to watch infomercials and the response to a particular infomercial can be measured quite accurately. For example, Lexus generated more than 40,000 telephone inquiries after launching its used-car program with an infomercial; 2 percent of those who called ultimately bought a Lexus automobile. Finally, the infomercial format is well adapted for communicating with prime prospects in small market segments who watch cable and special interest programs.

Because infomercials are typically 30 minutes in length and often feature studio audiences and celebrity announcers, many viewers believe they are watching regular talk-show programming. In fact, infomercials are sometimes called program-length commercials, or PLCs. It is precisely this blurring between commercial and regular programming that concerns some industry observers. For viewers who tune in late or slip out of the room during the brief disclaimer that differentiates infomercials from true entertainment-based programming, infomercials can be mistaken for "normal" programs.

Critics of infomercials also point out the format's potential to deceive consumers when advertisers make false or misleading product claims. Such criticism is often directed at traditional infomercial fare such as moneymaking schemes. Currently, the industry relies on self-regulation to address such concerns. ∎

IT'S YOUR TURN

1. Have you ever watched an infomercial? Have you ordered a product featured on an infomercial or do you know someone else who has? What affected the decision to buy or not to buy?
2. Watch (and videotape) a set of infomercials from cable or late-night TV. Which ones can be mistaken for programming? Will this confuse viewers? Are any of them using message techniques that might be criticized as misleading viewers? Identify the one that you believe is the least successful and prepare a proposal that would guide the revision of the infomercial to make it more effective.

Sources: Tim O'Leary, "Marketers Still Embrace Half Hour Programs," *DM News* (August 17, 1998): 12; Dena Levy, "Let's Find New Ways to Polish Our Image," *DM News* (August 17, 1998): 13; Kevin Whitelaw, "Not Just Slicing and Dicing," *U.S. News and World Report* (September 9, 1996): 43–44; Darren McDermott, "All-American Infomercials Sizzle in Asia," *Wall Street Journal* (June 25, 1996): B6; Andrew Miller and Michael Zapolin, "Does Your Product Have Infomercial Potential?" *Boston Business Journal* (June 14, 1996): 15.

Notes

1. Yumiko Ono, "Some Times Ad Agencies Mangle English Deliberately," *Wall Street Journal* (November 4, 1997): B1.

2. David Ogilvy, *Ogilvy on Advertising* (New York: Vintage, 1985).

3. Ibid.

4. Tim Nudd, "Shop Talk: Opening a Can of Whoop-Ass," *Adweek* (July 31, 2000): 21.

5. Sandra Dallas, "Road to Pave? Remember Burma-Shave!" *BusinessWeek* (December 30, 1996): 8; Frank Rowsome Jr., *The Verse by the Side of the Road* (New York: Dutton, 1965).

6. Peter Stasiowski and his work were nominated by Professor Tom Groth, University of West Florida (see "The Inside Story," Chapter 13).

7. This was used with permission from the Radio Advertising Bureau in my *Creative Advertising,* 2nd ed. (1991), 283.

8. Paul D. Bolls and Robert F. Potter, "I Saw It on the Radio: The Effects of Imagery Evoking Radio Commercials on Listeners' Allocation of Attention and Attitude toward the Ad," *Proceedings of the Conference of the American Academy of Advertising,* Darrel D. Muehling, ed. (Lexington, KY, 1998), 123–130.

9. Peter Hochstein, "Ten Rules for Making Better Radio Commercials," Ogilvy & Mather's Viewpoint (1981).

10. By Aaron Stern, a 1995 graduate of the University of Colorado, whose work as a copywriter at the Black Rocket agency was nominated by Professor Brett Robbs, University of Colorado.

11. Peter Hochstein, "Ten Rules for Making Better Radio Commercials," Ogilvy & Mather's Viewpoint (1981).

12. Bob Barrie, "Credits," *One* 2(1) (1998): 3.

13. Yumiko Ono, "Some Times Ad Agencies Mangle English Deliberately."

14. The Andy is an "award for creative excellence" given by the Advertising Club of New York.

15. Adapted from A. Jerome Jewler, *Creative Strategy in Advertising,* 4th ed. (Belmont, CA: Wadsworth, 1992), 164–65.

16. Adapted from John Burnett and Sandra Moriarty, *Marketing Communications: An Integrated Approach* (Upper Saddle River, NJ: Prentice-Hall, 1998), 296–97.

17. Blessie Miranda and Kuen-Hee Ju-Pak, "A Content Analysis of Banner Advertisements: Potential Motivating Features," Annual Conference Baltimore, AEJMC, August 1998.

CHAPTER 13

Design and Production

CHAPTER OBJECTIVES

When you have completed this chapter, you should be able to

1. Explain why visual communication is so important in advertising.
2. List the principles of layout and explain how design is affected by media requirements.
3. Describe how art and color are reproduced.
4. Explain how the art director creates TV commercials.
5. Identify the critical steps in planning and producing broadcast commercials.
6. Summarize the techniques of Web design.

The Work of a Lifetime: The Thomasville Hemingway Collection

Award: *EFFIE Silver, Household Furnishings category*

Company: *Thomasville Hemingway Collection*

Agency: *Long Haymes Carr*

Campaign: *"The Collection of a Lifetime"*

Ernest Hemingway was a writer, but when you think of him, you also think of bullfighting, foreign wars, deep-sea fishing, hunting, and safaris—of Barcelona, Paris, Kenya, Cuba, Key West, and Ketchum, Idaho. The Hemingway mystique is rich in imagery that reflects an exotic, adventurous lifestyle. And that was the reason North Carolina–based Thomasville Furniture chose to launch a collection of furniture designed to capture the spirit of Hemingway with its rugged leather, dark woods, and masculine detailing.

The challenge to the creative team at the Long Haymes Carr agency in North Carolina was to create a campaign titled "The Collection of a Lifetime" that reflected the craftsmanship of both the furniture and the legendary writer.

The strategy behind this EFFIE award–winning campaign was that the Ernest Hemingway Collection from Thomasville captured the spirit of Hemingway's life—his rugged individuality, his style of living on a legendary scale, his bigger-than-life personality, and his passion for his craft as a writer.

Two insights from an ethnographic study helped the creative team frame the strategy: (1) new items of furniture tended to be seen as devoid of meaning and viewed from a purely utilitarian or stylistic perspective; and (2) men were reluctant shoppers for furniture. A successful campaign, then, had to capture the imagination of men, as well as women, and somehow use the Hemingway lifestyle to make an emotional connection with the target audience.

In addition, although Thomasville had a healthy brand loyalty among an older (age 50+), more traditional market, the Hemingway collection was an opportunity to reach the younger, affluent "boomer" homeowners. These homeowners are more eclectic in their decorating tastes and want to make their homes an expression of their own creativity and style.

The design of the ads focused on settings reminiscent of Hemingway's travels. Cuba is suggested in an ad for a fruit-laden dining room table and chairs by positioning the furniture on an open-air patio with red tiled floors and white stucco arches and columns. In addition to the architecture, the Caribbean is also suggested by a palm tree and a tropical turquoise sea in the background. All the print ads in the campaign are framed by an archival black-and-white photo of Hemingway with a line that sets up the furniture featured in the color photo.

The campaign has a distinctive signature box in the lower right corner, which is designed to look like a pewter label with Hemingway's distinctive handwritten signature followed by the slogan, "The Collection of a Lifetime." The new furniture line—and campaign—were so successful, they brought in a record $100 million in its first year, the reason the campaign was an EFFIE-award winner, as well.

Source: Adapted from the EFFIE brief provided by Long Haymes Carr and Thomasville Furniture, and from Beth Snyder, "Thomasville Moves Hemingway into TV Ads," *Advertising Age* (August 23, 1999): 8; Sandra Dolbow "Literary License," *Brandweek* (July 24, 2000): 3.

VISUAL COMMUNICATION

In effective advertising, it's not just the words that need to communicate—it's the visuals, too. And they must work together to present the creative concept. Words and pictures accomplish different message effects. The visuals in the Thomasville ads, for example, link the image of Hemingway and the exotic places he liked with a style of furniture. But the words also add a depth to the rich imagery in the ad. For example, the headline under the Hemingway photo in the dining table ad says: "Hemingway had a tremendous appetite for life." The follow-up line, which the designer runs across the color photo in a typewriter typeface, continues the dining theme, "A quality we also bring to the table."

In most advertising the power lies with the visual, and its primary function is to get attention. In general, designers have found that a picture in a print ad captures more than twice as many readers as a headline does. Ads with pictures also tend to pull more readers into the body copy; initial attention is more likely to turn to interest with a strong visual. People notice ads and remember those with pictures more than those composed mostly of type. Furthermore, the bigger the illustration, the more the advertisement grabs consumers' attention.

These are the reasons that also help explain the visual impact of the Handgun Control ads. Chris Hutchinson (see Inside Story, Chapter 17), the art director for this *pro bono* campaign (all services, as well as time and space, are donated), which aimed at keeping guns out of the hands of children, explained that "Children killing children with guns is a very real issue and we wanted to communicate the horror of this. The visuals are meant to shock, juxtaposing toys with gun violence."

Similar experience with the design of television advertising has revealed that, in addition to attention, the pictorial elements of a television commercial are better remembered than are the words. Even radio can evoke mental pictures through suggestive or descriptive language and sound effects.

To learn how and when to use visuals effectively, art directors focus on five key points related to the effects of visuals in advertising:

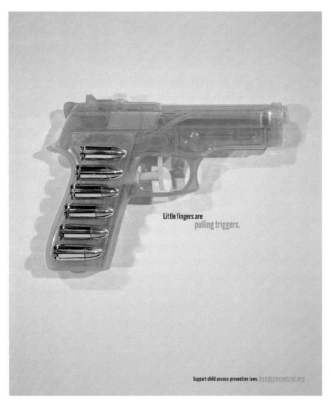

The pro bono Handgun Control campaign was designed as a wake-up call to this country following the Columbine High School shootings.

1. Visuals generally are better at getting and keeping attention.
2. Pictures communicate faster than words, as the Handgun Control ads demonstrate. A picture communicates instantly, while consumers have to decipher verbal/written communication word-by-word, sentence-by-sentence, line-by-line.
3. Many people remember messages as visual fragments, as key images that are filed easily in their minds.
4. Seeing is believing, as the IBM chick ad demonstrates, so visuals that demonstrate add credibility to a message.
5. To distinguish undifferentiated products with low inherent interest, advertisers often link the product with visual associations representing lifestyles and types of users.

The Art Director

The person who is most responsible for creating ad visuals is the *art director*. Artists may create the specific illustrations and renderings, but the art director is the chief designer. Art directors usually have a B.F.A. or M.F.A. (bachelor or master of fine art) from a design school or program. They are highly trained in graphic design, including art, photography, typography, the use of color, and computer design software such as Quark and Photoshop. The art director has a huge responsibility in the development of an effective advertisement.

In particular, the art director is in charge of the visual look of the message, both in print and TV, and how it communicates mood, product qualities, and psychological appeals. Specifically, the art director makes decisions about whether to use art or photography in print (film or animation in television), and what type of artistic style to use. The primary responsibility of the art director is to choose the visual elements used in the advertisement or commercial.

One of the most difficult problems that art directors—and those who work on the creative side of advertising—face is to transform a concept into words and pictures. During the brainstorming process, both copywriters and art directors are engaged in **visualization**, which means they are imagining what the finished ad might look like. However, some clients have a hard time visualizing, which can frustrate creative people who are trying to sell their ideas. "The Inside Story" shows how one art director has learned to handle this problem professionally.

IBM used a chick and an egg to demonstrate the smallness of its new hard disk drive, which is about the size of a large coin.

THE INSIDE STORY

WHAT YOU DON'T LEARN IN A TEXTBOOK: EVERYBODY'S AN ART DIRECTOR

Peter Stasiowski   Art Director, Gargan Communication, Dalton, Massachusetts

You finally land that art director's job you've worked so hard for, and you're going to be paid for your ideas! You dive into your first project with all the energy of a racehorse at the gate. You laugh and scream, you throw everything you've got into it, and when the smoke clears an idea for the visual is born. A tweak here, a touch-up there, and soon you're the proud owner of an idea ready to be seen. While presenting your idea to the client, however, you make a discovery: The client has ideas too.

"Oh, I love it! Just make that headline bigger, bolder, all-caps, and we've got a winner!" Your heart sinks. You've spent a lot of time getting that headline just right: the right type-face, the right size, the right everything. You visualize how the client's suggestion will look and nearly lose your lunch. But often, the client is on to something—even if the specific suggestion is dead wrong.

Your first reaction may be to defend your design with a detailed explanation of what thought processes were employed. Occasionally, a client will buy into such reasoning, but often this strategy comes across as argumentative or adversarial because making that headline bigger and bolder may seem like a very minor request. The smart move is not to react, but to *respond*.

Knowing your side of the story is only half the answer, because where your client's motivations are is the foundation of your response. Start with a simple question or two: "Do you like the way that headline looks but want to emphasize it more?" or "Do you think the way that headline looks is attractive, and making it larger will make it look more attractive?" The strategy is to respond by first determining your client's motivations. Then try to clarify those motivations while preserving the spirit of your original idea. Take solace in the fact that no matter how heated a presentation can get, the presenter and the client share the same goal of developing the most effective end product possible.

Peter Stasiowski, a Williamstown, Massachusetts native, graduated in 1991 from the University of West Florida in Pensacola, with a B.A. in Communication Arts, with an emphasis in advertising and public relations. He is presently an art director at Gargan Communication, a marketing and advertising agency in Dalton, Massachusetts.

Nominated by Professor Tom Groth, University of West Florida.

PRINT ART DIRECTION

The art director's toolkit for print advertising includes the photos, illustrations, typefaces, color, and layout of the proposed ad. There may be directions in the creative brief that specify the use of illustrations, photography, typefaces, and colors particular to the brand. Let's take a look at these and other elements of print ad design.

Illustrations and Photos

When art directors use the word "art," they usually mean photographs and illustrations. Photographs and illustrations can serve different purposes in ads. For instance, art directors know that photographs have more stopping power in advertising than illustrations, and that color attracts more attention than black-and-white images. In general, an illustration (or animation in television) is more fanciful; a photograph is more realistic. Illustrations, by definition, eliminate many of the details you see in a photograph, which can make it easier to understand since what remains are the "highlights" of the image that we use most often in recognizing what it represents. This ease of perception can simplify the visual message but it can also focus attention on key details of the image. Because it abstracts, it can communicate faster and more pointedly than a photograph. It can also intensify meanings and moods, making illustrations ideal for fantasy (think about comic books and animation).

Photography has an authenticity that makes it powerful, a dimension skillfully employed by the Hemingway campaign. Most people feel that pictures don't lie (even

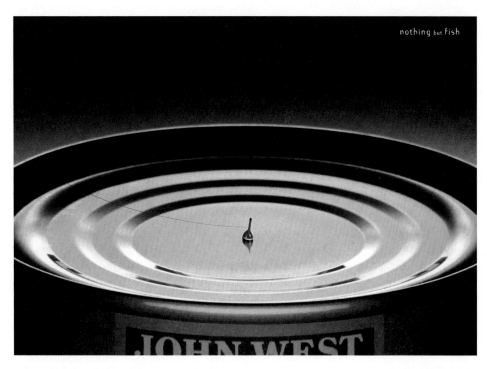

nothing but fish

A simple photograph of the top of a can takes on new meaning when the can's rings are associated with the rings in water from a fishing bobber.

though they can be altered). For credibility, then, photography is a good medium. The decision to use a photograph or an illustration is usually determined by the advertising strategy. If realism is important, then most art directors would use photographs; if a fanciful image is needed, then art directors would use illustrations or animation. The Thomasville ads use what we call a "beauty shot" of the furniture to establish the quality of the product. The historical photo of Hemingway is treated with a line screen technique that makes it more artful, symbolizing its historical qualities. The distinction between the two images is a visual statement of the strategy behind the ad campaign, which seeks to link Hemingway with the new furniture line created by Thomasville to reflect his tastes and style.

Photographs, of course, can also evoke fanciful images. For example, the billboard art for British beer brand John West is a close-up of the top of a can with just enough of the brand label showing for product identification. The visual is given a dramatic touch by making the rings on the can's top look like rings of rippling water cast from a fishing bobber.

Although art directors generally design the ad, they rarely create the finished art. If they need an illustration, they hire an artist. Usually, the artist is a freelancer. There are many different types of art and artists to choose from. There's fashion illustration, cartooning, photography, graphic arts, and technical illustrations. Both graphic artists and photographers tend to have personal styles or specialties, and the right person has to be found to create the right look. Newspaper and Web advertising visuals are often **clip art**, which are collections of copyright-free art that anyone can use who buys the clip-art service.

Art directors need to stay away from stereotyping and derogatory images when putting together an ad. For example, stereotypical images, such as those parodied in "The Good, the Bad, and the Ugly" Award show in Chapter 12, can cause problems. Sensitivity to local culture can become an issue. For example, a Utah ski area that was advertising its new quad lift in time for the Salt Lake City Olympics used copy that said, "Wife. Wife. Wife. Husband" under a picture of the quad lift. The visual was referring to polygamy, a sensitive issue in Utah. The ski area said it was trying to deliberately have fun with that perception and confront it in a humorous way. The company that owned the outdoor boards, however, refused to run the ad.[1]

The "A Matter of Principle" box discusses diversity, another issue in visual communication that contributes to or increases the effectiveness of advertising.

A MATTER OF PRINCIPLE
THE LINK BETWEEN DIVERSITY AND CREATIVITY

➤ Although stereotyped images may create ethical questions, diversity of images may be a positive factor in creative design, as the work of Sheri Broyles, a professor at the University of North Texas, has found.[2] She explains:

For decades the use of ethnic images—from Aunt Jemima to Uptown cigarettes, from Frito Bandito to taco-eating Chihuahuas—has been controversial. And the faces that appear in ads and commercials will become increasingly important as the faces across America become increasingly more diverse. One student in a creative advertising class at the University of North Texas made that point succinctly when commenting about an ad for Pantene Shampoo. The African American woman remarked that she didn't know this shampoo would work with her hair until she saw the black model.

This point—that diversity can increase the effectiveness of advertising—raises several questions: How does diversity relate to the execution of a creative strategy? And how does diversity relate to the perception, and ultimately the effectiveness, of the advertisement for younger consumers?

In a study, Professor Broyles asked echo boomers (children of baby boomers) questions concerning the faces found in magazine ads and the creative execution of the ads. She found that these echo boomers considered more diverse ads more creative, more positive, and more effective. Dr. Broyles suggests that ads showing the diverse ethnic faces of America may reach not only the growing ethnic population, but also the coveted youth market as well.

_____

Source: This feature was provided by Professor Sheri Broyles, Assistant Professor of Advertising, University of North Texas.

Color in Print

In addition to photos and illustrations, another important visual element that art directors manipulate in their design of print advertising is color. Art directors use color in print advertising when they want the ad to attract attention, provide realism, establish moods, and build brand identity. Art directors know that print ads with color, particularly those in newspapers, get more attention than ads without color.

Many ads are in full color, especially when art directors use photographs, such as the furniture shots in the Hemingway collection. However, note how the historical photo of Hemingway used in the panel on the left appears in contrast to the full-color photo. In this

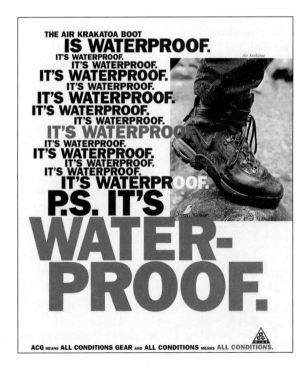

This ad, with an asymmetrical layout, uses spot color effectively as an accent to identify the product and the brand.

In an ad from the Hemingway® campaign for a Thomasville leather chair, the twist comes from the phrase "leather bound," a characteristic that is imagined for the book, but visualized by the art director in full color for the chair.

case, the black-and-white photo signifies a historical time in order to create the contrast between his time and the current furniture line.

Ads can also use **spot color**, in which they use a second color in addition to black (a black-and-white photo with an accent color) to highlight important elements. The use of spot color is highly attention-getting, particularly in newspaper ads. The ACG ad uses red spot color to accent the product and brand name.

When realism is important to convey in an ad, full-color photographs may be essential. Some products and ad illustrations just don't look right in black-and-white: pizza, flower gardens, and nail polish, for instance. These products are better presented in magazine ads and on posters and outdoor boards than in newspaper ads because newspapers do not show color well.

Color also can help an ad convey a mood. Color association can be an important part of a brand image. Warm colors, such as red, yellow, and orange, convey happiness. Pastels are soft and often bring a friendly tone to a print ad. Earth tones are natural and no-nonsense. Cool colors, such as blue and green, are aloof, calm, serene, reflective, and intellectual. Yellow and red have the most attention-getting power. Red may symbolize alarm and danger, as well as warmth. Black communicates high drama and can express power and elegance.

Color association can be an important part of a brand image. IBM uses the color blue so extensively that the company is often referred to as "Big Blue." In these cases, the art director has to honor the corporate identity program in the ad's color palette. Because color affects impressions of realism, as well as mood, and can be used to reinforce brand identity cues, its use is not only an aesthetic decision, but also a strategic one.

Typography

Not only do art directors have to carefully choose colors, they have to design the ad's **typography**—the appearance and arrangement of the ad's printed matter. Words in a print ad can be hand-drawn letters or the characters can be computer typeset. In most cases,

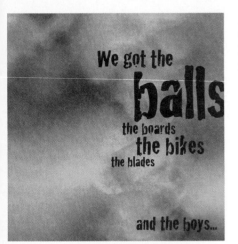

This is the cover for a four-page ad for Peterson publications inserted into advertising trade publications to dramatize that the group's magazines can deliver a youthful male audience. The message is in words, but it's also in the style of the type.

good typesetting does not call attention to itself because its primary role is functional: to convey the words of the message. That's usually the way typography should work. George Lois, chairperson and creative director at Lois Pitts Gershon Pon/GGK, once said, "It's important the typography doesn't get in the way of an idea."[3]

Type also has an aesthetic role and the type selection can, in a subtle or not so subtle way, contribute to the impact and mood of the message. The Petersen magazine group ad is an example of the use of typography as art. In this case, the heavy, bold, hand-drawn type has an attitude that reflects the readers of the Petersen's RAW Sport Group, which includes such publications as *Dirt Rider, Mountain Biker, MX Racer, BMX Rider, Inline,* and *sNoBoard.*

Print ad designers choose from among thousands of typefaces to find the right one for the ad's message. Next, we summarize the factors in typeface selection.

Families of Type There are two major typeface families—**serif** and **sans serif**. Serif means that the end of each stroke of a letter has a little flourish. A sans serif typeface is one that is missing this detail and the ends of the stroke tend to be more block-like. Serif letters are most often used for formal effects—invitations, for example—and when there is a lot of copy to be read; most books, for example, are set in serif faces. Sans serif is considered more "modern" in appearance. These faces also are used for copy that is consulted, rather than read—think about a phone book, or type in a diagram, because the look is "clean."

The basic set of letters in a particular typeface is known as the **font**. A font contains the alphabet for one typeface in all its various sizes plus the numerals and punctuation that go with that typeface, as Figure 13.1 shows. Here are some other variations that art directors specify and advertising managers should know (see Figure 13.1):

- *Uppercase* refers to the use of a capital letter, as in the capital U in the word Uppercase.
- *Lowercase* means small letters used without capitals.

FIGURE 13.1   TYPE VARIATIONS

Type has an aesthetic role in an ad. Art directors choose a serif or sans serif font, as well as a font's size and style.

A Font

> 14 pt
> ABCDEFGHIJKLMNOPQRSTUV
> abcdefghijklmnopqrstuvwxyz
> 1234567890

Serif (top) and Sans Serif (bottom)

> ABCDEFGHIJKLMNOPQRSTUVWXYZ ABCD
> ABCDEFGHIJKLMNOPQRSTUVWXYZ ABCD

All caps (top), lower case (middle), and u&lc (bottom)

> THIS IS TIMES ROMAN IN ALL CAPS.
> this is times roman in lower case.
> This Is Times Roman in Upper and Lower Case.

Typeface variations

> This is set in a light typeface.
> This is set in a normal weight.
> **This is set in a boldface.**
> *This is set in italic.*
> This is set in an expanded typeface.
> This is set in a condensed typeface.

FIGURE 13.2
TYPEFACE ALIGNMENT OPTIONS
Where the type sits on the ad has an
effect on the ad's overall look.

This is justified text. This is justified text. This is justified text. This is justified text. This is justified text. This is justified text. This is justified text. This is justified text. This is justified text. This is justified text.

This is centered text. This is
centered text.

This is left aligned text. This is
left aligned text.

This is right aligned text. This
is right aligned text.

- *All caps* is a design in which every letter in a word is a capital letter. (Uppercase refers to a type of letter, and all caps refers to how a word is set.)
- *U&lc* (upper- and lowercase) is a design in which the first letter of every word is capitalized and the others are lowercase.
- *Weight, posture,* and *width* of a typeface can vary using such elements as light, bold, italic, expanded, and condensed.

Justification How the lines align at the end is referred to as justification (see Figure 13.2). With **justified** type, also called *ragged right* (or *flush left*), the line endings on the right side of the column fall where they will. The opposite, which is rarely used, is *ragged left* (more often known as *flush right*) where the lines are aligned on the right but the beginnings of the lines vary. A final option is to center the type. Most of these justification patterns are used to specify the way body copy is typeset. There are more positioning options for headlines—the positioning of the words is arranged by the art director for artistic effect, as the Petersen's magazine ad illustrates.

Type Measurement There are a number of measurement systems used in graphic design. The smallest system of measurement units is called **points**, which designers use to indicate the size of typefaces. Figure 13.3 illustrates a variety of typeface sizes. There are 72 points in an inch. Display copy is usually 14 points or larger. Body copy in newspaper and magazine ads is usually 12 points or smaller. Designers also need to know the width of columns, which are measured in **picas**. The pica is a bigger unit of measurement than the point. There are 6 picas in an inch and 12 points in a pica. So 12-point type is exactly 1 pica high, or one-sixth of an inch. The column width used for the captions in this book is 10 picas. The text of the book is set on a 30–32 pica line length.

FIGURE 13.3   **DIFFERENT TYPEFACE SIZES**

Different sizes for the Times
Roman typeface

6 Point
ABCDEFGHIJKLMNOPQRSTUVWXYZABCDEFGHIJKLMNOPQRSTUVWXYZABCDEFGHIJKLMNOPQRSTUVWXYZABCDEFG
abcdefghijklmnopqrstuvwxyzabcdefghijklmnopqrstuvwxyzabcdefghijklmnopqrstuvwxyzabcdefghijklmnopqrstuvwxyz   1234567890

12 Point
ABCDEFGHIJKLMNOPQRSTUVWXYZABCDEFGHIJKLMNOPQ
abcdefghijklmnopqrstuvwxyzabcdefghijklmnopqrstuvwx 1234567890

18 Point
ABCDEFGHIJKLMNOPQRSTUVWXYZAB
abcdefghijklmnopqrstuvwxyzabc 1234567890

FIGURE 13.4

LEGIBILITY PROBLEMS
Research has shown that some
typography presentations, such as
those shown here, hinder the reading
process.

Legibility A major concern of designers in terms of the effectiveness of the type selection is **legibility** of type. If the type is difficult to read, most people will turn the page. Research has discovered a number of typography presentations that can hinder the reading process.[4] Figure 13.4 demonstrates some of these legibility concerns. Reverse type, for example, is hard to read because people are accustomed to reading type as black or dark shapes on a white or light background. We can recognize words when they are white letters reversed out of a dark surrounding area, but it's harder to do. Reverse works easiest for headlines and is more problematic for body copy. The same thing is true for all caps. We identify words by their distinctive shapes and when they are set in all caps, then the word's distinctive shape is obscured. It is less of a problem for headlines but really slows down the reading of body copy.

Layout and Design

Once art directors have chosen the images and typographic elements, they manipulate all of the visual elements on paper to produce a **layout**. A layout is a plan that imposes order and at the same time creates an arrangement that is aesthetically pleasing. The verb *lay out* means the process of arranging elements. Here are some common types of ad layouts the art director might use:

- *Picture window.* One of the most common layout formats is one with a single, dominant visual that occupies about 60 to 70 percent of the ad's space. Underneath it is a headline and a copy block. The logo or signature signs off the message at the bottom. The Dive ads in Chapter 12 (page 356) is an example.
- *All art.* The art fills the frame of the ad and the copy is embedded in the picture. The "Lost Innocence" ad for the Handgun Control campaign (page 365) is an example.
- *Panel or grid.* A layout that uses a number of visuals of matched or proportional sizes. If there are multiple panels all of the same size, the layout can look like a window pane or comic strip panel. The Thomasville ads use two panels of different size side by side to contrast Hemingway and his historical period with the contemporary furniture designed to reflect his style.
- *Dominant type or all copy.* Occasionally, you will see layouts that emphasize the type rather than the art, or even an all-copy advertisement in which the headline is treated as type art, such as the ACG ad (page 369). A copy-dominant ad may have art, but it is either embedded in the copy or placed in a subordinate position, such as at the bottom of the layout. Circus A layout combines lots of elements—art, type, color—to deliberately create a busy, jumbled image. This is typical of some discount store ads or ads for local retailers, such as tire companies.
- *Nonlinear.* A contemporary style of layout that can be read starting at any point in the image. In other words, the direction of viewing is not ordered, as in the "What a Ride" ad for Schwinn (page 373). This style of ad layout works for young people who are more accustomed to nonlinear forms; they are not as effective for older generations.
- *Grunge.* A style of layout that shows what is presumed to be a Generation X–inspired lack of concern for the formalities of art, design, type styles, and legibility. The Peterson magazine ad is moving in that direction.

Different layouts can convey entirely different feelings about a product. For example, look at the two ads for work boots. The ACG "Air Krakato" ad from page 369 screams "waterproof!" signaling the boots' ability to stand up to the most serious weather conditions.

This ad for Schwinn bicycles uses a plumbing drain motif to convey the industrial-strength features of the bike. It is a nonlinear design in that it doesn't matter where you start and what you read next.

In contrast, an ad campaign for the Dunham boot looks like a work of fine art. The reflective attitude of a serene outdoor scene (footprints in the snow) says these boots are for people who appreciate the beauty of nature. The difference between the two campaigns clearly lies with the visual impact that comes from the ads' layouts, as well as the imagery. Now let's look at the design principles that guide art directors as they seek to create effective layouts.

Design Principles A layout begins with a collection of miscellaneous elements: a headline and other display copy, one or more pieces of art, captions, body copy complete with subheads, a brand or store signature, and perhaps a trademark, slogan, or tagline. Local retail advertising also includes reminder information such as address, hours, telephone number, and credit cards accepted.

Arranging all these elements so that they make sense and attract attention is a challenge. The designer has both functional and aesthetic needs to fill for every ad. The functional side of a layout makes the message easy to perceive; the aesthetic side makes it attractive and pleasing to the eye. Here are some design principles that help artists know how to arrange a layout:

- **Direction.** Usually, designers create a visual path for the eye as it scans the elements. In Western countries most readers scan from top to bottom and from left to right. Most layouts work with these natural eye movements, although a layout can manipulate directional cues to cause the eye to follow an unexpected path. Figure 13.5 shows how the layout for one ad guides the eye.
- **Dominance.** The most emphasized element in an ad is the dominant element. Normally, the dominant element is a visual, but it can be a headline if the type is big

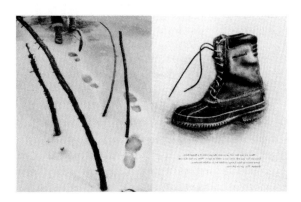

The layout in the ACG "Air Krakato" boot ad on p. 369 uses its copy and visuals to express the idea of tough boots for wet weather. The layout and art for the Dunham boot ad shown here speaks of the beauty of nature.

FIGURE 13.5

PORSCHE AD WITH TISSUE OVERLAY
The tracing on the tissue identifies
the starting point and the visual path
the eye takes when scanning this ad.

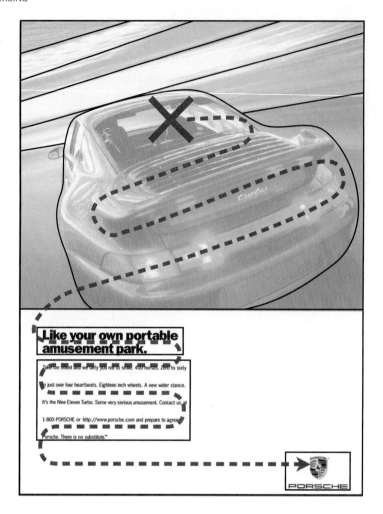

and bold enough to dominate other elements. By definition there can be only one
dominant element, one focal point; everything else must be subordinate. As in
Fig. 13.5 dominant elements are larger, more colorful, bolder, or positioned
in a more prominent spot, such as at the top of the page.

* *Unity.* With unity, all the elements in an ad fuse into one coherent image and the
  pieces become a whole. Neighboring elements that touch and align add unity and help
  with direction. An old axiom states the importance of grouping things: "Keep things
  together that go together." The two disparate photos in the Thomasville ad show a
  historical photo of Hemingway on the right joined to a current photo of a furniture
  arrangement on the left. The grouping works because the photos are aligned on the top
  and bottom and also because a light background screen made of lines is used behind
  both to link them visually.

* *White space.* Areas of the layout that aren't covered by art or type are called *white
  space* or negative space. White space can be a design element in itself—either to
  frame an element or to separate elements that don't belong together.

* *Contrast.* Contrast makes one element stand out from another and indicates
  importance. In the Hemingway ads, the furniture photos on the right are all bigger and
  in full color, to contrast with the smaller black-and-white photos of Hemingway.

* *Balance.* When an artist decides where to place an element, he is manipulating
  balance. There are two types of balance: formal and informal. Formal balance is
  symmetrical, centered left to right. Formal balance is conservative, it suggests
  stability, and it's used in more upscale product ads. Informal balance is asymmetrical
  and creates a visually exciting and dynamic layout, counterbalancing visual weights
  around an imaginary optical center. The Handgun Control ads are examples of
  informal balance.

- ***Proportion.*** Equal proportions of elements in a print ad are visually uninteresting because they are monotonous. Two visuals of the same size fight with one another for attention, and neither provides a point of visual dominance. Copy and art should be proportionately different. Usually, the art dominates and covers two-thirds to three-fifths of the page area (if the ad is not meant to be text-heavy).

- ***Simplify, simplify, simplify.*** This is truism but most art directors realize that less is more. Generally, the more elements that are crowded into a layout, the more the impact is fragmented. The fewer the elements, the stronger the impact. Clutter is the opposite of simplicity. It comes from having too many elements and too little unity. However, like all rules, this one is made to be broken. Art directors know that to create the effect they want in a circus layout or nonlinear layout, they have to sacrifice simplicity. Inevitably, that means the ad is more complex and harder to puzzle out; however, the trade-off may be worth it.

Layout Stages The stages in the normal development of a print ad may vary from agency to agency or from client to client. Figure 13.6 shows the six-stage development of

FIGURE 13.6   **ORLY "CHANTILLY PEACH" CREATIVE PROCESS**

(A) **Thumbnail Sketches.** These ideas for Orly were developed by the Wiley creative team late at night over Diet Coke and Chinese chicken salad. (B) **Rough Layout.** Transitioning to legs and painted toenails, the layout begins to give some glamour and personality to the product. (C) **Semicomps.** Type, color, and tagline still not finalized, but layout is more complete. (D) **Comprehensives.** Tagline approved. Illustrator has added more glitz to the layout. (E) **Mechanicals.** Quark file before retouching. Client still made small changes at this stage, but had approved the ad's layout and copy. (F) **Final High-Resolution Film.** Film house had to retouch, creating separate files for the legs and background image so that the proportion of the leg illustration would be correct.

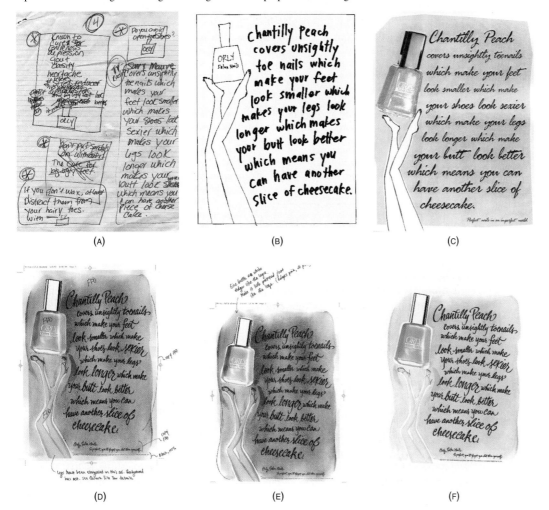

(A)   (B)   (C)

(D)   (E)   (F)

High-contrast graphics are the key to good reproduction in a newspaper. The art in these ads simulates an old wood engraving.

an Orly nail polish ad that agency Wiley & Associates created. This ad went through **thumbnail sketches**, which are quick, miniature preliminary sketches; **rough layouts**, which show where design elements go; **semicomps** and **comprehensives**, which are drawn to size and used for presentation either inside or to the client; and **mechanicals**, which assemble the elements in their final position for reproduction. The final product is a *high-resolution computer file* used for the actual production of the ad, which we will discuss shortly.

Print Media Requirements

Not only do art directors have to manage all the elements of an ad; they have to make sure that the elements will work with the ad medium. Different media put different demands on the design of the advertising.

Newspapers and Magazines Newspapers are printed at high speed on an inexpensive, rough-surfaced, spongy paper called **newsprint** that quickly absorbs ink on contact. Newsprint is not a great surface for reproducing fine details, especially color photographs and delicate typefaces. Most newspapers offer color to advertisers, but because of the limitations of the printing process, the color may not be perfectly **in register** (aligned exactly with the image). For that reason, ads such as the Oklahoma City ads are specifically designed for high-contrast black-and-white printing.

To catch the attention of the reader, who may be more absorbed in an article on the opposite page, magazine advertising often is more creative than newspaper advertising, using beautiful photography and graphics with strong impact. Magazines have traditionally led the way in graphic improvements because their paper is better than newsprint. Excellent photographic and color reproduction is the big difference between newspapers and magazines. Magazine advertisements are also turning to more creative, attention-getting devices such as pop-up visuals, scent strips, and computer chips that play melodies when the pages are opened.

Directories The design of Yellow Pages ads has changed during the last 60 years. Many advertisers design their ads to be not just listings but to stand out in a cluttered environment. Once users locate the category, most of them tend to browse through the listings, so the ad is designed to help the search. The "Practical Tips" shows some guidelines that designers follow when creating Yellow Pages ads.

Practical Tips

CREATING A YELLOW PAGES AD

- *Size.* The larger the ad, the more consumers notice it.
- *Image.* Graphics signal the reputation or image of the store. If possible, the headline, the illustration, the layout, and the use of type all should communicate the store's personality. A beauty shop ad will look different from an ad for auto parts.
- *Simplicity.* Keep the number of design elements to a minimum.
- *Art.* Illustrations work better than photographs.
- *Map.* If using a map, keep it simple to make the location clear.
- *The business.* Use graphics to convey the product category. Spell out the scope of service or product lines in the body copy.
- *Convenience cues.* Give prominence to location and hours because people look for stores that are open and easy to reach.
- *Critical information.* In addition to location and hours, the phone number must be included. Many consumers will call to see whether the product they want is available before making a trip. Note the multiple phone numbers listed in the IBM ad.

Outdoor Boards and Posters The key to an effective poster or outdoor board is a dominant visual with minimal copy.

Because billboards must make a quick and lasting impression from far away, their layout should be compact with a simple visual path. Usually, the path begins with a dominant graphic, followed by a catchy headline, and ending with some kind of product identification. The relationships between the elements should be clear and integrated so that consumers see them as one whole concept. For example, a billboard for a doughnut store announcing that it was also selling cookies featured a huge, one-word headline filling the entire board: "Goody." The two O's in the middle were both round cookies. The underline read: "Winchell's has gone cookies."

The Institute for Outdoor Advertising (IOA) recommends these tips for designers.

- *Graphics.* Make the illustration an eye-stopper.
- *Size.* Images in billboards are huge—a 25-foot-long pencil or a 43-foot pointing finger. The product or the brand label can be hundreds of times larger than life.
- *Colors.* Use bold, bright colors. The greatest impact is created by maximum contrast between two colors such as dark colors against white or yellow.[3]
- *Figure/ground.* Make the relationship between foreground and background as obvious as possible. A picture of a soft drink against a jungle background is hard to perceive when viewed from a moving vehicle at a distance. The background should never compete with the subject.
- *Typography.* Use simple, clean, uncluttered type that is easy to read at a distance by an audience in motion. The industry's legibility research recommends avoiding all-capital letters, fanciful ornamental letters, and script and cursive fonts.
- *Product identification.* Focus attention on the product by reproducing the label or package at a huge size.

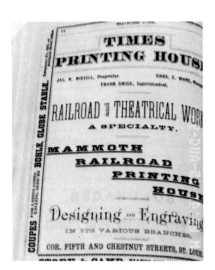

This series of Yellow Pages ads show the changes over the years.
Top row: (left) 1882, (right) 1920s
Bottom row: (left) 1930s, (right) 1990s.

- *Extensions.* Extend the frame of the billboard to expand the scale and break away from the limits of the long rectangle.
- *Shape.* For visual impact, create the illusion of three-dimensional effects by playing with horizons, vanishing lines, and dimensional boxes. Inflatables create a better 3-D effect than most billboards can, even with superior graphics. Made of a heavyweight, stitched nylon, inflatables can be free-standing, or they can be added to outdoor boards as an extension.
- *Motion.* Add motors to boards to make pieces and parts move. Disk-like wheels and glittery things that flicker in the wind create the appearance of motion, color change, and images that squeeze, wave, or pour. Use revolving panels, called kinetic boards, for messages that change.

PRINT PRODUCTION

Now we turn to a brief explanation of print ad production and what it means to the art director. Art directors need to understand print ad production not only because it affects the look of the ad, but also because it affects costs.

Art Reproduction

There are two general types of images: line art and halftone. A drawing or illustration is called **line art** because the image is solid lines on a white page, as in the Oklahoma City ads. Photographs, which are referred to as continuous tone or **halftone**, are much more complicated to reproduce because they have a range of gray tones between the black and white, as shown in Figure 13.7. Printers create the illusion of shades of gray by converting continuous-tone art and photos to halftones.

In the halftone process, the original photograph is shot through a fine screen. The image is converted to a pattern of dots that gives the illusion of shades of gray—dark

FIGURE 13.7   LINE ART AND HALFTONE ART
An example of a figure reproduced as line art (left) and as a halftone (right).

areas are large dots that fill the screen and light areas are tiny dots surrounded by white space. If you look closely at a photograph in a newspaper, you may be able to see the dot pattern. The quality of the image depends on how fine the screen is—a coarse screen, usually 65 lines per inch (called a 65-line screen), is used by newspapers while magazines use fine screens, which may be 120 and up to 200 lines per inch.

Screens are also used to create various **tint blocks**, which can either be shades of gray in black-and-white printing or shades of color. A block of color can be printed solid or it can be screened back to create a shade. These shades are expressed as a range of percentages, from 100 percent (solid) down to 10 percent (very faint). Figure 13.8 gives examples of screens in black and color.

Color Reproduction It would be impossible to set up a printing press with a separate ink roller for every hue and value in a color photo. How, then, are these colors reproduced? Full-color images are reproduced using only four distinctive shades of ink called **process colors**, in a process called four-color printing. These colors are *magenta* (a shade of pinkish purple), *cyan* (a shade of bright blue), *yellow,* and *black*. Printing inks are transparent, so when one ink overlaps another, a third color is created. For example, red and blue create purple, yellow and blue create green, yellow and red create orange. The black is used for type and, in four-color printing, adds depth to the shadows and dark tones in an image.

The process printers use to reduce the original color image to four halftone negatives is called **color separation**. The separation is done photographically or by laser from the original full-color images. A separate color filter screens out everything but the desired hue for each of the four process colors. Figure 13.9 illustrates the process of color separation.

Printing Processes

Here are the most common printing processes used in advertising and a general description of how they work:

- *Letterpress.* A process used for numbering items (such as tickets and so on) and specialty printing effects such as embossing. With letterpress printing, a raised surface gets inked; then when it strikes the surface of the paper, the image is transferred.
- *Offset lithography.* The most popular type of printing for newspapers and most magazines. Offset printing uses a smooth-surface and chemically treated plate to transfer the image. Based on the principle that oil and water don't mix, the oil-based ink adheres to parts of the image but not to other parts. The offset plates are produced photographically.
- *Rotogravure.* A process used for long print runs with high-quality photographic reproduction. Gravure printing uses an incised surface. The images are engraved into the plate and ink collects in these little wells. When the plate strikes the surface of the paper, ink is transferred from the wells to the paper.
- *Flexography.* A procedure that prints on unusual surfaces and shapes such as mugs and balls. Flexographic printing uses a rubber-surface printing plate that can be bent to print on irregular surfaces. The plate transfers ink similar to offset printing.
- *Silkscreen.* A type of printing used to print posters, T-shirts, and point-of-sale materials. Silk screen printing uses a porous screen of silk, nylon, or stainless steel mounted on a frame. A stencil image is made either by hand or using a photographic process and the stencil is adhered to the screen. The nonprinting areas are blocked by

FIGURE 13.8

SCREEN VALUES AND TINT BLOCKS
These are different screens for black and white image tints and for color tint.

(A)

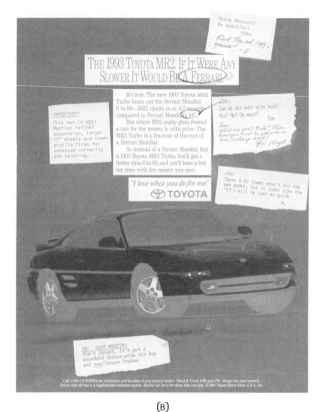

(B)

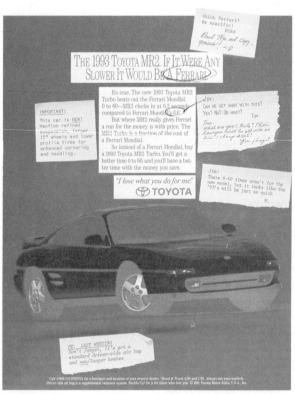

(C)

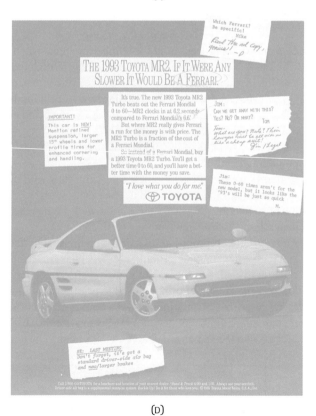

(D)

FIGURE 13.9   COLOR SEPARATIONS

The six photos starting here illustrate the process of creating four-color separations: (A) Yellow plate, (B)
Magenta plate, (C) Yellow and Magenta combined plate, (D) Cyan plate. (Note: After cyan is added, there
would also be combined plates showing it added first to yellow, then to magenta, then to the combined yellow
and magenta. These steps were left out to simplify the presentation.)

(E)

(F)

FIGURE **13.9**   CONTINUED

(E) Black plate, (F) the finished ad with all four process colors.

the stencil and the areas to be printed are left open. Using a squeegee, ink is forced through the screen onto the printing surface.

If an ad is going to run in a number of publications, there has to be some way to distribute a reproducible form of the ad to all of them. The duplicate material for offset printing is a slick proof of the original mechanical. These proofs are called photoprints or **photostats**, which are cheap to produce. Veloxes or C-prints are better-quality proof prints but are more expensive.

Art directors have to understand how these various printing processes work to know which one will be used for the advertisement or advertising materials. They all impact the design in some way.

Binding and Finishing   Art directors can use a number of special printing effects to further enhance their ads. For example, US Robotics, a maker of minicomputers, once used a small brochure the actual size of a Palm Pilot to demonstrate its minicomputer's size. The shot of the Palm Pilot was glued to a photo of a hand. As the ad unfolded it became a complete product brochure that visually demonstrated the actual size of the minicomputer. Other such mechanical techniques, used to embellish the advertising image, include:

*   ***Die cutting.*** A sharp-edged stamp, or die, used to cut out unusual shapes. A common shape you're familiar with is the tab on a file folder.
*   ***Embossing or debossing.*** The application of pressure to create a raised surface or depressed image in paper.
*   ***Foil stamping.*** The application of a thin metallic coating (silver, gold) molded to the surface of the image.

- *Tip-ins.* **Tip-ins** are separate preprinted ads provided by the advertiser to be glued into a publication as the publication is being assembled, or bound. Perfume manufacturers, for example, tip in samples that are either scratch-and-sniff or scented strips that release a fragrance when pulled apart.

Digitization The most recent trend in print production involves digitizing images that can then be transmitted electronically to printers or clients. Computer technology that relies on transmission by fiber optics or satellites makes computerized typesetting easy to transmit electronically. Art can be digitized (broken into tiny grids, each one coded electronically for tone or color) and then transmitted. Fiber optics can send type, art, or even complete pages across a city for local editions of newspapers. Satellites make national page transmission possible for regional editions of magazines and newspapers such as *USA Today*. However, the method can also be used for transmitting proofs of ads to a client, as well as a publication.

Desktop publishing, the process of producing print documents on personal computers with easy-to-use software, is taking over the low end (inexpensive printing) of typesetting. Designers, writers, and editors can create page layouts and advertising layouts on a personal computer, sometimes with very little training or understanding of design principles. At the higher end (higher quality) of typesetting, typesetting systems also use computer-based pagination equipment that combines computer typesetting with page layout capabilities. The art director can typeset the copy for and lay out a brochure, newsletter, or magazine, as well as a series of ads, on a desktop computer. More sophisticated computers and software can even produce the printing plates directly from the layout.

TELEVISION ART DIRECTION

Now that we've learned about print advertising art direction, let's move on to television art direction. Where does our art director start when putting together a commercial? A creative brief may have suggestions for bringing a television commercial to life, particularly if they are linked to the brand's identity. These suggestions might detail the casting, staging, setting, action, lighting, props, colors, sounds, and typography, all of the elements that can give a commercial a distinctive feel and look. Working within the framework of the creative strategy, art directors create the look of the TV commercial.

The look of the "Cat Herders" commercial that the Minneapolis-based Fallon agency created for Electronic Data Systems (EDS) was that of the American West, much like a John Ford movie or the *Rawhide* television show, with horses, craggy-faced cowboys, and stampeding animals. (See the "A Matter of Practice" box on page 385.)

The excitement and drama in a television commercial is created through the visuals—the moving images. Art directors are not dealing with static images but with visual storytelling. In the "Cat Herders" spot described in the "A Matter of Practice" feature, the felines were used for various scenes, including wranglers trying to coax the felines from a tree, a cat riding on a saddle, and a herd stampeding over a horse-thrown wrangler.

The Fallon art director, Dean Hanson, decided that the metaphor of herding cows means that the cats have to swim across a river, but is it possible? Here's how it was done for that EFFIE award–winning commercial: The trainers taught a few cats that weren't adverse to water to swim by starting them out in one-quarter inch of water and then gradually adding water to the pool until it was deep enough for the cats to swim. The "river" was actually a small pool warmed by a portable heater—art director Hanson described it as "a little kitty Jacuzzi." Multiple copies of the swimming kitties were made and manipulated using computer graphics until an entire herd had been created. And that's how this famous scene came about—from Hanson's unlikely vision of a herd of cats swimming a river.

Visual storytelling is important, even for abstract concepts such as the slogan for the Public Broadcasting Service (PBS): "Stay curious." Think about it: How would you visualize such a line in a television spot? The Fallon agency creative team came up with a series of fascinating commercials to bring that creative concept to life visually. Figure 13.10

Herding cats was the metaphor used by EDS for its information technology business.

Photo Booth

VIDEO: Open on a virtually black screen with one small circle. The aperture opens to reveal the whole scene. It's a photo booth in a mall. A man is behind the curtain gesturing wildly for each shot.

CUT to a close-up of one of the photostrips dropping down. We see his face is quite animated in each frame.

RAPID CUTS of him continuing to pose as the flash pops for each shot.

CUT to a hand placing the needle down on an old RCA record.

SFX (Sound Effects): The scratch of the needle at the beginning of a record. And then the tenor Enrico Caruso singing "Di Quella Pira" from Verdi's *Il Trovatore* under and throughout.

VIDEO: Cut to a hand cutting apart the photos from the strips. Dozens of photos lay underneath the hand. Cut back to the record going around on the turntable. CUT to a hand flipping through a series of the photos. The man in the photo booth has created a flipbook of himself lip-synching Caruso, and we watch as it matches the recording we hear, complete with gestures.

CUT to a wide shot of the man in his living room smiling as he flips through the book and watches himself "perform."

CUT back to the flipbook as the aria reaches its triumphant conclusion. The aperture closes.

SUPER: Stay curious.

LOGO: PBS

Dishwasher

SFX: The hum of a dishwasher.

VIDEO: Open on a virtually black screen. A small circle of film widens to reveal the scene. A young boy is sitting on a chair in a kitchen waiting for the dishwasher to finish. As soon as the cycle ends, the boy goes to it, unlocks the door, opens it, and pulls the bottom tray out. It's full of dishes, pots, and pans. He reaches in and pulls out something that's been placed in a large Ziploc bag. He opens the bag and pulls out a small camcorder. He rewinds it a bit, presses play, and watches what he's taped.

CUT to video footage of the inner workings of the dishwasher.

The aperture closes to a small circle.

SUPER: Stay curious.

LOGO: PBS

FIGURE 13.10 SCRIPTS FOR THE PBS "STAY CURIOUS" COMMERCIALS

shows the scripts for two of these Andy award–winning commercials. Notice that the commercials are essentially nonverbal.

In commercials like these, the art director imagines the characters and how they act in the scene, as well as the position and movement of the cameras recording the scene, a description of which is specified in the storyboard. For example, notice how the Photo Booth spot opens looking through the lens aperture of a camera at the subject who is taking pictures of himself as he pretends to direct a piece of music. The art director comes up with the visual idea for the scene and how it is shot, as well as how it links to the scenes that follow.

Video Graphics

Art directors are responsible for creating the graphic elements that appear on screen. The art director could arrange for filming, or choose to use **stock footage**—previously recorded images, either video, still slides, or moving film, used for scenes that aren't accessible to normal shooting. Typical stock footage files are shots from a satellite or rocket, historical scenes such as World War II battles, or a car crash. Other graphic elements such as words, product logos, and still photos are digitized or computer-generated right on the screen. A **crawl** is computer-generated letters that appear to be moving across the bottom of the screen. All of these are designed or specified by the art director.

In the Thomasville Hemingway ads, the association between Hemingway, his image, and the new furniture line was created using historical black-and-white (mostly) still photos of the writer interspersed with "Bold," "Romantic" and "Adventurous," which were

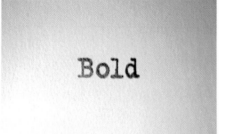

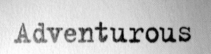

Stills and moving pictures of Hemingway® were edited together with key words that described his life followed by furniture from the Thomasville Hemingway® line.

on-screen graphics. Real-life, full-color shots of various furniture scenes—a desk with an old typewriter, a dining table, a couch and living room set, a bedroom set, and a patio set—followed the collage of photos and words.

Sophisticated computer graphics systems, such as those used to create the *Star Wars* special effects, have pioneered the making of film and video art on computers. Computer graphic artists brag that they can do anything with an image: They can make Mel Gibson look 80 or Bob Dole look 30. They can look at any object from any angle or even from the inside out. One of the most creative video techniques is called **morphing**, in which one object gradually changes into another. Photographs of real objects can change into art or animation and then return to life. The ability to manipulate images has brought an entire new world of creativity to video and film and has been an important innovation in television art direction in the last 10 years.

In the new computer-animated world, television images are changing dramatically, as the "Cat Herding" commercial in the "A Matter of Practice" feature demonstrates. Computer graphics specialists use tools such as the Paint Box software to create, multiply (that's how 50 cats can be made to look like hundreds), and manipulate video images. As costs have decreased and design technology has moved to personal computers, these computer programs are finding their way into the art director's office and expanding the graphics capabilities of the agency and production houses for both print and video.

TV and Film Requirements

The length of a TV commercial is important in its design. TV ads first got shorter (15 or 10 seconds) as television time got more expensive; then they got longer as advertisers discovered that longer commercials could be used in certain inexpensive time slots such as those used for infomercials. From a design standpoint, the short length means the ads must be simple enough for consumers to grasp quickly, yet visually intriguing to prevent viewers from switching channels.

Videos In addition to TV commercials, videos are also used for product literature, news releases, direct marketing, and training films and, like ads, these are also designed by art directors. The intention, however, is to tell a longer product story and sometimes the focus is as much on education as it is on selling the product. The car industry has been using videos for years as product "literature" to give potential customers a "test drive" on their television screens. The World Wildlife Fund has sent videos in membership renewal kits. In a neat piece of integration, WLIT-FM in Chicago used an 8½-minute video as a direct-response mailer to 250,000 local viewers. The video gave the station time to tell its story and build a relationship with its listeners. Because Viacom owns both the station and Blockbuster Video, sister retailer Blockbuster also distributed the video for customers to borrow free of charge. The station saw its Arbitron ratings jump from sixth to fourth place in the market after viewers received the mailing.[5]

Movie Trailers Most movie theaters accept filmed commercials to be run before the feature. Called **trailers**, these advertisements are similar to television commercials but are generally longer and better produced because they must compete with the beautiful images found in most movies. Trailer messages are usually 45 seconds, 1 minute, or 2 minutes in length. This gives more time for message development than the typical 30-second television spot.

The projection of larger-than-life images in a darkened theater is totally unlike the experience of watching television. The impact of the large screen makes for a compelling image that commands total attention. Some people, who see themselves as a captive audience, resent this form of advertising. However, in 1999, over 100,000 fans paid $7.50 to view the 12-minute trailer for *Star Wars: Episode I: The Phantom Menace.* Because of the potential resistance and the context in which the message is shown, this type of advertising needs to be highly entertaining.

A MATTER OF PRACTICE

KITTY SLICKERS AND CAT HERDERS

➤ EDS, a company that essentially invented the information technology (IT) industry back in the 1960s, found itself with an unhip Old Economy image as the New Economy exploded in the late 1990s. Although a leader in such New Economy areas as Web hosting, digital supply chain management, and networking, EDS got no respect from its would-be high-tech partners.

The assignment given to the Fallon agency (Minneapolis) was to change those perceptions and infuse energy and pride into the EDS workforce. Fallon's strategy was to leverage EDS's proven experience and its rock-solid infrastructure, which enabled it to tackle enormous IT problems. The strategy came together in the positioning statement: "EDS thrives on defeating complexity."

How do you depict an organization defeating complexity? A catch phrase popular in the Silicon Valley culture—"It's like herding cats"—was the perfect metaphor for how EDS wrangles technology and manages complexity. And that's what the Fallon creative team did—it filmed a team of rugged cowboys herding thousands of housecats across the Montana plains.

The commercial, which was designed to run on the Super Bowl, not only won an EFFIE award, it won every online poll ranking Super Bowl commercials that year. And it did so by erasing the company's image as rigid and unapproachable and supplanting it with a down-to-earth, tongue-in-cheek image that appealed to the cynical dot-com industry.

In addition to being the favorite Super Bowl commercial, the "Cat Herders" commercial started EDS's telephones ringing and its Web site overflowed with visitors. The company estimated it had 2 million hits on its Web sites the next day, 10 times the normal volume. In terms of Fallon's objectives, one of which was to create brand awareness and buzz

in the industry, EDS estimated that its $8 million investment in the ad and its supporting campaign netted an additional $12 million in PR. The campaign was also designed to generate sales and new business inquiries and EDS reported that its sales were up 20 percent and its new business leads grew by 40 percent.

The campaign was also designed to energize the workforce. "Cat Herders" gave EDS employees an inspiring image of themselves as wranglers in an epic undertaking whose message is: "No job is too tough." In addition to lowering the company's employee turnover rate, thousands of employees sent letters to the president thanking him for the inspiring symbol of the cat herder.

Sources: Adapted from the EDS EFFIE brief provided by EDS and Fallon. Also, from "Super Ad Has EDS Purring," *Washington Technology* 14(24) (March 20, 2000): 46; Becky Ebenkamp, "Creative: On Location: Kitty Slickers," *Adweek* (January 17, 2000): 24–26.

BROADCAST PRODUCTION

Most local retail commercials are simple and inexpensive, and are shot and taped at the local station or production facility. The sales representative for the station may work with the advertiser to write the script, and the station's director handles the taping of the commercial. The process is more complex for nationally released commercials. (Art directors are involved in the production of television commercials, but not radio.)

Creating a national TV commercial requires a number of people with specialized skills. The ad agency crew usually includes the copywriter, art director, and producer. The producer oversees the production on behalf of the agency and client and is responsible for the budget, among other things. The director, who is the person responsible for the recording or filming of the commercial, is usually someone from outside the agency. This person takes the art director's storyboard and makes it come to life on film. They work closely together and both are responsible for the "look" of the commercial that results.

TABLE 13.1	Who Does What in TV and Radio Production?
Copywriter	Writes the script, whether it contains dialogue, narrative, lyrics, announcements, descriptions, or no words at all.
Art Director	In TV, develops the storyboard and establishes the look of the commercial, whether realistic, stylized, or fanciful.
Producer (can be an agency staff member)	Takes charge of the production, handles the bidding and all production arrangements, finds the specialists, arranges for casting talent, and makes sure the expenses and bids come in under budget.
Director	Has responsibility for the actual filming or taping, including scene length, who does what, how lines are spoken, and the characters played; in TV determines how the camera is set up and records the flow of action.
Composer	Writes original music and sometimes writes the lyrics along with the music.
Arranger	Orchestrates music for the various instruments and voices to make it fit a scene or copy line. The copywriter usually writes the lyrics or at least gives some idea of what the words should say.
Editor	Puts everything together toward the end of the filming or taping process; evaluates how to assemble scenes and which audio elements work best with the dialogue and footage.

In the case of the "Cat Herders" commercial, director John O'Hagen, of the Hungry Man studio, took on the assignment because of his skill at coaxing naturally humorous performances from nonprofessional actors. In this commercial he worked with real wranglers on their semi-scripted testimonials about their work with kitties.

Table 13.1 summarizes the responsibilities of broadcast production personnel. The producer and director are the core of the production team. The commercial's effectiveness depends on their shared vision of the final commercial and their ability to bring it to life as the art director imagined it.

Producing TV Commercials

Producing a major national commercial may take the work of hundreds of people and cost as much as half a million dollars. The famous "1984" commercial for Apple Computer that ran only once (during the 1985 Super Bowl) used a cast of 200 and is estimated to have cost half a million dollars. Since then even more expensive commercials have been produced. There are a number of ways to produce a message for a television commercial. It can be filmed live or prerecorded using film or videotape. It can also be shot frame-by-frame using animation techniques. Let's look at these production choices.

Film or Videotape Directors shoot most television commercials on 16-mm or 35-mm film. The film is shot as a negative and processed, after which the editor transfers the image to videotape, a process called **film-to-tape transfer**. Film consists of a series of frames on celluloid; actually, each frame is a still shot. The film passes through a projector, and the small changes from frame to frame create the illusion of motion. Film is shot at 24 frames per second. In film-to-tape transfer the film is converted to videotape that uses 30 frames per second. To edit on film, editors cut between two frames and either eliminate a segment or attach a new segment of film. The term **cut**, which comes from this editing procedure, indicates an abrupt transition from one view of a scene to another. Art directors work closely with editors who assemble the shots and cut the film to create the right pacing and sequence of images as outlined in the storyboard.

Until the 1980s, art directors thought of videotape as an inferior alternative to film. Originally, it was used mainly by the television news industry because it records sound and images instantly, without a delay for film processing, and videotape can be replayed immediately. Videotape's "cheap cousin" image has changed dramatically as the quality of videotape has improved. Also, a number of innovations in editing have made the process more precise and faster; computer editing has improved accuracy and made special effects possible. Art directors who are creating high-end commercials will usually use film in production and then transfer the work to videotape for dissemination.

Animation The technique of **animation**, which means drawing the images on film, also records images on film one frame at a time. Cartoon figures, for example, are sketched and then resketched with a slight change to indicate a small progression in the movement of an arm or a leg or a facial expression. Animation is traditionally shot at 12 or 16 drawings per second. Low-budget animation uses fewer drawings, so the motion looks jerky. Because of the handwork, animation is labor-intensive and expensive. The introduction of computers has accelerated the process. Now illustrators draw only the beginning and the end of the action sequence; the computer fills in the frames in between.

Stop Motion and Claymation A particular type of animation is **stop motion**, a technique used to film inanimate objects like the Pillsbury Doughboy, which is a puppet. The little character is moved a bit at a time and filmed frame-by-frame. The same technique is used in **claymation**, which involves creating characters from clay and then photographing them one frame at a time. Both techniques are popular with art directors who create advertising where fantasy effects are desired.

The TV Production Process

For the bigger national commercials, there are a number of steps in the production process that fall into four categories: message design (which we've already discussed), preproduction, the shoot, and postproduction. Figure 13.11 shows the steps in the TV production process.

Preproduction The producer and staff first develop a set of production notes, describing in detail every aspect of the production. These notes are important for finding talent and locations, building sets, and getting bids and estimates from specialists. In the "Cat Herders" commercial, finding the talent was critical. Some 50 felines and their trainers were involved in the filming. Surprisingly, different cats have different skills—some were able to appear to be asleep or motionless on cue, others excel as runners or specialize in water scenes.

Before the commercial can be filmed or taped, the production team must handle a number of arrangements. Once the bids for production have been approved, the creative team and the producer, director, and other key players hold a preproduction meeting to outline every step of the production process and anticipate every problem that may arise. They also finalize a detailed schedule acceptable to all parties.

FIGURE 13.11 TV PRODUCTION PROCESS
In general, there are four steps in the production of a television commercial.

1. Message Design	2. Preproduction	3. Production (the Shoot)	4. Postproduction
• Get client approval on the advertising strategy • Choose the message format • Create a key frame • Write the script • Storyboard the action and scenes • Get client approval of script and storyboard	• Find the right director • Find the production house or animation house • Work out details in preproduction meeting • Locate or build the set • Cast the talent • Locate props, costumes, photographic stills • Get bids for all the production operations	• The director manages the shoot • Record the action on film • Record music, voices, and sound effects • Create the on-screen graphics • Create the computer graphics	• Edit the film • Mix the audio track • Synchronize the video and the audio • Give a presentation tape to client for approval • Duplicate videotapes for distribution

Surprisingly, cats can be trained to do a variety of things including sitting on a horse's saddle.

Then the work begins: The talent agency begins casting the roles, usually through a series of auditions. The production team has to find a location and arrange site use with owners, police, and other officials. If sets are needed, they have to be built. Finding the props is a test of ingenuity, and the prop person may wind up visiting hardware stores, second-hand stores, and maybe even the local dump. Costumes may also have to be made.

The Shoot Although the actual filming takes a relatively short time, the setup and rehearsal can take incredible amounts of time. The film crew includes a number of technicians. Everyone reports to the director. If the sound is being recorded at the time of shooting, a **mixer**, who operates the recording equipment, and a mic or boom person, who sets up the microphones, handle the recording. For both film and video recording, the camera operators are the key technicians.

Other technicians include the **gaffer**, who is the chief electrician, and the **grip**, who moves props and sets. The grip also lays tracks for the dolly on which the camera is mounted and pushes the camera dolly along the track at the required speed. The script clerk checks the dialogue and other script details and times the scenes. Crews of assistants support all the technicians. A set is a busy, crowded place. Table 13.2 offers definitions of terms common to television commercial production.

The director shoots the commercial scene-by-scene, but not necessarily in the order set down in the script. Each scene is shot and reshot until all the elements come together. If the director films the commercial on videotape, it is played back immediately to determine what needs correcting. Film has to be processed before the director can review it. These processed scenes are called **dailies**. **Rushes** are rough versions of the commercial assembled from cuts of the raw film footage. The director and the agency creative team view them immediately after the shoot to make sure everything's been filmed.

The five-day shoot for the "Cat Herders" commercial gives you an idea of some of the other unexpected factors that can affect even the most well-planned commercial. In this case, the shoot was a nightmare, not because of the difficulty of working with cats who have minds of their own, but because of the weather. Filmed at a ranch 70 miles north of Los Angeles, the crew had to suffer through wind and surprisingly cold weather for California, which didn't bother the cats as much as it did the two-legged crew.

The audio director records the audio either at the time of the shoot, or, in the case of the more high-end productions, separately in a sound studio. In the studio it is usually recorded after the film is shot so the audio is synchronized with the footage. Directors often wait to see exactly how the action appears before they write and record the audio track. However, if the art director has decided to set the commercial to music, then the music on the audio track may be recorded before the shoot and the filming done to the music.

Postproduction For film and video, much of the work happens after the shoot—when the commercial begins to emerge from the hands and mind of the editor. The objective of editing is to assemble the various pieces of film into a sequence that follows the storyboard.

In the "Cat Herders" commercial, Fallon could not film the cats and horses at the same time because of the National Humane Society regulations. The director had to film the horses, background, and kitties separately. An editor fused the scenes together during postproduction, editing seamlessly to create the illusion of an elaborate cat drive. In addition to streaming together a visual narrative, editing can condense, extend, and jumble time.

Another goal of editing is to manipulate time, which is a common technique used in commercial storytelling. Condensing time might show a man leaving work, then a cut of the man showering, then a cut of the man at a bar. The editor may have to extend time. Say a train is approaching a stalled car on the tracks. By cutting to various angles it may seem that the train is taking forever to reach the car—a suspense tactic. To jumble time, an editor might cut from the present to a flashback of a remembered past event or flash forward to an imagined scene in the future. All of these effects are specified by the art director in the storyboard.

TABLE 13.2	**Television Terminology**
Shot Information	
Distance (camera to image)	Long shot (LS), full shot (FS), medium shot (MS), wide shot (WS), close-up (CU), extreme close-up (ECU or XCU).
Camera Movement	
Zoom in or out	The lens on the camera manipulates the change in distance. As you zoom in, the image seems to come closer and get larger; as you zoom out, it seems to move farther away and get smaller.
Dolly in and out	The camera itself is wheeled forward or backward.
Pan right or left	The camera is stationary but swings to follow the action.
Truck right or left	The camera itself moves right or left with the action.
Boom crane shoot	Camera mechanism moves over a scene; scene is shot from above.
Shot Transitions	
Cut	An abrupt, instantaneous change from one shot to another.
Dissolve	A soft transition in which one image fades to black while another image fades in.
Lap dissolve	A slow dissolve with a short period in which the two images overlap.
Superimposition	Two images held in the middle of a dissolve so they are both on-screen at the same time.
Wipe	One image crawls across the screen and replaces another.
Action	
Freeze frame	Stops the scene in mid-action.
Stop motion	Shots are taken one at a time over a long period. Used to record animation, claymation, or something that happens over a long period of time, such as a flower blooming.
Slow motion	Suspends the normal speed of things by increasing the number of frames used to record the movement.
Speeded-up motion	Increases the normal speed by reducing the number of frames used to record the movement.
Reverse motion	The film is run backward through the projector.

Today, most editors use digital computer editing technology, including digital audio mixing. (Using this technology gives us some slightly different terms for the postproduction process.) They manipulate the audio and video images using Paint Box software. The result is a **rough cut**, a preliminary edited version of the story that is created when the editor chooses the best shots and assembles them to create a scene. The focus at this step is on assembling shots into scenes. The editor then joins the scenes together.

After the revision and reediting are completed, the editor makes an **interlock**, which means the audio and film are assembled together. The final version with the sound and film mixed together is called an **answer print**. The interlock could still be in a rough form (pieces of film snapped and taped together). The answer print is the final version printed onto a piece of film.

For the commercial to air on hundreds of stations around the country, the agency has to make duplicate copies—a process called **dubbing**. The dubbed copies are called **release prints** and are usually in video form.

EFFECTIVE WEB DESIGN

Web design involves more than just designing ads that run on the Web or even banner ads. That's because the Web site itself can be considered as a complex ad for a company or organization. The Web site may do other things as well, such as provide intranet communication within a company and between it and its business partners. The Web site that most people find when surfing fulfills some of the usual advertising functions—it attracts attention, provides information, and involves viewers, often leading them to some kind of action, such as placing an order. The Hemingway Collection on the Thomasville Web site displays the furniture in the collection as a visual catalog for people who search for furniture ideas on the Web.

Because of the magic of digitizing images, Web pages can combine elements and design styles from all different media: print, film, sound, and games. This medium's biggest challenge is ease of use. Let's see what advertising designers look for when designing Web pages and Web advertisements, then we'll talk about the design of a specific Web format called a banner.

The art on Web sites can be illustrations or photographs. Often the illustrations, as well as the photos, are obtained from clip art services, or rather click art, such as that provided by www.eyewire.com or www.1stoppictures.net. Actually, any image can be scanned and manipulated to create new images, which is causing a copyright problem for artists. One study of Web site artwork examined the impact of various types of color combinations on clip-art illustrations and photos. It found that, at least in terms of memory, color photos may not be worth their increased downloading time.[6] The study found that the subjects recalled more of the two- and four-color clip art illustrations than the black-and-white illustrations and color photographs.

Designers know that Web pages, particularly the first screen, should follow the same layout rules as posters: The graphics should be eye-catching without demanding too much downloading time; type should be simple, using one or two typefaces and avoiding all capitals and letter spacing that distorts the words. Because there is often a lot to read, black type on a high-contrast background usually is best; all the design elements—type and graphics—should be big enough to see on the smallest screen.

The Interactive Dimension

The combination of interactive navigation, live streaming video, online radio, and 360-degree camera angles creates Web pages that may be more complex than anything you see on TV. For example, Texture/Media, a Boulder Colorado–based Web design firm, created a seven-episode series over five months that detailed the journey of two men attempting to

The Hemingway® Collection is in the Lifestyle section of the Thomasville Furniture Web site (www.thomasville.com).

climb the Meru Sharksfin summit in India, for client Marmot Mountain Works. Called ClimbMeru.com, it chronicled the team's training and trip, and hosted contest giveaways that helped gather information about Marmot's customers. Texture/media's objective with its award-winning Web sites is to make the consumer a participant in its brand stories.[7]

Web advertisers are continuing to find ways to bring dramatic action to the small screen in order to make the imagery more engaging. For example, anyone logging on to the Yahoo! homepage on May 4 of 2001 saw nothing but a half-banner at the top of the screen with the familiar Ford oval and a bunch of little black birds on a wire. Then three of the birds flew down to the middle of the page and started pecking at what looked like birdseed, uncovering an image of the new Explorer 02. The link read: "Click to uncover the next territory." Those who did click probably expected a pop-up image, but instead the page shook, the birds scattered, and a big red Ford Explorer drove up to the front of the screen, replacing most of the content. It was a surprising, highly involving, and very effective announcement of the car.

Action has a dimension on the Web that it doesn't have in video or film, and that is the ability of users to control their viewing. Because users can create their own paths, designers have to make sure that their sites have sound **navigation**. Users should be able to move through the site easily and find the information they seek without getting stuck in a page or not knowing where they are on the site at all times. Ideally, users who visit a site regularly should be able to customize the site to fit their own needs.

Web designers use a completely different toolbox than other types of art directors. Animation effects, as well as sophisticated navigation paths, are designed using software programs such as Flash, Director, Blender, Squeak, and nonlinear editing tools such as Premier, FinalCut, and AfterEffects, among others. It's such a rapidly changing design world that it's difficult to keep track of the most recent innovations in Web design software.

Navigation, animation, and customization create a brand new set of design considerations. An example of a good Web site design is crewcuts.com, which was designated as the Best Web Site for February 2002 by the Internet Professional Publisher's Association. It's hard to convey here why the site is effective because of the animation, so check out www.crewcuts.com.

Interactivity is another element of good Web site and Web advertising design. Users should find it easy to contact the company with questions, suggestions, comments, and complaints. And on the company's side, there should be adequate staffing to ensure speedy answers to consumer questions. This feedback ability is one of the biggest strengths of the Web for companies looking to gather information from consumers. If a site is well designed, people may want to respond and interact with the organization sponsoring the site.

One source for tips on Web site design is www.eMarketers.com. Table 13.3 lists eMarketers' 10 rules for Web site design. For more examples of excellence in Web site design and reviews of the top Web sites, check out:

www.loudbrain.com	www.clioawards.com
www.imarvel.com	www.oneclub.com
www.topsiteslinks.com	www.ippa.org
www.netroadmap.com	www.momentumawards.com

Designing Banners

In addition to Web advertisements and Web sites, there is another format used on the Web—the banner ad—that has design considerations of its own. **Banners** are small space ads with limited words and graphics whose purpose is to tease viewers to click on the banner, which links them to the sponsor's Web site. They are ads on the screen but they function more like outdoor boards than more conventional ads because their small space puts intense requirements on the designer to make the ad communicate quickly and succinctly, and yet attract attention and curiosity in order to elicit a click-through response.

According to Michael T. Glaspie, author of *How to Sell Anything to Anyone, Anytime*,[8] grabbing attention with banners depends on copy, color, and graphics, in that order. For copy he recommends using free offers, fear, curiosity, humor, or a big promise. For color, use yellow, orange, blue, and green rather than reds and blacks. Animated banners are a value for the advertiser in that they increase ad space by rotating copy. But banners should not take too long to load or customers will lose interest.

TABLE 13.3	eRules for eDesign

Rule One: Manage your image. Projecting and protecting your brand identity are no less important online than in any other medium.

Rule Two: Simple navigation. Retail stores don't stay in business unless their customers can find what they want, easily. The same applies to Web sites. Remember K.I.S.S. (Keep It Simple, Stupid)?

Rule Three: Don't waste time. Do you like to wait in line? Do you go back to stores where sales clerks don't respond? Make sure your consumers find the information they're looking for–fast.

Rule Four: Keep your product fresh. Spiders may constantly comb the Web, but if anyone finds cobWebs on your site, they won't come back.

Rule Five: Give it away. If your site doesn't offer real value, there's no real reason for anyone to visit.

Rule Six: Information-in-the-end. When someone takes the time to link through to your site, don't let them come up empty. Reward them with content, content, content.

Rule Seven: Get interactive! Mass media are passive; the new media are interactive. In which direction do you think the world is going?

Rule Eight: Follow the rule of ten. Ten is enough for God and David Letterman, so learn from them. Keep your lists short, too.

Rule Nine: Promote your site. "Build it and they will come" was a nice theme for the movie *Field of Dreams*. But if you want customers, not virtual ghosts, on your site, get smart about promotion—in the real world.

Rule Ten: The rules will change. No one who does "business as usual" today is going to be in business tomorrow. So move often and as intelligently as possible. Keep up with fast-changing online business trends.

According to one study, banners that sit in the lower corner of the screen next to the scroll bar generate a 228 percent higher click-through rate than ads at the top of the page. Banner ads placed one-third down the page generate 77 percent more click-throughs than those at the top.[9]

Another study indicated that large, dynamic banners do not generate higher click-through rates than small, static banners, but incentive banners did increase click-throughs when compared to ads without incentives.[10]

IT'S A WRAP

IMAGINE A HEMINGWAY LIFESTYLE

The $60 billion furniture category is unusual in that there are more than 5,000 furniture manufacturers with very little brand differentiation among them. Thomasville Furniture is a key player but it, like all its competitors, struggles to create a brand identity for its products and a brand relationship with consumers.

The "Collection of a Lifetime" campaign for the Ernest Hemingway Collection generated $100 million in sales, which was six times the original sales objective and the largest launch in the company's history. Not only that, the Hemingway campaign also created a halo effect over the entire Thomasville line. Jim Adams, the senior vice president for marketing, commented, "We're a new company today."[11] Sales across all lines increased by 39 percent immediately following the Hemingway advertising.

In terms of effectiveness measures, the unaided brand awareness of Thomasville increased from 14 percent to 27 percent after the line's first year of advertising; however, the awareness of the Hemingway line jumped from zero to 41 percent during that same one-year period. That level exceeded the brand awareness levels of established competition, such as Henredon, which was at 28 percent awareness at the end of that same introductory year.

Furniture Today, a leading trade journal, declared that the Hemingway launch was "one of the most successful new lines in industry history."[12] And that was the reason "The Collection of a Lifetime" launch was selected as an EFFIE-award winner.

Summary

1. **Explain why visual communication is so important in advertising.** Visual communication is important in advertising because it is powerful. People tend to pay more attention to a photo and believe ads that contain them, thinking that "seeing is believing." In addition, research has shown that people find ads containing visuals easier to remember than ads that don't.

2. **List the principles of layout and explain how design is affected by media requirements.** A layout is an arrangement of all the ad's elements. It gives the reader a visual order to the information in the ad; at the same time, it is aesthetically pleasing and makes a visual statement for the brand. Principles that designers use in print advertising include direction, dominance, unity, white space, contrast, balance, and proportion.

   Newspaper ads accommodate the limitations of the printing process by not using fine details. Magazine ads, because they are printed on good paper, offer quality images and good color reproduction. For directory ads, designers keep in mind that people are searching for information, particularly about location and how to contact the company, and so these ads are focused on directional information. Visibility and the need for simple messages are the primary concerns of poster and outdoor board designers. Interior transit ads are designed for reading; exterior cards work like billboards.

3. **Describe how art and color are reproduced.** Illustrations are treated as line art and photographs are reproduced through the halftone process by using screens to break down the image into a dot pattern. Full-color photos are converted to four halftone images, each one printed with a different process color—magenta, cyan, yellow, and black—through the process of color separation.

4. **Explain how the art director creates TV commercials.** TV art directors are responsible for the "look" of a commercial. They also design the on-screen graphic elements as well as the presentation of the action through visual storytelling. Computer graphics are playing a more important role in the creation of special effects, particularly animation.

5. **Identify the critical steps in planning and producing broadcast commercials.** Commercials are planned using scripts (and storyboards for TV). Radio commercials are scripted, taped, and mixed. TV commercials are shot live, shot on film or videotape, or created "by hand" using animation, claymation, or stop action. There are four stages to the production of TV commercials—message design (scripts and storyboards), preproduction, the shoot, and postproduction.

6. **Summarize the techniques of Web design.** Web advertising can include ads and banners, but the entire Web site can also be seen as an advertisement. Art on Web pages can be illustrations or photographs, still images as well as moving ones, and may involve unexpected effects such as 360-degree images. When designers plan a Web page, they need to consider navigation—how people will move through the site. They also need to consider how to incorporate elements that allow for interaction between the consumer and the Web page company.

Key Terms

animation, p. 387	font, p. 370	morphing, p. 384	semicomps, p. 376
answer print, p. 389	gaffer, p. 388	navigation, p. 391	serif, p. 370
banners, p. 391	grip, p. 388	newsprint, p. 376	spot color, p. 369
claymation, p. 387	halftone, p. 378	photostats, p. 381	stock footage, p. 383
clip art, p. 367	in register, p. 376	picas, p. 371	stop motion, p. 387
color separation, p. 379	interlock, p. 389	points, p. 371	thumbnail sketches, p. 376
comprehensives, p. 376	justified, p. 371	process colors, p. 379	tint blocks, p. 379
crawl, p. 383	layout, p. 372	release prints, p. 389	tip-ins, p. 382
cut, p. 386	legibility, p. 372	rough cut, p. 389	trailers, p. 384
dailies, p. 388	line art, p. 378	rough layouts, p. 376	typography, p. 369
dubbing, p. 389	mechanicals, p. 376	rushes, p. 388	visualization, p. 365
film-to-tape transfer, p. 386	mixer, p. 388	sans serif, p. 370	

Questions

1. What does the visual contribute to an advertisement—what is its primary function in print and in television?

2. What does the art director do as a member of the team creating an advertisement for both print and TV?

3. What is visualization and why is it important?

4. What is the difference between using an illustration and using a photograph? Give an example of a product category where you would want to consider using an illustration and another example where you would want to consider using a photograph. Explain why.

5. What is the difference between full color and spot color? Why is color important in the design of advertising?

6. What is a font and what are the most common variations in a font that an art director has to specify?

7. What principles govern the design of a magazine ad? Collect two samples, one that you think is a good example of effective design and one that you think is not effective. Critique the two ads and explain your evaluation based on what you know about how design principles work in advertising layouts.

8. Choose an ad from this textbook that you think demonstrates a good layout with a clear visual path. Take a piece of tracing paper, as we have done with the Porsche ad in Figure 13.5, and convert the key elements to geometric shapes to see what kind of pattern emerges. Illustrate on your tracing how the eye moves around the page. Put an X on the dominant element on your tracing.

9. Think of a television commercial you have seen recently that you thought was creative and entertaining. Then find one that you think is much less creative and entertaining. Analyze how the two commercials work to catch and hold your attention. How do the visuals work? What might be done to make the second commercial more attention-getting? You can also use online sources to find commercials at www.adcritic.com and at www.badads.org.

10. One approach to design says that a visual image in an ad should reflect the image of the brand. Find a print ad that you think speaks effectively for the personality of the brand. Now compare the print ad with the brand's Web site. Does the same design style continue on the site? Does the site present the brand personality in the same way as the print ad?

11. Find a banner ad on the Web that you think can be improved. What recommendations would you make?

Suggested Class Project

Select a product that is advertised exclusively through print. Examples of such products are business-to-business and industrial products, school supplies, many over-the-counter drugs, and some food items. Your objective is to develop a 30-second television spot for this product. Divide the class into groups of four to six. Use a creative brief (see chapter 11) to summarize the ad's strategy. In your small groups, brainstorm about ways to develop a creative idea for the commercial. Then write a script and develop a storyboard to present your idea for this product. In the script include all the key decisions a producer and director would make. Present your work to the class.

Suggested Internet Class Project

You have been asked to design a Web page for a local business or organization (choose one from your local community). Go to www.1stoppictures.net and choose a visual to use to illustrate the Web site by trying to match the personality of the organization to a visual image. Then identify the primary categories of information that need to be included on the page. Develop a flow chart or map that shows how a typical user would navigate through the site. What other image could you find on 1stoppictures that might be used on inside pages to provide some visual interest to this business's online image? Now consider interactivity: How could this site be used to increase interactivity between this company and its customers? Turn in a plan for this site that includes the visual elements and a navigation flow chart.

Hallmark BUILD•A•CAMPAIGN Projects

Please review the Hallmark Case Appendix at the end of the text before responding to these questions.

1. Meet in small groups to discuss how Capitol Advertising used broadcast media to achieve its brand insistence goals and how those uses differed from its use of alternative media.

2. Should your local Hallmark store use broadcast or interactive media? If so, develop a proposal for a broadcast and interactive creative strategy and include a sample TV or radio script, storyboard (for TV), or color sketch of an Internet ad.

HANDS-ON

Case 13

DESIGNING ADS FOR THE SUBARU WRX

The 2002 Subaru Impreza WRX is an all-wheel-drive, four-door car. A wagon is available along with the coupe; both are available in six colors. The WRX is a performance-enhanced version of the Impreza: performance testing reveals the WRX can compete with the fastest cars in mass production. Competitors range from economy-class cars to SUVs, to high-performance sports cars. Prices for the WRX hover around $25,000 and approach $30,000 with all available options. Currently, the strongest selling point for the WRX is performance while maintaining Subaru's all-wheel-drive feature and a relatively low price.

The target audiences for the WRX are looking for a car that offers the best "bang for the buck." Relative to other cars offering similar performance (e.g., acceleration) and all-wheel-drive, the WRX is in a class by itself; no other automaker produces a similar car at a competitive price. Those who are on a budget and seeking high performance and all-wheel-drive will be interested in the WRX. These consumers may include young, active males interested in outdoor activities and sports. Those in wintry climates will be most interested; those in mountainous regions will also find some of the WRX's features beneficial.

The WRX promises to offer unhindered acceleration and the best traction, wet or dry, available in the market at a relatively low price. Considering the target, the tone of the advertising should reflect the tone of the product; a high-tech aura that represents the capability of all-wheel-drive.

The print campaign will appear in popular consumer magazines, full-page, headline, and limited body copy. ■

IT'S YOUR TURN

1. Given the information provided, what visual elements would be most attention getting? Describe a print ad for the launch of the WRX.
2. Convert the print ad to a Web ad.

Notes

1. Greg Burton, "Billboard Firm Rejects New Ad Spoofs on Polygamy," *Boulder Daily Camera* (November 8, 2001): 3B.

2. Personal communication from Sheri J. Broyles to the authorial team, October 7, 2001.

3. Noreen O'Leary, "Legibility Lost," *Adweek* (October 5, 1987): D7.

4. Rolf Rehe, *Typography: How to Make It Most Legible* (Indianapolis, IN: Design Research Publications, 1974).

5. "Video Helped the Radio Star," *Promo* (April 1996): 10.

6. Bruce Huhmann, Patrick Kelly, and Scott Muir, "Computerized Clipart versus Photographs in Internet Art: The Effect of Color and Image Complexity on Memory," *Frontiers in Direct Marketing Research,* vol. 2 1999 (New York: John Wiley, 1999): 51–52.

7. Matt Branaugh, "Dot-content: Marketing Tools Enhance Content," *Daily Camera Tech Plus* (October 20, 2001): 1E.

8. Michael T. Glaspie, "Web Site Promotion and Marketing Newsletter," *InternetDay* (October 1, 1998), retrieved online at http://internetday.com/archives/100198.html

9. Kim Doyle, Anastasia Minor, and Carolyn Weyrich, "Banner Ad Placement Study," retrieved online at www.webreference.com/dev/banners/.

10. Hairong Li, "What Makes Users Click on a Banner Ad: Two Field Experimental Studies of Banner Ad Size, Type, and Incentive," in *Proceedings of the 1998 Conference of the American Academy of Advertising,* Darrel Muehling, ed. (Lexington, Kentucky), 1998, pp. 289–90.

11. Sandra Dolbow, "Brand Builders," *Brandweek* (July 24, 2000): 19.

12. Ibid.

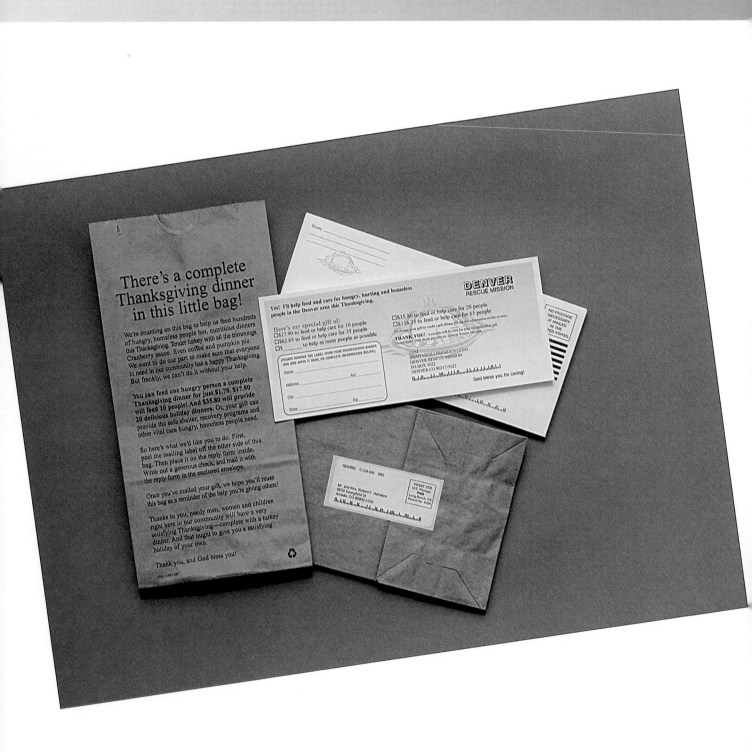

CHAPTER 14

Direct-Response Marketing

CHAPTER OBJECTIVES

When you have completed this chapter, you should be able to

1. Define and distinguish between direct marketing and direct-response advertising.
2. Explain some types of direct marketing.
3. Name the players in direct marketing.
4. Evaluate the various media that direct-response programs can use.
5. Explain how databases are used in direct marketing.
6. Discuss the role of direct marketing in integrated marketing programs.

Helping the Homeless Directly

Award: *Consumer Gold Echo Award 2001*

Organization: *Denver Rescue Mission*

Agency: *Russ Reid Company*

Campaign: *"Thanksgiving Dinner Bag"*

Throughout this book, we have introduced chapters with an EFFIE-award winning campaign. The direct marketing industry has its own award equivalent to the EFFIEs, called the Echo Award. You can read about the Echos at www.dma-echo.org, but for now we discuss how one organization won this award, which is given out for excellence in response rates, marketing strategy, and creative components.

The U.S. homeless population continues to grow. It's up to each city, town, and state to find solutions for this group of citizens. Many of these solutions are supported by government agencies, and can take the form of money or in-kind services. City-supported programs are the most common. One such example is the Denver Rescue Mission, established in 1987 and chartered to get the homeless men, women, and children off the streets of Denver and into programs that return them to society.

In the fall of 2000, The Rescue Mission's fundraising efforts faced competition from at least five other organizations serving the homeless in the Denver area at the time. Because eighty percent of the funds are collected in the last four months of the year, the Mission needed to create a unique campaign to help fund its annual Thanksgiving dinner for the homeless as well as the other year-long services.

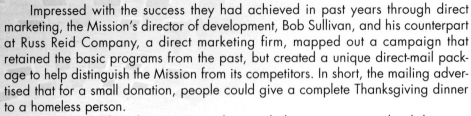

Impressed with the success they had achieved in past years through direct marketing, the Mission's director of development, Bob Sullivan, and his counterpart at Russ Reid Company, a direct marketing firm, mapped out a campaign that retained the basic programs from the past, but created a unique direct-mail package to help distinguish the Mission from its competitors. In short, the mailing advertised that for a small donation, people could give a complete Thanksgiving dinner to a homeless person.

The direct-mail package contained a simple brown paper sandwich bag, an outer envelope that explained how they could buy a Thanksgiving dinner for a homeless person for $1.79, and a peel-off label that donors could use to send their check to the Denver Mission. The mailing also worked to give the bag "a second life," to make it more than a direct-mail piece—and asked donors to reuse the bag for their own lunch as a reminder of the meals they were giving others. As noted in the "It's a Wrap" section at the end of this chapter, the campaign was a huge success.

DIRECT MARKETING

A big change is taking place in marketing and advertising as marketers are moving to more direct forms of communication with their customers. In the past, marketing communication was a monologue—advertisers talked to anonymous consumers through the mass media. Now communication is becoming a dialogue. Using computers and the Web, the mail, video, and the telephone, advertisers can talk directly with, rather than at customers. This advertising dialogue is achieved through direct marketing.

Direct Marketing is big business, with total expenditures in 2001 of $241.1 billion. Advertisers use direct marketing in every consumer and business-to-business category. IBM, Xerox, and other manufacturers selling office products use direct marketing, as do almost all banks and insurance companies. Airlines, hotels, and cruise lines use it. Packaged-goods marketers such as General Foods, Colgate, and Bristol Myers; household product marketers such as Black and Decker; and automotive companies use it. Direct marketing shows up in membership drives, fund-raising, and solicitation for donations by nonprofit organizations such as the Sierra Club and the Audubon Society, political associations, and the Denver Rescue Mission.

There is some confusion in marketing departments and the advertising industry over what people mean when they use the term "direct marketing." Although the direct-marketing industry continues to be in a state of flux, Figure 14.1 depicts the components that currently constitute direct marketing. **Direct marketing (DM)** occurs when a seller and customers deal with each other directly rather than through an intermediary, such as a wholesaler or retailer. As noted in Figure 14.1, it includes a strong focus on marketing research, to guide strategy; and database development, to better target customers. The strategic tools of direct marketing are: catalog, direct mail, telemarketing, and direct-response advertising. In turn, each of these tools provides an infrastructure whereby the transaction can actually take place.

When considering these four tools of direct marketing, there is recognition that catalog, direct-mail, telemarketing, and direct-response advertising are also types of communication devices. All four are delivering persuasive messages and the focus is on actually producing a sale. As noted repeatedly, producing a sale is the goal of all businesses, and identifies the primary reason why direct marketing is growing in popularity. And sales are measurable, meaning that the marketer always knows how it is doing relative to its investment in direct marketing.

Advantages of direct marketing over indirect marketing include the following:

1. Direct marketing technology allows for the collection of relevant information about the customer, contributing to the development of a useful database and selective reach, which reduces waste.
2. Products have added value, through the convenient purchase process and reliable/quick delivery mechanisms of direct marketing. Purchase is not restricted to a location.

Lands' End is a direct marketer, primarily selling to customers through its catalogs.

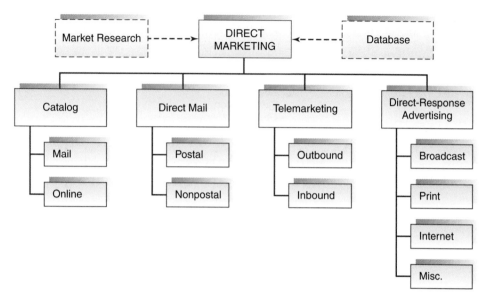

FIGURE 14.1

THE DIRECT-MARKETING INDUSTRY
The direct-marketing industry
focuses on research and database
building. Its main tools are catalogs,
direct mail, telemarketing, and
direct-response advertising.

3. The marketer controls the product (rather than the wholesaler or retailer) until delivery.
4. Advertising carrying direct-marketing components is more effective.
5. It affords flexibility both in form and timing.

As with all concepts, direct marketing has some weaknesses. Most notably, consumers are still reluctant to purchase a product sight unseen. This problem is changing with the increase in credible direct marketers, along with the ability of the Internet to simulate actual shopping and touching. The other weakness is the annoyances associated with direct marketing, such as too many catalogs, junk mail, and calls during dinner. Finally, direct-marketing strategies are unable to reach everyone in the marketplace. With improvement of **databases**, the problem is diminishing.

Since this text focuses on advertising, it is necessary to clearly distinguish between direct marketing and direct-response advertising. Essentially, direct-response advertising is a type of direct marketing, which combines the characteristics of nondirect advertising, such as copy, visuals, size, and timing, but also includes an element that allows the reader, viewer, or listener to make a direct response to the advertiser. The element can be an 800 or 900 phone number, an order coupon, a request-for-information device, and so forth.

Direct marketing makes an important contribution to advertising. It supplements the ad's value by including one or more components that allow for supplemental information, lead or traffic generation, and actual purchase. It also adds to the credibility of the ad and produces the most important outcome—sales. Advertising moves from a long-term implicit promise to a short-term explicit result. Therefore, the return-on-investment is significantly high for direct-response advertising. More will be said about direct-response advertising later.

Dell has built a huge business selling computers directly to consumers rather than through dealers, as its competitors do. Dell's success is evident in its market share, which hit 12 percent of desktop PCs worldwide in 2000, up from 6.9 percent at the end of 1997.[1] Why don't Compaq, Hewlett-Packard, and IBM copy the Dell model and sell computers directly? For one thing, dealers who deliver big sales to these companies would retaliate if they started experimenting with direct sales. Furthermore, it takes a lot of effort and infrastructure to set up a direct-marketing business. Rather than an army of sales reps, Dell employs an army of people in fulfillment who take the order, find the product, handle the money, and arrange for the shipping. Dell has a sound direct-marketing strategy, a topic that we turn to next.

DIRECT-MARKETING STRATEGY

As outlined in Figure 14.2, there are five basic steps in direct marketing: (1) setting objectives and making strategic decisions (research helps advertisers target, segment, prospect, and set objectives); (2) the communication of an offer (the message) by the

FIGURE 14.2

THE DIRECT-MARKETING PROCESS
The direct-marketing process has five main steps. The direct marketer's challenge is to manage these steps and build a relationship with the consumer.

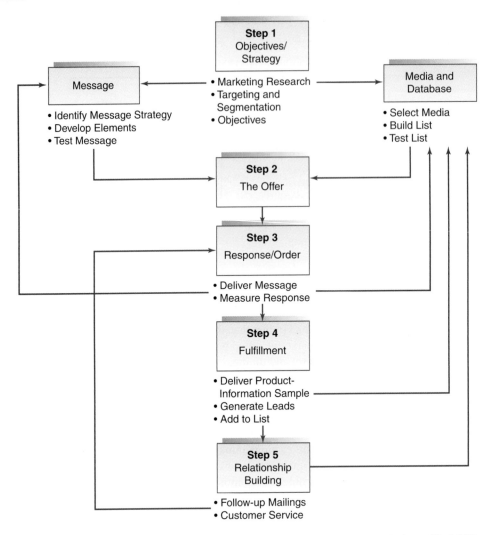

seller through the appropriate medium; (3) response, or customer ordering; (4) fulfillment, or filling orders and handling exchanges and returns; and (5) maintenance of the company's database and customer service.

Stating Objectives and Making Strategic Decisions

As is the case with all planning processes, we begin by delineating the specific objective we wish to achieve. Direct marketing has three general objective categories:

1. *Lead generation.* Providing basic information on companies or individuals who are potential customers.
2. *Traffic generation.* Motivating customers to visit an event, retail outlet, or other location.
3. *Purchase.* Order products and make payments.

These three basic objectives can then be made more specific with respect to such factors as timing, amount, and specific behavior. For example, a local Volvo dealership might expect its direct-marketing program to increase showroom traffic by 60 percent during the next 90 days.

The direct-marketing strategies employed to achieve these objectives are: direct-response advertising, catalog, direct mail, or telemarketing—separately or in some combination. Our Volvo dealer purchases a database of consumers who meet the criteria for a potential Volvo owner and sends out a direct-mail piece that offers $50 to anyone taking a test drive on a specific set of dates. This offer is repeated in the local newspaper. This whole process is also known as prospecting. **Prospecting** is a technique of mining the information in databases to uncover prospective buyers whose characteristics match those of users. Let's look more closely at "the offer."

The Offer

All direct marketing (DM) contains an offer, typically consisting of a description of the product, terms of sale, and payment and delivery terms. In its offer, a successful DM campaign must communicate benefits to buyers by answering the enduring question: "What's in it for me?" Direct marketers might tell potential buyers of product benefits by using buy-one-get-one-free tactics, or including product-related benefits in the offer. An effective DM offer, as with all marketing offers, clearly calls on the buyer to take some action. For the call to action to be effective, it should not be obscured by overly elaborate design elements, meaningless expressions, or other distractions. All the variables that are intended to satisfy the needs of the consumer are considered part of the offer. These variables include the price, the cost of shipping and handling, optional features, future obligations, availability of credit, extra incentives, time and quality limits, and guarantees or warranties. The offer is supported by a message strategy, a media strategy, and the database.

The Message Strategy There are general guidelines that apply to message development in direct marketing. First, the message is often longer and contains more detail; especially in light of the fact that DM products are often unavailable in traditional retail outlets. Messages must contain clear comparisons or characteristics such as price, style, convenience, and so forth. Second, copy tends to be written in a personal, one-to-one conversational style. Third, the message should reflect whether the offer is a one-step offer or a two-step offer. A **one-step offer** asks for a direct sales response and it is crucial that there is a mechanism for responding to the offer. A **two-step offer** is designed to gather leads, answer consumer questions, or set up appointments. The design of the message must account for all these possibilities.

The Media Strategy There are two types of media employed in direct marketing. In the case of direct-response advertising, traditional mass media are used to deliver the offer.

The cover of *Golf Day* magazine demonstrates a clear call to action, one component of an effective direct marketing offer.

Various print, broadcast, Internet, and other miscellaneous media are considered. The second kind of medium is called **controlled media**, in that the direct marketer either owns the medium or contracts for a company to deliver the message through carefully controlled criteria. These media include catalogs, telemarketing, and direct mail. They also differ from traditional mass media in their ability to better target the consumer, deliver longer messages, and deliver other salient information. Recall that these latter three DM media play a dual role of strategy and media. Each of them will be discussed in more detail later in this chapter.

The Database Direct marketers use databases as a segmentation tool for communicating their offers to customers and potential customers. Database technology became possible with computer technology, and became necessary to keep up with customers. People move, have children, marry, divorce, remarry, retire, change purchase behavior, and so forth. The purpose of the database is to produce up-to-date information on customers and potential customers. **Database marketing** is a tool and industry that uses databases to predict trends and monitor consumers to more effectively implement direct-marketing strategies. The database is simply a repository of information, having little value without a system for organizing and assessing it relative to direct-marketing strategies.

The database is at the heart of direct marketing. According to the Direct Marketing Association (DMA), a marketing database has four primary objectives, which we list in Table 14.1.[2]

Managing a database operation is difficult, and it is growing in complexity along with improvements in technology. The initial decision a company must make is whether it will gather data from internal sources, external sources, or both. Internal, or in-house databases are derived from customer receipts, credit card information, or personal information cards completed by customers. The internal approach is cost-effective as long as a company has the requisite expertise and resources.

If either expertise or resources are lacking, a company can obtain commercial databases from firms whose sole purpose is to collect, analyze, categorize, and market an enormous variety of detail about the American consumer. Companies such as National Decision Systems, Persoft, and Donnelly Marketing Information Systems are only a few of the firms that provide these relational databases (that is, their databases contain information useful in segmenting, as well as the contact information). Donnelly developed Hispanic Portraits, a database of households that segments the U.S. Hispanic population into 18 cluster groups.[3]

Direct-mail lists, a database of prospects, can be purchased or rented from list brokers, who manage a variety of lists from many different sources and can act as consultants to help you find a list or compile your own. Direct-mail list brokers have thousands of lists tied to demographic, psychographic, and geographic breakdowns. They have classified their data on Americans' households down to the carrier routes. For instance, one company has identified 160 zip codes it calls "Black Enterprise" clusters, inhabited by "upscale, white-collar, black families" in major urban fringe areas. If you want to target older women in New England who play tennis, most major firms would be able to put together a list for you by combining lists, called **merging**, and deleting the repeated names, called **purging**.

TABLE 14.1   **Objectives of a Marketing Database**

- To record names of customers, expires (names no longer valid), and prospects.
- To provide a vehicle for storing and then measuring results of advertising (usually direct-response advertising).
- To provide a vehicle for storing and then measuring purchasing performance.
- To provide a vehicle for continuing direct communication by mail or phone.

TABLE 14.2	**Types of Lists**
List Type	**Description**
House list	A list of the marketer's own customers or members, its most important target market, probably its most valuable list. Stores offer credit plans, service plans, special sale announcements, and contests that require customers to sign up to maintain this link. Some stores, such as Radio Shack, fill in customers' names and addresses at the cash register, and those customers join the list.
Response list	Derived from people who respond to something such as a direct-mail offer or solicitation, a response list is similar to the advertiser's target audience. For example, if you sell dog food, you might like a list of people who have responded to a magazine ad for a pet identification collar, usually available for rent from the original direct-mail marketer. Those on the list indicate a willingness to buy pet items, and possibly, by direct mail.
Compiled list	Compiled lists are rented from a direct-mail list broker. They are usually lists of some specific category, such as sports car owners, new homebuyers, graduating seniors, new mothers, association members, or subscribers to a magazine, book club, or record club.

Lists There are three types of lists: house lists, response lists, and compiled lists (see Table 14.2). New lists can be created by merging and purging. For example, you may want to develop a list of people who are in the market for fine furniture in your city. You could buy a list of new homebuyers and combine that with a list of people who live in a desirable census tract. These two lists together—a compiled list—would let you find people who have bought new homes in upscale neighborhoods.

Based on research conducted by John Cummings & Partners DBM/Scan, database marketing list usage had increased 30 percent by the mid-1990s, with 3,207 database programs noted in the packaged-goods industry alone. And the companies committed to using database marketing for the long term grew to approximately 42 percent.[4]

Today, computers and database software programs are getting smarter. Services such as Prodigy not only provide the user with online buying services, but also remember purchases and, over time, can build a purchase profile of each user. This kind of information is valuable to marketers, resellers, and their agencies. It's also scary to consumer activists and consumers who worry about their privacy.

Some grocery stores have computerized their grocery carts with displays that show individually selected advertised specials as the customer moves from one aisle to another. Customers at some of these stores have been issued bankcards to use in making purchases. When a customer makes a purchase using the card, the store's computer provides the retailer an item-by-item list of that customer's purchases and adds this to the demographic and income information on the customer's card application. The banks are so interested in this information that they are willing to waive the usual fees and charges to the store in exchange for the data.

Nintendo uses its 2-million-name database when it introduces more powerful versions of its video game system. The names and addresses are gathered from a list of subscribers to its magazine, *Nintendo Power.* The company believes that many of its current customers will want to trade up systems and this direct communication will make it possible for Nintendo to speak directly to its most important target market about new systems as they become available. Nintendo began its database in 1988 and credits database marketing with helping it to maintain its huge share of the $6 to $7 billion video game market.

Customer Relationship Management One of the most powerful tools to emerge from database marketing is a result of the in-depth exploration, classification, and improved management of information contained in customer databases. **Customer relationship management (CRM)** identifies and analyzes patterns in customer behavior to

As part of its direct marketing strategy, Nintendo maintains a two million-name database, compiled from subscribers to its magazine, *Nintendo Power.*

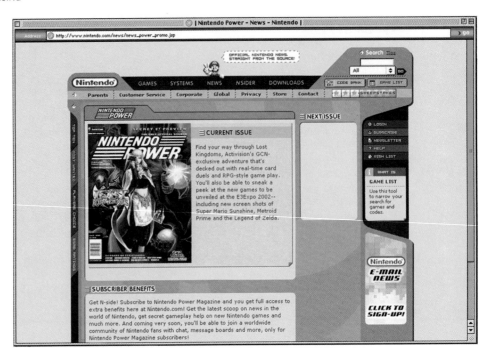

maximize the profitability of each relationship. (In Figure 14.2, customer relationship management is step 5, but notice that it begins at step 3—the response/order.) This management is accomplished through the use of highly developed database software that establishes links between transactions and the corresponding customers' characteristics. Armed with this knowledge, the company can pursue strategies to improve services that are important to their most profitable customers, attract new customers with similar characteristics, and identify and eliminate those customer relationships that drain company resources.

The use of CRM as a tool to selectively reduce a company's relationships with unprofitable customers has become quite pervasive, but this practice is not without its hazards. For example, several years ago, First Chicago Bank (later acquired by Bank One) recognized that it was losing money on certain transactions in its branches. For one thing, tellers were spending too much time on customers who held low bank accounts. It attempted to redirect these unprofitable customers to ATMs by charging lobby fees for teller-assisted transactions.

Unfortunately, what First Chicago failed to recognize, but the public seized upon immediately, was that these customers lived in predominantly poor neighborhoods and were largely African American. The negative PR caused by the ensuing public outcry was quite damaging to the company, and it shortly abandoned the policy. First Chicago learned a painful lesson: By using CRM to focus solely on profitability, a company may not recognize other intangible benefits generated by a particular group of customers. The experiences of First Chicago, and other similar incidents, have taught marketing professionals to carefully weigh other peripheral factors before implementing any plans to eliminate unprofitable customer relationships.

There are many examples of the successful use of CRM to improve customer relationships and services. The manufacturer of Lexus cars has a strong commitment to customer service and satisfaction. Each transaction is followed up with a letter, a phone call, and a survey—making each customer feel cared for and valued.

I know someone who flies nearly 2 million miles annually on American Airlines. While he was preparing to fly from San Diego to New York on a recent trip, the plane developed mechanical problems on the ground. Before my friend even started to inquire, an American Airlines' Special Services person came aboard, escorted him off the plane, handed him a ticket for another flight to San Diego, and sent him on his way. These positive experiences are based on the ultimate purpose of CRM: identifying a company's most profitable customers and giving them something that makes them feel prized and privileged. "The Inside Story" box describes techniques that enhance the success of a CRM strategy.

The database marketing process is illustrated in Figure 14.3. It begins with an initial collection point. This could be the completion of a warranty card, entering a contest or

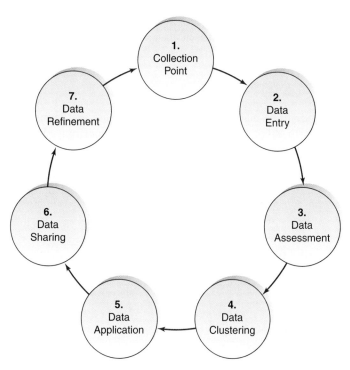

FIGURE 14.3

THE DATABASE MARKETING
PROCESS
Using database marketing,
advertisers can continually improve
the effectiveness of their campaigns.

sweepstake, opting in on a Web site, or filling out a card at a trade show, to name a few. The second stage is to enter the data into the computer to merge it with other information already in the file or added at the same time. Stage three allows the marketer to assess the data and determine the relevant level of detail. In stage four, the direct marketer can create clusters of characteristics and behaviors representing valuable consumer segments or target markets (audiences). Stage five applies the database to the specific marketing problems or strategies. An example might be sending coupons to a particular customer segment. In stage six, the direct marketer makes decisions about data sharing and partnerships. A manufacturer may decide his retail outlets could use the data. Finally, the database goes through a refinement process that includes corrections, updates, additions, and deletions.

Direct marketing (DM) is not a "shot-in-the-dark" approach. DM professionals are able to continually evaluate and accurately measure the effectiveness of various offers in a single campaign. By employing such measurement tools as tracking printed codes on mail-in responses that identify different offers, and using different telephone numbers for each commercial (by time slot, station, or length), the DM professional can clearly identify those offers that yield the best results, and modify the campaign to take advantage of them. Such accurate measurements and adjustments are largely responsible for DM's success.

The Response/Order

Unlike advertising, in which the initial objective is to generate awareness or brand awareness, and the ultimate objective is to contribute to sales, all direct marketing aims to generate a behavioral response, especially sales. Generating a response is the third step in the direct marketing process (Figure 14.2). Consumer response may take the form of direct action (purchase, donation, subscription, and membership) or behaviors that precede purchase (attending a demonstration, participating in a taste test, test driving a car, or asking for more information). DM prompts behavior by making a relevant offer and providing a mechanism for convenient purchase and fast delivery.

Fulfillment and Customer Maintenance

The next step in the direct marketing process, is called **fulfillment,** that is, getting the product to the customer who ordered it. It includes all the back-end activities that take place both before and after orders are received. The types of customer service offered, such as toll-free telephone numbers, free limited-time trials, and acceptance of several credit cards, are important techniques for overcoming customer resistance to buying through direct-response media.

The most critical aspect of successful direct marketing, however, is maintaining a customer relationship. Direct marketers use a database to track customer interactions and transactions, the last step in Figure 14.2.

THE PLAYERS

There are three main players in direct-response marketing: advertisers who use direct response to sell products or services by phone, mail, or the Web; agencies that specialize in direct-response advertising; and consumers, who are the recipients.

THE INSIDE STORY

THE FUTURE OF DIRECT RELATIONSHIP

Don Peppers and Martha Rogers, Ph.D.

Enterprises that are building successful customer relationships understand that becoming customer-focused doesn't begin with installing technology. It's not better-targeted and more efficient harassment (although you can't tell it when you look at a lot of the current efforts of "database marketing"). Becoming a customer-centric enterprise is about using insights into individual customers to gain a competitive advantage. It is an enterprise-wide approach to understanding and influencing customer behavior through meaningful communications, to improve customer acquisition, customer retention, and customer profitability.

Defined more precisely, however, and what makes "one-to-one" into a truly different model for doing business and competing in the marketplace, is this: It is an enterprise business strategy for achieving customer-specific objectives by taking customer-specific actions. In essence, one-to-one is about treating different customers differently. The overall business goal of this strategy will be to optimize the long-term profitability of the enterprise by increasing the value of the customer base. Building the value of customers increases the value of the "demand chain," the stream of business that flows from the customer up through the retailer all the way to the manufacturer. A customer-centric enterprise interacts directly with an individual customer.

Relationships are the crux of the customer-focused enterprise. The exchange between a customer and the enterprise becomes mutually beneficial, as customers give information in return for personalized service that meets their individual needs. This interaction forms the basis of the "learning relationship," an intimate, collaborative dialogue between the enterprise and the customer that grows smarter and smarter with each successive interaction. The learning relationship works like this:

> If you're my customer and I get you to talk to me, I remember what you tell me, and I get smarter and smarter about you. I know something about you my competitors don't know. So I can do things for you my competitors can't do, because they don't know you as well as I do. Before long, you can get something from me you can't get anywhere else, for any price. At the very least you'd have to start all over somewhere else, but starting over is more costly than staying with us.

Even if a competitor were to establish exactly the same capabilities, a customer already involved in a "learning relationship" with the enterprise would have to spend time and energy—sometimes a lot of time and energy—teaching the competitor what the current enterprise already knows. This creates a significant switching cost for the customer, as the value of what the enterprise is providing continues to increase, partly as the result of the customer's own time and effort. The result is that the customer becomes more loyal to the enterprise, because it is simply in the customer's own interest to do so. As the relationship progresses, the enterprise becomes more valuable to the customer, allowing the enterprise to protect its profit margin with the customer, often while reducing the cost of serving that customer.

Learning relationships provide the basis for a completely new arena of competition, quite separate and distinct from traditional, product-based competition. An enterprise cannot prevent its competitor from offering a product or service that is perceived to be as good as its own offering.

Don Peppers and Martha Rogers, Ph.D., are the founders of the Peppers and Rogers Group, a management-consulting firm that specializes in customer-based business strategy. Among their many accomplishments, Peppers and Rogers have authored numerous works, including the influential book The One to One Future.

| TABLE 14.3 | **Direct-Marketing Suppliers and Agencies** |

- **Advertising agencies.** Agencies whose main business is mass-media advertising either have a department that specializes in direct response or own a separate direct-response company.
- **Independent agencies.** The independent, full-service, direct-marketing agencies specialize in direct response, and many of them are quite large. The largest direct-marketing agencies include some firms that specialize in only direct response and others that are affiliated with major agencies.
- **Service firms.** Service firms specialize in supplying printing and mailing, and list brokering.
- **Fulfillment houses.** The fulfillment house is a type of service firm that is vital to the success of many direct-marketing strategies. This is a business responsible for making sure consumers receive whatever they request in a timely manner, be it a catalog, additional information, or the product itself.

The Advertisers

More than 12,000 firms are engaged in direct-response marketing. Their primary business is selling products and services by mail or telephone. This number does not include the many retail stores that use direct marketing as a supplemental marketing program. Traditionally, the types of companies that have made the greatest use of direct marketing have been book and record clubs, publishers, insurance companies, sellers of collectibles, manufacturers of packaged foods, and gardening firms.

The Agencies

The four types of firms in direct-response advertising include advertising agencies, independent direct-marketing agencies, service firms, and fulfillment houses, as Table 14.3 outlines.

The Consumers

Although people might dislike the intrusiveness of direct-response advertising, many appreciate the convenience. Former Postmaster General Preston Tisch observed that it is "a method of purchasing goods in a society that is finding itself with more disposable income but with less time to spend it."[5] Stan Rapp, an expert on direct marketing, described this type of consumer in a speech to an annual DMA conference as "a new generation of consumers armed with push-button phones and a pocket full of credit cards getting instant gratification by shopping and doing financial transactions from the den or living room."[6]

The push-button shopper now is joined by an even larger group of mouse-clicking shoppers. It takes some daring to order a product you can't see, touch, feel, or try out. These consumers are confident and willing to take a chance but don't like to be disappointed. Direct marketers establish sophisticated infrastructures to make sure requests/orders are received and accurately processed.

THE STRATEGIC TOOLS OF DIRECT MARKETING

Direct marketing (DM) employs four primary strategic tools to achieve objectives. These strategic tools are direct mail, catalogs, telemarketing, and direct-response advertising. We turn to each tool now.

Direct Mail

Direct mail is the granddaddy of direct response and still commands big marketing dollars. At the end of 2000 it accounted for some $44 billion in advertising expenditures. A direct-mail piece is a print advertising message for a product or service that is delivered by mail. It may be as simple as a single-page letter or as complex as a package consisting of a letter, a brochure, supplemental flyers, and an order card with a return envelope. A 2 to 5 percent response rate is considered typical.

TABLE 14.4   **Advantages and Disadvantages of Direct Mail**

Advantages	Description
Tells a story	The medium offers a variety of formats and provides enough space to tell a complete sales story.
Engages attention	Because direct mail has little competition when it is received, it can engage the reader's attention.
Personalizes the message	Because of the use of databases, it is now possible to personalize direct mail across a number of consumer characteristics, such as name, product usage, purchase history, and income.
Builds in feedback	Direct mail is particularly conducive to marketing research and can be modified until the message design matches the needs of the desired target audience.
Reaches the unreachable	Direct mail allows the marketer to reach audiences who are inaccessible by other media.

Disadvantages	Description
Negative perceptions	The main drawback of using direct mail is the widespread perception that it is junk mail. According to a Harris-Equifax Consumer Privacy Survey, about 46 percent of the public sees direct-mail offers as a nuisance, and 90 percent considers them an invasion of privacy.
Cost	Direct mail has a higher cost per thousand than mass media. A great deal of this high cost is a result of postage. (However, it reaches a more qualified prospect with less waste.) Another cost factor is the maintenance of the database.
Mailing list	To deliver an acceptable response rate, the quality of the mailing list is critical. It must be maintained and updated constantly.
Response rate	Because of the changing nature of mailing lists, as well as the difficulty of keeping relevant data in the database, the response rate can be as low as 2 or 3 percent. Even with that low response, however, database marketers can still make money.
Vulnerability	Direct-mail delivery is vulnerable to natural disasters as well as catastrophes such as the 9/11/01 terrorist attacks.

Most direct mail is sent using the third-class bulk mail permit, which requires a minimum of 200 identical pieces. Third class is cheaper than first class, but it takes longer for delivery. Estimates of nondelivery of third-class mail run as high as 8 percent.

Direct mail has a number of advantages and disadvantages. Table 14.4 summarizes these and suggests how advertisers can use direct mail most effectively.

Direct-Mail Message Design How it looks is as important as what it says. Progressive direct marketers, supported by research findings, have discovered that the appearance of a direct-response ad—the character and personality communicated by the graphics—can enhance or destroy the credibility of the product information.[7]

The functions of a direct-mail message are similar to the steps in the sales process. The message must move the reader through the entire process, from generating interest to creating conviction and inducing a sale. And it's all done with a complex package of printed pieces. (The Practical Tips box is a helpful guide for putting together direct-mail pieces.)

Direct mail can be anything and look like anything, but most pieces follow a fairly conventional format. The packaging usually includes an outer envelope, a letter, a brochure, supplemental flyers or folders, and a reply card with a return envelope. These can be one-page flyers, multipanel folders, multipage brochures, or spectacular **broadsheets** that fold out like maps to cover the top of a table.

The most critical decision made by the target is whether to read the mailing or throw it away, and that decision is based on the outer envelope. The envelope should state the

Practical Tips #1

CREATING EFFECTIVE DIRECT MAIL

- Get the attention of the targeted prospect as the envelope comes from the mailbox.
- Create a need for the product, show what it looks like, and demonstrate how it is used.
- Answer questions, as a good salesperson does, and reassure the buyer.
- Provide critical information about product use.
- Inspire confidence, minimize risk, and establish that the company is reputable.
- Make the sale by explaining how to buy, how to order, where to call, and how to pay for the purchase.
- Use an incentive to encourage a fast response.

offer on the outside and spark curiosity. (Actually, the industry estimates that consumers do read three-fourths of the pieces they receive.) The *Granta* direct-mail piece is comprised of an envelope and letter. The letter should explain the details of the offer, as the *Granta* letter does, and use a personal style.

Historically, the letter has been both the most important and the most difficult element in a direct-mail package.

Over the years many techniques have proven effective in getting consumers to read a direct-mail letter. Dean Rieck, an internationally respected direct-response copywriter, designer, and consultant, offers these hints for writing an effective letter.

- First, to grab attention or generate curiosity, use pictures and headlines that tout the product's benefits.
- Second, use a personalized salutation. If the individual's name is not available, the salutation should at least be personalized to the topic, such as, "Dear Cat Lover."
- Third, the best way to begin a letter is with a brief yet compelling or surprising statement—"Dear Friend: I could really kick myself!"
- Fourth, make the offer as early in the body of the letter as possible.
- Fifth, the letter should use testimonials or other particulars that clearly describe benefits to the customer.
- Finally, the closing of the letter should include a repetition of the offer, additional incentives or guarantees, and a clear call to action.[8]

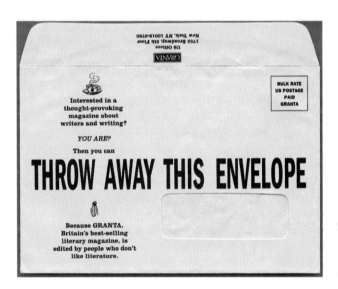

This direct-mail envelope for *Granta,* a British literary magazine, shows the power of an intriguing thought that sparks curiosity.

The Internet has made it easier for direct-mail companies to conduct business. USAMailNow provides several services for direct mail customers.

The Internet and Direct Mail The technology of the Internet has produced dramatic changes in the direct-mail industry. At a most basic level, the Internet has facilitated the ease in producing traditional direct mail and direct-mail companies are capitalizing on the technology. Take USA Direct, which introduced the USAMailNow Web site in early 2001. This company identified the most frustrating and time-consuming processes of direct-mailing campaigns and constructed a Web site that does these processes for companies (see its Web site shown here). USAMailNow's streamlined process allows a company of any size to point and click its way through a series of choices to make predesigned mailer templates priced and sorted by industry, mailing lists, and various mail media (postcards, letters, flyers, or newsletters), which customers can customize with their logo and other proprietary images or copy. Another benefit of their service is that it helps companies create uniform mailings to ensure a consistent public identity—a special challenge for organizations with several branches or locations that mail their own offers locally.

On a more sophisticated level, the Internet has begun to reconcile an ongoing conflict within the direct-mail industry: the debate over sending small, personalized mailings or big, mass mailings. Complete with long requisite letters, ornate brochures, free gift enclosures, and other attention-grabbing devices, personalized mailings were thought to grab consumers' attention. However, this attention came at a high per-unit price and so personalized mailings have a limited scope. In contrast, cheaper mass media (postcards, short form letters, flyers, and newsletters) were particularly well suited to boosting a company's reach and frequency. Unfortunately, they lacked much of the allure of their more personalized cousins.

How has the Internet helped reconcile this debate? Today, the utilization of extensive database information and innovative e-mail technology, combined with creative marketing strategies, has brought about a new era in direct electronic mail, which has the benefits of being highly personalized, inexpensive, and far-reaching. A report by a company called eMarketer, that tracks e-commerce activity, estimated the average cost per e-mail in the United States to be less than $0.01—compared to between $1 and $3 for telemarketing and $0.75 and $2 for direct mail. A sign of the growing popularity of e-mail among direct marketers, eMarketer forecasted that $2.1 billion would be spent on e-mail marketing in 2001; a 110 percent increase from the $1.1 billion spent in 2000 (the actual figure was $1.78 billion). Furthermore, the report provided evidence of targeted e-mail's superiority to the reach of Internet banner ads; citing that the click-through rate for e-mails was 3.2 percent and only 0.3 percent for the banner ads (for more information on the report, visit www.emarketer.com).[9]

Although e-mail marketing has enjoyed increased success, the practice has received intense criticism for generating too much unwanted e-mail, otherwise known as "spam." Direct marketers have responded to the criticism in two ways. For one, companies now search their rich databases for customers' buying habits or recent purchases. They then send these customers e-mail that offer deals on related products. This way, the company doesn't come across as predatory.

More recently, direct marketers have used an approach called "permission marketing" to reduce criticism about spam. **Permission marketing** gives customers an opportunity to "opt-in" to a notification service from a company. The e-mail will ask if the recipient wants further e-mails and wants to be on the mailing list. When opting-in, customers are often asked to complete a questionnaire about their purchasing habits or other information, which is used to personalize the service. Examples of these services include sending periodic newsletters, sending new offers that suggest items similar to those they have just purchased, and informing customers about upcoming sales or important dates.

Additionally, permission marketing gives customers an opportunity to opt-out of the service when they no longer need a company's product or services. They can sometimes even opt-down by reducing how frequently they receive messages. So customers gain control over the amount and type of e-mail messages they receive, and companies reduce wasted resources on marketing to uninterested individuals. They also gain valuable insight into their customers' habits and interests. The concept at the heart of permission marketing is that every customer who opts-in to a campaign is a qualified lead.[10]

The use of e-mail as a marketing tool has not been restricted to just the usual e-commerce companies. Well-known corporate brands such as BMW are getting into the act. Expanding its

Rich media, such as this example for buy.com, greatly increases advertising effectiveness.

Web presence, BMW has run some successful e-mail campaigns. In one such campaign, it requested existing and prospective customers to view a collection of Web movies about new BMW models. Another campaign notified BMW owners of a new section at BMW.com that was reserved strictly for their use. Called the "Owner's Circle," the section allowed owners to obtain special services and set up profiles that tracked maintenance items specific to their cars. Shortly after the mailing, enrollment in the Owner's Circle doubled, and participation in BMW's financial services program tripled.[11]

One of the most exciting developments in direct e-mail messaging is the use of **rich media**. Rich-media messages are effective in grabbing people's attention because of their novelty and entertainment value. They contain animated graphics, and/or streaming sound or video.

While rich-media messages can be quite dazzling, they have two major drawbacks. First, customers with dial-up modems may be turned off by the length of time it takes to download the message. Second, since most customers use their Internet service providers' systems to receive and store e-mail messages, the capacity of their e-mailboxes is severely restricted. Rich-media messages take up huge amounts of computer space, inconveniencing customers by taking up too much of their allotted mailbox resources. Notwithstanding these obstacles, many companies continue to believe that, as technological horizons expand, rich-media messaging will be the future standard of direct marketing on the Web.

Catalogs

A **catalog** is a multipage direct-mail publication that shows a variety of merchandise. The big books are those produced by such retail giants as JC Penney and L.L. Bean. The Spiegel Company is a major catalog merchandiser that doesn't have a retail outlet. Saks Fifth Avenue, Neiman Marcus, and Bloomingdale's are major retailers that support their in-store sales with expensive catalogs.

As databases have improved, catalog marketers are refining their databases and culling out consumers who receive catalogs but don't order from them. Even though catalog marketers are cutting back on the waste in their mailings, there are still a lot of catalogs in mailboxes. L.L. Bean still mails to 115 million customers and Lillian Vernon mails 175 million catalogs a year.[12]

The real growth in this field is in the area of specialty catalogs. There are catalogs for every hobby, as well as for more general interests, such as men's and women's fashions, sporting goods, housewares, gardening, office supplies, and electronics. There are catalogs specifically for purses, rings, cheese and hams, stained-glass supplies, garden benches, and computer accessories, to name just a few. Balducci's fruit and vegetable store in Greenwich Village, New York, produces a catalog promising overnight delivery of precooked gourmet meals.

Some of these retailers have their own stores, such as Williams-Sonoma and Tiffany's. Banana Republic, which began as a catalog marketer and then moved into retailing, is now launching its first catalog since 1988. Others, such as Hanover House and FBS, offer their merchandise only through catalogs or other retailers. Some of the merchandise is inexpensive, such as the Hanover line, which is usually $10 or less. In contrast, marketers such as Dell computer offer much more expensive products.

Catalogs are the chief beneficiaries of the social changes that are making armchair shopping so popular. However, the catalog marketer must make sure the ordering process is easy and risk free. Catalogs have become so popular that direct-response consumers receive mailings offering them lists of catalogs available for a fee. People pay for catalogs the way they pay for magazines and an increasing number of catalogs can be purchased at newsstands.

There are advantages and disadvantages of catalogs. They are listed in Table 14.5, and serve as input for the advertiser interested in using catalogs.

Electronic Catalogs

Catalogs are becoming available in videocassette and computer disk formats as well as online. Buick developed an electronic catalog on CD. The message is interactive and features animated illustrations. It presents graphic descriptions, and detailed text on the Buick line, including complete specifications, and lets you custom-design your dream car. The electronic catalog has been marketed to readers of computer magazines.

A number of advertisers are using video catalogs because it provides more information about their products. With more than half of American homes owning VCRs, this medium is increasingly important. Consumers no longer have to order catalogs or wait for them to arrive. They can go online and review several catalogs, make comparisons, and place orders. This convenience is hard for traditional catalogs to match.

A new addition to the catalog industry is digital imaging technology. With digital imaging, firms can improve their storage, management, and creative use of images in either traditional or online catalogs. Moreover, this technology saves money and generates high-quality images. In a recent agreement, Federated Department Stores replaced expensive traditional photography with digital imaging for their Bloomingdale's and Macy's

TABLE 14.5	**Advantages and Disadvantages of Catalogs**
Advantages	**Description**
Targeted	Can be directed at specific market segments.
Engages attention	Employs high-quality design and photography that is easy to read (see Alsto's cover).
Complete information	Extensive product information and comparisons are provided.
Convenience	Offer a variety of purchase options.
Disadvantages	**Description**
Negative perceptions	Catalogs are viewed as junk mail by many recipients.
Costs	The cost per thousand of catalogs is higher than mass media.
Response rate	The response is relatively low at 3 to 4 percent.
Mailing list	Databases must be constantly maintained.

Alsto's is an example of a catalog direct marketer that employs beautiful photography and high quality paper stock.

Direct online catalogs.[13] Federated is not alone in its strategy; this cost-effective approach to handling product images is quickly transforming the look of the entire catalog industry.

Telemarketing

More direct-marketing dollars are spent on **telemarketing**—ads delivered through phone calls—than on any other medium. That's because telemarketing is almost as persuasive as personal sales, but a lot less expensive. A personal sales call may cost anywhere from $50 to $100 after factoring in time, materials, and transportation. A telephone solicitation may range from $2 to $5 per call, or a CPM of $2,000 to $5,000. That is still expensive if you compare the cost of a telephone campaign to the CPM of an advertisement placed in any one of the mass media ($10–$50); however, the returns are much higher than those generated by mass advertising.

Telemarketing does have its drawbacks. Perhaps the most universally despised telemarketing tool is **predictive dialing**. Predictive dialing technology makes it possible for telemarketing companies to call anyone—even those with unlisted numbers. Special computerized dialing programs use trial-and-error to identify certain factors that increase the likelihood that they will actually reach someone, such as determining the optimal number of rings (usually two) before trying a new number. This explains why, from time to time, when you answer your phone you simply hear a dial tone; the predictive dialer has given up on trying to reach you. For many people, such an interruption is only a nuisance; but because some burglars have been known to call a house to see if anyone's home before they attempt a break-in, many people find such calls alarming.

Another problem associated with telemarketing, and one that has tarnished its reputation, is fraudulent behavior. Unfortunately, many scam artists see the ease with which they can trick people through telemarketing. A popular scam is to promise a product or service in exchange for an advance payment. Of course, after consumers send the money, they never receive anything. Another scam is to convince consumers they need some kind of financial or credit protection (something that the consumers' existing financial company

During the first five years of enforcement of the telemarketing sales rule (TSR) the Federal Trade Commission brought 121 actions alleging rule violations.

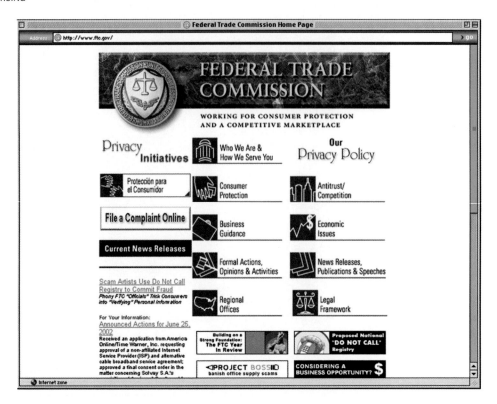

probably already provides). One final practice is to entice consumers to buy something by promising them prizes that are later discovered to be worthless.

In response to these abuses in telemarketing, the Federal Trade Commission enacted the Telemarketing Sales Rule (TSR) in 1995 to protect consumers. Among other things, the TSR prohibits telemarketers from calling before 8 A.M. or after 9 P.M.; it imposes strict informational disclosure requirements like the purpose of the call or the price of a product; it prohibits misrepresentative or misleading statements; and it provides for specific payment collection procedures. Violators of these rules can be prosecuted in federal court by the FTC or any of the states' attorneys general, and can face civil fines up to $10,000 for their misconduct.

Phone companies are also getting into the act and offering their customers a service called "Privacy Manager" that screens out sales calls.[14] For customers who have Caller ID, numbers that register as "unavailable" or "unknown" are intercepted by a recorded message that asks callers to identify themselves. If the caller does so, the call rings through.

Types of Telemarketing There are two types of telemarketing: inbound and outbound. An **inbound** or incoming telemarketing call originates with the customer. The consumer can be responding to an ad or a telemarketing message received earlier. L.L. Bean's telephone representatives handle inbound calls. The L.L. Bean ad draws attention to the representatives' friendly and helpful manner. Calls originating with the firm are outgoing or **outbound** and these are the ones that generate the most consumer resistance.

Most companies that use telemarketing hire a specialized company to handle the solicitations and order taking. They do this because most of the activity occurs in bunches. If a company advertises a product on television, for example, the switchboard will be flooded with calls for the next 10 minutes. Companies that do occasional direct-response advertising don't have the facilities to handle a mass response.[15]

Telemarketing Message Design The key point to remember about telemarketing solicitations is that the message has to be simple enough to be delivered over the telephone. If the product requires a demonstration or a complicated explanation, then the message might be better delivered by direct mail.

The message also must be compelling. People resent intrusive telephone calls, so there must be a strong initial benefit or reason-why statement to convince prospects to continue listening. The message also must be short; most people won't stay on the telephone longer than 2 to 3 minutes for a sales call. Of course, that is still a lot longer than a 30-second TV commercial.

Direct-Response Advertising

The common thread that runs through all types of direct-response advertising is that of action. That is, **direct-response advertising** seeks to achieve an action-oriented objective—such as an inquiry, a visit to a showroom, an answer to a questionnaire, or the purchase of a product—as a result of the advertising message and without the intervention of a sales representative. With brand or image advertising, a retailer or a sales representative who calls at the office or home usually makes the sale.

The elimination of the retail step is what makes direct-response advertising effective. However, some advertisers see direct response as less effective than brand or image advertising because it doesn't reach as many people or, if it does, the cost of reaching each individual is very high. This is because the objective is sales rather than a recall or an attitude change.

Today the high-cost argument is being reconsidered. Although it costs a lot per impression, direct-response advertising is well targeted. It reaches a prime audience; people who are likely, for reasons related to their demographics or lifestyles, to be interested in the product. Furthermore, although personal contact is lacking, which is an important element in closing some types of sales, newer forms of interactive media such as the Web are beginning to solve that problem. Still, direct-response advertising employs mass media more than any other type of advertising.

Print Media Ads in the mass media are less directly targeted than are direct-mail and catalog but they can still provide the opportunity for a direct response. Ads in newspapers and magazines can carry a coupon, an order form, an address, or a toll-free or 900 telephone number. The response may be either to purchase something or to ask for more information, which is the goal for the Clarinex magazine ad. In many cases the desired response is an inquiry that becomes a sales lead for field representatives.

In their book *MaxiMarketing,* direct-marketing experts Stan Rapp and Tom Collins discuss the power of double-duty advertising that combines brand-reinforcement messages with a direct-response campaign to promote a premium, a sample, or a coupon. American Express used this double-duty concept when it launched *Your Company,* a quarterly mailed to more than 1 million American Express corporate card members who own small businesses. Four sponsors launched *Your Company:* IBM, United Parcel Service, Cigna Small Business Insurance, and American Express Small Business Services. American Express also mails a magazine, *Connections,* to college students. Such efforts combine the editorial direction of a magazine with direct advertising's ability to target a narrow audience based on demographics and lifestyle. Magazines have been trying to do this with demographic editions and selective bindings as well.

In magazines, response cards may be either **bind-ins** or **blow-ins**. Both are freestanding cards that are physically separate from the ad they support. Bind-in cards are stapled or glued right into the binding of the magazine adjoining the ad. They have to be torn out to be used. Blow-in cards are attached to the magazine after it is printed by special machinery that puffs open the pages. These cards are loose and may fall out in distribution, so they are less reliable.

Broadcast Media Direct marketers can also use television and radio. Television is a good medium for direct marketers who are advertising a broadly targeted product and who have the budget to afford the ever-increasing costs of television advertising. A direct-response commercial would provide the necessary information (usually an 800 phone number or Web address) for the consumer to request information or make a purchase. Direct-response advertising on television used to be the province of the late-night hard sell with pitches for vegematics and screwdrivers guaranteed to last a lifetime. But as more national marketers such as Time Warner move into the medium, the direct-response com-

mercial is becoming more general in appeal, selling clothes, cable TV, and entertainment, to name a few.

Cable television lends itself to direct response because the medium is more tightly targeted to particular interests. QVC and the Home Shopping Network reach more than 70 million households.

Direct-response TV also makes good use of the infomercial format. The Salton-Maxim Juiceman infomercial took the company from $18 million to $52 million in sales overnight.[16] Infomercials blur the lines between retail and direct response. The Salton commercial made Juiceman the brand to buy, whether direct from television or from a local department store or mass merchant. Infomercials have been around since the emergence of the cable industry and have become a multibillion-dollar industry. An infomercial is typically 30 or 60 minutes long and tends to be played during non-prime-time periods. They were originally perceived as the equivalent of junk mail and appealed to

Television shopping networks handle sales orders by using hundreds of customer service agents.

consumers looking for a bargain or something unusual. Today, the infomercial is viewed as a viable medium. The reasons are as follows: (1) consumers now have confidence in infomercials and the products they sell; (2) with the involvement of upscale advertisers, the quality of infomercial production and supportive research has improved; (3) consumers can be better segmented and infomercials are coordinated with respect to these audiences; and (4) infomercials can easily be introduced into foreign markets. Finally, advertisers might use the infomercial format if their product needs to be demonstrated, is not readily available through retail outlets, and has a relatively high profit margin.

Radio Radio has not been a dynamic medium for direct-response advertising because the radio audience is too preoccupied with other things to record an address or a telephone number. However, some home listeners are able to make a note and place a call, and local marketers have had some success selling merchandise this way. Radio's big advantage is its targeted audience. For example, teenagers are easy to reach through radio. Also, radio has had some success selling products such as cellular phones and paging systems specifically to a mobile audience. Radio is often used to supplement other forms of direct response. For example, publishers use radio to alert people that a sweepstakes mailing is beginning and to encourage participation.

The Internet Although traditional advertisers have been looking for a way to use the Internet, direct marketers saw its potential immediately. Actually, direct marketing—particularly catalog marketing—is the model for e-commerce. Said James Rosenfield of Rosenfield & Associates, "Madison Avenue is trying to embrace the Internet as the next great advertising medium. They have it wrong. It's the next great commercial-information medium. It's not going to supplement TV. It's going to supplement direct mail and telemarketing."[17] So far, these predictions have turned out to be true. The Internet provides the same components found in direct mail and telemarketing. Amazon.com is the leader of the pack but other companies that sell merchandise direct include Columbia House Online (www.columbiahouse.com), L.L. Bean (www.llbean.com), Wal-Mart Online (www.wal-mart.com), Gridland (www.gridland.net), and CDNow (www.cdnow.com).

Another feature of Internet direct marketing is greater sampling opportunities. Online music stores now have 275,000 music clips for shoppers to listen to before making a purchase.[18] Eddie Bauer lets site visitors "try" on clothes. It also sends them e-mail messages offering special prices on items based on their past purchasing patterns.[19]

The Internet is also providing companies with new ways to gather information on consumers. One of the more ambitious is allowing consumers to create their own network of contacts for marketers to promote across. The giant bookseller Amazon.com owns PlanetAll, a Web-based address book, calendar, and reminder service. A subscriber enters friends' information and then Amazon can not only remind these subscribers about upcoming birthdays, but can also suggest books that those friends and relatives have indicated that they'd like to receive as gifts.[20]

The point is that the Web is moving marketers much closer to one-to-one marketing.[21] The Web not only offers merchants the ability to communicate instantly with each customer, but it also allows the customers to talk back, and that makes it possible to customize the offers and services. The campaign for stamps.com allows customers several options.

Lester Wunderman, the most recognized expert in direct marketing, recently offered these insights into the future of the Web as a direct-marketing tool.

- Despite all the news to the contrary, the Web is not a great shopping medium or a great browsing medium for shoppers. It's a great medium and works well if you know what to buy.
- The Web will change the way people shop and will eventually have an enormous impact on both branding and purchasing.
- What the Web does that no other medium ever did is put the consumer in charge.[22]

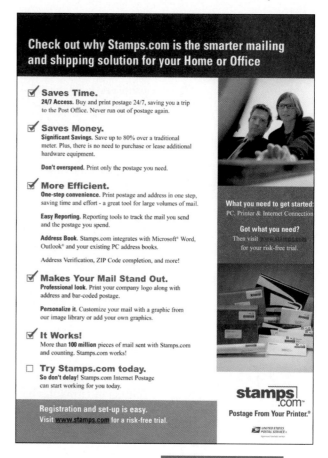

This stamps.com website allows consumers to purchase stamps through the Internet.

INTEGRATED DIRECT MARKETING

Historically, direct marketing is the first area of marketing communication that adopted an integrated marketing approach. In fact, it would be appropriate to rename direct marketing integrated direct marketing.

One reason integration plays so well in the direct-response market is because of its emphasis on the customer. By using databases, companies can become more sensitive to customer wants and needs and less likely to bother them with unwanted commercial messages. One expert defines **integrated direct marketing (IDM)** as "a systematic method of getting close to your best current potential customers."[23]

Linking the Channels

Many major advertising agencies that want to provide integrated, full-service promotional programs for their clients have bought direct-response companies. But traditional advertising agencies have found it difficult to integrate direct marketing into their operations. The reverse challenge also occurs when a direct-marketing company buys other marketing communication companies and tries to integrate into its operations. Apparently, the differences between direct and traditional advertising are greater than first envisioned.

Instead of treating each medium separately, as advertising agencies tend to do, integrated direct-marketing companies seek to achieve precise, synchronized use of the right mediums at the right time, with a measurable return on dollars spent.

Here's an example: Say you do a direct-mail campaign, which commonly generates a 2 percent response, a percentage long viewed as an average return. If you include a toll-free 800 number in your mailing as an alternative to the standard mail-in reply—with well-trained, knowledgeable people handling those incoming calls with a tight script—you can achieve a 3 to 4 percent response rate. If you follow up your mailing with a phone call within 24 to 72 hours after your prospect receives the mailing, you can generate a response two to eight times as high as the base rate of 2 percent. So, by adding your 800 number, you bring the response rate from 2 percent to 3 or 4 percent. By following up with phone calls, you bring your total response rate as high as 5 to 18 percent.

Same Message, Multiple Sources The principle behind integration is that not all people respond the same way to direct-response advertising. One person may carefully fill out the order form. Someone else may immediately call the 800 number. Most people, if an ad grabs them, tend to put it in the pending pile. That pile grows and grows, and then goes into the garbage at the end of the month. But, if a phone call follows the direct-mail piece, the marketer may get the wavering consumer off the fence. Hewlett-Packard, AT&T, Citibank, and IBM have all used integrated direct marketing to improve their direct-marketing response rates.

Safeway Stores have become interested in integrated direct marketing. Essentially, Safeway has signed up manufacturers such as the Quaker Oats Co. and Stouffer Food Corp. (owned by Nestlé) for a database marketing program that provides trade dollars for top-notch data. The program exemplifies the convergence of two trends: Grocers looking for manufacturers to supplement their own shrunken marketing budgets, and manufacturers eager to allocate new field marketing support dollars are shopping for local deals. Up to seven manufacturers fund Safeway's quarterly mailings in exchange for in-store support and sales data.[24]

One problem with direct marketing is its tendency not to mesh well with a company's operations, its distribution systems, communications, research, overall strategy, or even culture. For example, direct marketers have been part of programs that have failed because they are so successful: Catalog companies have run out of inventories, costing them not only short-term sales but long-term goodwill; and financial firms have generated too many leads for their salespeople to keep up with.

A MATTER OF PRACTICE

YAHOO! DIGS INTO ITS DATABASE

➤ According to the "Yahoo! Buzz Index," Britney Spears, Eminem, and Nelly were the most popular music artists on the Internet in July 2002. For anyone interested in trends, the Yahoo! Buzz Index (http://buzz.yahoo.com) provides information on the Internet's most popular subjects, ranking them on the number of queries generated by more than 210 million Yahoo! users monthly. Of those users, about 80 million have registered their demographic information somewhere on the site and 37 million have made Yahoo! their homepage. This means that Yahoo! has access to an astonishing amount of users' data plus the technology to track their online habits. The Buzz Index is one way that Yahoo! shows advertisers that it knows who is searching for what, and that it has the demographic data to supplement that information.

To make the Buzz Index easy to read, Yahoo! uses a rating system that grants a subject one point for every .001 percent of the unique users placing queries. A score of 1000 for Britney Spears means that 1 percent of all Yahoo! users performed a search with her as the subject. (A score of 1000 is almost unreachable; last look Britney had a score of 95, Eminem had 70 and Nelly had 60.)

The Buzz Index represents Yahoo!'s newest departure from its origins as a simple Internet search engine. Expanding its services to capitalize on such extensive access to user data and online habits is a logical progression for Yahoo! Touting a capability it calls "fusion marketing," Yahoo! provides a wide range of services to advertisers, including reports on the most frequently visited Web sites, targeted user data mining, research and analysis, and assistance in the development of online marketing campaigns. Subscribing clients can order periodic reports that monitor the activity within certain subject categories (toys, movies, sports, etc.) to be sent on a daily, weekly, or monthly basis. What's more, Yahoo! can provide advertisers with detailed information about its users, including age, gender, and professional or personal interests.

Advertisers can also obtain up-to-the-minute information on the number of times their ads have been seen by unique users, and how many of them clicked-through and made a purchase; valuable information for any company.

POINT TO PONDER

What could be some problems with Yahoo!'s services to advertisers?

Source: Joan Raymond, "The Engine that Could," *American Demographics* (June 2001): 38–39; http://www.business2.com/articles/mag/0,1640,34892,FF.html, accessed 7/12/2002.

Another common failure in direct-marketing integration is that direct-marketing messages and advertising messages often do not reinforce each other as well as they should because the two functions aren't combined under one roof. The advertising agency usually doesn't contain direct-marketing departments either. This will change, however, as clients demand more coordination of their marketing communication programs.

Creating Loyalty One of the historical truths about the direct-marketing industry is that merchandisers tend to view the relationship with the consumer as short term—that losing one unhappy consumer is okay because another one is right around the corner. Although some still follow this philosophy, most have realized, as have advertisers who practice integrated marketing, that maintaining a long-term relationship with the consumer is crucial.

Changing the attitude of the consumer toward direct marketing has not been easy because consumers resent companies that know too much about them. If the company can demonstrate that it is acting in the customer's best interest rather than just trolling for dollars, it might gain consumers' loyalty. Sprint has trained its sales force to look for ways to enhance customer loyalty. In one case, for customer Siptech Display, a Sprint representative recognized a phone number that might have been disconnected by mistake. The simple act of calling to verify the disconnect order so impressed the customer that Siptech decided to move its entire phone system to Sprint.[25] Saks Fifth Avenue identified the customers who account for half of all sales and offered the group exclusive benefits through a program call Saks First. The benefits include fashion newsletters and first crack at all sales.

Perhaps the most ambitious attempt to create consumer loyalty is through a concept called **lifetime customer value (LCV)**. LCV is an estimate of how much purchase volume companies can expect to get over time from various target markets. To put it formally, LCV is "the over-time volume/financial contribution of an individual customer or customer segment, based on known consumption habits plus future consumption expectations, where contribution is defined as return on investment, i.e., revenue gains as a function of marketing costs."[26] In simpler terms, by knowing a consumer's past behavior, you can decide how much you want to spend to get him to buy your product, and you can track your investment by measuring the response.

IT'S A WRAP
A WONDERFUL THANKSGIVING

Direct marketing and its various tactics have evolved from "junk mail" to a highly regarded, effective means of marketing communication. This chapter has introduced you to these new direct-marketing tactics along with the trends for the future.

The campaign for the Denver Mission proved to be very effective, with responses 51 percent higher than its campaigns for the previous three years. The cost of the mailing was under $50,000, while the average contribution was $26.20. In comparison, the campaigns for the three previous years cost nearly $70,000. The new campaign provided for over 2,600 dinners and was awarded a Gold Echo award for the most innovative use of direct mail in 2001.

Summary

1. **Define and distinguish between direct marketing and direct-response advertising.** Direct marketing always involves a one-on-one relationship with the prospect. It is personal and interactive and uses various media to effect a measurable response. Direct-response advertising can use

   any advertising medium, but it has to provide some type of response or reply device to facilitate action.

2. **Explain some types of direct marketing.** The direct-marketing industry includes direct-response advertising, database marketing, direct mail, catalog, and telemarketing.

3. **Name the players in direct marketing.** The three players in direct marketing are the advertisers, the agencies, and the consumers.

4. **Evaluate the various media that direct-response programs can use.** Direct-response media include direct mail, catalogs, telemarketing, print media, broadcast media, and the Internet.

5. **Explain how databases are used in direct marketing.** Direct-marketing advertising has benefited from the development and maintenance of a database of customer names, addresses, telephone numbers, and demographic and psychographic characteristics. Advertisers use this information to target their campaigns to consumers who based on demographics, are likely to buy their products.

6. **Discuss the role of direct marketing in integrated marketing programs.** Because direct marketing is close to the customer and is interactive, it fits very well into an integrated program. Direct marketers are accustomed to linking the channels of communication and delivering the same message using multiple sources that reinforce one another.

Key Terms

bind-ins, p. 416
blow-ins, p. 416
broadsheets, p. 408
catalog, p. 411
controlled media, p. 402
customer relationship
    management (CRM), p. 403
databases, p. 399

database marketing, p. 402
direct mail, p. 407
direct marketing (DM), p. 398
direct-response advertising,
    p. 415
fulfillment, p. 405
inbound telemarketing, p. 414

integrated direct marketing
    (IDM), p. 419
lifetime customer value (LCV),
    p. 421
merging, p. 402
one-step offer, p. 401
outbound telemarketing, p. 414

permission marketing, p. 410
predictive dialing, p. 413
prospecting, p. 400
purging, p. 402
rich media, p. 411
telemarketing, p. 413
two-step offer, p. 401

Questions

1. What principle separates direct response from other forms of advertising?

2. What are the major advantages and disadvantages of the various direct-response media? Develop a checklist that would help you in deciding which medium to use in advertising a computer, mountain bike, and DVD.

3. Most people hate telemarketing. Say you work for the local campus environmental organization. How could you conduct a campus and community telemarketing effort that would not generate resistance?

4. We know that copy and illustration are vital parts of a successful direct-mail campaign, but there must be some priorities. All of the components of creativity are important, but which are most important for direct-response creativity? What principles drive message design for direct marketing?

5. Hildy Johnson, a recent college graduate, is interviewing with a large garden product firm that relies on television for its direct-response advertising. "Your portfolio looks very good. I'm sure you can write," the interviewer says, "but let me ask you what is it about our copy that makes it more important than copy written for Ford, or Pepsi, or Pampers?" What can she say that will help convince the interviewer she understands the special demands of direct-response writing?

6. One of the smaller, privately owned bookstores on campus is considering a direct-response service to cut down on its severe in-store traffic problems at the beginning of each semester. What ideas do you have for setting up some type of direct-response system to decrease traffic?

7. Suppose you are the marketing director for a campus service organization that assists nearby needy people. How would you develop a telemarketing program to promote campus fund-raising? Would it be better to solicit money directly or indirectly by having people attend specially designed events? Your primary targets are students, faculty, and staff.

8. How does the recent fervor surrounding personal privacy affect direct marketing—specifically, telemarketing? In addition to legal issues, what consumer issues must media planners consider when designing a direct-marketing campaign? What do you believe will be future issues that direct marketers will face?

9. The success of infomercials helps validate direct marketing as a revenue generator. What characteristics of your product must you consider when determining whether to use a direct-marketing campaign?

10. Amazon.com is one of the most well-known direct marketers on the Internet. Browse the company's Web site and identify what direct marketing strategies the company employs. Which do you think are the most successful? Why? What are the least effective? Why? What does Amazon expect to gain from direct marketing?

Suggested Class Project

Divide the class into groups. Each group should select a consumer product that normally is not sold through direct marketing, but could be. Create a direct-marketing campaign for this product. Be sure to specify your objectives and indicate the parts of the offer as well as the medium used. Develop a mockup of some of the campaign's pieces that illustrates your ideas about message design.

Suggested Internet Class Project

Visit a few direct-marketing organizations online such as: The Direct Response Forum, Inc., www.directresponse.org; Direct Marketing Association, www.the-dma.org; and Direct Marketing News, www.dmnews.com.

Pick an issue that, judging from these sites, is a threat to direct marketing. Explain what you, as a direct-marketing firm, would do to overcome this threat.

Hallmark BUILD•A•CAMPAIGN *Projects*

Please refer to the Hallmark Case Appendix at the end of the text before responding to these questions.

1. Meet in small groups to discuss the type of direct-response marketing Capitol Advertising used in its campaign to create brand insistence for Hallmark. How might it have increased the use of direct-response marketing?

2. How can Gold Crown stores establish a relationship with their best customers through direct marketing techniques? Summarize your recommendations for a direct marketing proposal for your campaign plan.

Notes

1. Daniel Lyons, "Games Dealers Play," *Forbes* (October 18, 1998): 132–134.

2. Pradeep K. Korgaonkar, Eric J. Karson, and Ishael Akaah, "Direct Marketing Advertising: The Assents, the Dissents, and the Ambivalents," *Journal of Advertising Research* (September/October 1997): 41–45.

3. "WEFA Study Measures Direct Response Ad," *Direct Marketing* (November 1995): 6–9.

4. B. G. Yovovich, "Database 'Stealth' Adds to Marketing Arsenal," *Advertising Age* (October 16, 1995): 26.

5. "Outlook '87," *Target Marketing* (January 1987): 25–28.

6. Stan Rapp and Tom Collins, *MaxiMarketing* (New York: McGraw-Hill, 1987).

7. Korgaonkar et al., "Direct Market Advertising," 53.

8. Dean Rieck, "10 Basics for Writing Better Letters," *Direct Marketing* (April 2001, Vol. 63, No. 12): 52–53, 62.

9. "$2.1 Billion Will Be Spent on E-Mail Marketing by Year-End 2001," *Direct Marketing* (April 2001, Vol. 63, No. 12): 7.

10. Janis Mara, "E-Mail Direct," *Adweek* (April 10, 2001): 116–117.

11. Lance Arthur, "Clear Cut Lessons for Effective E-mail," *Direct Marketing* (May 2001, Vol. 64, No. 1): 62–63.

12. Lisa Brownlee, "Catalog Retailer's Turnaround Goes by the Book, Trumps Stores," *Wall Street Journal* (October 28, 1997): B10.

13. "Federated to Use Digital Imaging for Catalogs," *Direct Marketing* (August 2001): 17.

14. "Telemarketing Sales Rule Reaches Fifth Anniversary," *Direct Marketing* (June 2001, Vol. 64, No. 2): 8.

15. Carol Krol, "Levi Strauss Moves into Mail-Order Marketing," *Advertising Age* (September 14, 1998): 18.

16. Rick Cesari and Helen Kaplow, "Direct Response and Branding: How to Have Your Cake and Eat It Too," *Brandweek* (September 7, 1998): 10.

17. James R. Rosenfield, " 'Interactive' Helps Redefine Direct Niche," *Advertising Age* (September 7, 1998): 22.

18. Lynn Branigan, "The Internet: The Emerging Premier Direct Marketing Channel," *Direct Marketing* (May 1998): 46–48.

19. De' Ann Weimer, "Can I Try (Click) That Blouse (Drag) in Blue?" *BusinessWeek* (November 9, 1998): 86.

20. Rebecca Eisenberg, "The Net's Miracle Marketing," *San Francisco Examiner* (August 9, 1998): www.sfagate.com/cgi-bin/article.cgi?file= /examiner/achive/1998/08/09/ BUISNESS 1875.dtl&type= printable; Nancy Weil, "PlanetAll Keeps Online Masses Organized," *The Industry Standard* (August 14, 1998): www.thestandard.com/ articles/news_display/0,1270,1409,00.html?05.

21. Judy Strauss and Raymond Frost, *Marketing on the Internet* (Upper Saddle River, NJ: Prentice Hall, 1999), 5.

22. Lester Wunderman, "Going Strong: The Father of Direct Marketing Sees the Future in Cyberspace," *Advertising Age* (April 17, 2000): 25.

23. Fred R. McFadden and Jeffrey A. Hoffer, *Data Base Management* (Menlo Park, CA: Benjamin/Cummings, 1985), 3.

24. Betsy Spethmann, "Safeway Signs Up Marketers in New Deal," *Adweek* (May 8, 1995): 9.

25. Margery Tippen, "Building Customer Loyalty through Quality Telemarketing," *Direct Marketing* (September 1996): 14–15.

26. Barbara Jack, "There's No Rocket Science to 'Lifetime Customer Value,' " *Promo* (October 1992): 27.

Developing a Brand Campaign

You do not have to be a big brand with millions of dollars to have great advertising. The Chick-fil-A "Eat Mor Chikin" campaign is a great example of this. Chick-fil-A competes in one of the largest and most competitive industries: fast food. It is outnumbered in store count by 15 to 1 and outspent in media 60 to 1 by the likes of McDonald's, Burger King, and Wendy's.

Faced with these disadvantages in the marketplace, Chick-fil-A and its advertising agency set out to develop a brand campaign that would increase top-of-mind awareness, increase sales, and earn Chick-fil-A a spot in consumers' consideration list of fast food brands. To do this effectively, the campaign positioned Chick-fil-A chicken sandwiches as the premium alternative to hamburgers.

The company could not outspend the competition. It couldn't even afford a television campaign, which is how most of its competitors were advertising. So it decided to advertise where its competitors weren't—outdoor billboards. The challenge would then become: How does one build a brand using outdoor billboards as their primary medium? After all, common sense would indicate that billboards are used to let people know where to exit or how many miles to travel for the offering, not to build brands.

Well, for Chick-fil-A and its agency, overcoming the challenge would be easier than expected. Chick-fil-A's "Eat Mor Chikin" three-dimensional billboard campaign helped break the fast-food hamburger pattern. The witty use of a Holstein cow encouraging the target audience to "Eat Mor Chikin" instead of beef provided a bold personality that broke through industry clutter. Why? The message and execution were simple, the cows were funny, the creative idea was unexpected, and the call-to-action was powerful.

The lighthearted, unconventional campaign has helped increase sales every year it's been running. In 1995, when the campaign first began, Chick-fil-A reported $501,639,680 in sales. Today, the company reports over $1 billion in sales. In terms of brand awareness, Chick-fil-A's unaided brand awareness has grown 81 percent since 1996.

Chick-fil-A and its agency have found a creative way to use outdoor advertising successfully in building the Chick-fil-A brand without spending missions of media dollars.

IT'S YOUR TURN

1. Suggest other strategies Chick-fil-A could follow, given their strengths and weaknesses.
2. Identify possible problems this creative approach might face in the future.

CHAPTER

15

Sales Promotion

CHAPTER OBJECTIVES

When you have completed this chapter, you should be able to

1. Explain the principles that drive the use of sales promotion and discuss why advertisers are spending increasing sums of money on sales promotion.

2. List and explain the use of various consumer promotions.

3. Summarize the types and purposes of trade promotions.

4. Describe the use of other types of promotions: sponsorships, specialties, interactive promotions, loyalty programs, and co-marketing programs.

5. Explain the strategic use of promotions in marketing, in terms of brand building, new product launches, integration, and effectiveness.

Dreamcast Launches Assault on Gamers

Award: *EFFIE Silver, Entertainment category*

Company: *Sega of America, Sega Dreamcast*

Agency: *Foote, Cone & Belding*

Campaign: *"In the Box"*

At the end of the 1990s, Sega was a dying player in electronic games. Nintendo 64 and Sony PlayStation were fighting for leadership of the $6.3 billion worldwide category. At one time Sega controlled more than 50 percent of the video game market, but after the failure of its Saturn game system in 1995, Sega's share of market dropped to as little as 5 percent. To remain in the game Sega needed a new weapon.

The launch of Dreamcast in late 1999 was a stunning success. It was the most advanced video game system ever developed—with speed, jaw-dropping graphics, and a built-in connection to the Internet.

The "In the Box" launch campaign by Foote, Cone & Belding, San Francisco proved effective for Sega. Hardcore gamers couldn't wait to get their hands on Dreamcast and stood in line to get the first ones out of the boxes. But to rebuild Sega's competitiveness in gaming, the campaign had to sustain the momentum of the launch so Dreamcast could reach the critical mass that a video game system needs to keep new software coming.

The $100-million campaign included traditional print and television advertising, but it also used innovative promotions that delivered product trial with hands-on interaction.

In addition to advertising, the campaign included a guerrilla marketing effort that chalked the Dreamcast spiral logo on millions of sidewalks. There was also an online viral marketing push, using the Dreamcast Web site and those of its business partners to generate online buzz among gamers.

The promotional materials included T-shirts, postcards, stickers, and yo-yos, along with a video for employees. Several big media events were held for gaming journalists in various countries.

But Sega needed special promotions that created interactive experiences to engage the target market. The mobile marketing promotion put the Dreamcast system on wheels as "Mobile Assault Tour"—trucks designed like armored assault vehicles visited hip urban areas with a high concentration of gamers. The tour was linked to the "Dreamcast Family Values Tour," which was a traveling concert of alternative rock bands. Another special promotion was the Sega Dreamcast Championships, a game competition that ran in conjunction with the tour.

This promotional strategy for the launch of Dreamcast was so effective that it created a huge impact in the gaming world. Not only did the product achieve record sales levels, it also was selected as an EFFIE-award winner. The "It's a Wrap" box at the end of this chapter provides more information about the effectiveness of this campaign.

Sources: Adapted from the EFFIE brief provided by Sega and Foote, Cone & Belding, San Francisco. Other information came from news releases on www.sega.com/community/events/archives_events; http://network.artistdirect.com/corporate/pressreleases/1999_0817_familyvalues9.html; and articles on www.creativemag.com/sp0999.html; www.preimagames.com/news/article171/; www.salon.com/tech/log/1999/08/25/sega_dreamcast/; and www.mg.co.za/pc/games/1999/09/08Sep-segadreamcast.html.

SALES PROMOTION

Whenever a marketer increases the value of its product by offering an extra incentive to purchase a brand or product it is creating a sales promotion, which is the subject of this chapter. In most cases the objective of sales promotion is to encourage action, although promotion (we will use the word "promotion" to refer to sales promotion) can also help build brand identity and awareness, as the Dreamcast case illustrated.

Similar to advertising, sales promotion is one type of marketing communication. Although advertising is designed to build long-term brand awareness, sales promotion is primarily focused on creating action. To help you understand the concept of promotions, we explore consumer and trade sales promotions, as well as other programs, such as loyalty programs, tie-ins, and sponsorships, that cross the line between advertsing and promotion.

The Sega Dreamcast promotion built brand awareness through sales promotion.

As sales promotion has evolved, so too has the way experts define it. In 1988 the American Marketing Association (AMA) offered this definition of **sales promotion**: "media and nonmedia marketing pressure applied for a predetermined, limited period of time in order to stimulate trial and impulse purchases, increase consumer demand, or improve product quality."[1] More recently, the Council of Sales Promotion Agencies offered a somewhat broader definition: "Sales promotion is a marketing discipline that utilizes a variety of incentive techniques to structure sales-related programs targeted to consumers, trade, and/or sales levels that generate a specific, measurable action or response for a product or service."[2]

Let's examine the latter definition. First, it acknowledges that consumers are an important target for promotions, but so are other people, such as the company's sales representatives and members of the trade (distributors, retailers). Second, the definition recognizes that sales promotion is a set of techniques that prompts members of three target audiences—consumers, sales representatives, and the trade (distributors, retailers, dealers) to take action, preferably immediate action.

Simply put, sales promotion offers an extra incentive for consumers, sales reps, and trade members to act. Although this extra incentive usually takes the form of a price reduction, it also may be additional amounts of the product, cash, prizes and gifts, premiums, special events, and so on. It may also be just a fun brand experience, as the Sega Dreamcast tours and championship competition provided. Furthermore, sales promotion usually includes specified limits, such as an expiration date or a limited quantity of the merchandise.

Although an action response is the goal of most sales promotions, some programs, such as the Dreamcast campaign, are designed to build awareness first, but always with action as the ultimate goal.

Changes in the Promotion Industry

Until the 1980s, advertising was the dominant player in the marketing communication arena. But during the 1980s more marketers found themselves driving immediate bottom-line response through the use of sales promotion. As a result, in the 1980s and 1990s the budget share switched from 60 percent advertising and 40 percent sales promotion to the reverse: 40 percent advertising and 60 percent sales promotion.

That trend reversed again in the late 1990s as the dot-com companies spent huge sums on advertising to establish their brands, followed by a recessionary period as the economy saw the dot-com meltdown in the early 2000s. According to *Promo* magazines' 2001 Annual Report,[3] the industry trade publication, even though the promotion industry continued to grow with spending increasing 8.1 percent, that growth rate was slower than that of advertising, which saw spending increase by 9.8 percent to $236 billion.

In a survey reported in that same annual report issue of *Promo,* marketers said they allocated 53 percent of their total marketing communication budget to advertising and about 41 percent to sales promotion. Of that, 18 percent was for trade promotion and 23 percent was for consumer promotion. The other 6 percent of the total marketing communication budget went to other promotional areas such as public relations and customer service.

The marketers also used 18 percent of their ad budgets to support sales promotion messages—meaning a sales promotion, such as a rebate or special event, is announced through advertising. When you factor out that 18 percent that overlaps, then the advertising and sales promotion budgets are the same size. So over the years, advertising and sales promotion have been battling for their share of the marketing communication budget but they generally come out about equal in terms of budget.

Table 15.1 lists consumer sales promotion categories and their gross revenues as collected by *Promo* magazine. Premium incentives, which are free gifts given with a purchase, led the way at $26.9 billion; followed by point-of-purchase (POP) displays; and advertising specialties, such as T-shirts and mugs carrying a brand's logo, at $16.3 billion. We'll be explaining all these categories and tools in the discussion that follows.

TABLE 15.1 **Promotion Industry Revenues**				
Segment (000,000)	**1999**	**2000**	**% Change**	**% of Total**
Premiums	$26,300	$26,900	+ 2.3%	26.6%
Point-of-Purchase	14,400	17,000	18.1	16.1
Specialties	14,800	16,300	10.1	16.1
Sponsorships	7,600	8,700	14.5	8.6
Coupons	6,980	6,920	−0.9	6.9
Licensing	5,500	5,775	5.0	5.7
Interactive	1,471	1,800	22.4	1.8
Games, contests, sweeps	1,380	1,504	9.0	1.5
Sampling	1,120	1,200	7.1	1.2
In-Store	870	904	83.9	0.9
Administrative (printing, fulfillment, agency, research)	13,015	13,974	.07	13.8
Total	$93,436	$100,977	.07%	100%

Source: Adapted from 2001 Annual Report, *Promo* (May 1, 2001), as reported in http://www.industryclick.com/magazinearticle.asp?magazinearticleid=99739&.

Reasons for the Growth of Sales Promotion

Why are companies spending more money on sales promotion? The chief reasons are the pressure for short-term profits and the need for accountability for marketing communication efforts. There are also consumer factors.

In terms of the accountability issue, most U.S. companies focus on immediate profits, a drive that sales promotion satisfies. Product managers are under pressure to generate quarterly sales increases. Because advertising's benefits are often apparent in the long term only, companies invest more money in sales promotion when they want quick results.

Advertisers also cite economic reasons for the shift. Traditional media costs have escalated to the point where alternative types of media must be considered. As the networks raised their advertising prices, the networks' share of prime-time television viewers dropped to approximately 50 percent from a high of 92 percent.[4] Advertisers, therefore, are exploring marketing communication forms that cost less and produce immediate, tangible results. Sales promotion is able to deliver these results.

Another reason for sales promotion's accountability is that it is relatively easy and quick to determine whether a sales promotion strategy has accomplished its objectives because there is usually an immediate response of some kind. Providing accountability is critical at a time when marketers want to know exactly what they are getting for their promotional dollars.

From the consumers' perspective, sales promotion reduces the risk associated with a purchase by giving them something of added value such as a coupon, rebate, or discounted price. Promotions typically offer the consumer added value, or "more for less," as a Diet Coke ATM card promotion illustrates. Developed in conjunction with MasterCard International, it used ATM cash cards to reward consumers for buying Coke.

Other reasons for the move to sales promotion match changes in the marketplace, such as these:

- **Consumer Behavior.** Shoppers today are better educated, more selective, and less loyal to brand names than in the past, which means they are more susceptible to switching brands.
- **Pricing.** Retail prices soared during the inflationary 1970s because of the increased costs of labor, raw materials, and manufacturing. The increased costs led to low-priced, private-label brands and the emergence of generic products, particularly in the

highly volatile supermarket industry. Since then, consumers have come to expect constant short-term price reductions such as coupons, sales, and price promotions.

- *Market Share.* In most industries, the battle is for market share rather than general product growth. Sales promotion encourages people to switch products, increasing market share.
- *Parity Products.* Sales promotion is often the most effective strategy for increasing sales of a product, particularly when the products in the category are largely undifferentiated. In other words, the products are similar so promotions become the tie-breaker in the consumer's decision making.
- *The Power of the Retailer.* Dominant retailers, such as Safeway, Wal-Mart, Toys "R" Us, and Home Depot, demand a variety of promotional incentives before allowing products into their stores.

Categories of Sales Promotion

The three most common sales promotion strategies target the three audiences of promotions: consumer, trade, and sales force. The first two—to increase customer sales and to increase support of the trade—have direct implications for advertising and are the focus of this chapter.

In the third category, sales force promotions include two general sets of promotional activities directed at the firm's salespeople to motivate them to increase their sales levels. The first set of activities includes programs that better prepare salespeople to do their jobs, such as sales manuals, training programs, sales presentations, and supportive materials— training films, slides, videos, and visual aids. The second set of activities deals with promotional efforts or incentives that motivate salespeople to work harder. Contests dominate this category. We will include contests as part of our trade promotion discussion, but first we examine consumer promotions.

CONSUMER AND TRADE PROMOTIONS

In the late 1990s companies spent over 50 percent of their total promotion budget on promotions directed at the trade (distributors, dealers, retailers); however, that changed in 2000. The *Promo* magazine 2001 annual report found that companies directed 56 percent to the consumer market and 44 percent to the trade,[5] which is to say that although consumer promotion is highly visible, trade promotion is becoming more and more important. So let's look at these two major categories of promotions. We'll start with consumer promotions.

Consumer Promotions

Consumer sales promotions are directed at the ultimate user of the good or service. They are intended to provide an incentive so that when consumers go into a store they will look for a particular brand.

The primary strengths of consumer sales promotions are their variety and flexibility. There are many promotion techniques that a product manager can use and combine to meet almost any objective. Sales promotion works for all kinds of businesses.

Price Deals A popular sales promotion technique is a **price deal**, a temporary price reduction or a sale price. Here are the most common price deals:

- A *cents-off deal* is a reduction in the normal price charged for a good or service (for example, "was $1,000, now $500," or "50 percent off") announced at the point of sale or through mass or direct advertising.
- *Price-pack deals* provide the consumer with something extra through the package itself—a prize in a cereal box, for instance.

- *Bonus packs* contain additional amounts of the product free when consumers purchase the standard size at the regular price. For example, Purina Dog Food may offer 25 percent more dog food in the bag.
- *Banded packs* are more units of a product sold at a lower price than if they were bought at the regular single-unit price. Sometimes the products are physically packaged together, such as bar soap and six-packs of soft drinks.

Coupons There are two general types of **coupons**—retailer and manufacturer. Retailer-sponsored coupons can be redeemed only at the specified retail outlet. Manufacturer-sponsored coupons can be redeemed at any outlet distributing the product. They are distributed directly (direct mail, door-to-door), through media (newspaper and magazine ads, free-standing inserts), in or on the package itself, or through the retailer (co-op advertising). Manufacturers also pay retailers a fee for handling their coupons.

Refunds and Rebates A **refund** or **rebate** is a marketer's offer to return a certain amount of money to the consumer who purchases the product. Sometimes the refund is a check for a certain amount of money but other times it may be a coupon to encourage repeat use.

Sampling Allowing the consumer to try the product or service is called **sampling**. Advertisers can distribute samples to consumers in numerous ways. Products can show up with newspapers and on house doorknobs, in doctors' and dentists' offices, and, most commonly, through the mail. Advertisers can design ads with coupons for free samples, place samples in special packages, or distribute samples at special in-store displays

Special Events Marketers use special promotional events, such as a tour or the appearance of the product or its spokesperson at a mall or sporting event, to gain the attention and the involvement of people in the target audience who attend the event.

Contests and Sweepstakes Contest and sweepstakes promotions create excitement by promising "something for nothing" and offering impressive prizes. **Contests** require participants to compete for a prize or prizes based on some sort of skill or ability. **Sweepstakes** require only that participants submit their names to be included in a drawing or other chance selection. A game is a type of sweepstake. It differs from a one-shot drawing type of sweepstake because the timeframe is much longer, so it establishes a continuity, requiring customers to return several times to acquire additional pieces (such as bingo-type games) or to improve their chances of winning.

Premiums A **premium** is a tangible reward for a particular act, usually purchasing a product or visiting the point-of-purchase. Premiums are a type of incentive and they work by adding value to the product. Examples of premiums are the toy in Cracker Jacks, glassware in a box of detergent, and a transistor radio given for taking a real estate tour. Premiums are either free or quite low in price.

The two general types of premiums are direct and mail. Direct premiums award the incentive immediately, at the time of purchase. There are four variations of direct premiums: (1) store premiums, given to customers at the retail site; (2) in-pack premiums, inserted in the package at the factory; (3) on-pack premiums, placed on the outside of the package at the factory; and (4) container premiums, in which the package is the premium.

Mail premiums require the customer to take some action before receiving the premium. A **self-liquidator** premium usually requires that some proof of purchase and payment be mailed in before the customer receives the premium. The price of the item is sufficient to cover the cost, handling, mailing, packaging, and taxes, if any. Another type of mail premium requires the customer to save coupons or special labels attached to the product that can be redeemed for merchandise.

Specialties **Specialty advertising** presents the brand's name on something that is given away as a reminder—calendars, pens and pencils, T-shirts, mouse pads, tote bags, bottles, and so forth. The ideal specialty is an item kept out in the open for a long period of time where other people can see it, such as a coffee mug. Advertising specialties are similar to premiums, except that the consumer does not have to purchase anything to receive the specialty item.

How to Use Consumer Promotions

To demonstrate the strategy behind promotion's role in a new-product launch, let's suppose we are introducing a new corn chip named Corn Crunchies. Promotion is particularly useful to launch the corn chip because it has a number of tools designed to encourage trial, but it can also be used later in the brand's life to maintain or increase its share of market, as well as remind and reward its loyal customers.

Awareness Our first challenge is to create awareness of this product, which is the real strength of advertising and, you may remember from Chapter 6, the first step in consumer decision making. However, sometimes advertising can be combined with an appropriate promotion to call attention to the brand name in order to get people to try the product. Awareness-building promotion ideas for this new corn chip might include colorful point-of-purchase displays, sponsorship of a Corn Crunchies team, or a special event that will attract people in the target market. The Sega Dreamcast launch used the sponsorship of the "Family Values Tour" and a championship video game competition to get the attention of its hardcore gaming audience.

Trial Creating awareness will only take the product so far, however. Consumers must also perceive Corn Crunchies as offering some clear benefit compared to the competition. Sales promotion does this by arranging for experiences, such as special events where people can try the product or see it demonstrated. The Dreamcast's Mobile Assault Tour was designed to get hardcore gamers on the boxes so they could experience firsthand how much better the Dreamcast system was than its competition.

Sales promotion has other tools that lead to trial, such as sampling. An effective way to get people to try Corn Crunchies is to give away free samples at events, in stores, or through direct mail to the home. Sampling is an effective strategy for introducing a new or modified product or for dislodging an entrenched market leader by enticing potential users to try the product. The Maalox sample mailer shown here is an example of the use of a sample to encourage trial in a category where people may be reluctant to buy a product until they know it works.

Sega's Mobile Assault Tour promotion encouraged trial.

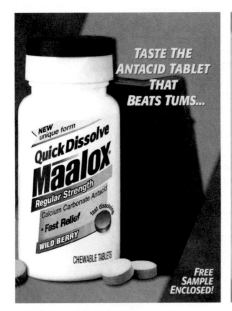

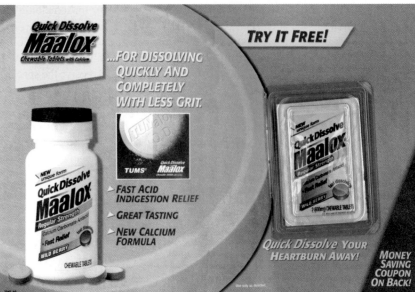

This direct mail piece contains a sample of Maalox chewable, quick-dissolve antiacid tablets. On the back is a coupon for $1.00 off the price of any size of Quick Dissolve Maalox.

In general, retailers and manufacturers maintain that sampling can boost sales volume as much as 10 times when used with a product demonstration and 10 percent to 15 percent thereafter. Sampling is generally most effective when reinforced on the spot with product coupons. Most consumers like sampling because they do not lose any money if they do not like the product. To be successful, the product sampled must virtually sell itself with minimal trial experience.

Another way sales promotion can motivate people to try a new product like Corn Crunchies is to make a price deal with them—you try this product and we will give it to you cheaper than the usual price or we may even give you a free gift. These price deals are usually done through coupons, refunds, rebates, or premiums. Refunds and rebates are effective because they encourage consumers to purchase a product before a deadline. In addition, refunds stimulate sales without the high cost and waste associated with coupons.

Coupons mainly encourage trial, induce brand switching, and reward repeat business. The main advantage of the manufacturer's coupon, such as those that run in consumer magazines, is that it allows the advertiser to lower prices without relying on cooperation from the retailer to distribute them. Announcements for cents-off deals include the package itself and signs near the product or elsewhere in the store. Advertising for these deals include sales, flyers, newspaper ads, and broadcast ads.

Maintain Market Presence In addition to encouraging trial of a new product, another purpose of price deals is to convince prospective users to switch from an established competing brand, such as Doritos in this case. Later, after the Corn Crunchies brand is established, a price deal can be used to reward loyal users in order to encourage their repeat business. Price deals are particularly effective in those situations where price is an important factor in brand choice or if consumers are not brand loyal.

To maintain a brand's presence or increase its market share after it is launched, markets use promotional tools such as premiums, special events, and contests and sweepstakes. In addition to serving as a reward, premiums, for example, can enhance an advertising campaign or a brand's image. Characters like the Campbell Soup Kids, Tony the Tiger, Cap'n Crunch, and Ronald McDonald are used on premiums, such as soup or cereal bowls, to reinforce the consumer's association of the brand with the character.

Cereal manufacturers are among the biggest users of in-pack premiums. Kellogg distributed millions of special anniversary promotions across its Corn Flakes, Rice Krispies, and Froot Loops brands to celebrate the company's ninetieth anniversary. The cereal boxes offered consumers commemorative Matchbox trucks, utensils, and other collectible items.

In addition, Kellogg's Special K cereal teamed with Reebok and Polygram to offer an on-pack, special-edition Reebok Versa Training exercise video; and a recipe and coupon offer good for free Sun Maid Dried Fruit appeared on packages of Kellogg's Low Fat Granola cereal. All of these special promotions were designed to increase excitement for the anniversary event.

A good contest or sweepstakes, such as the one described in the "A Matter of Principle" box, generates a high degree of consumer involvement, which can revive lagging sales, provide merchandising excitement for dealers and salespeople, give vitality and a theme to advertising, and create interest in a low-involvement product. Although contests and sweepstakes can be effective for many promotion objectives, they seem to work particularly well when a product or brand is not living up to its potential and needs a shot in the arm to stimulate sales.

Brand Reminder In addition to new product launches, promotions are also used in the reminder stage. This means that you change advertising copy to remind customers about the positive experience they had with the product, and use sales promotion to reinforce their loyalty with coupons, rebates, and other rewards. After the initial purchase we want the customer to remember the brand and repeat the purchase, so specialty items, such as a Corn Crunchies snack bowl, can serve as a brand reminder.

Specialty advertising serves as a reminder to the consumer—a reminder to consider the product—as the items in the photo illustrate. Specialties also build relationships, such as items given away as new-year or thank-you gifts (the calendar hanging in the kitchen). Advertisers use specialty items to thank customers for patronage, to reinforce established products or services, and to generate sales leads.

Trade Promotions

Unfortunately, consumer awareness and desire mean nothing unless Corn Crunchies is available where the consumer thinks it should be. Somehow the trade must be convinced

A MATTER OF PRINCIPLE

GOOD GAMES

➤ How would you like to win a walk-on role in a movie or music video? That's one of the prizes, along with a $1 million jackpot and various other prizes, found under a false lid on cans of Coke. The EFFIE-winning promotion designed by the St. Louis–based Momentum company and titled "It Could Be Your Next Coke" was used to create excitement for the brand, and at the same time spur increased sales. National TV and radio spots supported the promotional campaign.

Here's how it worked: Coke drinkers pop a false top (a top above the regular top) on a can of classic, regular, and caffeine-free Coke multipacks. Winners get a note sandwiched between the two lids. Losers just get a can of Coke (because there isn't a false top on most of them, only on the ones that have the note).

Called a "discover can," these new printing and packaging tricks give marketers like Coca-Cola the tools to deliver sweepstakes and games in the can or as part of the packaging. The technology that delivers these new printing and packaging tricks is sophisticated enough to make the games intriguing but also keep participation as simple as popping the top. These user-activated sweepstakes give a brand more play value, which increases the level of brand involvement.

Coca-Cola planned the promotion for two years after it discovered the technology at a German manufacturer's plant. Coca-Cola has exclusive U.S. rights to the flip-top can and its own packaging division designed the final version. In addition to a $1 million jackpot and a walk-on role in a Universal Studios film, Coke drinkers also won a recording session with a Universal artist, trips to Universal theme parks, shopping sprees, and smaller cash prizes.

The discover can was a huge success. Coca-Cola spokesperson Scott Williamson once said, "We've been in the promotions business a long time. We do a lot of research on what interests consumers. The "discover can" is a compelling promotion vehicle. It answers consumers' desires for instant gratification and simplicity." The involving experience is another plus, as Williamson points outs, "From a brand perspective, it's a real can of Coke; it's very experiential."

POINT TO PONDER

Why do you think this Coke promotion was selected as an EFFIE winner?

Source: Adapted from "Campaign Trail: Summer Splashes," *Promo* (May 2000); Betsy Spethmann, "Games, Contests, Sweepstakes Everybody Wins," *Promo* (August 2000): 70–76.

---

that the product will move off the shelves. Marketers know that if their promotional programs are to be effective, they must engage the trade in the program. In such programs, trade refers to all the people involved in the channel of distribution—buyers, brokers, distributors, wholesalers, dealers, franchisees, retailers, and so on.

Trade advertising directed at wholesalers and retailers is supposed to provide trade members with information about the new product and its selling points. In addition, trade promotion techniques, especially price discounts, point-of-purchase displays, and advertising allowances, help gain shelf space for products.

Resellers (the intermediaries in the distribution channel) are the 1.3 million retailers and 338,000 wholesalers who distribute the products manufacturers make. The Corn Crunchies manufacturer will be more encouraged that the product is acceptable only if resellers are willing to carry and push it. Sales promotion brings resellers to that point of conviction. There are two primary goals of a trade promotion:

1. To stimulate in-store merchandising or other trade support (for example, feature pricing, superior store location, or shelf space).
2. To create a high level of excitement about the product among those responsible for its sale.

In addition, trade promotion is also used to accomplish other marketing objectives, such as manipulating levels of inventory held by wholesalers and retailers and expanding product distribution to new areas of the country or new classes of trade.

The ultimate gauge of a successful trade promotion is whether sales increase. Many promotional devices designed to motivate resellers to engage in certain sales activities are available to the manufacturer. Here are the most common types of trade promotion tools.

Point-of-Purchase Displays A manufacturer-designed display distributed to retailers who use it to call their customers' attention to product promotions is known as a **point-of-**

TABLE 15.2	**Types of POP Displays**
Carton displays	Banners
Floorstands	Inflatables
Sidekicks	Product dispensers
Counter units	Chalkboards
Dump bins	Mirrors and clocks
Kiosks	Lightboxes
Literature holders	Posters
Neon signs	Decals
Menus and menuboards	CD listening stations
Table tents	Video units
Shelf talkers	Motion units
Signs (metal, cardboard, wood, paper, plastic, etc.)	

purchase (POP) display. Another popular POP form is the merchandising display, which retailers use to showcase their products and create a personality for their stores. Although POP forms vary by industry, they can include special racks, display cartons, banners, signs, price cards, and mechanical product dispensers, among other tools (see table 15.2).

Retailer (Dealer) Kits Materials that support retailers' selling efforts or that help representatives make sales calls on prospective retailing customers are often designed as sales kits. The kits contain supporting information, such as detailed product specifications, how-to display information, and ad slicks—print ads that are ready to be sent to the local print media as soon as the retailer or dealer adds identification, location, promotion price, or other information.

Trade Incentives and Deals Similar to consumer price deals, a manufacturer may reward a reseller financially for purchase of a certain level of a product or support of a promotion. These promotional efforts can take the form of special displays, extra purchases, superior store locations, or greater local promotion. In return, retailers can receive special allowances, such as discounts, free goods, gifts, or cash from the manufacturer. The most common types of **trade deals** are buying allowances for increasing purchases and advertising allowances, which include deals on cooperative advertising and display allowances, that is, deals for agreeing to use promotional displays.

Contests As in the case of consumer sales promotion, advertisers can develop contests and sweepstakes to motivate resellers. Contests are far more common than sweepstakes, mainly because resellers find it easy to tie contest prizes to the sale of the sponsor's product. A sales quota is set, for example, and the retailer or person who exceeds the quota by the largest percentage wins the contest.

Trade Shows and Exhibits The trade show is where companies within the same industries gather to present and sell their merchandise, as well as to demonstrate their products. Exhibits are the spaces that are designed to showcase the product, such as the military assault trucks designed for Dreamcast's Mobile Assault Tour. They can be moved and set up at different trade shows and other special events.

How to Use Trade Promotion

Trade promotions are primarily designed to get the cooperation of people in the distribution channel. To understand the role of trade promotion, let's first consider how sales promotion is used in push-and-pull strategies.

FIGURE 15.1

PUSH-AND-PULL STRATEGIES
Most marketers use a combination of push-and-pull strategies.

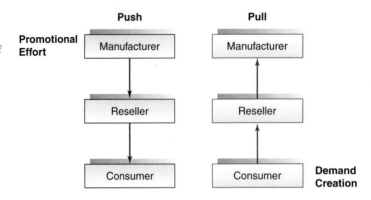

Demand: Push-and-Pull Strategies Consumer and trade promotions interact through complementing push-and-pull strategies (see Figure 15.1). Most marketers use some combination of push-and-pull strategies. Using one to the exclusion of the other would probably prove risky, given the need to appeal to both reseller and consumer.

If people really want to try Corn Crunchies, based on what they have heard about it in advertising and publicity stories, they will ask their local retailers for it, which is called a pull strategy; that is, by asking for it they will pull the product through the distribution channel. Sometimes the advertising and publicity are focused on a sales promotion, which can be used to intensify the demand for the product. By conducting a contest in conjunction with sampling, for example, we can increase the pull of a promotion at the same time we get people to try the new product.

However, you might use a push promotional strategy to convince members of the distribution network to carry and market Corn Crunchies by rewarding them. For example, we want grocery stores to not only carry them, but also allocate good shelf space in the crowded chip aisle. Table 15.3 summarizes the most common types of incentives and trade deals used with retailers.

TABLE 15.3	**Dealing with the Trade**

- **Bonuses.** A monetary bonus (also called push money or spiffs) is paid to a salesperson based on units that salesperson sells over a period of time. For example, an air conditioner manufacturer might give salespeople a $50 bonus for the sale of one model and $75 for a fancier model, within a certain timeframe. When time is up, each salesperson sends in evidence of total sales to the manufacturer and receives a check for the bonus amount.

- **Dealer loaders.** These are premiums (comparable to a consumer premium) that a manufacturer gives to a retailer for buying a certain amount of a product. A *buying loader* rewards retailers for buying the product.

    Budweiser offered store managers a free trip to the Super Bowl if they sold a certain amount of beer in a specified period of time. *Display loaders* reward retailers by giving them the display after the promotion is over. For example, Dr. Pepper built a store display for the July fourth holiday that included a gas grill, picnic table, basket, and other items. The store manager was awarded these items after the promotion ended.

- **Buying allowances.** A manufacturer pays a reseller a set amount of money, or a discount, for purchasing a certain amount of the product during a specified time period.

- **Advertising allowances.** The manufacturer pays the wholesaler or retailer a certain amount of money to advertise the manufacturer's product. This allowance can be a flat dollar amount or it can be a percentage of gross purchases during a specified time period.

- **Cooperative advertising.** In a contractual arrangement between the manufacturer and the resellers, the manufacturer agrees to pay a part or all of the advertising expenses incurred by the retailers.

- **Display allowance.** A direct payment of cash or goods is given to the retailer if the retailer agrees to set up the point-of-sale display. Before issuing the payment, the manufacturer requires the retailer's signature on a certificate of agreement.

Push-and-pull strategies reward retailers as well, with a predictable customer who will not only buy the product being promoted but will also purchase other products while in the store. Co-marketing and co-branding can get marketing partners involved in the product launch, and tie-ins, such as combining a promotion for Corn Crunchies with a salsa offer, can help spread the costs of the promotion.

Attention Some trade promotions are designed to not only get the attention of the trade members, but also to grab the attention of customers. POP displays, for example, are designed to get the attention of shoppers when they are in the store and to stimulate impulse purchases. They are used by retailers, but provided by manufacturers. As we move toward a self-service retail environment in which fewer and fewer customers expect help from sales clerks, the role of POP will continue to increase. The Point-of-Purchase Advertising International Association (POPAI) released a study in 2001 that examined the effect of various POP forms on sales. Topping the POP list were displays communicating a tie-in with entertainment, sports, or charities.[6]

In addition to getting attention in crowded aisles and promoting impulse purchases, marketers are designing POP efforts to complement other promotional campaigns. A POP display for Sega's Dreamcast would also contain information about the two tours and the championship. As part of getting attention, retailers appreciate POP ideas that build store ambience.[7] Club Med designed a floor display for travel agents that featured a beach chair with a surfboard on one side and a pair of skis on the other to show that Club Med has both snow and sun destinations. Advertisers must consider not only whether POP is appealing to the end user, but also whether the trade will use it—retailers will use a POP only if they are convinced that it will generate greater sales.

Motivation Most trade promotions are designed to in some way motivate trade members to cooperate with the manufacturer's promotion. Incentives such as contests and trade deals are used. If conducted properly with a highly motivating incentive or prize, contests can spur short-term sales and improve the relationship between the manufacturer and the reseller. They encourage a higher quantity of purchases and create enthusiasm among trade members who are involved with the promotion.

Trade incentive programs are common when the advertiser is introducing a new product like Corn Crunchies in a market, and trying to gain more space on store shelves or get retailers to stock more of a product. They are used to stimulate frequency and quantity of purchase and encourage cooperation with a promotion.

Information Trade shows display products and provide an opportunity to sample and demonstrate products particularly for trade buyers (people who buy for stores). The food industry has a number of trade shows for various product categories and the manufacturer of Corn Crunchies would want to make sure that there was an exhibit featuring the new corn chip at the appropriate food shows. Trade shows permit companies to gather information about their competition. In an environment where all the companies are attempting to give a clear picture of their products to potential customers, competitors can easily compare quality, features, prices, and technology.

Advertisers will use a POP display only when they are convinced it will lead to sales.

PROMOTIONS THAT CROSS THE LINES

So far we have looked at consumer sales promotions and trade promotions. But marketers have more promotion techniques at their disposal. In this section, we focus on sponsorships, event marketing, interactive and Internet promotions, licensing, loyalty programs, and co-marketing promotions. Many of these promotion techniques, such as sponsorships and event marketing, blur the lines between promotions, advertising, and public relations.

Event marketing means building a product's marketing program around a sponsored event, as Sega did with the Dreamcast championship competition.

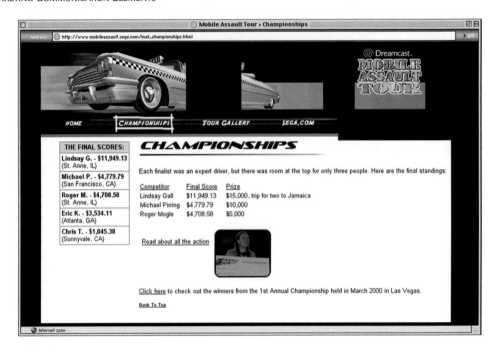

Sponsorships and Event Marketing

Sponsorships are when companies support an event, say a sporting event, concert, or charity either financially or by donating supplies and services. Event marketing means building a product's marketing program around a sponsored event, as Sega did with the Dreamcast championship competition. Sponsorships and event marketing include: sports sponsorships (events, athletes, teams), entertainment tours and attractions; festivals, fairs, and other annual events; cause marketing (associating with an event that supports a social cause); and supporting the arts (orchestras, museums, etc.).

An example of an innovative sponsorship is one by First USA Bank, which became the first corporation to sponsor college students when it agreed to pay the tuition of Chris Barrett and Luke McCabe at Pepperdine University and the University of Southern California. In return, these two men agreed to lend their names and faces to a college-student-focused marketing campaign that stresses financial responsibility.[8]

Sponsorships With $8.7 billion in revenues, sponsorship has moved from the sixth largest category of sales promotion in the 1990s to the third in 2000. The category grew at a rate of 14.59 percent, making it the third fastest-growing category of sales promotion, behind interactive and POP displays.

Regardless of title or place in the organization, companies undertake sponsorships to increase the perceived value of the brand in the consumer's mind. IBM, General Motors, and Sony spend millions of dollars to be official sponsors of the Olympics. Lipton sponsors golf tournaments. Texaco sponsors car races. Siemens sponsors international men's tennis, and 7-11 sponsors the Jerry Lewis Annual Telethon. These events also give sales representatives the opportunity to interact with prospective customers in a social environment as opposed to a less relaxed business setting, so it's building the image and reputation of the company.

In an EFFIE award–winning promotion, the Marines elected to sponsor the ESPN X-Games, as well as local related events. The idea was to use the "Xtreme" sports angle to show the connection between the Marines and youths' "can do" attitudes: The challenge of becoming a Marine and the challenge of Xtreme sports push people to limits they did not know they could reach. At the national level, the Marines sponsored ESPN's X-Games and X-Games Tour. In addition, a "Marines Xtreme" digital banner was placed on ESPN's "Sports Zone" home page and hot linked to the Marine Corps' home page. "Sports Zone" is a site their target age group visits often.

Scrabble celebrated its 50th anniversary and Big Mac celebrated its 30th with oversized versions of their products.

On the local level, the Marine Corps sought to use its larger-than-life image to engage prospects in an extreme challenge. It sponsored a "Hoop Camp" as a 50-city, three-on-three basketball tournament. The Corps also sponsored a "Chin-up Challenge" at fairs, concerts, and sporting events and produced an on-site video so that attendees could learn more about becoming a Marine. All of these events got prospective Marines involved with the Corps as part of its recruitment program.

Event Marketing The term "event marketing" has emerged in the last decade and describes the marketing practice of linking a brand to an event. The event usually matches the brand to the target market's lifestyle. For example, Sega's Dreamcast "Family Values Tour" linked the video game brand to the alternative music enjoyed by people in its target market. Some companies stage events to celebrate milestones, such as Scrabble's 50th anniversary and the 30th anniversary of the Big Mac. Special events such as Scrabble's 50th anniversary can also be the public relations manager's responsibility, as well as a sales promotion activity. For a company such as Reebok that is immersed in lifestyle marketing, there is even a director of events marketing.

An example of a promotional event is the Camp Jeep® which is held every summer. The event allows consumers to try off-road driving. Primarily a family vacation (a week in the mountains), Camp Jeep® offers Jeep 101® courses and miles of trails with different levels of difficulty. Beyond Camp Jeep®, the Jeep 101® course goes on the road to some 20 cities. It is designed to simulate trail conditions in the wilderness and features a number of off-highway driving challenges. Attendance is by invitation only from local dealers. Both events provide a combination of sales pitch and fun.

Aerial Advertising Support Advertisers will use blimps, balloons, and inflatables—even skywriting planes—to capture attention and create an aura of excitement at events. Everybody has probably heard of the Goodyear blimp, but other companies such as Fuji, Sea World, and Metropolitan Life Insurance also use aerial advertising. MetLife, for example, uses characters from the popular "Peanuts" comic strip in its advertising; and its two blimps, Snoopy I and Snoopy II, connect with the campaign to provide brand reminder messages.

Inflatables, giant models of products, and packages are used at all kinds of events, including grand openings, sporting events, parades, trade shows, beaches, malls, and other places where they can make an impression for a new-product rollout. Giant inflatables, such as the Whipper Snapple bottle by Boulder Blimp, demands attention and provides an entertaining and highly memorable product presentation. Its effectiveness comes from its huge size and three-dimensional shape.

Giant inflatables, such as the Whipper Snapple Bottle by Boulder Blimp, demand attention.

THE INSIDE STORY

MARKETING AN EVENT

Julie Blankinship   Manager of Marketing Communications, GE Access, Boulder, Colorado

Marketing is a critical component to any event, especially if it is a corporate event. Corporate events usually market to two distinct audiences: attendees and sponsors. In the case of the sponsors, event marketing needs to be directly connected to the needs and goals of that event sponsor. Most sponsors want exposure from an event. Their hope is that their sponsorship will build awareness and ultimately gain them a sale and a customer. Most sponsors want to use this opportunity to change attendees' perceptions of their organizations. If they plan their sponsorship correctly and understand their attendees' needs, they can achieve this goal.

Attendees, on the other hand, usually are looking to obtain education and networking opportunities from events. It is usually up to the sponsors to provide the pertinent information and networking opportunities that attendees want, so sponsors need to target their information appropriately toward the needs of their audience.

Achieving these goals and expectations for both groups requires advance planning and research for the event.

Julie Blankinship is manager of the marketing communications group at GE Access in Boulder, Colorado. Julie received her Master's Degree in Advertising from Denver University in May 2001. Her undergraduate degree is in Communications from the University of Colorado in Boulder.

Nominated by Professor John Burnett, Denver University.

Interactive and Internet Promotions

More and more companies are using the Internet as a promotional medium. According to Promo's 2001 Annual Report the interactive sales promotion category generated about $1.8 billion in promotion revenues. With increases of 22.4 percent, it was the fastest growing of all the sales promotion categories shown in Table 15.1. That growth was only half as great as 1999, but it's still impressive considering the crash of the dot-com industry.

There are a number of ways that advertisers can use the Internet for sales promotion programs, including sampling, sweepstakes and contests, price deals, and coupons.

Sampling has been a mainstay of interactive promotions on the Internet. Some companies offer samples from their own home pages; however, most farm out the efforts to online companies that specialize in handling sample offers and fulfillment. Some of these online sampling companies are: freesampleclub.com, startsampling.com, freesamples.com, and sampleville.com. There are also freebie portals such as amazingfreebies.com, nojunkfree.com, and the freesite.com that have endless offers for gratis goodies.

Sampling over the Internet is not cheap for companies, however. Although traditional store sampling costs 17 cents per sample and event sampling runs about 25 cents per sample, online sampling costs 75 to 90 cents.[9] The reason for the high cost is the money it takes to run the Web site.

Sweepstakes and contests are effective promotional tools for driving people to marketers' Internet sites, if that's the marketer's objective. America Online has conducted numerous promotions to drive users to its advertisers' sites. One recent promotion gives visitors a chance to win a $1-million drawing and one of the dozens of daily prizes including merchandise emblazoned with the online service's logo. To participate, members log onto the service and click on a number of icons.

The results from Internet sweepstakes can be huge. According to Seth Godin, president and founder of Yoyodyne, an online marketing and sweepstakes company, "We basically say, if you give us permission to e-mail you information about a product or a site, we'll give you a chance to win a house." He explains, "We get a 36 percent response rate every time we send an e-mail, which is about thirty times what you get with direct mail marketing." Steven Krein, president and chief executive of Webstakes, an online sweepstakes company, says, "Sweepstakes, combined with the Internet's direct marketing tools, equals sweepstakes on steroids. You're not just filling in information on a card. There's so much more interaction, that's why the results can be astronomical."[10]

Some sites offer price promotions only to online purchasers. The promotions might be discounted prices, rebates, or free offers such as frequent flier miles. *Promo* magazine has found that consumers are more receptive to rebates online than offline.[11] Incentive programs offered by online marketers CyberGold (www.cybergold.com), FreeRide Media (www.freeride.com), Intellipost (www.bonusmail.com), MotivationNet (www.mypoints.com), and Netcentives (www.clickrewards.com) offer discounts to customers who enroll with them before buying from other merchants.

Coupons can be delivered via the Internet. Several sites have been designed for this. Catalina's ValuPage Web site (www.valupage.com) allows users to print coupons that they can use at 7,000 supermarkets. The coupon is printed with a barcode and is used with the shopper's store card. If Corn Crunchies were to offer coupons this way, the site could link the shopper's Internet information with store card information, which the Corn Crunchies brand manager could use in determining whether the coupon strategy was effective.

Loyalty Programs

A second area for discussion in this section on programs that cross the line between advertising and promotion is frequency, or loyalty, programs. A **loyalty program**, also called a continuity or frequency program (such as airline frequent flyer programs), is a promotion to increase customer retention. Marketers typically define loyalty programs as ones created to keep and reward customers for their continued patronage. Thus, they are also called continuity programs. If customers have a reason to come back for more, the thinking goes, they'll spend more.[12] Typically, the higher the purchase level, the greater the benefits. The Practical Tips box lists the four mandates of loyalty programs.[13]

Practical Tips

FOUR MANDATES OF LOYALTY PROGRAMS

1. Identify your best customers.
2. Connect with those best customers.
3. Retain the best customers, usually by rewarding them for their patronage.
4. Cultivate new "best customers."

Today loyalty or continuity programs are synonymous with the word "frequent." Frequent-flier clubs, created by United and American Airlines in 1981, are the model for a modern continuity program. They offer a variety of rewards, including seat upgrades, free tickets, and premiums based on the number of frequent-flier miles accumulated. Continuity programs work in competitive markets in which the consumer has difficulty perceiving real differences between brands. TGI Friday's, for example, has used a "Frequent Friday's" program with several million members. Members receive 10 points for every dollar they spend in the restaurant. Bonuses include 500 enrollment points and double, triple, and double-triple points for special promotions. Members who accumulate 1,250 points receive a free appetizer and 5,750 points are good for a $15 dining certificate.

Marketers like membership programs because they also generate information for customer databases. The enrollment application at TGI Friday's, for example, captures name, address, telephone number, birth date, and average visit frequency. The database can also record the restaurant locations, date, time, purchase amount, and items you ordered for each visit. Marketers can then use this information to more specifically target customers with promotions and advertising materials.

Partnership Programs

Another promotion tool that crosses the lines is the partnership program. **Co-marketing** is where leading manufacturers develop marketing communication programs *with* their main retail accounts, instead of *for* them. If done right, they strengthen relationships between manufacturers and retailers. Co-marketing programs are usually based on the lifestyles and purchasing habits of consumers who live in the area of a particular retailer. The partnership means that the advertising and sales promotions build equity for both the manufacturer and the retailer. For example, Procter & Gamble and Wal-Mart might develop a spring cleaning promotion directed at Wal-Mart shoppers that features P&G cleaning products sold at reduced prices or with premium incentives.

Co-branding occurs when two companies come together to offer a product. An example of co-branding is when American Airlines puts its logo on a Citibank Visa card and awards AAdvantage points to Citibank Visa card users. Both companies are equally present in the product's design and promotion and both get to build on the other company's brand equity.

The PGA licenses the use of its logo to other advertisers who want to associate themselves with the PGA Tour golf audience.

Licensing With **licensing**, legally protected brand identity items, such as logos, symbols, and brand characters, must be licensed, that is, a legal contract gives another company the right to use the brand identity element. In brand licensing, a company with an established brand "rents" that brand to other companies, allowing them to use its logo on their products and in their advertising and promotional events. Fashion marketers such as Gucci, Yves St. Laurent, and Pierre Cardin have licensed their brand names and logos for use on everything from fashion accessories to sunglasses, ties, linens, and luggage, and they do this because it makes them money and extends their brand visibility.

PGA Tour is a golf brand that has become recognizable through an elaborate, integrated marketing campaign.[14] Charles Schwab, the financial investment house, has used the Tour logo as a part of its advertising. So has MasterCard and Anheuser-Busch for its Michelob brand. This lets these companies associate their brands with a golf event that has a lot of interest and positive associations for their target audiences.

Tie-Ins Another type of cooperative marketing program is a **tie-in**, which is proving to be an effective strategy for marketers who are using associations between complementary brands to make one-plus-one equal three. For example, Doritos may develop a tie-in promotion with Pace salsa in which bottles of salsa are displayed next to the Doritos section in the chip aisle (and vice versa). The intention is to spur impulse sales. Ads are also designed to tie the two products together and the sponsoring companies share the cost of the advertising.

The biggest tie-in deals are arranged around movies and other entertainment events. The launch of the movie series *Lord of the Rings* accompanied a Burger King global marketing program that was promoted by Burger King at more than 10,000 of its restaurants where "Rings" characters were offered for sale or as prizes to young customers.

The reason for the tie-in success stories is that brands can leverage similar strengths to achieve a bigger impact in the marketplace. Typically, marketers align themselves with partners that provide numerous complementary elements, including common target audiences, purchase cycle patterns, distribution channels, retailer penetration, and demographics to drive their products and promotions through retail channels and into the minds of consumers.

PROMOTION STRATEGIES

As we explained in Chapter 3, promotions are just one element of the marketing communication mix available to the marketer; others are personal selling, direct marketing, advertising, and public relations. Promotions can accomplish certain communication goals that the other techniques cannot. Here we discuss the strategy behind the use of promotions, as well as how advertising and promotions complement each other, particularly in building brands.

Promotion Objectives

Our earlier discussion of the use of promotion identified a number of reasons for using promotions. Many of them focused on the use of promotions in a new product launch, and

And the box said,
"Let me be free."

INTRODUCING
FREE SHIPPING
ON ORDERS OVER $99

Use Super Saver Shipping. Some restrictions apply. See Web site for details.

This amazon.com coupon seeks to induce consumers to buy more by giving a discount on large orders.

how they can deliver trial. Promotion can offer consumers an immediate inducement to buy a product, often simply by making the product more valuable. The amazon.com offer shown here makes purchases a better value by taking the cost of shipping off their price. Sales promotion can make consumers who know nothing about the brand develop awareness and trial, as well as persuade them to buy again once they've tried it. It can push the product through the distribution channel by generating positive brand experiences among resellers and buyers in many places along the channel and purchase continuum.

Promotions can help introduce a new product and create brand awareness or build a brand over time by reinforcing advertising images and messages. They can create an affinity between brands and buyers and provide new channels for reaching audience segments. They can create brand involvement and positive experiences that people associate with the brands.

There are some other things that promotions cannot do very effectively. Promotions alone cannot create an image for a brand, for example. They cannot compensate for lack of advertising and the broad awareness that it delivers. They cannot do much to change negative attitudes toward a product, overcome product problems, or reverse a declining sales trend. Brand building, however, is an interesting challenge, so let's look at it in more depth.

Brand Building

For years there has been a heated debate concerning sales promotion and brand building. Advertisers claim that the strength of advertising is creating and maintaining brand image and that sales promotion's price deals negate all their hard work by diverting the emphasis from the brand to the price. The result is a brand-insensitive consumer.

Consider McDonald's, which has long based its image on everyday value, one of the four pillars of McDonald's marketing mantra: Quality, Service, Cleanliness, and Value (QSC&V). Price promotions like a 99-cent Big Mac damage more than its bottom line because the price promotion undercuts the value pillar. In other words, if value is central to McDonald's pricing, then it wouldn't need to have special sale prices.[15]

Procter & Gamble's division manager of advertising and sales promotion, explains it this way: "Too many marketers no longer adhere to the fundamental premise of brand building, which is that [brand] franchises aren't built by cutting price but rather by offering superior quality at a reasonable price and clearly communicating that value to consumers. The price-cutting patterns begun in the early 1970s continue today, fostering a short-term orientation that has caused long-term brand building to suffer."[16] Critics point to a general decline in consumer brand loyalty as just one negative result of price-based promotions.

The problem is that brand building is a long and time-consuming process of establishing the brand's core values. Promotion, whether a sale price, a premium, a coupon, or some other incentive, is inherently short term, so the promotion undermines the brand's established values. But sales promotion experts argue that sales promotion can help to build brand image. They refer to many cereal brands, rental car companies, airlines, and hotels that have used a variety of well-planned sales promotion strategies (like loyalty programs, for example) to enhance their brand images. Second, they acknowledge that continuous promotion—particularly continuous price promotion—does not work well with brand building, except for discount marketers, whose image is built on the notion of sale prices.

According to one industry expert, the solution to the debate is to make advertising more accountable and promotion more brand-focused. He explained, "In isolation, neither traditional advertising nor promotion can deliver the level of long-term image and profitable volume-building that's now required."[17] In other words, the advertising and promotion need to work more closely together and, in particular, their short-term campaigns shouldn't be at odds with one another, which is why there is a need for more integration in the planning of marketing communication programs.

Promotion Integration

Advertising and promotion both contribute to the effectiveness of a marketing communication plan, primarily because they do different things and have different objectives. In an effective plan, the two work together, along with other marketing communication tools, to accomplish overall marketing communication objectives. For an example of advertising and promotion working side-by-side, see the "A Matter of Practice" feature on the launch of the Dreyer's Dreamery ice cream brand.

The major differences between advertising and sales promotion concern their methods of appeal and the value they add to the sale of the product or service. Advertising is primarily used to create an image and high levels of brand awareness and will take the time needed to do so; promotions are primarily used to create immediate action. To accomplish this immediate goal, sales promotion may rely heavily on rational appeals, such as price deals.

In contrast, advertising often relies on emotional appeals to promote the product's image. In other words, advertising tends to add intangible value—brand personality and image—to the good or service. Promotions add tangible value to the good or service and contribute greatly to the profitability of the brand. Table 15.4 summarizes the differences between these two marketing tools in terms of their primary orientations.

Some objectives advertising and promotion share include increasing the number of customers and increasing the use of the product by current customers. Both objectives attempt to change audience perceptions about the product or service, and both attempt to make people do something. Of course, advertisers accomplish these tasks in different ways.

In most cases, advertising must be used to support promotions. Price deals, for example, are advertised as a way to build traffic in a store. Contests, sweepstakes, and special events won't work if no one knows about them.

Another area needing cooperation and integration is the use of direct marketing to announce a promotion. For example, we mentioned earlier that marketers often choose direct mail when they want to deliver samples. An EFFIE-winning campaign by Sears titled "Umpteen Appliances" combined direct mail with an advertising specialty mailed to the home as part of its Home Central™ appliance repair service launch. The specialty was a branded refrigerator magnet that provided a visible daily reminder of the new Sears brand of appliance repair. This promotion was also supported with magazine advertising announcing this value-added program and the idea of one simple phone number, 1-800-4-REPAIR.

A MATTER OF PRACTICE

ICE CREAM DREAMS

➤ Competition in the $3.7 billion super premium ice cream market is heating up because of the image-building efforts of Ben & Jerry's and the award-winning advertising of Häagen-Dazs (see Chapter 6, p. 153). California-based Dreyer's increased competitive pressure in the ice cream category with the launch of its new brand, Dreamery, in 1999. (Dreyer's uses the Edy's brand in the East and Dreyer's in the West.) The "This Could Be a Problem" campaign not only effectively launched the Dreamery brand, it also won an EFFIE award.

In addition to a full array of TV, radio, outdoor, and print advertising materials by San Francisco–based ad agency Goodby, Silverstein & Partners, Dreyer's used a strong promotional plan by promotional agency Zipatoni of Chicago.

People who love ice cream really love it; in the super premium category fewer than 10 percent of consumers buy more than 45 percent of the volume. Prior to Dreyer's campaign, these consumers were loyal to the environmentally friendly Ben & Jerry's or the sophisticated Häagen-Dazs. So Dreyer's went after these loyal users, which is a hard sell in any market. The strategy was to reach them by positioning Dreamery as the ice cream lover's ice cream—for people who are so obsessive about their ice cream relationship, it's comical. As the EFFIE brief said about the research findings, "They dream about it, chatter on about it, and make late night trips to supermarkets for it. One woman flew to Dallas for her favorite ice cream. People talked of going to the supermarket with spoons so they could gobble it in line. Some had marked the inside of the carton so they could tell if others had partaken, while others stashed cartons behind frozen peas."

The campaign matched Dreamery's new exciting flavors (such as Hot Chilly Chili, Sticky Buns, Blue Ribbon Berry Pie, Banana Boogie, and Grandma's Cookie Jar) to the addiction-like response of the obsessive ice cream consumer, proclaiming the theme line: "This could be a problem."

The objective of the sales promotion effort was trial—what better way to lure in heavy users than to get them to taste? Zipatoni used sampling to get people to try this new brand and its exotic flavors at consumer events. In New York

The Dreamery commercials featured people obsessing over ice cream.

City, for example, which is a hard market to penetrate, the strategy was to take a mobile sampling program into this densely populated market. In San Francisco, the "Sweet Fleet" of 20 VW Bugs, each wrapped in a whimsical illustration of a Dreamery flavor, generated brand buzz and made appearances at local retail chains.

Between the advertising and the sales promotion, this campaign moved Dreamery to a 49 percent awareness level and a high level of brand involvement in the three-month summer launch period. Sales increased by as much as 30 percent in markets that received promotion over markets that didn't, which strongly suggests that the campaign was highly effective in reaching those who dream of ice cream.

POINT TO PONDER

What other sales promotion techniques might have been used in support of the launch of Dreamery? Identify five other tools that you would consider and give an idea for each one about how it could be used in this campaign.

Source: Adapted from the 2001 EFFIE brief provided by Dreyer's and Goodby, Silverstein & Partners.

In terms of the integration of promotion with other marketing communication activities, *Promo* magazine conducted a survey[18] in which it asked marketers how well sales promotion was integrated into their overall marketing communication plan. More than 82 percent said it was a part of the integrated effort and 31 percent of those marketers said it was the core component:

A component of our integrated marketing plan	51%
The core component of our integrated marketing plan	31.4%
A separate program not integrated into the overall plan	13.7%

In other words, most of them are planning promotion as part of an integrated marketing communication program.

| TABLE 15.4 | **The Differences between Advertising and Sales Promotion** |

Advertising	**Sales Promotion**
Creates a brand image over time	Creates immediate action
Relies on emotional appeals	Added value strategies rely on rational appeals; impulse appeals use emotion
Adds intangible value to the product or service through image	Adds tangible value to the product or service
Contributes moderately to short-term profitability	Contributes greatly to short-term profitability

Determining Promotion Effectiveness

Since promotions are so focused on action, it makes sense that sales is the primary measure of their effectiveness. After all, they are called "sales promotions." Response rate—consumers calling the company, sending back a card—is also important to sales promotion. So are redemption rates, which are the rates at which people redeem coupons, refunds, and rebates. These are used to evaluate the effectiveness of coupons and rebate programs. In another *Promo* magazine survey,[19] marketers reported that they used these evaluation measures as follows:

Measure	**% used**
Sales	45.8
Response Rates	19.4
Awareness	10.2
Other Mix	8.8
Redemption Rates	4.2

Marketers are finding that promotions are more effective when they catch consumers' interest. They are also finding that the best way to listen to consumers may be through qualitative tests.[20] By using focus groups and in-depth interviews, for example, researchers can identify the level of interest the target market has for certain sports and events and analyze how that interest might work in a future brand promotion.

Payout Planning Another way to evaluate the effectiveness of a sales promotion is in terms of its financial returns. Called a **payout plan**, the costs of the promotion are compared to the forecasted sales generated by the promotion. A type of payout plan called **breakeven analysis** seeks to determine the point at which the total cost of the promotion exceeds the total revenues, identifying the point where the effort cannot break even. Figure 15.2 depicts this analysis.

A famous example of poor payout planing comes from Maytag and its ill-fated U.K. promotion. It was a simple offer. Customers in Great Britain and Ireland were offered two free airline tickets to the United States or Continental Europe when they purchased at least $150 worth of Hoover products. Hoover planned to use the commissions it made from land arrangements, such as hotel reservations and car rentals, to help pay for the airline tickets.

How did the promotion turn into a catastrophe? Unfortunately, the commissions were less than anticipated and the ticket demand was far greater. Maytag's travel agents began attaching unreasonable demands to the free tickets, expensive extras, inconvenient airports, and undesirable departure dates to discourage acceptance of the offer. All of these strategies turned happy winners into complaining customers. In the aftermath, Hoover fired three top executives and set up a $30 million fund to pay for the airline tickets.

Design and Performance The trade press is full of stories about poorly designed or performing promotions. Such failures hurt companies' reputations, waste money, and

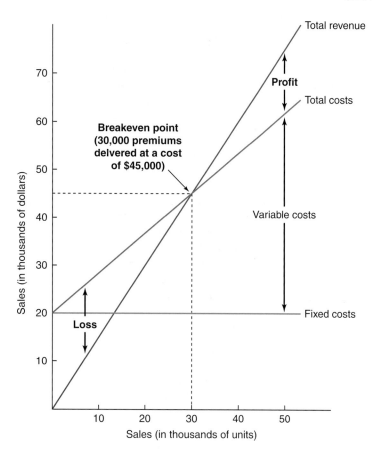

FIGURE **15.2**

A SALES PROMOTION BREAKEVEN ANALYSIS
At the breakeven point, where 30,000 premiums are delivered at a cost of $45,000, the sales revenues exactly cover, but do not exceed, total costs. Below and to the left of the breakeven point (in the portion of the diagram marked off by dashed lines) the promotion operates at a loss. Above and to the right of the breakeven point, as more premiums are sold and sales revenues climb, the promotion makes a profit.
Source: Adapted from Keegan, Moriarty, and Duncan, *Marketing* (Englewood Cliffs, NJ: Prentice-Hall, 1995): 511.

sometimes even hurt consumers. For example, in 2001, Burger King had to recall 400,000 toy boats given away with kids' meals after reports that children had been stuck with metal pins that came off the boats too easily. That recall came a week after McDonald's recalled a Happy Meal "Scooter Bug" toy. In 1999 the fast food industry reeled from the deaths of two infants who suffocated from containers used in a Pokémon promotion. About 25 million of those toys were recalled.

IT'S A WRAP
SURVIVOR ISN'T JUST A GAME

Sega designed the Dreamcast to recapture its share of the $6.3 billion worldwide gaming market, after reaching rock bottom in the late 1990s with a drop from 50 percent share of market to 5 percent. The launch of Dreamcast was a survival move for Sega.

The $1 million launch campaign created huge sales the first weekend; 1 million units were sold in the first two months in the United States. The original sales objective of 1.7 million consoles was reached within the first six months, which beat the target objective by 12 percent. Total software sales during the same period were 7 percent above the objective.

In terms of the visibility objective, Sega's unaided brand awareness grew from 48 percent to 77 percent in the first six months. Similarly, Sega's unaided advertising awareness grew from 40 percent to 55 percent during the same timeframe. Furthermore, Dreamcast's unaided advertising awareness was significantly higher than both competitors at 55 percent awareness (compared to 35 percent for PlayStation's and 28 percent for Nintendo 64's advertising).

(continues)

It was clear, shortly after the launch, that the campaign was a success. The bigger issue was whether Dreamcast could continue to sell at that rate until Sega could regain its competitive position, particularly since Dreamcast was outspent by a factor of four by PlayStation and twice the budget by Nintendo.

So how did it all come out? The editor of *Dreamcast Weekly* celebrated Dreamcast's first birthday with the comment, "If you're looking for sheer electronic entertainment, it seems you've backed a winning console." But it seems it wasn't a winner, as four months later Sega's executives announced that Dreamcast production was to end. A news story on a video game Web site explained that "the system never gained the market foothold necessary to compete against Sony and Nintendo."

This just proves the hard reality that, no matter how great the advertising and promotion might be, there may be other factors that make it impossible for a product to be successful, even when the campaign meets its objectives. Dreamcast was launched as a lifesaver for a brand that had lost almost all of its position in a highly competitive market. If this had been a normal marketing situation, a successful campaign might have led to a successful brand. In this case, the successful launch of Dreamcast simply wasn't enough to recoup Sega's huge lost market share. So instead of selling game systems, Sega turned its attention to its strength and refocused on selling the software for the games.

Summary

1. **Explain the principles that drive the use of sales promotion and discuss why advertisers are spending increasing sums of money on sales promotion.** Sales promotion offers an "extra incentive" to take action. It gives the product or service additional value and motivates people to respond. Sales promotion is growing rapidly for many reasons. It offers the manager short-term bottom-line results; it's accountable; sales promotion is less expensive than advertising; it speaks to the current needs of the consumer to receive more value from products; and it responds to marketplace changes.

2. **List and explain the use of various consumer promotions.** Sales promotions directed at consumers include price deals, coupons, contests and sweepstakes, refunds, premiums, specialty advertising, continuity programs, and sampling. Their purpose is to pull the product through the distribution channel. Trade promotions include point-of-purchase displays, contests and sweepstakes, trade shows, trade premiums, and trade deals. Their purpose is to push the products through the channel.

3. **Summarize the types and purposes of trade promotions.** Sales promotions directed at the trade include point-of-purchase displays, retailer merchandising kits, trade shows, and price deals such as discounts, bonuses, and advertising allowances. These are used to push the product through the channel.

4. **Describe the use of other types of promotions: sponsorships, specialties, interactive promotions, licensing, loyalty programs, and co-marketing programs.** Sponsorship is used to increase the perceived value of a brand by associating it with a cause or celebrity. The purpose of specialty advertising is to serve as a reminder. Internet promotions can be used to drive people to a sponsor's Web page. Licensing "rents" an established brand to other companies to use on their products. Loyalty programs are designed to increase customer retention. Co-marketing programs are designed to build stronger relationships between manufacturers and retailers.

5. **Explain the strategic use of promotions in marketing in terms of brand building, new product launches, integration, and effectiveness.** Promotion offers an incentive to action and it stimulates trial, which is important in launching a new product. In brand building it can reinforce advertising images and messages and encourage or remind consumers to buy the brand again. It can be used to push or pull a product through the distribution channel by creating positive brand experiences. Interactive promotions are more involving. Sales promotion is used with advertising to provide immediate behavioral action. It is effective when the return on the investment more than covers the cost of the promotion.

Key Terms

breakeven analysis, p. 448
co-branding, p. 444
co-marketing, p. 444
contests, p. 432
coupons, p. 432
licensing, p. 444
loyalty program, p. 443
payout plan, p. 448
point-of-purchase display (POP), p. 436
premium, p. 432
price deal, p. 431
rebate, p. 432
refund, p. 432
sales promotion, p. 429
sampling, p. 432
self-liquidator, p. 432
specialty advertising, p. 433
sponsorship, p. 440
sweepstakes, p. 432
tie-ins, p. 444
trade deal, p. 437

Questions

1. What basic principle drives sales promotion? What are the broad goals of sales promotion in terms of its three target audiences?

2. One agency executive was quoted as saying, "Advertising is on its way out. All consumers want is a deal. Sales promotion is the place to be." What do you think this executive meant? Do you agree or disagree?

3. You have just been named product manager for Bright White, a new laundry detergent that will be introduced to the market within the next six months. Would you use a push or pull strategy? Why?

4. Tom Jackson's marketing professor is covering some promotion methods, explaining that in selecting the consumer sales promotion, planners must know the brand situation and objectives before techniques are chosen. Some techniques tend to increase product use and others are used to get new consumers to try the product. "Which methods belong with which objective and why?" the professor asks. How should Tom answer this question?

5. Janice Wilcox is a brand manager for a new line of eye cosmetics. She is about to present her planning strategy to division management. Janice knows her company has been successful in using sales promotion plans lately, but she has strong misgivings about following the company trend. "This new line must create a consumer brand franchise, and promotion isn't the best way to do that," she thinks to herself. How is sales promotion weak in building and maintaining a brand? Should Janice propose no promotion, or is there a reasonable compromise for her to consider?

6. Jambo Products' promotion manager, Sean Devlin, is calculating the cost of a proposed consumer coupon drop for March. The media cost of a free-standing insert for the coupon and production charges is $125,000. The distribution will be 4 million coupons, with an expected redemption of 5 percent. The coupon value is 50 cents, and Devlin has estimated the handling and compensation to the store to be 8 cents per redeemed coupon. Based on these estimates, what will be the cost to Devlin's budget?

Suggested Class Projects

1. Look through your local newspaper and identify a retailer who is engaging in co-op advertising. Interview the store manager and determine the specific arrangements that exist between the advertiser and the retailer. What is the attitude of the retailer toward this arrangement? Write a two-page report.

2. Select a print ad for a national marketer. Redesign the ad, including the use of a consumer sales promotion. Show both the before version and the after version to five people. Assess whether the second version has increased their intention to buy.

Suggested Internet Class Project

Check the Web site for Camp Jeep® (www.jeep.com then type the "campjeep" keyword). Explain how the event works to build and reinforce customer relationships. Find another company that uses a special event to create a relationship building program. Explain that program and compare it to Camp Jeep®. Which do you believe is the most effective special event and why?

Hallmark BUILD•A•CAMPAIGN*Projects*

Please review the Hallmark Case Appendix at the end of the text before responding to these questions.

1. In small groups discuss how Capitol Advertising used promotions to create brand insistence for Hallmark. What other promotions might have enhanced the campaign?

2. What role should promotions play in an individual Gold Crown store's marketing and advertising mix? Summarize your recommendations in a sales promotion plan for next year's campaign.

HANDS-ON Case 15

IT SMELLS LIKE A WINNER

The packaged-goods giant Kraft Foods and the kids' cable network Nickelodeon recently teamed up for a sense-enhancing campaign called Smell-O-Vision. The interactive event was designed to increase sales of the 11 Kraft Kids brands while at the same time generating awareness and driving viewership for Nickelodeon's Nickel-O-Zone weekday prime-time programming.

Smell-O-Vision was designed to reinvent how children watch TV by incorporating their noses as well as their eyes. Kids who wanted to participate in the Smell-O-Vision experience had to obtain scratch-and-sniff cards and 3-D glasses from Kraft Kids packages. During the programs, icons appeared on the screen prompting kids to either put on their glasses or smell their cards. That required Nickelodeon to completely retool the Nickel-O-Zone series *Wild Thornberrys, Rocket Power, Cousin Skeeter,* and *Kablam* to include the interactive "play along" elements.

Kraft also sponsored a branded Smell-O-Vision Web site in conjunction with Nick.com that featured games utilizing the 3-D glasses and sniff cards. It was Kraft's first promotional Web site. Blockbuster supported the effort by distributing more than 500,000 Smell-O-Vision kits containing the glasses and cards.

The award-winning promotion, which took two years to plan, was successful because it was an involving experience supported by an integrated promotional effort. Kraft Marketing Services director Lisa Coker explained that "Smell-O-Vision enabled us to create a fully integrated event across all the touch-points in a kid's world." One of the most successful back-to-school programs in the history of Kraft and Nickelodeon, it built strong volume results for Kraft Kids brands and viewership increases for Nickelodeon.

The campaign was so successful that it drew a tremendous number of kids to the Nickelodeon programs and Web site. More importantly, the Smell-O-Vision promotion also gained a significant increase in sales of the 11 brands Kraft markets to kids. That success story was rewarded with an EMMA award by *Promo* magazine, an award designed for entertainment marketing efforts.

In terms of viewership for Nickelodeon, the promotion drew more than 20 million total viewers, including 5 million adults. More than 11 million children—nearly 40 percent of all kids age 2 to 11 in cable-equipped households participated in Smell-O-Vision. Ratings for Nickel-O-Zone shot up 12 percent over the four weeks prior to the promotion. The result of this increased viewership was a high level of awareness for Kraft Kids brands. But more importantly, for Kraft the effort yielded a 7.7 percent increase in total merchandising volume for the 11 participating brands. This high level of response was proof that the sales promotion, which was essentially designed to build awareness, could also drive sales. ■

IT'S YOUR TURN

1. What do you believe was the biggest factor in Smell-O-Vision's success—importance, relevance, or involvement? Justify your answer.

Source: Adapted from: "Smells Like A Winner," *Entertainment Marketing: Promo Special Reports* (May 1, 2001), as featured in (http://industryclick.com/Microsites/ Newsarticle.asp?newsarticleid=218986&srid=).

Notes

1. Russ Brown, "Sales Promotion," *Marketing & Media Decisions* (February 1990): 74.

2. Council of Sales Promotion Agencies, *Shaping the Future of Sales Promotion* (1990): 3.

3. 2001 Annual Report, *Promo* (May 1, 2001), as reported in www.industryclick.com/magazinearticle.asp? magazinearticleid=99739&.

4. Ibid.

5. Ibid.

6. "Entertainment Marketing Awards: Who's Who," *Promo Special Reports* (May 1, 2001) (www.industryclick.com/Microsites/Newsarticle.asp? newsarticleid=218986&srid=).

7. Matthew Kinsman, "The Last Stand," *Promo* (January 2001): 29–34.

8. "This Hangover is Brought to You By…," *Fortune* (September 3, 2001): 52.

9. Dan Hanover, "We Deliver," *Promo* (March 2001): 43–45.

10. Bob Tedeschi, "A Growing Ad Strategy: 'Click to Win!' " *New York Times* (August 21, 1998), retrieved online at www.nytimes.com/library/tech/98/08/cyber/articles/ 21advertising.html.

11. "Walking the Tight Rope," *Promo* (March 2001): 48–49.

12. Vicki Gerson, "Marketer's Best Friend," *Integrated Marketing and Promotion* (March/April 1998): 35.

13. Ibid.

14. Bill Gregory, "On Top of Its Game," *Integrated Marketing and Promotion* (March/April 1998): 17–20.

15. Jacques Chevron, "Branding and Promotion: Uneasy Co-habitation," *Brandweek* (September 14, 1998): 24.

16. Scott Hume, "Rallying to Brands' Rescue," *Advertising Age* (August 13, 1990): 3.

17. Jon Kramer, "It's Time to Tie the Knot with Promotion," *Integrated Marketing and Promotion* (September/October 1998): 77.

18. 2001 Annual Report, *Promo.*

19. Ibid.

20. Julie Zdziarski, "Evaluating Sponsorships," *Promo* (March 2001): 92–93.

CHAPTER 16

Public Relations

CHAPTER OBJECTIVES

When you have completed this chapter, you should be able to

1. Explain what public relations is and how it differs from advertising.
2. Identify the most common types of public relations programs.
3. Describe the key decisions in public relations planning.
4. Explain the most common types of public relations tools.
5. Discuss the importance of measuring the results of public relations efforts.

Teens Are Kicking Butts

Award: *2000 Gold CIPRA*

Organization: *Florida Department of Health*

Agency: *Porter Novelli; Crispin, Porter & Bogusky*

Campaign: *The "Truth" Campaign*

Award: *EFFIE Silver, Nonprofit category*

Organization: *American Legacy Foundation*

Agency: *Arnold Worldwide*

Campaign: *The "Truth" Campaign*

Rejected. Rebuffed. Returned! That's the message behind the "Truth" campaign by the Florida Department of Health, against teen smoking. The EFFIE award–winning effort, developed by the Porter Novelli public relations agency in partnership with Crispin, Porter & Bogusky, a Miami-based advertising agency, produced the largest single-year decline in teen smoking in nearly 20 years. The strategy was to get young people to rebel against the tobacco industry.

Tobacco use is the single leading preventable cause of death in the United States, and tobacco advertising is thought to be one of the problems. Cigarette companies spend over $5 billion a year selling tobacco, with much of that advertising reaching the youth market. In 1998, anti-smoking agencies estimated that every day in the United States 3,000 young people became regular smokers and that approximately 80 percent of them started smoking before the age of 18.

Porter Novelli's mission was to create an anti-tobacco brand that appealed to teens the way the major tobacco brands do. But how can a government agency tell today's teens not to smoke? The answer: It can't. However, Porter Novelli also found through research that teens listen to other teens, so the agency gave teenagers a leadership role in Students Working Against Tobacco (SWAT) teams, and the teens created the "truth" brand, the campaign, and Web site (www.wholetruth.com).

The campaign, begun in 1998, uses the slogan, "Our brand is truth, their brand is lies." The campaign's advertising uses an edgy humor that taps into teens' need to rebel and shows tobacco use as an addictive habit marketed by an adult establishment. Ad themes have ranged from an awards show set in hell—where the award for most deaths in a year goes to a tobacco executive—to a search for the Marlboro Man at Phillip Morris headquarters. Through the "Reel Truth" programs, the teens also took movie stars and the movie industry to task for irresponsibly depicting tobacco use in films and on television.

The Florida project was the model for a follow-up campaign in 2000 that took the "truth" brand nationwide. The $185 million campaign was developed by the Boston-based Arnold Worldwide agency for the American Legacy Foundation, the organization managing the tobacco settlement money nationwide (the money that came from the successful lawsuits filed against tobacco manufacturers by various states' attorneys general). The national campaign featured teens piling body bags outside Phillip Morris's New York headquarters. The campaign included a Teen Summit in Seattle attended by 1,000 teenagers, a mobile tour of 27 markets with 13 "truth" trucks, and a street-marketing promotion that distributed more than 300,000 pieces of "truth" apparel, gear, posters, and other materials. In addition, the campaign's Internet site (www.thetruth.com) became an electronic community for teenagers as well as an information resource. This national effort, which achieved a 78 percent awareness among people aged 12 to 17, won an EFFIE award in 2001.

Sources: Adapted from "Florida Department of Health Office of Tobacco Control 'Truth' Campaign," a report by Porter Novelli, September 2001; "Youth Tobacco Prevention in Florida: An Independent Evaluation of the Florida Tobacco Pilot Program," prepared by the University of Miami for the Florida Department of Health, December 15, 1999; "A Generation United against Tobacco," Florida Department of Health, 1998; John Franks, "The War on Smoking," *PRWeek* (March 5, 2001): 22–23; The 2001 EFFIE brief provided by Arnold Worldwide and the American Legacy Foundation.

THE PRACTICE OF PUBLIC RELATIONS

Handling a campaign assignment calls for extraordinary **public relations** skills and a well-thought-out plan. This chapter discusses many aspects of public relations, including marketing public relations (MPR), which is of particular importance to advertising. As we introduce these topics, we explore the award-winning anti-smoking idea that Porter Novelli and Crispin, Porter & Bogusky developed for the Florida Department of Health, its related campaigns for Mississippi, and a national effort referred to as the "Legacy" campaign.

Public goodwill is the greatest asset any organization can have. A well-informed public with a positive attitude toward an organization is critical to the organization's survival—creating goodwill is a goal of most public relations programs. This chapter considers the role of public relations in an organization and how this goodwill can be used effectively in a marketing communication program.

Although public relations has a distinguished tradition, people often mistake it for **publicity**, which refers to getting news media coverage. Public relations is broader in scope, as the official definition from the Public Relations Society of America (PRSA) suggests: "Public relations helps an organization and its publics adapt mutually to each other."[1] So public relations is focused on all the relationships that an organization has with its various publics. By publics, we mean all the groups of people with which a company or organization interacts—employees, media, community groups, shareholders, and so forth. Another term for this is "stakeholders," which refers more specifically to people who have a stake (financial or not) in a company or organization. Publicity, however, is focused on the news media and their audiences, which is just one aspect of public relations. The focus on bringing various interests into harmony is apparent in PRSA's Code of Ethical Practice, shown here.

Public relations is a management function practiced by a wide range of organizations: companies, governments, trade and professional associations, nonprofit organizations, the travel and tourism industry, the educational system, labor unions, politicians, organized sports, and the media. Its goal is to achieve positive relationships with various audiences (publics) in order to effectively manage the organization's image and reputation. Its publics may be external (customers, the news media, the investment community, the general public, government bodies) and internal (shareholders, employees).

Public relations programs are built on an understanding of **public opinion** regarding public affairs issues critical to the organization, such as ecology; how a company's practices impact on the environment and its local community; or workers' rights and how a company deals with its employees.

Public opinion, the label describing what a group of people think, is "a belief, based not necessarily on fact but on the conception or evaluation of an event, person, institution, or product."[2] The public relations strategist researches the answers to two primary questions about public opinion to design effective public relations programs. First, which publics are most important to the organization, now and in the future? Second, what do these publics think? Particular emphasis falls on understanding the role of **opinion leaders**, important people who influence the opinions of others.

Public relations is a growing industry that employs approximately 150,000 people and serves clients of every size and interest. Billings in the field are increasing by 20 to 25 percent each year. Clients pay annual fees to public relations practitioners and agencies ranging from a few hundred dollars to several million. In addition, many companies, such as Texas Instruments and IBM, have in-house public relations departments that handle most or all of the firms' public relations work.

Martin Sorrell, CEO of WPP Group, one of the largest advertising and marketing services groups in the world, believes that "public relations and public affairs are probably higher up the CEO's agenda than advertising, market research, or other forms of specialist communication." As Sorrell notes, public relations practitioners have "access to the CEO's office," which gives them more influence on corporate policies.[3]

Comparing Public Relations and Advertising

Designing ads, preparing written messages, and buying time or space are the key concerns of advertisers. Their objective is to create the consumer awareness and motivation that deliver sales. The goal of public relations specialists is communicating with various stakeholders, managing the organization's image and reputation, and creating positive public attitudes (goodwill toward the organization). The anti-smoking campaign illustrates how a public relations campaign can change attitudes.

Ultimately, the difference between advertising and public relations is that public relations takes a longer, broader view of the importance of image and reputation as a corporate competitive asset and addesses more target audiences.

If we believe in an integrated approach to mass communication, advertising and public relations should be complementary even though one focuses on products and the other on the organization. As one researcher observed, "In IMC, company assets and product assets are managed at the same time."[4] In integrated programs, advertising and public relations aim at different targets with different but complementary messages.

This postcard from the "Truth" campaign was mailed to Hollywood stars with a personal message on the back side asking them to protest smoking in movies. Several stars, including supermodel Christy Turlington, talk show host Leeza Gibbons, and Melrose Place star Antonio Sabato, Jr., publicly pledged their support in fighting the entertainment industry's depiction of tobacco use.

For example, consider how AT&T analyzed two different situations that generated news coverage affecting the company's customers—one on a Volunteerism Summit and one on switching customers' phone companies without their knowledge, a practice called *slamming*. The research discovered that AT&T's loyalty rate among its "high value" customer segment remained good when news coverage about the company was positive but the amount of advertising was low. When the amount of advertising was high and the media coverage about the company was largely negative—as in the slamming coverage— loyalty scores dipped below average.

This means that if a company, in this case a phone company, is working with a coordinated marketing communication plan, advertising would be dialed back when the company is in the news; but advertising would be a better tool for the company to use to maintain corporate awareness in between events like these that bring the company into the news.[5]

In many companies, advertising and public relations are separate, uncoordinated functions. This setup is due partly to tradition—"this is the way we've always done it"— and partly to differences in philosophy. People working in public relations are often trained as journalists, with little background in marketing, and they focus on corporate image rather than product sales. These different orientations can sometimes create inconsistencies in a company's communication efforts.

Public relations and advertising also differ in how they use the media, the level of control they have over message delivery, and their perceived credibility. Credibility was a major factor in the Florida "Truth" campaign.

- ***Media use.*** In contrast to *buying* advertising time and space, public relations people seek to *persuade* media gatekeepers to carry stories about their company. **Gatekeepers** include writers, producers, editors, talk-show coordinators, and newscasters. This aspect of public relations is labeled "publicity" and carries no direct media costs. There are indirect costs, however, such as the costs of production—printing, photography, and so on. Even when public relations uses paid-for media like

Using the familiar graphic style associated with movie ratings, this poster from the Truth campaign assigned a new rating—"L"—for lazy. The message is that the film's makers couldn't find a way to make their characters cool other than smoking, which confronted teens' attitudes about smoking being cool.

advertising the message focuses on the organization, with little or no attempt to sell a brand or product line. The effort to center on the company and not a product—is corporate, or institutional, advertising. The goal is to change the public's attitudes to favor the sponsoring organization.

- *Control.* In the case of news stories, the public relations strategist is at the mercy of the media gatekeeper, the editor, or reporter. There is no guarantee that all or even part of a story will appear. The PR person at the company writes up a story, ships it to a gatekeeper, and crosses his fingers in the hopes that this story will appear. In fact, there is the real risk that a story may be rewritten or reorganized by an editor so that it no longer means what the strategist intended. In contrast, advertising runs exactly as the client who paid for it has approved. And it runs as scheduled.

- *Credibility.* Successful public relations efforts bring a credibility not usually associated with advertising. Experts believe that consumers tend to trust the media more than they do advertisers. This consumer tendency is called the **implied third-party endorsement** factor. For example, when Tom Brokaw delivers a two-minute story on the *NBC Evening News* about an Eli Lilly pharmaceutical breakthrough, he is more credible than a print ad sponsored by Eli Lilly.[6] Thomas Harris, in his book *Value-Added Public Relations,* observes that today's sophisticated and skeptical consumers know when they are being informed and when they are being "sold to." He explains, "PR closes the marketing credibility gap because it is the one marketing communication tool devoted to providing information, not salesmanship."[7]

TYPES OF PUBLIC RELATIONS PROGRAMS

The word *relations* in public relations refers to relationships with various stakeholders. In fact, the main subspecialties in the field—public affairs, media relations, employee relations, and financial relations—call attention to important relationships with such groups as the general public, the media, employees, and the financial community. Figure 16.1 outlines the various publics, or stakeholders, for a multinational company. The term **relationship marketing** introduces a point of view in marketing planning that resembles that of public relations.[8]

The key publics addressed by relationship management programs in public relations are media, employees, the financial community—including a company's shareholders—government, and the general public.

- **Media relations** focuses on developing media contacts—knowing who in the media might be interested in the organization's story. When you say "public relations," most people immediately think about publicity, which indicates the importance of this media function. The organization initiates publicity and provides pertinent information to the media. A successful relationship between a public relations person and the editor is built on a PR person's reputation for honesty, accuracy, and professionalism. Once this reputation is tarnished or lost, the public relations person cannot function effectively as a liaison between a company and the media.

- **Employee relations** programs communicate information to employees. This function may belong to public relations, although it may also be the responsibility of human resources. A related program is called **internal marketing**, which is communication efforts aimed at informing employees about marketing programs and encouraging their support.

- **Financial relations** includes all the communication efforts aimed at the financial community, such as press releases sent to business publications, meetings with investors and analysts, and the annual report, which the federal government requires of publicly held companies.

- **Corporate relations** programs focus on an organization's image and reputation. The goal is to persuade the public to view the company in a positive light. Public relations expert Fraser Seitel warns in *The Practice of Public Relations,* that "it takes a great deal of time to build a favorable image for a corporation but only one slip to create a negative public impression." He continues, "In other words, the corporate image is a fragile commodity,"[9] as the beleaguered cigarette industry has found out.

TWENTY KEY PUBLICS OF A TYPICAL MULTINATIONAL CORPORATION

Of the twenty key publics of a typical multinational corporation, relationship management programs focus on the media, employees, the financial community, government, and the general public.

Source: Fraser P. Seitel, *The Practice of Public Relations* (Upper Saddle River, NJ: Prentice Hall, 1998), 10.

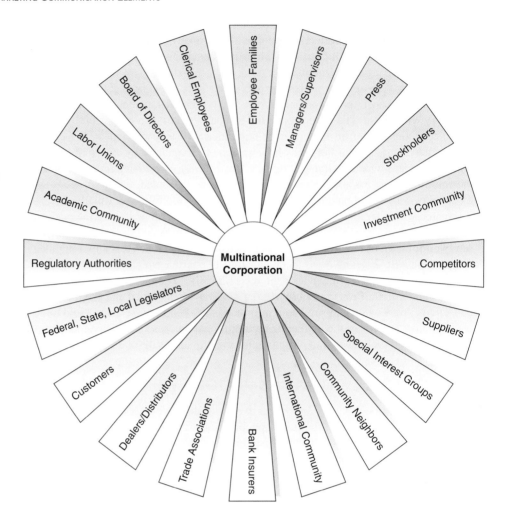

The overriding goal of **reputation** management in a corporate relations program is to strengthen the trust that stakeholders have in an organization. Since corporate reputation is a perception, it is earned through deeds, not created by advertising. In an article on Corporate Reputation Management, marketing consultant Prema Nakra says, "A company's reputation affects its ability to sell products and services, to attract investors, to hire talented staff, and to exert influence in government circles." She concludes that "once lost—or even tarnished—[it is] incredibly difficult to regain."[10]

- **Public affairs** focuses on corporate communication with government and with the public on issues related to government and regulation. For example, a company building a new plant may need to gain the approval of government health and public safety regulators. Public affairs also includes **lobbying**, when the company provides information to legislators in order to get their support and vote on a particular bill. It also includes communication efforts with consumer or activist groups who seek to influence government policies. **Issue management** is another term for this function. In addition to government relations, public affairs programs also monitor public opinion about issues central to the organization's interest and develop programs to communicate to and with the public about these issues.

Other areas of public relations, such as crisis management, marketing public relations, and social marketing, are distinctive because of their focus rather than their target audience.

Crisis Management

There is no greater test for an organization than how it deals with a crisis. The key to **crisis management** is to anticipate the possibility of a disaster and plan how to deal with the bad news and all the affected publics.

For example, Jack-in-the-Box restaurants may never recover from the public relations disaster it faced when a 2-year-old child ate a Kid's Meal from the Jack-in-the-Box restaurant in Tacoma, Washington, and ten days later died of kidney and heart failure. Soon reports came in that over 300 people had been stricken with the same E. coli bacteria responsible for the Tacoma death. Most victims had eaten recently at Jack-in-the-Box outlets in Idaho, Nevada, and Washington. Others apparently got sick after contact with restaurant customers.

The company's 12-person crisis team did some things right: It quickly scrapped nearly 20,000 pounds of hamburger patties prepared at meat plants where the bacteria were suspected of originating. It also changed meat suppliers, installed a toll-free number to field consumer complaints, and instructed employees to turn up the cooking heat to kill the deadly germ. But it took nearly a week for the company to admit publicly its responsibility for the poisonings. Even then, the admission seemed half-hearted. At a Seattle news conference, the company's president attempted to deflect blame, first criticizing state health authorities for not telling his company about new cooking regulations, then pointing a finger at the meat supplier. The damage to the company's reputation has been long-lasting.

An effective crisis plan can help to both avoid crises and ease the damage if one occurs. A plan outlines who contacts the various stakeholders who might be affected (employees, customers, suppliers, civic and community leaders, government agencies), who speaks to the news media, and who sets up and runs an on-site disaster-management center. Companies also should conduct unannounced crisis training during which staff must drop everything and deal with a simulated crisis as it unfolds.

Marketing Public Relations

One area where advertising and public relations overlap is **marketing public relations (MPR)**. Tom Harris, author of *The Marketer's Guide to Public Relations,* says MPR is the fastest-growing area of public relations. He defines MPR as the process of planning and delivering programs that encourage sales and contribute to customer satisfaction by providing communication that addresses the needs and wants of consumers.

MRP is different from a more general public relations approach in its consumer and sales focus. However, the need to establish a credibility platform is similar in both; that's what PR brings to marketing and is PR's greatest strength in an integrated marketing communication program. In other words, MPR supports marketing's product and sales focus by increasing brand credibility and the company's credibility with consumers, which the "A Matter of Principle" box demonstrates.

Social Marketing

Public relations activities designed to increase profits or create a positive company image are an important part of the PR picture, but such efforts are not the only type of public relations, as the Florida "Truth" campaign illustrates. **Social marketing** affects attitudes or behaviors toward some idea or cause, as in the "sexy model" billboard for the "Truth" campaign. Social marketing is also called public communication.

The anti-smoking campaigns are one type of a social marketing effort.

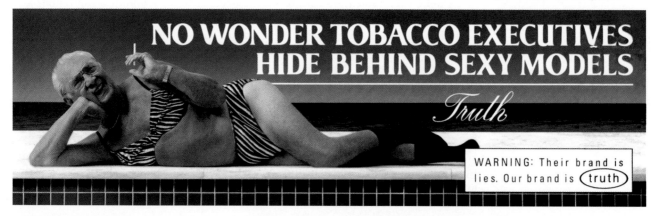

A MATTER OF PRINCIPLE

Target's Guest Card Targets Moms

➤ Selling the idea of a proprietary card (a credit card that is owned by a company and provided to its regular customers, such as a Sears charge card) is not easy for smaller chain companies such as Target. Competitors Kmart and Wal-Mart have bigger customer bases and larger media budgets to support their proprietary cards. Mass merchandisers prefer that their customers use these cards for the revenue they can get from the interest, but also because that lets them build a database of their customers for other types of promotions, such as direct-mail offers.

In order to increase the use of the Target Guest Card by acquiring 100,000 new users, the Martin/Williams agency of Minneapolis had to find a compelling reason for people to shop at Target and use the Target Guest Card.

Target's typical customer is female, aged 25 to 54. Her most important concern is her family. The Martin/Williams agency team proposed a campaign for Target that appealed to family through school education. Target Guest Card users would contribute to local schools under the "Take Charge of Education" theme, a simple fund-raising program for local schools with no labels to collect, no raffle tickets to buy, no fuss at all. Once parents, teachers, or community members enrolled, they would get a Target Guest Card. One percent of the value of the purchases made with the card would go to a qualifying K–12 school of their choice.

The fund-raising program for schools showcased Target's commitment to education, an area of great importance to Target customers. A cleaning supplies tie-in promotion with SC Johnson brands Vanish, Fantastik, Dow Bathroom Cleaner, and Windex also appealed to moms. The "Take Charge of Education" campaign and its various supporting programs built trust among people and demonstrated that Target is a good corporate citizen.

The Target "Take Charge of Education" campaign included a number of other public initiatives such as Arts in Education Grants, Good Neighbor Volunteers, and an environmental club for kids called EarthSavers®, all of which reflect a strong public affairs orientation.

POINT TO PONDER

Why does Target support a program like "Take Charge of Education?" What does the company get out of such a promotional effort?

Shop at Target and you'll also buy a child's education.

The Target Take Charge of Education™ program is part of an ongoing corporate commitment to our nation's children. We donate millions in scholarships to both students and teachers. We've begun a fundraising program that lets you direct 1% of Target purchases made with your Target Guest Card® directly to the school of your choice. And our Arts in Education Grants support organizations that help students appreciate art and music. Call 1-800-316-6142 for more information.

The Target Guest Card is a credit card issued by Retailers National Bank. This bull's-eye design is a registered trademark of Dayton Hudson Corporation.

⊙ TARGET

Source: Information for this case comes from the EFFIE brief provided by Target and Martin/Williams.

Public communication campaigns are undertaken by nonprofit organizations as a conscious effort to influence the thoughts or actions of the public. For example, the Ad Council is a group of advertising agencies, media, and suppliers who donate their services to create ads and campaigns on behalf of some socially important cause. The classic example is the long-running "Smokey the Bear" campaign, with its message about forest fire danger. Some more recent examples are the "Just Say No" anti-drug campaign by the Drug-Free America Council and the anti-smoking campaigns featured in this chapter.

"The Inside Story" explains how to plan a social marketing campaign.

Cause and Mission Marketing Customer attitudes of disrespect, disgust, and distrust toward advertising and marketing create marketplace challenges. If a company wants to increase its integrity among customers, it must prove that it is a good corporate citizen.

THE INSIDE STORY
The Strength of Evidence as a Campaign Asset

Edward Maibach
Worldwide Director of Social Marketing, Porter Novelli

Social marketing campaigns aim high. Increasing awareness and changing beliefs are often necessary steps, but the goal of social marketing is to change people's behavior. Getting people to change their behavior is rarely easy, especially when the size of the target audience is counted in millions or tens of millions rather than single or double digits.

One of the most important assets in a social marketing campaign is the strength of your marketing partners—the other companies, nonprofit groups, and government agencies that will help you achieve your objectives. And to build a strong network of marketing partners you need a strong "evidence base" to shape the campaign's objectives.

Consider the National Youth Anti-Drug Media Campaign, conducted by the Office of National Drug Control Policy (ONDCP). Congress funded this campaign in 1998 to reduce drug use among our nation's youth. At the time, little was certain about how to use an integrated marketing campaign to prevent drug use among adolescents. As a result, in planning the campaign we looked beyond the obvious (but inconclusive) literature on health campaigns and drew on exciting and largely new evidence from the fields of psychology, public health, and prevention research. These findings pointed us—quite unexpectedly—to parents as a key target audience for the campaign.

The "evidence base" we drew from indicated that adolescents who feel close to at least one of their parents are dramatically less likely to use drugs (and less likely to be involved in a variety of other risk behaviors) than are adolescents who do not feel close to a parent. The research literature also showed that parents—even parents of adolescents who were already having trouble—can learn "parenting strategies" that will improve their relationship with their child, and reduce their child's risk of drug use. Teaching parents these "strategies" became a major focus of the campaign.

Taking the campaign in this unexpected yet "evidence-based" direction became an enormous boon to ONDCP in that it attracted a large number of well-positioned marketing partners. These included the National Education Association, National PTA, Urban League, National Fatherhood Initiative, American Academy of Pediatrics, Society of Health Resource Managers, Oxygen Media, 100 Black Men, Hispanic Leadership Institute, and United Native Indian Youth, Inc. These groups and others became active partners in the campaign, adding to ONDCP's campaign resources, reach, and impact with the target audiences.

Ed Maibach holds a Ph.D. in Communication Research from Stanford University and a Master's in Public Health from San Diego State. In 1995 he joined Porter Novelli, a marketing-based public relations agency widely credited with having pioneered the field of social marketing, after having taught social marketing and public health communication at the Emory School of Public Health since 1990.

Nominated by Professor Bill Wells, University of Minnesota.

It can do this by practicing **cause marketing** (adopting a good cause and sponsoring its fund-raising and other community-oriented efforts) and by **mission marketing,** linking a company's underlying business philosophy and core values to a cause that connects with the company's interests.

Cause marketing—"sales promotion with a PR spin"[11]—is what people often think of as a company "doing good things and getting credit for it."[12] For example, American Express has made it possible for its card users to donate money to aid the homeless with each purchase. Carol Cone, president of the Cone agency, develops dramatic programs for her clients based on what Cone calls passion branding, because it links brands to causes that people feel passionately about.[13]

The September 11, 2001 attacks sparked a new interest in charitable giving. For example, the GAP's fall and holiday campaign featured the song "Give a Little Bit" by Supertramp. The GAP gave $100,000 to the New York City firefighters' benefit fund in return for the right to use the song; and it gave roughly $100,000 to the charity chosen by each celebrity who participated in this cause-marketing campaign.

Mission marketing is of a longer duration than cause marketing. Think of Tom's of Maine, Ben & Jerry's, and The Body Shop and their corporate commitment to social and environmental action—the way they design and produce their products, as well as market them.[14] These entire organizations and their stakeholders are committed to the effort. Although we know these cause- and mission-marketing programs affect the support and patronage of people who feel passionate about these causes, the activities are so new that it is difficult to evaluate how well they work to drive sales.[15]

PUBLIC RELATIONS PLANNING

Planning for a public relations campaign is similar to planning an advertising campaign. The plan should complement the marketing and advertising strategies so the organization communicates with one clear voice to its various publics. The plan also identifies the various key publics and the public relations activities that PR people use to address the interests of its various publics. In addition to identifying key targets, public relations plans also specify the objectives that give direction to the PR program or campaign. The campaign described in the "A Matter of Practice" box targeted a small group of high-tech writers, editors, and analysts in order to reposition (the objective) a technology company and its software product.

SWOT Analysis

A PR plan begins with background research leading to a situation analysis, or **SWOT analysis**, that evaluates a company's *strengths, weaknesses, opportunities,* and *threats.* This analysis creates a general understanding of the communication problem, such as the Linux positioning problem that affected Red Hat's business. Understanding the nature of the problem makes it easier to determine the appropriate communication objectives and the target stakeholder audiences, or publics, who will be addressed by the PR efforts.

In public relations planning, the situation can include such critical issues as changes in public opinion, industry and consumer trends, economic trends, governmental regulations and oversight programs, and corporate strategies that affect a company's relationships with stakeholders.

Objectives and Strategies

A variety of objectives guide a PR plan, and the company can use a number of strategies to carry out the plan. Public relations objectives are designed by PR planners to make changes in the public's knowledge, attitudes, and behaviors related to a company, brand, or organization. Usually, these objectives focus on creating credibility, delivering information, and building positive images. As Bettinghaus and Cody[16] explain, the ultimate goal of persuasive communication is to change behavior, and that is a difficult task. Before changing behavior, a PR effort must change people's beliefs, attitudes, and feelings.

Typical public relations objectives include:

- Creating a corporate brand
- Shaping or redefining a corporate reputation
- Positioning or repositioning a company or brand
- Moving a brand to a new market or a global market
- Launching a new product or brand
- Disseminating news about a brand, company, or organization
- Providing product or brand information
- Changing stakeholder attitudes, opinions, or behaviors about a brand or company
- Creating stronger brand relationships with key stakeholders, such as employees, shareholders and the financial community, government, members (for associations), and the media
- Creating high levels of customer (member) satisfaction
- Creating excitement in the marketplace
- Creating buzz (word of mouth)
- Involving people with the brand, company, or organization through events and other participatory activities
- Associating brands and companies with good causes

A MATTER OF PRACTICE
A High-Tech Hat Trick

➤ How do you reposition a high-tech company that few people have heard of—and why would you want to? That was the assignment Red Hat gave to Schwartz Communications, a public relations agency that specializes in handling high-tech clients.

Red Hat is a tiny software company, located in Research Triangle Park in North Carolina, that services the Linux operating system. Red Hat's communication problem is related to the unconventional marketing strategy of Linux, which is open-source software, meaning volunteer programmers create it and give it away free on the Internet. Red Hat makes its money from service and maintenance fees for the system. Linux is also a server software, not desktop software, and there was some confusion about the difference between the two in the minds of Linux's potential users.

Because of its unconventional business platform—giving it away—corporate information technology (IT) decision makers viewed Linux as a weird and risky system created by anti-establishment programmers. Schwartz Communications worked with Red Hat to change the reputation of open-source software with the business press and reposition Linux as a smart, safe choice for corporate operating systems, thus generating more opportunities for Red Hat's services. The idea was that the more companies used Linux, the more business Red Hat would get in servicing it.

Schwartz's media relations program included news releases sent to the business press, online press, and more general print and broadcast media that cover high-tech products and issues. In addition to press releases, the Schwartz team also conducted phone and e-mail briefings with analysts from major high-tech consulting companies, to ensure that the analysts were well-informed and enthusiastic about Linux when the media interviewed them.

Another part of the strategy was to clean up the misperceptions about the Linux product by positioning it as an alternative to Microsoft. By comparing the Linux open-source code to the software giant's operating systems, Schwartz was able to explain what Linux did well and add clout to the Linux image. At the time, the federal government was scrutinizing Microsoft, so its corporate reputation had lost some of its luster, which certainly played to Red Hat's advantage. Another tactic Schwartz used to overturn Red Hat's underground image was to feature Red Hat's media-savvy CEO, Bob Young, as a spokesperson. The team put the likeable leader in the spotlight as much as possible.

The campaign helped support a hugely successful IPO that tripled the value of Red Hat at the same time it provided more visibility in the media. The media relations campaign generated more than 1 billion media impressions. Red Hat's revenue more than doubled over the course of the campaign without a single dollar being spent on advertising.

The company's successful repositioning was obvious a year later, when a Harris Interactive survey ranked Red Hat as 17 on its Top 40 Best Regarded Technology Companies, beating out giants like Yahoo!, amazon.com, and Apple. This success arose because the mystery about Linux disappeared, more companies started using it, and Red Hat, then, had more business. The survey also named Red Hat to the tenth spot on the Top 10 list for Vision and Leadership and won many other awards.

POINT TO PONDER

How did public relations help reposition Red Hat? What was accomplished by this campaign?

Sources: Adapted from "Agency Opens Door for Open Space," *Phillips PR News* (June 12, 2000); "Red Hat Dominates Industry Awards in 2001," (Red Hat Press Release); "Linux in 2002: More Security, High-end Computing," CNN.com (December 27, 2001).

Building brands is an area where public relations, particularly marketing PR, is useful. Advertising builds brand by creating awareness but, as Larry Weber, CEO of Weber Public Relations Worldwide, explained, "what has moved to the center of branding is the relationship with the constituencies,"[17] and PR is particularly useful at building these brand relationships.

Changing the attitudes that drive behavior is central to public relations programs. For example, the objectives for the anti-smoking campaigns discussed in this chapter delivers a change strategy that, according to the Centers for Disease Control and Prevention (CDC), has three steps:

1. Generate awareness
2. Change attitudes
3. Change behaviors

FIGURE 16.2

FTPP CHANGE STRATEGY
The change strategy behind the
"Truth" campaign involved first
increasing youth awareness and
knowledge about tobacco use, then
empowering youth to lead anti-
tobacco efforts that would lead to
changing community norms. The
result would be a reduction in both
youth tobacco use and exposure to
second-hand smoke.
*Source: Youth Tobacco Prevention in
Florida,* a report prepared for the Florida
Department of Health by the University
of Miami (December 15, 1999): 3.

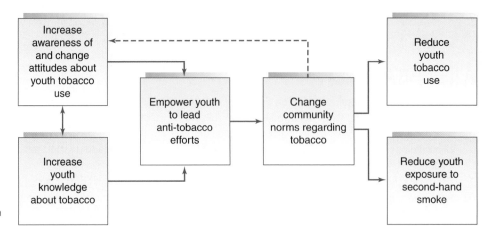

As noted earlier, the last step, changing behaviors, is the most difficult, but these anti-smoking behavior-change campaigns were award winners because they achieved their objective. Figure 16.2 diagrams the change strategy behind the "Truth" campaign, but this diagram describes many change strategies.

Getting people to participate in an action plan is one way to drive behavior change. For example, in the Florida "Truth" campaign SWAT members tore cigarette ads from magazines they read, plastered them with neon-orange "Rejected" stickers, and mailed them back to tobacco company CEOs along with a request to meet with SWAT team members to discuss youth marketing guidelines. Only one company, Brown & Williamson, accepted the invitation, but the campaign was still a highly successful effort because of the SWAT team's passion and the publicity they generated. The smoking rate among Florida teens dropped significantly because of this campaign.

Development Research

Research is used by an organization, the company itself, as well as an outside PR agency, throughout the planning and implementation of a PR plan to determine if the organization is spending its money wisely on the public relations efforts. The Institute for PR has developed a set of measurement standards to help evaluate the effectiveness of public relations. (See, for example, www.instituteforpr.com/measurement_tree.phtml.)

Background research, which is another way of looking at a SWOT or situation analysis, uses primary and secondary information to identify the communication problems that

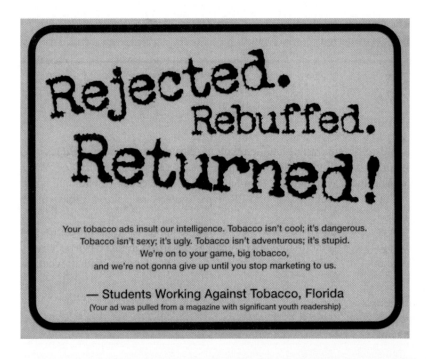

SWAT team members of the "Truth"
campaign sent cigarette ads back to
the ad companies' CEOs adorned
with a neon-orange "Rejected.
Rebuffed. Returned" sticker.

the PR plan needs to address. The PR effort may also begin with a more formal type of background research, called a **communication audit**, as a tool to assess the internal and external PR environment that affects the organization's audiences, objectives, competitors, and past results. An annual audit or a campaign-specific audit can be used to ensure that a program is on track and performing as intended.

Trend-tracking services such as The Intelligence Factory (www.intelligencefactory.com) uncover attitudes and monitor trends important to companies and organizations. Recognizing the significance of public attitudes to its clients, the Porter Novelli public relations agency annually tracks American institutions' credibility. Its survey has consistently found that the credibility of institutions such as government, the media, and corporations is continuing to decline. The agency interpreted these findings to mean that America "is deeply mired in the Age of Cynicism."[18]

Another aspect of the Porter Novelli study investigates consumers' concerns about health, nutrition, and their lifestyles. The company analyzes the findings in terms of seven different personality types, from "Hard-Living Hedonists" (people who smoke, drink, and eat cheeseburgers without even a twinge of guilt) to "Decent Dolittles" (people who pay attention to health issues but can't bring themselves to do much about it). The agency believes such information is useful in identifying people's orientation to health messages.[19] It's also helpful in targeting various types of publics based on their general attitudes toward key issues, such as anti-smoking.

PUBLIC RELATIONS TOOLS

The public relations practitioner has many tools, which we can divide into two categories: controlled media and uncontrolled media. **Controlled media** include house ads, public service announcements, corporate (institutional) advertising, in-house publications, and visual presentations. The sponsoring organizations pay for these media. In turn, the sponsor maintains total control over how and when the message is delivered. **Uncontrolled media** include press releases, press conferences, and media tours. The most recent new media are electronic and they can be categorized as semi-controlled. Corporate Web sites, for example, are controlled by the company, but other Web sites (particularly those that are set up by critics and disgruntled ex-employees) and chat rooms about the company are not controlled.

Likewise, special events and sponsorships are set in place by the company, but participation by the press and other important publics is not under the control of the sponsoring company. Word of mouth, or buzz, is important to PR programs because of the persuasive power of personal conversation. PR programs, particularly the employee communication programs, may be designed to influence what people say about the company, but ultimately the comments are outside the control of the company. Table 16.1 summarizes these tools.

House Ads

A company (or a medium, such as a newspaper, magazine, or broadcast station) may prepare an ad for use in its own publication or programming. Consequently, no money changes hands. For instance, a local television station may run a house ad announcing its new fall programming or a local promotional event within its evening news program; likewise, a company may run an ad advocating a point of view or promoting a special employee benefit program within its corporate magazine. These house ads are often managed by the public relations department.

Public Service Announcements

The ads for charitable and civic organizations that run free of charge on television or radio or in print media are **public service announcements (PSAs)**. The United Way, American Heart Association, and local arts councils all rely on PSAs. These ads are prepared just like commercials, and in many instances ad agencies donate their expertise to design them. They also appear on the Internet.

The Advertising Council is a private, nonprofit organization that creates public service advertising campaigns in the public interest. It has produced almost all the PSAs you see on network television, such as the "Just Say No" anti-drug campaign or the classic "Smokey the Bear" campaign.

The Ad Council creates public service ad campaigns such as these.

TABLE 16.1   **Public Relations Tools**

Controlled Media (company controls the use and placement)	**Uncontrolled Media** (media control the use and placement)
• House ads	• The news release (print, audio, video, e-mail, faxes)
• Public service ads	• Features (pitch letters)
• Corporate or institutional and advocacy advertising	• Fillers, historical pieces, profiles
• Publications: brochures, flyers, magazines, newsletters	• The press conference and media advisory (media kits, fact sheets, background information)
• Annual reports	• Media tours
• Speakers	• Bylined articles, op/ed pieces, letters to the editor
• Photographs	• Talk and interview shows
• Films, videos, CD-ROMs	• Public service announcements
• Displays, exhibits	**Semi-Controlled Media** (some aspects are controlled or initiated by the company, but other aspects aren't)
• Staged events	• Electronic communication (Web sites, chat rooms)
	• Special events and sponsorships
	• Word of mouth (Buzz)

Unfortunately, networks and publishers are flooded with requests to run public service announcements. Many PSAs never air at all or appear during very low-viewing times, which dilutes their effectiveness. Such severe competition has forced nonprofit organizations to better design the PSAs to have more impact or to run them at preferable times as paid commercials.

Studies of PSA effectiveness help guide nonprofit organizations. For instance, a look at PSAs to combat drunk driving, particularly among the college population, found that the usual anti-drunk-driving messages are not as relevant to this audience as they might be. They do not address the students' greatest fear: being pulled over and charged with a DUI. The study also found that a localized PSA, one that mentions or uses a local community angle, is more meaningful to the college-age group.[20]

Corporate Advertising

Corporate advertising promotes a **corporate image** or viewpoint. There is no attempt to sell a particular product. For that reason, the ad may originate in the public relations department rather than the advertising department. Corporate advertising sometimes tells the public about the company's position on some issue. For example, the United Technologies corporate image campaign uses advertising to deliver its corporate philosophy, make a statement about its corporate culture, and build its corporate brand equity. This ad, for example, is a message about corporate culture and employee attitudes.

Corporate identity advertising is another type of advertising that firms use to enhance or maintain their reputation among specific audiences or to establish a level of awareness of the company's name and the nature of its business. Johnson & Johnson targeted its "Healthy Start" institutional campaign at pregnant women to position itself as a concerned company. Companies that have changed their names, such as Nissan (formerly Datsun), have also used corporate identity advertising.

To polish its corporate image, the CIGNA insurance company has attempted to brand an intangible: a caring business philosophy. Edward A. Faruolo, CIGNA marketing communications vice president, stated: "If we could build our brand around the concept of caring, we could not only obtain a highly coveted position in the marketplace, but also earn the trust and loyalty of our customers and our employees."[21]

Sometimes companies deliver point-of-view messages called **advocacy advertising**. Oil companies, for example, will advertise that they support the environment and their extraction procedures do not do any lasting damage to the environment. To combat the anti-smoking campaigns, tobacco companies will run ads that explain their point of view—that they have a right to advertise a legal product.

Brighten Your Corner

Have you noticed the great difference between the people you meet? Some are as sunshiny as a handful of forget-me-nots. Others come on like frozen mackerel. A cheery, comforting nurse can help make a hospital stay bearable. An upbeat secretary makes visitors glad they came to see you. Every corner of the world has its clouds, gripes, complainers, and pains in the neck—because many people have yet to learn that honey works better than vinegar. You're in control of *your* small corner of the world. Brighten it. . . You *can.*

United Technologies used corporate image advertising to construct a corporate image that set it apart from its competitors.

Publications

Organizations may provide employees and other publics with pamphlets, booklets, annual reports, books, bulletins, newsletters, inserts and enclosures, and position papers.

The Securities and Exchange Commission (SEC) requires that each publicly held company publish an **annual report**. You can review annual reports at www.sec.gov. A company's annual report is targeted to investors and may be the single most important document the company distributes. Millions of dollars are spent on the editing and design of annual reports.

Another example of a publication is found in the education part of the Florida "Truth" campaign, which included a book for children in grades 1, 2, and 3 titled *The Berenstain Bear Scouts and the Sinister Smoke Ring.* A companion Student Activity Workbook took the prevention message into an interactive format. For fourth and fifth grade students a jazzy, high-tech "Science, Tobacco and You" program was incorporated into two *Crush It!* magazines, which integrated the anti-smoking message into science, math, language arts, and social studies classes.

Some companies publish material—often called **collateral material**—to support their marketing public relations efforts. Corning Fiberglass Insulation offers a free booklet on home insulation do's and don'ts as an integral part of its promotion effort. The booklet is highlighted in its advertising campaign.

Corporate publication, marketing, and sales promotion departments and their agencies produce training materials and sales kits to support particular campaigns.

Target's Coordinators Kit, for instance, was produced by Target for school representatives to help run the "Take Charge of Education" campaign. Target also used a number of different brochures, such as a series included in a "School Fundraising Made Simple" kit designed to train and support school representatives involved in the "Take Charge of Education" campaign.

Speakers, Photos, and Films

Many companies have a speakers' bureau of articulate people who will talk about topics at the public's request. Apple Computer, Harvard University, and the Children's Hospital in Houston, Texas, all have speakers' bureaus that will speak to local groups and classes.

Target, with the help of its agency, produced these in-house brochures and a "School Fundraising Made Simple" kit to train and support school representatives involved in the "Take Charge of Education" campaign.

Some publics—particularly the news media—may want pictures of people, products, places, and events. That's why PR departments maintain files of photographs that are accurate and well composed. The permissions for ads in this book were provided because they present the advertisers in a positive light. Companies seldom give permission to use ads that authors intend to criticize.

Films, especially videotapes, have become a major public relations tool for a great many companies. Costing $1,000 to $2,000 per minute to make, these videos are not cheap. However, for a company such as Target, mailing videotapes to schools as part of the "Take Charge of Education" announcement package was a worthwhile investment.

Displays, Exhibits, Events, and Tours

Displays, exhibits, tours, and staged events may be important parts of both sales promotion and public relations programs. A model of a new condominium complex, complete with a literature rack that has brochures about the development, is an example of a display. Exhibits tend to be larger than displays; they may have moving parts, sound, or video, and usually are staffed by a company representative. Booth exhibits are important at trade shows, where some companies may take orders for much of their annual sales.

Staged events include open houses, plant tours, and even birthday celebrations. For example, when Barnum's Animal Crackers turned 100, Nabisco invited people to decide what new critters should join the circus of 17 animals in the traditional box. Sidewalk events, which use messages chalked on the sidewalks in major urban areas, often called **guerrilla marketing**, reach customers where they walk. Table 16.2 summarizes some of these MPR activities.

The Florida "Truth" campaign featured a 10-day, 13-city whistle-stop train tour and concert series across the state of Florida. Governor Lawton Chiles rode the train, joining the teen spokespeople, who conducted their own press conferences at every stop. SWAT members trained their peers in advocacy and media relations along the way, empowering teens throughout the state to join in the movement's rebellion against the tobacco industry.

The use of fancier staged events has seen the most growth. Corporate sponsorship of various sporting events has evolved into a favorite public relations tactic. For example, *Sports Illustrated* magazine developed an elaborate events strategy to attract new advertisers. The centerpiece of that strategy is the Sports Festival, a 70,000-square-foot exhibition that tours Time Warner's Six Flags theme parks during the summers, spending 10 days at each park. The exhibition includes interactive games that allow participants to slam-dunk a basketball or race against Carl Lewis.

News Releases

Moving away from controlled messages, consider the **news release**, the primary medium used to deliver public relations messages to the various external media. Although the company distributing the news release controls its original form and content, the media decide

TABLE 16.2 **Marketing Public Relations Tours and Events**

Client	Agency	Event or Tour
Best Buy	Momentum Marketing	Uniformed Best Buy teams hit streets with branded CD samplers and store coupons; 30,000 people received tickets for a Sting concert in Central Park sponsored by Best Buy.
Intimo (men's underwear)	The Bromley Group	A "Thong-a-Thon" run featured some 10 guys in Intimo black thong underwear and a black Intimo running bib on a route through New York streets.
Häagen-Dazs Gelato	Aronow & Pollock	Three Italian chefs compete in an ice cream scoop-off; winner gets a $25,000 charity donation in his/her name; onlookers get to sample gelato.
Hasbro Shoezies (tiny shoes)	Alliance	A brand-wrapped van tours malls and teen hangouts; 20 girls in Shoezies gear dance and hand out samples of the tiny collectibles.
Levi Strauss & Co.	TBWA Chiat/Day	Old UPS trucks painted in Levi's colors, with mock college dorm rooms inside, toured raves, clubs, and other youth hangouts; and sold jeans from the truck.

what to present and how to present it. What the public finally sees, then, is not necessarily what the originating company had in mind, and so this form of publicity is uncontrolled by the originating company. The decision to use any part of a news release at all is based on an editor's judgment of its news value. Figure 16.3 illustrates how product categories rank in terms of news value to editors.

News releases must be written differently for each medium, accommodating space and time limitations. The more carefully the news release is planned and written, the better the chance it has of being accepted and published as written. Note the tight and simple writing style in the news release from the Florida "Truth" campaign.

The news release is usually delivered by a company that specializes in distribution, such as the U.S. Newswire. Originally sent by mail or delivery services, news releases are now distributed electronically through satellite and Web-based networks. PR Newswire, U.S. Newswire, and BusinessWire are services that provide targeted distribution to special interest media outlets or handle mass distribution of news releases, photos, graphics, video, audio, and other materials.

Video news releases (VNRs) contain video footage for a television newscast. They are effective because they show target audiences the message in two different video environments: first as part of a news report and then reused later in an advertisement. Of course, there is no guarantee that a VNR will be used. One study found that VNRs aired in the Miami market had high visual quality and simple stories.[22]

Press Conferences

A **press conference**—when a company spokesperson makes a statement to media representatives—is one of the riskiest public relations activities because the media may not see the company's announcement as being real news. Some companies have successfully introduced new products, such as Gillette's Sensor, Sensor for Women, and, more

High News Value	Low News Value
Computers Cars Entertainment	Beer Soft Drinks Athletic Shoes
A	**C**
B	**D**
Soup Cereal Aspirin	Cigarettes Car Mufflers Cookies

A High news value
B Less interesting than A, but still considered to have a high news value
C Low news value
D Lower interest value than C

FIGURE 16.3

MEDIA ASSESSMENT OF NEWS VALUE OF SELECTED PRODUCT CATEGORIES This figure shows how product categories rank in terms of news value to editors.
Source: Adapted from Thomas L. Harris, *The Marketer's Guide to Public Relations* (New York: Wiley, 1993), 58.

For Immediate Release   Contact: Carlea Bauman
February 12, 1999   850-488-5959
                                                                                                  Damien Filer
                                                                                              850-488-6809

Florida Teens Preparing Tobacco Industry Attack
at Second Annual Teen Tobacco Summit

(Tarpon Springs, FL) - More than 1,000 teenagers representing Florida's 67 counties will gather here at the second annual Teen Tobacco Summit, February 25 – 28, 1999. Their mission: Defending their generation from a lame addiction that kills.

Last year, 600 teenagers gathered in central Florida for the inaugural Summit. There, youth brainstormed on how to reach their peers with an effective anti-tobacco message. From that meeting, the "Truth" campaign and its activist organization, Students Working Against Tobacco (SWAT), were born. The goals for this year's Summit are just as ambitious.

"We've got a lot of strong momentum going against Big Tobacco," said SWAT Chairwoman Chrissie Scelsi, 17. "But we aren't through. The tobacco industry knows it is about to lose a lot of customers. They're going to turn up the heat on us. We have to be ready."

SWAT's teen leaders will lead the Summit. Participants will hold rallies, review SWAT's plans for the coming year and attend sessions on how to become more powerful advocates. The teens will be developing new advertising to publicize SWAT's role in the anti-tobacco movement. The heart of the counter-marketing effort, the "Truth" campaign, has already enjoyed remarkable success to date. In a survey taken six months after the launch of "Truth," more than 90 percent of Florida teens could identify at least one aspect of the campaign. What's more, teen attitudes about tobacco are already changing.

Additional sessions will give teens a chance to talk with professional athletes and coaches about how tobacco can make an athlete lose his or her edge. Other sessions will provide participants with the latest information on tobacco possession laws, cessation programs and the dangers of second-hand smoke. (See attached session descriptions and timelines for more detailed information.)

"The goal of the Summit is to inform and empower," said Susan Medina, a SWAT leader who has appeared in some of the "truth" commercials. "There is nothing more threatening to Big Tobacco than a teen who is armed with the truth and is feeling pretty mad about being lied to for so long."

While the Summit schedule includes serious activities, the weekend won't be all work for the teens.

- The opening session on Thursday, February 25th will focus on SWAT's project. "Reel Truth," which began during last summer's Truth Train. "Reel Truth" took the entertainment industry to task for irresponsibly depicting tobacco use in films and on television. Antonio Sabato, Jr., star of *Melrose Place* and *General Hospital,* will be on hand for a panel discussion on the issue and other celebrities, such as Leeza Gibbons, will send video-taped messages of support for the teens. Folk rock singer Leslie Nuchow, who received national attention for rejecting a Virginia Slims sponsorship offer, will also perform during the opening session.
- The teens will learn leadership and teamwork by tackling a ropes/obstacle course. As the teens face these challenges, they will gain the confidence, strength and leadership skills necessary to win the fight against Big Tobacco.
- On Saturday night, February 27th, teen participants will be treated to a live concert by the number one R & B band, Divine, who will perform their hit single, "Lately."

Several of the state's VIPs will also attend the Summit. Lt. Governor Frank Brogan will address the teens at breakfast and Secretary of Health, Robert G. Brooks, M.D., at lunch on Friday, February 26th. Following lunch, Secretary Brooks will tour the teen training sessions. Education Commissioner Tom Gallagher and Secretary of State Katherine Harris will be on hand for the closing ceremonies Sunday, February 28th. Also on Sunday, Ed Chiles, youngest son of the late Governor and Mrs. Chiles, will be on hand to announce the winners of the Lawton Chiles Youth Advocate of the Year Awards. The recipients, chosen for their anti-tobacco efforts, will receive scholarships to any public Florida university of their choosing. The scholarship is funded by the Lawton Chiles Foundation.

Foreign and national anti-tobacco experts will also be in attendance. Says Peter Mitchell, Acting Director of the Florida Tobacco Pilot Program: "As the 'Truth' campaign and SWAT become a bigger force in the tobacco war, more people want to study us; to see what works and why." Among the experts attending will be Bill Novelli, President of the Campaign for Tobacco Free Kids.

The Teen Tobacco Summit 2 is funded by the Florida Tobacco Pilot Program, which was created by the state's historic settlement with the tobacco industry in 1997.

For up to the minute information on Teen Tobacco Summit 2, check out our web site at www.state.fl.us/tobacco.

This is a typical news release. It has the
release information in the upper left
corner and contact information in the
upper right. A headline summarizes
the point of the news release.

recently, the Mach III, through press conferences and other publicity events, and then followed up the launch news events with an advertising campaign. Companies worry about whether the press will show up for a press conference. Will they ask the right questions, or will they ask questions the company cannot or does not want to answer?

To anticipate some of these problems, companies may issue a **media kit**, usually a folder that provides all the important background information to members of the press, either before or when they arrive at the press conference. The risk in offering media kits (also called press kits) is that they give reporters all the necessary information so that the press conference itself becomes unnecessary. The SWAT "Truth Tour" featured a "Watch Out" media kit, which the media found useful because it provided a more detailed explanation of the anti-smoking campaign and its events.

A **media tour**, like the Florida SWAT team whistle-stop tour, is a press conference on wheels. The traveling spokesperson makes announcements and speeches, holds press conferences to explain a promotional effort, and offers interviews.

Online Communication

The new electronic media are making the biggest change in the communication landscape. E-mail, **intranets** (which connect people within an organization), **extranets** (which connect people in one business with its business partners), Internet advertising, and Web sites have opened up avenues for public relations activities.

External Communication "The World Wide Web can be considered the first public relations mass medium in that it allows managed communication directly between organizations and audiences without the gatekeeping function of other mass media."[23] The Florida "Truth" campaign developed a Web site (www.wholetruth.com) based on ideas from the Teen Tobacco Summit. The site contains facts and statistics on cigarettes and chewing tobacco, as well as information on how to join SWAT teams. It also provides updates on the program's activities.

PR practitioner and author Fraser Seitel says, "No other area of public relations is 'hotter' in the new millennium than the development of Web sites, Internet operations, and the general harnessing of the Web to communicate with target publics."[24] Even the distribution of press releases is moving online, as well as pitching editors with story ideas. Ragan Communications, publisher of *Interactive Public Relations,* lists some tips for getting reporters and editors to read e-mail pitch letters.[25] (See the Practical Tips box.)

Practical Tips #1

HOW TO WRITE E-MAIL PITCH LETTERS

1. Never list all recipients in the "To:" line. No one wants to see all the reporters who received the pitch, since these story ideas are supposed to be made available to the medium on an exclusive basis—in other words, no other medium will be offered that story.
2. Avoid attachments. They take time to open and to read, and busy reporters often dismiss them. They can also carry viruses.
3. Keep your pitches less than a page in length. The first paragraph should capture the who, what, and why of the story.
4. Help reporters do their jobs. Some reporters won't rewrite a news release because they want to write the story their own way. For those reporters, provide them with a great story idea, including visuals and other resources, and with contacts, so they can round out the story.
5. Make it personal. Use their first names and mention the publication name.
6. Keep subject-line headers to fewer than four or five words. The header should be clear and to the point; don't waste the space running the term "press release" itself.
7. Never follow up an e-mail pitch by asking, "Did you get it?" Instead, call to ask reporters if they need more information and call within an hour (things move quickly in the online world).

Corporate Web sites have become an important part of corporate communication. These sites can present information about the company and open up avenues for stakeholders to contact the company. One study noted that the interactive dimension is particularly important: "If you built a highly interactive and informative Web site, then you can capitalize on building brand and corporate image through longer and more intense exposures than any other type of campaign." The study also found that interactivity—being able to contact the company—is more important than the actual information.[26]

Internal Communication E-mail is a great way for people in separate sites to communicate. You can get a fast reply if people on the other end are checking their mail regularly. It is also an inexpensive form of internal communication.

Internal company e-mail may have its public relations downside, however. It can be used in court. Some of the most damaging evidence the federal government presented against Microsoft in its antitrust suit came from e-mail messages exchanged within the company.[27]

Internal company networks do have great benefits. Internal company networks, such as intranets and corporate portals (an extensive collection of databases and links that are important to people working in a company), encourage communication among employees in general and permit them to share company databases, such as customer records and client information. Some companies urge employees to set up personal home pages as part of the company portal, which allows them to customize the material they receive and set up their own links to crucial corporate information such as competitor news, product information, case histories, and so forth.[28]

Web Challenges The Internet presents at least as many challenges to public relations professionals as it does opportunities.[29] On the one hand, the Internet makes it possible to present the company's image and story without going through the editing of a gatekeeper. On the other hand, it is much harder to control what is said about the company on the Internet. According to Parry Aftab, a lawyer specializing in computer-related issues, "It used to be that you could control the information because you'd have one spokesman who represented the company. Now where you have thousands of employees who have access to an e-mail site, you have thousands of spokesmen."[30] All employees have "an inside view" of their company, whether sanctioned by the PR department or not. Every employee becomes a spokesperson.

Gossip and rumors can spread around the world within hours. Angry customers and disgruntled former employees know this and have used the Internet to voice their complaints. A number of these people have set up Web sites such as the Official Internet AntiNike Web site; alt.destroy.microsft; I Hate McDonald's; ToysRUs Sucks, GTE Sucks; Why America Online Sucks; Packard Bell Is Evil; and BallySucks. As a defense against this negative press, some companies are registering domain names that might cause them trouble. For example, Chase Manhattan owns IHateChase.com, ChaseStinks.com, and ChaseSucks.com.

Some companies monitor the Internet to see what is being said about them so they can respond to protect their reputations. More than 600 companies have hired eWatch, a firm that provides Web-monitoring services, to collect such information.

Another thorny issue is whether a company's Internet presence is primarily a responsibility of the management information services or information technology (IT) departments, or a tool for communication managed through public relations. In a survey of the top 50 U.S. companies, the *PR Reporter* found that the responses suggest that MIS and IT personnel are setting the rules for management of communication in this realm. Building relationships isn't the main concern of IT people in managing their Web sites.[31]

For companies that do use their Internet sites as a public relations communication tool, another debate focuses on whether the company site is to be primarily an advertising medium, a direct-marketing medium, the key to a corporate identity, or a public relations tool. Paul Holmes, editor of *Inside PR* says, "We believe the Internet is primarily about those things public relations does well: dialogue rather than monologue; education rather than promotion; relationship-building rather than transaction; all a company's audiences rather than its customers only. But a quick survey of the firm's clients reveals that PR is not currently winning this battle."[32]

EFFECTIVENESS AND EXCELLENCE

As in advertising, public relations evaluation is based on setting measurable objectives in the beginning of the planning. Objectives that specify the impact the program seeks to have on the various publics can be evaluated by the PR manager if they contain benchmarks and target levels. Figure 16.4 illustrates how research company Delahaye Medialink evaluates the effectiveness of public relations programs' controlled, semi-controlled, and uncontrolled messages (www.delahayemedialink.com). The model identifies exposure, awareness, and understanding (which leads to behavior change) as categories of effects that need to be measured in an evaluation program.

Output and Outcome Evaluation

Public relations practitioners must track the impact of a campaign in terms of output (how many news releases lead to stories or mentions in news stories) and outcome (attitude or behavior change). Such tracking is done to prove the effectiveness of the PR program, and so that they learn from their efforts and fine-tune future campaigns. To get a comprehensive picture of PR's impact, practitioners evaluate process (what goes out) and outcome (effect on the target audience).

Process evaluation examines the success of the public relations program in getting the message out to the target audiences by asking such questions as: How many placements (news releases that ran in the media) did we get? How many articles were published? How many times did our spokesperson appear on talk shows? How much airplay did our public service announcements receive? The Burrelle's ad describes the difficulty of tracking such

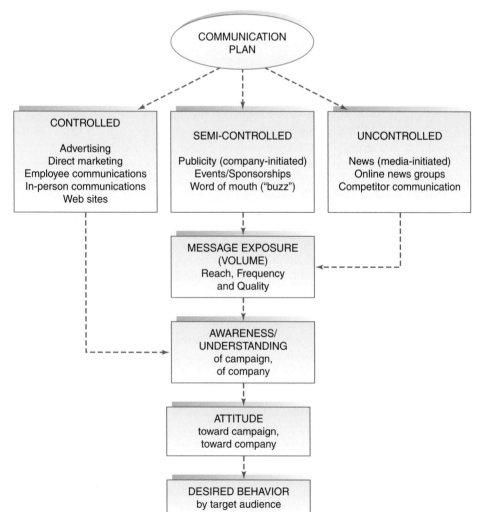

FIGURE 16.4

THE DELAHAYE MEDIALINK MODEL OF PUBLIC RELATIONS EVALUATION
Research company Delahaye Medialink uses this model to evaluate the effectiveness of PR programs.
Source: Adapted from Delahaye Medialink New Business Kit, Portsmouth, NH (www.delahayemedialink.com).

publicity and offers its services as an outside company (www.burrelles.com) that specializes in tracking and monitoring press coverage. The "Truth" campaign was deemed successful because it resulted in more than 590,476,000 "impressions"—the number of times a person in the target audience is reached by one or more of the messages. In this case, the target audience was teens, parents and influencers (teachers, role models).

The outcome evaluation considers such questions as: Has there been a change in audience knowledge, attitudes, or behavior (as measured in the pretesting and posttesting)? Can we associate behavior change (for example, product trial, repeat purchase, voting, or joining) with the public relations effort? The "Truth" campaign was effective because it touched the minds and hearts of a generation of Florida youth. One objective of the Florida "Truth" campaign, for example, was to involve teenagers and their community leaders in the tobacco rebellion. The campaign attracted 8,209 people to join the SWAT team and 10,503 Community Partnership people who supported them.

The "Practical Tips" box summarizes the most common measures of output and outcomes in public relations.

Let's look at some measures of the Florida "Truth" campaign. Only nine months after the campaign began, it had achieved a 92 percent awareness level among Florida teens. Research by the University of Florida and Florida Research Institute also found that youth tobacco attitudes where shifting to align with the campaign's message.

- Anti-tobacco attitudes among Florida youth under age 16 increased from 59 percent to 64 percent between 1998 and 1999. (During this same time, anti-tobacco attitudes among the nation's youth actually decreased.) A sample statement the studies used in their investigation: "Smoking has nothing to do with whether or not a person is cool."
- Forty-eight percent of nonsmoking but "susceptible" youth said that the anti-tobacco TV ads were important in their decision not to smoke, and 56 percent said their reason for not smoking was their learning that the tobacco industry was manipulating youth, a main message of the "Truth" campaign.

Practical Tips #2

HOW TO MEASURE PR EFFECTIVENESS

The following are common types of evaluation measures used in public relations:

- *Output Production.* Number of PR products, such as news releases or brochures, generated.
- *Distribution.* Number of media outlets (TV stations, newspapers) receiving PR products.
- *Coverage.* Number and size of clips, column inches, seconds, or minutes of time or space.
- *Impressions.* Media placements multiplied by circulation or broadcast reach.
- *Advertising value.* Equivalent ad costs for time or space.
- *Systematic Content Analysis.* Positive or valence (whether the story or mention seems to be more positive or negative), key messages (the idea in the story), sources, and prominence.

Outcome Objectives achieved:

- *Awareness.* Aided and unaided recall the target audience.
- *Attitudes.* Perceptions, preferences, and preference or intent to buy.
- *Behavior.* Did they do what you wanted them to do?

How was the campaign's critical behavioral success measured? In 1998, before the "Truth" campaign began, the state of Florida surveyed 11,865 middle school students and 10,675 high school students in 250 schools to determine a baseline of cigarette use. A follow-up survey a year later with students in 242 of the original schools found that cigarette use declined from 18.5 percent to 15 percent for middle school students and from 27.4 percent to 25.2 percent among high school students.

In addition to this important behavioral measure, a five-year follow-up study by Florida International University tracked students in grades four through seven. This survey found a connection between students' exposure to the "Truth" campaign and subsequent behavior change.

Relationship Evaluation

Relationship management has become another area where PR must focus its research efforts. In a study of PR practitioners and organization heads, PR expert Linda Hon found that managing relations and earning respect for the organization were two major variables in the evaluation of PR's effectiveness.[33]

Harvard professor Charles J. Fombrun recommends conducting a relationship audit.[34] He observes that most companies deal with their publics in a fragmented manner. A relationship audit would determine the state of affairs not only for employees and the general public, but also for customers, investors, the local community, government agencies, and the media. This type of audit tracks a company's interactions with all its various stakeholders. Fombrun predicts that an organization's stock price—its reputational capital—could be at least 20 percent higher if it managed its relationship portfolios the way investors manage their stock portfolios.

Excellence in Public Relations

Another aspect of PR evaluation was showcased in Professor James Grunig's mammoth study of excellence in PR, sponsored by the International Association of Business Communicators (IABC).[35] The study concluded that there are 14 factors of excellent PR, grouped into four categories: program level, departmental level, organizational level, and effects of excellent public relations. As an example of how Grunig's factors can be used, one study used the fourteen factors to investigate the forest industry. It found that based on these factors, the major companies investigated were making great efforts to identify and communicate effectively with their publics.[36]

IT'S A WRAP
DOES COUNTERMARKETING WORK?

Public communication campaigns are a way to change public opinion as well as discourage socially harmful behaviors. But can they work to counter advertising by one of the world's largest industries that spends billions promoting its product?

One of the best examples of successful countermarketing comes from California, where a confrontational anti-tobacco campaign that began in 1990 reduced sales of cigarettes by 232 million packs. In that state, 34.3 percent of smokers, about 200,000 people, said that tobacco-control advertisements influenced them to quit. Cigarette consumption in the state has dropped 38 percent since 1988, twice the national average.

Is it possible to challenge—and succeed in changing—the tendency of teens drawn to smoking as a way to rebel, to challenge authority, to take risks, and to assert control of their own behavior? As we mentioned in the opening story, the Florida "Truth" campaign produced the largest single-year decline in teen smoking in 20 years. Not only was the campaign successful in changing teen attitudes and behavior, it also won a number of awards for Porter Novelli, including the 2000 Gold CIPRA (Creativity in Public Relations Award) and the Silver Anvil Award of Excellence from the Public Relations Society of America (PRSA), among many others.

The national "Truth" campaign by the Arnold agency achieved its goal of creating a high level of national awareness, reaching 78 percent in six months. Because the EFFIE brief was written only six months after the national launch, behavioral data were not available. However, 86 percent of the intended audience sees the campaign as attention-getting, and 80 percent say it gives good reasons not to smoke. In comparison, the Florida "Truth" campaign was rated as convincing and believable by 88 percent of the audience; tobacco giant Phillip Morris's "Think, Don't Smoke" effort received only a 70 percent rating. Campaigns such as these were effective, particularly with their youth market targets, because they were able to change attitudes and behaviors.

Summary

1. **Explain what public relations is and how it differs from advertising.** Public relations is a management function that communicates to and with various publics to manage an organization's image and reputation. Advertising focuses on enhancing brand value and creating the awareness and motivation that deliver sales.

2. **Identify the most common types of public relations programs.** In addition to the key areas of government, media, employee, and investor relations, PR programs also include marketing public relations (MPR), corporate relations and reputation management, crisis management, and nonprofit public relations.

3. **Describe the key decisions in public relations planning.** Planning for a public relations campaign begins with a SWOT, or situation, analysis that is used as backgrounding for the development of objectives and strategies. Research is

needed when planning a PR program and evaluating its effectiveness.

4. **Explain the most common types of public relations tools.** Uncontrolled media tools include the news story that results from a news release or news conference. Controlled media are tools that the company uses to originate and control content. Semi-controlled tools are controlled in that the company is able to initiate the use of the tool, but also uncontrolled in that the content is contributed by others.

5. **Discuss the importance of measuring the results of public relations efforts.** Public relations evaluation usually focuses on outputs and outcomes and may include relationship management and excellence. The evaluation effort is made to determine how well a PR program meets its objectives.

Key Terms

advocacy advertising, p. 468

annual report, p. 469

cause marketing, p. 463

collateral materials, p. 469

communication audit, p. 467

controlled media, p. 467

corporate advertising, p. 468

corporate image, p. 468

corporate relations, p. 459

crisis management, p. 460

employee relations, p. 459

extranets, p. 473

Questions

1. How does the practice of public relations differ from the practice of advertising?

2. Why is public opinion so important to the success of public relations?

3. What is reputation management, and how does it intersect with advertising programs?

4. Dynacon Industries is a major supplier of packaging containers for industrial and food-service companies. Its research labs have developed a foam-polymer container with revolutionary environmental characteristics. The public relations department learns that the trade and consumer press is unwilling to give the product the coverage the company needs. Public relations proposes that paid space (news and trade magazines) be used. The message will feature product background and the story about the environmental implications. Public relations argues that half the media and creative costs come from the advertising budget. If you were in charge of these budgets, what would you recommend?

5. Wendy Johnson and Phil Draper are having a friendly disagreement before class. Wendy claims that she is not interested in advertising as a career because she dislikes the "crass commercialism" of promoting products and services that many people don't need. Phil counters by saying that public relations is doing the same thing by "selling ideas and images," and its motives are usually just as money-centered as those of advertising. If you overheard this discussion, would you take Wendy's or Phil's side? Could you offer advice on ethical considerations for both careers?

6. Suppose you belong to a campus group planning a special weekend event on campus to raise public support and funds for a local charity. This will cost your organization time and money. Although contributions at the event will be some measure of the effectiveness of your public relations program, what other steps could you take to evaluate your success?

Suggested Class Projects

1. Working in a team, locate library materials on two organizational crises: one whose outcome was positive and the other negative. Do a short (two- to three-page) report explaining the reasons for these outcomes. Be prepared to present your findings to the class.

2. Divide the class into groups of three to four people. Each group should adopt a local cause that operates on a low budget and needs public relations help. As a team, develop a public relations plan for that nonprofit organization.

Suggested Internet Class Project

Consult the three anti-smoking Web sites mentioned in the effectiveness stories in this chapter and compare them in terms of their appeal to a teen audience. Which one do you think is the most interesting to this age group? Which one is the least interesting? Compile the best ideas from all of them and write a report to your instructor on why their ideas are good and what else a Web site can do to reach a teen market.

www.wholetruth.com
www.thetruth.com
www.Questionit.com

Hallmark BUILD•A•CAMPAIGN*Projects*

Please review the Hallmark Case Appendix at the end of the text before responding to these questions.

1. In small groups, discuss how Capitol Advertising used public relations to extend the Hallmark advertising budget and meet objectives.

2. How can your local Gold Crown store build on Hallmark's brand image to garner positive publicity and loyalty? Develop a public relations plan for your local Gold Crown store.

HANDS-ON   Case 16

"WHOSE SIDE ARE YOU ON?"

The Advertising Council is a nonprofit group that creates public service advertising with funding provided by some of America's biggest corporations. Some of the Ad Council's slogans have become ingrained in America's consciousness, including "Friends Don't Let Friends Drive Drunk," "Only You Can Prevent Forest Fires," and "A Mind Is a Terrible Thing to Waste."

After advertising legend Alex Kroll resigned as chairperson of the Young & Rubicam advertising agency, he became director of the Ad Council. There he created what is sure to be his legacy: an advertising campaign designed to create awareness of and support for urban parents who are struggling to raise children in tough neighborhoods.

The slogan for the campaign was "Whose Side Are You On?" The campaign's tone was shaped by focus-group research that revealed the belief among the general public that irresponsible parents were contributing to the plight of urban kids. After hearing comments such as "What's wrong with parents who let this happen? I would never let this happen!" researchers were convinced that the campaign would only work if it helped viewers see past their stereotyped attitudes about urban parents. But the researchers also wanted viewers to empathize and identify with urban parents, who were doing their best under difficult circumstances. In fact, that empathy did materialize in the focus group when researchers read the following statement: "We hear a lot of news about welfare cheats, but what the news doesn't cover is all the millions of parents and kids who are struggling hard, often under circumstances that are so difficult they would wear down the best of us." As Kroll commented, "When [focus group participants] hear of these stories of people trying to help themselves, it's like the ice block melts."

Tom Shortlidge of Young & Rubicam helped create the first group of spots. Actual neighborhood residents appear in the ads rather than professional actors, and universal images of caring parents were used, such as a mother looking through a screen door to check on her children. As Shortlidge explained, "We were trying to make these cases all somebody's neighbor, and, as a result, have you feel for these people." To break stereotypes, one spot featured former gang members who had joined together in a neighborhood patrol group called "Mad Dads."

Kroll has committed the Ad Council to supporting the campaign for 10 years, an unusually long time in the world of public service announcements. In addition to television and print ads, a Web site on the Internet and a toll-free telephone number are sources of further information and practical, specific suggestions for activities supporting children. The council supplies its ads to the media, which air or print them free when time or space is available.

The Ad Council's efforts to focus on children are paying off. A massive study on children and families, initiated by the Ad Council and sponsored by the Ronald McDonald House, shows the majority of American adults now think our number-one national priority ought to be getting kids off to the right start. And 75 percent say the gravest threat to our national security is the plight and problems of children. Kroll concludes, "What's at stake is the future of a lot of innocent kids. We're talking about the future of America." ■

IT'S YOUR TURN

1. Why do AT&T and other companies support the Ad Council?
2. If you worked for the Ad Council, how would you extend the impact of this campaign? What other media, marketing communication tools, and PR tie-in programs would you suggest? Are there other corporate partners who might be enlisted?

Sources: "What Can We Do about Kids Today? Keep the Focus of Public Service Advertising on Helping Kids Get a Good Start," *Advertising Age* (April 27, 1998): 42; "The 'Whose Side Are You On?' Ad Campaign," *Nightline* video (August 19, 1996); Joseph Hanania, "Campaigning to Give All Kids a Fair Chance," *Los Angeles Times* (December 3, 1996): F5.

Notes

1. www.prsa.org/pressroom/aboutpr.html.

2. Doug Newsom, Alan Scott, and Judy Van Slyke Turk, *This Is PR: The Realities of Public Relations,* 4th ed. (Belmont, CA: Wadsworth, 1989), 99.

3. Martin Sorrell, "Assessing the State of Public Relations," *The Strategist* 3(4) (Winter 1998): 48.

4. Thomas L. Harris, *Value-Added Public Relations: The Secret Weapon of Integrated Marketing* (Lincolnwood, IL: NTC Business Books, 1998), flyleaf.

5. "AT&T with Delahaye Medialink—Understand How News Coverage and Advertising Interact," *PRWEEK* (February 21, 2000).

6. Kirk Hallahan, *"No, Virginia, It's Not True What They Say about Publicity's 'Implied Third-Party Endorsement' Effect,"* Association for Education in Journalism and Mass Communication Annual Conference (August 1998, Baltimore, MD): 13.

7. Harris, op. cit.

8. John A. Ledingham and Stephen D. Bruning, "Relationship Management in Public Relations: Dimensions of an Organization–Public Relationship," *Public Relations Review* 24(1) (1998): 55–65; Sandra Moriarty, "IMC Needs PR's Stakeholder Focus," *AMA Marketing News* (May 26, 1997): 7.

9. Fraser P. Seitel, *The Practice of Public Relations* (Upper Saddle River, NJ: Prentice Hall, 1998), 58.

10. Prema Nakra, "Corporate Reputation Management: 'CRM' with a Strategic Twist?" *Public Relations Quarterly* 45(2) (Summer 2000): 35.

11. Tom Duncan and Sandra Moriarty, *Driving Brand Value: Using Integrated Marketing to Manage Profitable Stakeholder Relationships* (New York: McGraw-Hill, 1997), 137.

12. John A. Koten, "The Strategic Uses of Corporate Philanthropy," in *The Handbook of Strategic Public Relations and Integrated Communications,* Clarke L. Caywood, ed. (New York: McGraw-Hill, 1997), 149.

13. "1999 Midsize Agency of the Year: Cone," *Inside PR* (Winter 1999): 11.

14. Duncan and Moriarty, 126–147.

15. Cynthia R. Morton, "Consciousness-Raising Advertising: Issue Promotion, Brand Building, or a Combination of Both?" in *The Proceedings of the American Academy of Advertising Conference,* Darrel D. Muehling, ed. (Lexington, KY, 1998), 233–240.

16. Erwin Bettinghaus and Michael Cody, *Persuasive Communication,* 5th ed. (Fort Worth, TX: Harcourt Brace, 1994), 7.

17. Schrage: 26.

18. "Survey Highlights 'Age of Cynicism' but Finds Most Keep an Open Mind," *Inside PR* (July 15, 1996): 1, 3.

19. "Porter Novelli Research Seeks to Identify Health Styles," *Inside PR* (March 11, 1996): 8.

20. Alyse R. Gotthoffer, "Exploring the Relevance of Localization in Anti-Drinking and Driving PSAs," in *The Proceedings of the American Academy of Advertising Conference,* Darrel D. Muehling, ed. (Lexington, KY, 1998), 214.

21. Edward A. Faruolo, "A Business of Caring," *The Advertiser* (October 1998): 36–40.

22. Anne R. Owen, "Avant-Garde or Passé: Using Video News Releases Internationally," in *The Proceedings of the American Academy of Advertising Conference,* Carole M. Macklin, ed. (St. Louis, 1997), 290.

23. Candace White and Niranjan Raman, "The World Wide Web as a Public Relations Medium," Association for Education in Journalism and Mass Communication Annual Conference, Baltimore, MD, August 1998.

24. Seitel, *The Practice of Public Relations,* 223–224.

25. "Seven Tips for Getting Your E-mail Pitches Read," direct mailing from Ragan Communications, September 2000.

26. Michelle O'Malley and Tracy Irani, "Public Relations and the Web: Measuring the Effect of Interactivity, Information, and Access to Information in Web Sites," AEJMC Conference, Baltimore, MD, August 1998.

27. Matt Richtel, "Companies Get Candid Criticism from Online Employee Forums," *New York Times* (September 7, 1998); retrieved online at www.nytimes.com/library/tech/98/09/biztech/articles/07tech.html.

28. "Is a Corporate Portal in Your Future?" *Ragan's Intranet Reports* 6:6 (June 2001): 1–2.

29. Robert Gustafson, "Merging the Teaching of Public Relations and Advertising onto the Information Superhighway," *Public Relations Quarterly* 2 (1996): 1–7.

30. Michael Markowitz, "Fighting Cyber Sabotage," *Bergen Record* (October 4, 1998); retrieved online at www.bergen.com/biz/online04199810041.htm.

31. Paul A. Holmes, "Going Unarmed into a Battle for Corporate Image," *Inside PR* (September 8, 1996): 2; "The Battle between MIS and PR for Internet Control," *Inside PR* (July 28, 1996): 8.

32. Ibid.

33. Linda Hon, "What Have You Done for Me Lately? Exploring Effectiveness in Public Relations," *Journal of Public Relations Research* vol. 9 (1) (1997): 1–30.

34. Charles J. Fombrun, *Reputation: Realizing Value from the Corporate Image* (Boston: Harvard Business School Press, 1996): 192–210.

35. James E. Grunig, *Excellence in Public Relations and Communication Management* (Hillsdale, NJ: Erlbaum, 1992).

36. Kimberly Gill, "Searching for Excellence in Public Relations," Association for Education in Journalism and Mass Communication Annual Conference, Public Relations Division, Baltimore, MD, August 1998.

CHAPTER 17

Retail and Business-to-Business Advertising

CHAPTER OBJECTIVES

When you have completed this chapter, you should be able to

1. Discuss retail advertising fundamentals.
2. Summarize the media options for retailers.
3. Explain business-to-business advertising objectives.
4. Identify the media used in business advertising.

Bug Killing at a New Site

Award: *EFFIE Gold 2001, Professional Services category*

Company: *Orkin*

Agency: *J. Walter Thompson*

Campaign: *"Q & A"*

If you think you have some scary critters crawling around your house, you should see the monsters that the Orkin exterminators face when calling on commercial clients.

Yes, businesses need pest control of the insect kind, too. However, a few years ago they weren't calling on the Orkin Exterminating Company as much as the company hoped. It seemed that potential business customers did not perceive Orkin, which was known for its residential expertise, to be experts in commercial pest control. Even though the company had improved its sales infrastructure to support commercial-focused direct sales, Orkin's growth in this area was flat. Said the company: "Prospects simply don't believe a company known for residential pest control services could provide the specialized level of expertise needed for their business."

Orkin decided to take a tremendous risk. Orkin management, along with its agency experts at J. Walter Thompson, decided to reposition the Orkin company from a residential generalist to a commercial specialist. The companies postulated that Orkin was so well-established in the minds of residential customers that it could keep this core target market regardless of what it did with the commercial market.

Generating interest among managers responsible for pest control at target companies—sanitation engineers, environmental services managers, property managers—wasn't easy. Orkin summed up these managers' typical attitudes as: "I have a lot of crap to deal with today. If no one is screaming about bugs, I could care less, and besides, my current pest control contract isn't up for another six months."

Orkin and J. Walter Thompson created a campaign titled "Q & A," to show that they were more than "bug zappers." One of its objectives was to communicate the specialized knowledge and technological effectiveness of the Orkin Commercial Division. The campaign included direct mail and public relations as well as ads such as the one shown here.

The campaign had another objective—to increase sales growth by 5 percent in 2000.

How did it work? Check the "It's a Wrap" box at the end of this chapter.

RETAIL ADVERTISING

This chapter covers two types of advertising—retail and business-to-business. The Orkin company has had success running campaigns in both types. It's important to recognize the changes these two types of advertising have gone through over the years, and the constraints faced by advertisers in both types. Just as advertising is part of the marketing mix for an international consumer brand such as Estée Lauder, it also plays a role in retail marketing and merchandising strategies. **Retail advertising**, used by merchants to sell products and services directly to consumers, accounts for nearly half of all the money spent on advertising. Let's examine the aspects of this form of advertising.

Local Retail Advertising

Retail advertising occurs on local, national, and international levels. Retailers such as Sears, Office Max, Macy's, and Home Depot advertise nationally. Some retailers, such as Toys "R" Us, advertise internationally, but most retail advertising is local. By local, we mean it is targeted at consumers who live within close proximity to a retail store. Sometimes consumers living in the region receive ads from stores that are many, many miles away. Consumers living in West Texas may get ads for stores as far away as Amarillo or Lubbock.

As Table 17.1 shows, many types of organizations use local retail advertising to reach consumer audiences. The types of organizations are diverse, ranging from independently owned stores to restaurant chains.

Retail advertising should perform several functions: sell a variety of products, encourage store traffic, deliver sales promotion messages, create and communicate a store image or personality, and establish a brand that resonates with the local audience. The ad for Sofa Mart is a regional retail ad.

Differences between Local Retailing and National Brand Advertising

Retail advertising at the local level differs from national or international brand advertising in various ways. First, local retail advertising, whether sponsored by an international chain or a local store, is targeted to people living in the store's community. So, such advertising is customized to match the needs, wants, culture, and idiosyncrasies of the target audience.

TABLE 17.1   **Types of Organizations That Use Local Retail Advertising**

Type	Examples
Locally owned stores	The local record or book store, auto parts shop, or bakery.
Service businesses	A local beauty salon, health clinic, or the local branch of a bank.
Local branches of retail store chains	Staples, Macy's, Wal-Mart.
Franchised retail businesses	Texaco, Holiday Inn, or Hertz.
Dealerships	Toyota or DaimlerChrysler auto dealerships, AT&T phone stores.
Restaurant and entertainment businesses	Applebee's, TGI Friday's, the local bagel shop, movie theaters, sports arenas and teams, theater troupes.

This ad for Sofa Mart focuses on price, convenience, and discounts.

In comparison, national and international brand advertisers (Sony, Calvin Klein, Levi's, Cadillac) typically deliver a standard, general message to a large audience. These general messages make appeals that are specific to the product sold by the national retailer, but local advertising can get even more specific.

Second, national brand advertising supports only the sponsor's brands, while retail advertising may promote several different brands or even competing brands. The retailer's loyalty gravitates to whichever brand is selling best.

Third, retail advertising directed at the local community has an inherent urgency. Everything about the ad pushes the consumer toward a behavior, typically visiting the store. As a result, the retail ad includes price information, address, telephone number, conditions of sales, colors, sizes, and so on. National retail brand advertising is more concerned with image and attitude change, so there tends to be less copy and fewer specifics.

The fourth difference is that local retail advertising is customized, to some extent, to reflect the local store. Usually, it includes basic information such as the store's name, address, telephone number, and business hours. National and international brand advertising usually is not customized this way.

To build and maintain store traffic, a retailer (and its advertisements) must meet four objectives:

1. Build store and brand awareness.
2. Create consumer understanding of items or services offered.
3. Convince consumers that the store's items and services satisfy needs.
4. Create consumer desire to shop at this particular store.

In addition, most retailers use advertising to help attract new customers, build store loyalty, increase the amount of the average sale, maintain inventory balance by moving out overstocks and outdated merchandise, and help counter seasonal lows (see Figure 17.1).

FIGURE 17.1

RETAIL ADVERTISING OBJECTIVES
To build and maintain store traffic, a retail ad strives to meet these objectives.

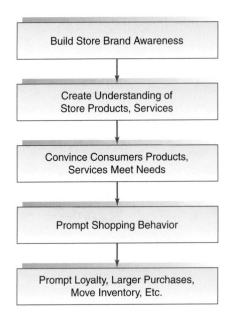

Build Store Brand Awareness

↓

Create Understanding of Store Products, Services

↓

Convince Consumers Products, Services Meet Needs

↓

Prompt Shopping Behavior

↓

Prompt Loyalty, Larger Purchases, Move Inventory, Etc.

For several reasons local retail advertising is less sophisticated and more utilitarian than national advertising (with a few exceptions). First, it is short term compared to national advertising. Most retail ads deal with price and run for only a few days, while a national ad may run for months or years.

In addition, local retail advertisers can't justify high production costs for advertising. National advertisers can easily justify spending $5,000 to produce a newspaper ad when they are paying $200,000 to run it in 100 large markets. A local retailer that places an ad in the city newspaper might have a media cost of only $400, making it difficult to justify spending $5,000 on production.

Most retailers have little formal training in advertising, so they are sometimes uncomfortable making professional advertising decisions. They often rely on their media sales representatives to design and produce their ads. Most media advertising departments turn out several dozen ads a day, rather than working on one ad for several days (or weeks) as ad agencies do. These ads look less polished than national and international ads, often using stock artwork and clip art services that are copyright-free.

Cooperative Advertising

One way businesses that use local retail advertising can compensate for their smaller budgets and limited expertise is to take advantage of **cooperative (co-op) advertising** (discussed in Chapter 3), in which the manufacturer reimburses the retailer for part or all of the advertising expenses. Most manufacturers, service providers, and franchisers have some type of ongoing promotional program that provides retailers with advertising support in the form of money and advertising materials. Funds for cooperative advertising are available, subject to certain guidelines, and generally are based on a percentage of sales to the retailer.

Co-op funds, sometimes called *ad allowances,* have become so common that most retailers won't even consider taking on a new brand, especially one in a heavily advertised category, without receiving some support.

Co-op advertising may be funded by the supplier in one of two ways. The supplier can give an ad allowance that varies from month to month depending on product sales figures. The higher the amount, the more the retailer is expected to run the manufactured ads. Or the supplier can set up an accrual fund for the retailer's advertising in which the supplier automatically sets aside money based on a certain percentage of a retailer's purchases.

Retailers may also seek reimbursement for local advertising from suppliers as part of a retailer's vendor support program. Large drug and discount chains, for instance, periodically schedule a special advertising supplement. Their suppliers are offered an opportunity to buy space in this supplement. Suppliers generally are promised that no competing brands will be included.

Some manufacturers also provide a **dealer tag**, time left at the end of a radio or television ad during which the local store is mentioned. Manufacturers also can provide window banners, bill inserts, and special direct-mail pieces, such as four-color supplements for the local paper that carry the store's name and address.

Large Specialty Retailers

Many retailers have begun to specialize in merchandising products, such as electronics, running shoes, tennis equipment, and toys. The largest of these retail specialists are called *superstores.* Examples include Home Depot, Sports Authority, Circuit City, and Toys "R" Us. The idea behind the superstore is fairly simple: Provide customers with the ultimate assortment in a product category (say, hardware) and they will come. In these cases retail advertising may be targeted at local, regional, national, or international audiences. The advertising is more like manufacturer advertising in that fewer products are highlighted and the emphasis is on image rather than a quick sale. Benetton ads, for instance, focus on image.

Nonstore Retailing

Nonstore retailing occurs when the exchange between the manufacturer or retailer and the consumer takes place outside the traditional retail store. This is also a type of direct marketing. Avon and Lands' End make their own products, which they offer through door-to-door and catalog selling, respectively. Lillian Vernon, in contrast, purchases products from a variety of manufacturers and sells the products through its catalog. Designer Checks used an offer in a Sunday newspaper supplement with an order form to convince people to call or mail their orders for customized checks. As discussed in Chapter 14, this is a form of direct marketing.

Designer Checks does not rely on a retail store to transact business with customers.

Vending machines are another type of nonstore retailing. Sales from vending machines generate over $25 billion annually. Products sold through vending machines are supported through manufacturer and retail advertising.

Nonstore retailing has grown for a variety of reasons; most notably, that the time-conscious consumer is no longer inclined to spend hours shopping for goods and services. Simultaneously, the quality and selection of the merchandise sold through nonstore retailing have improved greatly. Warranties and guarantees remove the risk associated with purchasing unseen merchandise. Finally, improvements in mailing lists have better matched the marketer with potential customers. The use of nonstore retailing has shifted a great deal of retail advertising toward direct marketing, direct mail, and now the Internet. We turn to Web retailing next.

Online Retailing and E-Commerce

Both store-based and nonstore retailers have moved online not only to advertise their products but to take orders as well. We call these retailers "e-tailers." Many e-tailers have opted to conduct **e-commerce**, which is the selling of goods and services (commerce) through electronic means, mostly the Internet.

The fuss over e-tailing is a bit overblown. Although the growth of retail sales through the Internet is large in actual dollars, it is quite small as a percentage of total retail sales (see Figure 17.2). E-tailing sales represented over $20 billion in 2001 sales, but almost 30 percent were sales of computers and computer-related products. Beyond technology, most additional sales are books/magazines, music, and clothing.[1]

FIGURE 17.2

CHARACTERISTICS OF NET SHOPPERS

Net shoppers have changed dramatically since the emergence of the Internet in the mid-1990s. *Sources:* PeopleSupport; Shepardson, Stem and Kaminsky; Digital Idea and GNS research.

Net grabs shoppers

E-commerce sales represent less than 1 percent of overall retail sales; much of that is being done by about 5 percent of the Internet's 100 million users.

Who they are...

Those who shop online several times a week...

By sex:

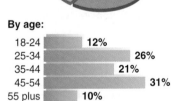

Women 40% 60% Men

By age:

18-24	12%
25-34	26%
35-44	21%
45-54	31%
55 plus	10%

By marital status:

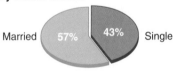

Married 57% 43% Single

By income (per year):

Under $35,000	22%
$35,000-$75,000	45%
Over $75,000	33%

...And how many feel about it.

A recent survey found many of these super shoppers are not happy with the customer service they get online:

Frustrated	**Alone**	**Invaded**
85 percent say they are frustrated with the level of customer service they get online.	68 percent want contact with a sales representative by phone or e-mail; 40 percent of sites don't provide it.	51 percent say they have bailed out of a purchase because it required too much personal information.

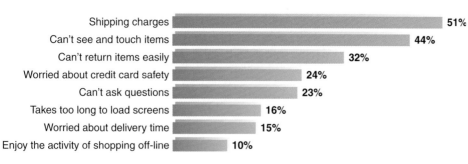

Shipping charges — 51%
Can't see and touch items — 44%
Can't return items easily — 32%
Worried about credit card safety — 24%
Can't ask questions — 23%
Takes too long to load screens — 16%
Worried about delivery time — 15%
Enjoy the activity of shopping off-line — 10%

FIGURE 17.3

REASONS FOR NOT SHOPPING ONLINE

Despite the increased popularity of the Internet, there are still reasons why consumers are reluctant to shop online.

Source: Greenfield Online, Inc.

Yet, the Internet does offer companies the ability to establish relationships with customers in a manner that has not been available to retailers since the 1950s. It used to be that a local retailer knew his customers' names, as well as the names of their spouses and kids, their birthdays, likes, and dislikes. To a certain extent, those are some of the benefits a good Web site can offer today, along with creating a compelling and convenient way to do business.

Despite the best efforts of e-tailers, there are still several reasons why consumers are reluctant to purchase online. As noted in Figure 17.3, research conducted by Greenfield Online Inc., indicates that "shipping charges," "can't see/touch items," and "can't return items easily" were the top three deterrents. But e-tailers are already addressing these deterrents. Companies such as amazon.com and FTD.com are addressing the shipping charges issue by paying for them. Many retailers have both an online and off-line facility that allows touching and trying. Best Buy is such a retailer. Nordstrom.com has a very generous, flexible return policy, without a receipt—no matter how long ago you bought it and what condition it's in when you return it.[2]

Practical Tips

Jonathan Palmer, a professor at the University of Maryland, suggests four factors that indicate your business would do well online:

1. You sell a product line that can be delivered economically and conveniently.
2. You have a desire to market to customers outside your own geographical location and you have a product that will appeal broadly.
3. There are significant economic advantages to going online, such as lower rent, labor, inventory, and printing costs.
4. You can economically draw customers to your site.

Source: Robert McGarvey, "Connect the Dots," *Entrepreneur* (March 2000): 82.

Many large retailers run advertising campaigns to promote e-commerce. The online trading company E*TRADE launched a multimedia television, print, cable, outdoor, and radio campaign designed to build its brand name. Chase Bank also advertises its online services.

Today, e-commerce appeals mainly to shoppers who value convenience above all else and those too time-starved to shop. Will online retailing replace traditional retailing completely? It's doubtful, but it's quickly becoming more prevalent. As the Web becomes more crowded with online retailers, even the smaller ones may have to advertise to draw customers to their cyberstores.

Institutional and Product Retail Advertising

Despite the great diversity in retailing, there really are two general focuses of a retail ad: the institution and the product. **Institutional retail advertising** is advertising that sells the retail store as an enjoyable place to shop. Through institutional advertising, the store helps to establish its image as a leader in fashion, price, and wide merchandise selection, as well as superior service, or quality, or whatever image the store chooses to cultivate.

Loyalty programs are a form of institutional retail advertising. Retailers are designing frequent-shopper programs to strengthen the relationship between the store and its regular customers. Similarly, grocery stores have card-based loyalty programs that reward shoppers who present the card at the cash register with discounts and special prices. When scanned electronically (swiped), the cards also register customer identification and shopping information into the store's database.

Product retail advertising presents specific merchandise for sale and urges customers to come to the store to buy it. This form of advertising helps create and maintain the store's reputation through its merchandise. **Nonpromotional product advertising** talks about merchandise that is new, exclusive, and of superior quality and designs. When the sales price dominates the ad, it is called promotional or **sales advertising**. When sales items are interspersed with regular-priced items in the ad, it is called **semipromotional advertising**.

Promotional advertising is the main form of product retail advertising. Many retailers now use any reason they can find to have a sale (President's Day, tax time, overstocks). There are also end-of-month (EOM) sales, even hourly sales (Ayre's 14-Hour Sales, Kmart's Midnight Madness). The Foley's ad features still another type of sale—the anniversary sale.

Aside from traditional newspaper ads, retailers can use a host of media to communicate their promotional ads. These media include banners, posters, shelf talkers (signs attached to a shelf that let the consumer take away some piece of information or a coupon), end-of-aisle displays, and shopping cart ads. New interactive electronic kiosks with touch-screen computers, CD-ROM databases, full graphics, and product photos are moving into the aisles in many stores, where they provide more information about more products than the store can ever stock on its shelves.[3]

This ad for Foley's department store demonstrates one way to create excitement: an anniversary sale.

Factors Affecting Retail Advertising

Retail advertising has been affected not only by new forms of retailing, but also by three business influences: consolidation, demographics, and heightened competition.

Ownership consolidation, especially among department stores and specialty chains, has brought mass merchandising to many stores that formerly operated on a smaller scale. This consolidation has given retailers much greater interest in both mass advertising and the use of different media, such as *free-standing inserts,* in lieu of traditional newspaper space.

Demographic changes that affect retail advertising include time stress, an aging population, geomarketing, and market fragmentation. For families in which both spouses work, time is a valuable commodity. As a result, retailers must reach consumers with messages that are short and sweet, delivered where and when the consumer group is most receptive to them. They must also appeal to women and various ethnic groups in ways that are devoid of unflattering stereotypes.

To reach elderly people, retailers must recognize that this market segment is knowledgeable, and has opinions on price and quality. Advertising copy must make price and quality comparisons readily available.

In targeting consumers, a retailer's first concern is geography: Where do my customers live? How far will they drive to come to my store? The next concern is consumer taste. **Geomarketing** is a practice geared to the increasing diversity in consumer tastes and preferences. Retailers are trying to develop offers that appeal to consumers in different parts of the country as well as in different neighborhoods in the same suburb. H.E.B. Supermarkets operates its stores in both central and south Texas. In San Antonio, the stores located in Mexican American neighborhoods carry a very different merchandise assortment than do stores in other locations.

Overriding all these demographic trends are the changes resulting from the events of 9/11. All forms of retailing suffered as consumers were reluctant to go out and shop. No one knew how long the reluctance would last, but retail advertisers knew they would need to ask a lot of questions. Does it mean that Internet retailing will become more popular as people might be afraid to go to malls? Does it mean that security-related copy (copy about safe parking lots, good lighting, security guards, etc.) will dominate retail ads?

Retailers such as Wal-Mart and Sears recognize that the store is first and foremost a brand. Retailers that want to build a brand identity must clearly and consistently communicate an identity to consumers, as does Home Depot through its name, logo, sign, and employees' orange aprons. A retail brand is not only what the company says it is but also what the customer thinks it is.[4] Relying on integrated marketing communications ensures that all the retailer's marketing messages—those sent through advertising, public relations, sales promotion, and so on—communicate the same brand image. As noted in the "A Matter of Practice" box, Kmart is trying to rebuild its brand.

Creating the Retail Ad

Prior to actually writing copy or drawing a layout, retail advertising experts Jeweler and Drewniany suggest that advertisers answer this question: Why would you shop in your store? Possible answers to this question can provide direction for the creative process. Jeweler and Drewniany suggest these answers:[5]

- store's personnel
- store's location
- store's pricing policy
- store's products
- store's history
- store's stand on issues

If the retailer wants to build store traffic, it typically creates ads either to emphasize a reduced price on a popular item or to promote the store image by focusing on unusual or varied merchandise, friendly and knowledgeable clerks, or prestige brands. Let's turn to how image plays a part in retail advertising.

A MATTER OF PRACTICE

THE BLUE LIGHT GLIMMERS THEN FADES

➤ Things had not been going well for Kmart for over a decade. Turnaround efforts had all failed, and stores remained dirty, shelves understocked. Competitors such as Wal-Mart and Target had steadily taken market share from Kmart, resulting in a $225 million net loss in fiscal 2000.

As a last-ditch effort, the Kmart board hired Charles Conaway at the end of 2000. Conaway, who was credited with turning around drug retailer CVS Corp., quickly created a management team from companies such as Wal-Mart, Target, and Coca-Cola. Their new marketing plan was unveiled on April 2, 2001.

Conaway decided to bring back the Blue Light Special. Made famous by Kmart during the 1960s, 1970s, and 1980s, the promotions directed shoppers to unadvertised bargains. The "Light" hadn't been in use since 1991. Conaway decided to modernize it a bit, hoping that the icon would resonate with customers, both old and new, and perhaps even create a sense of excitement.

Conaway and his team were smart enough to realize that the fundamental problems at Kmart needed to be solved first. Stores were remodeled, shelves were fully stocked, and employees were retrained. Satisfied with many of these changes, a $25 million advertising campaign was directed by a specific set of tactics: "(1) bathe stores in blue and debut an updated, 'Blue Light Special', (2) match Wal-Mart on pricing for thousands of items, (3) spend $2 billion to improve Kmart's inventory system, and (4) initiate employee incentives in order to raise customer satisfaction."

Did the plan to save Kmart work? In January 2002, Kmart filed for chapter 11 bankruptcy and Conaway and his team vacated the premises. Over 500 stores were closed and 100,000 employees were released.

POINT TO PONDER

Is there anything advertising can do to save Kmart?

Sources: Joanne Muller, "Kmart's Bright Idea," *BusinessWeek* (April 9, 2001): 48–51; Lorrie Grant, "CEO Rings Up Plan to Restore Kmart," *USA Today* (June 27, 2001): 3B; Matthew Kinsman, "The Corner ISP," *Promo* (May 2000): 55–56; Bruce Horovitz, "Kmart Hopes Spike Lee Ads Do the Right Things," *USA Today* (February 22, 2002): 3B.

Image or Price For retail operations that sell products and services that have little product differentiation, such as gasoline, banking, and car rentals, a positive, distinctive image is a valuable asset. The retailer can convey this image through advertising, other forms of marketing communication, pricing, location, and security.

Price also can be a factor in establishing a store's image. Most discount stores signal their type of merchandise with large, bold prices. Several specialty retailers emphasize price by offering coupons in their print advertising. Featuring prices doesn't necessarily apply only to ads that give the store a bargain or a discount image, however. Price can help the consumer comparison shop without visiting the store. Many customers appreciate this basic information.

Executing Retail Ads Because the main object of retail ads is to attract customers, store location (or telephone number, if advertising is a service) is essential. For merchandise that is infrequently purchased, such as cars, furniture, wallpaper, and hearing aids, the ad should include a map or mention a geographic reference point (for example, three blocks north of the state capitol building) in addition to the regular street address.

A mistake some retailers make is to place the owner as the star or key spokesperson in their advertising. Customers are interested in the merchandise, not the owner. This is especially noticeable in broadcast commercials, where a presenter needs acting talent or training. Although hiring big-time superstars is beyond the budgets of most retailers, competent and affordable actors are available in most cities. In fact, local celebrities typically have greater attention-getting potential to a local retail store than nationally known talent does.

However, the retail owner doesn't need to be invisible. Take a look at the three-page print ad for Kenneth Cole, a men's clothing retailer. The print ad conveys a brand image. It uses models to showcase the clothes, but the copy includes a quote from Kenneth Cole.

Small and medium-sized retailers often save money by using stock artwork. All daily newspapers subscribe to clip art services that provide a wide range of photographs and line

The copy in this image ad for Kenneth Cole features the retail owner in an effective, subtle way.

art drawings. Larger retailers or upscale specialty retailers, such as Tiffany's or Avon Cleaners of Dallas, generally have their art custom designed, which gives all of their ads a similar look and a distinct image.

Retailers have also found ways to make their television production more efficient by using a "donut" format in which the opening and closing sections are the same, while the middle changes to focus on different merchandise. Using this format, the retailer saves money by only having to create the middle section of the ad.

In Retail, Who Are the Creatives? Most retail advertising is created and produced by one or a combination of the following: in-house staff, media, ad agencies, and freelancers. The larger the retail operation, the more likely it is to have an in-house advertising staff.

All local media create and produce ads for retailers. With the exception of television, most provide this service free. The medium- and larger-sized newspapers and stations often have people whose only job is to write and produce ads.

Some retail ads are created by agencies. Generally, agency work is the most costly way to produce retail ads on a regular basis. Also, because agencies work for many different clients, they cannot always respond as quickly as an in-house agency can. Few agencies are prepared to handle the large number of day-to-day copy changes that are characteristic of major retail advertising. Featured products, prices, hours of operation, and special promotions may all change during the course of a few days.

What an agency can do well for a retailer on a moderate budget is develop an image or position and some ad formats that the store's in-house creative people can use for fast-breaking advertising. Television spots, particularly if they are more image oriented instead of focused on product or price, may also be created by outside agencies. For example, office superstore Staples used the Cliff Freeman agency to create an award-winning back-to-school campaign that used humor to distinguish Staples' brand image. In one broadcast ad that used the song, "It's the Most Wonderful Time of the Year," a deliriously happy father is skipping down the aisles, gleefully dropping school supplies into a shopping cart. His kids look on with unhappy faces.

Freelancers often are a good compromise between an in-house staff and an ad agency. Generally, freelancers charge a lower hourly rate than do ad agencies because they have less overhead.

In this section we have examined the types of retailing, retail advertising objectives, factors that affect retail advertising, and the basics of creating retail ads. Next we turn to the key media issue that affects retail advertising: buying and selling local media.

THE INSIDE STORY

FOREVER VIRGIN, FOREVER '70s

Chris Hutchinson

Art Director
Bulldog Drummond, San Diego

For a national campaign for Virgin Megastore's "Forever '70s" sale, I came up with the idea of a character who was stuck in the '70s but living in modern times. Ads would show him in various modern environments interacting with people in his "far-out" way, which would make consumers laugh and feel good about Virgin, and thus sell CDs. Everything about him would be straight out of the '70s; his music, his style, his lingo, his attitude. But where were we going to find this cool cat? We had to cast the perfect fellow. At a skinny 6'7", my creative director decided I would be perfect to play the part. Who better to play the character I created than myself? It cut out the middleman. Directing myself, I was able to get some pretty interesting stuff. My stylist (again me) and I worked out an excellent outfit: a huge real-hair Afro, tight bell bottoms and an "orange" leather jacket that my father had worn in the real 1970s.

We did a test shoot and pitched the idea to Virgin. Once we got approval, I was off to produce the campaign. I told the photographer we would run all over town causing trouble, shooting me doing random stuff, without actually setting up any shots. I wanted a candid documentary look, not too polished. The photographer would have to work without an assistant because of the speed with which we'd have to move. I planned to infiltrate several interesting places that we'd likely get kicked out of; he would be shooting on the run.

My height coupled with the Afro and outfit made me clash with everything. We shot me at a bar, at Starbucks, playing in a beach volleyball game, shopping, talking to people, leaning on a Camaro, and buying beer. We also made up and filmed the TV spots in real time. The sale was a huge success nationwide, and my modeling portfolio is now available.

Chris Hutchinson is an art director at Bulldog Drummond, a darn fine ad agency in San Diego. Chris's work has been featured in Archive, PDN magazine, and on his mom's fridge. He graduated from the University of Oregon in 1999.
Nosnihctuh@hotmail.com

Nominated by Professor Charles Frazer, University of Oregon.

BUYING AND SELLING LOCAL MEDIA

Perhaps the most rapidly changing area in retail advertising is the buying and selling of local media time and space. Local retailers are becoming more sophisticated about buying media. Why? They are being forced to work with tighter budgets, they are getting more advertising help and advice from their suppliers, they are being exposed to more media ideas at association workshops and seminars, and they are being educated by a growing number of media salespeople.

At the same time, media competition has increased significantly. At the local level, nearly all major markets now have at least one local independent station and a public television station, which solicits underwriting, a type of soft-sell advertising. These stations, along with local advertising that is now being sold by the national cable networks, have created many more television opportunities for the retailer advertising to a local audience.

Finally, most of the top-50 markets in the United States have at least one local magazine offering retailers' high-quality, four-color ads to reach the upscale consumer. Examples are *Los Angeles Magazine, Palm Springs Life,* and *Phoenix Homes & Gardens.*

The increase in competition for retailers' advertising dollars has resulted in a different type of selling. Salespeople increasingly emphasize advertising and promotion ideas rather than just rate cards and circulation figures. Unfortunately, many retailers still buy advertising strictly on price or number of spots. Some retailers don't realize that five spots during morning drive time on the market's leading radio station can reach more people than can 50 spots that run between 2:00 A.M. and 4:00 A.M.

Local Retail Media Strategy

Unlike national advertisers, local retailers generally prefer reach over frequency. A retailer with a "30 Percent Off All Women's Casual Shoes" ad doesn't have to tell this more than once or twice to women interested in saving money on a pair of casual shoes. In contrast, a national advertiser with an image campaign, such as Eveready Batteries, continually needs to remind consumers that its batteries "keep going and going and going."

Successful retailers use media that minimize waste. Direct mail, which is narrowly targeted, is now the second-largest advertising medium used by retailers.

Because retailers can choose from many local media, they must be careful not to buy a lot of wasted circulation. Consider a local bakery in Des Moines, Iowa, which can serve about 380,000 households and competes with 24 other bakeries. If the vast majority of the bakery's business comes from the three-mile radius surrounding the shop (which includes only 5 percent of Des Moines households), using television advertising that covers the entire city would waste almost all (95 percent) of its advertising dollars. Direct mail and outdoor media would prove more effective for the bakery.

Media Alternatives

Retailers may choose from the entire arsenal of media alternatives. In general, however, local retailers are interested only in local media and stay clear of media that reach an audience beyond their immediate markets. Several media are relevant to retailers.

Newspapers Newspapers have always made up the bulk of the retailer's advertising, probably because the local nature of newspapers fits the retailer's desire for geographic coverage, prestige, and immediacy. In addition, newspapers are a medium that people read in part for the advertising. In fact, many people use newspapers as a shopping guide. Also, retailers can gain some measure of audience selectivity by advertising in specific sections of the paper, such as the sports, society, and financial pages.

Most retailers that advertise regularly make space contracts with the newspaper. In the contract the retailer agrees to use a certain amount of space over the year and pay a certain amount per line, which is lower than the paper's "open" rate for the same space. The lower rate is simply a quantity discount.

In addition to special rates, newspapers have developed several other products or services to retailers. Many newspapers provide retail advertisers with their zip code circulation reports, which identify the circulation level for that newspaper in the various zip codes. This information, combined with zone editions of the paper (certain versions of the paper go to certain counties, cities, and so on), greatly reduces the wasted circulation often associated with large newspapers. Special advertising sections, such as preprints, can be inserted in these various papers.

Shoppers and Preprints Free-distribution newspapers (shoppers) that are dropped off at millions of suburban homes once or twice a week are becoming increasingly popular advertising outlets for retailers. More than 3,000 such papers are published in the United States, such as *Center Island Pennysavers,* distributed in Long Island, New York.

Preprints are advertising circulars furnished by a retailer for distribution as a free-standing insert in newspapers. In recent years preprinted inserts have also become popular with retailers striving for greater market coverage. For instance, preprints account for more than 80 percent of Wal-Mart's advertising budget.

Magazines Many magazines have regional or metropolitan editions. They enable local retailers to buy exposure to the audience within their trading area only. Sears, Kmart, and JCPenney advertise in monthlies targeted to particular audience segments and in weeklies to accommodate short-term sales patterns. Local retailers use magazines mainly for institutional or image ads.

Broadcast Media Local retailers advertise on television and radio, but these broadcast media usually are used to supplement newspaper advertising. Both offer important advantages over print media. Radio has a low cost and a high degree of geographic and audience selectivity. It also provides high flexibility in spot scheduling, and this flexibility carries over into creativity.

Many of the same advantages are found in local television. The cost of television is higher, however, as is the creative expertise needed to produce satisfactory commercials. Television stations produce commercials for a fee. The advent of cable TV has reduced the expense problem somewhat, because of its ability to show retail commercials in the local market only. Cable also offers the retailer the kind of selectivity that network television cannot. Undoubtedly, as more and more homes are hooked up to cable, retailers will view television as an affordable, effective media alternative.

Directories Telephone directories (the Yellow Pages) are important advertising media for retailers. In the Yellow Pages the retailer pays for an alphabetical listing (and a larger display ad, if desired) within a business category. Most retailers advertise in the Yellow Pages because they are so widely used by customers and the ads have a long life (1 year or more).

The disadvantages include limited flexibility and long lead times for new ads. Retailers that don't get their ads to the Yellow Pages in time (for example, a camera-ready ad often must be mailed by May or June for the September directory) have to wait an entire year. However, electronic versions of the Yellow Pages eliminate the limited flexibility and lead-time disadvantages.

Direct Response Retailers use direct-response advertising extensively to communicate their product offerings to a select group of consumers. The retailer creates its own advertisement and distributes it directly to consumers through the mail or the distribution of circulars, letters, handbills, samples, and other printed matter. Although direct-response advertising is expensive in terms of cost per thousand, it is the most selective medium because only people the retailer selects read the ads.[6]

Online Media The Web is still a less common medium for retailer advertising than newspapers, magazines, and TV, but that hasn't stopped ad agencies from creating new media divisions to explore its potential. Scores of startup companies do nothing but create Web advertising.

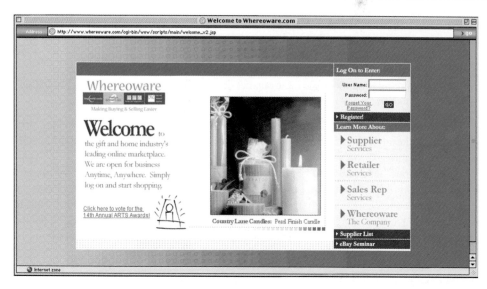

Web-based pitches come in two forms: A retailer can set up its own Web site or buy an ad on someone else's. What happens on the Net is narrowcasting: one-on-one, highly targeted marketing. And on the Web, it's interactive: Click on a picture of a camera and a more detailed description appears. Many retailers start with a $15,000 or so investment in a banner ad posted on a popular Web site.

As part of the effort to create a site people will return to, some advertisers are becoming their own publishers. Levi's Web site has a magazine about deejays, clubs, and other cool Web sites. L.L. Bean offers a database of national parks. Black & Decker's site offers home improvement tips. Whereoware.com facilitates retailers who want to sell online.

Another online medium is ATM technology. Imagine pulling up to an ATM, which simultaneously delivers instructions on how to access your cash as well as print and TV ads suggesting where you can spend this money. Even cents-off coupons can be part of your receipt. Companies that have used ATM ads include Compaq Computers, Sears, Paramount Pictures, and Food.com.[7]

Specialty Historically, retailers have been avid users of specialty media. Specialty media include a host of message-delivering items such as pens and pencils, hats, calendars, rulers, balloons, jackets, T-shirts, and clocks. These items are inexpensive, and in the case of retailers such as the Hard Rock Café, Planet Hollywood, and Nike, they are actually cost-free. The simple rule is this: If the customer values and uses the item, it is probably a good way to deliver basic retailer information. Now let's examine another form of advertising—business-to-business.

BUSINESS-TO-BUSINESS ADVERTISING

Advertising directed at people in business who buy or specify products for business use is called **business-to-business advertising**. Although personal selling is the most common method of communicating with business buyers, business advertising is used to create product awareness, enhance the firm's reputation, and support salespeople and other channel members.

A purchaser in the business market, like a consumer, goes through a search process beginning with gathering information about alternatives, processing this information, learning about valuable products, determining which alternatives match the perceived needs most closely, and carrying through by making a purchase.

Business marketing is the marketing of goods and services to business markets.[8] It differs from consumer marketing in two key ways: who buys a product and what the buying motive is.

- **Who buys.** In business markets, organizations buy products or services. In consumer markets, individuals or household consumers do the buying. The business market consists of all organizations, whether profit or nonprofit, public or private, that acquire goods or services to support their organizational needs. This includes all commercial enterprises, governments, and institutions.

- *Buying motives.* Organizations purchase goods or services to support (1) their production requirements or (2) their business needs. In contrast, consumers purchase products or services for personal consumption to satisfy a need or want.

In the business arena, many people can be involved in the purchasing decision: people from marketing, manufacturing, purchasing, or other different functional areas who have varying information needs.

To illustrate, let's say a purchasing decision might change the business consumer's product by altering the materials used to make the package. Marketing would want to know whether the change will help or hurt product sales. Manufacturing would want to know how much the change will affect production costs. Business advertising faces the challenge of reaching the various decision makers in a way that meets their specific information needs.

Types of Business-to-Business Advertising

Information needs also depend on the type of market the business advertiser is trying to reach. As we see in Figure 17.4, we can divide the business arena into five distinct markets, each of which tends to purchase products and services differently. These five markets are *industrial, government, trade, professional,* and *agricultural.*

Industrial Advertising Original equipment manufacturers (OEMs), such as IBM and General Motors, purchase industrial goods, services, or both that either become a part of the final product or aid business operations. **Industrial advertising** is directed at OEMs. Information needs depend on the reason the business is purchasing the product.

For example, when General Motors purchases tires from Goodyear, information needs focus on whether the purchase will contribute to a high-quality finished product. When Goodyear purchases packaging materials to ship the tires it manufactures, information needs focus on prompt, predictable delivery.

Government Advertising The largest purchasers of industrial goods in the United States are federal, state, and local governments. These government units purchase virtually every kind of good, from $15 hammers to multimillion-dollar Polaris missiles. Such goods may be advertised in *Federal Computer Week, Commerce Business Daily,* or *Defense News.* However, you seldom see advertisements targeted directly to government agencies. Because supplier reputation plays an important role in the selection decision, corporate image advertising is one way of influencing the government market.

Trade Advertising Trade advertising is used to persuade resellers, wholesalers, and retailers in the consumer market to stock the products of the manufacturer. *Chain Store Age, Florist's Review,* and *Pizza and Pasta* are examples of trade publications. Because resellers purchase products for resale to ultimate consumers, they want information on the profit margins they can expect to receive, the product's major selling points, and what the producer is doing in terms of consumer advertising and other promotional support activities.

Professional Advertising Advertising directed at a group of mostly white-collar workers such as lawyers, accountants, technology consultants, doctors, teachers, funeral directors, and marketing research specialists is known as **professional advertising**. Advertisers interested in attracting professionals advertise in publications such as the *Music Educators' Journal* and *Advertising Age.* Information needs depend on both the advertiser's product and the target audience.

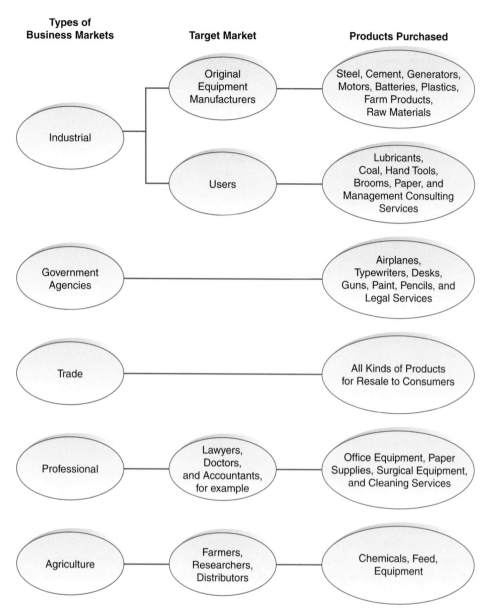

FIGURE 17.4

TYPES OF BUSINESS MARKETS AND PRODUCTS PURCHASED
The overall B-to-B market has five distinct markets, each purchasing products and services differently.

Agricultural Advertising Agricultural advertising promotes a variety of products and services, such as animal health products, seeds, farm machinery and equipment, crop dusting, and fertilizer. Large and small farmers alike want to know how industrial products can assist them in the growing, raising, or production or agricultural commodities. They turn to such publications as *California Farmer* and *Trees and Turf* for such assistance.

Business versus Consumer Marketing

Several characteristics differentiate business marketing from consumer marketing, including market concentration, decision makers, strategy, and purchasing objectives. As a result, the process of creating business-to-business advertising differs from the creation of consumer advertising.

Market Concentration The market for a typical business good is small compared to the market for a consumer good. In some cases the market may be geographically concentrated. Consider some examples. Most U.S. automakers are located in Detroit, the steel industry is located mainly in Pennsylvania and Illinois, and the majority of furniture makers are located in North Carolina. Businesses trying to supply the auto, steel, and furniture industries should recognize the geographic concentration and select and target media accordingly.

This ad for Daly & Wolcott touts the technical advantages of its integrated management software and targets potential users such as business managers and information system specialists—users who also would be decision makers.

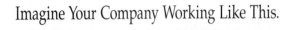

Application Plus® is the integrated enterprise software that makes all your systems work as one. Smoothly, and toward a single objective.

Application Plus turns complex functions into a simple operation. So that everyone in your organization can get the information they need, when and how they need it, and share it with those who need to know.

Application Plus gets to work quickly, managing your enterprise with proven, trouble-free reliability, no matter what your hardware, operating or database system.

Managing software has suddenly gotten a lot easier. Now what more could you ask?

Daly&Wolcott
INTEGRATED MANAGEMENT SOFTWARE

Daly & Wolcott, Inc., 21st Floor, One Hospital Trust Plaza, Providence, RI 02903
Telephone: (800) 343-2414, ext. 336, Fax: (401) 351-8484
Or visit us at http://www.dalywolcott.com
ATLANTA • CHICAGO • DALLAS • LOS ANGELES • PROVIDENCE

In addition to geographic concentration, businesses can be grouped according to the *Standard Industrial Classification* (SIC) system. The U.S. government established the SIC system to group organizations on the basis of the major activity or product or service provided. It helps the federal government to publish the number of establishments, number of employees, and sales volume for each group, designated by a commercial code. Geographic breakdowns are also provided where possible.

The SIC system, which classifies more than 4 million manufacturers into categories, allows a business advertiser to find its customers' SIC codes and then obtain lists that include the publications each SIC group uses. This information means the advertiser can select media that will reach the businesses in a certain SIC.

Decision Makers In general, those involved in making decisions for businesses are professionals who use rational criteria when comparing choices. These professionals often have technical knowledge and expertise about the advertised products and services. As many as 15 to 20 people may be involved in a particular purchase decision. Unfortunately, little is known about the inner workings of the decision process or the people involved.

Strategic Orientation Unlike the typical consumer who makes decisions based on partial information and sometimes irrational criteria, businesses tend to follow decision-making strategies that eliminate a great deal of decision-making autonomy available in personal decisions. Factors such as cost pressures, measures of advertising effectiveness, the agency–client partnership, customer concerns, and distribution may dictate what a business must do, regardless of the advertising message. Advertisers, then, must understand the business's strategy and adjust accordingly.

Government regulations affect many businesses. This AIG ad offers its insurance and financial services as safeguards against regulatory problems.

One major adjustment is accepting the timeframe of a typical business strategy. Buying decisions, as well as advertising decisions, are often made by committees and influenced by others in the organization from different functional areas. Every function may have its own timetable. This process can take days, weeks, or months. In the meantime, creative efforts and media buys may no longer be valid when approval is finally given.

Purchasing Objectives As you can see in the AIG advertisement, purchasing objectives in the insurance and financial services market center on rational, pragmatic considerations such as price, service, quality of the product or service, and assurance of supply. The AIG ad assures business purchasers that the company offers customized coverage to help the clients deal with government regulations.

- *Price.* Because of the size of most business purchases, buyers in the business arena are more concerned with the costs of owning and using a product than ordinary consumers. In evaluating price, then, businesses consider a variety of factors that generate or minimize costs, such as: What amount of scrap or waste will result from the use of the material? What will the cost of processing the material be? How much power will the machine consume?
- *Service.* Business buyers require multiple services, such as technical assistance, repair capability, and training information. Thus, the technical contributions of suppliers are highly valued wherever equipment, materials, or parts are in use.
- *Quality.* Business customers search for quality levels that are consistent with company standards, so they are reluctant to pay for extra quality or to compromise quality for a reduced price. The crucial factor is uniformity or consistency in product quality that will guarantee uniformity in end products, reduce the need for costly inspections and testing of incoming shipments, and ensure a smooth production process.

- *Assurance of supply.* Interruptions in the flow of parts and materials can shut down the production process, resulting in costly delays and lost sales. To guard against interruptions in supply, business firms rely on a supplier's established reputation for delivery, especially on-time delivery.

Business-to-Business Advertising Objectives

Although business advertising is an economical means of reaching large numbers of buyers, it is used primarily to assist and support the selling function. As a result, business-to-business advertising objectives center on creating company awareness, increasing overall selling efficiency, and supporting distributors and resellers. Well-planned business advertising assists the industrial salesperson by increasing customer awareness of and interest in the supplier's product. When buyers are aware of a company's reputation, products, and record in the industry, salespeople are more effective. Although salespeople may not know of or may not be able to contact all those who can influence a business purchasing decision, advertising in trade magazines and general business publications often can reach these influences.

Third, business advertising supplements personal selling by providing information to distributors, resellers, and end users and can answer the most common trade member questions, such as what profit they can expect on a product and what the producer is doing in terms of consumer advertising and other promotional support (see Figure 17.5).

Creating Business-to-Business Ads

As in consumer advertising, the best business-to-business ads are relevant and understandable and strike an emotional chord in the prospective client. However, business-to-business advertisers must keep in mind the differences between consumer and business audiences. Business-to-business advertisers follow these guidelines to create effective ads:

- Make sure the ad selects the strongest benefit and presents it prominently and persuasively.
- Dramatize the most important benefit, either by showing the product in action or by visualizing the problem and offering your product or service as a solution.

FIGURE 17.5

BUSINESS-TO-BUSINESS ADVERTISING OBJECTIVES

Business-to-business advertising has six main objectives.

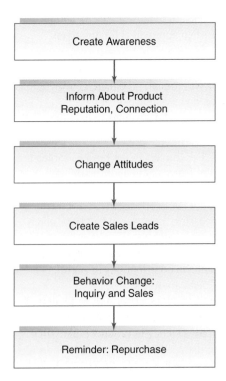

- Make sure your visual is relevant to the key message. It should help readers understand how your product or service works or instantly show that you understand the problem.
- The layout should have a sense of balance and flow. There should be a large visual that catches your eye, a headline that works with the visual, and a strong logo given its own space.
- The offer must be clear. What exactly do you want the reader to do as a result of seeing your ad?

BUSINESS-TO-BUSINESS ADVERTISING MEDIA

Although some business advertisers use traditional consumer media, most rely on general business or trade publications, industrial directories, direct marketing, or some combination of media. Because business-to-business advertisers have more media choices than ever before, media that offer advertisers a competitive advantage in reaching their customers are most appealing.

General Business and Trade Publications

General business and trade publications are classified as either horizontal or vertical. **Horizontal publications** are directed to people who hold similar jobs in different companies across different industries. For example, *Purchasing* is a specialized business publication that is targeted to people across industries who are responsible for a specific task or function. The magazines read by accountants or software engineers are other examples of horizontal publications. In contrast, **vertical publications**, such as *Iron Age* and *Steel,* are targeted toward people who hold different positions in the same industries. Advertisers select publications based on their target audience and their goals.

Directory Advertising

Every state has an industrial directory, and there are also a number of private ones. One of the most popular industrial directories is the New York-based *Thomas Register.* The 19-volume *Register* contains 50,000 product headings and listings from 123,000 industrial companies selling everything from heavy machine tools to copper tubing to orchestra pits.

Direct Marketing

Business advertisers use various direct-marketing vehicles, such as direct mail, catalogs, and **data sheets**, to reach their markets. They often use direct mail to prepare the groundwork for subsequent sales calls. Catalogs and data sheets support the selling function by providing technical data about the product and supplementary information concerning price and availability.

Direct mail has the capacity to sell the product, provide sales leads, and lay the groundwork for subsequent sales calls. Technology developments allow direct-mail marketers to personalize the message to specific customers, include highly technical information, and provide top-notch photography and designs. Long copy, illustrations, diagrams, or any other device can be carried through direct mail. In addition, dramatic improvements in mailing list accuracy have reduced the waste historically associated with direct mail.

Consumer Media

Consumer media can sometimes be effective because of the lack of competition from other business advertisers. Because the message exposure occurs away from the office, it also encounters less competition from the receiver's other business needs.

Although consumer media are also an excellent means of reaching the market in which coverage is limited geographically, they still are not used much. In general, consumer publications receive less than 5 percent of the total dollar amount spent on business-to-business advertising, and spot radio, spot television, and network television each receive less than 1 percent. Sometimes businesses advertise in consumer magazines (such as *Better*

Homes and Gardens, Golf, or *Newsweek*) in the hope of influencing consumers to pull the brand through the channel by requesting a brand at their retail store.

In addition to the use of traditional consumer media, there has been a tremendous growth in business television programming targeted at both businesspeople and consumers who are interested in business-related topics. For example, Financial Network News (FNN) not only produces its own business shows, but also provides the syndicated business shows *This Morning's Business* and *First Business.* Introduced in 1989, CNBC was conceived with the consumer in mind, and its programming focuses more on personal finance.

The Web and B-to-B Advertisers

The Internet is fast becoming a key medium for business-to-business advertisers. Company Web pages allow business clients to view product lists, place orders, check prices and availability, and replace inventories automatically. Promo City is a company that facilitates Web creation for businesses.

One of the most popular sites on the Web is FedEx, which allows its business clients all over the world to track their packages, obtain price information, and learn about FedEx software and services. It receives 1.7 million tracking requests a month, 40 percent of which probably would have been called in to the 800 number if the Web site had not been available. Because handling each call costs approximately $1, the Web site saves the company as much as $8 million in customer costs.[9]

The "A Matter of Principle" box provides suggestions to make Web B-to-B more effective.

A MATTER OF PRINCIPLE
"WOOING BUSINESS THROUGH THE WEB"

➤ Few areas of marketing have more eagerly adopted Web technology than business-to-business. In many respects it is a system that enhances all the marketing tasks found in B-to-B—research, buying, selling, communication, and support services. However, one must be careful with this technology. Site operators must be true experts in design and creating a requisite level of flexibility. Specifically, the site must offer additional services, such as help with logistics and credit, which provides a competitive advantage.

Recent reports offer three specific recommendations that enhance the effectiveness of Web in business-to-business. The first recommendation is one common to all facets of marketing—understand your customers. That's right, conduct research that will provide the insights that allow a marketer to create relevant value propositions that address the needs and wants of the consumer. One of the strengths of the Internet is its ability to customize consumer messaging. This is accomplished through relevant consumer information.

A second recommendation is for business-to-business marketers to look for strategically beneficial partnerships, such as creating a collaborative business model, where one party has the products to offer online and the other partner has the Internet technology. Microsoft (VericalNet) partnered with the Microsoft Corp. in 2001. AOL and amazon did the same at the beginning of 2002.

Finally, Internet business-to-business marketers must be able to move quickly and purposively. The industry is very dynamic and opportunities do not last long.

Ultimately, the biggest challenge is how an Internet company or a B-to-B company positions itself with clients and in the marketplace. The Internet has changed processes. In the past, business processes were kept behind the scenes, and were not the concern of customers. The Web now offers process improvements that position the company differently.

An example of a successful B-to-B Web site is Lennox Industries (www.davelennox.com), a manufacturer of residential and commercial air-conditioning and heating equipment. Lennox's network of more than 6,000 independent dealers has always relied on the company for vital business information, such as engineering documentation, service literature, and installation. Since the launch of Dave Net (named after company founder Dave Lennox) in 1999, dealers now use a single CD to access product information, technical data, and marketing literature. And because the Dave Net system connects to Lennox via the Internet, information is automatically updated the moment users log on to the site. In addition, the site allows dealers to process warranty claims online. Finally, the site provides for online ordering and price checks.

POINT TO PONDER
Can you think of other ways to enhance B-to-B online advertising?

Sources: Paula Lyon Andruss, "Choose or Lose," *Marketing News* (October 23, 2000): 1, 11; Dana James, "B-to-B Works Better Collaboratively," *Marketing News* (March 27, 2002): 4; Markley Harty, "To Be or Not to B," *Adweek* (December 4, 2000): 58–60.

Does Business Advertising Sell?

Although few business marketers today rely exclusively on their sales forces to reach potential buyers, many people have questioned the effectiveness of business advertising. The Advertising Research Foundation (ARF) and the Association of Business Publishers (ABP) have studied the link between business advertising, industrial product sales, and profits.[10] The researchers monitored product sales and the level and frequency of their advertising schedules for one year. To ensure that the study's findings could apply to a wide range in industries and products, three very different products were monitored: a portable safety device that sold for less than $10, a commercial transportation package that sold for around $10,000, and highly specialized laboratory equipment priced between $5,000 and $10,000.

Despite the diversity in price, product life, purchase complexity, and distribution channels, the study found that for all three products:

- Business-to-business advertising created more sales than would have occurred without advertising.
- Increased advertising often resulted in increased product sales.
- It paid to advertise to both dealers and end users when the product was sold through dealers.
- Increased advertising frequency increased sales leads and generated higher profits.
- It took 4 to 6 months to see the results of the advertising program.

Global company FedEx uses the Web to communicate with business clients from Brazil to China to Italy to the United States.

- The use of color in the advertising made a dramatic difference.
- The advertising campaign was effective long after the campaign had ended.
- Advertising favorably affected purchasers' awareness of and attitudes toward industrial products.

Business-to-business advertising has a reputation for being dull. The future of business-to-business advertising depends on how well it adapts to the following trends:

- Business-to-business marketers require more accountability and efficiency in marketing communication programs.
- Ad programs and staff, seen as marginal expenses in the business-to-business companies, are being pared down or eliminated.
- Business customers have many more product choices and less time to make decisions. Advertising must support customer sales and services and help build relationships with clients. Media choices must become more creative; they must break through the clutter and allow decision makers to gather information conveniently.
- Business-to-business marketing itself is becoming more people oriented, with the best television and print ads addressing a product's solution to human problems.

IT'S A WRAP
KILLING BUGS IS JUST THE BEGINNING

We began this chapter with the challenge facing the Orkin Commercial Division. Firmly established in the residential market, Orkin needed to increase its credibility among the myriad of businesses that need pest control. Orkin accounted for the unique requirements of business customers by focusing on its high level of knowledge and technology, and specialized applications.

In respect to its two primary objectives, the "Q & A" campaign proved very effective. First, Orkin's sales growth objective was exceeded by 300 percent. Second, its closure rate goal was exceeded by over 250 percent. All these successes were a direct result of Orkin's ability to reposition itself as a commercial exterminating expert. As hoped for, sales from the residential segment remained stable. Not bad for a business that had experienced a three-year downward trend.

Summary

1. **Discuss retail advertising fundamentals.** Retailers are merchants who sell directly to consumers. Most retail businesses are locally owned and advertise at the local level. However, retail advertising at the national and international levels is becoming more common. Co-op advertising with manufacturers and service providers is common. Retail advertising directed at a local audience typically focuses on attracting customers through price and promotion information. It may also focus on store image, product quality, and style. The advertising generally is less sophisticated and more utilitarian than national or international brand advertising. Many diverse businesses rely on local retail advertising, such as independently owned businesses, franchisees, and the local stores of national or international chains. Apart from traditional store retailing, some businesses engage in nonstore retailing, including use of the Web. Several trends affect retail advertising, including consolidation, changing demographics, and competition.

2. **Summarize the media options for retailers.** Retail advertising uses various media alternatives. The main medium is newspapers. However, retailers also use shoppers, preprinted inserts, magazines, television, radio, and the Web.

3. **Explain business-to-business advertising objectives.** Business-to-business advertising is used to influence demand and is directed at people in the business arena who buy or specify products for business use. Its objectives include creating company awareness, increasing selling efficiency, and supporting channel members. Compared to the consumer market, the market for business goods is limited; decision making tends to be shared by a group of people and purchasing decisions center around price, services, product quality, and assurance of supply.

4. **Identify the media used in business advertising.** Business-to-business media consist of general business and trade publications, directories, direct mail, catalogs, data sheets, the Web, and consumer media.

Key Terms

business-to-business advertising, p. 497
business marketing, p. 497
cooperative (co-op) advertising, p. 486
data sheets, p. 503

dealer tag, p. 487
e-commerce, p. 488
geomarketing, p. 491
horizontal publications, p. 503
industrial advertising, p. 498

institutional retail advertising, p. 489
nonpromotional product advertising, p. 490
product retail advertising, p. 490

professional advertising, p. 498
retail advertising, p. 484
sales advertising, p. 490
vertical publications, p. 503

Questions

1. You are developing an ad to reach chemists in the oil industry. Would you place this ad in a general business magazine or in a trade publication? Why?

2. How does retail advertising differ from national consumer brand advertising? Which is the more difficult to create?

3. Think of a restaurant in your community. What types of people does it target? Would you recommend that its advertising focus on price or image? What is (or should be) its image? Which media should it use?

4. Biogen Corporation's mission is to become a leading company in genetic research and development for health industries. Privately held at the time of incorporation, it decided to go public and have its stock traded. How would corporate advertising assist Biogen in its mission? What audience targets should be priorities for its communication programs? Should it develop more than one campaign?

5. Although personal selling is a vital marketing tool for industrial (business-to-business) companies, advertising also has a significant role in many marketing situations. What if a limited budget means expanding one at the sacrifice of the other? Suppose you were making a decision for a company that is beginning a marketing effort for a new set of products; you'll need approximately six new salespeople. If an advertising campaign to introduce the firm would mean hiring four salespeople instead of six, is the advertising worth it? Explain the strengths and weaknesses of this idea.

6. Tom and Wendi Promise have just purchased a sandwich shop. They found a good lease in a neighborhood shopping center, but the costs of franchising, leasing, and other charges have left them very little for advertising. With limited funds, Tom and Wendi can afford only one of the following options: a Yellow Pages display ad, a series of advertisements in the area's weekly "shopper" newspaper, or advertising in the area's college newspaper (the campus is six blocks from the store). Which of these mediums will best help Tom and Wendi get the awareness they need? Support your answer.

7. Abby Wilson, the advertising manager for a campus newspaper (published four times per week), is discussing ways to increase advertising revenues with her sales staff. She asks opinions on using sales time to promote a co-op program to interest campus-area businesses. One salesperson says the retailers won't want to bother with all the paperwork. Another explains that newspaper reps have to understand co-op well to sell it, and that none of Wilson's staff has experience. Would you be persuaded that promoting cooperative advertising is more trouble than it is worth?

8. What is cooperative advertising? How does it benefit the retailer? The manufacturer?

9. What are some of the concerns the consumer has with shopping on a retail Web site? How could these concerns be resolved?

10. How do retail advertising objectives differ from business-to-business objectives?

Suggested Class Project

Select a print retail advertisement. Think about how this ad could be converted into a television commercial. Give examples of when and on what channel this broadcast ad would be aired. Support your recommendations with an explanation.

Suggested Internet Class Project

Compare the speed, convenience, and content of the following three business-to-business sites: americanexpress.com, dell.com, officedepot.com. Write a one- to two-page report on what you find.

Hallmark BUILD•A•CAMPAIGN*Projects*

Please review the Hallmark Case Appendix at the end of the text before responding to these questions.

1. In small groups discuss the ramifications of Hallmark's decision to advertise directly to consumers versus competitors' decisions to establish distribution relationships through a push marketing strategy.

2. Recommend ways to build brand insistence, given Hallmark's decision to extend its Expressions line into major grocery and drug stores. Summarize your recommendations on these retail marketing issues in a proposal for a local Gold Crown store campaign.

HANDS-ON   Case 17

UNISYS TRIES AGAIN

On his second day as chief executive of Unisys Corp., Lawrence Weinbach ordered the marketing folks to dump their advertising pitch, which promoted the computer company as the "Information Management Company." Brought in to resuscitate Unisys, Weinbach was worried that it was perceived to be a dull, old-line maker of big, mainframe computers. Never mind that 63 percent of its $7 billion in annual revenue was coming from the red-hot computer services business. "Information management" was not only vague, but also didn't convey the youthfulness Weinbach was trying to portray.

The following week, Weinbach told nervous executives from Bozell Worldwide, Unisys's longtime ad agency, that he would let them keep the account if they came up with a campaign that would reflect a "new" Unisys and stand out amid the clutter of high-tech advertising. "Push the envelope in good taste," he said. "And make me smile."

In time for his first anniversary at the company, Bozell unveiled a global advertising blitz, designed to create a new image for Unisys. The $20 million print and television campaign featured offbeat, almost surreal ads that are clearly designed to look and sound different from most of the technology babble. They showcase young people like the ones seen in Gap commercials, golfing, dancing, and skiing. The people featured in the ads are supposed to be Unisys employees. But instead of having heads, computer monitors sit atop their shoulders.

The point? Unisys employees supposedly are thinking 24 hours a day about how to solve real-life problems for customers. The underlying premise is that computer services is a people business, and Unisys people are willing to roll up their sleeves. The new tagline: "We eat, sleep, and drink this stuff."

Weinbach concedes that Unisys can't compete with many of its deep-pocketed rivals, but he notes that in tests the ads resonated well with customers and employees. ■

IT'S YOUR TURN

1. Do you feel that the new strategy will work with a high-tech b-to-b company?
2. Should Unisys be concerned that some customers will feel let down when their sales rep doesn't match the youthful image of the salespeople portrayed in the ad? Explain your answer.
3. Why do you think Bozell and Unisys chose young people to represent the company in the ads?

Sources: Raju Narisetti, "Unisys Campaign Emphasizes Firm's Vigor," *Wall Street Journal* (September 24, 1998): B12; Leslie J. Nicholson and Jane M. Von Bergen, "Wanted: Changed Image for Deeply Changed Firm," *The Inquirer* (September 24, 1998): retrieved at Philadelphia Online, www.phillynews.com/inquirer/98/Sep/24/business/UNI24.htm.

Notes

1. William M. Buckley, "Clicks and Mortar," *Wall Street Journal* (July 17, 2000): R4–R5.

2. Rebecca Quick, "Returns to Sender," *Wall Street Journal* (July 17, 2000): R8.

3. Kate Maddox, "E-Commerce Becoming Reality," *Advertising Age* (October 16, 1998): S1–S2.

4. Leonard L. Barry, "Branding the Store," *Arthur Andersen Retailing Issues Letter* 9(5) (September 1997).

5. A. Jerome Jeweler and Bonnie L. Drewniany, *Creative Strategy in Advertising,* 7th ed. Belmont, CA: (Wadsworth, 2001): 240–244.

6. Phillip W. Mahin, *Business-to-Business Marketing* (New York: Allyn & Bacon, 1991), 5.

7. Marc Gunther, "Take Your $20, and a Coupon," *Fortune* (April 3, 2000): 48.

8. "From a Reporter to a Source: A New Survey of Selling Costs," *Sales & Marketing Management* (February 16, 1987): 12.

9. Lynn G. Coleman, "The Crunch Has Come," *Marketing News* (March 4, 1991): 16.

10. Ibid.

CHAPTER 18

International Advertising

Chapter Objectives

When you have completed this chapter, you should be able to

1. Explain the evolution of global marketing.
2. Summarize how international management affects international advertising.
3. Discuss the approaches to international advertising.
4. List the special problems international advertisers face.

P&G: A Leader in Global Branding

Award: *Winning Global Strategy*

Company: *Procter & Gamble's global brands*

At one time or another, you have used a Procter & Gamble (P&G) product. You probably have a number of P&G products in your home right now. With the dominance of P&G's brands, it's likely that you wash your clothes with Tide or Cheer, brush your teeth with Crest, drink Folgers coffee, eat Pringles chips, and clean your dishes with Dawn or Cascade. Although we may think of P&G as a U.S. company, it currently markets more than 250 products in more than 140 different countries. Its net sales in 2001 were nearly $40 billion. Moreover, P&G employs almost 106,000 people in approximately 80 countries worldwide.

It's not surprising to learn that P&G has a fully developed global branding strategy in place. Global Marketing Officer Jim Stengel, cogently expressed the philosophy of this global strategy (via satellite) at a conference for the International Advertising Association in Beirut: "Our goal is global brand leadership in the categories in which we choose to compete. Sometimes we can do that with one brand name and brand positioning, and sometimes it takes several brands with different positionings."

As you'll see in this chapter, there are two basic approaches to international marketing and advertising. Companies can either try to standardize their products (and, to a degree, their advertising) to work in many markets. Or, companies can tailor their products and advertising to local markets. The first approach is easier to manage, but runs the risk of not effectively reaching consumers. The second approach targets consumers more specifically, but is more expensive and complicated to implement.

The P&G approach toward global branding is flexible enough to accommodate global strategies at various points on this spectrum. For example, on one end of the spectrum, P&G's global laundry business markets several brands including Ariel, Cheer, Bold, Yes, Dreft, Gain, and Tide because consumer laundry habits are highly varied from country to country and region to region. On the other end of the spectrum, the company markets its Pampers brand in most of the countries in which P&G competes. Pampers' global equity is consistent around the globe: helping babies develop better. But when it comes to translating this equity into precise communications strategies and advertising executions, Pampers allows for regional and local variations. Mr. Stengel believes the right global branding decision must be made on a case-by-case basis. He points to the Safeguard brand as a past example of how P&G went too far in standardizing its global branding strategy. Named Escuda in Mexico for many years, P&G changed the name to Safeguard and watched sales and market share drop dramatically. Sales returned when P&G reinstated the Escuda name.

To ensure that P&G's marketing organization is savvy about global marketing, Mr. Stengel encourages marketing employees to serve in P&G's regional organizations at some point in their careers. And, he's created a number of internal programs that enable marketing employees from all around the world to share knowledge and best practices from their regions. He also expects P&G's advertising agencies to be strategic about how to reach consumers in key markets and build global brands. To enable its agencies to take a more global approach, P&G has moved to align each of its largest global brands with a single global agency, a move that has resulted in efficiency and effectiveness around the world.

The global branding challenges P&G faces are becoming more common in business as world markets open up. By the time you reach the "It's a Wrap" section at the end of this chapter, you should have a pretty good idea of the global strategies of a variety of companies.

Source: Procter & Gamble External Relations Department and Jack Neff, "P&G Flexes Muscle for Global Branding," *Advertising Age* (June 3, 2002): 53.

INTERNATIONAL BUSINESS

Since Wendell Wilkie coined the phrase "One World" in his 1940 presidential campaign, the distance between that vision and the reality has narrowed: The top worldwide markets began spending more than 50 percent of their advertising dollars outside the United States in the early 1990s. The non–U.S. gross income of the top 500 advertising agencies reached $9 billion as the twentieth century drew to a close. Interestingly, of the top 25 agencies almost half are headquartered in the United States (see Table 18.1).

In this chapter we explore the evolution of advertising from a local venue to a global one. We examine the tools of international management, the means of organizing for international advertising, creating and planning international advertising campaigns, and special problems in the international arena.

THE EVOLUTION OF GLOBAL MARKETING

In most countries markets are composed of local, regional, and international brands. A **local brand** is one marketed in a single country. A **regional brand** is one marketed throughout a region (for example, North America or Europe). An **international brand** is available virtually everywhere in the world.

Marketing emerged when the emphasis changed from importing products (tea, spices, silk, gold, and silver) to exporting products. Advertising was used to introduce, explain, and sell the benefits of a product—especially a branded product—in markets outside the

TABLE 18.1   **World's Top 25 Advertising Organizations**

Ranked by worldwide gross income in 2001 from all marketing-related activities.

Rank				Worldwide Gross Income		Billings
2001	**2000**	**Advertising Organization**	**Headquarters**	**2001**	**% CHG**	**2001**
1	2	WPP Group	London	$8,165.0	2.5	$75,711.0
2	1	Interpublic Group of Cos.	New York	7,981.4	−1.9	66,689.1
3	3	Omnicom Group	New York	7,404.2	6.0	58,080.1
4	4	Publicis Groupe (Includes Bcom3 Group)	Paris	4,769.9	2.0	52,892.2
5	5	Dentsu	Tokyo	2,795.5	−8.9	20,847.8
6	6	Havas Advertising	Levallois-Perret, France	2,733.1	−2.1	26,268.5
7	7	Grey Global Group	New York	1,863.6	1.7	12,105.7
8	8	Cordiant Communications Group*	London	1,174.5	−7.0	13,388.0
9	9	Hakuhodo	Tokyo	874.3	−13.0	6,862.2
10	10	Asatsu-DK	Tokyo	394.6	−8.7	3,500.6
11	11	TMP Worldwide	New York	358.5	−13.8	1,705.6
12	12	Carlson Marketing Group	Minneapolis	356.1	−8.7	2,611.1
13	17	Incepta Group	London	248.4	13.6	695.0
14	13	Digitas	Boston	235.5	−18.3	NA
15	15	Tokyo Agency	Tokyo	203.9	−11.3	1,782.6
16	16	Daiko Advertising	Tokyo	203.0	−10.2	1,585.0
17	14	Aspen Marketing Group	Los Angeles	189.2	−24.0	1,262.2
18	18	Maxxcom	Toronto	177.1	−0.1	386.7
19	20	Cheil Communications	Seoul	142.0	−5.6	796.0
20	23	Doner	Southfield, Mich.	114.2	4.0	1,070.8
21	19	Ha-Lo Industries	Niles, Ill.	105.0	−33.3	NA
22	22	Yomiko Advertising*	Tokyo	102.2	−7.7	1,022.2
23	21	SPAR Group	Tarrytown, N.Y.	101.8	−8.3	678.8
24	30	Cossette Communication Group	Quebec City	95.2	12.1	488.2
25	28	DVC Worldwide	Morristown, N.J.	92.6	4.4	680.9

Advertising Age April 23, 2001.

home country. The current patterns of international expansion emerged largely in the twentieth century. Advertising that promotes the same product in several countries is known as **international advertising**. It did not appear in any organized manner until the late nineteenth century.

Home Country Production

Figure 18.1 illustrates the development of product marketing from companies outside their home markets. It starts with a product that begins to reach the saturation point in its home market. Management tries to recapture sales by introducing new products in its home market or expanding into foreign markets.

Saturation of the home country market isn't the sole reason companies venture outside the home market. Research that shows market potential for products in other countries, mergers and acquisitions with foreign businesses, and moving into other markets to preempt development by competitors also prompt international marketing and advertising.

Exporting

The first step in Figure 18.1, exporting a product, requires placing the product in the distribution system of another country. The exporter typically appoints a distributor or importer,

FIGURE 18.1

THE TYPICAL LIFE CYCLE OF A PRODUCT'S MARKETING

Companies looking to enter foreign markets generally export their products first. Then, if the product gains momentum, it enters a growth phase and, finally, a maturity phase.

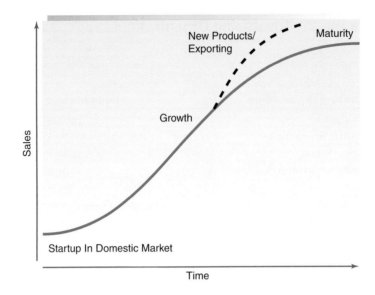

who assumes responsibility for marketing and advertising in the new country. As volume grows, the complexity of product sizes, product lines, pricing, and local adaptation increases. The exporter might send an employee to work with the importer to act as a liaison. Some companies prefer to appoint a local distributor who knows the language and the distribution system and can handle customers and government better than a foreigner could. Starbucks, for instance, appointed a local distributor in several Asian countries, including Thailand.

A few years ago the Brazil-based chocolate manufacturer, Garoto (which means "boy" in Portuguese), decided to export to other Latin American countries. Even though only $25 million of Garoto's $592 million sales come from exports, the company is already Latin America's biggest chocolate exporter. Although sales outside Latin America aren't big enough to merit media advertising beyond the region, Garoto does participate in promotional opportunities such as major food fairs.[1]

Export marketing and advertising are not the exclusive province of large companies. Bu Jin, an innovative company in Boulder, Colorado, creates and markets martial arts products. With only eight full-time employees, its products fill a high-end international niche market worldwide. Most of Bu Jin's business is driven by its catalog.

Many service providers also market internationally. Airlines and transportation companies that serve foreign markets, such as UPS, are in effect exporting a service. The UPS ads on page 516 ran in several countries.

Nationalization and Rationalization

If sales of the imported line grow even further, the exporter may want greater control or a larger profit share and may either buy back the importer's rights and handle distribution or set up assembly (or manufacturing) facilities in the importing country. In essence, management and manufacturing transfer from the home country to the foreign one.

At this point, key marketing decisions focus on acquiring or introducing products specifically for the local market, such as BMW setting up a U.S. manufacturing plant to build American versions of its German cars.

Once the exporter becomes nationalized in several countries in a regional bloc, the company often establishes a regional management center and transfers day-to-day management responsibilities from the home country to that office.

When a company is regionalized, it may still focus on its domestic market, but international considerations become more important. For instance, Coca-Cola has several international regional offices to support its international markets.

Colarado Company, Bu Jin promotes its martial arts products internationally, mainly through catalog distribution.

THE GLOBAL PERSPECTIVE

The company that has domestic operations and established regional operations in Europe, Latin America, North America, the Pacific, or elsewhere, faces the question of whether to establish a world corporate headquarters. Part of the reason for making such a decision is to give the company a truly **global perspective**: a corporate philosophy that directs products and advertising toward a worldwide market. This perspective means the company must internationalize the management group. Unilever and Shell (both of which have twin world headquarters in the United Kingdom and the Netherlands), IBM, Nestlé, and Interpublic have changed to a global management structure.

As mentioned earlier, virtually every product category can be divided into local (or national), regional (trading bloc), and international brands. International brands are those that are marketed in two or more of the four major regional market blocs: North America, Latin America, Europe, and Asia-Pacific. Although the Eastern European bloc will exist as a trading region for years, several of the western-most countries in this group have been subsumed into the European Union, and Russia and the Asian republics of the former Soviet Union may coalesce into a smaller fifth bloc. The sixth bloc—Africa, the Middle East and Southern Asia—is so much smaller economically than the others that it is often attached to Europe or Asia-Pacific.

The ultimate goal of any organization in attaining a global perspective is to leverage its operations in such a way that they benefit from advantages offered by each country's business environment. These advantages include: currency exchange, tax or labor rates; the education and skill base of the labor force; natural resources; and, industrial or government infrastructures.

For example, Toyota Motors began as a local Japanese car manufacturer, but has become a particularly successful global marketer. It achieved this by progressively expanding the reach of its export market; and eventually positioned itself to take advantage of the business environments of several countries. It opened manufacturing facilities in the United States, Great Britain, and Germany, with local skilled labor, and used regional advertising agencies who were sensitive to each market's needs.

Although there are thousands of companies that view themselves as selling a **global brand**, this designation requires a lot more than a self-proclamation. A report by market-research firm A.C. Nielsen, entitled "Researching the Billion Dollar Mark: A Review of

With these ads, UPS projected its image in several different markets.

Today's Global Brand," cites only 43 brands that qualify as global. To qualify, a brand needs to have "more than $1 billion in annual sales, with at least 5% coming outside the company's home region." Coca-Cola's, Philip Morris', Procter & Gamble's, and Wal-Mart's brands lead the way. Several companies did not make the list because they used different brand labels in different countries.[2]

THE GLOBAL DEBATE AND ADVERTISING

A 1983 *Harvard Business Review* article by Theodore Levitt, Professor of Business Administration and Marketing at Harvard Business School, ignited a debate over how to achieve global coverage. Levitt argued that companies should operate as if there were only one global market. Why? He argued that differences among nations and cultures were not only diminishing but should be ignored because people throughout the world are motivated by the same desires and wants. Levitt argued further that businesses would be more efficient if they planned for a global market.

Philip Kotler, marketing professor at Northwestern University, disagreed with Levitt's philosophy. According to Kotler, Levitt misinterpreted the overseas success of Coca-Cola, PepsiCo, and McDonald's. "Their success," he reasoned, "is based on variation, not offering the same product everywhere." However, Levitt did not back down. "It's a big mistake for advertisers to think that everything is becoming narrow. The challenge is to effectively come up with ways to communicate the same message to a homogenized audience all over the world."[3]

The outgrowths of this debate have been three main schools of thought on advertising in another country:

• *Standardization.* This school of thought contends that differences between countries are more a matter of degree than directions, so advertisers must instead focus on the similarities of consumers around the world.

Totally Standardized Strategy and Execution	Standardized Strategy, Translated Execution	Standardized Strategy, Modified Execution	Totally Localized Strategy and Execution

FIGURE 18.2

THE ADAPTABILITY CONTINUUM
Most global companies fall in the middle and right side of the continuum in their global advertising strategies.

- *Localization (adaptation).* This school of thought argues that advertisers must consider differences among countries, including culture, stage of economic and industrial development, stage of life cycle, media availability, research availability, and legal restrictions.
- *Contingency (moderate).* This school of thought reasons that neither complete standardization nor complete adaptation is necessary and that a combination of the evaluation of factors can affect the effectiveness of such advertising.

These three perspectives are further illustrated in the Adaptability Continuum shown in Figure 18.2. Note that most companies use the middle-of-the-road approach or lean toward localization. Starbucks uses localization. Tea is offered in stores in the far east, stronger coffees in Europe, and gourmet coffees in the United States. Accordingly, it has standardized its product name, logo, and packaging.

So which is the right approach? In actuality, no business has a completely global campaign. Even companies committed to globalization, such as Toyota and McDonald's, must translate many of their ads into other languages and conform to local standards and regulations. In contrast, a completely localized campaign could lead to chaos and inefficiency.[4]

The reality of global advertising suggests that the contingency approach is best. Marketers are restricted by language, regulations, and a lack of completely global media. Still, the trend toward global markets is inescapable. The challenge for advertisers is to balance Kotler's "variations" nationally or regionally with a basic Levitt-style global plan to maintain efficiency. See the "Practical Tips" box for the benefits of standardization and local strategies.

Starbucks follows a localization strategy by tailoring its offerings in different countries.

Practical Tips

REASONS TO GO GLOBAL OR STAY LOCAL

Reasons to Use a Standardization Strategy

* Standardization will lead to savings through economies of scale (advertising production, planning, control).
* Standardization ensures that advertising messages of a product are complementary and reinforcing.
* The company maintains control over the image projected by advertising for the brand.
* Global media create opportunities for global marketing.
* Converging buyer wants and needs means that buyers everywhere will increasingly want the same products.
* There is little or no competition in many foreign markets.
* Graphic and visual advertising approaches can be used to overcome cultural differences.

Reasons to Use a Local Strategy

* A better fit with local markets means the advertiser is less likely to overlook local variations that affect buyer behavior.
* As a general rule, the fewer the people who have to approve decisions, the faster they can be made.
* Getting local managers and employees involved and motivated is much easier if those people have a say in the advertising decisions.
* Any cost reductions resulting from globalization often are offset by mistargeted ads.
* The chance of cultural blunders decreases.
* Strategically sound advertising is more likely to be successful.

INTERNATIONAL MANAGEMENT

Regardless of the company's form or style of management, the shift from national to international management requires new tools for advertisers, including one language (usually English), one control mechanism (the budget), and one strategic plan (the marketing strategy).

Lingua Franca

Language affects the creation of the advertising. English normally requires the least space in printed material or air time. The range of words (estimated at over 900,000) and the ease with which English adopts words from other languages often make it more economical than many other languages. This creates a major problem when the space for copy is laid out for English and one-third more space is needed for French or Spanish. However, English does not have the subtlety of other languages such as Greek, Chinese, or French. Those languages have many different words for situations and emotions that do not translate precisely into English.

Headlines in any language often involve a play on words, themes that are relevant to one country, or slang. Because these verbal techniques often don't cross borders well, copywriters must remove them from the advertising unless the meaning or intent can be recreated in other languages. For this reason, international campaigns are not translated. Instead, a copywriter usually rewrites them in the second language.

Some languages simply do not have words equivalent to English expressions. Computer words and advertising terms are almost universally of English derivation. There are even problems translating British English in to American English, as Table 18.2's dictionary of BritSpeak illustrates.[5] However, there are some unexpected similarities between the United Kingdom and the United States, as the British road rage ad points out.

TABLE 18.2	**An English-to-American English Dictionary**

Rubber: an eraser	Estate car: station wagon
Ladder: a run in a stocking	Hoover, Hoovering: vacuum cleaner, to vacuum
Bonnet: a car's hood	Wind-up: a practical joke
Queue: to stand in line	
Freephone: a toll-free number	

Source: Adapted from "A Pitch with a New Angle," *Brandweek* (November 11, 1996): 20.

Since 1539 the French have had legislation to keep their language "pure" and now have a government agency to prevent words, especially English words, from corrupting the French language. The words *marketing* and *weekend,* unacceptable to the French government agency, are translated literally as "study the market" (or "pertaining to trade") and "end of the week," respectively. Neither quite captures the essence of the English word. Understanding language not only prevents mishaps; it also gives advertisers a greater cultural understanding. Getting Through Customs is one company that helps business people understand foreign cultures.

Here are two examples which show how a poor translation can send the wrong message.

- *From an ad for a Rome laundry:* "Ladies, leave your clothes here and spend the afternoon having a good time."
- *From a Moscow weekly:* "There will be a Moscow Exhibition of Arts by 1,500 Soviet Republic painters. These were executed over the past two years."

Experience suggests that the most reasonable solution to the language problem is to use bilingual copywriters who understand the full meaning of the English text and can capture the essence of the message in the second language. It takes a brave and trusting international creative director to approve copy he doesn't understand but is assured is right. A *back translation* of the ad copy from the foreign language into the domestic one is always a good idea, but never conveys a complete cultural interpretation.

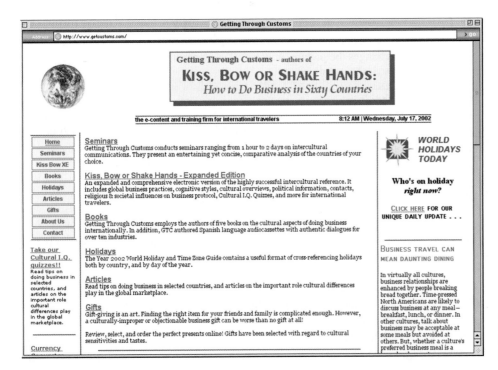

Advertisers can consult companies that specialize in helping business people understand foreign cultures.

An ad from the United Kingdom addresses road rage. Because of the power of the visual, it is understood easily in other countries.

The Global Advertising Plan

The strategic advertising plan usually is prepared in conjunction with the budget. Basically, the plan outlines the marketing strategy, while the budget allocates the funds. Two major approaches to strategic advertising in foreign cultures differ in their orientation: one is market oriented and the other is culture oriented. We discuss these contrasting approaches next.

The Market Analysis Model This model is based on data and observation from several countries. It recognizes the existence of local, regional, and international brands in almost every product category. The two major variables are the share of market of brands within a category and the size of the category. For example, the brand's percentage share of the category market might vary substantially in four countries:

Brands Percentage Share

	Country A	Country B	Country C	Country D
Global Brands	25%	30%	50%	20%
Regional Brands	60	30	10	55
Local Brands	15	40	40	25

According to this example, Country C looks very valuable for the global brand. The size of the market changes the picture, however. Assume that the size of the category market in the four countries is as follows:

Size of Category Market

	Country A	Country B	Country C	Country D
Number of Global Brands	200,000	100,000	50,000	300,000
Regional Brands	25,000	30,000	50,000	20,000
Local Brands	50,000	30,000	25,000	60,000

According to this market analysis, Country C actually is much less important. Half of this smaller market is already in global brands. Country D not only is a larger global brand market but also is a much larger total market. A marketing manager must look not only at share but also at market size, growth rates, and growth opportunities.

For instance, cola-flavored soft drinks are not nearly as dominant in Germany as they are in the United States. To generate sales in Germany, then, a soft drink company would have to develop orange and lemon-lime entries. McDonald's serves beer in Germany, wine in France, a local fruit-flavored shake in Singapore and Malaysia, and even a Portuguese sausage in Hawaii, in addition to the traditional Big Macs, fish sandwiches, and French fries to cater to local tastes.

The Culture-Oriented Model The second model of international advertising emphasizes the cultural differences among peoples and nations. This school of thought recognizes that people worldwide share certain needs, but it also stresses the fact that these needs are met differently from culture to culture.

Although the same emotions are basic to all humanity, the degree to which these emotions are expressed publicly varies. The camaraderie typical in an Australian business office would be unthinkable in Japan. The informal, first-name relationships common in North America are frowned on in Germany, where co-workers often do not use first names. Likewise, the ways in which we categorize information and the values we attach to people, places, and things depend on the setting in which we were raised.

How do cultural differences relate to advertising? According to the high-context/low-context theory, although the *function* of advertising is the same throughout the world, the expression of its message varies in different cultural settings.[6] The major distinction is between *high-context cultures,* in which the meaning of a message can be understood only within a specific context, and *low-context cultures,* in which the message can be understood as an independent entity. Figure 18.3 lists cultures from the highest to lowest context, with Japanese being the highest-context culture.

This model helps explain the difficulties of advertising in other languages. The differences between Japanese and English are instructive. English is a low-context language. English words have clearly defined meanings that are not highly dependent on the words surrounding them. In Japanese, however, a word can have multiple meanings. Listeners or readers will not understand the exact meaning of a word unless they clearly understand the preceding or following sentences, that is, the context in which the word is used.

Advertising messages constructed by writers from high-context cultures might be difficult to understand in low-context cultures because they may offer too much detail to make the point clearly. In contrast, messages authored by writers from low-context cultures may be difficult to understand in high-context cultures because they omit essential contextual detail.

Our tendency is to assume that, in the case of the United States, cultural differences are most likely between countries that are separated by thousands of miles. By that logic it would be surprising to identify different values between the United States and Canada. But, there are differences. Canadians are more conservative in respect to health and social issues, for example. As shown on their cigarette packaging, Canada requires tobacco companies to put graphic health warnings on packages. Pictures of rotting gums and diseased lungs are common, along with the tagline: "Tobacco Use Can Make You Impotent." In the United States the warning is much less dramatic and has remained the same for several years.

Agencies have to develop techniques to advertise brands that are marketed around the world. Some agencies exercise tight control, while others allow more local autonomy. All of these techniques fall into three groups: tight central international control, centralized resources with moderate control, and matching the client.

Henkel, a large German manufacturer of household and cleaning products, provides an example of how centralized management with similar products works. Henkel's international strategy was designed to accomplish three goals: eliminate duplication of effort among its national companies, provide central direction for new products, and achieve efficiency in advertising production and impact. It included these steps:

1. Identifying how a product fulfills a need or functions beneficially.
2. Determining the common need or product benefit for consumers in Europe or a larger area.
3. Assigning that specific need or benefit to one product with one brand name.
4. Assigning that brand to one brand manager and one advertising agency to develop and market.
5. Disallowing the use of that one brand's benefit, name, or creative campaign for any other brand in the company.

The organizational structure for managing international advertising depends heavily on whether the company is following a standardization or localization marketing and

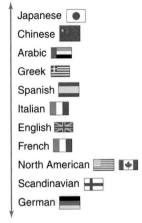

High-Context

Japanese
Chinese
Arabic
Greek
Spanish
Italian
English
French
North American
Scandinavian
German

Low-Context

FIGURE 18.3

HIGH- TO LOW-CONTEXT CULTURES
The language of advertising messages is not as easy to craft in high-context cultures as in low-context cultures, where the meaning of a sentence is not so dependent on surrounding sentences.

A MATTER OF PRACTICE

AGENCIES GO GLOBAL

➤ One way ad agencies establish a foothold in foreign markets is through agency partnerships. An example is the recent grouping of Interpublic Groups of Cos., McCann-Erickson Worldwide Group, and KidCom, the kid marketing unit of Campbell Mithun, Minneapolis. McCann currently manages two dozen General Mills dry cereal brands, including six brands in North America via Campbell Mithun, and sixteen brands for Cereal Partners Worldwide. The total media buy exceeded $450 million.

This sort of agency realignment has been spurred on by the need for U.S. companies to consolidate their communication efforts when they enter foreign markets. The U.S. cereal industry is in the forefront in this strategic realignment. There is a general belief that the only way to create market dominance in the world cereal business is by connecting with kids. Essentially, most Europeans are not cereal eaters, and adult habits are difficult to break.

KidCom was created through the joint venture of General Mills and Nestlé. It originated in London, and was later exported to Puerto Rico and Hong Kong. Its task is to serve as kids' cereal expert and assign brands and countries to the various agency partners.

It's clear that this type of arrangement will prove popular in other industries as well. The notion of U.S. marketing strategies translating easily into foreign markets is remote. Likewise, opening a foreign office is not always the answer for a U.S. ad agency. Placing a U.S. brand in the hands of a foreign agency may not be the answer either.

A consolidator, such as KidCom, becomes the product expert and makes agency assignments that make the most sense.

POINT TO PONDER

What problems would an industry face in trying to implement this type of structure?

Source: Kate MacArthur, "KidCom Goes to Paris," *Advertising Age* (December 10, 2001): 4, 70.

---

advertising strategy. For highly standardized advertising efforts, there may be one advertising plan for each product regardless of the number of markets entered. For a product using localized advertising, there probably will be a separate advertising plan for each foreign market.

Selecting an Agency

The choice of an advertising agency for international advertising is influenced not only by many of the same considerations as the choice of a domestic agency, but also by the standardized versus local decision. If the company wants to take a highly standardized approach in international markets, it is likely to favor an international agency that can handle advertising for the product in both the domestic and the international market. A localized advertising effort, by contrast, favors use of advertising agencies in many countries for both planning and implementation of the advertising.

As noted in the "A Matter of Practice" box, agencies must make adjustments when they go global.

APPROACHES TO THE INTERNATIONAL ADVERTISING CAMPAIGN

There is an old axiom, "All business is local." But this axiom should be modified to read "Almost all transactions are local." Although advertising campaigns can be created for worldwide exposure, the advertising is intended to persuade a reader or listener to do something (buy, vote, phone, order). That something is a transaction that usually is completed at home, near home, or in the same country if by direct mail. Even this will change as multinational direct-mail campaigns become possible in a unified common market.

As noted earlier, some advertisers develop tightly controlled global campaigns with minimum adaptation for local markets. Others develop local campaigns in every major

market. Most companies are somewhere in the middle, with a global campaign and a standardized strategy that is partially adapted as needed.

Centrally Controlled Campaigns

How are the campaigns, which can have nearly global application, created? International advertising campaigns have two basic starting points: (1) success in one country, and (2) a centrally conceived strategy, a need, a new product, or a directive.

In the first starting point, a successful advertising campaign, conceived for national application, is modified for use in other countries. "Impulse," the body spray, started in South Africa with a campaign showing a woman being pleasantly surprised when a stranger hands her flowers. That strategic idea has been used all over the globe, but in most markets the people and the setting are localized.

Wrigley, Marlboro, IBM, Waterman, Seiko, Philips, Procter & Gamble, Ford, Hasbro, and many other companies have taken successful campaigns from one country and transplanted them around the world. A strong musical theme, especially typical of Coke and Pepsi, makes the transfer even smoother because music is an international language.

Centrally Conceived Campaigns

The second starting point, a centrally conceived campaign, was pioneered by Coca-Cola and is now used increasingly in global strategies. Although the concept is simple, the application is difficult. A work team, task force, or action group (the names vary) assembles from around the world to present, debate, modify if necessary, and agree on a basic strategy as the foundation for the campaign.

Some circumstances require that a central strategy be imposed even if a few countries object. Cost is a huge factor. If the same photography and artwork can be used universally, this can save the $10,000 or more each local variation might cost. Or, if leakage across borders is foreseen, international management may insist on the same approach.

Colgate faced this problem before it standardized its red package and typography. Distributors in Asia bought shipments from the United States and Europe, depending on currency rates and shipping dates, so Asian consumers saw different packages for the same product, which led to consumer confusion.

A centralized campaign could include television, radio, newspapers, magazines, cinema, the Web, outdoor advertising, and collateral extensions (brochures, mailings, counter cards, in-store posters, handouts, take-one folders, or whatever is appropriate). The team can stay together to finish the work, or it can ask the writer or campaign developer to finish or supervise the completion of the entire project.

Variations on Central Campaigns Variations of the centrally conceived campaign also exist. For example, Xerox may handle its European creative development by asking the European offices of Young & Rubicam to develop a campaign for a specific product. The office that develops the approved campaign would be designated the lead agency. That agency office would then develop all the necessary elements of the campaign, determine the relationship of those elements to one another, shoot the photography or supervise the artwork, and prepare a standards manual for use in other countries. This manual would include examples of layouts and broadcast spots (especially the treatment of the logo or the product) and design standards for all elements.

Individual offices could either order the elements from the lead agency or produce them locally if that were less expensive. Because photography, artwork, television production, and color printing are very costly, developing these items in one location and then overlaying new copy or re-recording the voice track in the local language saves money; but advertisers must be careful to look local.

Local Application and Approval Assuming that the ad campaign has been approved centrally, its execution must be adapted to suit the local market. Every ad in every country cannot come back to regional and world headquarters for approval.

Within a campaign framework, most companies allow a degree of local autonomy. Some companies want to approve only pattern ads (usually the two or three ads that introduce the campaign) and commercials and allow local approval of succeeding executions. Others want to approve only television commercials and allow local freedom for other media. If headquarters develops common material (such as ad slicks or broadcast footage), it simplifies the approval process.

In any case, free-flowing communication is necessary. Senior officers travel, review work, and bring with them the best of what is being done in other countries. Seminars, workshops, and annual conventions all serve to disseminate campaign strategies, maintain the campaign's thrust, and stimulate development of new ideas. Today, companies must balance the globalization of concepts and strategy with the localization of application.

Determining Global Advertising Objectives

Just as every domestic advertising plan begins with a statement of objectives, global advertising plans originate with a similar statement. Global plans differ from their domestic counterparts in several key areas. These differences are largely responsible for limiting most global marketing objectives to awareness and recall, two effective yet easily attainable marketing measures. Below are some of the factors that advertisers must take into consideration when developing objectives:

1. There are often fewer customers in each foreign market; however, marketing materials must still be translated in a way that conscientiously addresses their market's culture and mores.
2. Business factors such as currency exchange rates and changes in tariffs influence the impact of an organization in any given market and therefore determine budgets.
3. Variations in the availability and cost of media and the effectiveness of certain types of media in some markets are a major consideration.
4. A global company cannot always obtain services from the best local advertising people; this creates a potential advantage for local competitors.
5. The often-smaller budgets allocated to global markets may hinder the achievement of long-term marketing effectiveness.
6. The availability of accurate and useful market research information is also often quite limited.

Positioning the Global Product

Research must be conducted to identify the problems and opportunities facing the product in each of the international markets to be entered. The normal approach of conducting consumer, product, and market analyses works well for international analysis. Emphasis should be placed on identifying local market differences to which the advertising programs must adjust.

The analysis portion of the advertising plan develops the information needed for positioning the product in the foreign markets. Particularly important is a good understanding of consumer buying motives in each market. This is almost impossible to develop without locally based consumer research.

If analysis reveals that consumer buying behavior and the competitive environment are the same across international markets, it may be possible to use a standardized positioning throughout. In exploring the international marketing opportunity for Gatorade, Quaker discovered that the active, outdoor lifestyle that created demand for sports beverages was an international, not a domestic phenomenon.

Starbucks' consumer research suggested that perceptions of a store such as Starbucks varied from market to market. In Japan, Starbucks was positioned as a daytime meeting place for business people and an evening place for socializing. The position of its Hawaiin stores was as a place to relax, any time of the day or night.

Setting the Budget

All the budgeting techniques discussed in Chapter 7 have possible application in foreign markets. However, several problems may affect this decision. Most notably, the exchange rate from country to country may affect not only the amount of money spent in a particular market, but also the timing of the expenditures. The cost of television time in Tokyo is approximately twice what it is on U.S. networks, and, rather than being sold during an up-front market every spring, Japanese TV time is wholesaled several times during the year.

Another factor is the budgetary tradition in a particular market. In the United States, the use of float is common, that is, bills do not have to be paid for 30, 60, or 90 days. In Denmark, everything is strictly cash. Likewise, the notion of barter, a common payment plan in many companies, is almost expected in Italy.

When a company is preparing a single advertising plan for multiple markets, many use an objective-task budgeting approach that makes advertising for each foreign market a separate objective with its own budget. (Remember that this approach looks at the objectives for each activity and determines the cost of accomplishing each objective.) This technique adds some flexibility to localize campaigns as needed. Alternatively, it can use other budgeting methods such as percentage-of-sales or the competitive method.

Selecting Media for International Campaigns

Advertising practitioners can debate global theories of advertising, but one fact is inescapable: Global media do not currently exist. Television can transmit the Olympics around the globe, but no one network controls this global transmission. An advertiser seeking global exposure must deal with different networks in different countries.

Satellite Transmission Satellite transmission now places advertising into many homes, but its availability is not universal because of the footprint (coverage area of the satellite), the technical limitations, and the regulations of transmission by various governments. Satellites beam signals to more than one country in Europe, the Asian subcontinent, North America, and the Pacific, but they are regional, not global, in coverage.

Despite its regional limitation, satellite transmission is still an enormous factor in the changing face of international advertising. The reach of satellite stations is based on a foundation of shared language, which is making national borders increasingly irrelevant in international markets.

The North American, European, Asian, and Latin American markets are becoming saturated with cable TV companies offering an increasing number of international networks. Such broadcasters include the hugely successful Latin American networks of Univision and Televisa, whose broadcasts can be seen in nearly every Spanish-speaking market, including the United States. One of Univision's most popular programs, Sabado Giganta, is seen by tens of millions of viewers in 16 countries.

Star TV, with an audience spanning 38 countries including Egypt, India, Japan, Indonesia, and Russia's Asian provinces, Star TV, was the first to reach this market of an estimated 2.7 billion people. It was closely followed by CNN and ESPN. Sky Channel, a U.K.-based network, offers satellite service to most of Europe, giving advertisers the opportunity to deliver a unified message across the Continent. The expansion of satellite television makes it possible to distribute a standardized message to extensive audiences, the potential of which presents international advertisers with new and unique challenges and powerfully enticing rewards.

The Web in International Advertising The Web is an international marketing and advertising medium but it faces access, legal, linguistic, currency, and technological barriers. First, not everyone around the globe has the access or ability to use the Internet via computer, but the number of Internet users is growing exponentially. The Internet audience is growing faster internationally than it is in the United States. Analysts had predicted that Europe's base of 9 million Internet users would top 17 million by the turn of the century. They also estimated that Asia and the Pacific Rim would double the 5 million households currently accessing the Internet by that time.[7] Figure 18.4 shows the state of global Internet use as of 2001.

Second, advertising and sales promotion laws differ from country to country.[8] Differences in privacy laws between Europe and the United States are expected to force American companies to change the way they collect and share consumer information.

FIGURE 18.4

THE NEW ECONOMY GOES GLOBAL
Web usage and users vary tremendously across the world. Advertisers need to track these trends to create and execute successful global campaigns.
Sources: Computer Industry Almanac, Gartner Group, Andersen Consulting, Taylor Nelson Sofres Interactive, Emarketer, Cyberatlas, and Dataquest. Research by Richard Rubin; graphic by Christoph Blumrich—*Newsweek.*

Databank: The United States led the first burst of e-commerce in the 1990s, but other nations are coming on strong. Especially in Europe and Asia, the Internet economy is growing rapidly and creating a virtual global marketplace.

Top 10 countries in Internet use
About 375 million people worldwide have online access, with more than a third located in the United States:

Country	Millions
United States	135.7
Japan	26.9
Germany	19.1
Britain	17.9
China	15.8
Canada	15.2
S. Korea	14.8
Italy	11.6
Brazil	10.6
France	9.0

E–Holidays
Online holiday sales will jump 85% this year, to $19.5 billion:

Region	%
Japan	184.8%
Europe	96.4
Asia/Pacific	90.5
North America	69.9
Rest of world	188.9

Around the world
- PC shipments to Latin America jumped **51%** over the second quarter of last year. Server shipments were up **17%**.
- The United States had **76%** of the global business-to-consumer market in 1999; Europe had just **14%**

Web browsing and buying
In some countries, almost everyone who thinks about buying online does so:
Considered buying online, but decided not to

Most		Fewest	
South Korea	32%	India	1%
Italy	26	Poland	4
Taiwan	25	Singapore	7
Thailand	23	Portugal	8
Indonesia	22	Germany	9
Australia	20	Britain	11
Hong Kong	19	Czech Republic	11
Norway	17	Malaysia	11
Philippines	16	Turkey	11
United States	15	Slovakia	12

E stands for Europe
A survey of European executives found differences in the extent of e-commerce:

Sales, Marketing / Purchasing

Country	Sales, Marketing	Purchasing
Netherlands	93%	33
Sweden	77	57
Britain	75	61
Germany	75	37
France	70	30

North of the border
- **64%** of retailers recognize that they lag behind the United States, but **50%** do not have a clear strategy to integrate the Internet into their businesses
- **17%** of Canadian homeowners have broadband access, while only **8.6%** of U.S. residents do
- **59%** of public-sector employees have Internet access, compared with just **28%** in the private sector

Language is another factor. Although English is the dominant language on the Internet, some advertisers who want to provide different Web sites for different countries have trouble ensuring consistency across all sites. The linguistic problem is evident when Web sites are in Japanese or Chinese, languages from high-context cultures, and in English, a language from a low-context culture. English has a few variations of the word "yes," for instance, while high-context cultures may have thousands of variations. Ensuring precise, accurate communication in these situations is tough.

Another issue is exchange rates. Companies must decide whether to offer prices in their own currency or in the local currency. For example, one Canadian shopper reported that books on a Canadian Web site were cheaper than the same books on Amazon.com.[9] In addition, some companies make different offers available in different countries. However, savvy Internet customers can see how pricing differs from country to country. If they find differences, they may become frustrated or disenchanted.

A final point to keep in mind when appealing to international audiences is the technological differences among the worldwide Internet audiences. Users in some countries have to pay per-minute charges and therefore want to get on and off quickly, which precludes sophisticated graphics that take a long time to load. In other countries, users have access to fast lines and may expect more sophisticated Internet programming as a result.

The dizzying number of rules, regulations, and conflicting requirements a company must understand to conduct international business on the Internet can be a barrier to entering the global electronic market. While Internet industries are lobbying global market participants to establish standardized regulations, it is widely believed that these regulations will bring additional burdens such as taxes, tariffs, and conflicting disclosure or competition requirements. Therefore, many international organizations are increasingly looking to the Internet for advertising—not direct sales.

One manufacturing company that uses this Internet-advertising approach to drive its store-supported sales is Waterford Crystal of Ireland. It is important to understand that it does not sell its product to customers directly online, but simply offers images and descriptions of its full product line, as well as information about retailers who offer its products. Waterford's goal is to channel potential customers to its retailers, like Bloomingdale's, from whom the customer can make a final purchase. Such an approach overcomes many of the overwhelming challenges to conducting business internationally on the Internet. And, it is widely supported by the retailers who benefit from the additional sales of Waterford's products as well as increased customer exposure and traffic.

Execution of International Campaigns

Media planning for an international campaign follows the same principles as those used for reaching a national target audience. The execution, however, is more complex.

International campaigns are not always centrally funded. The global corporation typically has operating companies locally registered in most major countries. Advertising might have to be funded through these local entities for maximum tax benefits or to meet local laws of origination. The media planner might only be able to establish the media strategy for the target audience and set the criteria for selecting media. In small agencies media planners often make the media buys as well. Otherwise, the media buy is too complicated for one individual. Greater latitude is allowed in media planning than in creative planning. For example, a media campaign in the Southern Hemisphere, especially for consumer goods and seasonal items, requires major changes from a Northern Hemisphere campaign. In the Southern Hemisphere, summer, Christmas, and back-to-school campaigns are all compressed from November through January.

Media Choices Once an international advertiser's overall strategy has been established, it is still faced with a daunting array of media possibilities or limitations within specific markets. In developing an optimal solution that addresses these differences, an organization must consider the availability, cost, coverage, and appropriateness of the media.

Availability. Two main characteristics define the availability of a medium to an international advertiser—quantity and accessibility. The quantity, or saturation, of different media types can be so high in some markets that no dominant medium emerges as the clear choice. Other markets may have such a narrow quantity of available media that it serves to limit the advertiser's potential message or reach.

Accessibility can be an issue as well when governments prohibit the use of certain media for the delivery of specific advertising messages. A domestic example of this kind of accessibility limitation is one in which cigarette manufacturers are prohibited by law from advertising on U.S. television.

Some markets have a highly fragmented distribution of newspapers or magazines. In such markets the costs of placing advertising with each distributor to obtain the desired market coverage would be prohibitive.

Costs. Of major consideration is the fact that, in many countries, media prices are not always firm, but vary widely because of bargaining customs. The bargaining expertise of an advertiser with its local agency in negotiating contracts, as well as the local agency's relationships and bargaining skills with media providers, can result in huge differences in marketing costs from country to country.

Coverage. The limited availability of media in a market has a direct effect on the coverage a company can hope to attain there. In many instances, a combination of a number of different media must be used to reach the majority of a given market. Sometimes advertisers are forced to become more creative and try new methods of reaching their targets. For example, in parts of India, with limited technologies and infrastructures, Colgate hires 85 vans during a single campaign to visit villages identified as potentially profitable by its market research.

Appropriateness of the Media. Unfortunately, while many countries do have agencies similar to the U.S. Audit Bureau of Circulation, they often lack the power to enforce their policies. This means the international advertiser is often faced with inaccuracies or misrepresentations of circulation figures by local media providers. Therefore, determining whether it is selecting the right mix of media is difficult, if not impossible. In response to vastly inflated circulation figures of local newspapers, the president of the Mexican National Advertisers Association suggested that advertising agencies divide the reported figure in half, and consider the resulting number with skepticism.

The Global Creative Effect

Global campaigns, like domestic campaigns, require ad work that addresses the advertising objectives and reflects the product's positioning. The opportunity for standardizing the campaign exists only if the objectives and strategic position are essentially the same.

The creative process requires three steps: to determine copy content, to execute the content through a central idea, and to produce the advertising. Standardizing the copy content by translating the appeal into the language of the foreign market is fraught with possible communication blunders. It is rare to find a copywriter who is fluent in both the domestic and foreign language and familiar with the culture of the foreign market.

It is best if the central creative idea is universal across markets, or at least can be converted easily from market to market. For Starbucks the central idea is high-quality products in a relaxing atmosphere. Although the implementation of this idea may vary from market to market, the creative concept is sound across all types of consumers.

Even if the campaign theme, slogan, or visual elements are the same across markets, it is usually desirable to adapt the creative execution to the local market. Adaptation is especially important if the advertiser wants its products identified with the local market rather than as a foreign import.

A MATTER OF PRACTICE

IKEA's GLOBAL WOES

➤ Despite its status as a retailer in 29 international markets—with 170 stores, each offering about 7,500 distinct inexpensive, Scandinavian-designed home furnishing items—the Netherlands' IKEA still can't seem to pick up enough momentum to capture a substantial share of any of its markets. Its lackluster presence in the United States is actually better than in its German and U.K. markets where, despite its European community appeal, IKEA's paltry performance prevents it from attaining even 5 percent of those key markets. Upon closer examination of the company's problems, two key factors emerge as the source of its disappointing operations: customer satisfaction and the ineffectiveness of its marketing.

IKEA's strategy of promoting inexpensive, flat-packed, assembly-required furniture to mass markets has been impaired by its retail stores' long checkout lines and consistently inferior customer service. There are seldom enough cashiers to handle the volume of customers, and the staff's sparse presence on the showroom floor makes it difficult for customers to get help. Also, the firm has failed to seek out and act on customer feedback on improving its service. Even IKEA's chief executive admitted, in an interview with London's *Financial Times,* that its level of service was "appalling." Negative customer experiences severely reduce potential same-store sales for the company—a requirement for any prosperous retail concern.

Compounding the company's customer service problems are its off-putting television advertisements. The quirky TV ads affronted some customers and even earned the company a recent U.K. television award for "Most Irritating Advertisement of 2000." The ad in question featured a rather obese man in a warehouse who, as he progressively removed his garments, revealed descriptions of the company's products tattooed on each newly exposed part of his anatomy.

IKEA's Web site also had problems. Rather than offering direct online sales that would increase accessibility to its merchandise, the site acts more like a guidebook to its product line, referring would-be customers to the already understaffed retail stores.

Further complicating matters for IKEA is its marketing strategy. Its target market of first-time homebuyers, 35 years of age and younger, is projected to shrink an estimated 14 percent in Europe by 2006. Considering IKEA's existing problems, it cannot be expected to overcome such a towering hurdle without first raising its operating standards.

POINTS TO PONDER

1. How do you think IKEA should change its targeting strategy?

2. Do you think it would be better off following a standardized or customized advertising strategy?

Sources: Allyson L. Steward-Allen, "IKEA Service Worst in Its Own Backyard," *Marketing News* (April 23, 2001): 11; Juliana Koranteng, "European Advertisers Find Web Ads Tangled," *Advertising Age* (July 17, 2001): 22.

Advertisements may be produced centrally, in each local market, or by a combination of both. With a standardized campaign, production usually is centralized and all advertisements produced simultaneously to reap production cost savings. Sometimes, as in IKEA's case, things don't work well (see the "A Matter of Practice" box).

Evaluating Effectiveness

A strong effectiveness evaluation program is particularly important for international advertising. Intuition serves the advertiser poorly as an evaluation method because of the lack of familiarity with foreign markets. International advertising most often takes place out of the advertising manager's sight and is difficult to control.

The effectiveness evaluation program for international advertising should focus, at least initially, on pretesting. Unfamiliarity with the culture, language, and consumer behavior can result in major miscalculations. Pretesting helps the advertiser correct major problems before damage is done.

SPECIAL INTERNATIONAL CONSIDERATIONS

International advertising, despite its glamorous image, is tough work because it poses formidable challenges. We have already discussed the problems that language creates. Other concerns relate to laws, customs, time, inertia, resistance, rejection, and politics.

THE INSIDE STORY

A CULTURAL INSIDER

Masaru Ariga   Dentsu Inc.

Masaru Ariga is responsible for planning international marketing communication strategies for clients of his agency, Dentsu Inc., one of the largest international marketing communication agencies in the world. Headquartered in Tokyo, Ariga travels extensively to work with strategic planners in overseas Dentsu offices. He has visited some 40 countries both as a student and later in his work with Dentsu.

Ariga is in charge of developing new marketing methodologies to cope with various market situations. For example, one project involved meeting with the creative and account teams for a new product launched in Thailand. The problem was to determine how to define the emerging "new urban middle class" in Thailand.

In addition, Ariga frequently takes charge of marketing communication campaigns on a pan-regional basis, particularly in Asia. He explains, "Coming from headquarters, I consider it my responsibility to identify what can be used in many countries and what needs to be country-specified."

Launching a brand in the Asian market can cause a complex communication issue, beginning with something as simple as the brand name. When a foreign brand name is translated into Chinese, the question arises as to whether its pronunciation should be adopted or its meaning should be translated. If the pronunciation is chosen, the meaning might be different due to the fact that the Chinese character symbols represent ideas rather than letters. If the meaning of the brand name is translated, it will be pronounced differently.

There is no correct answer to such a challenge. Rather, it is better to come up with a creative solution that meets the communication objectives on a case-by-case basis.

Ariga graduated with a B.A. in Political Science from Waseda University in Tokyo in 1985. In 1992 he was in the first graduating class from the new IMC Master's program at Northwestern University. His graduate education was sponsored by Dentsu and he has been working for that agency every since.

Laws and Regulations

International advertisers do not fear actual laws; they fear not knowing those laws. For example, a marketer cannot advertise on television to children under 12 in Sweden or Germany, cannot advertise a restaurant chain in France, and cannot advertise at all on Sunday in Austria. In Malaysia, jeans are considered to be Western and decadent, and are prohibited. A commercial can be aired in Australia only if it is shot with an Australian crew. A contest or promotion might be successful in one country and illegal in another.

Custom and Culture

Customs can be even stronger than laws. When advertising to children age 12 or over was approved in Germany, local customs were so strong that companies risked customer revolt by continuing to advertise. In many countries, naming a competitor is considered bad form.

Customs are often more subtle and, as a result, are easier to violate than laws. Quoting an obscure writer or poet would be risky in the United States, where people would not respond to the unknown author. In Japan the audience would respect the advertiser for using the name or become embarrassed at not knowing a name they were expected to recognize. A campaign that made such a reference might irritate U.S. audiences and engage Japanese consumers.

Companies that are starting to do business in the Middle East have to learn new selling methods because the region is so devoutly religious. There are major restrictions on how women are presented in advertising. Many Asian cultures emphasize relationships and context. To be effective, the advertising message must recognize these cultural differences.

Many oppose the move to a global perspective because of concerns about the homogenization of cultural differences. *Marketing* or *cultural imperialism* is a term used to describe what happens when Western culture is imposed on others, particularly cultures such as the Middle East, Asian, and African cultures.

Countries in Southeast Asia have advertising codes. Singapore has an ad code determined to prevent Western-influenced advertising from impairing Asian family values. Malaysia requires that all ads be produced in the country, which cuts back dramatically on the number of foreign ads seen by its public.

Time

Everything takes longer internationally—count on it. The New York business day overlaps for only three hours with the business day in London, for two hours with most of Europe, and for one hour with Greece. Normal New York business hours do not overlap at all with those in Japan, Hong Kong, the Middle East, or Australia. Overnight parcel service is dependable to most of Europe and other regions, if the planes are able to take off and land.

For these reasons e-mail that permits electronic transfer and telecopy transmission is a popular mode for international communication. E-mail and fax numbers have become as universal as telephone numbers on stationery and business cards in international companies.

Time is an enemy in other ways. France and Spain virtually close down in August for vacation. National holidays are also a problem. U.S. corporations average 14 to 15 paid legal holidays a year. The number is more than 20 in Europe, and more than 30 in Italy.

Inertia, Resistance, Rejection, and Politics

Inertia, resistance, rejection, and politics are sometimes lumped together as "not invented here" situations. Advertising is a medium for change, and change may frighten people. Every new campaign is a change. A highly successful campaign from one country might or might not be successful in another country. (Experience suggests that the success rate in moving a winning campaign to another country is about 60 percent.)

Creative directors often resist advertising that arrives from a distant headquarters in favor of advertising created within the local agency. This resistance is partially the result of a very real problem in local offices of international agencies: an inability to develop a good creative team or a strong creative reputation that means that most of the advertising emanating from the international office originates elsewhere.

Government approval of television commercials can also be difficult to secure in some countries. Standards may seem to be applied more strictly to international than to national products.

Flat rejection or rejection by delay or lack of support must be anticipated with every global strategy and global campaign. The best solution is to test two ads that are both based on the global pattern advertising: a locally produced version of the advertising and an original ad. As mentioned, the global strategy usually works 60 percent of the time. If the locally produced advertising wins, the victory must be decisive or the cost of the variation may not be affordable. Global companies must remain flexible enough to adapt the strategy that emerges as the winner.

At times the resistance and rejection are political. These may be the result of office politics or an extension of international politics. Trying to sell a U.S. campaign in a foreign country can be difficult if relations between the two nations are strained. To overcome local resistance and build consensus, companies should have frequent regional and world conferences, maintain a constant flow of communication, transfer executives, and keep their executives well-informed through travel, videotapes, e-mail, teleconferences, and consultation.

In addition, advertisers might ask local management for advice on a developing strategy or campaign. Their involvement often turns into support. Another proven axiom is always go to a problem, do not bring it to headquarters. Solutions worked out in the country that has a problem are seldom what either party anticipated and often are better than either could have hoped.

As demonstrated in this P&G commercial for Charmin in Mexico, a global strategy and campaign works most often for products and brands.

Despite its complexities and difficulties, international advertising is growing and will continue to grow in an increasingly interconnected world economy. Two of the largest agency groups are British-owned Saatchi & Saatchi and WPP, and one of the largest single agencies is Japanese (Dentsu), indicating how diverse the international advertising world is.

IT'S A WRAP
P&G WORKS GLOBALLY

Taking advertising global has led to a great deal of debate within the industry. Should an advertiser standardize strategy, design, and copy across international markets in order to achieve efficiencies in cost? Or, should its advertising be customized for each market? The answer appears to be a resounding—"It depends." This chapter delineated the variables that should be considered when the advertiser determines where to be on the global continuum. "Going global" is a complex process and mistakes in judgment can prove extremely costly. Moreover, it is a process that is in a state of continuous flux, requiring an infrastructure consisting of competent research and objectivity. The goal of effectiveness remains paramount, regardless of country.

Procter & Gamble understands how this assessment process works and has committed the necessary resources to do it correctly. It has created an approach to advertising globally that is inherently flexible yet highly strategic. Jim Stengel has logged time in four countries during his 18 years at P&G and is clearly comfortable with having a worldview. Marketing innovation can be found around the globe, and "a huge piece of my job is to connect these dots," he says. The lobby of P&G's Cincinnati headquarters features a faux home and a store, so the employees can view "the two moments of truth" when they arrive each day. P&G's results speak for themselves. The company's marketing and advertising work throughout the world.

Summary

1. **Explain the evolution of global marketing.** Marketing begins with a local brand, expands to a regional brand, and, finally, goes global. Advertising follows the same path. The strategic approach toward going global can be standardization, adaptation, or contingency. Likewise, three factors are considered: language, budget, and strategy.

2. **Discuss the approaches to international advertising.** The two basic approaches to global advertising are being market oriented or culture oriented. Ultimately, such campaigns should be centrally controlled and centrally conceived. There should also be local applications and approval.

3. **Summarize how international management affects international advertising.** International management affects international advertising in a number of ways, including how it handles language barriers, advertising planning, and selecting an agency.

4. **List the special problems international advertisers face.** Special problems international advertisers must face include, laws/regulations, customs/cultures, time inertia, resistance, rejection, and politics.

Key Terms

global brand, p. 515

global perspective, p. 515

international advertising, p. 513

international brand, p. 512

local brand, p. 512

regional brand, p. 512

Questions

1. What are the differences between local, regional, and international brands?

2. Why would an exporter of goods nationalize its operations in another country?

3. Give three examples of global brands and support your reasoning, as to why they are global.

4. What belief does Professor Levitt hold about international advertising? What belief does Professor Kotler hold?

5. How does international management affect international advertising?

6. Is Arabic a high-context or low-context language? French? English?

7. Name some impediments to international advertising.

Suggested Class Project

To demonstrate the problems of language in advertising, divide the class into teams of five or six. Each team should choose a print advertisement it believes would have universal appeal. Take the headline and one paragraph of body copy to a language professor or someone who is proficient in a language other than English. See whether you can do this for up to five different languages. Next, take that translation to another professor or native language speaker of the same language and ask for a back translation into English. Compare and report on how well the concept translated.

Suggested Internet Class Project

Go to www.tk.generactive.com. List the various services this agency provides. Is this is a local, regional, or global agency? How would it deal with a U.S. client?

HANDS-ON   Case 18

SIEMENS COMES TO AMERICA

Siemens faces an interesting problem. Despite the fact that the German engineering and electronic giant has been in the United States for nearly 50 years, few Americans know who it is. Recent company research shows that only 12 percent of Americans can identify Siemens, which is remarkable considering that Siemens technology sorts our mail.

Gerhard Schulemeyer, CEO of Siemens' U.S. operations, was put in charge of raising Siemens' visibility. Several initial strategies were implemented: for example, after a major restructuring in 2001, its stock was traded on the New York Stock Exchange. Also in 2001, it introduced its mobile phone in the United States. It acquired Westinghouse for $1.2 billion, Acuson for $700 million, and Efficient Networks, a dollar-based maker of modems, for $1.5 billion.

Siemens also engaged in a variety of activities to reflect its commitment to doing business in the United States. These include: making English its official business language, adopting U.S. accounting and financial reporting standards, and hiring a U.S. public relations firm.

Critics contend that Siemens' commitment of $20 to $25 million for a country-wide image campaign is inadequate to do the job. Moreover, the campaign was expected to present the entire produt line, including Internet technology, wireless communications, consulting, industrial automation, power mail systems, and auto parts. ■

IT'S YOUR TURN

Suggest a creative and media strategy that you feel would be effective for Siemens.

Source: James Cox, "Siemens Cultivates American Accent," *USA Today* (March 5, 2001): B1–B2.

Notes

1. Claudia Pentado, "Brazilian Sweets Marketer Tastes Success in Exporting," *Ad Age International* (September 1998): 40.

2. Shelly Branch, "AC Nielsen Gives 43 Brands Global Status," *Wall Street Journal* (October 31, 2001): B-8.

3. Karen Mitchell, "Samurai Spirit Lives in Boulder Company," *Business Plus* (January 7, 1997): 3.

4. Tom Duncan and Jyotika Ramaprasad, "Standardized Multinational Advertising," *Journal of Advertising* 24(3) (Fall 1995): 55–68.

5. "A Pitch with a New Angle," *Brandweek* (November 11, 1996): 20.

6. The high-context/low-context distinction is adapted from two books by Edward T. Hall, *The Silent Language* (New York: Doubleday, 1973), and *Beyond Culture* (New York: Doubleday, 1977).

7. Henry Heilbrunn, "Interactive Marketing in Europe," *Direct Marketing* (March 1998): 56.

8. Laura Rich, "A Sticky Web," *Brandweek* (April 6, 1998): 51–52.

9. Bob Garfield, "A Horrifying Result of Crossing Borders," *Advertising Age* (May 15, 1996): 123.

CHAPTER 19

The Integrated Campaign

CHAPTER OBJECTIVES

When you have completed this chapter, you should be able to

1. Describe an IMC campaign and explain why it is more complex than a one-shot ad.

2. Outline the structure of an IMC campaign plan.

3. Explain the purpose of evaluating a campaign.

Terrorism and Tourism: The Spokane Experience

A Winning IMC Campaign

Organization: *The Spokane Regional Convention and Visitors' Bureau*

Campaign: *"Spokane: The Real Deal"*

The situation: When you are in the tourism industry, how do you continue business after a major travel-related crisis, such as the September 11, 2001, terrorist attacks? The Spokane Regional Convention and Visitors' Bureau (CVB) responded with an emergency campaign—"Spokane: The Real Deal"—designed to stimulate local tourism in this sensitive time.

The CVB held a leadership summit and a series of mini-workshops immediately after September 11, with representatives from airports, hotels, restaurants, and retail partners to determine the impact on the travel industry. The CVB acted fast and created a SWOT analysis, which identified CVB's strengths, weaknesses, opportunities, and threats in this difficult time. While most cities were still moving forward with the marketing plans they had developed before the terrorist attacks, CVB was able to quickly adjust its programs to better address the new situation.

This short-term strategy for the "Spokane: The Real Deal" campaign focused on regional marketing programs for leisure, business, and group travel. The overall goal was to develop programs that attracted regional visitors to the city by increasing their top-of-mind awareness of Spokane as a travel destination.

After such a traumatic national crisis, the CVB believed travelers would stay much closer to home. The "See Spokane First" promotion for local people focused on nearby treasures to increase local spending as well as local pride in the area. Spokane County is the hub of the region and should retain its strong draw for local and regional travelers visiting friends and looking for entertainment and shopping.

A special "Visiting Friends and Relatives" (VFR) promotion asked Spokane residents to provide contact information for a mailing of event calendars and coupon books.

Shorter vacations by people in the nearby region mean trips that are closer to home, shorter planning and booking lead times, and an increase in impulse travel. Spokane had to increase its top-of-mind awareness to be considered by these consumers making quick travel decisions. Packaged programs had to be easy for consumers to plan and purchase, as well as easy for CVB partners to implement.

For business travelers, the goal was to showcase Spokane as a good city for meetings and conventions. Even before September 11, the trend was away from large national meetings and toward regional meetings in smaller markets. This trend would continue after September 11 because of safety issues and convenience.

The rest of the CVB plan for Spokane will unfold as you read through this campaign chapter. Our coverage may seem like a review of previous chapters—and it is. But in this chapter we pull everything together to show how the marketing communication activities are planned and executed as a complete communication package.

Source: Adapted from the "Short-Term Marketing Plan: October 2001–March 31, 2002," provided by John Brewer, President and General Manager of the Spokane Regional Convention and Visitors Bureau.

TOTAL COMMUNICATION: IMC

In this chapter we explore how all the activities we have covered in previous chapters—research, strategy and planning, media planning, message design, and the management of other marketing communication tools such as marketing public relations and sales promotion—are managed as part of an integrated campaign. The opening story demonstrates how one tourism bureau used integrated marketing communication (IMC) to keep its business healthy in the aftermath of the September 11 terrorist attacks. To better understand how that case worked, let's first look at integrated marketing communication as an approach to planning a campaign.

Integrated marketing communication (IMC) is the practice of unifying all marketing communication tools, as well as corporate and brand messages, to communicate in a consistent way to and with **stakeholder** audiences (that is, those who have a stake or interest in the corporation). An IMC campaign plan is more complex than a traditional advertising plan because it considers more message sources, more communication tools, and more audiences.

IMC programs coordinate all communication messages and sources of an organization or company. As Figure 19.1 shows, we can group communication as messages planned (or controlled) by the organization and as messages unplanned (or uncontrolled).[1] In addition, messages delivered by other aspects of the marketing mix (price, product design, distribution, and so on) and other contact points (such as how the store's parking lot appears) may communicate important information to stakeholders that may work against the advertising message.

An IMC campaign includes traditional marketing communication tools, such as advertising and sales promotion, but recognizes that other areas of the marketing mix also communicate. The price of the product signals a level of quality. The cleanliness of the store and helpfulness of the customer service department send powerful messages. The product's reliability also communicates.

These other messages may be as important as, if not more than, traditional marketing communications. IMC planners should consider all message sources and marketing communications that reach stakeholder audiences. Planning and managing these elements so they work together helps to build a consistent brand or company image.

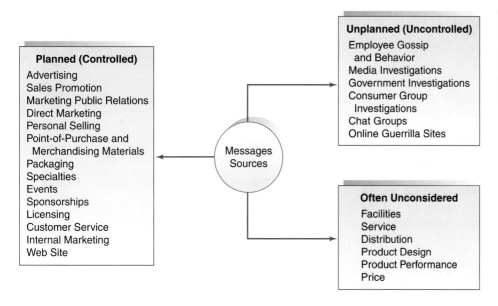

FIGURE 19.1
SOURCES OF MESSAGES
As this figure shows, messages are communicated through various sources, all of which must be considered in an IMC program.

Stakeholder Audiences

In addition to managing the total communication program, IMC campaigns also address a wide variety of stakeholders, all of whom have a different stake or interest in a company and its brand messages. Table 19.1 lists different stakeholder audiences in terms of the organization of the company—corporate, marketing, and marketing communication.

Stakeholders such as employees, investors, and suppliers come in contact with the company and its brands in more ways than through traditional marketing communication and advertising media. Why is IMC concerned with all these audiences? The support (or lack of it) that each stakeholder group gives to the company can affect that company's brands positively or negatively.[2]

The Spokane Regional CVB needed to consider a number of stakeholders. Let's start with travelers, as well as the people in the local community, who attend Spokane's events and attractions. And the local visitors also recruit still other people—friends and family—to spend time and money in Spokane.

The local travel and hospitality industries are important partners in CVB's operations, as well as regional and national travel and tourism companies, such as airlines, Amtrak, state travel and tourism organizations, and the American Automobile Association. In addition, local businesses and their employees, local government leaders, and leaders of organizations planning meetings need to be kept informed of Spokane's activities. The back of

TABLE 19.1   Types of Stakeholder Audiences

Corporate Level	Marketing Level	Marketing Communications Level
Employees	Consumers, customers, and target markets	Consumers, customers, and target audiences
Investors, financial community (analysts, brokers, and the financial press)	Retailers, distributors, dealers	Trade audiences
	Competition	Local community
Government regulators	Suppliers and vendors	Media (general, special interest, trade)
Business partners		Consumer activist groups, general public, optional leaders

The Spokane CVB has a number of stakeholders who had to be reached and kept informed about the campaign. An indication of the number of groups involved can be seen on the backside of the official Spokane map distributed by the CVB.

the Spokane map provided by the CVB lists the campaign's sponsors and companies affiliated with the CVB, which are just a few of the stakeholders in the "Spokane: The Real Deal" campaign.

In thinking about the varied stakeholders addressed by a tourism operation, one can imagine that maintaining consistent communication from all message sources to all stakeholders is particularly difficult because so many people and entities play a part. It works only if a company, brand, or organization has a focused business philosophy or mission, clearly understood core values, and a strong corporate culture.

What makes stakeholder communication management difficult is the inevitable overlap among stakeholder groups. An employee may be an investor, may serve on the local city council, and may belong to a special interest group whose concerns intersect those of the company. And, of course, that employee may also be a customer. People wear a lot of hats and the communication addressed to them by an organization may differ with the different roles, which creates potential problems in consistent communication. The human resources department, for example, may be threatening layoffs claiming that times are tight, but the company's annual report may be touting the financial health of the business in an effort to lure more outside investors. Or employees may learn through gossip that the business is planning to relocate, even though the company's press releases deny such plans.

As IMC experts Don Schultz, Stanley Tannenbaum, and Robert Lauterborn explain, IMC realigns marketing communication "to look at it the way the consumer sees it—as a flow of information from indistinguishable sources."[3] If the messages don't support some central core values and deliver a consistent image in a well-coordinated way to consumers in all their varied roles, they may conflict and create confusion.

Consistency and Coordination

Consistency grows from a strong creative idea that can hold a variety of messages together to create maximum impact. A strong theme such as the Marlboro cowboy, repeated across various marketing communication media and tools (print and broadcast advertising, special promotions, sponsorships, and so forth), creates a consistent message, which makes it more memorable. Consider the award-winning Batman campaign for GM's OnStar personal road assistance system, described in the "A Matter of Principle" feature.

A MATTER OF PRINCIPLE

"Where Does He Get All Those Toys?"

➤ That was the question the Joker (Jack Nicholson) asked about the first Batman film's techno gizmos. And techno gizmos is what GM is selling in an award-winning Batman campaign for its OnStar telematics system. Similar to the wonders in the legendary Batmobile, OnStar is a navigational and satellite personal assistance system for vehicles that provides safety, security, and information at the touch of a button.

The objective of the integrated campaign was to build awareness of OnStar, but almost as important was the need to explain what OnStar offered and how it worked. And the message had to present OnStar as a category leader with such characteristics as trusted, caring, responsive, approachable, and capable.

The Batman theme works because the character represents a bigger-than-life hero. This hero can overcome obstacles on the road as he goes about saving civilization with the help of information he gets from OnStar. Batman's personality (trusted, caring, and so on) and the technologically advanced Batmobile are a strategic fit with the brand personality desired for OnStar.

In the TV commercial that launched the IMC series, Batman's trusty personal assistant, Alfred, explains how he has improved the safety of the Batmobile.

> **Alfred:** "Should a villain steal it, someone will track it. If your air bag goes off, an advisory will assist you. If you're stranded, satellites will help locate you."
>
> **Batman:** "And where have you put all these things?"
>
> **Alfred:** "Just press the OnStar button sir."

Batman leaps into the Batmobile and blasts out of the Bat Cave as a female voice says, "OnStar. How can I help you, Batman?"

When the citizens of Gotham need Batman, they flash the Bat signal in the air to summon him and the Batmobile.

At auto shows, fans are attracted by Bat signals over the OnStar display, which is a 30 × 50-foot exhibit. It features an OnStar-equipped Batmobile, live demonstrations from within a portable Bat Cave, and interactive kiosks that display OnStar information and provide access to the OnStar Batmobile Web site. The Batmobile's presence at other high visibility events such as car races also generates press coverage. An "Adventure Sweepstakes" offered the winner a week in Los Angeles and a walk-on part in a Batman movie.

The campaign's Web site provided product information and links to other Web sites, including BatLinks, where Batman characters delivered OnStar messages. At another site enthusiasts could buy Batman merchandise. The campaign's Web site also carried a series of mini-adventures called "Batman Webisodes" that starred OnStar in Batman's encounters on the mean streets of Gotham. And to keep employees and sales representatives informed about all these marketing communication activities, the campaign also included a training program.

The OnStar Batman campaign has been highly successful over a number of years. It has won 2 gold EFFIE awards, New York Festival AME (Advertising and Marketing Effectiveness) awards, and recognition from the Advertising Research Foundation, and it has been listed in the "Best Spots" section in *Adweek*.

Source: Adapted from the EFFIE brief provided by Campbell Ewald and GM; the OnStar Web site (www.onstar.com); and the GM Web site (www.gm.com/cgi-bin/ pr_display.pl?1215). Batman and all related characters, names, and indicia are trademarks of DC Comics © 2002. © 2002 OnStar®. All rights reserved.

Organizing for Integration Coordinating all the messages in an IMC campaign is an organizational problem that is best solved through **cross-functional management**,[4] which means using teams of people from different parts of the company, outside agencies, or both to draw up the plan and monitor the way the plan is implemented.

Cross-functional management may even mean getting different agencies together who are producing the marketing communication. In an EFFIE case several years ago for the United Airlines' "Rising" campaign, the Fallon agency handled the domestic side of the account, and Young and Rubicam handled the international business. Fallon's creative director, Bill Westbrook, and Y&R's creative director, Ted Bell, had an inspirational experience when they met to devise a theme for the new campaign. Working together, they came up with the one-word slogan "Rising," which referred to United's redesigning the way it did business, that is, its operations as well as how it related to its customers. For United, the ability to get its domestic and international agencies on the same page was critical to its two-year plan to turn around the airline's image with consumers.

But developing a consistent advertising theme was not enough. To truly integrate the campaign, United had to integrate the management of its business operations first. United's employees and managers had to commit to the turn-around plan and communicate with each other. United knew it had to change its way of doing business, in support of the campaign. The campaign by itself was not enough—it was just an unsupported promise, because in the big picture of integrated marketing, advertising has to be supported by good business practices.

"It was a major culture change," said one former United executive. "In the past in-flight people did what they had to do. The marketing department did what it had to do. The top managers may have talked to each other, but the people who really were doing the work, day in, day out, never did."[5] Let's consider now how a campaign like that is created.

THE STRUCTURE OF A CAMPAIGN PLAN

Many advertisements are **single-shot ads**, free-standing ads unrelated to ads that preceded or followed them. Companies that create one ad at a time and constantly change the core message are not using a campaign.

In contrast, a **campaign** is a complex set of interlocking, coordinated activities strategically designed to meet a set of objectives and to solve some critical problem within a specified time period, usually a year or less. A campaign is designed around a creative theme that extends across time, and different advertising vehicles or marketing communication activities. Sometimes the audience groups may be different, as well. For example, Batman was used to help GM explain OnStar in an integrated campaign that used print and television commercials, Bat Cave exhibits and demonstrations at auto shows, a tour featuring the Batmobile, an OnStar Web site, direct mail, sweepstakes, Batman merchandise, and dealer training programs.

A campaign may focus on one specific product attribute or one audience or it may cover a variety of attributes and reach all the audiences. The initial Batman commercial focused on creating curiosity about OnStar and on the safety aspect of the telematics system. Later commercials focused on security and information.

A campaign plan summarizes the marketplace situation, the underlying campaign strategy, the main creative strategies and tactics, media, and the other marketing communication areas of sales promotion, direct marketing, and public relations. It concludes with a section on how to evaluate the effort's effectiveness.

The Hallmark campaign plan in the Appendix was developed by a student team from George Washington University. Please refer to it to see what a campaign plan looks like. It won the National Student Advertising Competition (NSAC), sponsored by the American Advertising Federation (AAF).

Table 19.2 outlines an IMC campaign. We examine each part of the outline in this section. Some of the terms may be unfamiliar to you, but we will discuss them in the section that follows.

Situation Analysis

The first section of most campaign plans is a **situation analysis**, which is a business review that summarizes all the relevant information available about the product, the com-

GM used Batman to help describe OnStar in an integrated campaign that used print and TV commercials, exhibits, sweepstakes, and other marketing tools.

TABLE 19.2	**An IMC Campaign Outline**

1. Situation analysis	**4. Communication strategy**
• Product and company research	• Message development research
• Consumer and stakeholder research	• The creative theme
• Market analysis	• Tactics and executions
• Competitive situation	**5. Media plan**
• Industry analysis	• Media mix
2. SWOT analysis	• Scheduling and timing
• Internal: strengths and weaknesses	**6. Other marketing communications activities**
• External: opportunities and threats	
• Problem identification	**7. The appropriation and budget**
3. Campaign strategy	**8. Campaign evaluation**
• Objectives	
• Targeting	
• Positioning	

pany, the competitive environment, the industry, and the consumers. This information is obtained using primary and secondary research techniques. The most important activity is analyzing the information—making sense of what has been found. The six most important research areas—product and company research, consumer and stakeholder research, market analysis, competitive analysis, industry analysis, and marketplace analysis—are outlined below. These areas provide a structure you can use when you conduct a situation analysis to obtain the needed background information to plan a campaign.

Background Research for a Situation Analysis

- *Conduct product and company research.* Conduct research that reviews a product in terms of its uses, packaging, quality, price, sales, brand image, distinctive features, distribution, positioning, and product life cycle. Also examine the company behind the product and its corporate reputation and image, resources, philosophies, mission, and culture.
- *Conduct stakeholder research.* Determine through research which key stakeholder groups the campaign must communicate with. How do these groups rank in importance? The consumer stakeholder should be described demographically and psychographically to answer questions such as: Who buys the product? When do they buy it? How often do they buy? How do they use the product? What are their attitudes and perceptions about the product? What is their buying behavior? Most campaign themes develop directly from some key consumer insight.
- *Analyze the market.* Find the best markets for the product by determining who and where the best prospects are with respect to demographic characteristics, geographic location, sociopsychological groupings (lifestyles, interests, attitudes), and product use (heavy, light, nonuser, switcher, loyal user). An analysis should also assess the market's accessibility. In the case of a direct-action advertising campaign, for instance, the availability of an extensive and accurate database is critical if messages are going to reach the target market.
- *Analyze the competitive situation.* Track the activities of competitors (direct and indirect). Look at their market share, product features, new products, positioning and targeting strategies, current and past advertising strategies, media expenditures, and advertising schedules. Find out what competitive advantages you have and what advantages your competitors have. What are the distinctive features of your product, your competitors' products, and how important are these features to consumers?
- *Analyze the industry.* What's the shape of the industry? Is the industry growing or is it stagnating? The dot-com industry, for example, was riding a wave of growth through the end of the 1990s, only to crash in 2000.

- *Analyze the marketplace.* What changes in the marketplace might positively or negatively affect your campaign? The tourism marketplace, for example, was dramatically affected by the September 11 terrorist attacks.

In 2000, through the situation analysis for OnStar, GM found that its navigation system, which had been introduced in 1996, was facing serious competition from new brands in the emerging telematics category and from a host of brands in wireless, Internet, computer software, and PDA (personal data assistants).

SWOT Analysis

The section that follows a situation analysis builds on it by evaluating the significance of the research. Some plans include a section called "Problems and Opportunities"; others call it a **SWOT analysis**, meaning the **S**trengths, **W**eaknesses, **O**pportunities, and **T**hreats the company or brand faces. Once the information is gathered and sorted into SWOT categories, the analysis begins. In this stage you are trying to make sense of all the information you have gathered and identify key areas on which you will build your campaign strategy. The "Inside Story" box explains how an understanding of a market situation led to the identification of a new position and logo for the Spokane Regional Convention and Visitors Bureau.

Problem Identification From the SWOT analysis, you should be able to focus on the serious communication problems that the campaign must address. For example, GM realized from its research and analysis of its marketing situation that it had a limited window of opportunity for OnStar to capture category leadership before more serious competition would develop.

With the Spokane campaign, the planners recognized that fear of travel would continue to play a role in the short term, causing many travelers to stay close to home and family. Developing a strong sense of nesting, community, family, and patriotism would likely increase Spokane's share of regional travelers.

Problems differ from year to year as an organization responds to different situations. For example, in one year's marketing plan, a brand may be introducing a line extension, which means the advertising will address the problem of launching a new product under a familiar brand name. The next year, the marketing plan may focus on increasing distribution, so the advertising will probably address opening up new territories where the brand is unknown.

Each problem calls for its own advertising and marketing communication strategy. Different communication objectives are set. Different marketing communication tools reach out to different audiences with different messages.

Campaign Strategy

After the situation analysis and the SWOT analysis, most advertising and IMC campaign plans focus on the key strategic decisions and programs that direct the campaign. The strategy section identifies the objectives that will solve the key problems identified at the end of the SWOT analysis. It will also specify the target stakeholder audiences and how the strategy will handle competitive advantage and the product's position. Other strategic decisions revolve around the scheduling and timing of the different phases of the campaign activities.

These fundamental decisions were discussed in detail in Chapter 7. They are relevant for all areas of marketing communication planning, from the creative plan to the media, sales promotion, and public relations plans.

Objectives Objectives guide the development of the campaign's strategy. These objectives are established based on an understanding of the hierarchy of effects and the various ways advertising can affect its audience (see Chapters 6 and 7). At the end of the campaign the company can compare its results against these objectives to measure the campaign's success.

The primary objective for the Spokane campaign, for example, was to raise the top-of-mind awareness of Spokane as a regional travel destination and meeting city. Supporting that goal was a set of measurable objectives that directed various programs, some of which we look at now.

THE INSIDE STORY

A Logo That Reflects Our Mission

John Brewer

President Spokane Regional Convention & Visitors Bureau

"Chris Rock, Barney the Dinosaur, and Bill Cosby; most performers focus on one audience and play well to them. Chris Rock isn't likely to be singing a chorus of "I love you" with Barney, and likewise, I can't see the purple dinosaur doing standup at the Improv. Bill Cosby, however, captivates both audiences. He knows how to speak the language of children and can just as easily amuse adults. Mr. Cosby's physical identity—his image—doesn't change when he speaks to different audiences, but his tone, mannerisms, and message do.

The Spokane Regional Convention and Visitors' Bureau was grappling with a similar issue. We have two distinct target markets—travelers and the local travel industry—with vastly different messages to be conveyed. As a nonprofit organization marketing the community to travelers around the world, we needed a brand identity that conveyed a warm and inviting message to potential travelers. It was also important that the CVB effectively communicate our value to the local community. Our primary stakeholders include city and county governments, and 600 regional businesses. Since our $1.5 million annual budget comes from their confidence in our being able to produce the desired results, it was important for them to have a clear understanding of who we are and the significant economic impact we produce.

We had an existing logo that simply said "Spokane." That identity was used throughout the county as well as locally. To dispel the misperception that Spokane must be a rainy destination (when in actuality we have over 260 days of sun), we made the sun a prominent element. Spokane possesses one of the largest urban waterfalls in the United States, so a water element was incorporated in the design. The CVB successfully encouraged community partners such as the Chamber of Commerce, the Economic Development Council, Downtown Spokane Partnership, and others to use this logo in their national marketing pieces. Before long, our organization lost its local identity because of these groups using the logo. This was not a problem in the national market since our objective was to create as many impressions as possible, and we understood that using the same logo aids in retention of our image if done with significant frequency.

After conducting primary research with our key stakeholders and consulting our advertising agency, we determined that the integrity and effectiveness of the "Spokane" logo and the identity it created were solid. So our focus became one of tweaking the existing logo in a way that would create a corporate identity for us in the local market.

At the same time we were repositioning our organization to be more regional. There is not a true convention and visitors' bureau within a 300-mile drive east of us and 150 miles west. Becoming regional in scope would allow us to better serve our visitors and to form partnerships with our regional tourism suppliers. So, it was also important that these regional suppliers, attractions, event coordinators, recreation outfitters, and so on, had a clear understanding as to who we were and what services we could provide them.

After months of meetings and numerous designs from our advertising agency, a design was chosen that would allow us to maintain the existing logo for tourism promotion, and, with a few added elements and color changes, give us the corporate identity we desired. The corporate look simply added the letters "CVB" to the end of "Spokane" and the word "Regional" above. We immediately began partnering with the local media to create an awareness of what a CVB was. We, didn't necessarily need everyone to know that CVB stood for Convention and Visitors' Bureau; we just wanted them to realize we were the organization responsible for driving revenue to our county from the traveling public. I'm not sure I could tell you right off what IBM stands for, but I know it helped revolutionize the computer industry. And how about that KFC? It won't be long before we forget their full names and just think of them as the chicken people. After all, Spokane Regional Convention and Visitors' Bureau is a long, bureaucratic name. CVB is easier to remember and say.

The new look has now allowed us to create the image we need in the mind of the travelling consumer, maintain continuity between that look and our corporate look, and differentiate us from the other organizations who use the "Spokane" logo. As Fat Albert would say (through Bill Cosby, of course), "Hey, Hey, Hey!" "

John Brewer is a 1992 communication arts graduate from the University of West Florida. He is currently the president and general manager of the Spokane Regional Convention & Visitors' Bureau in Spokane, Washington. John worked as an account executive, public relations specialist, and tourism director at agencies in Montana specializing in travel and tourism.

Nominated by Professor Tom Groth, University of West Florida.

Marketing Program Objectives

1. **"Spokane: The Real Deal" campaign:** A quick getaway program package discounted activities and accommodations as part of Spokane's stay, play, and shop season. The promotion focused on upcoming special events unique to the Spokane marketplace, with the discounted accommodations as the "deal closers." CVB partners AAA, American Express, and Ticketswest participated in the value packages aimed at people within driving distance.
   Objectives: 3,000 inquiries with 10 percent conversion for two nights (600 room nights) for an estimated $60,000 impact.

2. **"Visiting Friends and Relatives" (VFR) program:** The Spokane "Real Deal" campaign used program discounts (coupon books) at hotels, restaurants, retail stores, and attractions. Local advertising supported these discounts. Spokane residents were asked by CVB to give names of friends and family they would like to invite to Spokane. Then CVB sent those people introductory packages, including visitor guides and maps along with coupon books and letters from the mayor and county commission inviting them to visit. These mailings drove visitors to the CVB Web site, where there was a special page for these guests.
   Objectives: 4,000 households participated by providing names (1% of Spokane County) with a 10 percent conversion rate for three nights (1,200 room nights), for an estimated $120,000 in economic impact, meaning dollars spent in Spokane.

3. **"Bring It Home" campaign:** To generate conference leads through small group discussions and presentations, the CVB sales staff held meetings with local leaders. CVB encouraged these leaders to invite conference planners to hold their gatherings in Spokane. The convention service manager contacted local organizations and service clubs to set up speaking engagements to generate lead referrals. A response card was used in conjunction with these personal presentations. The effort targeted market segments that have the highest potential to produce short-term business through small to medium-sized meetings, such as religious, education, health/medical, and corporate planners.
   Objectives: Meetings with 30 leaders to generate seven bids, and four site inspections by meeting planners considering sites, four bookings bringing in 200 delegates (800 people at 3.5 nights for 2,800 room nights creating an impact of $504,000).

Targeting In the process of analyzing consumer behavior, potential target markets are pinpointed by campaign planners and segmented into groups, or segments, identified by certain demographic or psychographic characteristics, such as environmentalists, bike riders, or mall teens. In other words, within potential markets, such as the youth market, cer-

This coupon book was part of the "Visiting Friends and Relatives" promotion for Spokane's short-term marketing campaign.

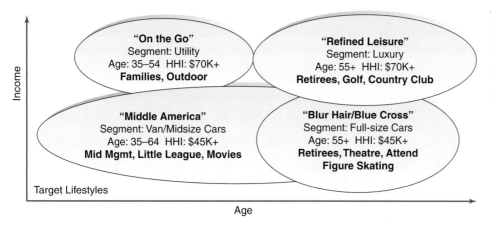

FIGURE 19.2

ONSTAR TARGET AUDIENCES
This figure illustrates how GM
analyzed its customers to determine
who would most likely be in the
market for the OnStar option.

tain groups of people, or segments such as "mall teens," are more likely than others to be targeted for advertising and other marketing communication messages because the situation analysis and SWOT analysis identified them as an opportunity (i.e., high potential that they would respond to the marketing communication).

GM's consumer research identified four types of car buyers who might be in the market for the OnStar option on their new GM cars. These types are identified in Figure 19.2. From this analysis, the campaign planners developed a description of OnStar's primary and secondary target audiences as:

- *Primary.* Buyers of medium/large SUVs and luxury car brands (Cadillac, Buick, Chevrolet, GMC) in the 35 to 64 age range with a household income of $75,000 or higher.
- *Secondary.* Buyers of other large or midsize cars, minivans, and trucks in the 35 to 64 age range with a household income of $50,000 or higher.

These target audiences (that is, groups of people to whom a marketing communication message is directed) shift with each campaign, its situation, key problems, and objectives. For example, if you are launching a line extension, you will probably target current users of the brand. However, if you are opening up new territory, there aren't current users, so you will have to target competitors' users. For both audiences, however, the objective may remain the same, which is to convince the target audiences to try a new product.

Positioning Although objectives and targeting differ from campaign to campaign, the product's positioning (at least for existing products) generally remains the same. However, you still need to identify the product's position and then analyze that position in terms of the campaign's impact on it.

Does the position mean the same thing to familiar brand users who are considering buying a new line extension, such as if Crest were to bring out a different type of toothpaste for, say, smokers? What would happen to the brand's position and what would it mean to entirely new users in a new market territory who are unfamiliar with the brand? They may not respond to the position in the same way, which means that the way the position is presented in the message strategy may need to be adjusted to the target audience's needs, interests, and level of knowledge.

Message Strategy

A campaign is a complex communication program that is tightly interwoven with all of an organization's marketing efforts. This total communication program reaches all stakeholders, all audiences, and all publics with the same promotional theme. Message variations related to that theme speak to the interests of the different audiences. For example, even though a campaign may be directed primarily at a consumer audience, there may be subsections of the campaign that focus on the sales force, dealers, or retailers.

The message strategy—and the choice of what type of creative approach (see Chapter 11) to use for the various stakeholder audiences—flows from an understanding of the key communication problems and the objectives. The message, or creative strategy outlines the impressions the campaign intends to convey to the target audience or audiences. Variations on the creative approach are tested through **concept testing**, which means a simple statement of the idea (usually a sketch with a key phrase) is tried out on people who are representative of the target audience to get their reactions to the Big Idea. The test seeks to determine if they understand the idea and if they find it interesting and engaging.

The "A Matter of Practice" box illustrates how a creative theme and strategy are built on a deep understanding of a brand's relationship to its customers, which is uncovered through research.

Creative Theme As we mentioned, a campaign is a series of ads built around one central theme, or Big Idea. Identifying this creative concept is an important element in the message strategy. In the White Castle case, the Big Idea is built on insight about how devoted customers crave the hamburger; the idea was expressed in the slogan, "What You Crave." Here is how a theme is developed and used in a campaign.

The creative concept is tested and retested through research used to try message ideas as they are developed. Later, after appropriate revisions, the finished work is copy-tested. Copy-testing is done on finished ads to predict their effectiveness or on ads that have run in the market to determine their effectiveness. The message strategy in a campaign includes this creative concept and its variations, known as **executions**, that carry the concept across different media, situations, stakeholder audiences, and times of the year.

The campaign theme that eventually wins out must be a strong concept, like the White Castle "Crave" idea in the "A Matter of Practice" box, and one that can hold all the diverse campaign efforts together as well as speak to the target audience. The creative strategy behind the "Crave" theme, for example, focused on the burger's indulgent qualities, which was expressed in the "What You Crave" line, which brings to mind the self-indulgence that comes from enjoying a guilty pleasure—such as consuming a sack of 10 burgers smothered with onions. The Craver's self-identity as an individualist who is loyal to a different kind of burger was linked to White Castle's image as a hamburger chain that makes its burgers in a nontraditional way. This resonated with the idea of consuming a sack of 10 Slyders® almost as a bragging right.

A creative theme also needs to be strategically sound. When Pepsi created the classic "Pepsi Generation" theme in the 1960s, it created a new position and an entirely new type of lifestyle advertising for the brand that resonated with its target audience. That theme has continued in subsequent campaigns even though the specific campaigns have changed. Notice in the following list how the youth appeal theme continues to show up over the years:

- 1961–1963: "Now It's Pepsi for Those Who Think Young"
- 1963–1967: "Come Alive! You're in the Pepsi Generation"
- 1967–1969: "The Taste That Beats the Others Cold"
- 1969–1973: "You've Got a Lot to Live, Pepsi's Got a Lot to Give"
- 1973–1975: "Join the Pepsi People Feelin' Free"
- 1975–1978: "Have a Pepsi Day"
- 1978–1981: "Catch That Pepsi Spirit"
- 1981–1982: Pepsi's Got Your Taste for Life!
- 1983: "Pepsi Now!"
- Late 1980s: "Pepsi, the Choice of a New Generation"
- Early 1990s: "Gotta Have It"
- Mid-to late 1990s: "Be Young. Have Fun. Drink Pepsi."

A strong umbrella theme not only holds the various ads in a campaign together, it creates synergy. **Synergy** means that the impact of the whole campaign is greater than the sum of the individual parts. For White Castle, the theme touched an emotional button in a way that was a bit irreverent, eccentric, rebellious, quirky, cool, fun, and funky. A strong theme creates synergy, which intensifies the impact and memorability of the message through repetition. Maintaining interest is the reason variations are built into a campaign.

Continuity devices, such as the Jolly Green Giant, the Pillsbury Doughboy, and the Aflac duck, are often used in campaigns to create a link from ad to ad. Slogans, such as White Castle's "What You Crave" are also important continuity devices. A good slogan

A MATTER OF PRACTICE

SO WHY DO YOU CRAVE WHITE CASTLE?

➤ Say you want a hamburger. What makes you stop at one fast-food chain or another? Some chains try to get your business with price discounts and premiums or by giving toys to kids. White Castle determined from its research that people who buy White Castle hamburgers really love them. They even crave them. And that's a strong point of difference in the highly competitive fast-food marketplace.

The Columbus, Ohio–based White Castle had a creative response to the business challenge of a soft market, bigger competitors, and a small advertising budget. That's because the company understands that its relationship with its customers is different from that of other fast-food chains. As ethnographic research (in which researchers do in-depth observational research of customers) revealed, people have an emotional attachment to the White Castle brand and the distinctive size, smell, and shape of its Slyders® burgers. Participants in the study said, "I crave White Castle more than anything else. When I get a craving, I just have to have it." What is it that drives the craving and what makes the burger such a self-indulgence? For one thing, it's the tiny juicy hamburger smothered with onions that people consider a treat, in spite of onion breath, a fact lampooned in some of the chain's commercials. But the real difference is in the production of the hamburger, which also has given White Castle an image different from the usual hamburger chain. In 1921, Walter Anderson, a professional cook, and Edgar "Billy" Ingram, a local real estate and insurance agent, created a different method of preparing a hamburger by cooking it with onions on a hot griddle for a short period of time. (Prior to that, hamburgers were cooked slowly on a griddle for a longer time.) The juicy, onion-laden, steam-grilled burger has a distinctive taste that brings its faithful back for sacks of Slyders®. (They are most often sold in sacks of 10.) Devoted cravers are a cult-like following united by their passion for the unusual burgers.

J. Walter Thompson's (JWT) Detroit agency recommended that the company leverage this emotional connection with its core target audience. This campaign would build on White Castle's strength, defending the company's unique position from encroachments by other players in the category. The campaign would also keep the brand fresh, interesting, and appealing to the hearts and minds of its core target market.

JWT's creative team used a simple brand idea that echoed what customers said about the brand: "White Castle: What You Crave," which represented their feelings of self-indulgence. This strong branding idea lent itself to a variety of quirky creative ideas, such as calling its customers "Cravers" and the restaurants "Crave Zones." Team members

who work there are "White Castle Crave Keepers." When a White Castle building is being remodeled, it is under "Cravestruction," and when staff members brainstorm, they are "Cravequesting."

Crave patches were distributed with the bags of hamburgers as brand reminders. The oniony taste was celebrated with Crave Air Fresheners for homes, cars, and cab companies, as well as After-Crave Mints provided to dating services. There's even an annual Crave Time Cook-Off contest. The Web site (www.whatyoucrave.com) is "The Epicenter of Crave" and features Crave-o-bilia, Cravitivity, Crave Culture surveys, and other craveable items.

White Castle has been able to connect with its customers on an emotional level through the "What You Crave" campaign, and sales have more than met the campaign's objectives, which brought it an EFFIE award as well.

POINT TO PONDER

What insights do you think the consumer research discovered about White Castle customers that led the campaign planners to create this "What You Crave" campaign? Summarize the key insights and relate each one to an element of the message strategy.

Sources: Adapted from the EFFIE brief provided by J. Walter Thompson, Detroit, and White Castle; other sources include "MSS 991–White Castle System, Inc. Records, 1921–1991," Ohio Historical Society (www.ohiohistory.org/resource/archlib/collections/msscoll/mss991/corphistory.html).

A set of decals with the "crave" theme were included in bags of 10 White Castle burgers.

generates its own excitement, but, more importantly, it is highly memorable and advertisers can use it in a variety of situations.

The creative theme can gain momentum through **image transfer**, which means that a presentation in one medium (such as radio) stimulates the listener to think about the presentation in another medium (such as television), which is another goal of campaign planners. When image transfer works successfully, a cheaper medium (radio, outdoor) can remind people of a message delivered in a more expensive way, and the links between the two help to create a more powerful synergy.

Creative Tactics and Executions We can divide the creative work on a campaign into two steps. The first is determining the creative strategy (what the message says). The second is determining the tactics (how to execute the message).

The means for carrying out the creative strategy are outlined in the creative tactics section of the campaign plan. The "Spokane: The Real Deal" campaign, for example, used a set of tactics designed to stimulate local travel in the aftermath of the September 11 terrorist attacks. They include the "Visiting Friends and Relatives" promotion, the "Bring It Home" program designed to enlist local leaders' help in recruiting more meetings and conferences, and the "See Spokane First" promotion that encouraged Spokane and nearby residents to visit local tourist sites and events. To encourage a sense of civic responsibility, the campaign also included Operation Spokane Heroes in support of local military bases and families and Spokane Loves NY, which provided assistance by Spokane residents at the World Trade Center cleanup site. These were all supported with press releases, advertising, brochures, and coupon books for discounts at local events.

As an example of how a creative theme and its executions were tested, consider a campaign for BellSouth Yellow Pages. At the theme stage, 21 different campaign concepts were presented to the client. Of those, BellSouth selected eight for concept testing in seven key markets, across various target segments, including ethnic markets. Only the one concept using a celebrity—Dixie Carter—performed well above all others in terms of intrusiveness, believability, and communication of the strategy. (Dixie Carter played a strongwilled owner of an interior design firm in the *Designing Women* television program, a personality that carried over to this campaign.)

The campaign executions were then copy-tested by a company called Diagnostic Research, Inc. (DRI), using three rough TV executions to evaluate the idea of a series of "episodes"—as Dixie Carter deals with the problems of renovating her country retreat on the Tennessee River. The campaign's executions achieved the highest copy-testing scores ever for the BellSouth Corporation. In fact, they were among the five highest scores ever tested by DRI, at 300 percent above norms for recall and message communication. They also beat norms for likability, believability, spokesperson suitability, and usage motivation.

Having a great idea is important, but producing it can either make or break it. Many advertisers pretest both concepts and executions to predict their effectiveness and eliminate approaches that don't work. Advertising pretesting helps avoid costly mistakes, predicts the relative strength of alternative approaches, and generally improves the advertising's efficiency.

Media Strategy

The media plan and the creative plan are equally important and are developed by the campaign planners simultaneously. The overall appropriation, or available money for the campaign, determines the media plan. Let's consider how a media plan might be put together for a campaign.

The Spokane short-term campaign, which was created rapidly after September 11, was designed to keep tourism alive during the six months after the attacks. It was a low-budget effort, so it demonstrates what can be done in a short time without a lot of money. The program was primarily driven by an ongoing flight of advertising designed to keep Spokane in the mind of people as they made impulse decisions about travel. Regional media—radio, television, and newspapers—were important, as well as newsletters, flyers, Web sites, postcards, and e-mail updates. The advertising effort was partnered with other local promoters and events to generate cooperative funding and extend the advertising budget.

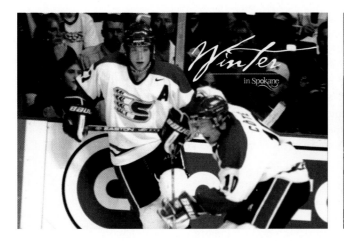

A variety of media was used in the Spokane campaign including postcards like these that carried a seasonal events schedule on the back side. These were mailed back to people who inquired about Spokane programs and activities, such as the "Visiting Friends and Relatives" program.

For White Castle, JWT used many different point-of-crave (POC) materials and media. In addition to traditional television and radio, it featured drive-through signs; three types of "Crave" patches; three types of pole banners (a tall narrow banner/poster mounted on a pole); an Onion Lover's Special meal package; 32-ounce Craverscope (horoscope) cups, and air fresheners; a dangler hung from the ceiling inside the Castles for the Crave Time cook-off; and recipe booklets.

Media planners created a tiered media strategy for the traditional media, which means markets were prioritized based on White Castle's penetration in the various markets where it had restaurants, and forecasted revenue for those markets. Because this is a David and Goliath situation, and White Castle has a small share-of-voice, under 5 percent (that is, White Castle's media expenditures account for only 5 percent of the total media spending by fast-food companies), the JWT media planners knew they couldn't compete on pure quantity of media. The White Castle media strategy had to be more efficient than the competition's.

The media plan called for television and radio in particular markets in dayparts centered on the key selling periods, when cravers were most likely to experience the "Crave." Other media vehicles, such as outdoor boards and transit signage, further intercepted Cravers with the "It's What You Crave" reminder message.

Media Mix The **media mix** is created by media planners by selecting the best combination of traditional media vehicles (print, broadcast, etc.), nontraditional media (electronic media, unexpected places like sidewalks and toilet doors), and marketing communication tools, such as PR, direct marketing, and sales promotion, to reach the targeted stakeholder audiences. If a product has an awareness problem, widespread mass media would probably increase the general level of awareness. If the problem is trial, sales promotion may be the most important tool. If the product appeals only to a small target, such as martial arts clothes for aikido devotees, direct mail (assuming, of course, that you can find a list or build one) and the Internet may be effective ways to reach that target. In fact, although there may be a lead tool, such as advertising, often a mix of supporting media will effectively reach different stakeholder groups.

Media planners allocate media dollars to accomplish reach and frequency objectives. In a high-reach campaign, money is allocated to get the message to as many people as possible. In a high-frequency campaign, the money is allocated to fewer media reaching fewer people, but message repetition increases.

Sometimes the media allocation will vary because of target audience considerations. In the BellSouth Yellow Pages campaign, for example, the media planners considered three segmentation groups: "Enthusiastic Brand Shoppers," "Product Value Shoppers," and "New Attitude Shoppers." Because these consumer groups vary in their use of media, the strategy was to buy specific TV programming and dayparts, radio formats, lifestyle magazines, and daily newspapers that appeal to the segments rather than to demographic targets. As a result, the WestWayne agency media planners made major shifts from the previous TV daypart mix by reducing prime-time buys, which represented most of the buys in previous schedules, and significantly increasing selected early morning, daytime, and news programming. Radio dayparts were balanced between morning and evening drive time and weekends. Sunday newspaper editions were added.

The media plan section in a campaign plan includes media objectives (reach and frequency), media strategies (targeting, continuity, timing), media selection (the specific vehicles), geographic strategies, schedules, and the media budget. A pie chart shows how the budget is allocated to the various media activities. A flow chart depicts the timing strategies and scheduling. A spreadsheet identifies the key expenditures and their budget figure total.

Scheduling Timing and scheduling are an important part of the media plan and tie into the overall campaign strategy.

There are also timing factors (such as a product or campaign launch) that determine the use of different types of marketing communication or media, such as public relations, advertising, sales promotion, or direct marketing. For example, news announcements usually start a campaign in order to capitalize on the newsworthiness of a new product or new product design. Once the ads start to appear, then the agency will no longer use news releases because the "news" is no longer new. In other situations where the objective is to build customer relationships, the agency uses advertising to elicit consumer responses that become a database of prospects for follow-up contact, either by direct mail or personal sales. This means that in that kind of situation, the advertising has to lead.

The opening story about the short-term Spokane campaign describes a plan developed in response to a current event and driven by timing, in this case how to keep tourism active after the September 11 attacks. The plan also had a seasonal element because it came at the end of the year, along with holiday promotions. The "Great Time to Invite" newspaper ad is part of the Friends and Relatives (VFR) promotion and features the event calendar for January.

Some campaigns must accommodate tragedies. For example, the Weight Watchers' campaign featuring Princess Diana's former sister-in-law, Sarah Ferguson, had to change after Princess Diana's death. The campaign had playfully used the line that losing weight was "harder than outrunning the paparazzi," and all the pieces—direct mail, as well as commercials—had to be yanked after Diana's tragic death.

Other Marketing Communication Activities

The concept of a communication mix in an IMC plan includes more than just traditional advertising media. In most cases, advertising campaigns are supported by other forms of marketing communication, such as sales promotion and public relations.

The Spokane campaign used a variety of marketing communication tools, such as sales promotions, direct marketing, and public relations, in addition to advertising and other forms of marketing communication. The objective was to better manage all points of contact with potential travelers and visitors that could deliver reminder messages about Spokane as a travel destination. Here are some of the marketing communication tools of this campaign.

Spokane Marketing Communication Mix

Sales Promotions

VFR: The Visiting Friends and Relatives program used coupon books to deliver
   discounted travel package to travelers.

Direct Marketing

The VFR Program: In addition to distributing the coupon books at hotels, restaurants,
   and other attractions, the books, along with an invitation letter and visitors' guide,
   were sent to people who were identified by locals as friends and family.

"See Spokane First": The campaign used a one-page flyer highlighting activities and
   special events in Spokane County during the winter and holidays. This was sent to the
   human resource and communications departments of the area's largest employers with
   a cover letter requesting that they insert the flyer in their own newsletter and pull facts
   and stories from it to use as filler in their employee communication pieces.

This newspaper ad was part of the Friends and Family promotion for the Spokane CVB. It invited people to contact the Bureau to get the "Visiting Friends and Relatives" kit, which included a calendar, a Spokane Visitor's Guide, and a coupon book for "Real Deals."

Group Business Travel: To support the group business travel effort, this program reached planners via a series of three direct-mail pieces sent by CVB through partnerships with area hotels. The key messages were safety, convenience, and the uniqueness of Spokane County as a meeting destination.

PR/Publicity: News releases supported all the specific programs, such as the VRF and Holiday promotions. Regional and local media were contacted every two weeks via news releases and/or phone calls to announce new promotions and events that would encourage travel to Spokane.

PR/Regional Media Blitz: This program identified the regional media in a three-state area of Montana, Idaho, and Washington. It used personal visits by CVB representatives to inform the media in the three states about seasonal travel promotions to the Spokane region; unique upcoming events, such as the USA vs. China women's hockey game; and new physical improvements, such as the opening of a new conference center.

PR/Civic Responsibility

"Operation Spokane Heroes": In partnership with the chamber of commerce and other local groups, the CVB Hospitality Committee developed packages and programs to give back support to local military families and to boost the family spirits of those serving in the military located at area bases. This good-neighbor campaign kicked off on Veterans' Day. One of the most effective elements of the "Real Deal" campaign occurred when over 100 local businesses gave significant discounts to people in the military. The governor also came to Spokane to proclaim November as Military Appreciation Month, which generated much publicity. Even local school children made signs and raised money for stress relief packages for families affected by the September 11 terrorist attacks.

"Spokane Loves NY": The "Spokane Loves NY" effort took a contingent of Spokanites to New York and raised funds for the Twin Tower Orphan Relief Fund. A very successful program, it created solidarity with those directly affected by the terrorist attacks. The Spokane folks worked at a café at ground zero, handing out free food to the workers. CVB is working with the New York mayor's office to bring back to Spokane large pieces of the World Trade Center debris to develop a monument in memory of those who lost their lives.

Personal Sales

"Bring It Home" Campaign: Sales presentations were made by CVB representatives to local organizations and service clubs to generate leads for people planning meetings in Spokane.

Group Business Travel: Following up on the direct-mail contact of meeting planners, personal sales calls were used by CVB to book group meetings.

Response Management: The goal was to provide immediate information to visitor inquiries. As travel decisions became more impulsive and distance of trips shortened, it was important that CVB respond immediately via telephone, fax, e-mail, and the Internet to get information in the hands of travelers before they moved on to consider alternative destinations.

Zero-Based Planning In IMC programs, advertising is just one of many tools that work together to deliver a comprehensive package of messages. Which IMC tool can best reach a mass audience (advertising), involve an audience (events), or build credibility and believability (public relations)? Making this decision is a process called **zero-based planning**, which means the decision about which marketing communication tool to use is based on an analysis of the year's situation analysis, SWOTs, and communication objectives, rather than just tweaking last year's budget with decisions based on what was done in the past. The "Practical Tips" explains how to do zero-based planning for marketing communication.[6]

Practical Tips

HOW TO DO ZERO-BASED PLANNING

1. Determine the key communication problem to be solved.
2. Identify the strengths and weaknesses of the marketing communication tools.
3. Match the problem to be solved to the tool with the most strength in that area.
4. Identify the other marketing communication areas and tools that need to be used in *support* of the lead program.

Source: Adapted from Tom Duncan and Sandra Moriarty, *Driving Brand Value* (New York: McGraw-Hill, 1997), p 155.

An example of building a campaign around one of the marketing communication areas comes from the White Castle case, which used a sales promotion to attract attention, capture the curiosity of its devotees, and serve as a long-term brand reminder. The "Craverscope" drink promotion involved 12 specially designed 32-ounce cups with Crave-related horoscopes. The Craverscope cups played with conventional horoscope signs, such as "Sagicravius" for Sagittarius. Advertising and in-store merchandising materials were used in support of this promotion. This is one of the many "Points-of-Crave" (POC) message tools used to remind customers of the theme.

Integration As we said earlier, when all the pieces work together, the whole is greater than the sum of its parts. That's called synergy, and it's the reason why advertisers run campaigns rather than one-shot ads. In addition to multiple message sources, a variety of communication tools, and a range of stakeholder groups, an IMC campaign also has to build on corporate elements, such as a company's mission and business philosophy, its corporate culture, and the performance of its products or services.

Integration starts with a company's business philosophy and its mission. The best campaigns grow from the company's approach to business, particularly when it is customer-

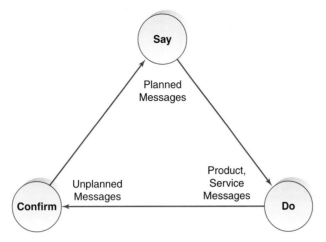

FIGURE 19.3

THE SAY, DO, CONFIRM MODEL
Source: Tom Duncon and Sandra
Moriarty, *Driving Brand Value* (New
York: McGraw-Hill, 1997), 91.

focused. Southwest Airlines, for example, has become the most profitable airline in the country on the basis of understanding its customers needs and serving them well. Integration also means matching up what a company says with what it does. In *Driving Brand Value,* which focuses on the importance of integrated marketing in building brand relationships, the authors describe the "integration triangle,"[7] which identifies three key elements that have to work together: what the company or brand says about itself (say, or planned messages), how the company or brand performs (do, or product and service messages), and what other people say about it (confirm, or unplanned word-of-mouth messages). Figure 19.3 shows these elements. A brand is integrated when there are no gaps between the say, do, and confirm messages.

A good example of the relationship among those three elements could be seen in the United Airlines "Rising" campaign, which was a multiyear commitment to significantly improve customer service. Campaign planners knew that if service lags, the campaign's "Rising" (which promises improvement) message would only irritate travelers more. United invested $400 million in a five-year customer service improvement program to deliver the performance its new theme promised. The gate-side improvements, at the time, included increased electronic ticketing, company agents with hand-held personal computers to check in passengers, and electronic gate readers that verify boarding passes. On board, the entire fleet was outfitted with more comfortable seats as well as adjustable head rests, individual reading lamps, plug-in power for laptop computers, individual TV screens that show videos, and 17 new lunch and dinner menus developed by a famous chef. A new position, the "onboard manager," oversees the service provided to frequent fliers, business travelers, and first-class guests. Since this campaign, most other airlines have made similar changes in an effort to keep up with United.

Gerald Greenwald, United's chairperson and CEO, said, "What we are really doing is narrowing the gap between what goes on in air travel and what we promise." He explained, "We do not want to only promise what we do today. We are trying to say to the flying public, we're honest and we empathize, and we'll talk about what it is you experience in our commercials and we are going to do our darnedest to raise your expectations."[8] However, in spite of all these efforts to make good on the promise, the "Rising" campaign was eventually stopped because United simply wasn't able to deliver the service it promised.

The Appropriation and Budget

The amount of money available from the client, or advertiser, governs all strategic decisions. Managers use their knowledge of the amount of money that has been appropriated for the campaign in planning the general scope and scale of the campaign effort.

After developing the plan, managers create a budget that estimates the costs of the various recommended campaign steps. If this budget exceeds the appropriation, either costs have to be shaved or the appropriation has to increase. Once the appropriation is set, the money can be allocated among the various advertising and marketing communication activities.

The budget size for advertising and marketing communication programs has a tremendous range. If you are working on a campaign for a major marketer, you may have

The "Craverscopes" cup promotion featured crave-related horoscopes as a Point-of-Crave (POC) brand reminder message.

plenty of money available. The United "Rising" campaign, discussed earlier, cost an estimated $100 million. Smaller companies can successfully run campaigns without spending as much money. Local companies buying local media may even succeed with a $250,000 budget. The Spokane campaign, which ran for six months, had a budget under $100,000.

Marketing experts remind campaign planners to build budgets based on the cost of reaching the target market rather than on the cost of certain kinds of marketing communication activities. Once the potential customer targets are identified in the campaign plan, then, according to marketing experts Dana Hayman and Don Schultz, it should be possible to quantify the value of the brand's customers and prospects so that "targets can be selected and prioritized based on what they are currently and potentially worth to the firm."[9] As Hayman and Schultz explain, that makes it possible to set return-on-investment goals—that is, to figure the expected profit returns based on the costs of reaching a customer or group of customers. This calculation is also called **breakeven analysis** or **payout planning**.

If you are working for a nonprofit campaign, such as the Spokane CVB, you may need to focus on inexpensive marketing communication, such as publicity and co-sponsorships, and try to stimulate as much word of mouth as possible. Most campaigns are somewhere in between big-budget and low-budget efforts, and their planners rarely have as much money as they feel they need to do the job right.

Fund-raising is another aspect of nonprofit marketing. One of the Spokane campaign's projects was to raise $76,500 to execute the campaign. Sources for this revenue included:

- Supplemental contributions from the city and county governments to help with the costs of the campaign.
- Nontraditional partners (groups that hadn't been affiliated in the past with financial support for the CVB) for specific programs, such as American Express, AAA Auto Club, Amtrak, and the Downtown Spokane Partnership.
- Partners from the inland of Washington state and other states in the Northwest for specific regional projects.
- In-kind contributions of supplies, time, or other services from vendors.

Evaluating the Campaign Plan

The last stage in the development of a campaign plan is to prepare a proposal stating how the campaign will be evaluated. Evaluation is the final and, in some respects, the most important step in an advertising campaign because it determines if the campaign effort was effective. The key part of an evaluation plan is to measure a company or brand's effectiveness against its stated objectives. If not done formally through a research project, some sort of evaluation is always done informally to determine whether the effort was successful.

A formal evaluation effort answers such questions as: Did the campaign work (based on its objectives)? What were the results? Did it build brand or corporate reputation? Was it cost-effective?

The Spokane campaign evaluated each facet of its program:

- ***Visiting Friends and Relatives Campaign.*** A conversion study (a study that determines how many people who say they intend to come actually do come) in March, six months after the September 11 attacks, surveyed a sample of the households that requested a kit to determine how many people actually traveled to Spokane.
- ***Getaway Value Package.*** A conversion study a month earlier surveyed a sample of the people who inquired about visiting Spokane to determine how many actually visited Spokane.

These measures provide the information necessary to determine the effectiveness of the campaign.

IT'S A WRAP
CAMPAIGNS THAT WORK MEET THEIR OBJECTIVES

An effective campaign delivers on its objectives, as the Spokane short-term marketing campaign, the OnStar campaign, and the White Castle campaign illustrated. Spokane's short-term marketing campaign effectively built a stronger top-of-mind awareness for Spokane, even in a difficult time for travel and tourism. The "Operation Spokane Heroes" and "Spokane Loves NY" programs were early successes covered in *USA Today,* on CBS radio, and in various regional publications.

How effective was OnStar's "Batman" campaign? It won an EFFIE for its performance measures, which included a 35 percent increase in awareness levels six months after the campaign was launched, accompanied by a 10 percent increase in brand familiarity. On the Web the number of monthly page hits increased from 24,000 to 165,000 six months after the campaign launched, an increase of almost 700 percent. The number of OnStar subscribers increased by 270 percent.

The White Castle "Crave" campaign was a clear success in terms of its objectives. For sales growth, the first objective, the campaign delivered a 10 percent increase compared to the industry average of 3 percent. The second objective—to outperform the category with annual sales-per-unit 50 percent greater than the industry average—was also met. Annual sales-per-restaurant unit for the campaign year was 59 percent greater than the industry average. The third objective—to maintain a 50 percent advertising awareness and association level (50% of consumers would reach that level of campaign theme awareness and 50% would associate the theme with White Castle) between White Castle and the "What You Crave" branding idea—was more than accomplished as White Castle achieved an 80 percent awareness and association level. And the campaign won an EFFIE.

Using an integrated marketing campaign backed by sound research, on-target strategy, and a variety of marketing communication tools sent effective messages in all three cases.

Summary

1. **Describe an IMC campaign and explain why it is more complex than on-shot advertising.** An IMC campaign unifies all marketing communication, corporate, and brand messages to communicate a consistent message to stakeholder audiences. The campaign message is based on a central theme or Big Idea. An IMC campaign plan is more complex than a traditional advertising plan because it has more message sources, more communication tools, and more stakeholder audiences to consider.

2. **Outline the structure of an IMC campaign plan.** A campaign outline includes a situation analysis, the campaign strategy, the communication strategy and tactics, a media plan, a plan for other marketing communication activities, a scheduling strategy, and a campaign budget.

3. **Explain the purpose of evaluating a campaign.** Companies evaluate IMC and advertising campaigns to gauge their effectiveness. The company measures how well the campaign met its objectives.

Key Terms

breakeven analysis (payout planning), p. 554
campaign, p. 540
concept testing, p. 546
cross-functional management, p. 540

executions, p. 546
image transfer, p. 548
Integrated Marketing Communication (IMC), p. 536

media mix, p. 549
single-shot ads, p. 540
situation analysis, p. 540
stakeholder, p. 536

SWOT analysis, p. 542
synergy, p. 546
zero-based planning, p. 552

Questions

1. Identify a local retailer that does a lot of marketing communication. List and analyze the store's message sources, its stakeholders, and its communication tools.

2. What is a situation analysis, and how does it differ from a SWOT analysis?

3. What are the four primary areas of campaign strategy?

4. What holds the messages in a campaign together? How is it developed?

5. Choose either Spokane, White Castle, or the OnStar "Batman" campaign and summarize the media strategy. What traditional advertising media are included, as well as other marketing communication areas? Think of at least one other advertising medium or marketing communication tool that might be used and explain why would you recommend it.

6. What principles are at work in IMC campaign planning that make it different from traditional advertising campaign planning? State and explain two.

Suggested Class Project

Interview a local advertiser about a local campaign. Write a report on how and why it was developed, its strategy, its creative theme, its media plan, and its evaluation. Use the integration triangle to analyze the campaign's say, do, and confirm messages.

Working in teams of four to six people, outline a research proposal for a program that you would recommend to evaluate the effectiveness of the most current campaign for Pepsi, Coca-Cola, Burger King, Taco Bell, Wendy's, or McDonald's.

Suggested Internet Class Project

Visit the White Castle Web site (www.whatyoucrave.com). Make a list of all the elements that tie in with the "Crave" theme, or that make up White Castle's current campaign.

Hallmark BUILD·A·CAMPAIGN Projects

Please review the Hallmark Case Appendix at the end of the text before responding to these questions.

1. In your small groups discuss how Capitol Advertising used an integrated marketing communication perspective in developing its campaign to build brand insistence.

2. How can Gold Crown stores use integrated marketing communications tactics to leverage Hallmark's existing campaign? Compile all the sections of the campaign plan that you developed in previous chapters. Using the Capitol Advertising case as a model, develop your own plan for next year's campaign for your local Gold Crown store.

Hallmark Case Analysis

(To be done in conjunction with or separate from the Build-A-Campaign projects at the end of each chapter.)

1. Summarize the marketing situation in which Hallmark found itself. Convert this information to a SWOT analysis. What was the key problem Hallmark needed to address with this campaign?

2. Develop a positioning statement for a local Hallmark Gold Crown Store that leverages Hallmark's positioning.

3. Develop a list of questions that you would need to ask to estimate the number of consumers at each level of the Brand Insistence Pyramid.

4. What consumer behaviors must a Hallmark Gold Crown Store alter to benefit from the brand inistence campaign? Write up a strategy for changing two of these behaviors.

5. How might a Hallmark Gold Crown Store establish customer loyalty for the local store? Write up a loyalty strategy for your local store.

6. Visit a Hallmark Gold Crown Store in your area. Develop two marketing and two communication objectives for the store you visited. Provide a clear rationale for setting these objectives.

7. What media mix would be most appropriate for your local Hallmark Gold Crown Store? Justify the choice of media and marketing communication tools in terms of their strengths and weaknesses and their ability to deliver the store's message to its target audience cost-effectively.

8. Based on what you understand about Hallmark's (and your local store's) market situation, positioning, targeting, and consumer behavior, develop a creative brief to give to a creative team (see Chapter 11).

9. Develop a sample print, radio, and TV ad that meets the demands of the creative brief.

10. How would you evaluate the effectiveness of this Hallmark campaign analysis?

Notes

1. Adapted from John Burnett and Sandra Moriarty, *Introduction to Marketing Communication: An Integrated Approach* (Upper Saddle River, NJ: Prentice Hall, 1998), 9.

2. Tom Duncan and Sandra E. Moriarty, "A Communication-Based Marketing Model for Managing Relationships," *Journal of Marketing* 62(2) (April 1998): 1–13.

3. Don E. Schultz, Stanley I. Tannenbaum, and Robert F. Lauterborn, *Integrated Marketing Communications* (Chicago: NTC Business Books, 1993), xvii.

4. Tom Duncan and Sandra Moriarty, *Driving Brand Value: Using Integrated Marketing to Manage Profitable Stakeholder Relationships* (New York: McGraw-Hill, 1997), 169.

5. Mary Ellen Podmolik and Jim Kirk, "United's New Flight Path; Upgrades Court Business Fliers," *Chicago Sun-Times* (May 12, 1997): 43.

6. Duncan and Moriarty, *Driving Brand Value,* 148–165.

7. Ibid., 91.

8. Jim Kirk, "Ad Agencies Rise to United's Challenge," *Chicago Tribune* (June 15, 1997): B1.

9. Dana Hayman and Don Schultz, "How Much Should You Spend on Advertising?" *Advertising Age* (April 26, 1999): 32.

PART-ENDING CASE

The "Eat Mor Chikin" IMC campaign continues to evolve.

Chick-fil-A and its advertising agency, the Richards Group, have developed one of the most successful integrated brand campaigns in the fast-food industry; an integrated brand campaign that was executed across all media.

For Chick-fil-A, the extendable brand idea was the "Eat Mor Chikin" campaign, which featured cows persuading consumers to eat more Chick-fil-A chicken. The campaign rolled out initially as a three-dimensional billboard. This medium provided Chick-fil-A with a unique platform for being heard and getting noticed. The billboard campaign was and still is very successful; however, the campaign didn't stop with just billboards. The "Eat Mor Chikin" campaign continues to evolve and make its way into every point of contact with the customer.

If cows could climb up on a billboard, why couldn't they stand in front of a Chick-fil-A restaurant encouraging people to "Eat Mor Chikin"? A seven-foot-tall, standup cow soon became part of a complete in-store point-of-purchase kit that also included banners, table tents, cups, bags, and register toppers. This marked the beginning of campaign integration.

From there, the campaign has been integrated into other print materials such as direct mail, FSIs, and ad slicks. In no time, the campaign found itself in promotions, events, TV, radio, the Web, clothing, and merchandise. In 1998, Chick-fil-A began producing calendars featuring the infamous "Eat Mor Chikin" cows. Due to high calendar demand, production numbers have jumped every year from 470,000 calendars in 1998 to more than 1.2 million in 2002. The cows and their quirky antics have become a key symbol of Chick-fil-

A's marketing communications. The calendars are yet another medium by which the cows are spreading their self-preservation message to "Eat Mor Chikin."

In addition to paid media, public relations has played a major role in the success of the campaign. The Chick-fil-A cows have received over $5 million in free media on both local and national levels.

Chick-fil-A may never have the advertising budgets of its competitors, but the influence and success of an integrated campaign is making up the difference.

ITS YOUR TURN

1. Has Chick-fil-A developed a truly integrated campaign? Why or why not?
2. Suggest how this campaign could be taken globally.

The Hallmark Brand Insistence IMC Campaign

The following case was written by Dr. Lynda M. Maddox, Professor of Marketing and Advertising, George Washington University. It reflects the work of her student team, Capitol Advertising, which won the American Advertising Federation's 25th Annual National Student Advertising Competition in 1998. The competition is the oldest and largest student advertising competition in the United States. For the past 25 years students, professors, and practitioners have looked to the NSAC to provide real-world experience to the best and the brightest students hoping to pursue careers in advertising and marketing.*

This IMC campaign case will serve as a model for a comprehensive case analysis. At the end of Chapters 3–19 several questions ask you to extend this case to local retailers, and questions on the text's Web site extend the case to online markets. By the end of the text, you will have created a version of the next Hallmark campaign plan.

WHY PEOPLE USE CARDS

The greeting card industry is built on relationships. Last year consumers purchased more then 6.6 billion cards, worth over $7 billion in retail sales, to help establish, sustain, and build relationships.

All consumers, but especially women, recognize the symbolic and tangible benefits of greeting cards. They provide a way to: (1) express feelings; (2) show caring through purchasing, signing, and sending a card; (3) save a feeling; and (4) add "specialness" to an occasion.

OVERALL INDUSTRY TRENDS

During the past decade, the greeting card industry has remained flat in terms of unit sales while growing in dollar volume. In 1996, units declined about 1 percent with dollars up 4 percent, due to increasing card prices. Dollar volume exceeded $7 billion for the first time.

"Everyday cards" mark personal occasions such as birthdays and anniversaries and represent 49 percent of the category dollars. Birthdays account for 60 percent of everyday cards. "Seasonal cards" comprise 51 percent of total category dollars. They include Christmas (47%), Valentine's Day (16%), Mother's Day (13%), Easter (8%), and Father's Day (7%). These holidays represent over 90 percent of seasonal dollar volume.

The Importance of Convenience

Over the past decade, however, time constraints, shifting social attitudes, and an ever-growing impersonal world have led to a decline in seasonal card sales and an increase in everyday cards, including humorous and alternative varieties. The

---

*Key recruiters from the advertising industry come to the district and national competitions to hire students who participate in this American Advertising Federation event. Approximately 140 universities are involvedin the NSAC each year. We thank Hallmark Cards, the winning Capitol Advertising team from the George Washington University, and the American Advertising Federation for providing the material for this case. Special appreciation goes to Steve Doyal at Hallmark and Mary Ellen Woolley at AAF for all their help.

consumer is often unwilling to spend 10 to 20 minutes writing a letter, but will spend the same amount of time looking for the perfect card.

Consumers have many choices as to where to shop for cards. In addition to card specialty shops, they also can be found at drug, department, and supermarket chains. Many consumers report that although they prefer to purchase at Hallmark's Gold Crown stores, they end up buying cheaper cards at more convenient mass merchandisers.

In 1997, Hallmark introduced its Expressions from Hallmark brand to bring the Hallmark name to mass merchandisers. As a result, many independent Gold Crown store owners have had to rethink their marketing efforts to remain competitive.

Electronic Challenges

Technological advances such as e-mail, the Internet, and mobile phones have contributed to convenience but also to the impersonal nature of the modern world. To develop a presence in these new markets, Hallmark has partnered with Microsoft to create Greetings Workshop Deluxe to provide users with electronic greetings from the Hallmark Connections shop.

The declining costs of electronic media have also prompted rethinking about pricing. With Hallmark's leadership, card price increases have begun to slow as consumers resist higher card prices. Research has shown that consumer price thresholds are $2 and $3.

Peculiarities of the Greeting Card Industry

The greeting card industry operates quite differently from most other product categories in three respects:

1. Generally, each outlet offers only one major brand of greeting card. This type of distribution means that consumers who purchase greeting cards at a favorite grocery or drug store for convenience do not have brand choice. If consumers do have a brand preference, they must decide if it is worth the inconvenience of going elsewhere to purchase the preferred brand. For most consumers, the answer is no.
2. Unlike virtually any other product, the brand name of the greeting card appears on the back. In addition, the brand name is small and insignificant. Card purchasers report looking on the back of the card for price, but not for the brand name.
3. The greeting card industry is one in which Hallmark is the only national advertiser. Its major competitors, American Greetings, Gibson, and the many small niche brands, have little brand name recognition or awareness. American Greetings, however, has recently begun to advertise its alternative line of cards.

Hallmark has nearly 100 percent brand name recognition and extremely high levels of expressed preference. However, the lack of awareness of competitive brands combined with the importance of convenience make attention to brand at the point-of-purchase almost nonexistent. Herein lies Hallmark's paradox. Consumers overwhelmingly prefer Hallmark but choose convenience at the point-of-purchase, resulting in low levels of brand insistence. This affects not only Hallmark but the individual Gold Crown retailers as well.

HALLMARK'S BRANDS AND RETAIL DISTRIBUTION

Hallmark has three major brands of greeting cards. Two include the Hallmark name, whereas the third does not.

1. The flagship Hallmark brand is distributed in Hallmark Gold Crown stores, card shops, bookstores, and selected drug stores.
2. The Expressions from Hallmark brand is a Hallmark branded mass-channel product for retailers who believe the Hallmark name will sell more product and build brand preference for their stores.
3. The Ambassador brand is a mass-channel brand for retailers who value terms-of-sale (such as price discounts) more than brand equity.

HALLMARK'S BRAND EQUITY

Hallmark is one of the strongest brand names in the United States. Of those who prefer a particular greeting card brand, three-quarters select Hallmark. Its brand equity was built through product leadership, high-quality retail distribution, and consistent advertising. Using the theme, "When You Care Enough to Send the Very Best," Hallmark has established itself as a wholesome, caring, traditional, tasteful, dependable, and friendly brand.

Wanting the perfect card and needing convenience often can seem at odds with one another—one is emotional, the other rational. Consumers favor Hallmark but shop at the closest store that sells cards.

Capitol Advertising realized that to create brand insistence for Hallmark, it had to marry these two aspects under the banner of "successful convenience." Consumers must believe that it is more convenient to find the perfect card the first time—and this can be done only with Hallmark.

PRIMARY RESEARCH

Capitol Advertising of the George Washington University conducted primary research to learn about the buying-decision process among card buyers, to assess current levels of brand insistence, and to better understand consumer attitudes toward Hallmark. The findings from nationwide focus groups, in-depth interviews among consumers and retailers, and a survey showed that consumers today are redefining convenience. They will pay more and become loyal to companies that save them the most time.

Capitol Advertising's research showed that consumers insist on Hallmark mostly when buying for special occasions or people. For example, a 50th wedding anniversary card for parents would warrant a Hallmark card, but a birthday card for an acquaintance might not.

Evolution of Brand Insistence

This research led Capitol Advertising to develop the Insistence Evolution Model, shown in Figure A.1. The base level of the model is "Hallmark Awareness." Current levels are over 90 percent. At this stage, consumers know about Hallmark but do not consider it. The next level is "Hallmark Acceptance." Consumers will buy Hallmark if it meets their needs. They have not developed preference yet, but see Hallmark as a possible part of the consideration set.

The third stage in the Insistence Evolution Model is "Hallmark Preference." Consumers say they prefer Hallmark, but price or convenience factors win out when they buy. Purchasers may not even think about the brand they are buying at the point of purchase. Consumers at the fourth level "Insist on Hallmark Most of the Time." They actively seek out Hallmark for important occasions or recipients. Finally, at the apex of the Insistence Evolution Model is "Always Insist on Hallmark." These shoppers refuse to purchase anything but Hallmark—the ultimate in brand loyalty.

Audience Prioritization Formula

Identifying Hallmark's primary target audience required calculation of market potential. The audience prioritization formula used data from primary research to identify the audience most likely to insist on Hallmark and increase purchases.

Although traditional marketing suggests that Current Insisters might be the primary group, Capitol Advertising's formula placed it third. This group is small and nearly saturated in terms of card purchasing.

The "Insist on Hallmark Most of the Time" group already demands Hallmark for special occasions or card recipients. Research suggests this group can be moved to insist on Hallmark for at least 16 other occasions per year. Its potential makes it Capitol Advertising's secondary target market.

The primary audience is Current Preferrers, the largest group. This group already believes Hallmark is best. If this large audience can be moved to insist on Hallmark at least 40 percent of the time, Hallmark will dramatically increase its market share and sales.

FIGURE AP.1
Insistence Evolution Model.

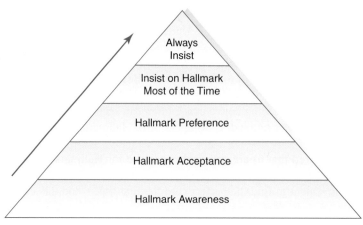

Insistence Evolution Model

Primary Target Market/Current Preferrers

The Current Preferrers market is comprised of 43.2 million adults (23 percent of the U.S. adult population). This group is predominantly female, aged 25 to 45, and is urban/suburban middle class. Members of this group purchase 46 greeting cards per year, 15 of which are Hallmark. The group spends a total of $2 billion per year on cards. Of that total, the Current Preferrers group spends $900 million on Hallmark cards. The group buys at grocery stores due to perceived convenience, and interprets Hallmark's tagline as, "When you care, you should send a card."

Secondary Target Market/Currently Insist Most of the Time

The "Currently Insist Most of the Time" group consists of 24.4 million adults (13 percent of the U.S. adult population). This target market is predominantly female, aged 45-plus, and is suburban and middle to upper class. Members purchase 47 greeting cards per year, 31 of which are Hallmark. The group spends a total of $1.2 billion per year on cards. Of that total, the group spends $1 billion on Hallmark cards. This market group seeks out Hallmark, but only for special people or occasions, and interprets Hallmark's tagline to mean, "When you care enough for the person or the occasion, you send a Hallmark; if not, just send a card."

Tertiary Market/Current Insisters

The Current Insisters target market consists of 3.75 million adults (2 percent of the U.S. adult population), mostly women, aged 45-plus, and is suburban and middle to upper class. On average, each member purchases 60 cards per year, all of which are Hallmark. This market, which spends a total of $300 million per year on Hallmark, always insists on Hallmark, and interprets Hallmark's tagline to mean, "When you care enough to send the very best . . . send a Hallmark."

CREATIVE STRATEGY

Capitol Advertising developed a brand insistence campaign that moves consumers up the brand insistence pyramid, creates higher brand loyalty, increases use of greeting cards, and produces higher satisfaction. It achieves the right balance of emotion and rationality. The emotion hooks, but it is the rationality of successful convenience that keeps them hooked.

Positioning Statement

Hallmark is the most convenient greeting card because it offers the best selection, most thoughtful verse, and emotional content that matches the sender's thoughts with the receiver's needs. This results in a successful card purchase without spending a lot of time looking. There is a sense of reliability, comfort, and confidence in knowing that Hallmark will have the right card. The consumer's choice can revolve around which card is best, rather than which card comes closest in either location or quality.

Creative Executions

Each creative execution focuses on a sender who needs to find the perfect card. Diverse situations—some poignant, some humorous—showcase Hallmark's extensive selection, quality, design, and verse. In each of these "perfect card profiles" the execution implies the importance of time and convenience. At the end of each ad, the sender is rewarded because the receiver thinks the card is absolutely perfect.

The format of each ad remains the same, adding continuity. Creative executions are tailored to the media and vehicles to add impact. Each ad ends with the tagline, "When You Care Enough to Send the Very Best … Send a Hallmark." This small, but subtle addition to Hallmark's tagline reflects the campaign's emphasis on brand insistence.

MEDIA

The media objective was to reach 90 percent of the primary target audience with a minimum frequency of six per month. To reach its target market, Capitol Advertising selected traditional and nontraditional media.

Traditional Media

Capitol Advertising places television, magazine, and radio ads in media that match the content of the creative advertising message. For example, television ads portraying poignant scenarios appear on shows such as *Touched by an Angel*. Humorous ads appear on comedies and radio spots run during traffic reports, to tie in with the consumer need for convenience and time saving.

Nontraditional Media

Capitol Advertising relies heavily on nontraditional media to increase frequency and provide reminders at the ready-now buying stage. Cash register receipts, peel-off strips on gift bows, and calendars carry the message, "Complete the perfect gift … send a Hallmark."

Ads in high-end catalogs, such as J. Crew, Pottery Barn, and Ballard Designs, urge consumers to remember to send a Hallmark, even when the catalog company wraps and mails their gift. These ads are unique and research shows consumers spend significant time looking through catalogs.

Other nontraditional media include advertisements on floor tiles and shopping carts in stores that carry Hallmark to remind consumers to think of the brand name they are purchasing. Mall advertising during peak holidays complements these and mass-media ads. Outdoor media include electronic "good news billboards," and bus shelters.

Internet tie-ins with the Microsoft Network include a trial version of Hallmark's Greeting Workshop Deluxe software that is bundled with other trial CDs that Microsoft sends. These are sent only to individuals within Hallmark's key demographics and are used to help build a better one-to-one relationship with consumers.

Promotions

Capitol Advertising's promotional cornerstone is the "Tell Us Your Story" contest in which Hallmark buyers submit their own perfect card story. Five winners are awarded $10,000 and given the chance to be the focus of a television commercial.

The "Perfect Year for the Perfect Card Calendar" uses Hallmark's print ads for each month to remind consumers to buy cards for all special occasions. Keepsake boxes are given to consumers who purchase at least $10.00 worth of cards to increase buying frequency and reinforce one of the key tangible values of greeting cards—the fact that they can be saved and cherished.

Public Relations

Key public relations activities reinforce the caring image of Hallmark and fit with Hallmark's corporate culture. For example, Hallmark sponsors Oprah's Angel Network by matching individual pledges up to $500,000. In addition, Hallmark's sponsorship of the Scripps-Howard Spelling Bee and a "Cards for Sick Kids" program reinforces the importance of children and relationships. The company's Golden Books division provides a donation of $200,000 to national literacy campaigns.

FIGURE AP.2
Hallmark Campaign Budget.

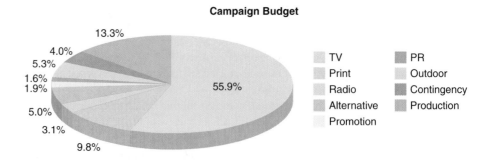

Campaign Budget

Budget

Hallmark's total budget for the year, shown in Figure A.2, is $75 million including media buys, creative development and production, promotions, and public relations.

Capitol Advertising, the George Washington University, Team Members: Student Team Members: Jeremy Beaver, Rachel Blut, Karl Carter, Kerri Grant, Jason Hagerman, Rikke Kasse, Kerry Krupsha, Arlene Lopez, Jaime Palmiotti, Sahar Sulayman Graduate Assistant Advisors: Lisa Foster, Jeff McKenna, Carolina Petrini

Please note: While Hallmark is delighted that it is the subject of this case, it regrets that it does not have the resources to field calls concerning the case. Please do not contact the company's head-quarters or individual stores for additional information, research, or interviews. Some current information is available on the company's Web site: www.hallmark.com.

A

Account management *(p.86)* People and processes at an ad agency that facilitate the relationship between the agency and the client.

Account planner *(p.129)* The person responsible for the strategy and its implementation in the creative work.

Account planning process *(p.129)* A process of using research to gain information about the brand in its marketplace, the consumer's perspective, or both, and to use that research to contribute directly to advertising development.

Adese *(p.333)* Formula writing that uses clichés, generalities, stock phrases, and superlatives.

Advertainment *(p.322)* A form of persuasive advertising in which the commercials look like TV shows or short films, and provide entertainment as opposed to high levels of information.

Advertiser *(p.16)* A person or organization that initiates the advertising process.

Advertising *(p.10)* Paid nonpersonal communication from an identified sponsor using mass media to persuade or influence an audience.

Advertising department *(p.84)* A department within the company that acts as a facilitator between outside vendors and internal advertising management.

Advertising plan *(p.189)* A plan that proposes strategies for targeting the audience, presenting the advertising message, and implementing media.

Advocacy advertising *(p.468)* A type of corporate advertising that involves creating advertisements and purchasing space to deliver a specific, targeted message.

Affiliate *(p.270)* A station that contracts with a national network to carry network-originated programming during part of its schedule.

Agency-of-record *(p.18)* An advertising agency that manages the business between a company and the agencies it has contracts with.

Aided recall *(p.171)* When one can remember an idea after seeing a cue.

Analysis *(p.190)* Making sense of all the data collected and figuring out what the information means for the future success of the brand or product.

Animation *(p.387)* A film or video technique in which objects or drawings are filmed one frame at a time.

Annual report *(p.469)* A financial document legally required of all publicly held companies.

Answer print *(p.389)* The finished version of the commercial, with the audio and video recorded together.

Aperture *(p.209)* The ideal moment for exposing consumers to an advertising message.

Art director *(p.331)* The person who is primarily responsible for the visual image of the advertisement.

Association *(p.169)* The process used to link a product with a positive experience, personality, or lifestyle.

Attitude *(p.112)* A learned predisposition that we hold toward an object, person, or idea.

Attribute trade-offs *(p.148)* An application of embedded research in which a list of most preferred products for an individual is generated from customer-provided quantitative ratings of their preferences for specific attributes, such as brand, price, and features.

Average frequency *(p.217)* The average number of times an audience has an opportunity to be exposed to a media vehicle or vehicles in a specified time span.

Awareness *(p.167)* The degree to which a message has made an impression on the viewer or reader.

B

Banners *(p.391)* See "banner ad."

Banner ad *(p.289, 355)* Small, often rectangular-shaped graphic that appears at the top of a Web page.

Benefits *(p.312)* Statements about what the product can do for the user.

Big Idea *(p.302)* A creative idea that expresses an original advertising thought.

Bind-ins *(p.416)* Cards bound into the binding.

Blind headline *(p.337)* An indirect headline that gives little information.

Blow-ins *(p.416)* Cards blown in loose between the pages of a publication.

Body copy *(p.334)* The text of the message.

Brainstorming *(p.308)* A creative thinking technique using free association in a group environment to stimulate inspiration.

Brand *(p.72)* A name, term, design, or symbol that identifies the goods, services, institution, or idea sold by a marketer.

Brand equity *(p.74, 176)* The value associated with a brand; the reputation that the brand name or symbol connotes.

Brand mark *(p.74)* The part of the brand that cannot be spoken, also known as the logo.

Brand name *(p.72)* The part of the brand that can be spoken, such as words, letters, or numbers.

Branding *(p.72, 175)* The process of creating a unique identity for a product.

Breakeven analysis (payout planning) *(p.448, 554)* A type of payout plan that seeks to determine the point at which the total cost of the promotion exceeds the total revenues, identifying the point where the effort cannot break even.

Broadband *(p.274)* A bandwidth that has more capacity to send data and images into a home or business through a cable television wire than the much smaller capacity of a traditional telephone wire or television antenna system.

Broadcast media *(p.270)* Media, such as radium television, and interactive media, which transmit sounds or images electronically.

Broadsheet *(p.240)* A newspaper with a page size eight columns wide and 22 inches deep.

Broadsheets *(p.408)* A full-size news page sheet.

Business marketing *(p.497)* The marketing of goods and services to organizations.

Business strategic plan *(p.184)* A business plan that deals with the broadest decisions of the organization.

Business-to-business advertising *(p.497)* Targets other businesses.

Buzz *(p.168)* Gossip created by people over a popular interest in something.

C

Cable television *(p.271)* A form of subscription television in which the signals are carried to households by a cable.

Call-out *(p.338)* A block of text separate from the main display copy and headline where the idea is presented.

Call to action *(p.339)* A concluding line that tells people how to buy the product.

Campaign *(p.540)* A comprehensive advertising plan for a series of different but related ads that appear in different media across a specified time period.

Captions *(p.337)* Text which explains what is happening in a corresponding photo or illustration.

Car cards *(p.264)* Small advertisements that are mounted in racks inside a vehicle.

Carryover effect *(p.214)* A measure of residual effect (awareness or recall) of the advertising message some time after the advertising period has ended.

Casting *(p.352)* Finding the right person for the role.

Cause marketing *(p.463)* Sponsoring a good cause in the hope that the association will result in positive public opinion about the company.

Catalog *(p.411)* A multipage direct-mail publication that shows a variety of merchandise.

Cease-and-desist order *(p.50)* An FTC remedy for false or deceptive advertising that requires an advertiser to stop its unlawful practices.

Central processing *(p.172)* When the brain is searching for information and evaluating it critically.

Channel of distribution *(p.76)* People and organizations involved in moving products from producers to consumers.

Circulation *(p.241)* The number of copies sold.

Claim *(p.312)* A statement about the product's performance.

Classified advertising *(p.243)* Commercial messages arranged in the newspaper according to the interests of readers.

Claymation *(p.387)* A stop-motion animation technique in which figures sculpted from clay are filmed one frame at a time.

Clip art *(p.367)* Generic, copyright-free art that can be used by anyone who buys the book or service.

Close *(p.339)* The last paragraph of the body copy that often refers back to the creative concept and wraps up the Big Idea.

Closing *(p.228)* Represents the last date to send an ad to production.

Closure *(p.172)* A gestalt principle which states that missing parts of a shape will automatically be added on perception.

Clutter *(p.161)* The excessive number of messages delivered to a target audience.

Co-branding *(p.444)* A product offered by two companies with both companies' brands present.

Cognitive dissonance *(p.108)* A tendency to justify the discrepancy between what you receive and what you expected to receive.

Cognitive learning *(p.169)* When advertisers want people to know something new after watching or hearing a message.

Collaborative filtering *(p.147)* An application of embedded research in which customers can see product recommendations based on predictive models that classify them with others who have similar profiles of attitude or behavior.

Collateral materials *(p.342, 469)* Brochures and other forms of product literature used in support of an advertising, public relations, or sales promotion effort.

Color separation *(p.379)* The process of splitting a color image into four images recorded on negatives; each negative represents one of the four process colors.

Co-marketing *(p.444)* Programs through which manufacturers partner with retailers in joint promotions.

Commercial speech *(p.44)* Our legal right to say what we want to promote commercial activity, as defined by the First Amendment.

Commission *(p.87)* The amount an ad agency charges to the client, often a percentage of media cost.

Communication audit *(p.467)* A type of background research that assesses the internal and external PR environment that affects the organization's audience, objectives, competitors, and past results.

Comprehensives *(p.376)* A layout that looks as much like the final printed ad as possible.

Concept testing *(p.546)* When a simple statement of an idea is tried out on people who are representative of the target audience in order to get their reactions to the Big Idea.

Conditional learning *(p.169)* Learning through association by connecting a stimulus to a reward through repeated exposure to a stimulus that eventually leads to the reward.

Consent decree *(p.50)* A formal FTC agreement with an advertiser that obligates the advertiser to stop its deceptive practices.

Consumer behavior *(p.97)* The process of an individual or group selecting, purchasing, using, or disposing of products, services, ideas, or experiences to satisfy needs and desires.

Contest *(p.432)* A form of promotion that requires participants to compete for a prize or prizes based on some sort of skill or ability.

Continuity *(p.214)* Even, continuous advertising over the time span of the advertising campaign.

Controlled media *(p.402, 467)* Media that the direct marketer either owns or has delivered through carefully controlled criteria by a contracted company.

Conviction *(p.172)* A particularly strong belief that has been anchored firmly in one's attitudes.

Co-op advertising *(p.244, 486)* Also called cooperative advertising; an arrangement between a retailer and manufacturer in which the manufacturer reimburses the retailer for all or part of the retailer's advertising costs.

Cooperative advertising *(p.77, 486)* See Co-op advertising.

Copy-testing *(p.323)* Evaluating the effectiveness of an ad, either in a draft form or after it has been used.

Copywriter *(p.331)* The person who writes the text for an ad.

Corporate advertising *(p.468)* A type of advertising used by firms to build awareness of a company, its products, and the nature of its business.

Corporate image *(p.468)* A perception of a company that its stakeholders create in their minds from messages and experiences with the company.

Corporate relations *(p.459)* Relations between a corporation and the public involving an organization's image and reputation.

Corrective advertising *(p.50)* An FTC directive that requires an advertiser to run truthful ads to counter deceptive ads.

Cost Per Rating (CPR) *(p.219)* A method of comparing media vehicles by relating the cost of the message unit to the audience rating.

Cost Per Thousand (CPM) *(p.219)* The cost of exposing each 1,000 members of the target audience to the advertising message.

Coupons *(p.432)* Legal certificates offered by manufacturers and retailers that grant specified savings on selected products when presented for redemption at the point-of-purchase.

Crawl *(p.383)* Computer-generated letters that move across the bottom of the screen.

Creative brief *(p.314)* The document that outlines the key strategy decisions and details the key execution elements.

Creative concept *(p.302)* A Big Idea that is original, supports the ad strategy, and dramatizes the selling point.

Creative director *(p.331)* The person responsible for managing the work of the creative team.

Creative platform *(p.198)* A document that outlines the message strategy decisions for an individual ad.

Crisis management *(p.460)* Management of people and events during times of great danger or trouble.

Cross-functional management *(p.540)* A practice that uses teams to coordinate activities that involve different areas in and outside a company.

Cultural and social influences *(p.98)* The forces other people exert on your behavior.

Culture *(p.261)* The complex whole of tangible items, intangible concepts, and social behaviors that define a group of people or a way of life.

Customary pricing *(p.78)* Using a single, well-know price for a long period of time.

Customer-focused marketing *(p.158)* All communication within an advertisement that is evaluated in terms of the consumer's response.

Customer relationship management (CRM) *(p.403)* A database process that identifies and analyzes patterns in customer behavior to maximize the profitability of each relationship.

Cut *(p.386)* An abrupt transition from one shot to another.

Cutouts *(p.255)* Irregularly shaped extensions added to the top, bottom, or sides of standard outdoor boards.

D

Dailies *(p.388)* Processed scenes on film that a director reviews to determine what needs correcting.

Databases *(p.399)* Lists of consumers with information that helps target and segment those who are highly likely to be in the market for a certain product.

Database marketing *(p.402)* A tool and industry that utilizes databases to predict trends and monitor consumers in order to more effectively implement direct-marketing strategies.

Data sheets *(p.503)* Advertising that provides detailed technical information.

Dealer tag *(p.487)* Time left at the end of a manufacturer's TV or radio commercial to insert local retail store information.

Demography *(p.102)* The study of social and economic factors that influence how individual consumers behave.

Demographics *(p.102)* Human traits such as age, income, race, and gender.

Directional advertising *(p.259)* Tells people where to go to find goods and services.

Direct mail *(p.407)* A type of direct marketing that sends the offer to a prospective customer by mail.

Direct marketing (DM) *(p.77, 398)* A type of marketing that uses media to contact a prospect directly and elicit a response without the intervention of a retailer or personal sales.

Direct-response advertising *(p.82, 415)* A type of marketing communication that achieves an action-oriented objective as a result of the advertising message.

Direct-response counts *(p.142)* Evaluative tests that count the number of viewers or readers who request more information or who purchase the product.

Discretionary income *(p.106)* The money available for spending after taxes and necessities are covered.

Display advertising *(p.243)* Sponsored messages that can be of any size and location within the newspaper, except the editorial page.

Display copy *(p.334)* Type set in larger sizes that is used to attract the reader's attention.

Dubbing *(p.389)* The process of making duplicate copies of a videotape.

E

E-commerce *(p.488)* Selling goods and services through electronic means, usually over the Internet.

Effective frequency *(p.219)* A planning concept that determines a range (minimum and maximum) of repeat exposures for a message.

Embedded research *(p.147)* Research that is measured through real purchase and use situations which benefits the consumer, manufacturer, and retailer.

Employee relations *(p.459)* Relations between the company and its workers.

Endorsement or testimonial *(p.48)* Any advertising message that consumers reasonably believe reflects the opinions, beliefs, or experiences of an individual, group, or institution.

Evaluative research *(p.132)* Research that determines how well the ad or campaign achieved its goals.

Exchange *(p.64)* The process whereby two or more parties transfer something of value to one another.

Exclusive distribution *(p.78)* When only one distributor is allowed to sell the brand in a particular market.

Execution *(p.317, 546)* The different variations used to represent the message of a campaign.

Extensions *(p.255)* Embellishments to painted billboards that expand the scale and break away from the standard rectangle limitations.

Exterior transit advertising *(p.257)* Advertising posters that are mounted on the sides, rear, and tops of vehicles.

Extranets *(p.473)* Networked systems of electronic communication that allow employees to be in contact with each other in one business with its business partners.

F

Family *(p.101)* Two or more people who are related by blood, marriage, or adoption and live in the same household.

Feature analysis *(p.193)* A comparison of your product's features against those of competing products.

Federal Communications Commission (FCC) *(p.53)* A U.S. government agency that regulates broadcast media and can eliminate ads that are deceptive or offensive.

Federal Trade Commission (FTC) *(p.45)* A U.S. government agency responsible for regulating several advertising issues including banning deceptive or misleading advertising.

Fee *(p.87)* An hourly amount charged to the client by the agency.

Film-to-tape transfer *(p.386)* A procedure by which film is shot, processed, and then transferred to videotape.

Financial relations *(p.459)* Communications with the financial community.

Flighting *(p.214)* An advertising scheduling pattern characterized by a period of intensified activity called a *flight,* followed by a period of no advertising called a *hiatus.*

Font *(p.370)* The basic set of letters in a particular typeface.

Food and Drug Administration (FDA) *(p.52)* A regulatory division of the Department of Health and Human Services that oversees package labeling and ingredient listings for food and drugs.

Frame-by-frame tests *(p.143)* Tests that evaluate consumers' reactions to the individual scenes that unfold in the course of a television commercial.

Free-standing insert advertisement *(p.244)* Preprinted advertisement placed loosely in the newspaper.

Frequency *(p.217)* The number of times an audience has an opportunity to be exposed to a media vehicle or vehicles in a specified time span.

Frequency *(p.295)* The number of radio waves produced by a transmitter in one second.

Frequency distribution *(p.218)* A media planning term describing exactly how many times each person is exposed to a message by percentage of the population (reach).

Fulfillment *(p.405)* The back-end operations of direct marketing, which include receiving the order, assembling the merchandise, shipping, and handling returns and exchanges.

Full-service agency *(p.84)* An agency that provides clients with the primary planning and advertising services.

G

Gaffer *(p.388)* Chief electrician on a film shoot.

Gatekeepers *(p.458)* Individuals who have direct relations with the public such as writers, producers, editors, talk-show coordinators, and newscasters.

Geodemographic clusters *(p.279)* Distinct types of neighborhoods.

Geomarketing *(p.491)* Marketing that is geared to increasing diversity in consumer tastes and preferences.

Global brand *(p.515)* One that is marketed with the same name, design, and creative strategy in most or all of the major regional market blocs.

Global perspective *(p.515)* A corporate philosophy that directs products and advertising toward a worldwide market.

Globalization *(p.24)* The deepening relationships and broadening interdependence among people from different countries.

Grip *(p.388)* Individual who moves the props and sets on a film shoot.

Gross impressions *(p.215)* The sum of the audiences of all the media vehicles used within a designated time span.

Gross Rating Points (GRPs) *(p.216)* The sum of the total exposure potential of a series of media vehicles expressed as a percentage of the audience population.

Guerrilla marketing *(p.470)* A form of unconventional marketing, such as chalk messages on a sidewalk, that is often associated with staged events.

H

Habit *(p.110)* Something learned so well, it has become second nature.

Halftone *(p.378)* (Continuous tone): Image with a continuous range of shades from light to dark.

Hard sell *(p.311)* A rational, informational message that emphasizes a strong argument and calls for action.

Headline *(p.334)* The title of an ad; it is display copy set in large type to get the reader's attention.

Hierarchy-of-effects *(p.191)* A set of consumer responses that moves from the least serious, involved, or complex up through the most serious, involved, or complex.

High involvement *(p.172)* Perceiving a product or information as important and personally relevant.

High-involvement decision process *(p.116)* A decision process that relates to higher-risk products purchased infrequently.

Horizontal publications *(p.248, 503)* Publications directed at people who hold similar jobs.

Household *(p.101)* All those people who occupy one living unit, whether they are related or not.

I

Image *(p.82)* The use of intangible attributes to create a specific perception.

Image transfer *(p.548)* When the presentation in one medium stimulates the listener or viewer to think about the presentation of the product in another medium.

Impact *(p.154)* The effect of the message on the audience.

Implied third-party endorsement *(p.459)* When the media endorse a product and the public finds it credible.

Inbound telemarketing *(p.414)* Incoming calls initiated by the customer.

Industrial advertising *(p.498)* Advertising that targets original equipment manufacturers (OEM).

Indirect advertising *(p.40)* Advertising that features one product instead of the primary (controversial) product.

Indirect marketing *(p.77)* Distributing a product through a channel structure that includes one or more resellers.

In-house agency *(p.18, 83)* An agency within an advertiser's organization that performs all the tasks an outside agency would provide for the advertiser.

In-market tests *(p.143)* Tests that measure the effectiveness of advertisements by measuring actual sales results in the marketplace.

In register *(p.376)* When the color layers align with each other in a printed image.

Institutional retail advertising *(p.489)* Advertising that focuses on the image of the store rather than selling merchandise.

Integrated direct marketing *(p.419)* A method of achieving precise, synchronized use of the right mediums at the right time, with a measurable return on dollars spent.

Integrated marketing *(p.70)* The process of meeting customers' needs through the coordination of the marketing mix and the other business functions.

Integrated Marketing Communication (IMC) *(p.22, 80, 536)* The practice of unifying all marketing communication efforts so they send a consistent, persuasive message to target audiences.

Integrated media strategy *(p.261)* A media strategy in which advertisers understand which media fit particular advertising needs, which media are complementary, and which detract from each other.

Intensive distribution *(p.78)* Stocking the product in as many outlets as possible.

Interactive technology *(p.261)* Technology such as the Internet.

Interconnects *(p.272)* A special cable technology that allows local advertisers to run their commercials in small geographic areas through the interconnection of a number of cable systems.

Interest *(p.168)* Activities that engage the consumer.

Interior transit advertising *(p.257)* Advertising posters that are mounted inside vehicles such as buses, subway cars, and taxis.

Interlock *(p.389)* A version of the commercial with the audio and video timed together, although the two are recorded separately.

Internal marketing *(p.459)* Providing information about marketing activity and promoting it internally to employees.

Internal service departments *(p.87)* Departments such as the traffic department, print production, financial services, and human resources or personnel, which serve the operations within the agency.

International advertising *(p.513)* Advertising designed to promote the same product in a number of countries.

International brand *(p.512)* A brand or product that is available in most parts of the world.

Intranets *(p.473)* Networked systems of electronic communication that allow employees to be in touch with one another from various locations.

Involvement *(p.172)* The intensity of the consumer's interest in a product.

Issue management *(p.460)* The practice of advising companies and senior management on how public opinion is coalescing around certain issues.

J

Justified *(p.371)* A form of typeset copy in which the ends of the lines in a column of type are forced to align by adding space between words in the line.

K

Kiosks *(p.257)* Multisided bulletin board structures designed for public posting of messages.

L

Layout *(p.372)* A drawing that shows where all the elements in the ad are to be positioned.

Lead *(p.339)* The first paragraph of the body copy.

Legibility *(p.372)* How easy or difficult a type is to read.

Licensing *(p.444)* The practice whereby a company with an established brand "rents" it to another company.

Lifestyle *(p.101)* The pattern of living that reflects how people allocate their time, energy, and money.

Lifestyle analysis *(p.113)* Examining the ways people allocate their time, energy, and money.

Lifetime customer value *(p.421)* An estimate of the revenue coming from a particular customer (or type of customer) over the lifetime of the relationship.

Line art *(p.378)* Art in which all elements are solid, with no intermediate shades or tones.

Lobbying *(p.460)* A form of public affairs involving corporations, activist groups, and consumer groups who provide information to legislators in order to get their support and to get them to vote a certain way on a particular bill.

Local brand *(p.512)* A brand that is marketed in one specific country.

Local cable *(p.272)* Cable scheduling that allows advertisers to show their commercials to highly restricted geographic audiences through interconnects.

Locking power *(p.170)* Creative approach that captures the attention of the consumer.

Low-involvement *(p.172)* Perceiving a product or information as unimportant.

Low-involvement decision process *(p.116)* A decision process that relates to products purchased frequently with low risk.

Loyalty program *(p.443)* A program designed to increase customer retention by rewarding customers for their patronage.

M

Makegoods *(p.228)* Compensation that media give to advertisers in the form of additional message units. These are commonly used in situations involving production errors by the medium and preemption of the advertiser's programming.

Market *(p.65)* An area of the country or a group of buyers.

Market segmentation *(p.67)* The process of dividing a market into distinct groups of buyers who might require separate products or marketing mixes.

Market selectivity *(p.239)* When the medium targets specific consumer groups.

Market tracking studies *(p.138)* Studies that follow the purchase activity of a specific consumer or group of consumers over a specified period of time.

Marketing *(p.12, 64)* Business activities that direct the exchange of goods and services between producers and consumers.

Marketing communications *(p.12, 65)* The element in the marketing mix that communicates the key marketing messages to target audiences.

Marketing communication mix *(p.80)* A combination of marketing communication activities, such as personal selling, advertising, sales promotion, marketing public relations, and packaging, to produce a coordinated message strategy.

Marketing concept *(p.69)* An idea that suggests that marketing should focus first on the needs and wants of the customer, rather than finding ways to sell products that may or may not meet customers' needs.

Marketing mix *(p.64)* A blend of four main activities: designing, pricing, distributing, and communicating about the product.

Marketing mix modeling *(p.213)* A modeling technique that allows marketers to determine the precise impact of the media plan on product sales.

Marketing plan *(p.184)* A written document that proposes strategies for using the elements of the marketing mix to achieve objectives.

Marketing Public Relations (MPR) *(p.461)* A type of public relations that supports marketing's product and sales focus by increasing the brand's and company's credibility with consumers.

Marketing research *(p.124)* Research that investigates all elements of the marketing mix.

Mass customization *(p.25)* A product development process that relies on flexible manufacturing to customize products for select markets or individuals.

Mechanicals *(p.376)* A finished pasteup with every element perfectly positioned that is photographed to make printing plates for offset printing.

Media *(p.18)* The channels of communication that carry the ad message to target audiences.

Media-buying services *(p.85)* Service providers that specialize in the purchase of media for their clients.

Media kit *(p.473)* Also called a press kit, a packet or folder that contains all the important information for members of the press.

Media mix *(p.157, 206, 549)* Selecting the best combination of media vehicles, nontraditional media, and marketing communication tools to reach the targeted stakeholder audiences.

Media objective *(p.228)* A goal or task a media plan should accomplish.

Media planning *(p.206)* A decision process leading to the use of advertising time and space to assist in the achievement of marketing objectives.

Media relations *(p.459)* Relationships with media contacts.

Media tour *(p.473)* A traveling press conference in which the company's spokesperson travels to different cities and meets with the local media.

Media vehicle *(p.206)* A single program, magazine, or radio station.

Medium *(p.206)* A single form of communication (television, billboards, online media).

Merging *(p.402)* The process of combining two or more lists of data.

Mission marketing *(p.463)* Linking the mission of the company to a good cause and committing support to it for the long term.

Mixer *(p.388)* The individual who operates the recording equipment during a film shoot.

Morphing *(p.384)* A video technique in which one object gradually changes into another.

Motive *(p.111)* An unobservable inner force that stimulates and compels a behavioral response.

N

Navigation *(p.391)* The action of a user moving through a Web site.

Needs *(p.111)* Basic forces that motivate you to do or to want something.

Network *(p.270)* When two or more stations are able to broadcast the same program that originates from a single source.

Network cable *(p.272)* Cable scheduling that runs commercials across an entire subscriber group simultaneously.

Network radio *(p.284)* A group of local affiliates providing simultaneous programming via connection to one or more of the national networks through AT&T telephone wires.

Newsprint *(p.376)* An inexpensive paper with a rough surface, used for printing newspapers.

News release *(p.470)* Primary medium used to deliver public relations messages to the media.

Niche markets *(p.25)* Subsegments of the general market which have distinctive traits that may provide a special combination of benefits.

Noise *(p.161)* Anything that interferes with or distorts the advertising message's delivery to the target audience.

Nonpromotional product advertising *(p.490)* A form of advertising that talks about merchandise that is new, exclusive, and of superior quality and design.

Nontraditional delivery *(p.249)* Delivery of magazines to readers through such methods as door hangers or newspapers.

Norms *(p.98)* Simple rules that each culture establishes to guide behavior.

O

Objective *(p.183)* The goal or task an individual or business wants to accomplish.

Objective-task method *(p.197)* Budgeting approach based on costs of reaching an objective.

One-order, one-bill *(p.244)* When media companies buy newspaper advertising space for national advertisers and handle the rate negotiation and billing.

One-step offer *(p.401)* A message that asks for a direct sales response and has a mechanism for responding to the offer.

On location *(p.352)* Commercials shot outside the studio.

Open pricing *(p.224)* A pricing a method in which prices are negotiated on a contract-by-contract basis for each unit of media space or time.

Opinion leaders *(p.457)* Important people who influence others.

Outbound telemarketing *(p.414)* Telemarketing sales calls initiated by the company.

Out-of-home advertising *(p.254)* All advertising that is displayed outside the home, from billboards, to blimps, to in-store aisle displays.

Overlines *(p.335)* Text used to set the stage and lead into the headline of copy.

P

Pace *(p.352)* How fast or slowly the action progresses in a commercial.

Painted bulletin *(p.255)* A type of advertisement that is normally created on-site and is not restricted to billboards as the attachment.

Participation marketing *(p.24)* A method of direct marketing in which the company knows its customers, generates feedback at every opportunity, involves the customers and prospects as much as possible, markets according to the customer's schedule, and makes the customer feel vested in the company's success.

Participations *(p.276)* An arrangement in which a television advertiser buys commercial time from a network.

Payout plan *(p.448)* A way to evaluate the effectiveness of a sales promotion in terms of its financial returns by comparing the costs of the promotion to the forecasted sales of the promotion.

Percentage-of-sales method *(p.197)* A budgeting technique based in the relationship between the cost of advertising and total sales.

Perception *(p.107)* The process by which we receive information through our five senses and acknowledge and assign meaning to this information.

Peripheral processing *(p.172)* Quick decision making based on simple factors for low-involvement purchases such as smell or a catchy slogan.

Permission marketing *(p.23, 410)* A method of direct marketing in which the consumer controls the process, agrees to receive communication from the company, and consciously signs up.

Personal selling *(p.80)* Face-to-face contact between the marketer and a prospective customer that intends to create and repeat sales.

Persuasion *(p.171)* Trying to establish, reinforce, or change an attitude, touch an emotion, or anchor a conviction firmly in the potential customer's belief structure.

Persuasion test *(p.141)* A test that evaluates the effectiveness of an advertisement by measuring whether the ad affects consumers' intentions to buy a brand.

Photostats *(p.381)* Photoprint proofs that are cheap to produce.

Pica *(p.371)* A unit used to measure width and depth of columns; there are 12 points in a pica and 6 picas in an inch.

Point *(p.371)* A unit used to measure the height of type; there are 72 points in an inch.

Point-of-Purchase (POP) display *(p.436)* A display designed by the manufacturer and distributed to retailers to promote a particular brand or line of products.

Positioning *(p.69, 194)* The way in which consumers perceive a product in the marketplace.

Poster (panels) *(p.255)* A type of advertisement that is created by designers, printed, and shipped to an outdoor advertising company who prepastes and applies it in sections to the poster panel's face on location.

Predictive dialing *(p.413)* Technology that allows telemarketing companies to call anyone by using a trial and error dialing program.

Preferred frequency *(p.217)* The percentage of audience reached at each level of repetition (exposed once, twice, and so on).

Preferred positions *(p.224)* Sections or pages of print media that are in high demand by advertisers because they have a special appeal to the target audience.

Premium *(p.432)* A tangible reward received for performing a particular act, such as purchasing a product or visiting the point-of-purchase.

Press conference *(p.471)* A public gathering of media people for the purpose of establishing a company's position or making a statement.

Price *(p.78)* An amount a seller sets for a product that is based not only on the cost of making and marketing the product, but also on the seller's expected profit level.

Price copy *(p.78)* A term used to designate advertising copy devoted to information about the price and the associated conditions of a particular product.

Price deal *(p.431)* A temporary reduction in the price of a product.

Price lining *(p.79)* A strategy where a company offers variations of a particular product and prices them accordingly.

Primary research *(p.125)* Information that is collected from original sources.

Primary research suppliers *(p.126)* Research firms that specialize in interviewing, observing, recording, and analyzing the behavior of those who purchase or influence the purchase of a particular good or service.

Process colors *(p.379)* Four basic inks—magenta, cyan, yellow, and black—that are mixed to produce a full range of colors found in four-color printing.

Product differentiation *(p.68)* A competitive marketing strategy that tries to create a competitive difference through real or perceived product attributes.

Product placement *(p.49)* The use of a brand name product in a television show, movie, or event.

Product retail advertising *(p.490)* Advertising that focuses on selling merchandise.

Professional advertising *(p.498)* Advertising that is targeted at professionals.

Profile *(p.193)* A composite description of a target audience using personality and lifestyle characteristics.

Program preemptions *(p.228)* Interruptions in local or network programming caused by special events.

Promise *(p.312)* Found in a benefit statement, it is something that will happen if you use the product.

Prospecting *(p.400)* In database marketing, this is the process of identifying prospects based on how well they match certain user characteristics.

Psychographics *(p.113)* All psychological variables that combine to share our inner selves and help explain consumer behavior.

Psychological pricing *(p.78)* A strategy that tries to manipulate the customer's purchasing judgment.

Public affairs *(p.460)* Relations between a corporation, the public, and government involving public issues relating to government and regulation.

Public communication campaigns *(p.462)* Social issue campaigns undertaken by nonprofit organizations as a conscious effort to influence the thoughts or actions of the public.

Public opinion *(p.457)* People's beliefs, based on their conceptions or evaluations of something, rather than on fact.

Public relations *(p.81, 456)* A management function enabling organizations to achieve effective relationships with various publics in order to manage the image and reputation of the organization.

Public Service Announcements (PSAs) *(p.467)* A type of public relations advertising that deals with public welfare issues and typically is run free of charge.

Publicity *(p.456)* Information that catches public interest and is relayed through the news media.

Puffery *(p.34)* Advertising or other sales representation that praises a product or service using subjective opinions, superlatives, and similar techniques that are not based on objective fact.

Pull strategy *(p.77)* A strategy that directs marketing efforts at the consumer and attempts to pull the product through the channel.

Pulsing *(p.214)* An advertising scheduling pattern in which time and space are scheduled on a continuous but uneven basis; lower levels are followed by bursts or peak periods of intensified activity.

Purging *(p.402)* The process of deleting duplicative information after lists of data are combined.

Push strategy *(p.77)* A strategy that directs marketing efforts at resellers, where success depends on the ability of these intermediaries to market the product, which they often do with advertising.

Qualitative data *(p.129)* Research that seeks to understand how people think and behave and why.

Quantitative data *(p.129)* Research that uses statistics to describe consumers.

Reach *(p.217)* The percentage of different homes or people exposed to a media vehicle or vehicles at least once during a specific period of time. It is the percentage of unduplicated audience.

Reason why *(p.312)* A statement that explains why the feature will benefit the user.

Rebate *(p.432)* A sales promotion that allows the customer to recover part of the product's cost from the manufacturer in the form of cash.

Recall test *(p.141)* A test that evaluates the memorability of an advertisement by contacting members of the advertisement's audience and asking them what they remember about it.

Recognition *(p.170)* An ability to remember having seen something before.

Recognition test *(p.141)* A test that evaluates the memorability of an advertisement by contacting members of the audience, showing them the ad, and asking whether they remember having seen it before.

Reference group *(p.100)* A group of people that a person uses as a guide for behavior in specific situations.

Refund *(p.432)* An offer by the marketer to return a certain amount of money to the consumer who purchases the product.

Regional brand *(p.512)* A brand that is available throughout a regional trading block.

Relationship marketing *(p.71, 459)* The ongoing process of identifying and maintaining contact with high-value customers.

Release prints *(p.389)* Duplicate copies of a commercial that are ready for distribution.

Reputation *(p.460)* A general estimation in which a company is held by the public, based on its practices, policies, and performance.

Retail advertising *(p.484)* A type of advertising used by local merchants who sell directly to consumers.

Rich media *(p.411)* Messages are effective in grabbing people's attention because of their novelty and entertainment value.

Rough cut *(p.389)* A preliminary edited version of the commercial.

Rough layout *(p.376)* A layout drawn to size but without attention to artistic and copy details.

Rushes *(p.388)* Rough versions of the commercial assembled from unedited footage.

S

Sales advertising *(p.490)* Advertising in which the sales price dominates the ad.

Sales promotion *(p.80, 429)* Marketing activities that add value to the product for a limited period of time to stimulate consumer purchasing and dealer effectiveness.

Sampling *(p.432)* Allowing the consumer to experience the product at no cost.

Sans serif *(p.370)* A typeface that does not have the serif detail at the end of the strokes.

Script *(p.347)* A written version of a radio or television commercial.

Secondary research *(p.125)* Information that already has been compiled and published.

Secondary research suppliers *(p.126)* Research firms that gather and organize information around specific topic areas for other interested parties.

Selective distortion *(p.108)* The process of interpreting information in a way that is consistent with the person's existing opinion.

Selective distribution *(p.78)* The use of more than one, but fewer than all, of the intermediaries who are willing to carry the company's product.

Selective exposure *(p.108)* The ability to process only certain information and avoid other stimuli.

Selective perception *(p.108)* The process of screening out information that doesn't interest us and retaining information that does.

Selective retention *(p.108)* The process of remembering only a small portion of what you are exposed to.

Self-liquidator *(p.432)* A type of mail premium that requires a payment sufficient to cover the cost of the item.

Selling premise *(p.312)* The sales logic behind an advertising message.

Semicomps *(p.376)* A layout drawn to size that depicts the art and display type; body copy is simply ruled in.

Serif *(p.370)* Typeface in which the end of each stroke is finished off with a little flourish.

Set *(p.352)* A constructed setting in which the action of a commercial takes place.

Share of voice *(p.211)* One brand's percentage of advertising messages in a medium compared to all messages for that product or service.

Signal *(p.272)* A series of electrical impulses used to transmit radio and television broadcasting.

Single-shot ads *(p.540)* Ads that are designed to work alone rather than as part of an ongoing campaign.

Single-source data tests *(p.144)* A test that is run after an ad campaign is introduced, is small in scope, and has more controls.

Situation analysis *(p.540)* The first section in a campaign plan that summarizes all the relevant background information and research and analyzes its significance.

Slogans *(p.337)* Frequently repeated phrases that provide continuity to an advertising campaign.

Social class *(p.100)* A way to categorize people on the basis of their values, attitudes, lifestyles, and behavior.

Social marketing *(p.34, 461)* Marketing with the good of society in mind.

Soft sell *(p.311)* An emotional message that uses mood, ambiguity, and suspense to create a response based on feelings and attitudes.

Sound effects *(p.346)* Lifelike imitations of sounds.

Source credibility *(p.161)* Belief in a message one hears from a source one finds most reliable.

Specialty advertising *(p.433)* Free gifts or rewards requiring no purchase and carrying a reminder advertising message.

Sponsorship (Cause or Event) *(p.440)* An arrangement in which a company contributes to the expenses of a cause or event to increase the perceived value of the sponsor's brand in the mind of the consumer.

Sponsorship (Television) *(p.276)* An arrangement in which the advertiser produces both a television program and the accompanying commercials.

Spot announcements *(p.276)* Ads shown during the breaks between programs.

Spot color *(p.369)* The use of an accent color to call attention to an element in an ad layout.

Spot radio advertising *(p.285)* A form of advertising in which an ad is placed with an individual station rather than through a network.

Stakeholders *(p.536)* Groups of people with a common interest who have a stake in a company and who can have an impact on its success.

Stereotyping *(p.36)* The process of positioning a group of people in an unvarying pattern that lacks individuality and often reflects popular misconceptions.

Stock footage *(p.383)* Previously recorded film, video, or still slides that are incorporated into a commercial.

Stop motion *(p.387)* An animation technique in which inanimate objects are filmed one frame at a time, creating the illusion of movement.

Storyboard *(p.352)* A series of frames sketched to illustrate how the story line will develop.

Strategic planning *(p.183)* The process of determining objectives, deciding on strategies, and implementing the tactics.

Strategic research *(p.125)* All research that leads to the creation of an ad.

Strategy *(p.183)* The means by which an individual or business accomplishes objectives.

Structural analysis *(p.313)* Developed by the Leo Burnett agency, this method evaluates the power of the narrative or story line, evaluates the strength of the product or claim, and considers how well the two aspects are integrated.

Subheads *(p.337)* Sectional headlines that are used to break up a mass of "gray" type in a large block of copy.

Subliminal message *(p.42)* A message transmitted below the threshold of normal perception so that the receiver is not consciously aware of having viewed it.

Supplements *(p.244)* Syndicated or local full-color advertising inserts that appear in newspapers throughout the week.

Support *(p.313)* The proof, or substantiation needed to make a claim believable.

Survey research *(p.134)* Research using structured interview forms that ask large numbers of people exactly the same questions.

Sweepstakes *(p.432)* Contests that require only that the participant supply his or her name to participate in a random drawing.

SWOT analysis *(p.184, 464, 542)* An analysis of a company or brand's strengths, weaknesses, opportunities, and threats.

Syndication *(p.273)* This is where local stations purchase television or radio shows that are reruns or original programs to fill open hours.

Synergy *(p.546)* The principle that when all the pieces work together, the whole is greater than the sum of its parts.

T

Tabloid *(p.240)* A newspaper with a page size five to six columns wide and 14 inches deep.

Tactic *(p.183)* The specific techniques selected to reflect the strategy.

Taglines *(p.337)* Clever phrases used at the end of an advertisement to summarize the ad's message.

Talent *(p.352)* People who appear in television commercials.

Target audience *(p.98, 193)* People who can be reached with a certain advertising medium and a particular message.

Target market *(p.20, 67)* The market segment(s) to which the marketer wants to sell a product.

Telemarketing *(p.413)* A type of marketing that uses the telephone to make a personal sales contact.

Test market *(p.136)* A group used to test some elements of an ad or a media mix in two or more potential markets.

Testimonial *(p.48)* See endorsement.

Thumbnail sketches *(p.376)* Small preliminary sketches of various layout ideas.

Tie-ins *(p.444)* A promotional tool that promotes two products together to increase both brands' visibility.

Tint blocks *(p.379)* A screen process that creates shades of gray or colors in blocks.

Tip-ins *(p.382)* Preprinted ads that are provided by the advertiser to be glued into the binding of a magazine.

Trade deal *(p.437)* An arrangement in which the retailer agrees to give the manufacturer's product a special promotional effort in return for product discounts, goods, or cash.

Trademark *(p.74)* When a brand name or brand mark is legally protected through registration with the Patent and Trademark Office of the Department of Commerce.

Traditional delivery *(p.249)* Delivery of magazines to readers through newsstands or home delivery.

Trailers *(p.384)* Advertisements shown in movie theaters before the feature.

Two-step offer *(p.401)* A message that is designed to gather leads, answer consumer questions, or set up appointments.

Typography *(p.369)* The use of type both to convey words and to contribute aesthetically to the message.

U

Unaided recall *(p.171)* When one can remember an idea all by oneself.

Uncontrolled media *(p.169, 467)* Media that include the press release, the press conference, and media tours.

Underlines *(p.335)* Text used to elaborate on the idea in the headline and serve as a transition into the body copy.

Understanding *(p.169)* A conscious mental effort to make sense of information.

Undifferentiated or market aggregation strategy *(p.67)* A view of the market that assumes all consumers are basically the same.

Unique selling proposition (USP) *(p.312)* A benefit statement about a feature that is both unique to the product and important to the user.

V

Values *(p.98)* The source of norms; values are not tied to specific objects or behavior, are internal, and guide behavior.

Vendors *(p.19)* A group of service organizations that assist advertisers, ad agencies, and the media; also known as freelancers.

Vertical publications *(p.248, 503)* Publications targeted at people working in the same industry.

Video News Releases (VNRs) *(p.471)* Contain video footage that can be used during a television newscast.

Virtual research *(p.147)* Measures the effectiveness of ads through interactive media.

Visualization *(p.365)* Imagining what the finished copy will look like.

Voice-over *(p.351)* A technique used in commercials in which an off-camera announcer talks about the on-camera scene.

W

Web page *(p.289)* Computer-generated information, usually sponsored by one company or institution, that provides information about the entity and is accessible via the Web.

Z

Zero-based planning *(p.552)* The practice of analyzing the strengths and weaknesses of the various marketing communication tools and then matching them to the problem identified in the situation analysis.

CREDITS

CHAPTER 1

2 Courtesy of Volkswagen of America, Inc., and Arnold Worldwide; **5** Courtesy Holiday Inn and Fallon; **8** An unconventional trophy case: Awards in Trash Cans from Ground Zero Advertising. Reprinted by permission; **10** Courtesy of Worldspan and The Martin Agency; **11** Courtesy of Arnold Worldwide. Photograph copyright © Russ Quackenbush, www.russquackenbush.com; **12** Reprinted by permission of Interland; **13** Courtesy of American Pharmaceutical Co.; **14** Courtesy of National Cattleman's Beef Association; **16** Reprinted with permission from the September 24, 2001 issue of *Advertising Age*. Copyright, Crain Communications Inc. 2001; **17** Courtesy of Tammie DeGrasse, McCann-Erickson; **18** Courtesy of Arnold Worldwide; **19** Courtesy of Ford Motor Company; **20** (Left) Alex Groner, *The American Heritage History of American Business and Industry* (New York: American Heritage Publishing Co., 1972): 17. (Right) Courtesy of Warshaw Collection, Smithsonian Institution; **19** Courtesy of William Heinemann; **20** (Left to Right) Reprinted by permission of the Garry Moore Estate and Kellogg Company. KELLOGG'S FROSTED FLAKES® is a registered trademark of Kellogg Company. All rights reserved. Copyright © 2002 Kellogg Company. Courtesy of Dreyfus Fund Inc. Courtesy of PepsiCo, Inc. And Courtesy of Computer Associates; **23** AOL screenshot © 2002 America Online, Inc. Used with permission.

CHAPTER 2

28 Courtesy of Cigna; **31** (Left) Reprinted by permission of Beach'N Billboard. (Top) AP Photo/Matt Moyer. Reprinted by permission. (Bottom) Courtesy of CarroSell, Inc.; **32** (Left) Courtesy of Alliance Capital. (Right) © 1997 American Express Financial Corporation. Reprinted with permission; **33** Courtesy of Connecticut Department of Public Health; **34** Courtesy of Connecticut Department of Public Health; **38** Courtesy of Pfizer, Inc.; **39** Courtesy of Commercial Closet Association. Courtesy of the Better Business Bureau; **42** Courtesy of the Association of American Advertising Agencies; **49** Courtesy of Quantex®; **50** Courtesy of Nike, Inc.; **51** Courtesy of Volvo; **55** Courtesy of Bob Witek; **57** Courtesy of the Better Business Bureau.

CHAPTER 3

62 Courtesy of General Motors and Mullen; **66** Courtesy of Procter & Gamble; **70** Courtesy of MasterCard International Incorporated; **72** Courtesy of Procter & Gamble; **73** (Left) Reprinted by permission of the Famous Amos Chocolate Chip Cookie Company. (Right) Reprinted by permission of Unilever United States, Inc. and Broadcast Business Consultants. Photo by Michael O'Neill; **74** (Ad) Courtesy of Intel Corporation. (Table) Reproduced from the August 6, 2001, issue of *Business Week* by special permission, copyright © 2001 by The McGraw-Hill Companies, Inc.; **75** (Photo) Courtesy of Andrew Goldberg. (Ad) Courtesy of Margeotes/Fertitta & Partners and The National Football League; **76** Courtesy of Celestial Seasonings; **79** Rolex Watch U.S.A., Inc.; **81** Courtesy of Stonyfield Farm; **82** Courtesy of Louisville Slugger; **84** Reprinted with permission from the April 23, 2001 issue of *Advertising Age*. Copyright, Crain Communications Inc. 2001; **88** (Top) Army materials courtesy of the U.S. Government. (Right) Stills from United States Air Force commercial. Reprinted by permission. (Bottom) Courtesy of The United States Navy; **93** Courtesy of Chick-fil-A.

CHAPTER 4

94 Courtesy of Holiday Inn Express and Fallon; **100** Courtesy of Procter & Gamble; **101** Courtesy of Snowboarding-Online, www.snowboarding-online.com; **102** Courtesy of Sony; **103** (Top) Reprinted with permission from the February 26, 2001 issue of *Advertising Age*. Copyright, Crain Communications Inc. 2001. (Bottom) Reprinted by permission of Radio-Locator.com (a division of Theodric Technologies); **104** (Left) Courtesy of Subaru of America, Inc. (Right) Courtesy of Do Tell, Incorporated; **106** From "Going for That Gold Watch" from *ADWEEK*, October 9, 2000, p. 35. Reprinted by permission of VNU Business Media, Inc.; **109** Reprinted by permission of The Humane Society of the United States; **110** Reprinted by permission of Shell; **111** Courtesy of Fox Sports. Copyright © Fox Sports; **114** Copyright © 2001 by SRI Consulting Business Intelligence. All rights reserved. Reprinted by permission; **115** Courtesy of Cheri L. Anderson;

CHAPTER 5

122 Courtesy of Delta Airlines and Leo Burnett, USA; **130** Courtesy of Land Rover; **131** Courtesy of AT& T Wireless; **132** Courtesy of Delta Airlines and Leo Burnett, **134** Courtesy of Michael Newman/PhotoEdit, and Ron Chapple/Getty Images, Inc.; USA; **137** Courtesy of Neutrogena Corporation; **140** Courtesy of Hauser & Associates, Inc; **143** Courtesy of Arm & Hammer; **148** Courtesy of Delta Airlines and Leo Burnett, USA.

CHAPTER 6

152 Courtesy of Häagen-Dazs and Wolf New York; **155** Courtesy of Florida's Natural Growers and WestWayne, Inc.; **158 - 159** Courtesy of Ingvi Logason, principal, HÉR & NÚ Advertising; **162** (Top) © 2002 General Motors Corporation. Used with permission of GM Media Archives. (Bottom) Courtesy of Carfax, Inc. and The Martin Agency, Inc.; **163** Courtesy Noah K. Murray/The Star-Ledger and Beach'n Billboard; **165** (Top) Courtesy of the Los Angeles Fire Department. (Bottom) Courtesy of Red Lobster Restaurants; **167** Courtesy of Carfax, Inc. and The Martin Agency, Inc.; **168** Courtesy of Ingvi Logason, principal, HÉR & NÚ Advertising; **170** Courtesy of Ingvi Logason, principal, HÉR & NÚ Advertising; **174** Courtesy of Florida's Natural Growers and WestWayne, Inc.; **175** © Teri Stratford; **176** Courtesy of and © Teri Stratford.

CHAPTER 7

180 Courtesy of FootJoy, Arnold Worldwide, Matt Griesser, and Culverton Group; **183** Courtesy of Rockport and photographer Lorenzo Agius; **184** *Marketing Management: The Millennium Edition 10/E* by Kotler, Philip, © 2000. Reprinted by permission of Pearson Education, Inc., Upper Saddle River, NJ; **185** Courtesy of Tom's of Maine; **190** Courtesy of The American Dairy Association; **192** Courtesy of FootJoy and Arnold Worldwide, Matt Griesser, and Culverton Group; **195** Courtesy of GE Exchange; **196** Courtesy of Carol Fletcher; **202** Courtesy of Chick-fil-A.

CHAPTER 8

204 Courtesy of Polaroid Corporation and Goodby, Silverstein & Partners; **208** Reprinted with permission from the September

24, 2001 issue of *Advertising Age*. Copyright, Crain Communications Inc. 2001; **212** Courtesy David Young-Wolff/PhotoEdit; **222** Courtesy of the American Advertising Federation. Photo by Geoffrey Spotts. Ad design by Anh-Thu Cunnion; **225** © Copyright by Meredith Corporation 1988. All rights reserved; **226** Reprinted by permission of SaveOnTV.com.

Chapter 9

236 Courtesy of The United States Marine Corps and J. Walter Thompson U.S.A.; **239** Newspaper Association of America; **240** Reprinted with permission from the May 31, 2001 issue of *Advertising Age*. Copyright, Crain Communications Inc. 2001; **241** (Top) Copyright © 1996 Newsday, Inc. Reprinted with permission. (Bottom) Courtesy of *el Nuevo Herald*; **242** (Bottom) Courtesy of Marston Webb International; **243** Courtesy Interep/Research Division; **246** Courtesy of The News & Observer; **247** Reprinted with permission from the February 19, 2001 issue of *Advertising Age*. Copyright, Crain Communications Inc. 2001; **248** Courtesy of Hachette Filipacchi Magazines; **249** Courtesy of Campbell Soup Company; **250** Reprinted by Permission of *Forbes* Magazine © 2002 Forbes Inc.; **251** Courtesy of *The Wall Street Journal*; **253** Courtesy of Merck; **255** (Top) Courtesy of Tiger Truck Media, Inc. (Bottom) Courtesy of the Workers Compensation Fund; **256** Courtesy of Ken Lubas/Los Angeles Times Syndicate International; **258** Courtesy of TDI Primetime Media; **262** Courtesy of Jane Dennison-Bauer; **263** Courtesy of The United States Marine Corps and J. Walter Thompson U.S.A.

Chapter 10

268 Courtesy of drugstore.com, inc., and Fallon; **273** Photograph of the cast from *Everybody Loves Raymond*. CBS Photo Archive. Copyright © CBS Worldwide, Inc. All Rights Reserved. Reprinted by permission; **275** © 2000 TiVo, Inc. All Rights Reserved; **278** Reprinted with permission from the September 24, 2001 issue of *Advertising Age*. Copyright, Crain Communications Inc. 2001; **280** Courtesy of Nielsen Media Research; **281** KELLOGG'S® and NUTRI-GRAIN® are registered trademarks of Kellogg Company. All rights reserved. © 2002 Kellogg Co.; **286** Courtesy of Arbitron; **290** Courtesy of Sears, Roebuck and Co. Copyright © 2002. All rights reserved; **297** Courtesy of Chick-fil-A.

Chapter 11

298 Copyright © Nissan 2000. Nissan and the Nissan logo are registered trademarks of Nissan; **301** Copyright © Nissan 2000. Nissan and the Nissan logo are registered trademarks of Nissan; **302** (Top) Courtesy of 3M. (Bottom) Courtesy of Dairy Management, Inc.; **303** (Top)Courtesy of Michelin. (Bottom) Courtesy

of Wm. Wrigley Jr. Company; **304** Courtesy of Harley-Davidson Motor Company; **306** All photos courtesy of CORBIS; **309** (Top) Courtesy of the American Advertising Federation. (Bottom) © Nissan 2000. Nissan and the Nissan logo are registered trademarks of Nissan; **312** Courtesy of Ingvi Logason, principal, HÉR & NÚ Advertising; **314** Courtesy of Maytag; **316** Photo courtesy of Tony Martin; **317** KELLOGG'S® SPECIAL K® and KELLOGG'S® SMART START® are registered trademarks of Kellogg Company. All rights reserved. © 2002 Kellogg Co.; **320** Ad Courtesy of General Motors; **321** Courtesy of Maytag; **322** Courtesy of American Airlines. Image © Abrams Lacagnina/Getty Images/The Image Bank. Reprinted by permission of Getty Images.

Chapter 12

328 Courtesy of Cisco and Hill Holliday; **331** Courtesy of NYNEX Yellow Pages; **335** Courtesy of Corporate Angel Network, Inc.; **335** Courtesy of DuPont; **337** Courtesy of Motorola; **338** Courtesy of Cisco and Hill Holliday; **340** Courtesy of Delta Airlines; **341** Courtesy of Coffee Rush and Coates Kokes; **342** Courtesy of Karl Schroeder; **343** Courtesy of Boyd; **354** Courtesy of Bell Atlantic; **355** Courtesy of Oxygen Media, LLC; **356** Reprinted by permission of Bulldog Drummond; **357** Courtesy of Oxygen Media, LLC.

Chapter 13

362 Ernest Hemingway Æ is a trademark of Hemingway, Ltd. and licensed exclusively through Fashion Licensing of America, Inc., 212-370-0770; **365** Reprinted by permission of Bulldog Drummond; **365** Courtesy of AP/Wide World Photos; **367** Reproduced with the permission of John West Foods Limited; **369** Courtesy of Thomasville Furniture Industries, Thomasville, NC. Ernest Hemingway Æ under exclusive license with Hemingway Limited through Fashion Licensing of America, Inc., 212-370-0770; **368** Courtesy of the Dunham Company; **370** Courtesy of EMAP Peterson Publishing Co.; **373** Courtesy of Schwinn; **373** Courtesy of the Dunham Company; **376** Greater Oaklahoma City Chamber of Commerce. Reprinted with permission; **377** Courtesy of Yellow Pages; **377** Courtesy of IBM; **382** Courtesy of Electronic Data Systems and Fallon; **384** Ernest Hemingway Æ is a trademark of Hemingway, Ltd. and licensed exclusively through Fashion Licensing of America, Inc., 212-370-0770; **385** Courtesy of Electronic Data Systems and Fallon; **388** Courtesy of Electronic Data Systems and Fallon; **390** Ernest Hemingway Æ is a trademark of Hemingway, Ltd. and licensed exclusively through Fashion Licensing of America, Inc., 212-370-0770.

Chapter 14

396 Courtesy of The Russ Reid Company; (ph.14.01) Courtesy of and © Teri Stratford; **398** Six–Cats Research, Inc.; **401** Courtesy Trend Lines, Inc./Golf Day; **404** Courtesy of Nintendo; **406** Courtesy of Don Peppers and Martha Rogers; **409** Courtesy of Granta; **410** Courtesy of USAMailNow.com, a division of USA Direct, Inc.; **411** Courtesy of Think Big Media; **413** Cover and photograph courtesy of Alsto's; **414** Courtesy of the Federal Trade Commission; **415** Courtesy of L.L. Bean; **416** Reproduced with permission of Schering Corporation and Key Pharmaceuticals, Inc. All rights reserved; **417** PEANUTS reprinted by permission of United Feature Syndicate, Inc.; **417** Courtesy of Home Shopping Network; **419** Courtesy of Donnelley Marketing; **419** Courtesy of Stamps.com; **425** Courtesy of Chick-fil-A.

Chapter 15

426 Courtesy of Monster.com; **428** Courtesy of Sega of America; **433** Courtesy of Sega of America; **434** Courtesy of Novartis Consumer Health; **435** Courtesy of Pearle Vision; **439** Courtesy of Club Med; **440** Courtesy of Sega of America; **441** Reed Saxon/AP/Wide World Photos; **441** Greg Baker/AP/Wide World Photos; **442** Courtesy of Julie Blankmanship; **441** Courtesy of Boulder Blimp Company; **444** Courtesy of PGA TOUR; **445** Courtesy of Amazon.com, Inc.; **447** Courtesy of Dreyer's and Goodby, Silverstein & Partners.

Chapter 16

454 Reprinted by permission of the Florida Department of Health; **457** Reprinted by permission of the Florida Department of Health; **458** Reprinted by permission of the Florida Department of Health; **462** Courtesy of Target and Martin/Williams; **461** Reprinted by permission of the Florida Department of Health; **463** Courtesy of Edward Maibach; **466** Reprinted by permission of the Florida Department of Health; **467** Courtesy of the National Fatherhood Initiative; **467** Courtesy of the Coalition on Donation; **469** © United Technologies Corporation; **470** Courtesy of Target and Martin/Williams; **472** Reprinted by permission of the Florida Department of Health; **476** NewsClip Analysis, Burrelle's Information Services.

Chapter 17

482 Courtesy of J. Walter Thompson; **485** Courtesy of Sofa Mart. Material may not be copied or reproduced in any manner; **487** Courtesy of Designer Checks, Inc.; **490** Courtesy of Foley's; **493** Courtesy of Kenneth Cole and photographer Nathaniel Goldberg; **494** Courtesy of Chris Hutchinson; **494** Reprinted by permission of Bulldog Drummond; **497** Courtesy of Whereoware.com; **499** From *Forbes*, March 6,

2000. Reprinted by Permission of Forbes Magazine © 2002 Forbes Inc.; **500** Courtesy of Daly & Walcott; **501** Reprinted by permission of American International Group, Inc., and Jose Azel/Aurora; **505** © 2002 Courtesy of FedEx Corp. All rights reserved; **506** Courtesy of J. Walter Thompson.

CHAPTER 18

510 Courtesy of The Procter & Gamble Company; **513** Reprinted with permission from the April 22, 2002 issue of *Advertising Age.* Copyright, Crain Communications Inc. 2002; **515** Geoffrey Wheeler Photography, Art Director Troy Farrow © Bu Jin™ Design; **516** UPS and UPS shield design are registered trademarks of the United Parcel Service of America, Inc. Used by permission; **517** Greg Baker/AP/Wide World Photos; **519** Courtesy of Getting Through Customs, www.getcustoms.com; **520** Courtesy of J. Walter Thompson London, "Anti-Aggressive Driving" Campaign, 1996; **523** Reprinted by permission of Unilever Group. Impulse® is a registered trademark of Unilever Group. All rights reserved. Copyright © 2002 Unilever Group; **531** Courtesy of The Procter & Gamble Company.

CHAPTER 19

534 Courtesy of The Spokane Regional Convention and Visitors Bureau; **538** Courtesy of The Spokane Regional Convention and Visitors Bureau; **539** Batman and all related characters, names and indicia are trademarks of DC Comics © 2002. © 2002 OnStar Æ. All rights reserved. Reprinted by permission; **540** Batman and all related characters, names and indicia are trademarks of DC Comics © 2002. © 2002 OnStar Æ. All rights reserved. Reprinted by permission; **544** Courtesy of The Spokane Regional Convention and Visitors Bureau; **547** Reprinted by permission of White Castle; **548** Reprinted by permission of White Castle; **549** Courtesy of The Spokane Regional Convention and Visitors Bureau; **551** Courtesy of The Spokane Regional Convention and Visitors Bureau; **554** Reprinted by permission of White Castle; **555** Courtesy of The Spokane Regional Convention and Visitors Bureau; **558** Courtesy of Chick-fil-A.